Cyber Warfare and Cyber Terrorism

Lech J. Janczewski
University of Auckland, New Zealand

Andrew M. Colarik
AndrewColarik.com, USA

INFORMATION SCIENCE REFERENCE

Hershey · New York

Acquisitions Editor:	Kristin Klinger
Development Editor:	Kristin Roth
Senior Managing Editor:	Jennifer Neidig
Managing Editor:	Sara Reed
Copy Editor:	Ann Shaver and Heidi Hormel
Typesetter:	Sharon Berger and Jennifer Neidig
Cover Design:	Lisa Tosheff
Printed at:	Yurchak Printing Inc.

Published in the United States of America by
Information Science Reference (an imprint of IGI Global)
701 E. Chocolate Avenue, Suite 200
Hershey PA 17033
Tel: 717-533-8845
Fax: 717-533-8661
E-mail: cust@igi-pub.com
Web site: http://www.igi-pub.com/reference

and in the United Kingdom by
Information Science Reference (an imprint of IGI Global)
3 Henrietta Street
Covent Garden
London WC2E 8LU
Tel: 44 20 7240 0856
Fax: 44 20 7379 0609
Web site: http://www.eurospanonline.com

Library of Congress Cataloging-in-Publication Data

Cyber warfare and cyber terrorism / Andrew Colarik and Lech Janczewski, editors.

p. cm.

Summary: "This book reviews problems, issues, and presentations of the newest research in the field of cyberwarfare and cyberterrorism. While enormous efficiencies have been gained as a result of computers and telecommunications technologies, use of these systems and networks translates into a major concentration of information resources, creating a vulnerability to a host of attacks and exploitations"-- Provided by publisher.

Includes bibliographical references and index.

ISBN 978-1-59140-991-5 (hardcover) -- ISBN 978-1-59140-992-2 (ebook)

1. Information warfare. 2. Computer crimes. I. Colarik, Andrew M. II. Janczewski, Lech, 1943-

U163.C946 2007

355.3'43--dc22

2006102336

British Cataloguing in Publication Data
A Cataloguing in Publication record for this book is available from the British Library.

All work contributed to this book set is new, previously-unpublished material. The views expressed in this book are those of the authors, but not necessarily of the publisher.

Table of Contents

Section I
Terms, Concepts, and Definitions

Section II
Dynamic Aspects of Cyber Warfare and Cyber Terrorism

Section V
Identification, Authorization, and Access Control

Section VI
Business Continuity

Section VII
Cyber Warfare and Cyber Terrorism: National and International Responses

Preface

INTRODUCTION

So many things come in sets of five. The five senses consisting of sight, hearing, touch, smell, and taste; the five elements consisting of water, earth, air, fire and ether; and even the Lorenz cipher machine that uses two sets of five wheels that generate the element obscuring characters—these are but a few examples of independent items that merge together to create a genre of function. Let us now take a look at a number of factors, which on their face value may seem to be totally independent but together create something worth contemplating.

Factor 1

In mid-1960s a group of scientists called the "Rome Club" published a report, which at that time was read and commented on widely around the world. This report was the result of analysis of computer-based models aimed at forecasting the developments of our civilization. The overall conclusions were dim. In the 21st century, human civilization would start facing major difficulties resulting from the depletion of natural resources. The conclusions of the report were discussed and rejected by many at that time. However, without any doubt the Rome Report was the first document trying to address the impact of our civilization on the natural environment.

Factor 2

At the end of the 20th century, the whole world was fascinated with the Y2K computer bug. Due to the limited space used for storing a date in computer records of legacy systems, it was discovered that switching from the year 1999 to 2000 may result in software failures. These failures then may trigger chain reactions due to the fact that computers drive public utility systems (i.e., power supply, water, telecommunications, etc.). As a matter of fact, some people went so far as to hoard food and other supplies to avoid any possible society-wide disturbances that may result. The information technology sector responded with mass action aimed at tracing all possible systems that could generate problems during the switch to a new millennium. As a result, no significant accidents occurred at that time around the world. Interestingly, some mass media outlets clearly were disappointed that nothing had happen.

Factor 3

Telecommunication networks come in many forms; whether they are for the use of businesses, governments, social organizations, and/or individuals, they have great value for improving people's lives. A network is essentially the connecting of two or more entities with the ability to communicate. Utilizing a multitude of telecommunication technologies, such as the Public Switched Telephone Network (PSTN), Public Switched Data Network (PSDN), Cable Television (CATV) network, and orbiting satellite networks (i.e., commercial and military), people from around the globe can communicate and share information virtually in an instant. The real-time services that this infrastructure provides include regular telephone calls, videoconferencing, voice over Internet protocol (VOIP), and a host of other analog, digital, and multimedia communications. Connecting these networked systems and facilitating their communications are high-speed switches, routers, gateways, and data communication servers. Combined, these technologies and infrastructures comprise the global information infrastructure, which is primarily used for the sharing of information and data. This infrastructure serves communications between communities, businesses, industrial and distribution interests, medical and emergency services, military operations and support functions, as well as air and sea traffic control systems. The global information infrastructure sustains our westernized economic and military superiority as well as facilitating our shared knowledge and culture.

It provides national, international and global connectivity through a vast array of systems. The services overlay that facilitate voice and data transfers support the globalization of western values, business, and cultural transfers by creating a smaller, highly responsive communication space to operate and interact with any interested participants. All of this is facilitated by the massive network of servers known as the Internet, and managed by thousands of organizations and millions of individuals. The global information infrastructure is utilized to improve organizations' and individuals' respective efficiencies, coordination and communication efforts, and share and consolidate critical data for maintaining ongoing efforts. This is why such an infrastructure is so important to our western way of life, and also why it is a viable target for those seeking to assert their influence and agendas on the rest of humanity.

Factor 4

Every year the Computer Security Institute, an organization based in San Francisco, California, produces, in cooperation with the FBI, a report called the CSI/FBI Computer Crime and Security Survey. It is a summary and analysis of answers received from more than 600 individuals from all over the United Stated representing all types of business organizations in terms of size and operation. This survey is known around the world as the most representative source of assessment of the security status of businesses. Some of the key findings from the 2006 survey were:

- Virus attacks continue to be the source of the greatest financial losses.
- Unauthorized access continues to be the second-greatest source of financial loss.
- Financial losses related to laptops (or mobile hardware) and theft of proprietary information (i.e., intellectual property) are third and fourth. These four categories account for more than 74% of financial losses.
- Unauthorized use of computer systems slightly decreased this year, according to respondents.
- The total dollar amount of financial losses resulting from security breaches had a substantial decrease this year, according to respondents. Although a large part of this drop was due to a decrease in the number of respondents able and willing to provide estimates of losses, the average amount of financial losses per respondent also decreased substantially this year.

The overall tone of the survey is optimistic. We, as a society, have put a curb on the rising wave of computer-based crime. The survey's findings confirm that.

Factor 5

The mass media reports everyday on terrorist attacks around the world. These attacks may be launched at any time in any place and country. The method of attack in the overwhelming majority of cases is the same: an individual or a group triggers an explosion at a target. It could be done remotely or in suicidal mode. The common dominator of these tragic events is that the attackers are representing only a small part of society and most of the victims are innocent people who just happen to be in the proximity of the explosion.

The important conclusions that may be drawn from these five factors:

- Lack of symptoms of certain phenomena does not imply that the phenomena do not exist. But if such a phenomenon may eventuate and would be damaging to us, we need to take preventive measures.

- All the technology that we have created could be used for the benefit of all of us, but also could be used as a tool of attack/destruction against all of us.
- Information technology, and networking in particular, is a marvel of 20th/21st-century civilization. It dramatically changes all aspects of human behavior. Information technology is beneficial for humanity but may also be (and is) used by individuals to pursue their own objectives against the interest of the majority of people.
- These jagged individuals have started creating significant damages to information technology applications and their respective infrastructures. To counter this new discipline, information/computer security emerged. At present, the efforts of security specialists have started to pay off, and the overall percentage of computer-based crime has leveled off.
- Currently, terrorism has become the most widespread form of violence for expressing public discontent. Thus far, terrorism has stayed within its traditional form of violence, but it has already begun to migrate into using computer technology and networks to launch such attacks. As in the case of Y2K, we need to build awareness among information technology professionals and people alike that terrorism based on the use of computers and networks is a real threat.

All of the above has laid the foundation to the discipline called cyber terrorism. So what are the objectives of cyber terrorism, or rather, why do we need to worry about it?

Because of the enormous efficiencies gained over the past 25 years due to the introduction of computers and telecommunications technologies, organizations have a vested interest to maintain and sustain their deployment regardless of any residual issues. The use of these systems and networks means that there now is a major concentration and centralization of information resources. Such a consolidation creates a major vulnerability to a host of attacks and exploitations. Over the past 35 years, electronic economic espionage has resulted in the theft of military and technological developments that have changed the balance of power and continue to threaten the safety and stability of the world. In 2005 alone, more than 93 million people in the United States were subjected to the potential of identity theft as a result of information breaches and poor information security. When viewed globally, organizations of all kinds are obviously doing something terribly wrong with the security of proprietary and personal information. This is why it is so important to re-energize the need to protect these systems and re-examine our underlying organizational processes that may contribute to future breaches. The emergence of cyber terrorism means that a new group of potential attackers on computers and telecommunications technologies may be added to "traditional" cyber criminals.

The use of technology has impacted society as well. Due to automation technologies, organizational processes are becoming similar around the world. Governments are sharing information and aligning legal frameworks to take advantage of these synergies. Businesses are operating in distributed structures internationally to expand global reach, as well as outsourcing services requiring the use of information to less expensive centers around the world. This has created an extended communication structure between functional units, vendors, and suppliers in order to maintain an efficient value chain of products and services. This facilitated the capabilities of attacking targets wherever they may be located.

Individuals now have access to a vast storage of information resources for the creation of new thought, ideas, and innovations. This includes technological as well as political ideas and innovations. Cultures are becoming closer through shared communications, and as a result are changing at faster rates than previously seen in recorded history. While these technologies have inherent benefits to unify disparate groups and nationalities, this is also creating ultra-minorities that may be inclined to engage in extremism in order to control these changes and compete in this unifying environment. The facilitation of the underlying technologies is also being utilized by these groups to form solidarity and global reach for those of similar mindset and means. Thus, the underlying infrastructures are allowing small groups of people to gain their own form of scales of economies. People and organizations are realizing that in order to be able to compete in a globally connected world, they must master the underlying infrastructure that supports this connectivity. Whether this is to gain access to the opportunities that lie ahead from its mastery or it is to undermine and/or destroy these opportunities for others is still an emerging issue we are all facing today and into the future. Therefore, the exploitation of its inherent strengths (i.e., communication and coordination of global activities, and intelligence gathering) and vulnerabilities (i.e., protocol weaknesses and people processes) can be considered one of the primary sources of attacks today and in the future. This is why we cannot ignore the societal and organizational influences that create the motivations to commit cyber warfare and cyber terrorism in addition to the technological requirements to securing our systems and eliminating any inherent vulnerability.

This book a compilation of selected articles written by people who have answered the call to secure our organizational, national, and international information infrastructures. These authors have decided to come together for this project in order to put forth their thoughts and ideas so that others may benefit from their knowledge and experience. They are dedicated people from around the world who conduct research on information security, and develop and/or deploy a host of information security technologies in their respective fields and industries, and have brought forward a host of key issues that require greater attention and focus by all of us. It is our sincerest hope that the readings provided in our book will create new lines of thought and inspire people around the world to assist in improving the systems and processes we are all now dependent on for our sustained futures.

Following this prologue, there is a chapter *Introduction to Cyber Warfare and Cyber Terrorism* formulating an overview with basic definitions of cyber terrorism and information warfare. Basic recommendations on how to handle such attacks are also presented. The main part of the book follows, containing more detailed discussions of the topics mentioned in the first chapter and other relevant issues. The articles are grouped roughly following the content of the most known security standard ISO 17799, which is entitled "Code of practice for information security management." In each chapter, the reader will find two types of articles: summaries of a given method/technology or a report on a research in the related field. An epilogue is then presented to conclude the content.

The purpose of this book is to give a solid introduction to cyber warfare and cyber terrorism, as we understand it at the beginning of the 21st century. Our book is not a guide to handling issues related to these topics but rather a review of the related problems, issues, and presentations of the newest research in this field. Our main audience is information technology specialists and information security specialists wanting to get a first-hand brief on developments related to the handling of cyber warfare and cyber terrorism attacks.

AC & LJ

Acknowledgment

First of all, we would like to thank all the contributing authors, who in the course of preparing this manuscript for publishing supported us in this task. This project would not be possible without their substantial efforts.

We are directing special thanks to the reviewers of the papers included in this book:

- Dr. Brian Cusack from AUT University, New Zealand
- Prof. Ronald Dodge from the West Point United States Military Academy, USA
- Prof. Peter Goldschmidt from the University of Western Australia, Australia
- Prof. Dieter Gollmann from Hamburg University of Technology, Germany
- Prof. Kai Rannenberg from Frankfurt University, Germany
- Prof. Matthew Warren from Deakin University, Australia
- Prof. Hank Wolf from the Otago University, New Zealand
- Prof. Dennis Viehland from Massey University, New Zealand

What we really appreciate is not only the high quality of their reviews, but their very timely responses to all of our queries and requests.

Special thanks are also directed to our families who were deprived of our mental presence during the time of writing this book.

LJ & AC

Introduction to Cyber Warfare and Cyber Terrorism

Andrew M. Colarik, AndrewColarik.com, USA

Lech J. Janczewski, University of Auckland, New Zealand

ORIGINS AND DEFINITIONS OF CYBER WARFARE AND CYBER TERRORISM

The number of publicized terrorist attacks started to escalate beginning in the mid-1990s. From the attacks that received wide coverage by the world press, we have arrived to the point where not a single day passes without a terrorist committing such acts. It is the spectacular that is getting first-page coverage by the mass media. The basic mechanics of these attacks is usually through the use of explosives detonated remotely or by a suicidal person intent on taking others with them into the next life.

An obvious question must be asked: Is it easy or difficult to plan and execute such attacks? In 2006, Bruce Schneier set up an unusual competition. The goal of this competition was to write a scenario for a terrorist attack against a major component of the United States' critical infrastructure. After an analysis of the possible plots that were submitted, he came to the conclusion that it is not as easy a task as many might think. The fact is that no major terrorists' attacks have happened on U.S. soil since 9/11, despite the fact that there are myriads of groups around the world with this one major objective. Their failure to inflict another attack may be related to the extensive security measures introduced after the 9/11 events.

As a result, a follow-up question may be formulated: Could the consequential damages (i.e., political, economic, and cultural) of 9/11 be created using information technology? Several studies indicate that in the early 1990s, the American society was not well prepared against electronic attacks. As a result, major information system users such as government agencies, military installations, major banks, and so forth began to prepare for the handing of such electronic attacks.

The word "terrorism" brings to mind a picture of bearded men throwing a pouch filled with explosives. But in the context of IT security, terrorists can come in many forms such as politically motivated, anti-government, anti-world trade, and pro-environmental extremists. If given the opportunity, such activists would gladly disrupt trade and legislative agendas by attacking a facility's communication server, especially if the media were standing by to report what just happened. Also, a terrorist could try to interfere with IT resources controlling critical national infrastructures (like water supply, power grid, air traffic, etc.) through the manipulation of SCADA systems. As a matter of fact, such attacks have already been carried out. In 2000, someone hacked into Maroochy Shire, Australia's waste management control system and released millions of gallons of raw sewage into the town. Given the political orientation, cyber warfare and cyber terrorism are realities that our civilization are now facing.

The term cyber terrorism was coined in 1996 by combining the terms cyberspace and terrorism. The term has become widely accepted after being embraced by the United States Armed Forces. A report generated in 1998 by the Center for Strategic and International Studies was entitled Cybercrime, Cyberterrorism, Cyberwarfare, Averting an Electronic Waterloo. In this report, the probabilities of such activities affecting a nation were discussed, followed by a discussion of the potential outcomes of such attacks and methods to limit the likelihood of such events. We will use the term cyber terrorism as:

Cyber terrorism means premeditated, politically motivated attacks by sub national groups or clandestine agents, or individuals against information and computer systems, computer programs, and data that result in violence against non-combatant targets.

Parallel to the term of cyber terrorism is an older term known as information warfare:

Information warfare is defined as a planned attack by nations or their agents against information and computer systems, computer programs, and data that result in enemy losses.

The practical difference between these two terms is that cyber terrorism is about causing fear and harm to anyone in the vicinity (i.e., bystanders), while information warfare has a defined target in a war (ideological or declared). Along with these terms there is a phenomenon of *cyber crime* used frequently by law enforcement agencies. Cyber crime is a crime committed through the use of information technology. We must point out that the physical forms of cyber terrorism, information warfare, and cyber crime often look very much alike.

Imagine that an individual gains access to a hospital's medical database and changes the medication of a pro-business, anti-environmental executive of a Fortune 100 company to one that he or she is dangerously allergic to and also removes the allergy from his or her digital record. The nurse administers the drug and the patient dies. So, which definition applies? The answer lies not in the mechanics of the event, but rather in the intent that drove the person's actions. If it was intentionally done, for instance as a result of poor relations between these two people, then it would be murder in addition to a cyber crime. If the executor later would announce that he or she is ready to commit more such acts if their demands would not be met, then it could be labeled as cyber terrorism. If the activities were carried out by an agent of a foreign power, then it could be labeled as information warfare. We believe the most important aspect of cyber attacks that have physical consequences is determining the intention of the attacker.

The distinction between these terms is extremely important because there are non-technology-related issues and solutions that will impact any strategy in combating cyber warfare and cyber terrorism. We would like to make it clear to our readers though that this book in no way attempts to cover the issue of what philosophical, political, or religious reasons would lead people to become cyber terrorists or cyber warriors. What we are putting forward is that societal and cultural orientations and their resulting motivations are important towards resolving the people component of such attacks. They cannot be ignored or disregarded just because we are exploring technological and organizational solutions.

CORRELATIONS BETWEEN CYBER AND CORPOREAL CONFLICTS

There are several important correlations between cyber attacks and current national and international corporeal situations. Any IT manager should be aware of the following existing consistencies:

- Physical attacks are usually followed by cyber attacks: Immediately after the downing of an American plane near the coast of China, individuals from both countries began cyber attacks against facilities of the other side. Similarly, an increased wave of cyber attacks was observed during the Pakistan/India conflict, throughout the Israeli/Palestinian conflict, and the Balkans War (i.e., the collapse of Yugoslavia).
- Cyber attacks are aimed at targets representing high publicity value: Cyber attacks are carried out in such way that they could either inflict serious losses and/or generate high publicity. All installations attached to top administrative and military units are primary targets. Apart from government organizations, cyber attacks are launched against the most visible and dominant multi-national corporations. Favorite targets by attackers are top IT and transportation industry companies such as Microsoft, Boeing, and Ford.
- Increases in cyber attacks have clear political/terrorist foundations: Available statistics indicate that any of the previously mentioned conflicts resulted in a steady increase of cyber attacks. For instance, attacks by Chinese hackers and the Israeli/Palestinian conflict show a pattern of phased escalation.

Because no one person can prevent world events, unless you have connections most mortals do not, you need to know why and how cyber warriors and terrorist strike. The follow section offers some context.

WHY AND HOW CYBER WARRIORS AND CYBER TERRORISTS STRIKE?

When building protections against cyber attacks, we must understand why they launch their attacks and what they are counting on. Understanding is the first step in reducing or eliminating attacks. The most probable reasons for cyber attacks are:

- **Fear factor:** The most common denominator of the majority of terrorist attacks is a terrorist wishes the creation of fear in individuals, groups, or societies. Perhaps the best example of this drive was the bombing of a Bali nightclub in 2002. This nightclub was nothing other than a watering hole for foreign tourists (Australians in particular), and inflicting casualties and fear among them was the main objective of the attackers. The influx of foreign tourists to Bali was significantly reduced after this attack. The same applies to attacks against IT installations.
- **Spectacular factor:** Whatever is the actual damage of an attack, it should have a spectacular nature. By spectacular we consider attacks aimed at either creating huge direct losses and/or resulting in a lot of negative publicity. In 1999, the Amazon.com Web site was closed for some time due to a denial of service (DOS) attack. Amazon incurred losses due to suspended trading, but the publicity the attack created was widespread.
- **Vulnerability factor:** Cyber activities do not always end up with huge financial losses. Some of the most effective ways to demonstrate an organization's vulnerability is to cause a denial of service to the commercial server or something as simple as the defacement of an organization's Web pages, very often referred to as computer graffiti.

Cyber attacks may be carried out through a host of technologies, but have an attack pattern that may be modeled. Despite using the most advanced technology, the phases of a cyber attack generally follow the same pattern as a traditional crime. These are as follows:

The first phase of an attack is reconnaissance of the intended victim. By observing the normal operations of a target, useful information can be ascertained and accumulated such as hardware and software used, regular and periodic communications, and the formatting of said correspondences.

The second phase of an attack is penetration. Until an attacker is inside a system, there is little that can be done to the target except to disrupt the availability or access to a given service provided by the target.

The third phase is identifying and expanding the internal capabilities by viewing resources and increasing access rights to more restricted, higher-value areas of a given system.

The forth stage is where the intruder does the damage to a system or confiscates selected data and/or information.

The last phase can include the removal of any evidence of a penetration, theft, and so forth by covering the intruder's electronic trail by editing or deleting log files.

Ultimately, an intruder wants to complete all five stages successfully. However, this is entirely dependent on the type of attack method utilized, the desired end result, and the target's individual defensive and/or monitoring capabilities.

According to the CSI/FBI 2006 Computer Crime and Security Survey, virus attacks continue to be the source of the greatest financial losses. Unauthorized access continues to be the second-greatest source of financial loss. Financial losses related to laptops (or mobile hardware) and theft of proprietary information (i.e., intellectual property) are third and fourth. These four categories account for more than 74% of financial losses. These types of attacks occurred despite the fact that most of the respondents had security policies and mechanisms in place as part of their prevention and response plans. Just imagine the number of successful attacks that went unnoticed and/or unreported, and by entities that were not even part of the survey.

In general, today's cyber attacks consist primarily of:

- Virus and worm attacks that are delivered via e-mail attachments, Web browser scripts, and vulnerability exploit engines.

- Denial of service attacks designed to prevent the use of public systems by legitimate users by overloading the normal mechanisms inherent in establishing and maintaining computer-to-computer connections.
- Web defacements of informational sites that service governmental and commercial interests in order to spread disinformation, propaganda, and/or disrupt information flows.
- Unauthorized intrusions into systems that lead to the theft of confidential and/or proprietary information, the modification and/or corruption of data, and the inappropriate usage of a system for launching attacks on other systems.

The goals of these attacks can vary. Some are to show the weaknesses inherent in the systems. Some are political statements about the conduct of the entities being attacked, while others are about the theft of information for a variety of reasons. These can include target intelligence, internal process observations, or wholesale theft. As previously stated, the perpetrator's reasons (i.e., why he or she decided to penetrate a system) have a lot to do with the extent of the damages that may be incurred. The perpetrator may wish to have a look around in an attempt to "case" the system, or may simply be looking for high-value data items (i.e., something that satisfies his or her penetration goal) that can be used for other internal and/or external operations. Some intrusions may be to do some damage to a system in that an underlying system or sub-process would be disrupted or modified as the end result of the intrusion or as a step in a series of penetration activities. Intruders may also seek to change important data in an attempt to either cover their tracks (i.e., such as delete/modify an audit log) or to cause people or other processes to act on the changed data in a way that causes a cascading series of damages in the physical or electronic world.

The means (i.e., course, process, etc.) of an attack has a lot to do with the approach taken to execute the attack and its related characteristics. If someone wants to damage a system with a virus, then he or she needs to consider how the virus will be delivered and what capabilities said virus is to be empowered with in order to create the damage done (i.e., delete data, monitor activities, steal intellectual property or identities, etc.). The design of an attack requires an appropriate delivery method and an appropriate device to perform the damage once it is delivered. Because an attacker does not control the basic choice of systems and protective mechanisms of any given network, he or she is left to choose from a variety of approaches that have both advantages and disadvantages for any given attack. At the highest level of these choices is whether to penetrate a system internally or externally.

It is a common fact that insiders can gain greater access to system resources than outsiders in most configured systems and networks. This is because certain service levels within a network rely on users and developers to be attentive to procedures, methods, and policies for the organization's overall benefit. Restrictions on users tend to reduce the overall capability of a given system. Thus, reliance on users to conduct themselves appropriately may lead to vulnerabilities, damaged systems and data, and future attacks. When it comes to access control, system programmers and developers ultimately tend to have the highest level of internal access of systems because it is they who create the hidden structures that provide services to users.

Periodically, operating systems and application programs have overlooked weaknesses built into their software. This is not uncommon, as pressure to reduce the time-to-market development cycle has created many dysfunctions in the computer software industry. The current paradigm of software development is to get the product to the customer as fast as possible with as few defects as feasible, and then to correct the software as defects surface. Would-be attackers may then exploit such weaknesses before they have been fixed. At first glance, this approach would be considered an external attack, except when the vulnerability has been deliberately created by those in the development process. Recently, it was discovered that Aum Shinrikyo cult members, the same cult that killed 12 people and injured 6,000 after releasing sarin gas in the Tokyo subways, had worked as subcontractors for firms developing classified government and police communication hardware and software. As a result, the cult was able to procure and further develop software that allowed them to track police vehicles. In addition, there may yet be undiscovered capabilities that were created as a result of their development contributions to more than 80 Japanese firms and 10 government agencies.

The above example shows that internal systems have an inherent weakness where users must rely on the quality control levels of the supplying company for their foundational security. In today's environment, people are forced to trust the secure operation of fabricated and pre-packaged hardware and software systems. An attack may or may not originate from inside a given network or system, but the execution of the attack is facilitated by the internal systems such as in the case of an e-mail virus that does some damage but also propagates itself internally and/or to externally connected systems and recipients. The following section presents the facilities that could be the primary target of the attackers.

PRIMARY TARGET FACILITIES

Usage Portals

Usage portals are application programs that comprise the bulk of a user's daily computer usage where he or she interacts with the outside world. These include applications such as e-mail, Web browsers, chat clients, video streaming, remote software, Web-enabled application software, and a host of other applications. These and other usage portals are utilized by attackers to turn a system against itself or hijack its applications to attack its host system or other connecting systems.

E-Mail

It is said that the most ubiquitous application in use for communication today is electronic mail (e-mail). We use e-mail to write letters and send attached files such as pictures and spreadsheets, and depending on the e-mail client's configuration, it can even receive Web page content inside a received e-mail. This particular usage portal reputably caused between US$3-15 billion in damages worldwide when a university student in the Philippines developed and released the Love Bug virus. Now this is no small matter when it is considered that Hurricane Andrew caused US$25 billion in damage when it went through the state of Florida. Essentially, this small e-mail virus was programmed to infect the computer of whoever opened the message and send itself to everyone in the user's address book. The deliverable was a virus, the portal was the e-mail client, the choice of target was anyone associated with an initial victim, and the damage was to distribute itself and then damage the host computer system.

This is but one application of what a virus can do with this portal. Such viruses now are being used to inundate targeted installations (i.e. military, government, corporate, etc.) with tens of thousands of e-mails that are intended to flood the organization's e-mail server with more messages than it can handle while attempting to spread itself to connecting systems (i.e., a cascading damage effect). Because care is not always taken in the proper use of e-mail clients, e-mail servers do not always have properly configured filtering systems, and users are not always selective in what they open and read, e-mail will continue to be a choice portal for conducting attacks.

Web Browsers

Web browsing has allowed the Internet to prosper and flourish by providing a point-and-click approach to informational Web sites about everything from basket weaving to building roadside bombs. With more than 8 trillion Web pages, the statistical probability that some of them are designed to disrupt, hijack, or damage a connecting computer cannot be ignored. Built into a Web browser are the tools and scripts (i.e., small executable programs that execute requested resources such as Install on Demand, Java Script, VB Script, etc.) that can be turned against a user's computer. The same tools that allow a browser to execute the playing of a video at a news site can be used to trigger remote executions of other programs and sub-routines that can allow a Web site's host server to take control of parts of the visitor's system. These tools can then be used to read and execute files on the visitor's system in order to access information such as user account details (i.e., full user name, logon name, e-mail addresses, permission levels, last time a password was changed, IP address, etc.), gather previously accessed sites and files stored in the operating system and application program working folders, determine configuration settings such as version levels and the settings of the operating system and/or application programs, as well as many more details that are stored on a user's computer.

In addition, by using executable code that are stored inside a digital picture, malicious sites can make use of these built-in tools and execute malicious code when a picture is opened and/or viewed. Browsers also have application program interfaces and plug-ins to security protocols such as Secure Socket Layer and mechanisms such as digital certificates that enable more secure browsing and communications. When vulnerabilities are discovered in browser applications, caustic Web site servers can be geared to take advantage of these resulting in site redirections, server authenticity spoofing (i.e., deliberate identity falsification), and the installation and execution of malicious code. The above issues and others not mentioned regarding Web browsers can be reduced or eliminated if a Web browser is properly configured and regularly updated, and therefore must be taken seriously. Unfortunately, the inherent design orientation of most Web browsers is geared towards an "open systems approach" for complete compatibility and interconnectivity with available Web services. This fundamental weakness makes this portal ripe for exploitation.

Chat Clients

Computer-user-to-computer-user communications is sometimes facilitated with the use of Internet relay chat (IRC) software such as MSN Messenger, AOL Instant Messenger, mIRC, and a host of others. Some chat clients allow a direct, dedicated connection between two computers, while others utilize a centralized server to log into and chat with others on the server both in individual chat sessions and in the groups forums. An extension of this basic approach is with the inclusion of voice and/or video feed via a microphone and/or video camera. This combined approach combines text messaging, Voice Over Internet Protocol, and video streaming using software such as Apple's iChat AV. The vast majority of the products in this usage portal have no privacy protection (i.e., encryption, IP address obscuring, etc.) and are subject to monitoring, hijacking, and substitution of communication content attacks in addition to any relevant information that can be ascertained from a given conversation.

Also, an intruder can use this class of software to obtain configuration information to remotely use a computer's microphone and video camera at a later date to see/listen in on the room in which the computer resides. Care must be taken in the choice of software, chat server, and those who are to be chatted with when using this portal. However, the basic nature of people to become comfortable with systems and trust previous relationships will lead to this portal being taken advantage of by technical savvy intruders and social engineers.

Remote Software

Remote software allows a user to take control of an existing computer or server remotely through another computer. This is usually accomplished via a modem or network connection. This usage portal is used to remotely manage servers (i.e., similar to telnet) and access limited or shared resources on a network such as databases, application software, work files, and the like. Sometimes, the remote connection is completed in such a way that the user's computer acts as a terminal for keystrokes and screen shots that are being performed on the remote computer using software such as Laplink or pcAnywhere, or the computer being remote is actually a virtually, fully functioned, created desktop that emulates the look and feel of an actual desktop as in the case of Microsoft's Terminal Services. When remote services are enabled and made available, intruders can use the modems and/or network address ports to gain access to the internal structure of a network. These access points tend to be user name and password protected only with little or no privacy protection (i.e., encryption), and therefore can be subject to external monitoring, and brute force (i.e., incremental generation of characters until a match is found) and dictionary password attacks (i.e., a dictionary list of potential passwords). Presumably, this portal is by far the least protected and one of the easiest to penetrate when present in an organization.

Web-Enabled Applications

Everyday applications such as word processors and spreadsheets are designed to be Web enabled to allow the sending and reading of files and work-in-process projects between systems (i.e., integrated applications and collaboration systems). It is quite common to attempt to insert clip art into a document and be prompted if you would like to browse additional clip art at the manufacturer's Web site. Other applications are integrated directly with e-mail and Web browser software as a result of being part of the same software suite such as Microsoft Office so that these associated applications are launched and executed when specialty functions are requested. Additionally, many applications and utility software periodically check to see if an Internet connection is available and if so may contact the manufacturer's server for update information and/or registration validation. Some software is still more intrusive in that when a connection is not present, it instructs the computer to dial or connect to the Internet without permission from the user.

Web-enabled applications can be used by an intruder's malicious code to transfer information about a system (i.e., via File Transfer Protocol, etc.), execute successive activities of an initial attack (i.e., transitive capabilities), and facilitate the spread of additional malicious code. Care must be taken in the selection and configuration of these types of software, as well as the source manufacturer. The use of shareware and freeware sources for Web-enabled software can sometimes have additional built-in communications and backdoors that can be exploited by its creators and/or are the result of a poor software development process. It is one thing to have software with the ability to access the Web outside of its hosting system; it is another completely different issue when such software is designed to accept connections from the Internet without notifying the user, such as in the case of many of Microsoft's Office products. Because users have been given the ability to integrate applications with the Web (willingly or not), the problems associated with this approach will be around for some time to come.

Updates

As previously discussed, the current software development paradigm is to get a product to market as quickly as feasible. When security faults become known as a result of this paradigm, patches (i.e., software fixes) are usually issued by the manufacturer. Whether the patch is for an operating system, utility program, or application package, a process is required for developing a new patch, notifying users of the patch's existence, making the patch available in a timely manner, and finally delivering said patch. Throughout this process, vulnerabilities can be created and/or bypassed by users and intruders alike. As an example, most antivirus software has provisions for updating the virus definition files to protect against new viruses as they are developed and deployed. Some attacks are directed at the virus software itself in that if the virus scanner can be disabled in some way, then a greater threat can be activated without the user being made aware of it. Therefore, updating the definition files and antivirus software is critical to maintaining a good virus defense. When the update process is circumvented (i.e., not renewing the subscription, disabling part of the update process, corrupting the software or definition files, etc.), a host of security issues emerge usually resulting in a breached system.

With regards to operating systems and enterprise level software such as SAP, the update process has additional complexities that provide additional opportunities for intruders. One method of corruption that continues to be utilized is to send a system administrator an official-looking e-mail detailing an actual new security vulnerability that provides a link to download the appropriate patch. This patch may actually be a piece of malicious code such as a worm, the actual patch with the addition of an attached malicious program (i.e., virus), or a combination of the two. Care must be taken not only to install patches in a timely fashion, but also to secure the entire process. Since system administrators tend to be very busy, they may not take the time to check the authenticity of the e-mail or the integrity of the patch itself before installing it. Even when an administrator is knowledgeable enough not to fall for this ploy, he or she may delay in getting the new patch, and as a result, not install a needed security patch quickly enough. The Code Red I and II worms and others like them have disabled as many as 25% of Internet servers in one attack because of poor patch management.

DELIVERABLES

Using the mechanisms described above, attackers try to infect the attacked systems with malicious code which will be used next to carry out their malicious intentions. These deliverables have enormous implications for the results of an attack. The deliverable may seek to gain information on the intended target system. It may create a backdoor into the penetrated system that can be exploited at a later date for a variety of purposes. The deliverable may also be used to force a system to execute malicious code or instructions to modify or delete data and other programs. For internal penetrations (i.e., internal usage with outbound capabilities), the vast majority of deliverables will be viruses, worms, and executable scripts (i.e., program instructions). Other attack deliverables having more external nature will be discussed later in the chapter.

Viruses and Worms

Viruses have been plaguing systems since the 1960s. Essentially, a computer virus is a self-replicating program that attaches itself to another program or file in order to reproduce. When a given file is used, the virus will reside in the memory of a computer system, attach itself to other files accessed or opened, and execute its code. Viruses traditionally have targeted boot sectors (i.e., the startup portion of a computer disk) and executable files, and have hidden themselves in some very unlikely memory locations such as in the printer memory port. Like computers, viruses have evolved in capabilities. These include the ability to conceal an infection by letting an executable program call the infected file from another location or by disabling the definition file (i.e., digital fingerprint used to detect a virus), by encrypting itself to prevent a discernable virus "signature," and/or by changing its digital footprint each time it reproduces (i.e., polymorphism).

Worms are a type of malicious software that does not need another file or program to replicate itself, and as such, is a self-sustaining and running program. The primary difference between viruses and worms is that a virus replicates on a host system while a worm replicates over a network using standard protocols (i.e., a type of mobile code). The latest incarnation of worms make use of known vulnerabilities in systems to penetrate, execute their code, and replicate to other systems such as the Code Red II worm that infected more than 259,000 systems in less than 14 hours. Another use of worms that are less destructive and more subversive has been designed to monitor and collect server and traffic activities, and transmit this information back to its creator for intelligence and/or industrial espionage.

Trojans

A Trojan horse is a malicious program that is intended to perform a legitimate function when it in fact also performs an unknown and/or unwanted activity. Many viruses and worms are delivered via a Trojan horse program to infect systems, install monitoring software such as keyboard loggers (i.e., a program that records every keystroke performed by a user) or backdoors to remotely take control of the system, and/or conduct destructive activities on the infiltrated system. It is very common for intruders to make available free software (i.e., games, utilities, hacking tools, etc.) that are in fact Trojan horses. In the commercial realm, it is also not unheard of to attach monitoring software (i.e., spyware) to a 30-day trial versions of "free" software that reports the activities of the user back to the manufacturer with the consent of the user when they agree to the terms and conditions when the software is first installed. The notification of the so-called intended monitoring is buried deep within such agreements. This spyware can also be monitored and hijacked by intruders to gather additional intelligence about a potential target, and in our opinion should be considered a Trojan horse regardless of the licensure agreement.

Malicious Scripts

Throughout the course of using the previously mentioned portals, a user will encounter the usage of scripting languages and macros that automate various calls and functions with connecting software modules and components. These scripts are designed to run in the background, and provide a means to communicate and execute legitimate code seamlessly between connecting/communicating modules and systems. These include Java Applets, Active X, and application software macros. Java Applets are programs designed to be executed within an application program such as a Web browser and do not get executed by the user's operating system directly. This allows applets to be operating system independent and instead rely on the application program to execute the commands through its resident operating system. Active X is a combination of Object Linking and Embedding (OLE) and Component Object Model (COM) technologies that allow information to be shared between applications, and can perform any action a user would normally be able to perform. This allows applications to use Active X to eliminate the restrictions imposed by application-specific formats for the processing and storage of data (i.e., they can be automated regardless of program dependencies). Macros are a series of stored keystrokes that can be sequentially executed at one time and repeatedly re-executed. This allows redundant tasks within applications to be automated and executed. Java Applets, Active X, macros, and similar scripting mechanisms have become a regular part of Web browsing, multi-player gaming, and business automation, and provide a foundation for streamlining computing functions for improved services.

When the above technologies are used for executing commands and activities that are unwanted by a user, they can be considered malicious scripts. When Java Applets are misused, they can be employed to read the system properties directories and files of the user's machine, create a socket to communicate with another computer, send e-mail from the user's account, and a host of other functions. When Active X is misused, it can be utilized to instruct accounting software to write an electronic check to someone's bank account, and a host of other automated attack sequences. Macros have been used by attackers from their beginnings to perform virus-like functions and as a result have been dubbed macro viruses. These are executed whenever an infected document is opened. They reproduce by adding themselves to the application's "normal" or base blank document. Whenever a new or existing document is opened, the macro duplicates itself into that document. It is then transported to new systems when an infected file is transferred and opened on another machine.

EXTERNAL PENETRATION

In this section, an examination of the more common approaches to penetrating a system externally will be presented.

Social Engineering

When we were young, there was a standard notion that stated it never hurt to ask a question. If one is being polite, sounds as if they are well versed in a topic or environment, and can communicate a sense of purpose in their voice, questions asked in a professional environment can be used to hurt organizations and individuals by convincing them to disclose confidential details. This information in turn can be used for future attack attempts. The aim of social engineering is to get people to disclose confidential information such as user names, passwords, points of entry, working hours, and so forth as the first step in penetrating a system. Traditional approaches to social engineering have included official-sounding telephone calls from so-called bank personnel or an intruder posing as an employee or system administrator, or even an official visitor using an employee's phone to call technical support while the employee steps out of his or her office for a few minutes. The knowledge gained from this type of deception may very well bring an intruder much closer to gaining an initial access point into an information system or network. Such information can also greatly enhance other methods discussed in previous sections as well as later in this section.

Physical

The simplest access method to system resources may very well be physical access. Because of the small size of computers, it is not uncommon to have a computer server placed directly within easy reach for maintenance by a given department or individual. This is especially true of small to medium-sized businesses that give more responsibility to individuals directly involved in using and managing the system. As a result, an intruder or visitor may be able to access the terminal while in proximity of it. This allows for the quick installation of software such as a keyboard logger or a monitoring device such as a wireless transmitter attached to a keyboard or video screen. The information collected by whatever means can be retrieved or transmitted to the intruder for supporting later intrusion activities. Such an approach is not the only means that physical access can be used. Physical access can also provide the following opportunities to an intruder:

- **Primary unit:** The intruder may unplug a computer unit's peripherals (i.e., monitor, keyboard, etc.) and walk away with it. Once this equipment has been examined and/or modified, it may be able to be plugged back into the system and used for future surveillance and/or attacks. This is one reason why better-organized facilities keep such systems in restricted, locked rooms and govern the access of their facility by guests and intruders alike by enforcing security policies and alarms.
- **Cabling:** The physical cabling of an organization's network is another point of vulnerability that must be carefully considered. Transmission wires come in twisted-pair telephone wire, coaxial cable, and fiber optic. In many cases these internal wires traverse through walls and conduits, and eventually terminate at wall plugs and/or switch racks or hubs. The ability to tap into these wires is related to their ease of access in the case of twisted pair and coaxial, and a higher level of skill and equipment in the case of fiber optic. In many cases they are encased in conduits, but in many other cases they are openly exposed. Also, these wires eventually must exit a building, and as such, become susceptible to outside splicing.
- **Equipment disposal:** The proper disposal of older equipment is an aspect of physical security. Hard drives contain details and configuration settings of a once operational computer that was connected to an internal network. In many cases, these retired computers are given away to employees or tossed in a dumpster after their hard drives have been reformatted. The problem with this approach is that computer forensic techniques that are readily available today can recover lost or formatted data of a hard drive that has been formatted up to six times. What is required is permanent eraser software that writes and re-writes a hard drive repeatedly in a fashion that makes such a recovery impossible. In addition, old backup tapes and CD-ROMs must also be securely disposed.

Having physical access to facilities and equipment provides a huge advantage in gaining additional access to a system. User histories, activities, and data can be retrieved in a major step towards additional penetrations. Therefore, physical intrusions will continue to be an effective step in gaining additional access and knowledge by intruders.

Wireless Communication Medium

Wireless devices are appearing everywhere a landline, cable, or cord served the same purpose. Wireless devices utilize laser, radio frequencies, and infrared technologies to imprint data on its frequency wave as a means of transmission. These technologies range from line-of-sight connectivity as in the case of laser transmissions, radio frequencies as in the case of cellular phones and networking equipment, to satellite control systems and broadcast transmissions. The basic nature of wireless communications makes this transmission medium accessible from any point within its broadcast range or point-to-point path. This is both its greatest strength and weakness. Generally, when two devices initially wish to connect, a handshake protocol establishes the two devices' connection and/or any security mechanisms that will be used throughout the connection. This link is maintained until discontinued or interrupted. Devices communicating via a wireless link sometimes experience environmental conditions that cause signal degradation and/or data corruption that can result in the retransmissions of previously sent data. These two issues provide intruders with the foundation for piercing such systems and any security that may be present or prevent the communication connection from being maintained. While there are numerous standards in existence for securing wireless communications, the underlying notion that the transmission can be openly monitored makes this transmission medium vulnerable to eavesdropping. Research conducted in 2004 in Auckland, New Zealand, showed that more than 60% of wireless office systems work without any protection—that is, anybody with a laptop and wireless antenna would be able to use a network as an authorized user. This allows an intruder to observe and record communications for examination of content, security keys, and/or decryption of the transmission. Such communications are also subject to jamming devices that flood the wavelengths with "white noise" and therefore preventing a device-to-device connection.

One last major security vulnerability of wireless devices has to do with having its source location ascertained. A transmitting device can have its physical location be deduced through a host of detection methods (i.e., triangulation, etc.) because all such devices have a point of origin for their transmission. While military versions of wireless devices have additional protective security mechanisms such as frequency hopping and spread spectrum, most commercial facilities continue to be shown as vulnerable to disruptions, monitoring, and intrusion.

User Access Points

Users of data communications utilize data pathways to access systems and resources on computer systems. In nearly all cases, users are assigned user accounts that specify the level and domains that the user is permitted to access. These accounts may be generic as in the case of an anonymous user or based on an access control list (i.e., a predetermined list of users and their corresponding access levels). The user traditionally enters his or her user account name and a password. The connecting computer then establishes a session (i.e., the period of time that a communication link is maintained) with the connected system. All activities that occur on the connected system are performed at the access control rights assigned to the user account. Therefore, one of the fundamental attack methods by intruders is to identify any user names and passwords to access a system.

One method of achieving this information is through the use of packet sniffing. As previously discussed, packet sniffing is a method of examining every packet that flows across a network in order to gain information on the communication content. When a sniffer is placed on an attached computer within a network, that computer may then anonymously monitor the traffic coming and going on that particular network. Essentially, a sniffer creates a socket stream on the network, has its network interface card configured to promiscuous mode, and begins reading from the open socket stream. When data is sent over communication channels in clear text form, reading it becomes quite simple. When a user seeks to connect to a system, that system usually prompts the user for a user name and password. This information is then entered and transmitted over the communication channel to the server for authentication. It is at this point that a sniffer may capture this information for later use by an intruder if not encrypted. The attacker can then gain access to the system with all the access rights of the legitimate user, and may even be capable of elevating these access rights once he or she has access to a given system or network. Because not all systems encrypt these transactions, sniffers continue to be an issue in securing user accounts.

Another approach that is used by intruders is to use direct attacks on the password of a user account. Sometimes, a user name is known or can be deduced from other transactions (i.e., social engineering, similar formatting of other users, etc.). All that is then needed is the corresponding password. This can be accomplished using brute force and dictionary attacks on the user's account. Brute force attacks rely on sheer computing power to incrementally try all of the possible password combinations for a given user account name. Dictionary attacks utilize the most common words that can be found in a dictionary such as names, places, and objects as the password for any given user account. Both approaches are typically automated using cracker exploit software. More secure systems provide a user a limited number of attempts at entering a correct password before they disable the account for a specified period of time. After this delay, a user account may generally then be logged into when the correct password is entered. However, many systems still do not provide or activate this security feature, leaving it open to such attacks.

Another well-established user access point is the dial-up connection to an Internet service provider (ISP) such as AOL or AT&T. Throughout the intruder community, it has been very common to trade accessible or cracked user accounts for other software cracks and specialty exploits. Gaining access to such an account grants the user the capability to use the account for spamming (i.e., unsolicited mass e-mailing), anonymous browsing, penetrating other accounts without direct traceability to the intruder, and also the use of the account's access rights within the ISP. In order to check for e-mail, initiate a session outside the ISP, or other seemingly harmless activities of a legitimate user, the user account must be granted certain access rights within the ISP in order to view files and execute activities. These access rights while restricted are still greater than non-subscriber rights, and assume a measure of responsibility and accountability on behalf of a legitimate user. When an account has been hijacked, such responsibility fails to influence activity decisions. Use of such an account by an intruder may allow the intruder to view other subscribers' e-mails, access server folders and configuration settings in order to elevate access rights, reconfigure various system components to attack other networks, or even turn the breached system into a proxy server as an anonymous staging point for other remote activities and/or attacks.

DNS and Routing Vulnerabilities Attacks

Domain name system (DNS) is a mechanism of recognizing Internet addresses. One can imagine the consequences if messages would be forwarded to the wrong IP address. The existing technology and system procedures have limited authentication capabilities, and a well-designed DNS attack can create havoc to the world network. Due to the lack of strong authentication within DNSs, the mechanisms controlling the flow of packages could be changed and therefore unauthorized information may be received and/or acted upon.

STARTING POINTS FOR PREPARATIONS

Awareness of the possibility of such attacks can lead to the preparation of a program of activities aimed at setting up effective defenses against potential threats. These fortifications generally fall into the following four categories:

- Physical defenses that control physical access to facilities
- System defenses that limit the capabilities of unauthorized changes to data stored and transmitted over a network
- Personnel defenses that limit the chances of inappropriate staff behavior
- Organizational defenses that create and implement an information security plan

Physical Defenses

Physical security as it applies to information security considers the activities undertaken, and the equipment installed to accomplish the following objectives:

- **Protection against unauthorized persons to penetrate the designated off-limit areas of the company premises:** This definition implies that there may be several classes of "unauthorized persons" and the company premises may have security zones with different access rights. Some areas, like the reception area, could be open to virtually anybody, while other areas are accessible only to a limited number of company employees.
- **Protection against the theft of company IT equipment, especially that containing sensitive information:** This protection extends to company equipment that may be physically outside the company's premises.
- **Protection against the physical destruction of company IT equipment:** This can include the protection against such acts as the planting of explosives within company premises. This also covers the protection measures against such events as fire, floods, and earthquakes.
- **Protection against unauthorized reading of information, regardless of its form (i.e., visual, acoustic, or analog signals):** Security measures have to prevent unauthorized persons from reading sensitive data from a computer screen, the interception of spoken messages, the tapping of telephone lines, or similar acts.

The security measures discussed here do not include security breaches such as the unauthorized system access to data through a broken password subsystem or the breaking of a cryptographic message. It also does not cover the breaches resulting from wrongly deployed mobile telecommunications systems, such as a mobile local area network.

System Defense Mechanisms

Firewalls

As part of the basic defense for intrusions within a system, firewalls provide basic barriers against penetrations. Firewalls tend to be a combination of hardware and software that acts as a partition between an internal network and the outside electronic world. Essentially, a firewall performs two primary functions. The first of these is hiding the IP address of the internal network from any connecting telecommunication networks that may wish to observe and/or connect to a system inside the firewall. This is like making all of the telephone numbers and mailing addresses of a business unlisted. In this way, an intruder must first know the destination IP address before proceeding to additional steps in an attack. The second function that a firewall performs is the control of packets through its communication ports in both directions. A port is the end point to a logical connection in a communication path, and as such, can be set to accept packets that are inbound, outbound, and/or both for a given port. For instance, if a system administrator wanted to prevent files from being transferred in an outbound direction, then ports 20 and 21 (i.e., used for File Transfer Protocol) would need to be configured to reflect these wishes among other additional ports (i.e., there are many ways of transferring files indirectly). Firewalls are commonly remotely accessed using a username and password from a specified IP address in order to configure and maintain them. This makes them susceptible to previously discussed attacks. Also, because many firewalls are not self-contained systems and therefore use a given system's operating or network operating system, any vulnerability that exists in the operating system provides a means for bypassing some of its protective mechanisms.

Virus Scanner

The name implies what the virus scanner does: search for all malicious software. Various scanners are available on the market. They operate on one or many principle likes these:

- Search for a given type of code, indicating existence of malicious software
- Search for unauthorized changes to the original software
- Detect unauthorized activities of a given system operating under given conditions

Due to the fact that everyday brings definitions of new malware, any virus scanner to operate properly must be updated frequently.

Vulnerabilities and Penetration Tools

This is a vast group of products which work as automated systems for collection end evaluation of information about properties of devices connected to the network. These devices, extremely useful for a security manager. must be used extremely carefully. Launching such a system without proper authority may result in official persecution. Such a case was reported during 2005 in the UK. A security expert noticed a strange occurrence regarding a charity Web site, to which he is a donator. As an interested party, he launched a vulnerability diagnostic tool and ended up facing several thousands of British pounds in penalties that were imposed by the court. There are now countries where even the possession of such software may lead to persecution, such as is the case in New Zealand.

Personnel Defenses

The importance of security issues relating to personnel policies has and continues to be a factor in the overall protection of organizational systems. These are mainly the security issues related to contractual agreements between companies and their employees, plus their implications. These include:

- Personnel screening prior to employment
- Application of the security policy and establishing confidentiality agreements
- Establishment and execution of a user training program in security
- Establishment and execution of a policy dealing with handling security incidents and malfunctions

Organizational Defenses

All the defense mechanisms outlined above must be implemented in an organized way. This means every organization should set up a plan on how to develop and implement security measures. An integral part of that procedure is formulating an information security policy—a document that would inform the staff what security measures are introduced and what is expected staff behavior. We would also like to emphasize that when dealing with cyber terrorist and cyber warfare attacks, the most effective mode of operation is the system approach, when all major decisions are done from the point of overall advantage to the whole of an organization.

PLANNING SECURITY SYSTEMS, OVERALL PRINCIPLES

To protect installations against possible attacks, including terrorist attacks, we must define all the possible threats, estimate the potential losses resulting from the materialization of these threats, design a line of defense, and implement it.

Cyber terrorism and information warfare are becoming new and important threats against information technology resources and must be a part of the overall planning, design, and implementation process aimed at providing overall protection. The most significant part of building an overall protection plan is founded in risk management analysis. It is feasible to secure all assets from all parties given highly restrictive access and unlimited resources. However, the real world must embrace a set of priorities that has a rational foundation to deciding priorities and any subsequent decisions based on that rationale.

This process is derived from a basic understanding that is easiest to explain by asking some simple questions such as:
- How important is it that our operations not be disrupted?
- How much is our proprietary and personal information worth to us and others?
- What will it cost to replace our systems and information?
- What are the consequences of not protecting our systems?
- How much are we willing to spend to protect our assets?

The reality is that it is nearly impossible to fully assess the business loss in value resulting from information being destroyed or made public. This is due to two reasons:

1. It is hard to associate value to an event which may not happen and has never happened before. Imagine a case where a company's marketing plan was stolen. This is a first occurrence, and as such, who can predict the financial consequences of such a theft even though there will likely be far-reaching consequences?
2. The intent of the act can greatly impact the loss-in-value factor. At the beginning of the 1990 Gulf War, a laptop containing detailed information on the Allied Forces' plans for the liberation of Kuwait was stolen. Fortunately, the information on the machine did not reach the Iraqi government. One can imagine the possible costs of changing battle plans or human losses resulting from the Iraqi military acquiring these plans.

All of the above leads us to a conclusion that prior to launching the development of any security program, a thorough information technology risk analysis must be performed. It should be performed to justify the implementation of controls; provide assurance against unacceptable risk; assess compliance with regulations, laws, and corporate policy; and balance the controls of the risks. The results of the risk analysis are then used to develop and implement organizational security programs, including issues related to countering cyber terrorist and cyber warfare threats.

CONCLUSION

The end of the 20th century and the beginning years of the next century have brought a rising wave of terrorist attacks. These attacks are influencing the IT domain, and the most probable attacks now are collateral effects (i.e., destruction of a building housing the organization's HQ resulting in the destruction of its IT facilities). Up until now, we have not witnessed any spectacular, worldwide cyber terrorist attacks, but the probability of such attacks continues to be on the rise. This real threat is forcing us to find answers to obvious questions:

- "To what extent is my installation vulnerable to cyber warfare and cyber terrorist attacks?"
- "What do I need to do to protect my systems from this growing threat?"

These are unknown territories. Finding the answers to these questions may be done by following the line of thoughts of terrorists and examining their connections between traditional terrorist attacks and cyberspace.

The threat of cyber terrorism and cyber warfare still may not change the procedures of a typical risk analysis, nor may it result in introducing new security controls. However, these threats have brought a new dimension to classical risk analysis and have elevated some issues related to information security that were not very popular in the past.

Traditional risk assessment analysis examines the results of possible activities carried out mainly by individuals driven by curiosity, a lust for wealth, and/or individuals having a grudge against a given organization. Cyber terrorists add a new dimension to this process. We must predict the foundational nature of their actions and setup a plan to deal with it.

In this chapter, among the other items brought forward, we have outlined the possible behavioral drivers of the attackers. We think that the predominant wish of a terrorist of any type is to create fear and harm among the widest possible spectrum of society. We also suggested some of the more important activities that should be undertaken to reduce the possibility of cyber-based attacks and/or their resulting consequences. We have identified the most probable types of cyber warrior and cyber terrorist attacks, and hope that this will serve as a foundation to understand and effectively take action in a prevention, detection, and responsive manner.

REFERENCES

CAIDA. (2005). *Analysis of Code Red.* Retrieved from http://www.caida.org/analysis/security/code-red/

Center for Strategic and International Studies. (1998). Cybercrime, cyberterrorism, cyberwarfare, averting electronic Waterloo.

CERT Coordination Center. (2000, December). Results of the Security in ActiveX Workshop. Software Engineering Institute, Carnegie Mellon University, USA.

Colin, B. (1996). The future of cyberterrorism. *Proceedings of the 11th Annual International Symposium on Criminal Justice Issues*, Chicago.

Computer Security Institute. (2006). *2005 CSI / FBI computer crime and security survey.* Retrieved from http://i.cmpnet.com/gocsi/db_area/pdfs/fbi/FBI2006.pdf

Convention on Cybercrime, Council of Europe. (2001). Proceedings of Convention.

Denning, D. (1999). *Information warfare and security.* Boston: Addison-Wesley.

Elmusharaf, M. (2004). *Cyber terrorism: The new kind of terrorism computer.* Retrieved April 8, 2004, from http://www.crime-research.org/articles/Cyber_Terrorism_new_kind_Terrorism

Journal of Information Warfare, Australia, since 2001.

Molander, R., Riddle, A., & Wilson, P. (1996). *Strategic information warfare, a new face of war*. Rand National Defense Institute.

National Security Telecommunications and Information Systems. (n.d.). Security policy no. 11. Retrieved from http://niap.nist.gov and http://nistissc.gov

President's Critical Infrastructure Protection Board. (2002). National strategy to secure cyberspace.

Schneier, B. (2006). *Counterpane Newsletter,* (April).

ADDITIONAL READINGS

Alexander, D., Arbaugh, W., Keromytis, A., & Smith, J. (1998). Safety and security of programmable network infrastructures. *IEEE Communications Magazine*, (October).

Alvey, J. (2002). Digital terrorism: Hole in the firewall? *Public Utilities Fortnightly*, (March).

Anagnostakis et al. (2002, April). Efficient packet monitoring for network management. *Proceedings of the IEEE/ IFIP Network Operations and Management Symposium.*

Bih, J. (2003). Internet snooping. *IEEE Potentials*, (October/November).

Burge et al. (1997, April). Fraud detection and management in mobile telecommunications networks. Proceedings of the European Conference on Security and Detection.

Chakrabarti, A., & Manimaran, G. (2002). Internet infrastructure security: A taxonomy. *IEEE Network*, (November/December).

Colarik, A. (2003, November). *A secure patch management authority*. PhD Thesis, University of Auckland, New Zealand.

Crocker, S. (2004). Protecting the Internet from distributed denial-of-service attacks: A proposal. *Proceedings of the IEEE, 92*(9).

Dotti, P., & Rees, O. (1999, June). Protecting the hosted application server. *Proceedings of the IEEE 8ᵗʰ International Workshops on Enabling Technologies: Infrastructure for Collaborative Enterprises.*

Edwards, M. (2001, March). *FBI finds secret U.S. source code on computer in Sweden*. InstantDoc #20178.

Ernst & Young. (2004). Global information security survey 2004. Assurance and Advisory Business Services.

Harper, H. (2002). Cyberterror: A fact of life. *Industrial Distribution*, (January).

Haugh, R. (2003). Cyber terror. *Hospitals & Health Networks*, (June).

Institute for Information Infrastructure Protection. (2003, January). *Cyber security research and development agenda.*

Joint Inquiry of the Senate Select Committee on Intelligence and the House Permanent Select Committee. (2002, October). Statement for the record by Lieutenant General Michael V. Hayden, USAF, Director, National Security Agency.

Karrasand, M. (2003, June). Separating trojan horses, viruses, and worms: A proposed taxonomy of software weapons. *Proceedings of the 2003 IEEE Workshop on Information Assurance.*

Langnau, L. (2003). Cyberterroism: Threat or hype? *Material Handling Management*, (May).

Levack, K. (2003). The E-Government Act of 2002: A stab at cyber security. *EContent*, (March).

Magoni, D. (2003). Tearing down the Internet. *IEEE Journal on Selected Areas in Communications, 21*(6).

Mavrakis, N. (2003). Vulnerabilities of ISPs. *IEEE Potentials*, (October/November).

Maxion, R., & Townsend, T. (2004). Masquerade detection augmented with error analysis. *IEEE Transactions on Reliability, 53*(1).

McCollum, T. (2003). Report targets U.S. cyber-security. *The Internal Auditor*, (February).

Mearian, L. (2002). Wall Street seeks cyberterror defenses. *Computerworld*, (March).

Misra, S. (2003). High-tech terror. *The American City & Country*, (June).

Mukhtar, M. (2004). *Cyber terrorism: The new kind of terrorism*. Retrieved April 8, 2004, from http://www.crime-research.org/articles/Cyber_Terrorism_new_kind_Terrorism

Nasir, B. (1994, October). Components, modeling and robustness of network management for telecommunications systems. *Proceedings of the IEE Colloquium on Network Management for Personal and Mobile Telecommunications Systems.*

NATO Parliamentary Assembly, Science and Technology Sub-Committee on the Proliferation of Military Technology. (n.d.). Draft interim report: Technology and terrorism. Retrieved from http://www.nato-pa.int/publications/comrep/2001/au-121-e.html#3

NATO Parliamentary Assembly, Science and Technology Sub-Committee on the Proliferation of Military Technology. (n.d.). *Draft report: Technology and terrorism: A post-September 11 assessment.* Retrieved from http://www.nato-pa.int/publications/comrep/2002/av-118-e.html#3

Ollmann, G. (2004, September). *The phishing guide: Understanding & preventing phishing attacks*. NGSSoftware Insight Security Research.

Pescape, A., & Ventre, G. (2004, April). Experimental analysis of attacks against routing network infrastructures. *Proceedings of the 2004 IEEE International Conference on Performance, Computing, and Communications.*

President's Critical Infrastructure Protection Board. (2002, September). *The national strategy to secure cyberspace.*

Reed, M., Syverson, P., & Goldschlag, D. (1998). Anonymous connections and onion routing. *IEEE Journal on Selected Areas in Communications, 16*(4).

Rennhard, M., Rafaeli, S., Mathy, L., Plattner, B., & Hutchinson, D. (2002, June). Analysis of an anonymity network for Web browsing. *Proceedings of the 11ᵗʰ IEEE International Workshops on Enabling Technologies: Infrastructures for Collaborative Enterprises.*

Rietscha, E. (2003, September). *Buffer overrun vulnerabilities in Microsoft programs: Do you really need to apply all of the security patches?* SANS Institute.

Sabeel, A., Rajeev, S., & Chandrashekar, H. (2002/2003). Packet sniffing: A brief introduction. *IEEE Potentials*, (December/January).

Shimeall, T., Williams, P., & Dunlevy, C. (2001/2002). Countering cyber war. *NATO Review*, (Winter).

Solomon, H. (2003). War in Iraq could cripple Internet, IDC. *Computing Canada*, (January).

Spencer, V. (2002). Cyber terrorism: Mass destruction or mass disruption? *Canadian Underwriter*, (February).

Thibodeau, P. (2001). War against terrorism raises IT security stakes. *Computerworld*, (September).

Thuraisingham, B. (2000). Understanding data mining and applying it to command, control, communications and intelligence environments. *Proceedings of COMPSAC 2000.*

U.S. Commission on National Security. (1999, September). *New world coming: American security in the 21st century: Major themes and implications.*

U.S. General Accounting Office. (2003, January). *Critical infrastructure protection: Efforts of the financial services sector to address cyber threats.*

Vatis, M. (2001, September 22). *Cyber attacks during the war on terrorism: A predictive analysis.* Institute for Security Technology Studies at Dartmouth College.

Verton, D. (2002). Experts predict major cyberattack coming. *Computerworld*, (July).

Voyiatzis, A., & Serpanos, D. (2003). Pulse: A class of super-worms against network infrastructure. *Proceedings of the 23rd International Conference on Distributed Computer Systems Workshops.*

Wan, K., & Chang, R. (2002). Engineering of a global defense infrastructure for DDOS attacks. *Proceedings of the 10th IEEE International Conference on Networks.*

Weaver, N., Paxson, V., Staniford, S., & Cunningham, R. (2003). A taxonomy of computer worms. *Proceedings of the 2003 ACM Workshop on Rapid Malcode.*

Wheatman, V., & Leskela, L. (2001, August). *The myths and realities of 'cybersecurity' in China.* Gartner.

Section I
Terms, Concepts, and Definitions

In the introductory chapter, we defined cyber terrorism and cyber warfare. We have also presented a brief history of this phenomenon, as well as some of the major issues related to handling cyber attacks.

Cyber terrorism and cyber warfare have existed for over 10 years. In this relatively short period of time, it has undergone a significant metamorphosis. These changes resulted from progress in information technology, developments in the regional and global politics, as well as changes to moral and ethical principles of contemporary society.

These changes are the subject of interest to many researchers and practitioners alike. They continue to examine these trends, reports on them, set up taxonomies, design tools for further investigations and formulate a prognosis response. It is these and similar topics that form the main part of this chapter.

Cryptography, steganography and other technologies are major contributors to carrying out cyber warfare and cyber terrorist activities. Knowledge of these techniques and the methods of battling them is an essential part in formulating a strategy against these activities. As this book is a review of many of the issues related to cyber warfare and cyber terrorism, for the convenience of our readers, we have included in this chapter to provide a brief review of these techniques.

Therefore, in this section the following opinions and views are presented:

Chapter I
Cyber Terrorism Attacks

Kevin Curran
University of Ulster, UK

Kevin Concannon
University of Ulster, UK

Sean McKeever
University of Ulster, UK

ABSTRACT

Cyber terrorism is the premeditated, politically motivated attacks against information, computer systems, computer programs, and data which result in violence against non-combatant targets by sub-national groups or clandestine agents. The possibilities created for cyber terrorism by the use of technology via the internet are vast. Government computer networks, financial networks, power plants, etc are all possible targets as terrorism may identify these as the most appropriate features to corrupt or disarm in order to cause havoc. Manipulation of systems via software with secret "back doors", theft of classified files, erasing data, re-writing web pages, introducing viruses, etc are just a few examples of how terrorism can penetrate secure systems. This chapter provides a brief overview of previous cyber terrorism attacks and government responses.

INTRODUCTION

Terrorism can be defined as "The unlawful use or threatened use of force or violence by a person or an organized group against people or property with the intention of intimidating or coercing societies or governments, often for ideological or political reasons" (Denning, 2000, pp. 54-55). To date there has been no serious act of cyber terrorism, but computer networks have been attacked in recent conflicts in Kosovo and the Middle East. As terrorists have a limited amount of funds, cyber attacks are more tempting as they would require less people and less resources (meaning less funds). Another advantage of cyber attacks is that it enables the terrorist to remain unknown, as they could be far away from the actual place where the terrorism is being carried out. As terrorists normally set up camp in a country with a weak government, the cyber terrorist could set up anywhere and remain anonymous (Oba, 2004). A combination of both physical terrorism and cyber terrorism is thought to be the most effective use of cyber terrorism. For example, disrupting emergency services in which the emergency was created by physical terrorism would be a very effective way to combine both. The possibilities created for cyber terrorism by the use of technology via the Internet are vast. Government computer networks, financial networks, power plants, and so forth, are all possible targets as terrorists may identify these as the most appropriate features to corrupt or disarm in order to cause the most havoc. Manipulation of systems via software with secret "back doors," theft of classified files, erasing data, rewriting Web pages, introducing viruses, and so forth, are just a few examples of how terrorism can penetrate secure systems. Terrorist attacks made possible by the use of computer technology could also be demonstrated via air traffic control hijacking systems, or corrupting power grids from a remote destination (Gordon & Loeb, 2005).

Terrorist groups are increasingly using new information technology (IT) and the Internet to formulate plans, raise funds, spread propaganda, and communicate securely. In his statement on the worldwide threat in the year 2000, Director of Central Intelligence, George Tenet testified that terrorist groups, "including Hezbollah, HAMAS, the Abu Nidal organization, and Bin Laden's al Qa'ida organization were using computerised files, e-mail, and encryption to support their operations." Convicted terrorist Ramzi Yousef, the mastermind of the World Trade Center bombing, stored detailed plans to destroy U.S. airliners on encrypted files on his laptop computer (Kosloff, Moore, Keller, Manes, & Shenoi, 2002, p. 22).

Terrorist organizations also use the Internet to target their audiences without depending on overt mechanisms such as radio, television, or the press. Web sites are presented as a way of highlighting injustices and seeking support for political prisoners who are oppressed or incarcerated. A typical site will not reveal any information about violent activities and will usually claim that they have been left with no choice but to turn to violence. They claim they are persecuted, their leader's subject to assassination attempts and their supporters massacred. They use this tactic to give the impression they are weak, and they portrait themselves as the underdog (Berinato, 2002). This public relations exercise is a very easy way of recruiting supporters and members. Alongside the propaganda aspect terrorists often present Web sites with information on how to build chemical and explosive weapons. This allows them to identify frequent users who may be sympathetic to their cause and therefore it is a cost effective recruitment method. It also enables individuals who are acting on their own to engage in terrorist activity. In 1999, a terrorist called David Copeland killed 3 people and injured 139 in London. This was done through nail bombs planted in three different locations. At his trial it was revealed the he used the *Terrorist Handbook* (Forest, 2005) and *How to Make Bombs* (Bombs, 2004) which were simply downloaded from the Internet.

CYBER TERRORIST ATTACKS

Terrorists use cyber space to cause disruption. Terrorists fight against governments for their cause, and they use every means possible to get what they want. Cyber attacks come in two forms; one against data, the other, control systems (Lemos, 2002). Theft and corruption of data leads to services being sabotaged and this is the most common form of Internet and computer attack. Attacks which focus on control systems are used to disable or manipulate physical infrastructure. For example, the provision of electrical networks, railroads, or water supplies could be infiltrated to have wide negative impacts on particular geographical areas. This is done by using the Internet to send data or by penetrating security systems. These weak spots in the system were highlighted by an incident in Australia in March 2000 where a disgruntled employee (who failed to secure full-time employment) used the Internet to release 1 million litres of raw sewage into the river and coastal waters in Queensland (Lemos, 2002).

Actually, it took him a total of 44 failed attempts to breach the system and his 45th attempt was successful. The first 44 were not detected. Following the attacks on September 11, auditors for public security were concerned that critical infrastructure is owned by primarily private companies, which are not always geared to high security practices (Lemos, 2002).

In 1998, a terrorist guerrilla organization flooded Sri Lankan embassies with 800 e-mails a day for a two-week period. The messages simply read "We are the Internet Black Tigers and we're doing this to interrupt your communications." Intelligence departments characterized it as the first known attack by terrorists against a country's computer systems. Internet saboteurs defaced the Home Page of, and stole e-mail from, India's Bhabha Atomic Research Center in the summer of 1998. The three anonymous saboteurs claimed in an Internet interview to have been protesting recent Indian nuclear blasts (Briere, 2005). In July 1997, the leader of a Chinese hacker group claimed to have temporarily disabled a Chinese satellite and announced he was forming a new global cracker organization to protest and disrupt Western investment in China.

In September 1998, on the eve of Sweden's general election, saboteurs defaced the Web site of Sweden's right-wing moderates political party and created links to the home pages of the left-wing party and a pornography site. That same month, other saboteurs rewrote the home page of a Mexican government Internet site to protest what they said were instances of government corruption and censorship. Analysts have referred to these examples of cyber crime as low-level information warfare (Berinato, 2002). Some countries such as the U.S. and Australia have recommended setting up a cyber space network operations center which will include Internet service providers and computer hardware and software developers. Their task is to develop secure technology, such as intelligence analysis software, which will be capable of sifting through and analysing existing data, both public and private, in order to uncover suspicious activity (Simons & Spafford, 2003).

GOVERNMENTAL RESPONSES TO CYBER TERRORISM

The European Commission has pursued a provision requiring all European Union members to make "attacks through interference with an information system" punishable as a terrorist offense if it is aimed at "seriously altering or destroying the political, economic, or social structures." France has expanded police powers to search private property without a warrant. Spain now limits the activities of any organization directly or tangentially associated with ETA—the armed Basque Homeland and Freedom group (similar to UK legislation). The European Council has taken steps to establish a Europe-wide arrest warrant and a common definition of "terrorist crime." Germany's government has loosened restrictions on phone tapping and the monitoring of e-mail and bank records and freed up once proscribed communication between the police and the secret services. In June 2002, the UK attempted to introduce regulations under the pretext of antiterrorism that would have mandated almost all local and national government agencies to gain access without warrant to communications traffic data (Kamien, 2006).

Australia introduced a terrorist law to intercept e-mail (giving powers to the nation's chief domestic spy agency, the Australian Security Intelligence Organization), creating an offense related to preparing for or planning terrorist acts, and will allow terrorist property to be frozen and seized. New Zealand commenced similar legislation in keeping with the bilateral legal harmonization agreements of the two countries. India also passed its Prevention of Terrorism Ordinance allowing authorities to detain suspects without trial, impose capital punishment in some cases, conduct wiretapping, and seize cash and property from terrorist suspects—despite concerns it would be used to suppress political opponents (Taylor, Krings, & Alves-Foss, 2002).

RISKS OF TOTAL SURVEILLANCE

There are those however who oppose some of the counter terrorism programs put in place by our western governments. One such lobby group is the U.S. Public Policy committee of ACM (USACM) who are concerned that the proposed Total Information Awareness (TIA) program, sponsored by the Defense Advanced Research Projects Agency, will fail to achieve its stated goal of "countering terrorism through prevention." They also believe that the vast amount of information and misinformation collected may be misused to the detriment of the public (Simons & Spafford, 2003). They recommend a rigorous, independent review of TIA which should include an examination of the technical feasibility and practical reality of this vast database surveillance system. They claim that the databases proposed by TIA would increase the risk of identity theft by providing a wealth of personal information to anyone accessing the databases, including terrorists masquerading as others. Recent compromises involving about 500,000 military-relevant medical files and 30,000 credit histories are harbingers of what may be in store. They also point out that the secrecy inherent in TIA implies that citizens could not verify that the information about them is accurate and shielded from misuse. Worse yet would be the resulting lack of protection against harassment or blackmail by individuals who have inappropriately obtained access to an individual's information, or by government agencies that misuse their authority. As the entire population would be subjected to TIA surveillance, even a very small percentage of false positives would result in a large number of law-abiding Americans being mistakenly identified as suspects (Yen, 2003).

The Federal Bureau of Investigation (FBI) runs an Internet surveillance tool called Carnivore, which was changed to DCS1000 to make it more innocuous sounding, that allows American law enforcement agents to intercept and collect e-mail and other electronic communications authorized by a court order. Due to the nature of packet networks it is a lot harder to identify particular target information compared with traditional telephone systems. FBI personnel only receive and see the specified communications addressing information associated with a particular criminal subject's service, concerned which a particular court order that has been authorized. Recently, according to an FBI press release, the FBI uncovered a plot to break into National Guard armoires and to steal the armaments and explosives necessary to simultaneously destroy multiple power transmission facilities in the southern United States.

After introducing a cooperating witness into the inner circle of this domestic terrorist group, it became clear that many of the communications of the group were occurring via e-mail. As the investigation closed, computer evidence disclosed that the group was downloading information about Ricin, the third most deadly toxin in the world. Without the fortunate ability to place a person in this group, the need and technological capability to intercept their e-mail communications' content and addressing information would have been imperative, if the FBI were to be able to detect and prevent these acts and successfully prosecute.

With all these potential disastrous scenarios it is strange that anyone could deny that there is a need for monitoring. The problem may be that the line between monitoring and invasion of privacy becomes very blurred. It is easy to understand why people feel uneasy about Carnivore. The installation of Carnivore at an ISP facility is carried out only by FBI technicians and all the traffic on the ISP goes through the surveillance system which can leave it open to unauthorized surveillance (Hughes, 2002). The system is a risk however as any hacker with the correct password can gain access to sensitive information on the public. Compared with traditional wire tapping systems where the provider of the service gathers the information that is required by a court order and hands it over to the agency that requests it, the FBI system can bypass this. This leaves them open to the claim that they break one of the American amendments that prohibits law enforcement agencies from gathering more information than is required although the bureau says that future systems will have audit trails and features to guard against abuse (Verton, 2003).

FUTURE TRENDS

It can be said that our entertainment industry has popularized the notion of an electronic doomsday scenario in which terrorist groups penetrate critical nodes of the Internet or government and are able to launch nuclear weapons, crash the communications system, cause mayhem on the railways or in the air, or bring the financial sector to a catastrophic halt however it is difficult to erase such a fear (Berinato, 2002).

Dancho Danchev in his *Mindstreams of Information Security* blog (Danchev, 2005) mentions a scenario related to U.S. RFID passports, namely a bomb which could automatically detonate, given a certain number of "broadcasted," terms such as U.S. citizens in a specific location.

Security expert Rob Rosenberger believes that a realistic common scenario may simply be cyber terrorist attacks that destroy critical data such as Parasites—tiny computer programs that live in databases and slowly corrupt the data and its backup which could wreck a crucial database like Social Security (Gavrilenko, 2004; McClure, Scambray, & Jurtz, 2003). Terrorists could also penetrate a hospital database, causing fatal medical errors when a patient takes a prescription drug. "If you want to raise hell on airlines, you hack the reservation system," says Schneier. "If you want to cyberterrorize airlines, you hack the weights and measures computers that control planes' fuel and payload measurements" (Berinato, 2002, p. 2).

CONCLUSION

Cyber terrorists are creating increasingly clever methods and tools to attack computer systems and governments in order to get their political views across. Issues of national and worldwide safety are at risk here. The reason this risk exists is due to the fact that the Internet offers little or no regulation, potentially huge audiences, anonymity of communication, and a fast flow of information. These four critical features require further research in order to combat cyber terrorism.

REFERENCES

Berinato, S. (2002, March). The truth about cyberterrorism. *CIO Magazine*.

Bombs. (2005). Retrieved from http://www.bluemud.org/article/11606

Briere, D. (2005). *Wireless network hacks and mods for dummies* (for Dummies S.). Hungry Minds, Inc.

Danchev, D. (2005, December 19). Cyberterrorism—don't stereotype and it's there! *Mind streams of information security knowledge blog*. Retrieved from http://ddanchev.blogspot.com/2005/12/cyberterrorism-dont-stereotype-and-its.html

Denning, D. (2000, May 23). Cyberterrorism. *Testimony before the Special Oversight Panel on Terrorism, Committee on Armed Services U.S. House of Representatives*, Georgetown University.

Forest, J. (2005). *The making of a terrorist: Recruitment, training and root causes*. Westport, CT: Praeger Publishers.

Gavrilenko, K. (2004) *WI-FOO: The secrets of wireless hacking*. Addison Wesley.

Gordon, L., & Loeb, M. (2005). *Managing aging cybersecurity resources: a cost-benefit analysis* (1st ed.). McGraw-Hill.

Hughes, B. (2002, November 21). A functional definition of critical infrastructure: making the problem manageable. *ACM Workshop on Scientific Aspects of Cyber Terrorism (SACT)*, Washington DC.

Kamien, D. (2006). *The McGraw-Hill homeland security handbook*. McGraw-Hill.

Kosloff, T., Moore, T., Keller, J., Manes, G., & Shenoi, S. (2002, November 21). SS7 messaging attacks on public telephone networks: Attack scenarios and detection. *ACM Workshop on Scientific Aspects of Cyber Terrorism (SACT)*, Washington DC.

Lemos, R. (2002, August 26). What are the real risks of cyberterrorism? *ZDNet*.

McClure, S., Scambray, J., & Jurtz, G. (2003). *Hacking exposed: network security secrets and solutions* (4th ed.). McGraw-Hill; Osborne Media.

Oba, T. (2004, April). *Cyberterrorism seen as future threat* (Computer Crime Research Centre Tech. Report). Retrieved from http://www.crime-research. org/news/2003/04/Mess0103.html

Simons, B., & Spafford, E. H. (2003, March). Inside Risks 153. *Communications of the ACM, 46*(3).

Taylor, C., Krings, A., & Alves-Foss, J. (2002, November 21). Risk analysis and probabilistic survivability assessment (RAPSA): An assessment approach for power substation hardening. *ACM Workshop on Scientific Aspects of Cyber Terrorism (SACT)*, Washington DC.

Verton, D. (2003). *Black ice: The invisible threat of cyber-terrorism* (1st ed.). McGraw-Hill; Osborne Media.

Yen, J. (2003, September). Emerging technologies for homeland security. *Communications of the ACM, 46*(9).

TERMS AND DEFINITIONS

Cyber Terrorism: Any premeditated, politically motivated attack against information and data which results in violence against non-combatant targets by sub-national groups or clandestine agents.

Denial-of-Service: A denial-of-service (DoS) attack is an incident in which a user or organization is deprived of the services of a resource they would normally expect to have. Typically, the loss of service is the inability of a particular network service, such as e-mail, to be available or the temporary loss of all network connectivity and services.

Hacker: Commonly used to refer to any individual who uses their knowledge of networks and computer systems to gain unauthorized access to computer systems.

Information Warfare: IW can be seen as societal-level conflict waged, in part, through the worldwide interconnected means of information and communication.

Security: Computer security is the effort to create a secure computing platform, designed so that agents can only perform actions that have been allowed. This involves specifying and implementing a security policy.

Virus: A self-replicating program that spreads by inserting copies of itself into other executable code or documents. In essence, a computer virus behaves in a way similar to a biological virus, which spreads by inserting itself into living cells.

Vulnerability: This refers to any flaw or weakness in the network defence that could be exploited to gain unauthorized access to, damage or otherwise affect the network.

Chapter II
Knowledge Management, Terrorism, and Cyber Terrorism

Gil Ariely
Interdisciplinary Center Herzliya, Israel

ABSTRACT

This chapter applies the conceptual framework of knowledge management (and vehicles familiar from that discipline) to analyze various aspects of knowledge as a resource for terrorist-organizations, and for confronting them, in the post-modern era. Terrorism is a societal phenomenon, closely integrated with changes in our knowledge society. Terrorist organizations became knowledge-centric, networked organizations, with a post-modern approach to organizational paradigms. Cyberspace is habitat for knowledge and information, and terrorists are knowledge-workers proficient in it. Cyber terrorism is the convergence of cyberspace and terrorism, and is closely entwined with "nonvirtual" terrorist activities and global terrorism. IT allows terrorists similar societal power-shift - from large organizations to small groups and individuals. The chapter reviews the changing nature of terrorism towards postmodern terrorism and towards "learning terrorist organizations" implementing knowledge, cyber terrorism and cyberplanning. Since it takes a network to beat a network, the chapter discusses knowledge and knowledge management (KM) in counterterrorism. Through 'NetWar,' conducted also in cyberspace (not necessarily aimed at the IT systems it uses as a platform—but rather at human lives), implementing familiar vehicles from the KM toolkit such as social network analysis (SNA), to KM in intelligence and KM in low intensity conflicts. Knowledge management proves salient both for terrorism and for countering it in a knowledge society.

INTRODUCTION

Terrorist organizations are going through fundamental changes that other organizations went through in the postindustrial age, as Mcluhan (1960) and Toffler (1970)

predicted. Many of these changes are derived from implementation and management of knowledge and innovation, towards devastating action and effective knowledge centric networks. This understanding is the key to confront them, since terrorism is a societal phenomenon, and as such is closely integrated with changes in our knowledge society. Terrorists themselves are *knowledge-workers*, with the skills and abilities to leverage technology and information technology (IT) towards their goals.

Thus, *cyber terrorism* goes beyond the phenomenon of implementing IT to interfere with other IT systems (harmful as it may be) that is widely covered in other chapters in this book. Cyber terrorism is the convergence of cyberspace and terrorism, and is closely entwined with "nonvirtual" terrorist activities and global terrorism. Cyberspace and IT allows the terrorists the same advantages that the postindustrial (or postmodern) information era allows any knowledge-worker, and any global (or "virtual") organization. The societal power-shift from large organizations to small groups and individuals gives the terrorist the ability to maximize their ability to communicate, collect intelligence, learn, plan, and inflict terror through a network of operatives and cells. It expands the concept of cyber terrorism: cyberspace as an infrastructure to support terrorism that is nonrelated to IT.

BACKGROUND

Knowledge is acknowledged as a resource by terrorists in manifest. Stewart (1997, p. ix) in his seminal book on intellectual capital, refers to "Knowledge as a thermonuclear weapon." Undeniably it has become so for terrorists in the information age. As the events of September 11, 2001 have proven, more efficient than any bomb is the knowledge which incorporates skills (such as flight) and competences, original and creative thinking, some understanding of engineering, learning, and integration of many context insights (Ariely, 2003), such as effect on communication and economy (Hoffman, 2003a). The smartest bomb that fighting forces ever invented, is the human one—the only bomb that adapts to a changing situation (in addition to being "preprogrammed"), charging a psychological price too.

And it is Stewart (2001) who mentioned Al-Qaida's networked organizational structures and knowledge-based operations, vs. the difficulties of hierarchies in the large organizations confronting it. Knowledge and information are intangibles, for which IT and the cyber arena are natural habitat. Smuggling tangibles (like a bomb) is more difficult than sending instructions over the Web or posting a lesson online.

THE CHANGING NATURE OF TERRORISM

Postmodern Terrorism

Insight into this new nature of terrorism shows it is no longer an agent of change through "proxies" and secondary mediums (such as public opinion or decision makers), but rather a devastating instrument able to cause direct change, effecting 1,000s and even whole populations.

The most sophisticated weapons (WMDs) are implemented (through highly technical knowledge) vs. the most sophisticated usage of the most primitive weapons (Ganor, 2001b). Suicide bombers become precision weapons (WMDs), through knowledge and innovation.

The Economic Jihad

Furthermore, new forms and dimensions of global terrorism implement *economic knowledge* both for internal conduct and for economic effect in the globalization era.

Research work in the last few years analyzing Al-Qaida documents (Fighel & Kehati, 2002), shows understanding of economic knowledge implemented explicitly towards an "economic Jihad." The Al-Qaida author confirms:

that the attack against the Twin Towers (September 2001) and against the French oil tanker (October 2002) are part of the economic Jihad. These attacks are meant to signal to the West under US leadership, that this type of Jihad, if it continues, will bring upon the West an economic holocaust. (Fighel & Kehati, 2002)

In the words of the author on the bombing of the French oil tanker by the "Yemen lions" (translated): "Striking the Western culture a blow, aimed at one of the pillars of its foundation, meaning: oil—on which modern Western civilization is based ..." This determination is seen in recent Al-Qaida attacks on oil production installations.

Furthermore, *Hammas* published a written statement on its official Web site "calling on Muslims all over the world to wage an *economic Jihad* against the United States" (Fighel, 2003). Indeed economic education and knowledge is projected towards terror, particularly when the global economy itself is interpreted as yet another front, as well as a vehicle for internal conflict. Bruce Hoffman refers to Bin Laden as a terrorist CEO: "He has essentially applied the techniques of business administration and modern management, which he learned both at university and in his family's construction business, to the running of a transnational terrorist organization" (Hoffman, 2003a). But it is as impractical to try to locate terrorists in business schools as it can be to track and manage other critical knowledge (e.g., flight schools since 9/11).

The "Learning Terrorist Organization"

Terrorists themselves are knowledge-workers, enjoying the global Internet infrastructure for secure knowledge exchange independent of geographical location. This brought about the "evolution" in smuggling tangibles (such as explosives via sea) by Hizbulla from Lebanon, to smuggling tangible information media (e.g., "Knaana brothers" case in Israel, attempting to smuggle "how-to" manuals and terrorism guidebooks on memory chips hidden in electrical appliances) and to contemporary cyber terrorism online "knowledge-centers." *Hammas* can now openly give technical classes in preparing bombs over the Web, and significance of knowledge transfer and learning is apparent in Al-Qaida media found in Afghanistan. The persistent "cyber-learner" may even find voluminous WMD-related knowledge online. Terrorist organizations are by nature intuitive "learning organizations: (Ariely, 2003; Jackson et al., 2005).

Cyber Terrorism and Cyber Planning

The more sophisticated a nation's infrastructure—the more vulnerable it may become. Interdependencies of electrical power grids, accessible computerized systems and other "soft" targets, allow potential for terrorist intruders. "By relying on intricate networks and concentrating vital assets in small geographic clusters, advanced Western nations only amplify the destructive power of terrorists—and the psychological and financial damage they can inflict" (Homer-Dixon, 2002). Indeed cyber terrorism poses a threat not yet fulfilled (Shahar, 1997) despite some initial attempts.

Cyber terrorism may be used not only to inflict damage in itself, but in combination with conventional or nonconventional terrorism.

Had Shoko Asahara and the Aum Shinrikyo group been able to crack the Tokyo power system and stop the subways, trapping passengers on the trains, the number of casualties caused by their 1995 Sarin gas attack might have been significantly larger. (Noble, 1999)

The U.S. Central Intelligence Agency (CIA), working with the Federal Bureau of Investigation (FBI), the Department of Homeland Security (DHS), and the Pentagon, published in 2004 the first classified National Intelligence Estimate (NIE) on the threat of cyber terrorism against U.S. critical infrastructures (first requested in March 2000). Recently, Keith Lourdeau, deputy assistant director of the FBI's Cyber Division, said the FBI's assessment indicates that the cyber terrorist threat to the U.S. is "rapidly expanding," and predicted that "terrorist groups will either develop or hire hackers, particularly for the purpose of complementing large physical attacks with cyber attacks" (Verton, 2004).

Since much of the Internet infrastructure usage so far was for "cyber planning" Thomas (2003) refers to different applications of the Internet which could be used for terrorism:

... in warfare as well as in business, IT is the great equalizer. Its low financial barrier to entry relative to heavy industry allows even the poorest organizations an IT effectiveness equal (or nearly equal) to large corporations. (Noble, 1999)

This infrastructure is used for covert, anonymous communication, for intelligence and information gathering, and even for actual online classes and training (including how to conduct computer attacks). It is also used for propaganda and could eventually become a recruiting tool.

The War on Consciousness and Public Education

Terrorism, as the term implies, is aimed *to terrorize*. Hence it is first and foremost a war on consciousness. Since fear is of the unknown, knowledge manangement (KM) is crucial in reducing fear (thus crippling terrorism), through extensive knowledge transfer to the public. Such public education programs are invaluable as proven in Israel, where suicide bombers in buses, restaurants, and malls tested public resilience on a daily base (see the International Policy Institute for Counter Terrorism (ICT) education program, in schools and for first-responders). Since media coverage is inherent to terrorism, self-restraint and an educated media (including online) is important. Sites identified with Al-Qaida approach their potential audiences for building support and the other audiences for building fear. Implementing KM on the widest scale possible—we should do at least as well, building public resilience and winning the war on consciousness.

The bigger challenge for KM (and for the whole world) is involvement in education (knowledge transfer) on the other side, identifying, renouncing, and confronting online schools ("Madrassas") preaching for Jihad and martyrdom. Once more, since media coverage is inherent to terrorism, full exploitation of it (including the Internet) by terrorists shows competency in information warfare. This second audience for terrorist organizations is what they perceive as the backbone—supportive communities. Sites identified with Al-Qaida approach their potential audiences for building support and aiming towards eventual recruitment. Cyber terrorism is salient in the evolution of the war on consciousness and education. This is crucial as it thwarts the next generation of terrorism. For instance, the MEMRI Institute monitors militant Islamic groups that educate and preach Jihad and martyrdom in mosques, school systems, and in the media. Those scholars and schools, who praise death rather than life, create a foundation for future terrorism by nurturing and promoting other children to become future terrorists. Identifying such dangerous trends, bravely renouncing and confronting them, is the best investment. Indeed there are contemporary cases in the U.S., UK, and so forth, of such attempts—however lagging after cyber terrorism. Since, a global Jihad ("Holy war") preacher taken off-bench becomes immediately online.

However before discussing KM and counter terrorism, it should be mentioned that cyberspace is also used as a platform for terrorist "command & control" (Whine, 1999), even up to the level of recent real-time involvement in incidents in Iraq.

KNOWLEDGE, KNOWLEDGE MANAGEMENT, AND COUNTERTERRORISM

Knowledge is (and always was) a main resource for countering terrorism. Sharing and "managing" knowledge (not just information and not just intelligence) as a resource within the international counterterrorism (CT) communities is essential—as is depriving terrorists of that resource where possible. That has been a concern mainly where the knowledge was part of the weapon itself, like in the case of WMD-related knowledge. However, acknowledgement derived from our profound understanding of the role of knowledge in society brings further insights and operational possibilities, as knowledge may act in some cases as a WMD in itself.

It follows that organizational forms and theories, familiar to us from the postindustrial (or postmodern) corporate world, of networked or virtual organizations, are being adapted by terrorist organizations—and should be understood in that context. When the other side plays soccer, we as hierarchies continue playing American football, while these are two different ball games. The strategic lessons learned in the last decade in the industry should be projected onto postmodern CT. (i.e., keep the strategic planning, advantages and defense gear of one ball game, while playing another, in fact not seeking to rigidly define that ball game paradigm). In this new form of warfare—the "NetWar" (Arquilla, Ronfeldt, Rand Corporation, & National Defense Research Institute, 2001), it takes a network to beat a network.

NetWar and Social Network Analysis (SNA)

This new form of warfare, the "NetWar," is an "emerging mode of conflict in which the protagonists ... use network forms of organization, doctrine, strategy, and technology attuned to the information age" (Arquilla et al., 2001).

One of the tools implemented in it is a familiar one to the KM community from knowledge mapping—the *social network analysis*. It is the "mapping and measuring of relationship and flow between people, groups, organizations ... the nodes are the people while the links show relationships or flows ... [SNA provides] a visual and a mathematical analysis of complex human systems" (Krebs, 2002).

A step further in analyzing terrorist knowledge networks—and breaking them requires a different focus than using SNA to locate links and target them—a focus on the transfer of knowledge itself. Hence mapping the sensitive knowledge based on a combination of:

- **Core type** (e.g., nuclear related knowledge, biological, chemical, etc., but also other unique knowledge).
- **Knowledge manageability** (i.e., terrorist KM skills, IT skills, acknowledgment of knowledge as resource)

This allows targeting the transfer of knowledge itself (e.g., cases in Israel, attempting to smuggle digital manuals and terrorism guidebooks on memory chips hidden in electrical appliances).

Yet a revolutionary approach to the "Net War" and terrorist networks comes from innovative research by Dave Snowden, who introduced complexity theory into KM. Snowden (one of the originators of "Organic KM") rather than analytically going through SNA, proposes a dissimilar projection of complexity insights from KM to the field of counterterrorism. By understanding the nature of a network and the attractors that affect its behavior, we can either aim to detect weak signals or to intervene with the attractors, rather than specific nodes, which the effect of is difficult to predict and might be counterproductive (D. Snowden, personal communication, 2004).

Knowledge Management in Counterterrorism Intelligence

Knowledge management in CT intelligence is relevant both for implementation in analyzing the opponent (as SNA has shown), but it is of seminal value to the conduct of intelligence organizations countering terror as well. Better implementation of information is what transforms it to knowledge and action. Relevancy of information existing in the system at the required point is paramount as the analysis of 9/11 shows (records of some of the terrorists activity did exist but were not implemented).

The inherent tension between the basic principle in intelligence of "the need to know" (an intelligence culture cornerstone) vs. "the need to share" (a KM culture cornerstone) is a polemic focal point, requiring a fine balance (Nolte, 2000; Varon, 2000).

Indeed in intelligence work the IT support for CT is paramount since the voluminous data arriving through intelligence channels and sources (in particular SIGINT—Signal Intelligence) are endless. For it to become information, and then knowledge aimed at action—intelligent IT systems allow narrower focus for human intervention of the analyst. Further progress may allow automatic translation raising the resources limit.

However even the chief knowledge officer (CKO) of the NSA emphasizes that "Knowledge management is not about introducing information technology (IT) into an organization, contrary to much of the writing ..." although "there clearly has to be an underlying IT infrastructure to enable the capturing, transfer, and use of the information to help people create knowledge" (Brooks, 2000, p. 18).

It is also the very nature of terrorists that obliges shorter response time and hence to implement KM towards more efficient, short-cycle knowledge work. Terrorist organizations shift their positions and adapt quickly, as intuitive learning organizations, so that information and knowledge must be quickly implemented towards action. This brings us directly to the discussion of KM in low intensity conflicts (LIC)—since current global terrorism is highly involved in this common warfare.

Knowledge Management in Low Intensity Conflicts

No clear delineation exists between terrorism and LIC—due to the lack of an agreed upon definition of terrorism.

The statement, "One man's terrorist is another man's freedom fighter," has become not only a cliché, but also one of the most difficult obstacles in coping with terrorism. The matter of definition and conceptualization is usually a purely theoretical issue—a mechanism for scholars ... However, when dealing with terrorism and guerrilla warfare, implications of defining ... transcend the boundaries of theoretical discussions ... in the at-

tempt to coordinate international collaboration, based on the currently accepted rules of traditional warfare. (Ganor, 2001a)

So here we aim not to coerce such delineation (one the opponent does not impose) in our global era, of state sponsored terrorism and postmodern terrorism. Both organizations and individuals involved in situations of LIC are those later involved in clear acts of terrorism—by *any* civilized definition. This postmodern approach of the opponent views these as methods in a methodological array.

And indeed the military is deeply involved in the global war on terrorism mainly through various low intensity conflicts. Hence, further attention to LIC is due.

The learning curves and learning cycles (->Learning->Action->) (Baird & Henderson, 2001) of the hierarchical organizations that confront terrorism, and of the terrorist organizations, can be described as part of the asymmetric molding factors of the low intensity conflict in general; since the apparently "stronger," larger organizational side cannot implement its advantages—there is an asymmetric power shift, relating to learning too.

One can imagine two Sinus-waves, each accounting for the learning curve of each organization, where every change in the curve represents an event that involves learning, adaptation, and change, and when any learning on one side causes the other side to adopt its own learning curve accordingly (Nir, Or, Bareket, & Ariely, 2002).

By their nature, it is more difficult for complex organizational hierarchies to deal with fast, responding, smaller networked organizations, with a faster learning curve and immediate realization of it.

This is why the only weapon we can implement on the organizational level is learning how a networked, knowledge centered organization is built and what the patterns of behavior are, to imitate its strengths and exploit its weaknesses.

This is similar to the way we imitate or "benchmark" on the tactical level the advantages and principles of guerilla warfare to our forces, in order to implement them better than the guerilla or terrorist organization—but within a military organizational framework (i.e., special forces) (Gordon, 2002).

In the low intensity conflict, the learning cycles are short, and contrary to conventional war when the main learning is done before and after—in LIC that is a long process, of varying intensities—the learning must be conducted throughout fighting. The other side understands that and acts accordingly, thus creating a process of continuous improvement and a learning curve (Ariely, 2006).

FUTURE

Terrorism is increasingly becoming an international and multi-disciplinary activity, carried out by networks, rather than classic organizations. In order to counter such terrorism, security agencies must adapt themselves to operate at least as efficiently as do the terrorists themselves ... Just as the terrorists have formed networks, so must counter-terrorists learn to network between like-minded organizations. (Ganor, 2004)

Such an attempt is ICTAC (the International Counter-Terrorism Academic Community) a community of practice (CoP) combining research institutions from some 14 nations defined as "a Post-Modern Counter-Terrorism Measure vs. Post-Modern Terrorism."

"Communities of practice" and many other familiar KM vehicles should be implemented to counterterrorism on a global scale. Knowledge management is at the heart of the confrontation. Such global cooperation, which in the past was rather bi-lateral or narrow-sighted, must now confront ultimate devotion and passion in the opposite side—belief in belonging to something bigger than self (e.g., global Jihad). That passion will always be difficult to equate even by the best, working in counterterrorism. Knowledge management supports cultural issues in organizations (such as common language and values), which in terrorist organizations are inherent. The "toolkit" and insights taken from the domain of knowledge management,

emerge salient as a counterterrorism measure, whereas so far international KM was a neglected instrument (Benjamin, McNamara, & Simon, 2004).

CONCLUSION

Terrorism is a societal phenomenon, and as such is closely integrated with changes in our postindustrial society, namely:

- Structural changes towards networked, knowledge centric organizations
- The understanding (and implementation) of knowledge as a resource
- An intuitive "learning organization" culture in terrorist organizations
- Postmodern terrorism trends able of a direct change of reality

It takes a network to beat a network. Terrorist organizations became knowledge-centric, networked organizations, with a post-modern approach to organizational paradigms. They see no more a need to use "organizational ID cards" (Hoffman, 2003b). Now, "the mother of all knowledge management projects" was launched in the form of creating the "Department of Homeland Security" in the U.S., integrating some 22 agencies (Datz, 2002). Underscoring the critical role that KM plays in the effort, two of the four foundations of the strategy are information sharing and systems, and international cooperation (the other two are science and technology, and law).

Much of the "NetWar" is conducted in cyberspace, although it is not aimed at the IT systems that it uses as a platform but rather at human lives—through suicide attacks in New York, London, Madrid, Bali, Cairo, and Tel-Aviv. Thus we should not confine cyber terrorism to any classic paradigm, creating artificial borderlines that terrorists do not.

Terrorism as a societal phenomenon is here to stay and shadow our knowledge society. Waging decisive war on terror demands all resources and a vigilant view ahead. Knowledge Management is salient both for terrorism and for countering it in a knowledge society—it is a postmodern measure vs. postmodern terrorism.

REFERENCES

Ariely, G. (2003). Knowledge is the thermonuclear weapon for terrorists in the information age. In *ICT at the Interdisciplinary Center Herzlia.*

Ariely, G. (2006) Operational Knowledge Management in the Military. In Schwartz, D. G. (Ed.) *Encyclopedia of Knowledge Management.* Hershey: Idea Group Inc. pp. 713-720.

Arquilla, J., Ronfeldt, D. F., Rand Corporation, & National Defense Research Institute (U.S.). (2001). *Networks and netwars : The future of terror, crime, and militancy.* Santa Monica, CA: Rand.

Baird, L., & Henderson, J. C. (2001). *The knowledge engine : How to create fast cycles of knowledge-to-performance and performance-to-knowledge.* San Francisco: BK.

Benjamin, D., McNamara, T. E., & Simon, S. (2004). *The neglected instrument: Multilateral counterterrorism. Prosecuting terrorism: The global challenge.* Presented at the Center for Strategic and International Studies (CSIS), Florence, Italy.

Brooks, C. C. (2000). Knowledge management and the intelligence community. *Defense Intelligence Journal 9*(1), 1524.

Datz, T. (2002, December 1). Integrating America. *CIO Magazine.*

Fighel, J., & Kehati, Y. (2002). *Analysis of al-qaida documents.* ICT Website, ICT.

Fighel, J. (2003). *Hamas calls for "economic Jihad" against the US.* ICT Website, ICT.

Ganor, B. (2001a). *Defining terrorism: Is one man's terrorist another man's freedom fighter?* www.ict. org.il

Ganor, B. (2001b). *The world is not coming to an end, however ... .* ICT.

Ganor, B. (2004). The international counter-terrorism academic community. In *Proceedings of the ICTAC Inauguration Conference*, Athens, Greece. ICT.

Gordon, S. L. (2002). *Israel against terror—A national assessment.* Efi Meltzer.

Hoffman, B. (2003a). The leadership secrets of Osama bin Laden: The terrorist as CEO. *The Atlantic Monthly.*

Hoffman, B. (2003b). Modern terrorism trends: Re-evaluation after 11 September. In *Proceedings of the ICT'S 3rd International Conference on Post Modern Terrorism: Trends, Scenarios, and Future Threats*, Herzliya. ICT.

Homer-Dixon, T. (2002). The rise of complex terrorism. *Foreign Policy.*

Krebs, V. (2002). Mapping networks of terrorist cells. *Connections 24*(3), 4352.

Jackson, O. A., Baker, J. C., Cragin, K., Parachini, J., Trujillo, H. R. & Chalk, P. (2005) *Aptitude for destruction: Organizational learning in terrorist groups and its implications for combating terrorism.* RAND.

McLuhan, M. (1960). Effects of the improvements of communication media. *The Journal of Economic History 20*(4), 566575.

Nir, S., Or, S., Bareket, Y., & Ariely, G. (2002). Implications of characteristics of low intensity conflict on the issue of learning and operational knowledge management. In *Learning throughout fighting.* School of Command, IDF.

Noble, J. J. I. (1999). Cyberterrorism hype. *Jane's Intelligence Review.*

Nolte, W. M. (2000). Information control is dead. What's next? The knowledge management challenge for the intelligence community in the 21st century. *Defense Intelligence Journal 9*(1), 513.

Shahar, Y. (1997). *Information warfare.* Retrieved from www.ict.org.il

Stewart, T. A. (1997). *Intellectual capital: The new wealth of organizations.* New York: Doubleday/Currency.

Stewart, T. A. (2001). Six degrees of Mohamed Atta. *Business 2.0.*

Thomas, T. L. (2003). Al Qaeda and the Internet: The danger of "cyberplanning". *Parameters,* 11223.

Toffler, A. (1970). *Future shock.* New York: Random House.

Varon, E. (2000). The Langley files. *CIO Magazine.*

Verton, D. (2004). CIA to publish cyberterror intelligence estimate. *ComputerWeekly.com.*

Whine, M. (1999). *Cyberspace: A new medium for communication, command and control for extremists.* ICT.

TERMS AND DEFINITIONS

Counterterrorism (CT): Any and all measures and efforts to confront different layers and different phases of terrorism, through intelligence, military operations, public education, protection, and "hardening" of targets, and so forth. Although purely defensive in its ultimate goals of protecting innocents, successful CT must form an offensive and be aggressive in nature, in order to precede the terrorists.

Cyber Planning: "The digital coordination of an integrated plan stretching across geographical boundaries that may or may not result in bloodshed. It can include cyberterrorism as part of the overall plan" (Thomas, 2003). The Internet is widely being used as a "cyber planning" tool for terrorists. "It provides terrorists with anonymity, command and control resources, and a host of other measures to coordinate and integrate attack options."

Cyber Terrorism: The "intentional use or threat of use, without legally recognized authority, of violence, disruption, or interference against cyber systems, when it is likely that such use would result in death or injury of a person or persons, substantial damage to physical property, civil disorder, or significant economic harm" (from http://www.iwar.org.uk/cyberterror/).

Knowledge: Since "data" are any signals, and "information" is putting the data in-a-formation, which gains it meaning in order to inform; knowledge is information in a context. Thus, it is always dynamic, contextual, and difficult to "manage". Knowledge is commonly divided into tacit knowledge inherent in people (hence processes or people can be managed rather than knowledge directly), and "explicit" knowledge; that is more easily managed directly. This is a working definition for the sake of this chapter (not dealing in epistemology per se).

Knowledge Management (KM): Out of various definitions of KM, the APQC define knowledge management as "strategies and processes to create, identify, capture, and leverage vital skills, information, and knowledge to enable people to best accomplish the organization missions." (Brooks, 2000, p. 17)

Low Intensity Conflict (LIC): A military confrontation in which at least one side is either not a regular army (e.g., guerilla forces, insurgents) or not deployed in full scale. Hence it is usually characterized by asymmetric forces—with contradictious symmetry in the ability to implement force advantages, on a prolonged time-axis.

NetWar: An "emerging mode of conflict in which the protagonists…use network forms of organization, doctrine, strategy, and technology attuned to the information age" (Arquilla et al., 2001).

Postmodern Terrorism: Terrorism that transcends previous paradigms of organizational affiliation or hierarchy, and is able to affect directly the change of reality, rather than through proxies (like public opinion or policy makers).

Signal Intelligence (SIGINT): Quantifiably, most of the intelligence data comes from SIGINT sources. These may include electronic signatures (ELINT) or communications content analysis (COMINT). The field of SIGINT forms acute challenges for both for MIS and for knowledge management due to the vast amount of data accumulated daily and the need to "find the needle in a haystack."

Social Network Analysis (SNA): Drawing from social network theory, a social network analysis in CT allows mapping visually the invisible dynamics of a terrorist-networked community, obtained through their communications. This helps portray specific "node" individuals and clusters that deserve attention.

State Sponsored Terrorism: Terrorism that is either directly sponsored by, or builds on infrastructure supported in, a defined and recognized national entity.

Terrorism: "Terrorism is the intentional use of, or threat to use violence against civilians or against civilian targets, in order to attain political aims" (Ganor, 2001a).

Weapons of Mass Destruction (WMD): Weapons used by terrorist organizations that are aimed to inflict maximum casualties, in crowds or large number of civilians. Although in literature and media the term is used foremost to more sophisticated weapons (i.e., chemical, biological, or radioactive) in fact conventional weapons may become weapons of mass destruction through suicide bombers as precision weapons.

Chapter III
Ten Information Warfare Trends

Kenneth J. Knapp
United States Air Force Academy, USA

William R. Boulton
Auburn University, USA

ABSTRACT

This chapter discusses the rapid entry of information conflicts into civilian and commercial arenas by highlighting 10 trends in information warfare. The growing societal reliance on cyber technologies has increased exposure to dangerous sources of information warfare threats. Corporate leaders must be aware of the diversity of potential attacks, including from high-tech espionage, organized crime, perception battles, and attacks from ordinary hackers or groups sponsored by nation-states or business competitors. Based on a literature review conducted by the authors, we offer an information warfare framework that contains the ten trends to promote a greater understanding of the growing cyber threat facing the commercial environment.

INTRODUCTION

Commonly regarded as a military concern, information warfare is now a societal issue. While the bulk of the cyber war literature addresses the military dimension, information warfare has expanded into non-military areas (Cronin & Crawford, 1999; Hutchinson, 2002). After reviewing 16 years (from 1990 to 2005) of literature, this chapter identified ten important trends. While individually the trends are not surprising, we integrate the trends into a framework showing how information warfare has moved beyond the military dimension and into the commercial world as well. This expansion into the commercial world presents a growing threat to information managers who are responsible for protecting commercial information assets.

Given the high availability of Internet-based, low-cost cyber weapons that can target civilian information assets, there is a growing threat to the economic stability of modern societies that depend on today's commercial infrastructures. Because conventional military missions are often not available and do not traditionally include the defense of commercially operated infrastructures (Dearth, 1998), business managers should accept this responsibility and plan to defend themselves against growing cyber threats. The trends described in this chapter together provide an integrated framework that helps us understand the ways which information warfare is spreading into civilian and commercial arenas.

INFORMATION WARFARE IN CONTEXT

Information warfare is a relatively new field of concern and study. The late Dr. Thomas Rona reportedly coined the term *information warfare* in 1976. Since then, many definitions emphasized the military dimension. Libicki (1995) offered seven categories of information warfare that are replete with military terminology: command and control warfare, intelligence-base warfare, electronic warfare, psychological warfare, hacker warfare, economic information warfare, and cyber warfare. Webster's New World Dictionary defines *conflict* as (1) a fight or war and as (2) a sharp disagreement, and defines *warfare* as (1) the action

of waging war; armed conflict and as (2) a conflict or struggle of any kind. In this chapter, we use *conflict* and *warfare* interchangeably.

Today, we use the terms *information war* and *cyber war* to explore a range of conflict types covering political, economic, criminal, security, civilian, and military dimensions. Testifying before Congress in 1991, Winn Schwartau stated that poorly protected government and commercial computer systems were vulnerable to an "electronic Pearl Harbor" (Schwartau, 1998, p. 56). Others describe information warfare as the actions intended to protect, exploit, corrupt, deny, or destroy information or information resources in order to achieve a significant advantage, objective, or victory over an adversary (Alger, 1996). Cronin and Crawford (1999) proposed an information warfare framework that extends beyond military dimensions. They argue that information warfare will intensify, causing potentially serious social problems and creating novel challenges for the criminal justice system. Cronin and Crawford (1999) consider four spheres where information warfare may become commonplace: military, corporate-economic, community-social, and personal.

Table 1. Information warfare framework

Information Warfare Characteristic	1990	2005
1. Computer-related security incidents reported to CERT/CC	252 incidents	137,529 incidents (year 2003)
2. Entry barriers for cyber attackers	High barriers	Low barriers
3. Forms of cyber-weapons	Few forms, lower availability	Many forms, high availability
4. Nations with information warfare programs	Few nations	> 30 nations
5. Economic dependency on information infrastructures	Partial, growing dependency	Heavy dependency
6. Primary target in information conflicts	Both military & private targets	Increasingly private targets
7. Cyber technology use in perception management	Global TV, radio	Ubiquitous, global multi-media
8. Cyber technology use in corporate espionage	Less substantial	Substantial & increasing
9. Cyber technology use in organized crime	Less substantial	Substantial & increasing
10. Cyber technology use against individuals & small businesses	Less substantial	Substantial & increasing

INFORMATION WARFARE TRENDS

A review of the information warfare literature for major trends suggests that a paradigm shift has taken place. The framework of ten trends illustrated in Table 1 demonstrates that information warfare has moved beyond the military arena and into civilian contexts in a way consistent with the four spheres suggested by Cronin and Crawford (1999). The following paragraphs describe each of the ten trends in more detail:

1. **Computer-related security incidents are widespread:** Two highly referenced security incident measures come from the CERT/CC[1] and the annual CSI/FBI[2] survey. Based on CERT and CSI information: (1) security incidents are prevalent, (2) private institutions are the target of a large number of cyber attacks, and (3) many incidents receive no public acknowledgement. The number of incidents reported to the CERT/CC has risen from 6 in 1988 to 137,529 in 2003.

    While the security incident numbers appear large, these numbers may actually be under-reported. Respondents to the annual CSI/FBI survey indicate that more illegal and unauthorized cyber space activities occur than many corporations admit to their clients, stockholders, and business partners or report to law enforcement. For example, in 2005 only 20% of respondents reported incidents to law enforcement, primarily because of concerns with negative publicity (Gordon, Loeb, Lucyshyn, & Richardson, 2005).

2. **Entry barriers are low for cyber attackers:** Early generations of cyber weaponry (i.e., hacker tools) required technical knowledge for effective use. For instance, some hackers of the 1960s were students at MIT (*PCWorld*, 2001). In the 1970s, system hackers were profiled as highly motivated, bright people with technical knowledge who often worked in university or business computer centers (Parker, 1976). The hacker environment began changing in the early 1990s. Technical barriers began to fall as down-

loadable and graphic-interfaced tools became widely available.[3] A notorious incident occurred in the late 1990s. In an incident called Solar Sunrise, a group of teenage hackers, under the guidance of an eighteen-year-old mentor, gained access to numerous government computers including military bases. Solar Sunrise served as a warning that serious hacking capabilities were within the grasp of relative nonexperts. Testifying before Congress in 1999, CIA Director George Tenent stated that terrorists and others are recognizing that information warfare tools offer a low cost way to support their causes. Many of these tools are Windows-based, require minimal technical understanding, and are available as freeware. By 2002, one IS security professional maintained a database of over 6,000 hacker sites believed to contain only a part of the better hacker tools (Jones, Kovacich, & Luzwick, 2002).

3. **Dangerous forms of cyber weapons have emerged:** The first electronic message boards for hackers appeared around 1980. Once available, these boards allowed the rapid sharing of hacker tactics and software, including distributed denial-of-service (DDOS) tools. This software was responsible for the February 7, 2000 attack which effectively shut down major Internet sites such as Yahoo, eBay, Amazon, E*Trade, and CNN.

    Over the past 20 years, wide ranges of formidable cyber weapons have become more affordable and available from keystroke and eavesdropping devices to high-energy radio frequency (HERF) and electromagnetic pulse (EMP) generators. An attacker can build an e-bomb, designed to "fry" computer electronics with electromagnetic energy, for as little as $400 (Wilson, 2001). A demonstration of an e-bomb occurred in 1994. According to a London *Sunday Times* report, the Defense Research Agency believed HERF guns initially blacked out computers used by London's financial houses. Cyber terrorists then extorted millions of British pounds by threatening to totally knock out these financial computer systems (*Sunday Times*, 1996). As technology advances, we can expect smaller, affordable, and more dangerous cyber weapons to emerge.

4. **Many nations have information warfare capabilities:** In the early 1990s, few nations had organized information warfare capabilities. By 2001, more than 30 nations were believed to have information warfare programs, including India, China, Taiwan, Iran, Israel, France, Russia, and Brazil (Adams, 2001). In the 2003 CSI/FBI survey, 28% of respondents identified foreign governments as a likely source of attack against their systems.

China is an example of a nation that is improving its information warfare capabilities (Rhem, 2005). Some attribute the following 1995 statement to Chinese Major General Wang Pufeng:

In the near future, information warfare will control the form and future of war. We recognize this developmental trend of information warfare and see it as a driving force in the modernization of China's military and combat readiness. This trend will be highly critical to achieving victory in future wars. (Jones et al., 2002, p. 221)

While militaries are concerned with state-sponsored information warfare programs, commercial businesses should pay attention as well. With at least 30 countries suspected to be actively pursuing cyber weaponry, business and government executives alike should assess their vulnerabilities from a concerted attack.

5. **Increased economic dependency on information infrastructures:** Our society has evolved from an agrarian to an industrial to an information-based culture. References to the "digital economy" and "third wave" (Toffler, 1981) describe our growing dependence on information technology. With rising anxiety about potential disruptions (Meall, 1989), the U.S. government seriously addressed the deepening economic dependency on computers in the National Research Council's 1991 report, *Computers at Risk*. This

report expressed concern over a dependence on computers that "control power delivery, communications, aviation, and financial services. They are used to store vital information, from medical records to business plans to criminal records" (National Research Council, 1991, p. 7). This dependence has continued to the point where the 2003 U.S. *National Strategy to Secure Cyberspace* recognized that:

By 2003, our economy and national security became fully dependent upon IT and the information infrastructure. A network of networks directly supports the operation of all sectors of our economy—energy, transportation, finance and banking, information and telecommunications, public health, emergency services, water, medical, defense industrial base, food, agriculture, and postal and shipping. (p. 6)

6. **The private sector is the primary target:** Many high profile cyber attacks initially targeted the military. The 1986 *Cuckoo's Egg* incident had Clifford Stoll tracking German hackers who were scouring American military systems. In 1994, hackers infiltrated Griffis Air Force Base computers to launch attacks at other military, civilian, and government organizations.

With the growing economic dependency on IT, civilian infrastructures are increasingly the primary targets of cyber attacks. Headline-grabbing cyber attacks such as SQL Slammer, MyDoom, MSBlast, and Sasser have targeted widely used commercial products and Web sites. Slammer penetrated an Ohio nuclear power plant's computer network and disabled a safety monitoring system for nearly five hours. This attack prompted a congressional call for U.S. regulators to establish cyber security requirements for the 103 nuclear reactors operating in the U.S. (Poulsen, 2004).

Some scholars are concerned that an enemy of the United States will launch an information warfare attack against civilian and commercial firms and infrastructures (Strassmann, 2001). Seeking to avoid a direct military confrontation with U.S. forces, foreign attackers can shift their assaults to the private sector and infrastructure in a way that can make military retaliation very difficult. Mentioned earlier, electromagnetic pulse (EMP) represents a serious and emerging threat to societies that are heavily dependent on electronics. Unfortunately, many commercial systems have little or no protection against an EMP. If an aggressor nation detonates a nuclear bomb a few hundred miles above a target country, the EMP resulting from the blast could seriously damage commercial electronic components throughout a large geographic region (Chisholm, 2005). The private and public sectors now form the front line of twenty-first century warfare, and private citizens and commercial infrastructures are likely to be the primary target (Adams, 2001).

7. **Cyber technology is increasingly used in perception management:** Perception management has been called a "catchall phrase" for the actions aimed at influencing public opinion, or even entire cultures (Callamari & Reveron, 2003) and can cross the spectrum of corporate, political, civilian, cultural, and military realms. An emerging characteristic of modern perception management is the key role of technology in influencing public perception through new technologies that increase the speed of media reporting. The rise of global television and Internet technologies makes perception management a crucial dimension in many types of conflicts (Rattray, 2001).

    Perception wars target the court of public opinion. Consider the electronic perception battles during the Iraq War. In 2003, antiwar activists used the Internet to organize and promote marches and rallies. Embedded wartime reporters traveling with military units provided favorable news coverage for the campaign. The Qatar-based news agency Al-Jazeera transmitted images of dead and wounded Iraqi civilians to the Arab world. Al-Jazeera then launched an English Web site in part to counter what some believed to be U.S. military censorship of the American-based media. At one point, the Al-Jazeera Web site itself was hacked and taken off-line (Svensson, 2003). In 2004, images propagated on the Internet of prisoner abuse at Abu Ghraib influenced world opinion regarding American conduct. One report called the Internet dissemination of a video depicting terrorists beheading western hostages a new form of cyber terrorism that comes right into the home (Smith, 2004). The use of technology to manipulate public perceptions will assuredly persist.

8. **Cyber technology is increasingly used in corporate espionage:** While forms of espionage have been around for thousands of years, increased global competition, advances in IT, and the proliferation of tiny, embedded storage devices have added considerably to espionage dangers. For example, in March 2001, former U.S. Defense Secretary William Cohen identified the former director of French intelligence as publicly admitting that French intelligence secretly collects and forwards to French companies information about their competitors in the United States and elsewhere. He gave several examples of French espionage against American companies. One incident involved the theft of proprietary technical data from a U.S. computer manufacturer by French intelligence who then provided it to a French company (Cohen, 2001). While the average cost of a hacking attack or denial of service is roughly $150,000 to a company, according to the FBI, the average loss of a corporate espionage incident is much larger (Cohen, 2001).

    Espionage can occur in e-mail communications between employees of business competitors. One survey of 498 employees from a variety of organizations reported that 40% of respondents admitted to receiving confidential information about other companies via the Internet, a 356% increase since 1999 (Rosenoer, 2002). In

2004, the Justice Department announced that Operation Web Snare identified a wide range of criminal activity on the Internet including credit card fraud and corporate espionage. Investigators identified more than 150,000 victims with losses in excess of $215 million (Hansell, 2004). As organizations open their internal networks and make more company information available to employees and vendors, the occurrence of corporate espionage will likely increase.

9. **Cyber technology is increasingly used by organized crime:** The Internet explosion has introduced innovative forms of cyber crime. In May 2003, the U.S. Justice Department announced Operation E-Con to help root out some leading forms of online economic crime (Federal News Service, 2003). The Department claims that Internet fraud and other forms of online economic crime are among the fastest growing crimes. One type of crime involves Web site scams. For example, Australian scammers targeted Bank of America customers by implementing a look-alike Web site. Customers were sent scammed e-mails that linked to a fake site that requested an account name and password. This *phishing* scam compromised nearly 75 customer accounts (Legard, 2003).

    Other forms of global cyber crime include extortion schemes from gangs often based in Eastern Europe and Russia (O'Rourke, 2004). In one case, Russian cyber gangs targeted nine betting companies in a denial-of-service attack coinciding with a major sporting event. The Russian Interior Ministry that fights cyber crime broke up the extortion ring after two of the victim companies agreed to pay the gangs $40,000 each (The Australian, 2004). In another area, antivirus researchers are reporting large increases in organized virus and worm development activity. This underground criminal activity is powering what some call an underground economy specializing in identity theft and spam (Verton, 2004).

10. **Cyber technology is increasingly used against individuals and small businesses:** One threat facing individuals and small businesses is the use of spyware and adware. These monitoring programs can be legitimate computer applications that a user agrees to or can be from third-parties with nonlegal intentions (Stafford & Urbaczewski, 2004). An estimated 7,000 spyware programs reportedly exist and, according to Microsoft, are responsible for half of all PC crashes (Sipior, Ward, & Roselli, 2005). One study indicates that 91% of home PCs are infected by spyware (Richmond, 2004).

    Another growing problem is identity theft, which has been called a new form of cyber terrorism against individuals (Sterling, 2004) and often takes the form of a doppelgänger: in this case the pervasive taking of a victim's identity for criminal purposes (Neumann, 1998). This crime affects individuals and businesses alike. The Federal Trade Commission reported that 9.9 million Americans in 2003 were victims (Gerard, Hillison, & Pacini, 2004). The majority of cases result from cyber thieves using an individual's information to open new accounts with the average loss at $1,200 (Sterling, 2004). Falsified accounts have cost businesses $32.9 billion and consumers $3.8 billion (DeMarrais, 2003).

    In addition to vulnerabilities linked to identity theft, one recent study stressed that small businesses face many of the same vulnerabilities of the larger corporations. The leading perceived threats by small businesses include: internal threats (intentional and accidental), Trojans, hackers, viruses, password control, system vulnerabilities, spyware, and malware (Keller, Powell, Horstmann, Predmore, & Crawford, 2005). Likewise, many of the cyber warfare threats discussed in this chapter should concern smaller organizations as well (e.g., organized crime, espionage).

CONCLUSION

This chapter demonstrates the rapid entry of information conflicts into civilian and commercial arenas by highlighting ten trends of information warfare. Yet historically, information security concerns have not had a high priority with most managers. Many seemed willing to risk major losses by permitting their information systems to be either lightly protected or entirely open to attack. Yet, the growing reliance on information technology has increased exposure to diverse sources of cyber war threats. Corporate leaders must be aware of the diversity of attacks, including high-tech espionage, organized crime, perception battles, and attacks from ordinary hackers or groups sponsored by nation-states or business competitors. Our aim is that the information warfare framework presented in this chapter will promote a greater understanding of the growing cyber threat facing the commercial environment.

NOTE

Paper revised and abridged from Knapp & Boulton (2006), "Cyber Warfare Threatens Corporations: Expansion into Commercial Environments" *Information Systems Management, 23*(2).

Opinions, conclusions and recommendations expressed or implied within are solely those of the authors and do not necessarily represent the views of the USAF Academy, USAF, the DoD or any other U.S. government agency.

REFERENCES

Adams, J. (2001). Virtual defense. *Foreign Affairs, 80*(3), 98112.

Alger, J. I. (1996). *Introduction*. In W. Schwartau (Ed.), *Information warfare: Cyberterrorism: Protecting your personal security in the information age* (2nd ed., pp. 814). New York: Thunder's Mouth Press.

Australian, The. (2004, August 3). Officials break up Russian extortion ring. *The Australian,* p. C03.

Callamari, P., & Reveron, D. (2003). China's use of perception management. *International Journal of Intelligence & Counter Intelligence, 16*(1), 115.

Chisholm, P. (2005, December 19). *Protect our electronics against EMP attack*. Retrieved from www.csmonitor.com/2005/1219/p25s02-stct.html

Cohen, W. (2001, March 6). *Former Defense Secretary Cohen's remarks at the 2001 summit*. George Mason University. Retrieved August 10, 2005, from http://www.gmu.edu/departments/law/////techcenter/programs/summit/cohen's_2001_remarks.html

Cronin, B., & Crawford, H. (1999). Information warfare: Its applications in military and civilian contexts. *Information Society, 15*(4), 257264.

Dearth, D. H. (1998). Imperatives of information operations and information warfare. In A. D. Campen & D. H. Dearth (Eds.), *Cyberwar 2.0: Myths, mysteries, and reality*. Fairfax, VA: AFCEA International Press.

DeMarrais, K. (2003, September 4). Identity theft on the rise, FTC warns. *Knight Ridder Business News,* pp. 14.

Federal News Service. (2003, May 16). Press Conference with Attorney General John Ashcroft, FBI Director Robert Mueller, and FTC Chairman Timothy J. Muris. *Federal News Service Inc.*

Gerard, G., Hillison, W., & Pacini, C. (2004, May/June). What your firm should know about identity theft. *The Journal of Corporate Accounting & Finance,* 311.

Gordon, L. A., Loeb, M. P., Lucyshyn, W., & Richardson, R. (2005). *Tenth Annual, 2005 CSI/FBI Computer Crime and Security Survey*. San Francisco: Computer Security Institute (www.gocsi.com).

Hansell, S. (2004, August 26). U.S. tally in online-crime sweep: 150 charged. *New York Times*.

Hutchinson, W. (2002). Concepts in information warfare. *Logistics Information Management, 15*(5/6), 410413.

Jones, A., Kovacich, G. L., & Luzwick, P. G. (2002). *Global information warfare: How businesses, governments, and others achieve objectives and attain competitive advantages*. New York: Auerbach Publications.

Keller, S., Powell, A., Horstmann, B., Predmore, C., & Crawford, M. (2005). Information security threats and practices in small businesses. *Information Systems Management, 22*(2), 719.

Legard, D. (2003, May 14). *Fake bank web site scam reaches U.S.* Retrieved August 10, 2005, from http://www.itworld.com/Tech/2987/030514fakebank

Libicki, M. C. (1995). *What is information warfare?* Washington, DC: National Defense University, Institute for National Strategic Studies.

Meall, L. (1989). Survival of the fittest. *Accountancy (UK), 103*(1147), 140141.

National Research Council. (1991). *Computers at risk*. Washington, DC: National Academy Press.

Neumann, P. G. (1998). Identity-related misuse. In D. E. Denning & P. J. Denning (Eds.), *Internet Besieged*. Reading, MA: ACM Press.

O'Rourke, M. (2004). Cyber-extortion evolves. *Risk Management, 51*(4), 1012.

Parker, D. B. (1976). *Crime by computer*. New York: Scribners.

PCWorld. (2001, November 19). Timeline: A 40-year history of hacking. *IDG News Service*. Retrieved August 10, 2005, from http://www.cnn.com/2001/TECH/internet/11/19/hack.history.idg/

Poulsen, K. (2004, September 27). U.N. warns of nuclear cyber attack risk. *SecurityFocus*. Retrieved

August 10, 2005, from http://www.securityfocus.com/news/9592

Rattray, G. J. (2001). *Strategic warfare in cyberspace*. Cambridge, MA: MIT Press.

Rhem, K. T. (2005, July 20). China investing in information warfare technology, doctrine. *American Forces Press Service*. Retrieved August 10, 2005, from http://www.pentagon.gov/news/jul2005/20050720_2171.html

Richmond, R. (2004, January 22). Netware associates to attack spyware with new products. *Wall Street Journal*, p. B5.

Rosenoer, J. (2002). Safeguarding your critical business information. *Harvard Business Review, 80*(2), 2021.

Schwartau, W. (1998). Something other than war. In A. D. Campen & D. H. Dearth (Eds.), *Cyberwar 2.0: Myths, mysteries, and reality*. Fairfax, VA: AFCEA International Press.

Sipior, J. C., Ward, B. T., & Roselli, G. R. (2005). The ethical and legal concerns of spyware. *Information Systems Management, 22*(2), 3949.

Smith, L. (2004, June 30). Web amplifies message of primitive executions. *Los Angeles Times*.

Stafford, T. F., & Urbaczewski, A. (2004). Spyware: The ghost in the machine. *Communications of the Association for Information Systems, 14*, 291306.

Sterling, B. (2004, August). The other war on terror. *Wired, 12*(8). Retrieved August 10, 2005, from http://www.wired.com/wired/archive/12.08/view.html?pg=4

Strassmann, P. A. (2001). *Government should blaze global information warfare trails*. Retrieved August 10, 2005, from http://www.strassmann.com/pubs/searchsecurity/2001-8.php

Sunday Times. (1996, June 9). Secret DTI inquiry into cyber terror. *The (London) Sunday Times*, pp. 18.

Svensson, P. (2003, March 25). Al-Jazeera site experiences hack attack. *The Associated Press.*

Toffler, A. (1981). *The third wave.* New York: Bantam Books.

Verton, D. (2004, August 30). *Organized crime invades cyberspace.* Retrieved August 10, 2005, from http://www.computerworld.com/securitytopics/security/story/0,10801,95501,00.html

Wilson, J. (2001). E-bomb. *Popular Mechanics, 178*(9), 5054.

TERMS AND DEFINITIONS

Computer Emergency Response Team (CERT): The CERT® Coordination Center (CERT/CC) is a center of Internet security expertise, located at the Software Engineering Institute. Established in 1988, the CERT/CC is a U.S. federally funded research and development center operated by Carnegie-Mellon University.

Computer Security Institute (CSI): Established in 1974, CSI is a membership organization dedicated to serving and training information, computer, and network security professionals.

Cyber Warfare: A synonym for information warfare that emphasizes the computer or network intensive aspects of information warfare.

Electromagnetic Pulse (EMP): Is an intense burst of electromagnetic energy. It may be caused from a lightning strike, an EMP gun, or from the detonation of an atomic bomb. A powerful enough EMP can cause temporary or permanent damage to computer and electronic devices.

Espionage: The practice of spying or obtaining secrets from rivals or enemies for military, political, or business advantage. Advances in IT and the proliferation of tiny, embedded storage devices have added considerably to espionage dangers.

High-Energy Radio Frequency (HERF): A HERF gun can disrupt computer equipment by exposing them to damaging HERF emissions. See also, *electromagnetic pulse.*

Information Warfare: The actions intended to protect, exploit, corrupt, deny, or destroy information or information resources in order to achieve a significant advantage, objective, or victory over an adversary (Alger, 1996).

Organized Crime: Unlawful activities carried out systematically by formal criminal organizations. Advanced IT has introduced innovative forms of organized cyber crime.

Perception Management: Describes the actions aimed at influencing public opinion, or even entire cultures and can cross the spectrum of corporate, political, civilian, cultural, and military realms. Increasingly, Internet technologies are used to influence public perception through the media.

ENDNOTES

[1] The Software Engineering Institute at Carnegie-Mellon University operates the Computer Emergency Response Team Coordination Center (CERT/CC). Given that attacks against Internet-connected systems have become so commonplace and for other stated reasons, as of 2004, the CERT no longer publishes incident numbers (see www.cert.org/stats/cert_stats.html).

[2] The Computer Security Institute annually conducts the Computer Crime and Security Survey with the participation of the San Francisco Federal Bureau of Investigation's (FBI) Computer Intrusion Squad (see www.gocsi.com).

[3] A list of 75 security tools is provided at http://www.insecure.org/tools.html. This list is derived in part from a hacker mailing list. Many of the listed tools are free hacker tools that have been around for years.

Chapter IV
Bits and Bytes vs. Bullets and Bombs:
A New Form of Warfare

John H. Nugent
University of Dallas, USA

Mahesh Raisinghani
Texas Woman's University, USA

... attaining one hundred victories in one hundred battles is not the pinnacle of excellence. Subjugating the enemy's army without fighting is the true pinnacle of excellence. ~ Sun Tzu, The Art of War

There are but two powers in the world, the sword and the mind. In the long run the sword is always beaten by the mind. ~ Napoleon Bonaparte

ABSTRACT

This chapter examines briefly the history of warfare, and addresses the likelihood that in the future wars may well be fought, and won or lost not so much by traditional armies and/or throw weights; but rather based upon digital offenses and defenses that are not constrained by geographic limitations or necessarily having overwhelming national resources. This changing landscape may well alter how nations or groups heretofore not a major threat to world powers, soon may pose an even larger threat than that posed by conventional weapons, including weapons of mass destruction (WMD), or at least approach parity with the destructive power of such weapons.

MACRO HISTORY OF WARFARE

The topic of warfare may be examined from different vantage points.

In examining warfare from various viewpoints, we see a progression from conflicts of a limited nature (scale, location, destructive power, etc.) to one where technology has mitigated to a large degree the linear

Figure 1. Historical analyses of warfare (Source: The University of Dallas Center for Information Assurance, 2005)

Warfare Defined
- By era or period
- By duration
- By scale or level of destruction
- By theater, geographic region, or weather
- By type (tribal, civil, extraterritorial, guerilla, declared, undeclared, hot, cold, etc.)
- By form (land, sea, air, space, Internet, some of or all five)
- By weapons, technology, or intelligence
- By national resources or national ages or stages
- By leader personalities
- By government forms or structures
- By strategies and tactics
- By drivers or reasons for, etc.

---

constraints of time, distance, and potential destruction. That is, where small groups, tribes or armies fought wars with weapons of a relatively limited capability in the past (pre-1945); today, we have powerful nations with significant resources that have strategic missile systems capable of delivering tremendous destructive power (nuclear, biological, chemical) virtually anywhere in the world at the push of a button in a matter of minutes.

The one constant in conflicts throughout the millennium has been that the victors almost universally were the adversary with the superior intelligence and command, communication, and control infrastructures (C3I). And while large nation-states have such strategic WMDs in their arsenals today, there is a new threat which all need to be cognizant of, that of the digital weapon where parties with significantly fewer resources than a super power may pose threats of an equally destructive nature. As James Adams has pointed out, "The United States may be the uncontested military superpower, but it remains defenseless against a new mode of attack: information warfare" (Adams, 2001).

No less than Nicholas Negroponte has pointed out that the nature of our assets is changing from the physical to the virtual (Negroponte, 1995). A sign of this fact is the growth in the amount of digital or digital information being stored today. Estimates of this growing volume of stored information ranges from one to two exabytes of new data a year, or approximately 250 megabytes of data for every man, woman, and child on earth (Sims, 2002).

Moreover, most systems, operations, and infrastructure today are run via digitally controlled systems ranging in degree of capability and security. Additionally, with technological advances in digital communications, most have come to recognize that telecommunications is a subset of information technology, and not vice versa.

Therefore, today our current state is such that our information base, control systems, and communications modes are all moving to a digital state that is even more interconnected. This movement creates a digital Achilles' heel where, the most digitally advanced party may also be the most vulnerable, or if adequately protected, possibly the most dangerous.

That is, "the anatomy of the Internet allows computer viruses [or other attacks] to spread much more effectively than was previously thought" (Pastor-Satorras, 2001). Moreover, the Internet lacks what Pastor-Satorras identifies as the "epidemic threshold," which in human terms naturally limits the spread of diseases across large segments of the population. And, "the very feature of the Internet that makes it so robust against random connection failures might leave it vulnerable to intelligent attack" (Barabasi, 2000).

An attempt to deal with this pervasive security, and to address the need for more IP addresses, as well as, mobility issues, is the development of IPv6 (Internet Protocol version 6). This new IPv6 architecture uses a 128-bit IP address (vs. a 32-bit IPv4 address capability) not only to provide significantly more IP addresses ($3.4*10^{38}$), but also to address communication security from the ground up. This means that in the IPv6 architecture, security is being designed from the ground up, vs. being treated as an after thought. However, issues still remain during the transition from IPv4 to IPv6 architectures; such as transitioning tools that can be exploited by creating a way for IPv4 applications to connect to IPv6 servers, and IPv6 applications to connect to IPv4 services (Ironwalker, 2004). Moreover, since many firewalls permit UDP traffic, IPv6 over UDP may transgress certain firewalls without an administrator's knowledge. At present, the IETF is addressing such issues.

THE NEW DIGITAL THREAT

Today the world's population is larger and more integrated than ever before. Today we have world organizations and religious groups, international trading partners, international bodies such as the United Nations and its many agencies, the World Court, treaty organizations, multinational corporations, and so forth, that all traverse traditional nation-state boundaries in one form or another. This geographically diverse but integrated world has, to a large degree, evolved via technology advancements in land, air, and sea transportation, technology breakthroughs,

and communications technology enhancements and deployments.

This increasing world integration, especially digital integration, becomes apparent when examining the world population and the number of Internet users there are now and will be in the near future as seen in Table 1.

The counts and estimates of future Internet users may well be on the low side however. With the introduction of the $100 laptop by Nicholas Negroponte of MIT's Media Lab through his One Laptop per Child (OLPC) organization in 2005, coupled with wireless Internet access, the numbers of Internet users may well surpass the estimates presented thereby exacerbating the digital threat even further (Kahn, 2005).

Robert Metcalfe, the "father of the Ethernet," has postulated that the value of the network increases at a square of the number of nodes connected to the network (Green, 2003). And just as value increases with the number of interconnected users, so do threats, vulnerabilities, risks, and attacks.

This interconnected landscape presents the condition where one or a few can reach, and potentially cripple, many.

Moreover, just as access and "digital connectivity" have increased, the time to react to digital threats, risks, vulnerabilities, and attacks has decreased. That is, there is an inverse relationship relative to the number and capability of threats and attacks, and the time to react to such attacks.

In 1990, it only took the Nimda virus 22 minutes to become the number one virus ever (ICSA/TruSecure, 2002). In January 2003, the Slammer worm became the fastest spreading worm ever, infecting 75,000

Table 1. Number of people (Source: ITU [www.itu.org], 2001; U.S. Census Bureau [www.census.gov], 2005)

	Year		
	1990	2005	2015 (E)
World population estimates:	5.3 billion	6.4 billion	7.2 billion
Internet user estimates:	2.6 million	1.0 billion	2.0 billion
Users as a percent of world population:	<1%	15.6%	27.8%

Figure 2. CERT incidents report (Source: www.cert.org, 2003)

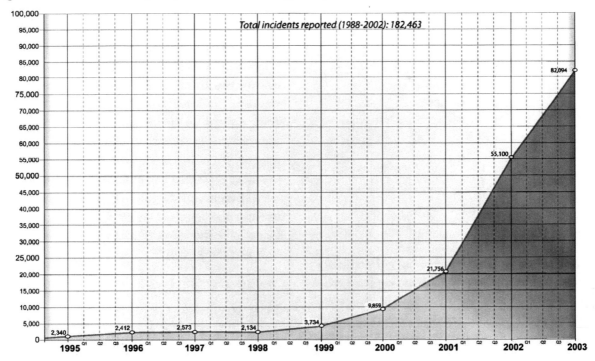

Figure 3. CERT vulnerabilities report (Source: www.cert.org, 2003)

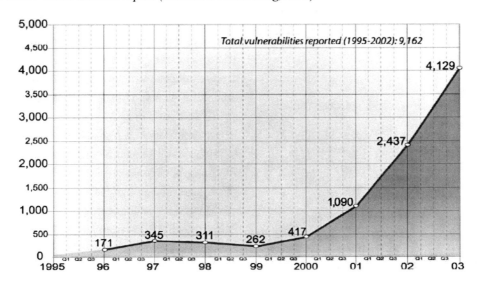

computers in approximately 10 minutes, doubling in numbers every 8.5 seconds in its first minute of infection (Pearson Education, 2005). However, in 2004 the Sasser virus was launched and the world was faced with what has been coined the Zero Day response time as this virus reached virtually every core Internet router in less than an hour while causing an estimated $3.5 billion in damages (CipherTrust, 2004).

Figure 4. Incidents and response times: An inverse relationship

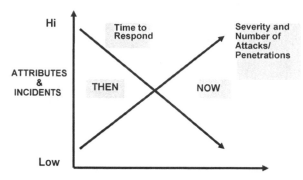

And just as the number and severity of attacks has increased, so has the negative financial consequences. But the costs of creating this financial damage are relatively small; principally being limited to the costs of developing and/or launching a digital attack; as the network to deliver an attack—the Internet and potentially compromised servers wherever—is already in place and available to all with the desire and skill necessary to execute such an action.

As alarming as the numbers in Table 2 are, in June 2001 Charles Neal, an FBI cyber-crime leader stated,

Table 2. Financial impact of virus attacks (Source: Computer Economics, 2006)

Worldwide Impact in Billions of U.S. Dollars	
YEAR	IMPACT
2005	14.2
2004	17.5
2003	13.0
2002	11.1
2001	13.2
2000	17.1
1999	13.0
1998	6.1
1997	3.3
1996	1.8
1995	.5

"Only 2% of the companies that discovered their sites had been compromised reported the incidents to investigators" (Smetannikov, 2001). Moreover, Neal continued, "We have identified thousands of compromised sites, and we identified so many so quickly we couldn't tell all the victims they were victims ..." (Smetannikov, 2001). Hence, it is likely a fair assumption that the reported number of incidents and the losses associated with those incidents is low. Additionally, it is also probably a safe bet that a number of government, criminal, terrorist, or other bodies have been testing their attack techniques to see just how fast they could invade nodes on the Internet; for example, the Slammer Worm in 2003, a basically harmless attack.

THE NATURE OF THE NEW THREAT: SOME EXAMPLES

In 1997 the Department of Defense under an exercise titled "Eligible Receiver," found significant digital weaknesses in the U.S. critical infrastructure (GlobalSecurity, 2005). But perhaps even more striking was finding no fewer than 30,000+ Web sites which provided either attack tools or techniques to penetrate others' systems. Such a proliferation of attack tools and techniques shifts leverage to potential attackers, even those relatively resource constrained and unsophisticated attackers.

As noted in a *U.S. News and World Report* article in 1992, and subsequently refuted to be an April Fools Day hoax, it was reported that the U.S. National Security Agency had embedded software in a chip placed in a French printer connected to the Iraqi Air Defense System, such that the Iraqi Air Defense System could be controlled remotely by the U.S. Government (Arkin, 1999). Whether this story has veracity or not, it highlights the likelihood that many governments employ technology exploitation practices of either an active or passive nature. And with much of the world's electronic devices being made in Asia today, the opportunity for a large manufacturer, or manufacturers, working in conjunction with its host government in the realm of technology exploitation, is a real likelihood.

In September 1999, the U.S. Central Intelligence Agency issued a warning to U.S. businesses that sent their software offshore to be remediated relative to Y2K software issues (Messmer, 1999). The Agency listed the countries where the software remediators were working hand in hand with the host governments to not only fix the Y2K software issues, but to also place a trap door in the code so those governments could later enter the systems on which this software was reloaded.

And just recently, an employee working for Sandia National Laboratories, Shawn Carpenter, was reported to have tracked down a crack Chinese hacker team code named the "Titan Rain," that had penetrated and copied copious amounts of data from some of America's most classified sites (Thornburgh, 2005). Carpenter reported that this team was so efficient that they stayed on a site only 10 to 30 minutes, and usually left an almost undetectable "beacon" (rootkit), so they could reenter the respective system at will. Carpenter reported these hackers left no audit trail of their activities, and represented one of the most sophisticated attacks he had ever seen.

This Titan Rain episode begs the question; if these attackers were so competent, were these attacks perhaps a country or party attacking the U.S. systems via servers commandeered remotely while located in China (known as a false flag attack)?

A FUTURE WAR SCENARIO

A future war and its outcome is likely to be based on strategic and tactical digital thrusts and defenses across geographical boundaries where assets are taken electronically, are remotely controlled, or destroyed by compromising their digital brains or storage medium.

Communications technologies will become the means for massive digital attacks that compromise all matter of an adversary's command, control, communications, operations, and stored information.

Comprehensive attacks will be carried out by relatively few skilled professionals in a time sensitive manner across an interconnected Internet and other networks.

New technologies such as specifically pulsed RF energy will be employed to destroy digitally stored information at significant distances while requiring relatively little power, and which can bepositioned long before being activated (Nugent, 2005).

CONCLUSION

As the world becomes even more digital and interconnected, and as the number and capability of users increases, it is likely that adversaries will develop the skills and abilities to implement both offensive and defensive digital strategies, and develop capabilities that support such strategies.

In this regard, it appears future wars may well result in one adversary capturing via rapid downloading another adversary's national digital assets, including its digital economy, and then destroying that adversary's copy, while digitally controlling the adversary's means of command, control, and communications. That is, an adversary will likely be able to make the other digitally dumb, blind, deaf, and mute.

Moreover, the leading super powers of today may well be challenged by second or third tier resource constrained nations or technology capable groups, such that a virtual shift in power takes place. Such a threat may also lead to first strike strategies, thereby increasing the threat level for all.

It is also likely that nation-states will have a more difficult time in identifying adversaries launching an attack, especially if such adversaries are groups smaller than nation-states, and they use false flag digital disguises to hide their true identities. This occurrence would also complicate reactive, offensive, and defensive measures.

Such likely threats or actions require the development and deployment of a new Internet architecture more resilient to wrongful use for destructive purposes, more powerful encryption, significantly more powerful intrusion prevention systems, more securely developed operating and applications software, better and more timely patch capabilities, and intelligent digital agents residing on the networks of the world that can sense and mitigate digital threats.

REFERENCES

Adams, J. (2001, May/June). Virtual defense. *Foreign Affairs*. Retrieved May 11, 2007 from http://www.foreignaffairs.org/20010501faessay4771/james-adams/virtual-defense.html

Arkin, W. (1999, January 26). Phreaking hacktivists *The Washington Post*. Retrieved from http://www.washingtonpost.com/wp=srv/national/dotmil/arkin.htm

Barabasi, A.-L. (2000, July 26). *Strength is weakness on the internet*. Retrieved from http://physicsweb.org/articles/news/4/7/10/1

Bosworth, S., & Kabay, M. E. (2002). *Computer security handbook* (4th ed.). John Wiley & Sons.

CipherTrust. (2004, November 18). *Maximizing Email Security ROI*. Retrieved from http://www.ciphertrust.com/resourses/articles/articles/roi_2_virus.php

Computer Economics. (2005). Retrieved from http://http://www.computereconomics.com/article.cfm?id=1090

GlobalSecurity. (2005). *Eligible receiver*. Retrieved from http://www.globalsecurity.org/miliatary/ops/eligible-receiver.htm

Green, H. (2003, August 25). We all knew better. *BusinessWeek Online*. Retrieved from http://www.businessweek.com/magazine/toc/03_34/B38460333futuretech.htm

ICSA/TruSecure. (2002). *Virus stats*. Retrieved from http://www.ICSAlabs.com; also at http://www.cit.cornell.edu/computer/security/seminarspast/virus

Ironwalker, (2004). *Does IPv6 introduce new security vulnerabilities?* (#9464). Retrieved from http://www.dslreports.com/faq/9464

Kahn, A. (2005, December 13). *Quanta computer to manufacture $100 laptop*. Retrieved from http://www.laptop.org/2005-1213.olpc.pdf

Kaspersky. (2006). *Virus statistics*. Retrieved from http://www.kasprsky.com/press?chapter=146437529

Messmer, E. (1999, September 13). Threat of "infowar" brings CIA warnings. *Network World Fusion*. Retrieved from http://www.nwfusion.com/archive/1999/75306_09-13-1999.html

Negroponte, N. (2005). *Being Digital*, p. 11, New York: Alfred A. Knopf, Inc.

Nugent, J. (2005). *RF energy as an attack medium for digitally stored data*. Unpublished working conceptual research paper, University of Dallas Center for Information Assurance, Irving, TX.

Pastor-Satorras, R., & Vespignani, A. (2001, April 4). *Internet aids the spread of computer viruses*. Retrieved from http://www.physicsweb.org/article/news/5/4/2/1

Pearson Education, Inc., Information Please Database. (2005). *History of viruses*. Retrieved from http://www.factmonster.com/pages/copyright.html

Sims. (2002). *How much info 2000?* Retrieved from http://sims.berkeley.edu/research/projects/how-much-info/summary.html

Smetannikov, M. (2001, June 4). Cyberspies protect the virtual business world. *Interactive Week*. Retrieved from http://www.zdnet.com/zdnn/stories/news/0,4586,2767657.00.html

Thornburgh, N. (2005, August 29). The Invasion of the chinese cyberspies (and the man who tried to stop them). *Time Magazine*. Retrieved from http://www.time.com/time/magazine/article/0,9171.1098961,00html

TERMS AND DEFINITIONS

Achilles' Heel: Achilles' heel refers to a fatal weakness that leads or may lead to a downfall.

Beacon: See *rootkit*.

Bits: A bit refers to a digit in the binary numeral system (base 2). For example, the number 1001011 is 7-bits long.

Bytes: A contiguous sequence of a *fixed* number of bits. On modern computers, an 8-bit byte or octet is by far the most common.

C3I: Command, control, communications, and intelligence.

Cyberspace: The global network of interconnected computers and communications systems.

Cyber War: A synonym for information warfare.

Digital: A digital system is one that uses numbers, especially binary numbers, for input, processing, transmission, storage, or display, rather than a continuous spectrum of values (an analog system) or non-numeric symbols such as letters or icons.

Eligible Receiver: A network penetration test run by the U.S. Department of Defense in 1997 that highlighted significant defensive computer security weaknesses. This test also identified over 30,000 Web sites that provided attack tools or techniques.

Exabyte: An exabyte is a billion gigabytes, or ten to the eighteenth power.

False Flag: False flag operations are covert operations conducted by governments, corporations, or other organizations, which are designed to appear as if they are being carried out by other entities.

Hacker: A person who either breaks into systems for which they have no authorization, or who exceeds their authority levels in accessing information, in an attempt to browse, copy, alter, delete, or destroy such information.

IETF: The Internet Engineering Task Force is a large open international community of network designers, operators, vendors, and researchers concerned with the evolution of the Internet architecture and the smooth operation of the Internet. It is open to any interested individual (www.ietf.org).

Information Warfare: The offensive and defensive use of information and communication systems to gain adversarial advantage by denying use of information or the systems on which such information is created, resides, or is transmitted, by copying, altering, or destroying information or the means to communicate by electronic means.

IPv4 and IPv6: IPv4 is the Internet Protocol (version 4) primarily in use in 2006. It is a 32-bit address architecture that permits up to 4 billion IP addresses. A new Internet Protocol, IPv6 (version 6), permits trillions of addresses ($3.4*10^{38}$), and has security designed into its architecture from the initial design. Moreover, IPv6 has designed in the capability to efficiently and effectively pass mobile communications. A transition architecture pathway has also been developed such that IPv4 networks may communicate with IPv6 compliant networks.

Nimba: See *virus*.

NSA: The U.S. National Security Agency.

Phreaker: A synonym for a *hacker*.

Rootkit: "Rootkits are one of the many tools available to hackers to disguise the fact that a machine has been "rooted." A rootkit is not used to crack into a system, but rather to ensure that a cracked system remains available to the intruder. Rootkits are comprised of a suite of utilities that are installed on the victim machine. The utilities start by modifying the most basic commonly used programs so that suspicious activity is cloaked. Rootkits are extremely difficult to discover since the commands and programs appear to work as before" (Bosworth & Kabay, 2002) Some common utilities included in a rootkit are: Trojan horses, backdoors, beacons, trapdoors, log wipers, and packet sniffers.

Sasser: See *virus*.

Slammer: See *virus*.

Technology exploitation: The clandestine masking of a hidden function in a component, hardware, software, or system that also provides a declared overt function.

Titan Rain: The name given to penetrations of highly classified U.S. governmental and institutional databases emanating from servers in China in 2005.

Trapdoor: See *rootkit*.

Virus: A virus is a self-replicating program that spreads by inserting copies of itself into other executable code or documents. A computer virus behaves in a way similar to a biological virus, which spreads by inserting itself into living cells. Well known viruses have been named: Nimba, Slammer, and Sasser.

WMD: Weapons of mass destruction generally include nuclear, biological, chemical, and, increasingly, radiological weapons. The term first arose in 1937 in reference to the mass destruction of Guernica, Spain, by aerial bombardment. Following the bombing of Hiroshima and Nagasaki, and progressing through the Cold War the term came to refer to more non-conventional weapons.

Zero Day: A term that has come to mean zero response time to a posed attack.

Chapter V
Infrastructures of Cyber Warfare

Robert S. Owen
Texas A&M University, USA

ABSTRACT

Discussions of cyber warfare tend to focus on weakening or disrupting a physical critical core infrastructure. Critical infrastructures are systems and assets that if destroyed, would have an impact on physical security, economic security, and/or public health or safety. Some have argued that meaningful, sustainable damage to critical infrastructures is unlikely through cyber warfare tactics. However, damage to non-critical infrastructures could inflict considerable economic damage and could cause an existing or emerging technology to lose acceptance in a targeted region or society. War planners with goals of economic damage or decreased quality of life could achieve these ends at relatively low cost without attempts to physically attack the critical infrastructure itself. Much of the work to carry out attacks on non-critical infrastructures could be done by a worldwide network of volunteers who might not even be aware of the motivations of the war planners or cyber terrorists. Non-critical infrastructures that are vulnerable to damage are outlined and discussed. Greater concern for and attention to the vulnerabilities of these non-critical infrastructures is advocated.

INTRODUCTION

This chapter makes an appeal for greater attention to non-critical infrastructures that are vulnerable to cyber warfare. Cyber warfare discussions sometimes debate the extent of damage that can or cannot be caused to a critical infrastructure or if the infrastructure is even vulnerable. The focus of these discussions tends to presume a focus on weakening or disrupting a critical core infrastructure of some sort, such clogging the bandwidth of an Internet connection or crashing

a server in the case of the Internet infrastructure. Evidence, however, seems to suggest that it is unlikely that cyber terrorists or other war planners could cause meaningful damage to critical infrastructures through cyber warfare tactics (Lewis, 2003).

Additional non-critical infrastructures are proposed here as necessary to the diffusion and continued use of a technology: customer infrastructures that include a social infrastructure and a commercial infrastructure, and a political/regulatory infrastructure that moderates the customer infrastructures. Tactics that target these accompanying infrastructures could be part of a larger strategy to disrupt the core technological or physical infrastructure in order to cause economic damage or a decrease in quality of life. Although such tactics are not likely to be useful for immediate mass destruction of a technology or associated physical infrastructure, they could be effective in blocking the diffusion of an emerging technology or of causing an existing technology to lose acceptance in a targeted region or society.

BACKGROUND

Discussions of "cyber terrorism" tend to work from a definition something like:

The use of computer network tools to shut down critical infrastructures for the purpose of coercing or intimidating a government or civilian population. (cf., Caruso, 2002; Lewis, 2002)

"Critical infrastructures" are systems and assets that if destroyed, would have an impact on physical security, national economic security, and/or national public health or safety (HR 3162, 2001) and includes such industries or operations as (to name only a few) energy, food, transportation, banking, communication, government, and cyberspace itself (cf., DHS, 2003a, 2003b). "Cyberspace" refers to the interconnected computers, servers, routers, switches, and cables that make critical infrastructures work (cf., DHS, 2003a).

Although the sudden debilitating failure of some critical piece of the cyberspace infrastructure might be an objective of terrorism, the impact of smaller incidents that could be used by cyber warfare strategists to merely temporarily "cripple" critical infrastructures are perhaps more possible and more likely, and, in aggregate, are perhaps much more costly overall. Failures of critical infrastructures occur naturally in ordinary every day life, causing power outages, flight delays, and communication disruptions, and societies that depend on these critical infrastructures seem to be resilient to these events; cyber attacks on these critical infrastructures are likely to be less effective than nature (cf., Lewis, 2002).

The perspective of the article is that while a digital 9/11 is unlikely, smaller, perhaps individually insignificant, incidents can serve two useful strategic functions: they can erode public confidence in systems that rely on cyberspace, and they can be used by cyberwar planners to prepare for future attacks. In preparing for later attacks, cyberwar planners can map information systems, identify key targets, and lace an infrastructure with "back doors" that create future points of entry (DHS, 2003a). Of greater interest in the present chapter, erosion of public confidence in a system is likely to cause less reliance on that system; decreased use of a system due to lack of confidence is in many ways the same end result as if a part of the system had been destroyed by a single huge attack. The primary difference is that a huge attack on a critical infrastructure might be impossible to implement; many seemingly insignificant attacks, on the other hand, could be easily implemented at low cost.

This chapter proposes that infrastructures other than critical core infrastructures are vulnerable, important, and deserving of greater attention. A gang of thugs does not have to blow the foundation out from under the house to force a resident out of the neighborhood. Giving candy to neighborhood children to throw rocks whenever the windows are replaced could be every bit as effective. From that perspective—that an important asset can be easy to cripple with a thousand stones even though impossible to kill with a single boulder—the goal of the present chapter is to propose infrustructures that might be associated with critical infrastructure vulnerability. In addition to a critical core infrastructure—servers, routers, switches, cables, and such in the case of the Internet—this article proposes that we conceptually consider a social infrastructure, a commercial infrastructure, and a political/regulatory infrastructure in devising strategies to defend against cyber warfare.

THE MOST ECONOMICALLY DESTRUCTIVE CYBER EXPLOITS

Physical destruction of the Internet infrastructure is extremely unlikely. Instead, there are a number of other exploits that might be classed by some as merely "weapons of temporary annoyance," but as we will see, these "annoyance" tactics can, and indeed do, result in billions of dollars in damage. Such damage—which actually occurs - should collectively be considered just as noteworthy in cyber warfare as is the damage from a single large infrastructure attack. An Internet infrastructure attack—an attack on network systems on which many users depend—is only one kind of cyberspace exploit or incident. Other "lesser" incidents could be weapons used in waging an infrastructure attack (e.g., a denial of service attack), but as we will see later, these could be conceptually associated with other kinds of infrastructures that lead to a crippling of a technological infrastructure.

Other cyber exploits or incidents could include (NIAC 2004a):

- **Probe:** An attempt to gain access to a system
- **Scan:** Many probes done using an automated tool
- **Account compromise:** Unauthorized use of a computer account
- **Root compromise:** Compromise of an account with system administration privileges
- **Packet sniffing:** Capturing data from information as it travels over a network
- **Denial of service attack:** Deliberately consuming system resources to deny use to legitimate users
- **Malicious programs and malware:** Hidden programs or programs that do more than is expected, causing unexpected, undesired results on a system

In a recent survey of 700 organizations conducted by the Computer Security Institute and the U.S. Federal Bureau of Investigation, virus attacks were found to be the greatest source of business financial loss, amounting to losses of $42.8 million for survey respondents in 2005. Unauthorized access amounted to $31.2 million in losses, and theft of proprietary information amounted to $30.9 million. Denial of service was a distant fourth source of financial loss for survey respondents, amounting to only $7.3 million in losses (Gordon et al., 2005).

From this survey, then, we can see that malicious software exploits were the most annoying financially, being six times more costly than denial of service attacks that more directly affect the Internet infrastructure. Cashell et al. (2004) report that the total cost of financial loss due to malicious software was around $13 billion in 2003. Although the collective $13 billion/year cost of malicious software might seem small in contrast to the estimated $50 billion cost of the 9/11 terrorist attack (Hutchings, 2004a), the latter is likely to forever be difficult to repeat, while the former is likely to be an easy repeat performance year after year. While idealistic terrorists might prefer to draw attention to a political agenda, war planners bent on economic damage or decreased quality of life might realize that cyber warfare can achieve economic destruction with relatively low cost – without attempts to attack the critical infrastructure itself.

NON-CRITICAL INFRASTRUCTURE ATTACK

If viruses and worms result in six times the losses of denial of service attacks, then there certainly is reason to focus on malicious software exploits as either a weapon that is currently being used in cyber warfare —whether or not we realize it—or as a weapon that is so easy to use that it becomes a desirable weapon to use in cyber warfare – even if cyberwar planners don't yet recognize its potential. In considering the propagation of such attacks, we have to consider an Internet infrastructure that exists on two levels (cf., NIAC 2004b):

- **Core infrastructure:** Routers, name servers, and backbone links that make up the interconnected network: what is typically discussed as a critical infrastructure
- **Customer infrastructure:** Personal computers and organizational networks that are part of this interconnected network

The point here is that personal computers in homes and business desktops become part of the physical network that spreads malicious applications that caused $13 billion in financial damage in 2003. A war-waging state does not need to develop a nuclear warhead or fly an airplane into a building in order to cause billions of dollars in economic damage; a campaign using malicious software could do the job if economic damage rather than political attention is the primary objective.

ECONOMICS AND POTENTIAL FOR NON-CRITICAL ATTACK

Cyber attacks enjoy several advantages over physical attacks. Cyber attacks can be done from a distance without the necessity of being near a physical target and without the necessity of possessing the mechanism to carry a payload to a target. This allows the attackers to obfuscate their identities, locations, and paths of entry. In many cases, the work requires only commodity technology that is widely available. Carrying out attacks could be subcontracted to individual hackers who have the necessary technical expertise, where the hacker does not necessarily share or even know the motivation of the terrorist (cf., DHS, 2003a; Warren & Furnell, 1999).

Hutchings (2004a, 2004b) notes that there is a sizeable worldwide "youth bulge" that creates a lot of "unemployed young guys," including 21 of the 54 countries with large Muslim populations; he further notes that half of the Saudi population is under the age of 15. The worldwide pool of "unemployed young guys" probably contains a few brilliant people who

have nothing better to do than to develop malicious cyber exploits as an intellectual outlet. Even without a political reason to do so, members of this group could very well harness a coordinated effort to cause havoc. Under the influence of a social of political movement, they are more likely to do so.

NON-CRITICAL INFRASTRUCTURES

The above discussion suggests that substantial economic damage can be had without necessarily causing damage or disruption to the core or critical infrastructure - the backbone computers, routers, cables, and such. Economic damage to a society can be gained through attacks on other infrastructures. Below is an expansion on the idea of the core + customer infrastructure idea of NIAC (2003b).

Below, the customer infrastructure of NIAC is broken out into two component parts: a social infrastructure and a commercial/competitor infrastructure. An additional political/regulatory infrastructure is added to that model as a factor that can moderate environmental effects on the other three infrastructures.

Core Technical Infrastructure

In cyberspace, this is the critical Internet infrastructure of backbone computers, routers, cables, and such.

Social Infrastructure

In order for the core technical infrastructure of cyberspace to diffuse into common use, a social infrastructure is also required (cf., Rogers 1995). In cyberspace, if consumers hadn't adopted the microcomputer as a household appliance, hadn't adopted Web surfing as a pastime, and hadn't adopted online information gathering or shopping as a trustworthy way of doing business, retail Internet commerce could not have diffused.

Although cyberspace is diffused, cyber warfare can be waged that constricts the social infrastructure.

If people lose confidence in the reliability or safety of cyberspace, then cyber warmongers win the battle. If consumers are afraid that "sniffing" is commonly used in identity theft, then they might disengage from the conduct of Internet commerce. If business users continually lose valuable email messages in the noise of spam that doesn't even advertise anything, then they will decrease reliance on that mode of communication. The core critical infrastructure itself does not have to be attacked in order to suffer effects that cripple it.

Competitive / Commercial Infrastructure

The role of marketing actions and the role of competitive actions are also important in the diffusion of a social infrastructure (cf., Frambach, 1993; Gatignon & Robertson, 1985; Robertson & Gatignon, 1986). For cyberspace to evolve, commercial enterprises had to start putting goods or information up for sale or distribution through the Internet before consumers could become accustomed to and accepting of Internet based commerce. The competitive infrastructure and the social infrastructure are interdependent: consumers had to start buying in order for commercial business to become motivated to conduct Internet commerce, and Internet commerce had to exist before consumers would adopt this form of promotion and distribution.

As with the social infrastructure, it is not unthinkable to consider that the commercial infrastructure is vulnerable to constriction even though it has already diffused. If probes, scans, account compromise, and such are seen as costly vulnerabilities, then less Internet access might be offered to consumers or commercial partners. If the threat of malicious software is an issue, then business could restrict the use of email for employees. There is the same loss of use of a technology whether a cyber terrorist permanently blows up a piece of the core infrastructure or if commerce voluntarily disengages in some uses of the technology due to the "less critical" annoyances that cyber warfare has created.

Political / Regulatory Infrastructure

Finally, without a regulatory infrastructure, Internet commerce could not diffuse. Communication protocols had to exist; a way for business to lay claim to IP addresses and domain names had to exist. A way to resolve disputes in this process had to exist. Rules of civility in the conduct of business had to exist.

An incomplete set of enforceable rules and sanctions, however, leaves the various non-core cyberspace infrastructures vulnerable. For example, email users receive spam that has no commercial message, whereby the intention of the sender might be to create noise in email boxes or to see if the messages are received for future attacks. Without sanctions to the senders, without sanctions to service providers who allow senders to conduct such operations, and without sanctions to nation-states that permit such activities, the current state of this kind of spam will only get worse as the brightest of the "unemployed young guys" look for ways to use their time. Regulation of cyber activities on a worldwide level would seem to be implementable (cf. Grove et al., 2000).

FUTURE TRENDS

Current thought seems to be that cyber attacks on critical infrastructures are not an especially large threat. Incidents in cyberspace tend to be considered either as issues of crime or as issues of pranks. These non-critical incidents, whatever the motive behind them, are nonetheless costly from an economic sense. If the objective of a war planner is to cause economic hardship and decreased quality of life, then attacks on non-critical infrastructures might one day attract the attention of war planners. Cyber attacks, while probably not effective on critical infrastructures, are easy to implement and might eventually become useful weapons even if currently being ignored. A growing population of young, educated, but unemployed people will be readily available in the future to deploy in cyber war tactics. When that happens, an understanding of the vulnerabilities in non-critical infrastructures would be helpful in defending against cyber war tactics.

CONCLUSION

Attack on the critical core technological infrastructure of the Internet is not likely but also is not necessary in waging a cyber war. Although the intention of a terrorist organization might be to cause harm in a way that is noticeable, a person, organization, or state could have interest in conducting warfare that causes economic or quality of life damage, whether or not it is suddenly noticed. Damage does not have to occur through disruption of a critical core infrastructure; it can occur through disruptions of the customer infrastructures: a social infrastructure and a commercial infrastructure.

Attacks on the social and commercial customer infrastructures are enabled or inhibited through a regulatory infrastructure. If attacks on cyberspace infrastructures emanate from a particular place, then that place could be held liable. For example, denial of service attacks might have been instigated by individuals who cannot be traced because the attack was by stealing access to a compromised account. Although these individuals might not be easily found, the owner of the compromised account could be held responsible for not updating applications that allowed the compromise, or the server owner could be held responsible for not monitoring unusual activities in accounts on that server. Viruses and worms can be spread by household computers that are using outdated operating systems and protection applications. If laws can be passed that require automobile drivers to maintain auto safety and emissions standards, then the safety standards could be required of those who use the information superhighway. If nation-states can be scrutinized in association with nuclear or bioterrorism activities, then it should be thinkable to scrutinize those who associate with cyber activities.

REFERENCES

Caruso, J.T. (2002). Congressional Testimony. Testimony before the House Subcommittee on National Security, Veterans Affairs, and International Relations, March 21, 2002. Last accessed electronically January 30, 2006, from http://www.fbi.gov/congress/congress02/caruso032102.htm

Cashell, B., Jackson, W. D., Jickling, M., & Webel, B. (2004). *The economic impact of cyber-attacks.* CRS Report for Congress, Congressional Research Service, The Library of Congress. April 1, 2004.

DHS (2003a). *The national strategy to secure cyberspace.* Department of Homeland Security, February 2003. Last accessed January 30, 2006, from http://www.dhs.gov/interweb/assetlibrary/National_Cyberspace_Strategy.pdf

DHS (2003b). *The national strategy for the physical protection of critical infrastructures and key assets.* The United States Whitehouse, February, 2003. Last accessed January 30, 2006, from http://www.dhs.gov/interweb/assetlibrary/Physical_Strategy.pdf

Frambach, R. T. (1993). An integrated model of organizational adoption and diffusion of innovations. *European Journal of Marketing, 27*(5), 22-41.

Gatignon, H., & Robertson, T. (1985). A prepositional inventory for new diffusion research. *Journal of Consumer Research, 11*(March), 849-867.

Gordon, L. A., Loeg, M. P., Lucyshyn, W., & Richardson, R. (2005). *2005 CSI/FBI computer crime and security survey.* Computer Security Institute. Last accessed January 30, 2006, from http://i.cmpnet.com/gocsi/db_area/pdfs/fbi/FBI2005.pdf

Grove, G. D., Goodman, S. E., & Lukasik, S. J. (2000). Cyber-attacks and international law. *Survival, 42*(3), 89-103.

HR 3162 (2001). Uniting and Strengthening America by Providing Appropriate Tools Required to Intercept and Obstruct Terrorism (USA PATRIOT ACT) Act of 2001. United States Senate.

Hutchings, R. (2004a). *Terrorism and economic security.* Talk given at the International Security Management Association meeting, Scottsdale, AZ, 14 January 2004. Last accessed January 30, 2006, from http://www.cia.gov/nic/PDF_GIF_speeches/terror_and_econ_sec.pdf

Hutchings, R. L. (2004b). *Looking over the horizon: Assessing America's strategic challenges.* Talk given at the Department of State/INR/World Affairs Council Seminar, Washington, DC, March 9, 2004. Last accessed January 30, 2006, from http://www.cia.gov/nic/PDF_GIF_speeches/strategic_challenges.pdf

Lewis, J. A. (2002). Assessing the risks of cyber terrorism, cyber war and other cyber threats. Center for Strategic and International Studies, December 2002. Last accessed January 30, 2006, from http://www.csis.org/media/csis/pubs/021101_risks_of_cyberterror.pdf

Lewis, J. (2003). Cyber terror: Missing in action. *Knowledge, Technology, & Policy, 16*(2), 34-41.

NIAC (2004a). Prioritizing cyber vulnerabilities: Final report and recommendations by the Council. National Infrastructure Advisory Council. October 12, 2004.

NIAC (2004b). Hardening the Internet: Final report and recommendations by the Council. National Infrastructure Advisory Council. October 12, 2004.

Robertson, T. S., & Gatignon, H. (1986). Competitive effects on technology diffusion. *Journal of Marketing, 50*(July), 1-12.

Rogers, E. M. (1995). *Diffusion of innovations* (4th ed.). New York: The Free Press.

Warren, M.J., & Furnell, S.M. (1999). *Cyber-terrorism: The political evolution of the computer hacker.* Australian Computer Ethics Conference, July 1999. Last accessed January 30, 2006, from http://www.cissr.com/whitepapers/cyberterrorism4.pdf

TERMS AND DEFINITIONS

Cyber Terrorism: The use of computer network tools to shut down critical infrastructures for the purpose of coercing or intimidating a government or civilian population.

Cyber Warfare: The use of exploits in cyberspace as a way to intentionally cause harm to people, assets, or economies.

Cyberspace: The interconnected computers, servers, routers, switches, and cables that make critical infrastructures work.

Critical Infrastructure: Systems and assets that if destroyed, would have an impact on physical security, national economic security, and/or national public health or safety.

Core Infrastructure: A physical or technological infrastructure; this is probably the critical infrastructure in most cases.

Customer Infrastructure: An infrastructure that depends on or is an outgrowth of the core infrastructure.

Social Infrastructure: A customer infrastructure of people who decide to use or not use a core infrastructure.

Commercial / Competitive Infrastructure: A customer infrastructure of organizations that use or don't use a core infrastructure.

Political / Regulatory Infrastructure: Government, industry, and political entities which can provide incentives and sanctions to enable or inhibit an infrastructure.

Exploit: An action that takes advantage of weaknesses or vulnerabilities in software or hardware.

Chapter VI
Terrorism and the Internet

M. J. Warren
Deakin University, Australia

ABSTRACT

The new millennium has had a major impact, the world in which we live is changing. The information society is becoming a global society, the growth of electronic businesses is developing new industrials markets on a global basis. But the information society is built on a very fragile framework—the Internet. The Internet is at risk from attacks, historically it was sole hackers, but we are now seeing the development of cyber terrorist organisations. This chapter will explore the ways in which terrorist organizations use the Internet and builds upon a number of case studies focusing upon the middle east.

INTRODUCTION

Many aspects of our modern society now have either a direct or implicit dependence upon information technology (IT). As such, a compromise of the availability or integrity in relation to these systems (which may encompass such diverse domains as banking, government, health care, and law enforcement) could have dramatic consequences from a societal perspective.

In many modern business environments, even the short-term, temporary interruption of Internet and e-mail connectivity can have a significantly disruptive effect, forcing people to revert to other forms of communication that are now viewed as less convenient. Imagine, then, the effect if the denial of service was over the long-term and also affected the IT infrastructure in general. Many governments are now coming to this realisation.

The term terrorist or terrorism is a highly emotive term. But the general term, terrorist, is used to denote revolutionaries who seek to use terror systematically to further their views or to govern a particular area (Wilkinson, 1976).

Cyber terrorism is a different form of terrorism since physical systematic terror does not occur (unless, for example, the attack causes a critical system to fail), but systematic wide spread destruction of information resources can occur. The problem relates to the fact that a terrorist group could easily be perceived as a resistance group carrying out lawful actions. In the context of this chapter all groups will be defined as terrorist/resistance groups in order to give a neutral perception of their activities and aims.

This chapter sets out to consider the scenario in which technology infrastructures or services are targeted deliberately by "cyber terrorists."

THE CYBER TERRORIST

Recent years have seen the widespread use of information technology by terrorist-type organisations. This has led to the emergence of a new class of threat, which has been termed *cyber terrorism*. This can be viewed as distinct from "traditional" terrorism since physical terror does not occur and efforts are instead focused upon attacking information systems and resources. (Hutchinson & Warren, 2001).

When viewed from the perspective of skills and techniques, there is little to distinguish cyber terrorists from the general classification of hackers. Both groups require and utilise an arsenal of techniques in order to breach the security of target systems. From a motivational perspective, however, cyber terrorists are clearly different, operating with a specific political or ideological agenda to support their actions. This in turn may result in more focused and determined efforts to achieve their objectives and more considered selection of suitable targets for attack. However, the difference does not necessarily end there and other factors should be considered. Firstly, the fact that cyber terrorists are part of an organised group could mean that they have funding available to support their activities. This in turn would mean that individual hackers could be hired to carry out attacks on behalf of a terrorist organisation (effectively subcontracting the necessary technical expertise). In this situation, the hackers themselves may not believe in the terrorist's

"cause," but will undertake the work for financial gain (Verton, 2003).

Propaganda and Publicity

Terrorist groups have difficulty in relaying their political messages to the general public without being censored: They can now use the Internet for this purpose. Different terrorist groups and political parties are now using the Internet for a variety of different purposes. Some examples are:

- **Tupac Amaru Revolutionary Movement (MRTA):** In 1997, a Peruvian terrorist group know as MRTA took over the Japanese embassy in Peru taking a number of hostages. During this time, the Web Site of the MRTA contained messages from MRTA members inside the embassy as well as updates and pictures of the drama as it happened.
- **Chechen rebels:** Chechen rebels have been using the Internet to fight the Russians in a propaganda war. The rebels claimed to have shot down a Russian fighter jet, a claim refuted by the Russians until a picture of the downed jet was shown on www.Kavkaz.org, the official Web site of the Chechen rebels. The Russians were forced to admit their jet had in fact been shot down.
- **Fundraising:** Azzam Publications, based in London and named after Sheikh Abdullah Azzam, a mentor of Osama bin Laden; is a site dedicated to Jihad around the world and linked to Al Qaeda. It is alleged that the Azzam Publications site, which sold Jihad related material from books to videos, was raising funds for the Taliban in Afghanistan and for guerrillas fighting the Russians in Chechyna. After September 11, Azzam Publications came under increased pressure to the point where its products could no longer be purchased through their site. In a farewell message published on their site they

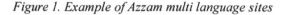

Figure 1. Example of Azzam multi language sites

provide alternatives to ensure that funds can still be raised and sent around the world to fight the "struggle." In 2002 the main Azzam site went back online, offering the same fundraising options. The new site also mirrored itself around the world and provides its content in a number of languages including: Arabic, English, German, Spanish, Indonesian, Bosnian, Turkish, Malay, Albanian, Ukranian, French, Swedish, Dutch, Italian, Urdu, and Somalian (as shown in Figure 1). The reason for doing this according to the Azzam site "is to protect against Western Censorship Laws." It will probably prove to be difficult to close the Azzam site in the future, when the information is mirrored around the Internet in a variety of languages.

- **Information warfare:** Cyber terrorism or the more appropriate term information warfare as discussed earlier is becoming a common technique used to attack organisations. Cyber terrorist groups employ what is known as *hacktivism*. Hacktivists are activists involved in defacing the site of an enemy for a political cause for example, a cyber terrorism group or

a group acting on behalf of a cyber terrorism group (Meikle, 2002; Warren & Hutchinson, 2002).

CASE STUDY 1

Terrorist organisations are organisations, that have the ability to reflect and learn (Warren, 2005). An example of this is the Hezbollah group, their initial Internet presence was focused upon a Web site that contains just limited information. This Web site simply represents a propaganda tool for them to get their message to the outside world without any political constraint or censorship.

The group developed their basic site into something much more advanced. It contains extensive information about their military campaigns and political activities. The site also contains extensive information about their operations from all around the world, not only their own resources.

The site also includes readers letters, where individuals can openly support the aims of Hezbollah, it also offers cartoons, various images, multimedia,

Figure 2. Early

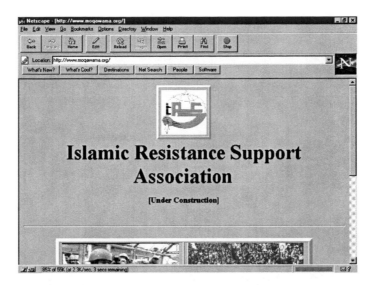

Figure 3. Later Hezbollah site (2001)

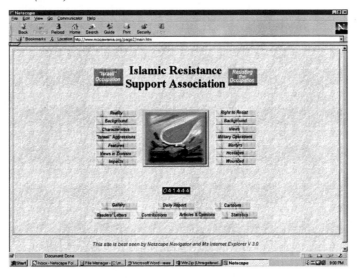

e-mail access to the organisation and so forth. Figures 25 show the steps in their progression.

The multimedia aspect of the site includes pictures taken of combat situations, video clips, news reports, and audio recordings of Hezbollah speeches.

CASE STUDY 2 FUTURE TRENDS: IRAQI WAR CASE STUDY, 2003

In the example of the Iraqi War during 2003 you had a situation that included hackers, viruses, and online propaganda. What makes this different to the previous

Figure 4. Current Hezbollah site (2006)

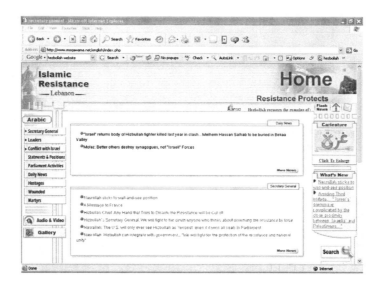

Figure 5. Sample selection of multimedia content found on the Hezbollah site

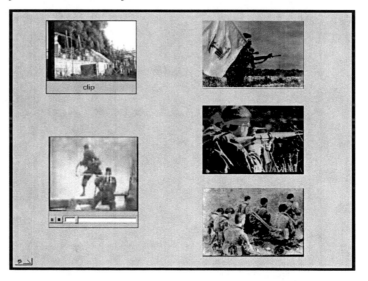

cyber wars for example, the Serbian-NATO cyber war, is the fact that more than two parties are involved and the motivation is based upon ideologies—religious and political. What also makes this cyber war of interest are the three parties involved. These included (Warren, 2003):

- U.S. based hackers who are inspired by patriotism and wish to attack anything that can be considered as an Iraqi target
- Islamic-based hackers who are trying to carry out an online Jihad against perceived allied targets

• Peace activists who are trying to use the Web to promote a peaceful message via Web sites—but what would have been the next step for the radical peace activists if the war had continued?

The situation was very confusing as you had the U.S. government NIPC releasing an advisory on February 11, 2003, trying to restrain "patriotic hacking" on behalf of the U.S. government (NIPC, 2003). They defined that attacks may have one of several motivations (NIPC, 2003):

• Political activism targeting Iraq or those sympathetic to Iraq by self-described "patriot hackers"
• Political activism or disruptive attacks targeting United States systems by those opposed to any potential conflict with Iraq
• Criminal activity masquerading or using the current crisis to further personal goals

During this period there were active pro-Islamic hacking groups such as the Unix Security Guard (USG), their strategy was trying to deface sites with their pro-Iraqi political messages (Warren, 2003). A typical antiwar successful hack is illustrated in Figure 6.

Following the defeat of Iraqi forces and the restoration of a democratic government, Iraqi resistance groups formed to fight new government and occupying military forces. These new resistance groups turned to the Internet (see Figure 7) for the reasons described previously, but with some differences, these are (Warren, 2005):

• Recruitment of volunteers
• Focus on Arabic rather than English Web sites and content
• Mirroring information around the world, making it harder to remove
• Spreading information on making explosives, how to use captured foreign firearms, and so forth

A final point to note is that cyber terrorist activity could also be used in conjunction with or to sup-

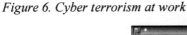

Figure 6. Cyber terrorism at work

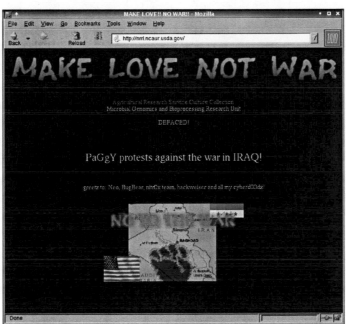

Figure 7. Iraqi resistance groups at work

port more traditional attacks. For example, hacking techniques could be employed to obtain intelligence information from systems, which could then be used as the basis for a physical attack.

CONCLUSION

Another observation is that cyber attacks offer the capability for terrorist activities with wider-reaching impacts. With traditional terrorist activities, such as bombings, the impacts are isolated within specific physical locations and communities. In this context, the wider populous act only as observers and are not directly affected by the actions. Furthermore, acts of violence are not necessarily the most effective way of making a political or ideological point–the media and public attention is more likely to focus upon the destruction of property and/or loss of life than whatever "cause" the activity was intended to promote. The ability of cyber terrorism activities to affect a wider population may give the groups involved greater leverage in terms of achieving their objectives, whilst at the same time ensuring that no immediate long-term damage is caused which could cloud the issue. For

example, in a denial of service scenario, if the threatened party was to accede to the terrorist demands, then the situation could (ostensibly at least) be returned to that which existed prior to the attack (i.e. with service resumed). This is not the case in a "physical" incident when death or destruction has occurred.

Cyber terrorists operate with a political agenda. This motivation (which could often be more accurately described as fanaticism) will mean these types of attacks will be more specifically targeted and aimed at more critical systems. This collective action would do more harm than the action of a single hacker. There is also the issue of funding, since terrorist groups could have substantial funds available, they could easily employ hackers to act on their behalf.

Whether we like it or not, we have developed a significant (and increasing) dependence upon information technology. The Internet is available 24 hours a day and cyber terrorist groups that view developed countries as a target will be able to attack 24 hours a day. This means that all organisations could feel the impact as their sites are attacked just because they happen to be in Australian, Japan, USA, and so forth. Only the future will show the risks that we face from the threat of cyber terrorism

REFERENCES

Hutchinson, W., & Warren, M. J. (2001). *Information Warfare: Corporate attack and defence in a digital world*. London: Butterworth-Heinemann.

Meikle, G. (2002). *Future active: Media activism and the internet*. Routledge.

NIPC. (2003).*Encourages heightened cyber security as Iraq—US tensions increase* (Advisory 03-002). Washington, DC.

Verton, D. (2003). *Black ice: The invisible threat of cyber terrorism*. McGraw Hill.

Warren, M. J. (2003). *The impact of hackers*. Presented at the Second European Information Warfare Conference, Reading, UK.

Warren, M. J. (2005). *Cyber terrorism*. Presented at the Annual Police Summit, Melbourne, Australia.

Warren, M. J., & Hutchinson, W. (2002). *Will new laws be effective in reducing web sponsorship of terrorist groups*. Presented at the Third Australian Information Warfare and Security Conference, Perth, Australia.

Wilkinson, P. (1976). *Political terrorism*. MacMillan Press Ltd.

TERMS AND DEFINITIONS

Note: Definitions from Dictionary.Com (http://dictionary.reference.com/browse)

Cyber Terrorism: Terrorism conducted in cyber space, where criminals attempt to disrupt computer or telecommunications service.

Hacker: One who uses programming skills to gain illegal access to a computer network or file.

Internet: An interconnected system of networks that connects computers around the world via the TCP/IP protocol.

Risk: The possibility of suffering harm or loss; danger.

Security: Something that gives or assures safety, as: (a) Measures adopted by a government to prevent espionage, sabotage, or attack; (b) Measures adopted, as by a business or homeowner, to prevent a crime.

Terrorist: One that engages in acts or an act of terrorism.

Terrorism: The unlawful use or threatened use of force or violence by a person or an organized group against people or property with the intention of intimidating or coercing societies or governments, often for ideological or political reasons.

Chapter VII
Steganography

Merrill Warkentin
Mississippi State University, USA

Mark B. Schmidt
St. Cloud State University, USA

Ernst Bekkering
Northeastern State University, USA

ABSTRACT

Steganography, the process of hiding information, can be used to embed information or messages in digital files. Some uses are legitimate, such as digital watermarking or the combination of text with medical images. But the technique can also be used for criminal purposes or by terrorists to disguise communications between individuals. We discuss some commonly available steganographic tools, the detection of stegonography through steganalysis, and future challenges in this domain. In the future, the legality of steganography may depend on legal issues and challenges. Jurisdictional differences may play a role. Privacy will have to be balanced by the duty of authorities to safeguard public safety, both from threats by criminals and terrorists. Techniques for steganalysis will become increasingly important, and will be complicated by the use of the Internet and emerging technologies such as VOIP. Packet routing complicates analysis of files, and new data streams offer new opportunities for hiding information. An internationally coordinated response to threats may be necessary.

INTRODUCTION

Steganography is the process of hiding information. In the digital environment, steganography (which literally means "covered writing") involves hiding data or messages within files, so that the files, which might appear to be legitimate, would be ignored by authorities. Steganography has been practiced since the times of ancient Greece. Ancient steganographic methods where simple yet effective; for example, a message in a wooden tablet was covered with wax thereby hiding the message. Another method was to shave a messenger's head, tattoo a message on his scalp, and let the hair grow back only to shave it again when the messenger arrived at his destination (Jupitermedia Corporation, 2003). More technical forms of steganography have been in existence for several years. In fact, international workshops on information hiding and steganography have been held regularly since 1996 (Moulin & O'Sullivan, 2003). However, the majority of the development and use of computerized steganography has occurred since 2000 (Cole, 2003). Steganography does not necessarily encrypt a message, as is the case with cryptography. Instead, the goal is to conceal the fact that a message even exists in the first place (Anderson & Petitcolas, 1998), so that anyone intercepting and viewing the file (image, document, e-mail, etc.) would not be readily aware of the hidden bits. Modern technologies have enabled the embedding of hidden messages efficiently and easily. These computerized tools encode the message, and then hide it within another file.

BACKGROUND: LEGITIMATE USE OF STEGANOGRAPHY

There are several useful applications for steganography. Much like "watermarks" and embossing have been used for many years to identify banknotes or other important documents, "digital watermarks" can be introduced into files to identify the ownership of the digital content, such as an image or music file. This tool for preserving intellectual property rights (copyright, trademark, etc.) enhances the ability of the creator to safely distribute his or her work without fear of copyright infringement (Nikolaidis & Pitas, 1996). It also enables legitimate monitoring of the use of such files. Intelligent software agents ("bots") can be used to search the Web for files (JPG-image files, for example), which might encompass the embedded string of ownership information (the digital watermark). In this way, for example, a journalist or artist might ensure that their digital signature (typically a

unique serial number used as a virtual "fingerprint") is found only in images displayed on Web pages that have licensed their use and not for unauthorized uses (Moulin & O'Sullivan, 2003).

Another use of steganography involves sending a secret message (Anderson & Petitcolas, 1998). Other uses include hiding messages in radio advertisements to verify that they are run as contracted, embedding comments in a file, embedding a patient's name in medical image data, and embedding multilingual soundtracks in pay-per-view television programs (Anderson & Petitcolas, 1998; Moulin & O'Sullivan, 2003). Embedded digital watermarks also have been used to identify copyrighted software (Hachez, 2003) and to prevent music and video files from being illegally copied.

RISKS POSED BY STEGANOGRAPHY

Though most individuals generally utilize the benefits of modern technology to increase productivity or for other positive outcomes, other individuals will use technology for detrimental activities, such as cyber theft and the planning of terrorist attacks. One need look no further than Osama bin Laden and his terrorist network, Al Qaeda, to see evidence of the latter. U.S. intelligence has evidence that Al Qaeda uses the Web to conduct operations (Cohen, 2001). Known examples include Mohamed Atta making airline reservations on Americanairlines.com, members using Yahoo e-mail, and members using the Web to research crop dusters in an effort to determine how effective they could be in chemical attacks. A more recent example concerns the use of steganography by a radical Muslim infiltrator of the Dutch Intelligence Service (Reporter, 2004). Similarly, steganography has been used for criminal purposes. An extortionist in The Netherlands demanded that the victim, a food producer, hide information regarding a bank account with the ransom in a picture placed on the Web site of a major newspaper (Ringelestijn, 2004).

Table 1. Examples of steganography tools

Tool	File Types	Cost	ADDRESS
Camouflage	Several	Free	http://www.downseek.com/download/5746.asp
Invisible Secrets v4.0	JPG, PNG, BMP, HTML, and WAV	$39.95	http://www.stegoarchive.com/
SecurEngine 2.0	BMP, JPG, and TXT	Free	http://www.freewareseek.com
Camera/Shy	GIF and Web pages	Free	http://sourceforge.net/projects/camerashy/
Stegdetect (XSteg)	Detects the presence of steganography in JPG images.	Free	http://packages.debian.org/cgi-bin/download.pl
MP3Stego	MP3	Free	http://www.petitcolas.net/fabien/software/index.html
Hydan	Executables	Free	http://www.crazyboy.com/hydan/

STEGANOGRAPHIC SOFTWARE TOOLS

The availability of simple steganography tools has made it relatively easy for terrorists and other criminals to hide data in files. In fact, law enforcement is concerned with steganography as an easy-to-use, readily-available method for the exchange of illicit material (Jajodia & Johnson, 1998).Steganography tools are readily available on the Web; many are even available for free (interested readers can see sites such as http://www.pcworld.com/downloads/ for more information). Not only can terrorists and other criminals use steganographic tools to hide messages inside files on their own Web sites and e-mail, but they also can use hacking techniques to invade other Web sites and hide their messages there. It is theorized (Cohen, 2001) that Al Qaeda uses porn sites to hide their messages because porn sites are so prevalent and because they are among the last places Muslims would be expected to visit. Therefore, porn sites might provide an extra level of protection from detection.

For example, SpamMimic is a method for disguising hidden messages within e-mail and other communications. Someone wishing to disguise a message can visit http://spammimic.com and type a message. The Web site will then translate that text into a seemingly innocuous e-mail message that looks like spam, but can be sent as a regular e-mail. (The sender can cut and paste this bogus message into an e-mail client.) The recipient can then visit spammimic.com to decode the message, thus revealing the original unencoded message. Although the legitimacy of this software is questionable (i.e., do other people have access to the messages turned into spam or is spammimic.com actually run by a government agency?), it is an interesting concept and perhaps will be further developed in the future. User-friendly steganographic resources, such as spammimic.com, increase the workload for government monitoring programs, such as Carnivore and Echelon, by making them process spam rather than simply discarding it (Clark, 2001).

There are other, arguably less technical, methods of using the Web to disseminate secret information. The content and placement of items on a Web site could be used to convey secret meaning. An example of this low-tech version of steganography could be as straightforward as displaying a Web site image of a man wearing a blue shirt. This image may tip off operatives that a certain attack is scheduled for Tuesday. For terrorists, the benefits of using the Web to convey information include the speed, reach, and clandestine nature of the Web. According to Matthew Devost of the Terrorism Research Center, using steganography "avoids the operational security issues that exist anytime conspirators have a physical meeting" (Cohen, 2001).

STEGANOGRAPHY TOOLS AVAILABLE TO THE PUBLIC

Certain steganographic tools are available only to select government agencies, but there are many tools available on the Web—many are available free of charge. Table 1 presents some examples of steganography tools. For a more inclusive list, the interested reader is directed to http://www.jjtc.com/Steganography/toolmatrix. htm. This site, maintained by Neil F. Johnson, lists and describes approximately 150 examples of steganographic software.

Initially, steganography tools were only capable of hiding information in image files. Recently, however, steganography programs have emerged that can hide files in many other types of files, including sound, text, executables, and even unused portions of disks.

STEGANALYSIS: THE DETECTION OF HIDDEN DATA IN FILES

Steganalysis is the process of hunting for small deviations in the expected patterns of a file (Cohen, 2001) and utilizes a process of detecting steganographic carrier files. "Most current steganalytic techniques are similar to virus detection techniques in that they tend to be signature-based, and little attention has been given to blind steganography detection using an anomaly-based approach, which attempts to detect departures from normalcy" (Claypoole Jr., Gunsch, & Jackson, 2003). A current area of research focuses on genetic algorithms to detect steganography using statistics (Claypoole Jr. et al., 2003). As law enforcement agencies take steganography more seriously, there will certainly be increased efforts to efficiently and effectively detect and isolate potential carrier files.

STEGANOGRAPHICALLY EMBEDDED DATA ARE BRITTLE

Files containing steganographic data are brittle; the embedded data are fragile. The embedded data may be altered or deleted purposefully or accidentally. One simple way to eliminate steganographic data in a host file is to save the file in another format and either leave the file in the new format or resave it in the original format. Even slight changes in compression (or other file transformations) will destroy the hidden message (Cole, 2003). For example, converting the JPG file into another graphics file format, then back to JPG would result in a file with substantially similar visual characteristics, but with the embedded information surely scrambled or otherwise destroyed.

FUTURE LEGAL ISSUES AND CHALLENGES

As with other new technologies, there are issues that existing laws do not address. However, even when laws involving the Internet are enacted, they are typically difficult to enforce. The issue of jurisdiction will need to be decided because most Internet communications cross state lines and international borders. What may be illegal in one country may not be so in another.

In 1952, the United States enacted section 1343 of the Federal Criminal Code. Section 1343 included a wire fraud provision, which was extended to encompass the Internet. It is a federal offense to use any part of the telecommunications system in a criminal act (Cole, 2003). In order to monitor phone conversations, a court order must be obtained from a judge. The court order applies to a specific phone number only. Criminals could easily bypass this by using disposable cell phones (Charny, 2001). Another challenge is the emergence of new technologies, such as the voice over Internet protocol (VoIP), which breaks phone conversations into data packets, sends them over the Internet, and reassembles them at the destination. To monitor this traffic, a few central locations would have to be set up where voice streams could be diverted and then be copied before resending them to the intended destination (*Wired News*, 2003). It would be much more effective to monitor right after the starting point when packets are not separated over different routes or right before the destination, when all packets follow a single path.

There is a delicate balance between loss of personal privacy and the greater good of society. Indeed, groups, such as the American Civil Liberties Union (ACLU), are fighting to maintain privacy and to prevent law enforcement agencies from monitoring communications. The following is a summary of the ACLU's position on privacy and technology:

The United States is at risk of turning into a full-fledged surveillance society. There are two simultaneous developments behind this trend:

- *The tremendous explosion in surveillance-enabling technologies. George Orwell's vision of 'Big Brother' has now become technologically possible.*
- *Even as this technological surveillance monster grows in our midst, we are [weakening] the legal restraints that keep it from trampling our privacy.* (American Civil Liberties Union, 2003)

Although government agencies typically are presumed to be acting in the best interests of the public, there is always the possibility that legislation is used for other purposes than intended. For instance, a Michigan state law enacted March 31, 2003, based on the Digital Millennium Copyright Act (DMCA) and originally intended to protect cable TV operators and broadband providers, contained the provision "A person shall not assemble, develop, manufacture, possess, deliver, or use any type telecommunications access device by doing, but not limited to, any of the following: ... (b) Conceal the existence or place of origin or destination of any telecommunications service." (Act 328 of 1931, 2004) The law had to be amended in 2004 because in its original form, the legitimate use of technologies, such as steganography, was clearly prohibited. Similarly, the possibility exists that some information gathered by authorities will be used for illegitimate purposes.

In recent years, the U.S. government has pushed for increased access to communications and restrictions of the use of encryption technology. Similar to the Communications Assistance for Law Enforcement Act of 1994 (CALEA) in the United States, the European Parliament passed the Communications Data Protection Directive in 2002. When implemented by the individual member states, authorities can order telecommunications companies to store all electronic communications, including phone calls, e-mails, and Internet use, for indefinite periods. With regard to specific technologies to hide data, the European Union takes a more permissive approach. Neither continent has enacted laws restricting the use of steganography specifically, nor is likely that legal restrictions on the use of steganography will be implemented.

Even if efficient and effective steganography monitoring can be implemented, it remains to be seen whether or not the potential loss of privacy is worth the potential thwarting of criminal activities and terrorist plots.

FUTURE NEED: STEGANOGRAPHY DETECTION SYSTEMS

Publicly available sources do not currently address how files with steganographic contents can and should be detected, other than that specific software tools are available to check for steganographic content. Considering the large volume of files sent over the Internet, it would be impossible or impractical to check all traffic. Rather, a manageable number of files to be examined must be selected in order to make detection feasible. It is entirely possible that government systems, such as Carnivore and Echelon, have already implemented techniques to achieve this goal.

The Internet has indeed increased the potential for both legitimate and illegitimate parties to communicate efficiently, effectively, and secretly. The Internet offers several communication protocols, including e-mail, FTP, IRC, instant messaging (IM), P2P (e.g., Napster and Kazaa), HTTP (Web sites), and WSDL (Web services). By some accounts, there will soon be trillions of files transmitted each year over the Internet (Cole, 2003). Herein lies the difficulty—how will law enforcement agencies and security officials identify, isolate, intercept, and address files that contain criminal or terrorist intent? There are no easy answers to this question. A comprehensive solution will require cooperation between Internet access providers (such as, Internet service providers [ISPs]) and agencies such as law enforcement agencies, the Department of Defense, and the new Department of Homeland Security. Access providers can be a first line of defense against criminal activity on the Internet, because they carry nearly all traffic at the starting points and destinations of any network traffic. But monitoring transmissions between sender and recipient is much more resource intensive, if not impossible, due to the very nature of the Internet as a medium where packets are routed over any available path.

SUMMARY

Though computerized steganography has legitimate uses, such as watermarking, copyrighting, and digital fingerprinting, it also has the potential to be a very effective tool for terrorists and other criminals to conduct covert communications. Specifically, there is evidence that terrorist groups, such as Al Qaeda, are using steganography to facilitate communications. Therefore, continued research of methods to identify carrier files and (temporarily) block Internet-based data traffic with illegal messages is strongly indicated, Steganographic data can be hidden in graphics, video, sound, text, e-mail, executable files, and empty sectors of disks. Improved methods for identifying these altered files must be developed and disseminated. An international consortium of nations allied against terrorism could be established to share knowledge related to steganography and steganalysis methods.

REFERENCES

Act 328 of 1931, Michigan Penal Code. §750.540c (2004).

American Civil Liberties Union. (2003). *Privacy and technology.* Retrieved October 29, 2003, from http://www.aclu.org/Privacy/PrivacyMain.cfm

Anderson, R. J., & Petitcolas, F. A. P. (1998). On the limits of steganography. *IEEE Journal on Selected Areas in Communications, 16*(4), 474-481.

Charny, B. (2001). *Disposable cell phones spur debates.* Retrieved October 29, 2003, from http://news.com.com/2102-1033_3-273084.html?tag=st_util_print

Clark, E. (2001). A reason to love spam. *Network Magazine, 16,* 20.

Claypoole Jr., R. L., Gunsch, G. H., & Jackson, J. T. (2003). Blind steganography detection using a computational immune system: A work in progress. *International Journal of Digital Evidence, 4*(1), 1-19.

Cohen, A. (2001, November 12). When terror hides oOnline. *Time, 158,* 65-69.

Cole, E. (2003). *Hiding in plain sight: Steganography and the art of covert communication.* Indianapolis, IN: Wiley Publishing, Inc.

Hachez, G. (2003). *A comparative study of software protection tools suited for e-commerce with contributions to software watermarking and smart cards.* Unpublished doctoral dissertation, Louvain-la-Neuve.

Jajodia, S., & Johnson, N. F. (1998). Exploring steganography: Seeing the unseen. *IEEE Computer, 31*(2), 26-34.

Jupitermedia Corporation. (2003). *Steganography.* Retrieved August 31, 2003, from http://www.webopedia.com/TERM/S/steganography.html

Moulin, P., & O'Sullivan, J. A. (2003). Information-theoretic analysis of information hiding. *IEEE Transactions on Information Theory, 49*(3), 563-593.

Nikolaidis, N., & Pitas, I. (1996). Copyright protection of images using robust digital signatures. *IEEE International Conference on Acoustics, Speech and Signal Processing, 4*, 2168-2171.

Reporter. (2004, November 14). Mol in AIVD gaf tekens op website. *De Telegraaf.*

Ringelestijn, T. V. (2004, March 23). *Technologie buiten schot in zaak toetjesterrorist.* Retrieved June 30, 2006, from http://www.netkwesties.nl/editie86/artikel3.php

Wired News. (2003). *Internet phone calls stymie FBI.* Retrieved October 27, 2003, from http://www.wired.com/news/print/0,1294,58350,00.html

TERMS AND DEFINITIONS

Carnivore: This is an FBI system that is used to analyze the e-mail packets of suspected criminals.

Digital Watermarks: Much like a watermark on a letterhead, a digital watermark is used to assist in identifying ownership of a document or other file. It includes embedded unique strings of data that do not alter the sensory perception of the image file, music file, or other data file.

Echelon: This is a putative system of analysis of international communications. The details of the system are difficult to obtain because many government officials often deny or ignore reports regarding the existence of Echelon.

Encryption: This is a reversible method of encoding data, requiring a key to decrypt. Encryption can be used in conjunction with steganography to provide another level of secrecy.

SpamMimic: A Web site located at http://www.spammimic.com can be used to send a message that appears to be spam when in reality the message is just a cover for sending secret content. The use of spam as a cover will likely increase the workload of FBI systems, such as Carnivore and Echelon.

Steganalysis: This is the process of detecting hidden data in other files. Steganalysis is typically done by searching for small deviations in the expected pattern of a file.

Steganography: In general, it is the process of hiding information or "covered writing." More specifically, in the digital environment, steganography involves hiding data or images within other files, so they appear unaltered to persons unaware of the secret content.

Virtual Fingerprint: This is a unique digital watermark that can be used to uniquely identify a particular file.

Chapter VIII
Cryptography

Kevin Curran
University of Ulster, UK

Niall Smyth
University of Ulster, UK

Bryan Mc Grory
University of Ulster, UK

ABSTRACT

One of the main methods of security is cryptography encrypting data so that only a person with the right key can decrypt it and make sense of the data. There are many forms of encryption, some more effective than others. Cryptography works by taking the original information and converting it with ciphertext, which encrypts the information to an unreadable form. To decrypt the information we simply do the opposite and decipher the unreadable information back into plain text. This enciphering and deciphering of information is done using an algorithm called a cipher. A cipher is basically like a secret code, but the main difference between using a secret code and a cipher is that a secret code will only work at a level of meaning. This chapter discusses a little of the history of cryptography, some popular encryption methods, and also some of the issues regarding encryption, such as government restrictions.

INTRODUCTION

The art of cryptography reaches back as far as 1900 BC, when an Egyptian scribe used a derivation of hieroglyphics to communicate. Throughout history, there have been many people responsible for the growth of cryptography. Many of these people were quite famous and one of these was Julius Caesar. He used a substitution of characters and just moved them about. Another historical figure who used and changed cryptography was Thomas Jefferson. He developed a wheel cipher that was made in 1790. This cipher was then to be used to create the Strip cipher, which was used by the U.S. Navy during the second World

War. During World War II, several mechanical devices were invented for performing encryption, this included rotor machines, most notably the Enigma cipher. The ciphers implemented by these machines brought about a significant increase in the complexity of cryptanalysis. Encryption methods have historically been divided into two categories: substitution ciphers and transposition ciphers. Substitution ciphers preserve the order of the plain-text symbols but disguise them. Transposition ciphers, in contrast, reorder the letters but do not disguise them. Plain text is the common term for the original text of a message before it has been encrypted (Cobb, 2004). In this chapter, we discuss a little of the history of cryptography, some popular encryption methods, and also some of the issues regarding encryption, such as government restrictions.

BACKGROUND

Possibly the earliest encryption method was developed by a Greek historian of the 2nd century BC named Polybius, and it is a type of substitution cipher (Burgess, Pattison, & Goksel, 2000). This method worked with the idea of a translation table containing the letters of the Greek alphabet. This was used for sending messages with torch telegraphy. The sender of the message would have 10 torches, five for each hand. He would send the message letter by letter, holding the number of torches representing the row of the letter in his left hand, and the number of torches representing the column of the letter in his right hand. For example, in the case of the letter "s," the sender would hold three torches in his left hand and four in his right hand. Polybius wrote that "this method was invented by Cleoxenus and Democritus but it was enhanced by me" (Dénes, 2002, p. 7). This method, while simple, was an effective way of encrypting telegraphic messages. The table could easily be changed without changing the method, so as long as both the sender and receiver were using the same table and no one else had the table they could send messages that anyone could see being sent, but which would only be understood by

the intended recipient. This is a form of private key encryption—where both the sender and the recipient share the key to the encrypted messages. In this case, the key is the letter table.

Another type of substitution cipher is the Caesar cipher, attributed to Julius Caesar (Tannenbaum, 1996). In this method, the alphabet is shifted by a certain number of letters; this number being represented by k. For example, where k is 3, the letter A would be replaced with D, B would be replaced with E, Z would be replaced with C, and so forth. This is also a form of private key encryption, where the value of k must be known to decrypt the message. Obviously this simple form of encryption is not difficult to crack, with only 26 possible values of k; it is only a matter of shifting the encrypted message with values of k until you get a comprehensible decrypted message. There are also more complex methods of cracking this encryption, such as using letter frequency statistics to work out some likely letters from the message. For example, E is the most common letter in the English language, so the most common letter in the encrypted message is likely to be E. Replacing the most common letters in the encrypted message with the most common letters of the language may help to make sense of some words. Once a word is partially decrypted, it may be easy to guess what the word is, which will then allow more letters to be substituted with their decrypted versions. For example, if E and T had been used to replace the most common letters and one of the partially decrypted words is "tXe," then the X is likely to be H forming the word "the," so replacing all occurrences of X in the message with H may provide some more words that can be guessed easily (Garrett & Lieman, 2005).

A common transposition cipher, the columnar transposition, works with a private key. The private key is a word or phrase not containing any repeated letters, for example, "HISTORY." This key is used to number columns, with column 1 being under the letter closest to the start of the alphabet and so forth. The plain text is written in rows under the key, and the encrypted text is read in columns, starting with column 1. An example is shown in Figure 1.

Figure 1. Common transposition cipher

H	I	S	T	O	R	Y
1	2	5	6	3	4	7
a	_	p	r	i	v	a
a	t	e	_	p	h	r
a	s	e	_	t	o	_
b	e	_	e	n	c	r
y	p	t	e	d		_

Original message:
a_private_phrase_to_be_encrypted

Encrypted message:
*aaaby_tsepiptndvhoc_pee_tr__eear_r_*

The recipient of this message will then put the encrypted message back into the table with the key providing the column numbers.

Cryptanalysis is the study of methods for obtaining the plain text of encrypted information without access to the key that is usually required for decryption. In lay-man's terms, it is the practice of code breaking or cracking. The dictionary defines cryptanalysis as the analysis and deciphering of cryptographic writings/systems, or the branch of cryptography concerned with decoding encrypted messages. A cryptanalyst is the natural adversary of a cryptographer, in that a cryptographer works to protect or secure information and a cryptanalyst works to read date that has been encrypted. They also complement each other, because without cryptanalysts or the understanding of the cryptanalysis process, it would be very difficult to create secure cryptography. So when designing a new cryptogram, it is common to use cryptanalysis in order to find and correct any weaknesses in the algorithm. Most cryptanalysis techniques exploit patterns found in the plain text code in order to crack the cipher; however compression of the data can reduce these patterns and, hence, enhance the resistance to cryptanalysis (Stallings, 2005).

POPULAR ENCRYPTION METHODS

Cryptography works by taking the original information and converting it through an algorithm into an unreadable form. A key is used to transform the original information. This unreadable information is known as ciphertext. To decrypt the information, we simply do the opposite and decipher the unreadable information back into plain text. This enciphering and deciphering of information is done using an algorithm called a cipher. A cipher is basically like a secret code, but the main difference between using a secret code and a cipher is that a secret code will only work at a level of meaning. This basically means that the secret code could be made up with the same letters and words but just rearranged to mean something else. Ciphers work differently; they can target individual bits or individual letters and design a totally unrecognizable representation of the original document. Another interesting thing about ciphers is that they are usually accompanied by the use of a key (Gritzalis, 2005). Depending on the type of key, different forms of encrypting procedures can be carried out. Without the key, the cipher would be unable to encrypt or decrypt (Jakubowski & Venkatesan, 2000).

One-Time Pads

The previous traditional forms of encryption discussed can be broken by someone who knows what to look for, but there is another method known as the one-time pad that can create unbreakable encrypted messages. A random bit string is used as the key. The message to be encrypted is then converted into a bit string, for example, by using the ASCII codes for each character in the message. Then the EXCLUSIVE OR of these two strings is calculated, bit by bit. For example, take the key to be 0100010 and the message to be A. The ASCII code for A is 1000001. The resulting one-time pad would be 1100011 (Trappe & Washington, 2005). A one-time padded message cannot be broken, because every possible plain text message is an equally probably candidate (Tanenbaum, 2002). The message can only be decrypted by someone who knows the correct key. There are certain disadvantages to this. Firstly, the key must be at least as long as the bit string to be encrypted. Since the key will be a long random bit string, it would be very difficult to memorize. So both the sender and the receiver will need written copies of the key, and having written copies of keys is a security risk if there is any chance of the key falling into the wrong hands. Also, if the sender and the recipient have a previously agreed key to use, then the sender will be limited as they will not be able to send a message too long for the key. With computer systems, the one-time pad method is more useful, as the key could be stored digitally on something like a CD and, therefore, could be extremely long and relatively easy to disguise. Also, it is worth noting that in one-time pads, the key is only used once and never used again.

Advanced Encryption Standard

The advanced encryption standard (AES), also known as Rijndael, is a block cipher adopted as an encryption standard by the U.S. government. It is expected to be used worldwide and analyzed extensively. This was also the case with its predecessor, the data encryption standard (DES). AES came about after it became apparent that with the availability of cheaper and faster hardware, DES would be rendered untenable in a short time. To address this problem, the National Institute of Standards and Technology (NIST) issued a request for comment (RFC) in 1997 for a standard to replace DES (Wikipedia, 2006). NIST worked closely with industry and the cryptographic community to develop this next-generation private-key algorithm. The cipher was developed by two Belgian cryptographers, Joan Daemen and Vincent Rijmen, and submitted to the AES selection process under the name "Rijndael," a portmanteau comprising the names of the inventors (McCaffrey, 2003).

Security was the top priority for the AES algorithm. With security in mind, the algorithm also had to account for future resiliency. Moreover, the algorithm design, contrary to conventional wisdom, had to be simple so that it could be successfully cryptanalyzed.

The AES algorithm is based on permutations and substitutions. Permutations are rearrangements of data, and substitutions replace one unit of data with another. AES performs permutations and substitutions using several different techniques. Basically, there are four operations that are at the heart of the AES encryption algorithm. AddRoundKey substitutes groups of 4 bytes, using round keys generated from the seed-key value. SubBytes substitutes individual bytes using a substitution table. ShiftRows permutes groups of 4 bytes by rotating 4-byte rows. MixColumns substitutes bytes using a combination of both field addition and multiplication. AES-encrypted data is unbreakable in the sense that no known cryptanalysis attack can decrypt the AES cipher text without using a brute-force search through all possible 256-bit keys.

As of 2006, the only successful attacks against AES have been side-channel attacks. Side-channel attacks do not attack the underlying cipher, but attack implementations of the cipher on systems that inadvertently leak data. Some cryptographers, however, worry about the security of AES. They feel that the margin between the number of rounds specified in the cipher and the best-known attacks is too small for comfort. The risk is that some way to improve these attacks might be found and that, if so, the cipher could be broken (McCaffrey, 2003).

DES

IBM developed a method of encryption known as DES, which was adopted by the U.S. government as its official standard for unclassified information in 1977. According to Tanenbaum (2002, p. 103), the standard "is no longer secure in its original form, but in a modified form it is still useful." When IBM originally developed DES, they called it Lucifer, and it used a 128-bit key. The National Security Agency (NSA) discussed the system with IBM, and after these discussions IBM reduced the key from 128 bits to 56 bits before the government adopted the standard. Many people suspected that the key was reduced so that the NSA would be able to break DES on encrypted data that they wished to view, but organizations with smaller budgets would not be able to. As with most forms of encryption, it is possible to break DES encryption by means of a brute-force approach, where a computer is used to attempt to decrypt the data using possible keys one after the other until the correct key is found. Due to the constant speed increase of computers, it takes less time to break DES encryption with every passing year. The key size of DES is no longer big enough for it to stand up to brute-force attacks long enough to make the attacks pointless, so, in its original form, DES is no longer safe for use. Many other encryption methods, which also work on block ciphers akin to DES, have been proposed since, including the international data encryption algorithm (IDEA), which uses a 128-bit key and is still safe from brute force attacks due to the length of time required to find the correct key from the huge key space.

All of the encryption methods discussed so far have been private key methods—meaning they depend on data being encrypted with a key known both to the sender and the recipient. This means that an unencrypted key must somehow be transferred between the sender and the recipient and finding a secure method of doing that can present a problem in many situations. For example, there is no point in encrypting an e-mail to a business partner and then e-mailing him the encryption key, as this defeats the purpose of making the original e-mail secure (Minami & Kasahara, 2005). Next we will discuss another type of encryption that solves this problem and is known as public key encryption.

Public Key Encryption

The idea of public key cryptography was first presented by Martin Hellman, Ralph Merkle, and Whitfield Diffie at Stanford University in 1976 (Mollin, 2002). They proposed a method in which the encryption and decryption keys were different, and in which the decryption key could not be determined using the encryption key. Using such a system, the encryption key could be given out publicly, as only the intended recipient would have the decryption key to make sense of it. A common use of this system is for a person to give out a public key to anyone who wishes to send private information, keeping the private key to themselves. Of course, the encryption algorithm also will need to be public. There are three important requirements for a public key encryption method (Garrett, 2005):

1. When the decryption process is applied to the encrypted message, the result must be the same as the original message before it was encrypted.
2. It must be exceedingly difficult (ideally impossible) to deduce the decryption (private) key from the encryption (public) key.
3. The encryption must not be able to be broken by a plain text attack. Since the encryption and decryption algorithms and the encryption key will be public, people attempting to break the encryption will be able to experiment with the algorithms to attempt to find any flaws in the system.

The RSA Algorithm

One popular method for public key encryption was discovered by a group at the Massachusetts Institue of Technology (MIT) in 1978 and was named after the initials of the three members of the group: Ron Rivest, Adi Shamir, and Leonard Adleman (Tanenbaum, 2002). Shortly before the details of RSA encryption were to be published, the U.S. government reportedly "asked" the inventors to cancel the publication. However, copies of the article had already reached the public. A. K. Dewdney of *Scientific American* had a photocopy of the document explaining the algorithm, and photocopies of this quickly spread. The RSA algorithm was patented by MIT, and then this patent was handed over to a company in California called Public Key Partners (PKP). PKP holds the exclusive commercial license to sell and sublicense the RSA public key cryptosystem. They also hold other patents that cover other public key cryptography algorithms. There is a recognized method of breaking RSA encryption, based on factoring numbers involved, although this can be safely ignored due to the huge amount of time required to factor large numbers. Unfortunately, RSA is too slow for encrypting large amounts of data, so it is often used for encrypting the key used in a private key method, such as IDEA (Sun & Wang, 2003). This key can then be transferred in public securely, resolving the key security problem for IDEA.

Pretty Good Privacy

Published for free on the Internet in 1991, pretty good privacy (PGP) was a public key e-mail encryption software package. It was originally designed by Philip R. Zimmermann as a human rights tool, allowing human rights activists to protect sensitive information from the prying eyes of opposing forces (Zimmermann, 2004). At the time of its development, there were laws against the export of cryptography software from the United States, so when PGP spread worldwide after its release on the Internet, Zimmermann came under criminal investigation. Despite this, PGP spread to become the most widely used e-mail encryption software in the world. PGP used a combination of IDEA and RSA encryption to allow e-mails to be transferred securely under public key encryption. Eventually in 1996, the U.S. government dropped its case against Zimmermann, and so he founded PGP Inc. to continue development of the software. PGP Inc. bought up ViaCrypt and began to publish new versions of PGP. Since the U.S. export restrictions on cryptography software were not lifted until early 2000, PGP Inc. used a legal loophole to print the PGP source code and export the books containing the code outside the United States, where they could then scan it in using optical character recognition (OCR) software and publish an international version of the software legally. In 1997, PGP Inc. was acquired by Network Associates Inc. (NAI), where Zimmermann stayed on for three years as a senior fellow. In 2002, the rights to PGP were acquired from NAI by a new company called PGP Corporation, where Zimmermann now works as a consultant. The PGP Corporation carries on the tradition of publishing the source code of its software for peer review, so that customers and cryptography experts may validate the integrity of the products, and satisfy themselves that there are no back doors in the software, allowing easy decryption (PGP Corporation, 2005).

Steganography

Steganography refers to hiding a secret message inside a larger message in such a way that someone unaware of the presence of the hidden message cannot detect it. Steganography in terms of computer data works by replacing useless or unused data in regular files (such as, images, audio files, or documents) with different, invisible information. This hidden information can be plain text, encrypted text, or even images (Hook, 2005). This method is useful for those who wish to avoid it being known that they are sending private information at all; with a public key encryption method, although the data is safe, anyone viewing it will be able to see that what is transferring is a private encrypted message (Bailey, Curran, & Condell, 2004). With steganography, even this fact is kept private, as you can hide a message in a simple photograph, where no one will suspect its presence. This leads onto an important issue of cryptography: the involvement of governments (Venkatesan & Jakubowski, 2000).

Cryptography and steganography are different, however. Cryptographic techniques can be used to scramble a message, so that if it is discovered, it cannot be read. If a cryptographic message is discovered it is generally known to be a piece of hidden information (anyone intercepting it will be suspicious), but it is scrambled so that it is difficult or impossible to understand and decode. Steganography hides the very existence of a message, so that if successful, it generally attracts no suspicion.

Governments and Cryptography

Many governments try to suppress usage of encryption, as they wish to be able to spy on potential criminals. If these criminals use secure encryption to send information between each other, law enforcement agencies will not be able to tap in to what is being said. The U.S. government at one point developed what is known as a key escrow system, and the British government was rumored to be working on a similar system, which never came to fruition. The idea of a key escrow system is that you can use it as a public key encryption system, with the addition that certain government agencies will hold a "spare key," allowing them to decrypt your private messages, if they were suspicious of illegal activities being discussed in the messages' contents. There are some obvious flaws with such a system; for one, the only people who would use the key escrow encryption would be those with nothing to hide from the government (Yamaguchi, Hashiyama, & Okuma, 2005).

As cybercrime technologies become more sophisticated, governments need to implement new and more powerful technologies to fight this new breed of criminals. Identification systems that use biometrics will help to secure trust in the online world but so also will cryptography. This places cryptography beyond its traditional role in mainframe computing, but also in securing data across every touch point on the network. The result will be to build robust security into the design and development of computer systems, rather than bolting it on as an after thought (IBM, 2005).

CONCLUSION

Cryptography is a powerful tool, both for keeping important information private and, when in the wrong hands, for keeping illegal activities hidden from government agencies. As computers grow faster and methods for breaking encryption become more viable, encryption algorithms will need to be constantly strengthened to stop them from becoming insecure. There is little that can be done about the use of cryptography to keep illegal activites hidden—short of making all forms of strong encryption illegal, which would create an outrage in Western countries used to freedom in such matters. The benefits of the government key escrow or key recovery program seem to benefit them solely in that they can track who they want, when they want. It can, however, if used properly and without abuse, aid law enforcement. It has the potential to meet the needs of users' confidentiality. The most

obvious downside of key escrow, or the clipper chip, is that its main purpose is for law enforcement, but why would a criminal or terrorist use a technology that the government can decipher? This could only lead to the terrorists turning to stronger forms of cryptography, and then all the benefits of the model are gone. It is only likely to be successful to capture or monitor petty criminals.

REFERENCES

Bailey, K., Curran, K., & Condell, J. (2004). An evaluation of automated stegodetection methods in images. *International Conference on Information Technology and Telecommunications*. Limerick Institute of Technology.

Burgess, J., Pattison, E., & Goksel, M., (2000) *Public key cryptography*. Stanford University. Retrieved from http://cse.stanford.edu/classes/sophmore-college/projects-97/cryptography/history.html

Cobb, C. (2004). *Cryptography for dummies*. Dummies Series.

Dénes, T. (2002). *Cardan and cryptography—The mathematics of encryption grids*. Hungary. Retrieved from http://www.komal.hu/lap/2002-ang/cardano.e.shtml

Garrett, P., & Lieman, D. (2005). Public-key cryptography. In *Proceedings of Symposia in Applied Mathematica*.

Gritzalis, S. (2005). Public key infrastructure: Research and applications. *International Journal of Information Security, 5*(1), 1-2.

Hook, D. (2005). *Beginning cryptography with Java*. Wrox.

IBM. (2005). *The future of crime*. Retrieved from http://www.306.ibm.com/innovation/us/pointofview/cybercrime/jan23/IBM_Future_Crime.html

McCaffrey, J. (2003, November). Keep your data secure with the new advanced encryption standard. *MSDN*

Magazine. Retrieved from http://msdn.microsoft.com/msdnmag/issues/03/11/AES/

Minami, N., & Kasahara, M. (2005). A new decoding method for digital watermark based on error correcting codes and cryptography. *Electronics and Communications in Japan (Part III: Fundamental Electronic Science), 88*(8), 9-17.

Mollin, R. (2002). *RSA and public-key cryptography.* Chapman & Hall/CRC.

PGP Corporation. (2005). *PGP Corporation source code.* Retrieved from http://www.pgp.com/downloads/sourcecode/index.html

Stallings, W. (2005). *Cryptography and network security* (4th ed.). Prentice Hall.

Sun, Z., & Wang, R. (2003). Research on mixed encryption authentication. *The Journal of China Universities of Posts and Telecommunications, 10*(4), 90-94.

Tannenbaum, A. (1996). *Computer networks* (3th ed.). Prentice Hall.

Trappe, W., & Washington, L. (2005). *Introduction to cryptography with coding theory* (2nd ed.). Prentice Hall.

Venkatesan, R., & Jakubowski, M. H. (2000). *Image watermarking with better resilience.* Presented at the IEEE International Conference on Image Processing (ICIP 2000).

Venkatesan, R ., Koon, S. -M., Jakubowski, M. H., & Moulin, P. (2000 September). *Proceedings of the IEEE ICIP.* Vancouver.

Wikipedia. (2006). Retrieved from http://en.wikipedia.org/wiki/Cryptography

Yamaguchi, T., Hashiyama, T., & Okuma, S. (2005). The proposal of power analysis for common key cryptography implemented on the FPGA and its countermeasure. *Electronics and Communications in Japan (Part III: Fundamental Electronic Science), 88*(8), 28-37.

Zimmermann, P. (2004). *Philip Zimmermann—Creator of PGP*. Retrieved from http://www.philzimmermann.com

Zimmermann, P. (2005). *Why do you need PGP?* Retrieved from http://www.pgpi.org/doc/whypgp/en/

TERMS AND DEFINITIONS

Application Encryption: Cryptographic functions built into the communications protocols for a specific application, like e-mail. Examples include PEM, PGP, and SHTTP.

Authentication: The ability to ensure that the given information is produced by the entity whose name it carries and that it was not forged or modified.

Certificate, Public Key: This is a specially formatted block of data that contains a public key and the name of its owner. The certificate carries the digital signature of a certification authority to authenticate it.

Cryptography: The practice and study of encryption and decryption—encoding data so that it can only be decoded by specific individuals. A system for encrypting and decrypting data is a cryptosystem.

Private Key: Key used in public key cryptography that belongs to an individual entity and must be kept secret.

Public Key System: A public key system is one which uses two keys, a public key known to everyone and a private key that only the recipient of message uses.

RSA: A popular, highly secure algorithm for encrypting information using public and private keys, obscurely named for the initials of its creators (Massachusetts Institute of Technology (MIT) professors Ron Rivest, Adi Shamir, and Leonard Adleman).

Secure Sockets Layer (SSL): Cryptography protocol applied to data at the socket interface. It is often bundled with applications and widely used to protect World Wide Web traffic.

Chapter IX
A Roadmap for Delivering Trustworthy IT Processes

Kassem Saleh
American University of Sharjah, UAE

Imran Zualkernan
American University of Sharjah, UAE

Ibrahim Al Kattan
American University of Sharjah, UAE

ABSTRACT

Due to the proliferations of computers and networks, organizations are providing many of their services online. Consequently, organizations are becoming more vulnerable to attacks by cyber criminals, in addition to attacks by insiders. Ultimately, these attacks lead to reducing the trust in the organization and the trustworthiness of its provided services. Online services are mainly provided using internal IT processes. In this chapter, we provide a systematic roadmap that addresses the delivery of trustworthy IT processes at the strategic, tactical and operational levels. This roadmap is based on a defensive and preventive approach to ensure the trustworthiness of the services provided by an organization. We argue that to deliver trustworthy services, the IT processes used must be trustworthy themselves. The requirements for implementing and delivering trustworthy IT processes in an organization are discussed. For each IT process, we discuss how confidentiality, integrity, availability, accountability, reliability, privacy and business integrity requirements can be satisfied.

INTRODUCTION

The proliferation of computers and networks and the need to provide network-based online services is making organizations more vulnerable to attacks by malicious users, among which are cyber terrorists and cyber criminals. In this chapter, we propose a defensive and preventive countermeasure approach against cyber terrorism and cyber warfare that can be adopted by organizations. Information technology (IT) departments within such organizations are responsible for the delivery of trustworthy IT services, and consequently, fending off malicious users and attackers. IT services are delivered through the execution of processes at the strategic, tactical, and operational levels. Our proposed approach relies on ensuring that these IT processes are themselves trustworthy. In this chapter, we first refine Microsoft's definition of trustworthiness (Mundie, deVries, Haynes, & Corwine, 2002) and refine the 38 IT processes identified by Luftman (2003). Then, we discuss how each of the refined trustworthiness requirements, which obviously includes security requirements (Firesmith, 2003), can be considered in the engineering and management of each of the refined IT processes. The result of this chapter can be used as a generic roadmap to achieve trustworthiness in delivering IT processes. Organizations of different sizes and different IT budgets can adapt and use this generic roadmap for their own situations. This roadmap can also be extended and used for the qualitative and quantitative assessment of service trustworthiness.

The rest of this chapter is organized as follows. First, we provide some preliminary background on trustworthiness and IT processes, and their refinements. Then we will provide an introduction to defensive measures against cyber attacks and the need to embed security and trust in the way we engineer and manage IT systems. Next we present the generic requirements for trustworthiness of IT processes at the strategic, tactical and operational levels. We conclude by providing some ideas for further investigation.

BACKGROUND

Trust in IT-based systems is a topic of current interest among researchers and practitioners. Delivering high assurance and trustworthy services has been subject to long-term initiatives by Microsoft, Cisco, the Software Engineering Institute (SEI), among others (Mundie et al., 2002). According to Microsoft, the four pillars of trustworthy computing are security, privacy, reliability, and business integrity. Security addresses issues related to confidentiality, integrity, availability, and accountability. Privacy is related to the fair handling of information. Reliability is related to the dependability of the system to offer its services. Finally, business integrity is related to the responsiveness and ethical responsibility of the service provider.

Luftman identifies 38 IT processes and categorizes them into three layers (Luftman, 2003). First, the strategic layer consists of three processes focusing on the long-term goals and objectives of the organization and considering the strategic alignment of IT and business objectives. These three processes are: business strategic planning, architecture scanning and definition, and IT strategic planning and control. Second, the tactical layer consists of 14 processes focusing on medium-term goals contributing to the strategic goals. Finally, the operational layer consisting of 21 processes providing guidance for day-to-day activities contributing to the tactical processes. Many of the tactical and operational processes can be clustered together since they can be dealt with similarly when considering their trustworthiness requirements. We have clustered the tactical processes into: IT financial management, IT human resource management, IT project management, IT systems development and maintenance, and finally, IT service engineering and management. Figure 1 shows the three layers of Luftman's IT processes.

Next we refine the four pillars of Microsoft's trustworthy computing by adapting them to trustworthy processes and trustworthy services:

- **Security:** Service clients expect that the provided services are protected from malicious attacks on their confidentiality (C), integrity (I), and availability (AV). Confidentiality implies that all data, information and knowledge are kept in confidence. Integrity means that data, information, and knowledge will only be shared with and provided to entities that are allowed to have access to it according to organizational rules. Finally, availability means that the service is available when required. At the strategic level, for example, confidentiality implies that

Figure 1. The three layers of Luftman's IT processes

Business Strategic Planning		Architecture Scanning & Definition		IT Strategic Planning & Control	
Management planning: • Monitoring and planning • Project planning	**Development planning:** • Application planning • Data planning • Network planning • System planning	**Resource planning:** • Capacity planning • Skills planning • Budget planning • Vendor planning		**Service planning:** • Service level planning • Recovery planning • Security planning • Audit planning	
Financial management: • Asset management • Financial performance	**Human resource management:** • Staff performance • Education and training • Recruiting, hiring, and reception	**Project management:** • Assignment and scheduling • Requirements control • Controlling and evaluating	**Systems engineering & management:** • Software dev. & maintenance • S/w and h/w procurement • Systems maintenance • Tuning and systems balancing • Problem and change control	**Services engineering & management:** • Service evaluating • Service marketing • Production and distribution scheduling	

all data, information, and knowledge used in strategy formulation is kept confidential. Moreover, care should be taken to enforce its integrity. This means information provided to individuals involved in the strategy formulation process is consistent with their rights and roles. Availability at the strategic level is the degree to which the strategy formulation process is available to provide strategic directions to other IT processes. Finally, accountability (AC) can also be considered as a security requirement, since holding a legitimate user accountable for their actions enhances security and avoids nonrepudiation.

- **Reliability (R):** Service clients can depend on the provided service to fulfill their functions when required to do so. This feature relates to the "correctness" of the provided service. The smaller number is the failure rate and the mean time between failures, the higher number is the service reliability. At the strategic level, reliability deals with the ability of a strategic process to arrive at the "correct" strategic decisions and directions. Reliability at this level can therefore be measured by the number of times the strategy is "incorrect."

- **Privacy (P):** Service clients are able to control their own personal or institutional data collected by the process delivering the service. Moreover, the use of this data must not be shared with external processes without the consent of the service clients. At the strategic level, for example, this means that the data that went into making the strategic choices such as productivity records, failure rates, and so forth, is controllable by the client who provided such data.

- **Business integrity (BI):** The service owner behaves in a responsive and responsible manner. This means that requests from service clients are handled ethically while keeping the interest of the client and the organization in balance. In addition, such service is provided in a reasonable amount of time. At the strategic level, for example, the strategic process has business integrity if it appropriately addresses both the business and IT sides of issues in an even-handed manner.

TRUSTWORTHINESS REQUIREMENTS FOR IT PROCESSES

Here we present the trustworthiness requirements for the strategic, tactical, and operational level processes. For each IT process providing services, we should recognize the different service stakeholders, including, service owners, service clients, and service providers. Service clients can be either internal or external clients. Internal clients include other entities within an organization such as other units. External clients include outside agencies such government, external auditors, compliance agencies, and so forth.

Strategic Processes

IT has three types of strategic processes: business strategic planning, architecture scanning and definition, and IT strategic planning. The trustworthiness of each of these processes is summarized in Table 1.

Business strategic planning process defines a business strategy that is enabled and driven by IT. The primary client for the business strategic planning process is the IT strategic planning process. All aspects of trustworthiness apply to the strategic planning processes. For example, as Table 1 shows, confidentiality dictates that information about business scope, structure, markets, and competitors needs to be controlled.

Architecture scanning and definition is the process of defining data, information, and knowledge architectures for the enterprise. The primary direct client of the architecture scanning and definition process are internal IT organizations and the suppliers and customers. For example, as Table 1 shows, privacy constraints dictate that business, IT, customers, and suppliers have control over the data they have provided for the process.

IT strategic planning process is concerned with defining the IT strategy to support a business strategy. The IT planning process has recently been driven by alignment models that formulate the strategic planning process as an alignment between the business and IT (Handerson & Venkatraman, 1993). The primary clients for a strategic management process are the higher management who need to implement and approve an IT strategy for a business and its alignment with business goals, and the IT deployment function that needs to implement the strategy. As Table 1 shows, for example, the reliability constraint for this process is that business is correctly aligned with the IT.

Table 1. Trustworthiness of strategic IT processes

Process	C	I	AV	AC	R	P	BI
Business Strategic Planning	Business scope, structure, markets, competitors	Limit access to those with access rights	When business or IT strategy changes	Decisions are traceable	Strategy is correct	Business and IT data is protected	True business demands are taken into account
Architecture Scanning and Definition	IT capabilities, standards, data from suppliers, partners, and customers	Same	Same	Same	Architecture is accurate	Customer and supplier data is also involved	The capabilities are not under- or over-stated
IT Strategic Planning and Control	Scope, competencies, governance, processes, skills, etc.	Same	Same	Same	IT is aligned with Business	Business and IT is protected	Correct balance is maintained between IT and business

Table 2. Trustworthiness of management planning process

Process	C	I	AV	AC	R	P	BI
Monitoring and planning	All information from data, resource, services, and security planning	Data from varied services only shared when allowed	When any tactical processes changes	All decisions are traceable	Correct monitoring schedule and planning	Of all the privacy processes	Adequate allocation of resources across services
Project planning	Organizational resources, goals, and development schedules	Data restricted to those with access rights	With operational or strategic changes	All decisions are traceable to data and teams	Project schedules are adequate and consistent with strategic goals	Strategic and operational processes	All stakeholder needs are considered

Tactical Processes

Tactical processes consist of management planning, development planning, resource planning, and service planning processes. Table 2 summarizes the trustworthiness aspects of the management planning process.

The management systems planning process uses the strategic processes, reviews the existing IT plans, and defines a new prioritized portfolio of projects that is matched to the organizational objectives. The primary client of this process are other IT planning processes. Finally, project planning is concerned with defining the feasible and manageable projects that reflect organizational goals and objectives. As Table 2 shows, for example, the business integrity constraint for this process needs to ensure an equitable distribution of resources among the other tactical processes. The trustworthiness of development planning processes is summarized in Table 3.

Table 3. Trustworthiness of development planning processes

Process	C	I	AV	AC	R	P	BI
Application planning	Portfolio and schedule	Data restricted to those with access rights	With operational or strategic changes	All decisions are traceable to data and teams	Portfolio and schedule are appropriate	Strategic and operational processes	Portfolio is not biased
Data planning	Data needs and schedule	Same	Same	Same	Date planning and schedule are correct	Same	All stakeholder needs are considered
Network planning	Network needs and schedule	Same	Same	Same	Network planning and schedule are correct	Same	Same
System planning	Hardware, software, networking requirements, strategic goals	Same	Same	Same	Strategic goals are met	Same	Same

Table 4. Trustworthiness of resource planning

Process	C	I	AV	AC	R	P	BI
Capacity planning and management	Financial capability, technical capacity	Data is shared only with those who have access	Needs of the operations or strategy changes	Decisions are traceable	Capacity planning is adequate	Internal IT capacity data	Fairness between operational processes
Skills planning and management	Skill profiles and capacity	Same	Same	Same	Skills planning is correct	Skill profiles of individuals	Same
Budget planning and value management	Fiscal constraints	Same	Same	Same	Budget is appropriate	Financial data	Same
Vendor planning and management	Contracts, pricing, relationships, service levels	Same	Same	Same	Correct vendor relationships are established	Vendor profiles and contracts	Same

Application planning process defines a portfolio and schedule of applications to be built or modified within a set period of time. Data planning process works in conjunction with an application plan and determines the data needs that are planned. Network planning focuses on the network connectivity demands of the enterprise. System planning consists of translating the enterprise's strategic goals into a combination of hardware, software, networks, and people. The primary client for the development planning processes are the operations level IT processes that actually implement projects and services. As Table 3 shows, for example, the application portfolio and schedule needs to be kept confidential for the application planning process. Table 4 summarizes the trustworthiness requirements for the various resource planning processes.

Table 5. Trustworthiness of service planning

Process	C	I	AV	AC	R	P	BI
Service level planning and management	Service needs and service levels	Planners who need access should have it	When contracts are negotiated, continuous monitoring	Planning decisions should be traceable	Service levels are maintained	Customers, vendors, service providers	Business needs are not violated
Recovery planning and management	Business continuity requirements and plans	Same	When significant changes in IT/business requirements	Same	Recovery plans are robust	Everyone in the organization	Adequate resources are allocated for continuity
Security planning and management	Security strategies, needs, and plans	Same	Same	Same	Security is not violated	Same	Processes are not misused
Audit planning and management	Audit requirements and plans	Same	Same	Same	Adequate audit trace is established	Same	Audit is not used for personal gain

Table 6. Trustworthiness of financial management processes

Process	C	I	AV	AC	R	P	BI
Asset management	Proper identification and authentication, Role-based access control	Planners who need access should have it	Access should be granted within reasonable delays	Audit logs to trace back activities	Use of reputable asset management package	Privacy of vendors must be protected	Relationship transparency with vendors
Financial performance	Same	Same	Same	Same	Use of reputable financial performance package	None	Awareness of ethical and professional conduct

Capacity planning and management determines how resources will support the demands of IT. Skills planning and management determines the staffing levels and profile based on the requirements defined in the service and project plans. Budget planning and management converts individual plans into monetary terms and determines how funds will be sourced, allocated, and distributed to support the various projects and services. Vendor and planning management deals with outsourcing of IT services and with the management of external vendors. These processes have a variety of clients. For example, capacity planning has an impact on the IT operational processes in determining the resources available to execute specific projects. Skill planning process affects the human resource and training functions within the organization. Finally, the budget process effects the financial planning processes of the company. As Table 4 shows, from a trustworthiness perspective, the privacy requirements of the skills planning and management process dictates that employees have control over their skill profiles. Table 5 summarizes the trustworthiness of service planning processes.

Service planning process defines, negotiates, deploys, and monitors service level agreements. Service planning is also concerned with recovery planning and management, security planning and management, and audit planning and management. These processes have a variety of clients. For example, service management processes can have both internal and external clients. As Table 5 shows, for example, the business integ-rity requirements for service level planning process dictate that the business needs are not violated while formulating service level agreements.

Operational Processes, Financial Management (FM) Processes

IT provides support for asset management and financial performance management. Clients of these two FM-related IT processes are mainly internal organization clients. However, the financial performance process may allow for direct interactions and interfacing with vendors for the settlement of purchase orders and for the administration of contracts, and the calculation of charges for the provided IT services. The asset management process provides internal services including the identification and management of system assets, and the reporting and control of the status of the inventories. In addition to the external services, the financial performance process provides internal services including the execution of cost accounting procedures, the reporting on the accounting and financial status, and the tracking of vendor performance. Table 6 shows trustworthiness requirements for financial management processes.

Project Management (PM) Processes

IT provides support for PM-related processes, including assignment, scheduling, control, evaluation, and requirements control. Clients of these PM-related IT

Table 7. Trustworthiness of project management processes

Process	C	I	AV	AC	R	P	BI
Assignment and scheduling Controlling and evaluating	Proper identification and authentication, role-based access control	Access rights reflecting role	Access should be granted within reasonable delays	Audit logs collected to provide backward traceability	Use of reputable and reliable project management tool	None	Adhere to professional ethics of project managers
Requirements control	Same	Same	Same	Same	Use of reputable and reliable requirements engineering tool	Private clients requirements concerns must be protected	Ethical and professional dealing with clients requests

processes are mainly internal organization clients. However, only the project requirements control process deals with external clients with respect to the reception, analysis, and decision making regarding external clients' requests for requirements changes. Table 7 summarizes the trustworthiness of project management processes.

Human Resources Management (HRM) Processes

IT provides support for HRM-related processes, including staff performance, education and training, and recruiting, hiring, and retention of personnel. Clients of these HRM-related IT processes are mainly internal

organization clients. However, the recruiting, hiring, and retention process deals with external clients with respect to the recruitment of personnel. Also, the education and training process interfaces with either external or internal training services providers. Table 8 shows trustworthiness requirements for human resources management processes.

Systems Engineering and Management (System E&M) Processes

These IT processes support the delivery of IT services to both internal and external clients. These processes include software and hardware procurement, software

Table 8. Trustworthiness of human resources management processes

Process	C	I	AV	AC	R	P	BI
Staff performance Recruiting, hiring, and retention	Proper identification and authentication, Role-based access control	Integrity constraints dictated by access rights and role	Access should be granted within reasonable delays	Audit logs collected to provide backward traceability	Use of reputable and reliable tools for HR management	Privacy of clients' information must be protected	Meeting the ethical and professional standard in human resource mgmnt.
Education and training	Same	Same	Same	Same	Use reputable external training services providers	Privacy of trainees' and trainers information must be protected	Meeting professional and quality standards for training

Table 9. Trustworthiness of systems engineering and management processes

Process	C	I	AV	AC	R	P	BI
Software development and maintenance **Systems maintenance**	Proper identification and authentication, Role-based access control	Integrity constraints dictated by access rights and role	Access should be granted within reasonable delays	Audit logs collected to provide backward traceability	Use of reliable development/ maintenance tools, highly trained professionals	Private clients data must be protected	Professionals meeting software engineering code of ethics
Software and hardware procurement	Same	Same	Same	Same	Use professionally sound procurement decisions	Private vendors / suppliers info must be protected	Ethical and professional dealing with vendors
Tuning and systems balancing	Same	Same	Same	Same	Highly trained professionals dealing with tuning and balancing decisions	None	Faithful, timely response to tuning and balancing requests
Problem and change control	Same	Same	Same	Same	Use of reliable configuration management tools	Private clients data must be protected	Professional, ethical and responsive dealing with problem / change requests

development and maintenance, systems development and maintenance, tuning and balancing, and finally, problem and change controls. Clients of these processes are mainly internal ones. Service managers recognize the problems and report them to the system managers. These problems may require software and hardware changes, including development and maintenance activities, and possibly system tuning and balancing actions. As a result, testing and deployment of an updated system will take place. Project managers, financial managers, and human resource managers can also initiate requests needing software development or maintenance. External clients may interface with these processes in the software and hardware procurement activities. These clients may include vendors, contractors, external quality auditors, standard compliance authorities, and government regulators. Table 9 shows trustworthiness requirements for systems engineering and management processes.

Services Engineering and Management (Service E&M) Processes

These service E&M processes support the delivery of IT services to both internal and external clients. These processes include service evaluating and marketing, and production and distribution scheduling. Clients of these processes are both internal and external clients. Service managers are responsible for the assessment of collected operational field service data and comparing them with service level agreements. As a result, requests for changes are initiated and passed to the system E&M processes. Service managers are also responsible for the reporting on the status of existing services and the identification of new service requests. New services can also be requested by interacting with existing or potential service clients. Prior to the deployment of new services, service managers are

Table 10. Trustworthiness of services engineering and management processes

Process	C	I	AV	AC	R	P	BI
Service evaluating	Proper identification and authentication, role-based access control	Integrity constraints dictated by access rights and role	Must be performed for timely service improvement	Audit logs collected to provide backward traceability	Engage highly trained professionals	Private clients' information must be protected	Meeting professional standards for services professionals
Service marketing	Same	Same	Same	Same	Engage highly trained marketing professionals	Same	Meeting ethical standards for marketing professionals
Production and distribution scheduling	Same	Same	Access should be granted within reasonable delays	Same	Use reliable tools, engage trained professionals	None	Meeting ethical behavior standards for service production and distribution

responsible for the marketing of these new services by interfacing with public relations and with human resources should additional service providers be needed to support new services, such as help desk managers and information and support managers. Moreover, service managers map service level agreements into a schedule for production and distribution activities. Service managers must monitor the progress of these activities and make necessary adjustments if needed to meet these agreements. Finally, service managers must monitor and report on production and distribution status, and if needed, oversee the execution of the necessary incidence response or recovery procedures by coordinating with the appropriate system managers. Table 10 shows the trustworthiness requirements for services engineering and management processes.

FUTURE TRENDS

As an extension to this chapter, we are planning to adapt and use this roadmap for the assessment of existing IT processes in different organizational contexts. A quantification of the level of IT processes trustworthiness would provide a good indicator on how the organization is performing with respect to its trustworthiness, and would pinpoint the areas of weaknesses that can be addressed. Consequently, we plan to develop a trustworthiness maturity model for services-based organizations. We are also planning to apply our roadmap to knowledge management systems and define the concept of knowledge trustworthiness. It is also interesting to check and confirm the direct relation between processes trustworthiness, clients' trust level, and the reported incidents of computer crimes and attacks.

CONCLUSION

The proliferation of computers and networks, and the increase in users accessing them have led to an increase in reported computer-related attacks and crimes. In this chapter, we propose a defensive and preventive solution to counter these attacks based on increasing the organization's awareness with respect to the trustworthiness of its IT processes. We argue that the organization's readiness to deal with computer attacks is strongly related to the level of trustworthiness of its internal IT processes. We also suggest that trustworthiness involves, in addition to the operational level IT processes, both tactical and strategic level planning and decision making processes. Having "trustworthiness-aware" IT processes leads to higher readiness to counter computer crimes and hence leading to higher internal and external users' trust in the delivered IT services.

REFERENCES

Firesmith, D. (2003). Engineering security requirements. *Journal of Object Technology, 2*(1), 53-64.

Handerson, J. C., & Venkatraman, N. (1993). Strategic alignment: Leveraging information technology for transforming organizations. *IBM Systems Journal, 32*(1), 472-483.

Luftman, J. (2003). *Managing the information technology resource*. Prentice Hall.

Mundie, C., de Vries, P., Haynes, P., & Corwine, M. (2002). *Trustworthy computing*. Microsoft White Paper.

TERMS AND DEFINITIONS

Business Integrity Requirement: Service providers meeting the highest ethical and professional standards when dealing with clients.

Privacy Requirement: Service providers ensuring that clients' private information is protected and clients have control over the access to their private information.

Preventive Control: A prescribed defensive measure to prevent a crime from being committed.

Trust: Trust is a relative user's perception of the degree of confidence the user has in the system they use.

Trustworthy Service: A trustworthy system is a system that gains a high level of trust by its users by satisfying the specified security, privacy, reliability, and business integrity requirements.

Section II
Dynamic Aspects of Cyber Warfare and Cyber Terrorism

Cyber attacks by definition are conducted by or against electronic data processing facilities. But as it has been outlined previously, they may have additional objectives. A good example of this is the banking/financial sector. We could easily predict that an effective cyber terrorist attack against, for instance, the New York Stock Exchange may result not only in generating substantial loses to NYSE traders but may create a domino effect that may decrease the volume of trades on other international stock exchanges.

The banking and financial sector is without any doubt the first totally computerized sector of human activity that encompasses and is integrated into everything we know. The SWIFT financial network was the first truly international commercial network, long before the ARPANET was conceived. When viewed in the above context, the saying that "money rules the world" has an enormous impact on the digital world. This is the underling reason why in this chapter there a number of papers discussing aspects of attacks on financial systems. Through various forms of attacks, these financial systems and others may be subjected to a host of criminal abuses.

In order to gain access to a system, various forms of deception may be employed on legitimate users. Several papers addressing this problem have been included. Closely associated with deception are ethical problems and this too has been included. Finally, the use of software as a transport mechanism in carrying out cyber attacks that may have severe security consequences hare included. In this section, the following opinions and views are being presented:

Chapter X
An Introduction to Key Themes in the Economics of Cyber Security

Neil Gandal
Tel Aviv University and CEPR, Israel

ABSTRACT

Software security is an important concern for vendors, consumers, and regulators since attackers who exploit vulnerabilities can cause significant damage. In this brief paper, I discuss key themes in the budding literature on the economics of cyber-security. My primary focus is on how economics incentives affect the major issues and themes in information security. Two important themes relevant for the economics of cyber security issues are (i) a security externality and (ii) a network effect that arises in the case of computer software. A nascent economics literature has begun to examine the interaction between vulnerability disclosure, patching, product prices and profits.

INTRODUCTION

It has become commonplace to receive warnings about killer viruses. Some of these are hoaxes, but several real viruses have done significant damage. According to the *Economist* magazine,[1] the Blaster worm and SoBig.F viruses of 2003 resulted in $35 billion in damages. Weaver and Paxson (2004) suggest that a worst case scenario worm could cost anywhere from $50 billion to $100 billion. And it appears that the time between the announcement of a software vulnerability and the time in which an attack is launched has declined significantly. According to the *Economist*,[1] the time from disclosure to attack was six months for the Slammer worm (January 2003), while the time from disclosure to attack for the Blaster worm (August 2003) was only three weeks.

The Slammer, Blaster, and Sobig.F worms exploited vulnerabilities even though security patches or updates eliminating the vulnerabilities had been released by Microsoft. That is, although the security updates were widely available, relatively few users applied them. Indeed, a 2004 survey found the following:[2]

- 80% of the computers connected to the Internet are infected with spyware.
- 20% of the machines have viruses.
- 77 of those surveyed thought that they were very safe or somewhat safe from online threats, yet 67% did not have updated antivirus software.
- Two-thirds of all computer users had no firewall protection.

In this chapter, I discuss key themes in the budding literature at the "intersection" of computer science and engineering issues, and the economic incentives associated with cyber security and software provision. My primary focus is on how economic incentives affect the major issues and themes in information security.[3] A quick introduction to the topic can be found at Ross Anderson's *Economics and Security Resource Page*.[4] Another source of information is the annual Workshop on Economics and Information Security (WEIS).[5]

TWO KEY PHENOMENA: SECURITY EXTERNALITIES AND NETWORK EFFECTS

Two key phenomena relevant for the economics of cyber security issues are (1) a security externality and (2) a network effect that arises in the case of computer software.

Security Externality

Unprotected computers are vulnerable to being used by hackers to attack other computers. There is a lack of incentive for each user in the system to adequately protect against viruses in their system, since the cost of the spread of the virus is borne by others. That is, computer security is characterized by a positive "externality." If I take more precautions to protect my computer, I enhance the security of other users as well as my own. Such settings lead to a classic *free-rider* problem. In the absence of a market for security, individuals will choose less security than the social optimal. Solutions to the free-rider problems have been addressed in many settings.

Network Effects

A *network effect* arises in computer software. The benefits of computer software typically depend on the number of consumers who purchase licenses to the same or compatible software. A direct network effect exists when increases in the number of consumers on the network raise the value of the goods or services for everyone on the network. The most common examples are communication networks such as telephone and e-mail networks.

A network effect also exists when individuals consume "hardware" and complementary software. In such a system, the value of the hardware good increases as the variety of compatible software increases. Increases in the number of users of compatible hardware lead to an increase in demand for compatible software, which provides incentives for software vendors to increase the supply of software varieties. This in turn increases the benefit of all consumers of the hardware, software, or virtual network. Examples of markets where virtual network effects arise are consumer electronics, such as CD players and compact discs and computer operating systems and applications programs.

Given the importance of interconnection in information technology networks, the economics of compatibility and standardization has become mainstream economics. For an introduction to network effects and policy issues, see Gandal (2002) and Church and Gandal (2006).

Network effects are typically thought to benefit consumers and firms that have coalesced around a standard. However, network effects may contribute to security problems. Large networks are more vulnerable to security breaches, precisely because of the success of the network. In part because of its large installed base, Microsoft's Internet Explorer is likely more vulnerable to attack than the Mosaic's "Firefox" Browser. This is because the payoff to hackers from exploiting a security vulnerability in Internet Explorer is much greater than the payoff to exploiting a similar vulnerability in Firefox.

RESEARCH ON THE ECONOMICS OF CYBER SECURITY

A significant portion of the research in the economics of cyber security focuses on the creation of markets. I first briefly survey this research and then discuss research on the incentives of software vendors regarding the provision of security.

Intermediaries and Markets for Software Vulnerabilities

The Computer Emergency Response Team/Coordination Center (CERT/CC) is a center for Internet security in the Software Engineering Institute at Carnegie-Mellon University. Although CERT/CC is not a public agency, it acts as an intermediary between users who report vulnerabilities to CERT/CC and vendors who produced the software and the patches. When informed by a user about a vulnerability, CERT/CC conducts research into the matter. If the user has indeed uncovered a security vulnerability, CERT/CC then informs the software vendor and gives it a 45 day "vulnerability window." This allows the firm time to develop a security update. After the 45 day period, CERT/CC will typically disclose the vulnerability even if a security update has not been made available.

Recently, a private market for vulnerabilities has developed where firms such as iDefense and Tipping Point/3Com act as intermediaries, paying those who report vulnerabilities and providing the information to software users who have subscribed to the service.

There is growing literature on markets for vulnerability. Camp and Wolfram (2004) heuristically discuss this issue of markets for vulnerabilities. Schechter

(2004) formally models the market for vulnerabilities and Ozment (2004) shows how such a market can function as an auction. Kannan and Telang (2004) develop a model with four participants—an intermediary, a benign agent who can identify software vulnerabilities, an attacker, and software users–and ask whether a market based mechanism is better than the setting in which a public agency acts as an intermediary.

In the work discussed here, there is no role for software vendors. Software vendors that deal directly with benign agents would likely reduce the need for such intermediary markets.

Examining Incentives for Software Vendors

In this section, I discuss research that includes software vendors in the models. Arora, Telang, and Xu (2004) theoretically examine the optimal policy for software vulnerability disclosure. The software vendor strategy is limited to whether it will release a patch and if so, when to release the patch. August and Tunca (2005) have a strategic software vendor as well, but the vendor strategy is limited to pricing the software. Nizovtsev and Thursby (2005) examine the incentives of software firms to disclose vulnerabilities in an open forum.

Choi, Fershtman, and Gandal (2007) examine how software vulnerabilities affect the firms that develop the software and the consumers that license software. They model three decisions of the firm: An upfront investment in the quality of the software to reduce potential vulnerabilities, a policy decision whether to announce vulnerabilities, and a license price for the software. They also model two decisions of the consumer: whether to license the software and whether to apply a security update. The paper differs from the literature because it examines the interaction between vulnerability disclosure, patching, product prices and profits. While this model provides a base, further research is needed to examine incentives for software vendors to invest in security.

Empirical Work in the Economics of Cyber Security

To the best of my knowledge, there are only a few empirical papers in the economics of cyber security. Here I briefly mention a few recent studies. Arora, Nandkumar, Krishman, Telang, and Yang (2004) examined 308 distinct vulnerabilities and showed that disclosure of vulnerabilities increases the number of attacks per host and installing security updates decreases the number of attacks per host. Arora, Krishman, Telang, and Yang (2005) find that disclosure deadlines are effective. They find that vendors respond more quickly to vulnerabilities that are processed by CERT/CC than to vulnerabilities not handled by CERT/CC.

Data for Empirical Work

In many fields, theoretical work progresses much more quickly than empirical work, in part due to the dearth of data. There is clearly an untapped potential for empirical work in the economics of Internet security, since the National Vulnerability Database (NVD), which is assembled by the Computer Security Division of the National Institute of Science and Technology (NIST) and is available online at http://nvd.nist.gov/statistics.cfm.

High quality data are available at the level of the vulnerability as well as at the industry or firm level. The data include information about severity of the vulnerability, the impact of the vulnerability, as well as information on the vulnerability type. This database was employed by Arora, Nandkumar, Krishman, Telang, and Yang (2004) and Arora, Krishman, Telang, and Yang (2005).

Suggestions for empirical work can be found by examining the summary statistics available from the NVD. They show that while the number of vulnerabilities in the NVD increased from 1,858 in 2002 to 3,753 in 2005, the number of "high severity" vulnerabilities has roughly stayed the same during that period.[6] According to the NVD, severe vulnerabilities constituted about 48% of all vulnerabilities in 2002, 33% of all vulnerabilities in 2004, and 23.5% of all

vulnerabilities in 2005. These data suggest a fall in the percentage of high severity vulnerabilities as a percentage of all vulnerabilities.

The data further show that vulnerabilities that enable unauthorized access and derive from input validation error, that is, from either buffer overflow or boundary condition error, account for a large and growing percentage of all high severity vulnerabilities. While they accounted for approximately 50% of all high severity vulnerabilities during 19952001, they accounted for 60% of all high severity vulnerabilities in 20022004. In 2005, they accounted for 72% of all high severity vulnerabilities.

It would be helpful for researchers to try to determine what is driving these and other trends. These simple statistics suggest that interdisciplinary empirical is likely to be quite fruitful. Economists may be able to identify trends in the data, but without collaboration with computer scientists and engineers, it will not be possible to understand the implications of these numbers. Hopefully such work will be forthcoming in the not too distant future.

ACKNOWLEDGMENT

I thank Jay P. Choi, Chaim Fershtman, Jacques Lawarree, Shlomit Wagman, several anonymous reviewers from WEIS 2005 and this book, for their helpful comments. A research grant from Microsoft is gratefully acknowledged. Any opinions expressed are those of the author.

REFERENCES

Anderson, R. (2001). *Why information security is hard.* Mimeo.

Arora, A., Krishman, R., Telang, R., & Yang, Y. (2005). *An empirical analysis of vendor response to software vulnerability disclosure.* Mimeo.

Arora, A., Nandkumar, A., Krishman, R., Telang, R. & Yang, Y. (2004, May 13-15). *Impact of vulnerability disclosure and patch availability—An empirical analysis.* Presented at the Third Workshop on Economics and Information Security, Minneapolis, MN.

Arora, A., Telang, R., & Xu, H. (2004). *Optimal policy for software vulnerability disclosure.* Working paper, Carnegie-Mellon.

August, T., & Tunca, T. (2005). *Network software security and user incentives.* Mimeo.

Camp, L. J., & Wolfram, C. (2004). Pricing security. In L.J. Camp & S. Lewis (Eds.). *Economics of information security* (Vol. 12). *Advances in information security.* Springer-Kluwer.

Choi, J., Fershtman, C., & Gandal, N. (2007). *Network Security: Vulnerabilities and Disclosure Policy* (CEPR Working Paper #6134).

Church, J., & Gandal, N. (2006). Platform competition in telecommunications. In M. Cave, S. Majumdar, & I. Vogelsang (Eds.), *The handbook of telecommunications* (Vol. 2, pp. 117-153). Elsevier.

Gandal, N. (2002). Compatibility, standardization, & network effects: Some policy implications. *Oxford Review of Economic Policy, 18,* 8091.

Grady, M., & Francesco, P. (2006, in press). *The law and economics of cybersecurity: An introduction.* Cambridge University Press.

Kannan, K., & Telang, R. (2004). *Market for software vulnerabilities? Think again.* Working paper, Carnegie-Mellon.

Nizovtsev, D., & Thursby, M. (2005). *Economic analysis of incentives to disclose software vulnerabilities.* Mimeo.

Ozment, A. (2004). *Bug auctions: Vulnerability markets reconsidered.* Mimeo.

Schechter, S. (2004). *Computer security, strength and risk: A quantitative approach.* Mimeo.

Weaver, N., & Paxson, V. (2004). *A worst case worm.* Mimeo.

ENDNOTES

[1] http://www.economist.co.uk/science/displayStory.cfm?story_id=2246018

[2] From the article *Home Web Security Falls Short, Survey Shows* by John Markoff, October 25, 2004, available at http://www.staysafeonline.info/news/safety_study_v04.pdf

[3] Legal issues are surveyed by Grady and Francesco (forthcoming 2006). Readers interested in the economics of privacy should see the web page maintained by Alessandro Acquisti: http://www.heinz.cmu.edu/~acquisti/economics-privacy.htm

[4] See http://www.cl.cam.ac.uk/users/rja14/econsec.html. For a wealth of articles on computer security, see Bruce Schneier's web page at http://www.schneier.com/essays-comp.html

[5] The first conference was held in 2002.

[6] The NVD defines a vulnerability to be "high severity" if (1) it allows a remote attacker to violate the security protection of a system (i.e., gain some sort of user, root, or application account), (2) it allows a local attack that gains complete control of a system, or (3) it is important enough to have an associated CERT/CC advisory or US-CERT alert. See http://nvd.nist.gov/faq.cfm

Chapter XI
Role of FS–ISAC in Countering Cyber Terrorism

Manish Gupta
M&T Bank Corporation, USA

H. R. Rao
The State University of New York (SUNY) – Buffalo, USA

ABSTRACT

In recent times, reliance on interconnected computer systems to support critical operations and infrastructures and, at the same time, physical and cyber threats and potential attack consequences have increased. The importance of sharing information and coordinating the response to threats among stakeholders has never been so great. Information sharing and coordination among organizations are central to producing comprehensive and practical approaches and solutions to combating threats. Financial services institutions present highly financially attractive targets. The financial services industry, confronts cyber and physical threats from a great variety of sources ranging from potentially catastrophic attacks launched by terrorist groups or other national interest groups to the more commonly experienced extremely targeted attacks perpetrated by hackers and other malicious entities such as insiders. In this chapter we outline structure, major components, and concepts involved in information sharing and analysis in the financial services sector. Then we discuss the relevance and importance of protecting financial services institutions' infrastructure from cyber attacks vis-à-vis presentation of different issues and crucial aspects of current state of cyber terrorism. We also discuss role and structure of ISACs in counterterrorism; and constituents, functions, and details of FS-ISAC.

INTRODUCTION

The pervasive nature of the Internet coupled with recent threats of cyber terrorism makes Internet infrastructure security an area of significant importance (Devost & Pallard, 2002). Beyond isolated and annoying attacks on official Web sites, potential targets for a hypothetical cyber-terrorist act in the United States include most of the nation's critical infrastructure, including utilities such as electricity, water, and gas facilities and their supply systems; financial services such as banks, ATMs, and trading houses; and information and communication systems (Estevez-Tapiadoe, 2004). Hacking as part of cybercrime is definitely moving forward, with new tools to hack and new viruses to spread coming out every day (Sukhai, 2004). One of the major challenges in counterterrorism analysis today involves connecting the relatively few and sparse terrorism-related dots embedded within massive amounts of data flowing into the government's intelligence and counterterrorism agencies (Popp et al., 2004). On the Internet, an attacker has an advantage. He or she can choose when and how to attack (Schneier, n.d.). However, at the operational level, how cyber terrorists plan to use information technology, automated tools, and identify targets may be observable and to some extent, predictable (Chakrabarti & Manimaran, 2002). Figure 1 shows the general framework within the operational context of financial services-information sharing and analysis centers (FS-ISAC).

In recent times, reliance on interconnected computer systems to support critical operations and infrastructures and, at the same time, physical and cyber threats and potential attack consequences have increased. The importance of sharing information and coordinating the response to threats among stakeholders has never been so great. Information sharing and coordination among organizations are central to producing comprehensive and practical approaches and solutions to combating threats. In addition, comprehensive, timely information on incidents can help federal and nonfederal analysis centers determine the nature of an attack, provide warnings, and advise on how to mitigate an imminent attack (*Homeland security,* 2003).

National critical infrastructure protection (CIP) policy for the United States as covered in Presidential Decision Directive (PDD) 63 and confirmed in other national strategy documents, including the *National Strategy for Homeland Security* issued in July 2002, called for a set of strategies and actions to establish a partnership between the public and private sectors protecting national critical infrastructure. For these

sectors, which now total 14, federal government leads (sector liaisons) and private-sector leads (sector coordinators) were to work with each other. Federal CIP policy also encourages the voluntary creation of information sharing and analysis centers (ISACs) to serve as mechanisms for gathering, analyzing, and appropriately sanitizing and disseminating information to and from infrastructure sectors and the federal government through NIPC (*Homeland security,* 2003). ISACs, today, control over 80% of nation's critical infrastructures.

The financial services industry, confronts cyber and physical threats from a great variety of sources ranging from potentially catastrophic attacks launched by terrorist groups or other national interest groups to the more commonly experienced extremely targeted attacks perpetrated by hackers and other malicious entities such as insiders. A concerted, industry-wide effort to share attack information and security best practices offers the best hope of identifying, responding to, and surviving the very real threats facing both the industry and the country (*Financial service-information sharing and analysis centers (FS-ISAC) brochure,* n.d.).

In this chapter we outline structure, major components, and concepts involved in information sharing and analysis in the financial services sector. Then we discuss the relevance and importance of protecting financial services institutions' infrastructure from cyber attacks. The next section elaborates and illustrates information sharing as a key element in developing comprehensive and practical approaches to defending against potential cyber and other attacks. In following section, we present different issues and crucial aspects of current state of cyber terrorism. Then, we discuss role and structure of ISACs in counterterrorism, using information sharing as an operational tenet. Next we discuss, in detail, constituents, functions, and details of FS-ISAC. The final section concludes the chapter with a summary and discussion.

FINANCIAL SERVICES INSTITUTIONS

Some financial services institutions present highly financially attractive targets. Cyber attacks against them occur with increased frequency and complexity when compared to other sectors. A report from U.S. General Accounting Office (GAO) shows that financial services firms received an average of 1,108 attacks per company during the six-month study period. During that same period, 46% of these companies experienced at least one attack they considered to be "severe." In its 2004 Global Security Survey (Deloitte Global Security Survey, 2004), Deloitte and Touche reported that 83% of financial services firms acknowledged that their systems had been compromised in the past year, compared to only 39% in 2002. Of this group, 40% stated that the breaches had resulted in financial loss. The fact that the financial services industry relies so heavily on public trust puts it at even greater risk from all manner of cyber attacks. Any act that undermines the confidentiality, integrity, and availability of financial data or transactions negatively impacts the affected institution and the industry (Deloitte Global Security Survey, 2004).

Increased exposure of the financial services sector is due to following characteristics of the industry (www.fsisac.com/tour.htm):

- **The "target":** 50% of cyber attacks are financial services firms
- **"Vulnerable":** Online presence (subject to software vulnerabilities of Internet)
- **In the business of "trust":** Bedrock of business
- **Highly "regulated":** Regularly examined for compliance; and
- **"Interconnected":** To settle payment and securities transactions globally.

Over the last year, attacks on financial institutions have been on the rise. Financial services institutions are targets because they hold people's money and have copious amounts of personal data. Many global financial institutions have been subject to phishing attacks over the last year (Deloitte Global Security Survey, 2005). Corporate executives are relatively on par with those of last year in that they are willing to take a direct investment in security preparedness against physical disasters, cyber terrorism, and other potential threats (Deloitte Global Security Survey, 2004). A Deloitte and Touche 2005 survey (Deloitte Global Security Survey, 2004) shows that the distribution of cyber attacks on financial institutions across the globe ranges from 16% in the APAC region to 50% in Canada.

INFORMATION SHARING

Information sharing is a key element in developing comprehensive and practical approaches to defending against potential cyber and other attacks, which could threaten the national welfare. Information on threats, vulnerabilities, and incidents experienced by others, while difficult to share and analyze, can help identify trends, better understand the risks faced, and determine what preventive measures should be implemented. The effective pursuit of counterterrorism activities requests the rapid and semantically meaningful integration of information from diverse sources (Choucri, Madnick, Moulton, Siegel, & Zhu, 2004). For counterterrorism information sharing, just like for many other government and military operations in the post-September 11, 2001, world, the traditional mindset of "need to know" is being overtaken by the "need to share" among dynamic communities of interests (COIs) (Yuan & Wenzel, 2005). Financial services is one the communities of *highest* interest.

The private sector has always been concerned about sharing information with the government and about the difficulty of obtaining security clearances. Both congress and the administration have taken steps to address information sharing issues in law and recent policy guidance. The Homeland Security Act of 2002, which created the Department of Homeland Security

Table 1. Cyber threats to critical infrastructure observed by the FBI (Source: GAO-03-715T Report, 2003)

Threat	Description
Criminal groups	**Criminal groups who attack systems for purposes of monetary gain.**
Foreign intelligence services	Foreign intelligence services that use cyber tools as part of their information gathering and espionage activities.
Hackers	Hackers sometimes crack into networks for the thrill of the challenge or for bragging rights in the hacker community. Thus, while attack tools have become more sophisticated, they also have become easier to use.
Hacktivists	Hacktivism refers to politically motivated attacks on publicly accessible Web pages/resources or e-mail servers.
Information warfare	Several nations are aggressively working to develop information warfare doctrine, programs, and capabilities to enable a single entity to have a significant and serious impact by disrupting the supply, communications, and economic infrastructures that support military power.
Insider threat	The disgruntled organization insider is a principal source of computer crimes.
Virus writers	Virus writers are posing an increasingly serious threat.

(DHS), brought together 22 diverse organizations to help prevent terrorist attacks in the United States, reduce the vulnerability of the United States to terrorist attacks, and minimize damage and assist in recovery from attacks that do occur (*Homeland security*, 2003). To accomplish this mission, the act established specific homeland security responsibilities for the department, which included sharing information among its own entities and with other federal agencies, state, and local governments, the private sector, and others. The GAO was asked to discuss DHS's information sharing efforts, including (1) the significance of information sharing in fulfilling DHS's responsibilities; (2) GAO's related prior analyses and recommendations for improving the federal government's information sharing efforts; and (3) key management issues DHS should consider in developing and implementing effective information sharing processes and systems (*Homeland security*, 2003).

CYBER TERRORISM

With the terrorist attacks of September 11, 2001, the threat of terrorism rose to the top of the country's national security and law enforcement agendas. As stated by the president in his *National Strategy for Homeland Security* in July 2002, our nation's terrorist enemies are constantly seeking new tactics or unexpected ways to carry out their attacks and magnify their effects, such as working to obtain chemical, biological, radiological, and nuclear weapons. In addition to traditional threats, terrorists are gaining expertise in less traditional means, such as cyber attacks. To accomplish the mission of DHS, as outlined in the previous section, it is directed to coordinate its efforts and share information within DHS and with other federal agencies, state, and local governments, the private sector, and other entities. This information sharing is critical to successfully addressing increasing threats and fulfilling the mission of DHS.

Information technology (IT) is a major contributor and enabler within counterterrorism communities that provides capabilities and mechanisms to anticipate and ultimately preempt terrorist attacks by finding and sharing information faster; collaborating across multiple agencies in a more agile manner; connecting the dots better; conducting quicker and better analyses; and enabling better decision making (Jonietz, 2003; Secretary of Defense, 2003). There are many technology challenges, but perhaps few more important than how to make sense of and connect the relatively few and sparse dots embedded within massive amounts of information flowing into the government's intelligence and counterterrorism apparatus. As noted in the *National Strategy for Combating Terrorism* (2003) and *Report of the Joint Inquiry into the Terrorist Attacks of September 11, 2001* (2003), IT plays a crucial role in overcoming this challenge and is a major tenet of the U.S. national and homeland security strategies. The U.S. government's intelligence and counterterrorism agencies are responsible for absorbing this massive amount of information, processing and analyzing it, converting it to actionable intelligence, and disseminating it, as appropriate, in a timely manner. Table 1 summarizes the key cyber threats to our infrastructure (*Homeland security*, 2003).

Government officials are increasingly concerned about cyber attacks from individuals and groups with malicious intent, such as crime, terrorism, foreign intelligence gathering, and acts of war. According to the FBI, terrorists, transnational criminals, and intelligence services are quickly becoming aware of and are using information exploitation tools, such as computer viruses, Trojan horses, worms, logic bombs, and eavesdropping sniffers that can destroy, intercept, degrade the integrity of, or deny access to data. As larger amounts of money are transferred through computer systems, as more sensitive economic and commercial information is exchanged electronically, and as the nation's defense and intelligence communities increasingly rely on commercially available IT, the likelihood increases that cyber attacks will threaten vital national interests (*Homeland security*, 2003).

ISACS

The PDD-63 of 1998 resulted in creation of ISACs. The directive requested the public and private sector create a partnership to share information about physical and cyber threats, vulnerabilities, and events to help protect the critical infrastructure of the United States. PDD-63 was updated in 2003 with Homeland Security Presidential Directive/HSPD-7 to reaffirm the partnership mission. To help develop ways of

better protecting our critical infrastructures and to help minimize vulnerabilities, the DHS established ISAC's to allow critical sectors to share information and work together to help better protect the economy. Today there are 14 ISACs for critical infrastructures (*FS-ISAC FAQ*, n.d.), presented as follows:

1. Agriculture
2. Food
3. Water
4. Public health
5. Emergency services
6. Government
7. Defense industrial base
8. Information and telecommunications
9. Energy
10. Transportation
11. Banking and finance
12. Chemical industry and hazardous materials
13. Postal and shipping
14. Real estate

Their activities could improve the security posture of the individual sectors, as well as provide an improved level of communication within and across sectors and all levels of government (*Homeland security*, 2003). While PDD-63 encouraged the creation of ISACs, it left the actual design and functions of the ISACs, along with their relationship with NIPC, to be determined by the private sector in consultation with the federal government (*Homeland security*, 2003).

PDD-63 did provide suggested activities that the ISACs could undertake (*Homeland security*, 2003), including:

- Establishing baseline statistics and patterns on the various infrastructures
- Serving as a clearinghouse for information within and among the various sectors
- Providing a library for historical data for use by the private sector and government
- Reporting private-sector incidents to NIPC

Table 2. Sector-wise participation of firms in FS-ISAC (Source: FS-ISAC)

Sector	Percentage
Commercial banks	72%
Savings institutions	12%
Securities firms	2%
Insurance companies	2%
Exchange/sector utilities	3%

FS-ISAC

FS-ISAC was established by the financial services sector in response to 1998's PDD-63. The FS-ISAC is a not-for-profit organization formed to serve the needs of the financial services industry for the dissemination of physical and cyber security, threat, vulnerability, incident, and solution information. Later, Homeland Security Presidential Directive updated the directive. The update mandates that the public and private sectors share information about physical and cyber security threats and vulnerabilities to help protect U.S. critical infrastructure.

The FS-ISAC offers eligible participants the ability to anonymously share physical and cyber security information. The FS-ISAC gathers threat, vulnerability, and risk information about cyber and physical security risks faced by the financial services sector. Sources of information include commercial companies, which gather this type of information, government agencies, CERTs, academic sources, and other trusted sources. FS-ISAC also provides an anonymous information sharing capability across the entire financial services industry. Upon receiving a submission, industry experts verify and analyze the threat and identify any recommended solutions before alerting FS-ISAC members. Table 2 shows sector-wise participation in FS-ISAC within financial services. This assures that member firms receive the latest tried-and-true procedures and best practices for guarding against known and emerging security threats. After analysis by industry experts, alerts are delivered to participants based on their level of service (*FS-ISAC FAQ*, n.d.). FS-ISAC, recently, successfully concluded a critical infrastructure notification system (CINS) that enables near-simultaneous security alerts to multiple recipients, while providing for user authentication and delivery confirmation. Some of the common and critical services offered by FS-ISAC include an industry platform to share security information, such as biweekly threat conference calls, crisis conference calls, member meetings and a secure portal. The membership to FS-ISAC is open to regulated financial services firms and utilities. The tiered membership options provide for participation of any firm.

FS-ISAC membership is recommended by the U.S. Department of the Treasury, the Office of the Comptroller of Currency, DHS, the U.S. Secret Service, and the Financial Services Sector Coordinating Council, and comes in a range of service levels, providing key benefits to organizations of all sizes and security profiles. Based on level of service, FS-ISAC members take advantage of a host of important benefits, including early notification of security threats and attacks, anonymous information sharing across the financial services industry, regularly scheduled member meetings, and biweekly conference calls (*FS-ASAC dashboard*, n.d.). By 2005, the FS-ISAC's goal was to be able to deliver urgent and crisis alerts to 99% of the more than 25,000 members of the financial services sector within one hour of notification. Figure 2a and 2b (*FS-ISAC dashboard*, n.d.) show current and projected membership statistics. FS-ISAC is currently composed of members who maintain over 90% of the assets under control by the industry.

CONCLUSION

"We are at risk. Increasingly, America depends on computers. They control power delivery, communications, aviation, and financial services" (National Research Council, 1991, p. 7). A proactive approach to protecting information infrastructure is necessary to prevent and combat cyber attacks. The Internet has become a forum and channel for terrorist groups and individual terrorists to spread messages of hate and violence, to communicate and to attack computer-based information resources. The effective pursuit of counterterrorism activities mandates a rapid and semantically meaningful integration of information from diverse sources. IT plays a crucial role in sharing information across diverse domains of counterterrorism effort and has evolved as a major tenet of the U.S. national and homeland security strategies. The U.S. government's intelligence and counterterrorism agencies are responsible for correlating the extensively distributed and scattered information, converting it to actionable intelligence, and disseminating it in a timely manner. Through FS-ISAC, many of the nation's experts in the financial services sector share and assess threat intelligence provided by its members, enforcement agencies, technology providers, and security associations.

REFERENCES

Chakrabarti, A., & Manimaran, G. (2002, November/December). *Internet infrastructure security: A taxonomy.* Iowa State University, IEEE Network.

Choucri, N., Madnick, S. E., Moulton, A., Siegel, M. D., & Zhu, H. (2004). Activities: Requirements for context mediation, MIT Sloan School of Management. In *IEEE Aerospace Conference Proceedings Information Integration for Counter Terrorism.*

Cousins, D. B., & Weishar, D. J. (2004, March). Intelligence collection for counter terrorism in massive information content. In *2004 IEEE Aerospace Conference Proceedings* (pp. 3273-3282) Vol.5

Deloitte Global Security Survey. (2004). *Global financial services industry.*

Deloitte Global Security Survey. (2005). *Global financial services industry.*

Devost, M., & Pollard, N. (2002). *Taking cyber terrorism seriously—Failing to adapt to threats could have dire consequences.* Retrieved from http://www.terrorism.com

Estevez-Tapiador, J. M. (2004). The emergence of cyber-terrorism. *IEEE Distributed Online System, 5*(1).

Financial services information sharing and analysis centers (FS-ISAC) brochure. (n.d.). Retrieved January 28, 2006, from http://www.fsisac.com/docs/FSISAC.pdf

FS-ISAC dashboard. (n.d.). Retrieved January 29, 2006, from https://core.fsisac.com/dashboard/

FS-ISAC FAQs. (n.d.). Retrieved January 29, 2006, from http://www.fsisac.com/faqs.htm

Homeland security: Information sharing responsibilities, challenges, and key management issues [GAO-03-715T]. (2003, May 8). Presented to Committee on Government Reform, House of Representatives.

Jonietz, E. (2003). Total information overload. *MIT Technology Review, 106*(6), 68.

National Research Council. (1991). *Computers at risk.* National Academy Press.

National strategy for combating terrorism. (2003, February) Submitted by the White House.

Popp, R., Pattipati, K., Wille, P., Serfaty, D., Stacy, W., Carley, K., et al. (2004). Collaboration and modeling tools for counter-terrorism analysis. *CIHSPS2004— IEEE International Conference on Computational Intelligence for Homeland Security and Personal Safely*, Venice, Italy.

Report of the joint inquiry into the terrorist attacks of September 11, 2001. (2003, July). Submitted by the House Permanent Select Committee on Intelligence (HPSCI) and the Senate Select Committee on Intelligence (SSCI).

Schneier, B. (n.d.). *Natural advantages of defense: What military history can teach network security* (Part 1).

Sukhai, N. B. (2004). Hacking and cybercrime. *Computer Society, 5*(10), 128-132.

Yuan, E., & Wenzel, G. (2005, March). Assured counter-terrorism information sharing using: Attribute based information security (ABIS). In *Proceedings of IEEE Aerospace Conference* (pp. 1-12). 5-12 March 2005.

TERMS AND DEFINITIONS

Critical Infrastructure Protection: This means security of those physical and cyber-based systems that are essential to the minimum operations of the economy and government by ensuring protection of information systems for critical infrastructure, including emergency preparedness communications, and the physical assets that support such systems.

Department of Homeland Security (DHS): The Homeland Security Act of 2002, which created the Department of Homeland Security (DHS), brought together 22 diverse organizations to help prevent terrorist attacks in the United States, reduce the vulnerability of the United States to terrorist attacks, and minimize damage and assist in recovery from attacks that do occur.

Financial Services Information Sharing and Analysis Centers (FS-ISAC): The FS-ISAC, established in response to PDD-63, is a not-for-profit organization formed to serve the needs of the financial services industry for the dissemination of physical and cyber security, threat, vulnerability, incident, and solution information.

Hacktivism: This refers to politically motivated attacks on publicly accessible Web pages/resources or e-mail servers.

Information Sharing and Analysis Centers: Presidential Decision Directive 63 (PDD-63) in 1998 resulted in creation of information sharing and analysis centers to allow critical sectors to share information and work together to help better protect the economy.

Information Warfare: This means the use and management of information in pursuit of a competitive advantage over an opponent.

Presidential Decision Directive (PDD) 63: In 1998, the Clinton Administration issued Presidential Decision Directive 63 (PDD-63), to meet the demands of national security interests in cyberspace and to help protect the critical infrastructure of the United States.

Chapter XII
Deception in Cyber Attacks

Neil C. Rowe
U.S. Naval Postgraduate School, USA

E. John Custy
U.S. Naval Postgraduate School, USA

ABSTRACT

Cyberspace, computers, and networks are now potential terrain of warfare. We describe some effective forms of deception in cyberspace and discuss how these deceptions are used in attacks. After a general assessment of deception opportunities in cyberspace, we consider various forms of identity deceptions, denial-of-service attacks, Trojan horses, and several other forms of deception. We then speculate on the directions in which cyber attacks may evolve in the future.

INTRODUCTION

Any communications channel can convey false information and, thus, be used for deception (Miller & Stiff, 1993). The communications resources of cyberspace have several characteristics that make them attractive for deception. Identity is hard to establish in cyberspace. So mimicry is easy and often effective, as with the false e-mail addresses used in spam, the fake Web sites used for identity theft, and software "Trojan horses" that conceal malicious functions within. The software-dependent nature of cyberspace also encourages automated deceptions. So the infrastructure of cyberspace itself can fall victim to denial-of-service attacks that overwhelm sites with massive numbers of insincere requests for services.

Amateur attackers (hackers) are attacking sites on the Internet all the time. These attacks can range from vandalism and sabotage to theft and extortion. The rate of attack incidents reported to the Computer Emergency Response Team (CERT) at Carnegie Mellon University continues to grow due to the increased use of automated attack tools (CERT/CC, 2005). Most attack techniques involve deception in some form, since there are many possible countermeasures against attacks in general. Hacker attack techniques can be adopted by information-warfare specialists as tools of warfare (Hutchinson & Warren, 2001; Yoshihara,

2005). Attacks generally exploit flaws in software; and once flaws are found, they get fixed, and the corresponding attacks no longer work. Web sites, such as www.cert.org, serve as up-to-date clearinghouses for reports of security vulnerabilities used by attackers and how to fix them. So information-warfare attacks either need to find software that is not current with vulnerability fixes (something rare for important infrastructure sites) or else develop new techniques that no one knows about (for which the results are only useful for a limited time given the pace of the development of fixes). Since these things are difficult, deception is often used to improve the chances of a successful attack.

DECEPTION IN CYBERSPACE

Deception can be defined as an interaction between two parties, a deceiver and a target, in which the deceiver successfully causes the target to accept as true a specific incorrect version of reality, with the intent of causing the target to act in a way that benefits the deceiver. Because conflicts of interest are almost inevitable whenever humans interact, many deceptions are commonly encountered in everyday life. Though familiarly associated with income taxes, politics, and the sale of used cars, deception can occur in any financial or economic interaction, as well as in advertising, in sports, and other forms of entertainment, in law, in diplomacy, and in military conflicts (Ford, 1996). Deception carries a stigma because it violates the (usually unspoken) agreement of cooperation between the two parties of an information exchange, and thus represents a misuse of and threat to the normal communication process. However, the moral status of deception can sometimes be unclear, as it has been justified in crisis situations, to avoid a greater evil, against enemies, for the public good, or to protect people like children from harmful truths (Bok, 1978).

Cyberspace differs in many ways from our natural environment, and two differences hold special rel-

evance for deception in cyber attacks. First, cyberspace communications channels carry less information than channels of normal "face-to-face" interactions (Vrij, 2000). Cues that we normally use to orient ourselves during a face-to-face interaction may not be available or may be easily forged in cyberspace. For instance, body language, voice inflections, and many other cues are lost in e-mail messages, which permit "spoofing," where a message appears to come from someone other than the author. Second, information in cyberspace can quickly and easily be created or changed so there is little permanence. For instance, Web sites and e-mail addresses can appear and disappear quite fast, making it difficult to assign responsibility in cyberspace, unlike with real-world businesses that have buildings and physical infrastructure. The link between labels on software objects and their human representatives can be tenuous, and malicious users can exploit this. Also, it is difficult to judge the quality of a product in cyberspace, since it cannot be held in the hand and examined, which permits a wide range of fraudulent activities. An example is an antivirus product made available for a free trial that actually harbors and delivers malicious code.

Rowe (2006) and Rowe and Rothstein (2004) identify 23 categories of possible deceptions in attacks in cyberspace, based on case grammar in linguistics. Arranged in decreasing order of their estimate of suitability and effectiveness in cyberspace, these categories are deception in agent (deceiving the target about who performs an action), accompaniment (what the action is accompanied by), frequency (of the action), object (of the action), supertype (category of the action), experiencer (who observes the action), instrument (used to accomplish the action), whole (to which the action belongs), content, external precondition (environmental effects on the action), measure, location-from, purpose, beneficiary, time-at, value (of data transmitted by the action), location-to, location-through, time-through, internal precondition (self-integrity of the action), direction, effect, and cause. We elaborate on these major categories in the following sections.

IDENTITY DECEPTION

Since impersonation is easy in cyberspace, many attacks exploit it. These are generally deceptions in object, whole, instrument, supertype, and agent. Military personnel are tempting targets for "social engineering" attacks involving impersonation of one person by another. Social engineers assume a false identity to manipulate people into providing sensitive information or performing tasks (Mitnik & Simon, 2002), often by deceiving as to purpose and beneficiary. An example is pretending to be a representative of the information-technology staff so as to steal a password from a new employee.

Phishing is a particularly dangerous kind of impersonation for social engineering that has increased in frequency and severity recently (MessageLabs, 2005). A perpetrator sends e-mail to a large group of potential targets, urging them to visit a Web site with a familiar-sounding name to resolve some bogus issue. For example, a bogus e-mail from "PayPal, Inc" may urge that "Security updates require that you re-enter your user name and password." The information provided by the victim is used to commit identity theft or enable espionage. Organizations are increasingly being targeted by "spear phishers," who carefully tailor their attacks to specific victims to obtain specific secrets from them, as a form of espionage.

A more subtle category of identity deception in cyberspace is "privilege escalation," where an attacker gains access to a system through a vulnerable account, and then exploits additional vulnerabilities to parlay their limited privileges up to those of a full system administrator (Erbschloe, 2005). This is analogous to what human spies try to do in improving upon their access abilities. Privilege escalation can be accomplished by certain buffer overflows in software. A buffer overflow occurs when a piece of information provided by a user is larger than the space allocated for it by the program, and, under the right circumstances, when there is a flaw in the software, this can allow a malicious user to overwrite parts of the operating system and execute arbitrary code at a higher level of privilege. Buffer overflows are common because some popular programming languages, like C and C++ and some common software products, do not automatically enforce bounds on data placed in memory. Another technique for escalating privileges is to steal a password table, try passwords systematically until a correct one is found, and then impersonate the owner of the password on the system. Usually passwords are stored in a "hashed" form that cannot be decrypted, but the hashing algorithm is often known and attackers can just try to match the hashes repeatedly on a fast machine of their own.

Knowledgeable attackers who successfully escalate privileges may try to install a "rootkit" to conceal or camouflage their presence and actions from system administrators (Kuhnhauser, 2004). A rootkit is a replacement for critical parts of the operating system of a computer to provide clandestine access and total control of the computer by the attacker. This is analogous to occupying the adversary's terrain in conventional warfare. Rootkits usually include specially modified file-listing and process-listing commands that hide the attacker's files and processes from administrators and other users (Denning, 1999). A rootkit can provide a "back door" by surreptitiously listening on a port for (possibly encrypted) control commands from an attacker.

Other common identity deception on the Internet involves impersonating computers. This includes "spoofing" of Internet addresses by faking the header information on Internet packets to make it look like it came from someplace other than where it really came from. During an impersonation of computers, spoofing can screen or camouflage the origin of an attack. That is, a machine on which an attacker has gained unauthorized access can serve as a launching point for further unauthorized accesses, concealing the attacker's identity because it is difficult to trace a connection backwards through many intermediate machines with most Internet protocols. Intervening computers also may be located in many countries throughout the world, and legal coordination between jurisdictions can be difficult (Stoll, 2000).

DENIAL-OF-SERVICE ATTACKS

A denial-of-service attack slows or stops the operation of a cyberspace resource or service by overwhelming it with insincere requests. Denial-of-service attacks are deceptions in frequency and purpose as per Rowe and Rothstein (2004). They can occur if large numbers of coordinated computers try to access the same Web site simultaneously. These attacks are easy to do and have been used successfully against big companies like Amazon and the U.S. presidential site. Another example is a "SYN flood attack" against the commonly used TCP protocol (McClure, Scambray, & Kurtz, 2005), which involves the attacker starting, but not completing, a large number of interactions called "three-way handshakes" with a victim computer. This forces the victim to maintain many half-open connections that prevent valid connections from being established. Denial of service also can be achieved by a "smurf" attack, which involves flooding a network with many ICMP echo (or "ping") requests to different machines. The requests have their source addresses forged as that of the victim machine, which is flooded with echo responses and overwhelmed.

Denial of service is quite valuable militarily as a way to disable adversary's computer systems. Potential targets could include command-and-control networks, file servers holding mission plans, Web servers holding enemy communications intercepts, and domain name service (DNS) sites that serve as the Internet's indexes.

TROJAN HORSES

Attacks can be concealed inside otherwise innocent software. These are called "Trojan horses" (Erbschloe, 2005) and are instances of deception in accompaniment and content. To trick a user into running them, they can be provided for free at Web sites, sent as e-mail attachments with forged addresses, hidden in storage media, or even embedded when the software is manufactured. The "cover" software can be a useful utility, a game, or a "macro" (embedded code) within a document file. Running a piece of software is insufficient to confirm it is malicious, since its sabotage or espionage may be subtle, or it may be set to trigger later according to the clock or on instructions from a remote attacker. Sabotage can range from changing numbers in data to causing programs to fail completely. Computer viruses and worms are important forms of Trojan horses, but they are usually too obvious to be effective for military use.

An important category of Trojan horses is spyware, or automated espionage in cyberspace. These programs covertly pass useful information back to an attacker about the activities on a computer and so are deception in experiencer. Spyware is currently an epidemic, although its incidence is decreasing as antivirus and antispyware software is now looking for it. Commercial spyware usually just reports what Web sites a user visits, but the techniques can be adapted for espionage to record everything a user types on a keyboard, enabling theft of passwords and encryption keys. Spyware uses "covert channels" to communicate back to its controller; these can use encryption (messages transformed into unintelligible codes) (Pfleeger, 1997) or "steganography" (concealed messages in what appears to be innocent messages or data) (Wayner, 2002). For instance, an encryption of the password "foobar" might be "&3Xh0y," whereas the steganographic encoding might be "find our own bag at Rita's," using the first letter of every word. Steganography also can use subtle features like the number of characters per line, the pattern of spaces in a text document, or every 137th letter.

MISCELLANEOUS DECEPTIONS

Other deceptions from the taxonomy of Rowe (2006) can be used in cyberspace:

- Buffer overflows can be done by sending insincere large inputs to programs.
- To achieve surprise, attacks can involve rarely used software, ports, or network sites.

- Attacks can have surprising targets, such as little-used software features.
- Attacks can occur at surprising times (but everyone knows the Internet is always active).
- Attacks can occur from surprising sites (but everyone knows attacks can come from anywhere).
- To maximize concealment, attacks can be done very slowly, as by sending one command a day to a victim computer.
- Attacks can modify file or audit records in time and details to make attackers appear to have been doing something different at a different time.
- Attackers can claim abilities that they do not possess for purposes of extortion, such as the ability to disable a computer system.

FUTURE TRENDS

As defenses to cyber attack improve, we can expect amateur cyber attacks to show more deception, and information-warfare attacks can be expected to show more too. Attacks are increasing in technical sophistication as easier attacks are being blocked or foiled. Deception can be a useful "force multiplier" for mission plans in cyberspace, just as in real battle spaces (Dunnigan & Nofi, 2001). But we do not expect many new deceptions, since most of the possible ploys have already been explored. And it will become more difficult for deceptions to succeed. Defenses are improving; and defenders are becoming more aware of deceptions being practiced, so that the pool of potential victims for many attacks is decreasing.

The diversity of deceptions should increase in the future as the continued development of automated tools will permit attackers to try many methods at once. But diversity in defenses against deceptions also should increase. Deception will be increasingly common in asymmetric cyber war, as it is in asymmetric conventional warfare (Bell & Whaley, 1991), for tactics and strategies by the weaker participant.

CONCLUSION

Deception occurs in all military conflicts, and as more military activity shifts to cyberspace, we will see more deception there too. An analysis of how deception is used in attacks can help in understanding them, with the goal of developing effective defenses for future attacks. The deception methods we have described here are not difficult to use. While there have not been confirmed instances of cyber war using deception, information-warfare specialists are developing cyber weapons using these methods. However, a wide variety of methods can be used to ensure that particular cyber attack deceptions against a particular target are totally ineffective.

REFERENCES

Bell, J., & Whaley, B. (1991). *Cheating and deception.* New Brunswick, NJ: Transaction Publishers.

Bok, S. (1978). *Lying: Moral choice in public and private life.* New York: Pantheon.

CERT/CC. (2005). *CERT/CC Statistics, 1988-2005.* Retrieved February 15, 2006, from www.cert.org/stats/cert_stats.html

Denning, D. (1999). *Information warfare and security.* New York: Addison-Wesley.

Dunnigan, J. F., & Nofi, A. A. (2001). *Victory and deceit: Deception and trickery in war* (2nd ed.). San Jose, CA: Writers Press Books.

Erbschloe, M. (2005). *Trojans, worms, and spyware: A computer security professional's guide to malicious code.* Amsterdam: Elsevier.

Ford, C. V. (1996). *Lies! Lies!! Lies!!! The psychology of deceit.* Washington, DC: American Psychiatric Press.

Hutchinson, W., & Warren, M. (2001). *Information warfare: Corporate attack and defense in a digital world.* London: Butterworth-Heinemann.

Kuhnhauser, W. (2004). Root kits: an operating systems viewpoint. *ACM SIGOPS Operating Systems Review, 38*(1), 12-23.

McClure, S., Scambray, J., & Kurtz, G. (2005). *Hacking exposed* (5th ed.). New York: McGraw-Hill Osborne.

MessageLabs. (2005). *Annual security report*. Retrieved February 8, 2006, from www.messagelabs. com/publishedcontent/publish/threat_watch_dotcom_en/intelligence_reports/2005_annual_security_report/DA_123230.chp.html

Miller, G. R., & Stiff, J. B. (1993). *Deceptive communications*. Newbury Park, UK: Sage Publications.

Mitnick, K. D., & Simon, W. L. (2002). *The art of deception: Controlling the human element of security*. Indianapolis, IN: Wiley.

Pfleeger, C. P. (1997). *Security in computing* (2nd ed.). Upper Saddle River, NJ: Prentice Hall PTR.

Rowe, N. (2006, March). *A taxonomy of deception in cyberspace*. Presented at the International Conference on Information Warfare and Security, Princess Anne, MD.

Rowe, N., & Rothstein, H. (2004). Two taxonomies of deception for attacks on information systems. *Journal of Information Warfare, 3*(2), 27-39.

Stoll, C. (2000). *The cuckoo's egg: Tracking a spy through the maze of computer espionage*. New York: Pocket Books.

Vrij, A. (2000). *Detecting lies and deceit: The psychology of lying and the implications for professional practice*. Chichester, UK: Wiley.

Wayner, P. (2002). *Disappearing cryptography: Information hiding: Steganography and watermarking*. San Francisco: Morgan Kaufmann.

Yoshihara, T. (2005). *Chinese information warfare: A phantom menace or emerging threat?* Retrieved December 2005 from www.strategicstudiesinstitute. army.mil/pubs/display.cfm?PubID=62

TERMS AND DEFINITIONS

Buffer Overflow: This means techniques by which large inputs are given to software to induce it to do things it normally does not.

Covert Channel: This is a concealed communications channel.

Denial of Service: This refers to an attack that overwhelms a cyberspace resource with requests so as to prevent authorized persons from using the resource.

Encryption: This is a systematic and reversible way of making a message unintelligible by using secret keys.

Escalation of Privileges: This is exploiting security weaknesses to increase one's abilities on a computer system.

Hacker: This refers to an amateur attacker of computers or sites on the Internet.

Phishing: This type of e-mail tries to steal secrets by directing users to a counterfeit Web site.

Rootkit: This replacement code for the operating system of a computer is placed on a compromised system by an attacker to ensure that their malicious activities will be hidden and to simplify future access to the system by them.

Social Engineering: This refers to methods to trick or manipulate people into providing sensitive information or performing a task.

Steganography: This means concealed messages within others.

Chapter XIII
Deception in Defense of Computer Systems from Cyber Attack

Neil C. Rowe
U.S. Naval Postgraduate School, USA

ABSTRACT

While computer systems can be quite susceptible to deception by attackers, deception by defenders has increasingly been investigated in recent years. Military history has classic examples of defensive deceptions, but not all tactics and strategies have analogies in cyberspace. Honeypots are the most important example today; they are decoy computer systems designed to encourage attacks to collect data about attack methods. We examine the opportunities for deception in honeypots, and then opportunities for deception in ordinary computer systems by tactics like fake information, false delays, false error messages, and identity deception. We conclude with possible strategic deceptions.

INTRODUCTION

Defense from cyber attacks (exploits) in cyberspace is difficult because this kind of warfare is inherently asymmetric with the advantage to the attacker. The attacker can choose the time, place, and methods with little warning to the defender. Thus a multilayered defense (defense in depth) is important (Tirenin &

Faatz, 1999). Securing one's cyberspace assets by access controls and authentication methods is the first line of defense, but other strategies and tactics from conventional warfare are also valuable, including deception.

Dunnigan and Nofi (2001) provide a useful taxonomy of nine kinds of military deception similar to several other published ones: concealment, camouflage, disinformation, ruses, displays, demonstrations, feints, lies, and manipulation of the adversary by insight into their reasoning and goals. Rowe and Rothstein (2004) propose an alternative taxonomy based on case theory from linguistics. Table 1 shows those categories of deceptions they argue are feasible for defense from cyber attack, with revised assessments of suitability on a scale of 1 (unsuitable) to 10 (suitable). Some of these deceptions also can be used in a "second-order" way, after initial deceptions have been detected by the adversary. An example is creating inept deceptions with obviously false error messages, while also modifying attacker files in a subtle way.

HONEYPOTS

Honeypots are the best-known example of defensive deception in cyberspace (The Honeynet Project, 2004; Spitzner, 2003). These computer systems serve no purpose besides collecting data about attacks on them. That means they have no legitimate users other than system administrator; anyone else who uses them is inherently suspicious. Honeypots record all their activity in secure audit files for later analysis, and the lack of legitimate traffic means this is a rich source of attack data. Honeypot data is one of the few ways by which new (zero-day) attacks can be detected. Honeypots also can serve as decoys that imitate important systems like those of command-and-control networks.

Honeypots are often used in groups called "honeynets" to provide plenty of targets for attacks and to study how attacks spread from computer to computer. Software for building honeynets is provided by the Honeynet Project (a consortium of researchers that provides open-source software) as well as some commercial vendors. Honeypot and honeynets can be "low-interaction" (simulating just the first steps of network protocols (Cohen & Koike, 2004)) or "high-interaction" (permitting logins and most resources of their systems, like Sebek (The Honeynet Project, 2004)). Low-interaction honeypots can fool attackers into thinking there are many good targets by simulating many Internet addresses and many vulnerable-looking services, as "decoys." For instance, low-interaction honeypots could implement a decoy military command-and-control network, so adversaries would attack it, rather than the real network. Low-interaction honeypots, like HoneyD, provide little risk to the deployer but are not very deceptive, since they usually must be preprogrammed with a limited set of responses. High-interaction honeypots, like Sebek, are more work to install and entail more risk of propagating an attack (since countermeasures cannot be perfect), but will fool more attackers and provide more useful data. A safer form of high-interaction honeypot is a "sandbox," a simulated environment that appears to be a real computer environment; it is important for forensics on malicious code.

Counterdeception and Counter-Counterdeception for Honeypots

Deception is necessary for honeypots because attackers do not want their activities recorded: This could permit legal action against them as well as learning of their tricks. So some attackers search for evidence of honeypots on systems into which they trespass; this is a form of counterdeception (McCarty, 2003). Analogously to intrusion-detection systems for cyberspace (Proctor, 2001), this counterdeception can either look for statistical anomalies or for features or "signatures" that suggest a honeypot. Anomalies can be found in statistics on the types, sizes, and dates of files and directories. For instance, a system with no e-mail files is suspicious. Counter-counterdeception in designing good honeypots then requires ensuring realistic statistics on the honeypot. A tool that calculates statistical metrics on typical computer systems is useful (Rowe, 2006). One good way to build a honeypot is to copy its file system from a typical real computer system. However, exactly identical file systems are suspicious so it is important to make at least random differences among honeypots.

Honeypot signatures can be found in main memory, secondary storage, and network packets (Holz &

Table 1. A taxonomy of deception in cyberspace

Deception method	Suitability in cyberspace	Example
Agent	4	Pretend to be a naive consumer to entrap identity thieves
Object	7	Camouflage key targets or make them look unimportant; or disguise software as different software
Instrument	1	Do something in an unexpected way
Accompaniment	4	Induce attacker to download a Trojan horse
Experiencer	8	Secretly monitor attacker's activities
Direction	3	Transfer Trojan horses back to attacker
Location-from	2	Try to frighten attacker with false messages from authorities
Location-to	6	Transfer attack to a safer machine, like a honeypot
Frequency	7	Swamp attacker with messages or requests
Time-at	2	Associate false times with files
Time-from	1	Falsify file-creation times
Time-to	1	Falsify file-modification times
Time-through	8	Deliberately delay processing commands
Cause	7	Lie that you cannot do something, or do something unrequested
Effect	9	Lie that a suspicious command succeeded
Purpose	8	Lie about reasons for asking for an additional password
Content	9	Plant disinformation, redefine executables, or give false system data
Material	3	"Emulate" hardware of a machine in software for increased safety
Measure	6	Send data too large or requests too difficult back to the attacker
Value	7	Systematically misunderstand attacker commands, as by losing characters
Supertype	5	Be a decoy site for the real site
Whole	2	Ask questions that include a few attacker-locating ones
Precondition	10	Give false excuses why you cannot execute attacker commands
Ability	6	Pretend to be an inept defender, or have easy-to-subvert software

Raynal, 2005). The Honeynet Project has put much thought into signature-concealing methods for honeypots, many of which involve deception. Since good honeypots should log data through several independent methods (packet dumps, intrusion-detection system alerts, and keystroke logging), it is especially important to conceal logging. Sebek uses specially-modified operating systems and applications software rather than calling standard utilities, such as implementing the UDP communications protocol directly, rather than calling a UDP utility. It specially conceals the honeynet software when listing operating-system files. It also implements a firewall (protective network filter) that deceptively does not decrement the "time to live" of packets traversing it as most firewalls do, helping to conceal itself. Honeypots also can conceal logging by sending data by indirect routes, such as to nonexistent computer addresses, where it can be picked up in transmission by network-packet "sniffers." Honeypots implemented in hardware can be even better at avoiding software clues. Signatures of honeypots also can be concealed by putting key data in unusual places, encrypting it, or frequently overwriting it with legitimate data. But steganography (concealed messages) is unhelpful with honeypots since just sending log data is suspicious, not its contents.

Deception to Prevent the Spread of Attacks from Honeypots

Honeypots must try to protect attacks on them from spreading to legitimate computers, since attackers frequently use compromised systems as bases for new attacks. This means honeypots should have a "reverse firewall" that just controls data leaving them. Deception is essential for reverse firewalls because they are rarely found on legitimate systems and are obvious clues to honeypots. Sebek and other "Gen II honeynets" use several deception tactics. They impose a hidden limit on the number of outbound connections. They can drop (lose) outgoing packets according to destination or the presence of known malicious signatures. They also can modify packets so known malicious code can be made ineffective and/or more visible to its targets. Modification is particularly good when packets an attacker is sending are malformed or otherwise unusual, since a good excuse to the attacker for why they do not work is that a new signature has been recognized.

DISINFORMATION

Deception can be used by ordinary computer systems, too. As with print media, disinformation (false information) can be planted on computers for enemy spies to discover, as a counterintelligence tactic (Gerwehr, Weissler, Medby, Anderson, &Rothenberg, 2000). This includes fake mission plans, fake logistics data, fake intelligence, and fake orders; it also can include fake operating-system data, such as fake temporary files and fake audit logs, constructed to make it appear that a system is being used for normal purposes, analogous to the fake radio messages used by the Allies

before D-Day (Cruikshank, 1979). Disinformation can work well in cyberspace because, unlike handwritten materials, electronic data does not provide clues to deception in style and provenance (how it was obtained), and methods for detecting text inconsistencies (Kaza, Murthy, & Hu, 2003; Zhou, Twitchell, Qin, Burgoon, & Nunamaker, 2003) do not work well for fixed-format audit records. While operating systems do record who copied a file and when, the author may be masquerading as someone else, and dates can easily be faked by changing the system clock. Since timing and location are often critical to military operations, a useful tactic for creating disinformation is to copy a previous real message but change the times and/or places mentioned in a systematic way.

Disinformation can be used to fight spam with "spam honeypots" (Krawetz, 2004). These sites collect large amounts of e-mail traffic to detect identical messages sent to large numbers of addresses, which they then identify as spam, and quickly report to e-mail servers for blacklisting. Spam honeypots can deceive in publicizing their fake email addresses widely, as on Web sites. Also, sites designed for phishing, or identity theft via spam, can be counterattacked by overwhelming them with large amounts of false identity data.

Since attackers want to avoid honeypots, other useful disinformation could be false indicators of a honeypot (Rowe, Duong, & Custy, 2006). For instance, one can put in secondary storage the executables and data files for monitoring software, like VMWare, even if they are not being run. Disinformation also could be a false report on a Web page that a site uses honeypots, scaring attackers away. Amusingly, hackers created disinformation themselves when they distributed a fake journal issue with a fake technical article claiming that Sebek did not work (McCarty, 2003).

DECEPTIVE DELAYS

Deceptive delaying is a useful tactic when a defender needs time to assemble a defense or await reinforcements. It can mean just waiting before responding, or giving an attacker extra questions to answer or information to read before they can proceed. Delaying helps a defender who is suspicious about a situation but not certain, and it gives time to collect more evidence. Deception is necessary to delay effectively in cyberspace because computers do not deliberate before acting, though they may seek authorizations (Somayaji & Forrest, 2000). One possible excuse for deceptive delays is that a computation requires a long time. This can be done, for instance, in a Web site (Julian, Rowe, & Michael, 2003): If input to a form is unusually long or contains what looks like program code, delays will simulate a successful denial-of-service attack while simultaneously foiling it. Delays also are used in the LaBrea tool (www.hackbusters.net) to slow attacks that query nonexistent Internet addresses. Plausible delays should be a monotonically increasing function of the expected processing time for an input, so they seem causally related to it. A delay that is a quadratic or exponential function of the expected processing time is good because it penalizes very suspicious situations more than it penalizes mildly suspicious situations.

DEFENSIVE LIES

Lies also can be an effective way to defend computer systems from attack. While not often recognized, software does deliberately lie to users on occasion to manipulate them. For instance, most Web browsers will suggest that a site is not working when given a misspelled Web link, apparently to flatter the user. Information systems can lie to protect themselves against dangerous actions. Useful lies can give excuses for resource denial, like saying "the network is down," in response to a command requiring the network—much as a lie "the boss just stepped out" can be used to avoid confrontations in a work place. Attackers must exploit certain key resources of a victim information system like passwords, file-system access, and networking access. If we can deny them these by deception, they may conclude that their attack cannot succeed and just go away without a fight. False resource denial has an advantage over traditional mandatory and discretion-

ary access control of resources in that it does not tell the attacker that their suspiciousness has been detected. Thus, they may keep wasting time trying to use the resource. Resource denial also can be fine-tuned to the degree of suspiciousness, unlike access control, permitting more flexibility in security.

Deception planning is essential to the use of deliberate lies because good lies require consistency. So cyber-deception planners need to analyze what attackers have been told so far to figure what lies to best tell them next; decision theory can be used to rank the suspiciousness of alternative excuses (Rowe, 2004). For attacks that are known in advance, one can construct more detailed defensive plans. Michael, Fragkos, and Auguston (2003) used a model of a file-transfer attack to design a program that would fake succumbing to the attack, and Cohen & Koike (2004) used "attack graphs" to channel the activities of attackers with situation-dependent lies about the status of services on a virtual honeynet.

DECEPTION TO IDENTIFY ATTACKERS

A serious problem in defense against cyber attack is finding its source (attribution) so that one can stop it, counterattack, impose sanctions, or start legal proceedings. But the design of the Internet makes it very difficult to trace attacks. Military networks do generally track routing information by using modified networking protocols; but it is often impossible to get civilian sites to do this, since it requires significant storage, so an attacker that comes in through a civilian network can remain anonymous.

"Spyware" that remotely reports user activities (Thompson, 2005) is useful for source attribution. "Trojan horses," or programs containing concealed processing, can be used to insert spyware onto attacker machines by offering free software (like attack tools) through "hacker" sites or via e-mail; or spyware can be installed by surreptitious loading onto attacker computers. Spyware can track when a user is logged in, what programs they run, and what Internet sites they visit. Spyware also can be designed to delay or impede an adversary when they attempt attacks. But then it is likely to be discovered, and once it is discovered, any subsequent deceptions are much less effective.

One also can try common cyber scams (Grazioli & Jarvenpaa, 2003) on an attacker. One can plant "bait" like passwords and track their use or plant credit-card numbers and watch to where the goods are delivered. One may be able to fool an attacker into submitting a form with personal data. Or one can just try to chat with an attacker to fool them into to revealing information about themselves, since many hackers love to boast about their exploits.

STRATEGIC DECEPTION

Deception also can be used at a strategic level to make the enemy think you have information-system capabilities you do not have or vice versa. Dunnigan and Nofi (2001) argue that the Strategic Defense Initiative of the United States in the 1980s was a strategic deception. Since it was then infeasible to shoot down missiles from space, and it served only to panic the Soviet Union into overspending on its military. Something similar could be done with information technology by claiming, say, special software to find attackers that one does not have (Erdie & Michael, 2005). Conversely, one could advertise technical weaknesses in one's information systems in the hope of inducing an attack that one knows could be handled. Dissemination of reports that an organization uses honeypots could make attackers take extra precautions in attacking its systems, thereby slowing them down, even if the organization does not use honeypots. Strategic deceptions can be difficult to implement because they may require coordination of numbers of people and records.

CONCLUSION

Deception has long been an important aspect of warfare, so it is not surprising to see it emerging as a defensive tactic for cyber warfare. Honeypots have pioneered in providing a platform for experimentation with deceptive techniques, because they need deception to encourage attackers to use them and show off their exploits. But any computer system can benefit from deception to protect itself, since attackers expect computers to be obedient servants. However, deceptions must be convincing for attackers and cost-effective considering their impact on legitimate users.

REFERENCES

Cohen, F., & Koike, D. (2004). Misleading attackers with deception. In *Proceedings of the.5th Information Assurance Workshop*, West Point, NY (pp. 30-37).

Cruikshank, C. G. (1979). *Deception in World War Two*. New York: Oxford.

Dunnigan, J., & Nofi, A. (2001). *Victory and deceit: Deception and trickery in war* (2nd ed.). San Jose, CA: Writers Club Press.

Erdie, P, & Michael, J. (2005, June). Network-centric strategic-level deception. In *Proceedings of the 10th International Command and Control Research and Technology Symposium*. McLean, VA.

Gerwehr, S., Weissler, R., Medby, J. J., Anderson, R. H., & Rothenberg, J. (2000). *Employing deception in information systems to thwart adversary reconnaissance-phase activities* (Project Memorandum, PM-1124-NSA). National Defense Research Institute, Rand Corp.

Grazioli, S., & Jarvenpaa, S. (2003). Deceived: Under target online. *Communications of the ACM, 46* (12), 196-205.

Holz, T., & Raynal, F. (2005). *Defeating honeypots: System issues* (Parts 1 and 2). Retrieved October 25, 2005, from www.securityfocus.com/infocus/1826

The Honeynet Project. (2004). *Know your enemy* (2nd ed.). Boston: Addison-Wesley.

Julian, D., Rowe, N., & Michael, J. (2003). Experiments with deceptive software responses to buffer-based attacks. In *Proceedings of the IEEE-SMC Workshop on Information Assurance* (pp. 43-44). West Point, NY.

Kaza, S., Murthy, S., & Hu, G. (2003). Identification of deliberately doctored text documents using frequent keyword chain (FKC) model. In *Proceedings of the IEEE International Conference on Information Reuse and Integration*, Las Vegas, NV (pp. 398-405).

Krawetz, N. (2004). Anti-honeypot technology. *IEEE Security and Privacy, 2*(1), 76-79.

McCarty, B. (2003). The honeynet arms race. *IEEE Security and Privacy, 1*(6), 79-82.

Michael, J. B., Fragkos, G., & Auguston, M. (2003). An experiment in software decoy design: intrusion detection and countermeasures via system call instrumentation. In *Proceedings of the IFIP 18th International Information Security Conference*, Athens, Greece (pp. 253-264).

Proctor, P. E. (2001). *Practical intrusion detection handbook*. Upper Saddle River, NJ: Prentice-Hall PTR.

Rowe, N. (2004). Designing good deceptions in defense of information systems. In *Proceedings of the Computer Security Applications Conference*, Tucson, AZ (pp. 418-427).

Rowe, N. (2006). Measuring the effectiveness of honeypot counter-counterdeception. In *Proceedings of the Hawaii International Conference on Systems Sciences,* Koloa, HI.

Rowe, N., Duong, B., & Custy, E. (2006). Fake honeypots: A defensive tactic for cyberspace. In *Proceedings of the 7th IEEE Workshop on Information Assurance,* West Point, NY.

Rowe, N., & Rothstein, H. (2004). Two taxonomies of deception for attacks on information systems. *Journal of Information Warfare, 3*(2), 27-39.

Somayaji, A., & Forrest, S., (2000). Automated response using system-call delays. In *Proceedings of the 9th Usenix Security Symposium*, Denver, CO (pp. 185-198).

Spitzner, L. (2003). *Honeypots: Tracking hackers.* Boston: Addison-Wesley.

Thompson, R. (2005). Why spyware poses multiple threats to security. *Communications of the ACM, 48*(8), 41-43.

Tirenin, W., & Faatz, D. (1999). A concept for strategic cyber defense. In *Proceedings of the Conference on Military Communications* (Vol. 1, pp. 458-463).

Zhou, L., Twitchell, D., Qin, T., Burgoon, J., & Nunamaker, J. (2003). An exploratory study into deception detection in text-based computer-mediated communication. In *Proceedings of the 36th Hawaii International Conference on Systems Sciences*, Waikoloa, HI (p. 10).

TERMS AND DEFINITIONS

Deception: This means misleading someone into believing something that is false.

Disinformation: This is false information deliberately planted for spies to obtain.

Exploit: This is an attack method used by a cyber attacker.

Honeypot: This is a computer system whose only purpose is to collect data on trespassers.

Honeynet: This refers to a network of honeypots, generally more convincing than a single honeypot.

Intrusion-Detection System: This software monitors a computer system or network for suspicious behavior and reports the instances that it finds.

Lie: This means deception by deliberately stating something false.

Low-Interaction Honeypot: This honeypot simulates only the initial steps of protocols and does not give attackers full access to operating systems on sites.

Reverse Firewall: This computer controls outgoing traffic from a local-area computer network; important with honeynets to prevent attacks from spreading.

Sniffer: This is software that eavesdrops on data traffic on a computer network; essential for network-based intrusion-detection systems but also useful to attackers.

Spyware: This software secretly transmits information about what a user does to a remote Web site.

Chapter XIV
Ethics of Cyber War Attacks

Neil C. Rowe
U.S. Naval Postgraduate School, USA

ABSTRACT

Offensive cyber warfare raises serious ethical problems for societies, problems that need to be addressed by policies. Since cyber weapons are so different from conventional weapons, the public is poorly informed about their capabilities and may endorse extreme ethical positions in either direction on their use. Cyber weapons are difficult to precisely target given the interdependence of most computer systems, so collateral damage to civilian targets is a major danger, as when a virus aimed at military sites spreads to civilian sites. Damage assessment is difficult for cyber war attacks, since most damage is hidden inside data; this encourages massive attacks in the hopes of guaranteeing some damage. Damage repair may be difficult, especially for technologically primitive victim countries. For these reasons, some cyber war attacks may be prosecutable as war crimes. In addition, cyber-war weapons are expensive and tend to lose effectiveness quickly after use as they lose the element of surprise, so the weapons are not cost effective.

CRITERIA FOR ETHICAL ATTACKS

Ethics starts with laws. International laws of war ("jus in bello") try to regulate how wars can be legally fought (Gutman & Rieff, 1999). The Hague Conventions (1899 and 1907) and Geneva Conventions (1949 and 1977) are the most important. While most cyber war attacks do not appear to fall into the category of "grave breaches" or "war crimes" as per the 1949 Geneva Conventions, they may still be illegal or unethical. Article 51 of the 1977 Additional Protocols of the Geneva Conventions prohibits attacks that employ methods and means of combat whose effects cannot be controlled or whose damage to civilians is disproportionate. Article 57 says "Constant care shall be taken to spare the civilian population, civilians, and civilian objects"; cyber weapons are difficult to target and difficult to assess in their effects. The Hague Conventions prohibit weapons that cause unnecessary suffering; cyber-attack weapons can cause mass destruction to civilian computers that is difficult to repair. Arquilla (1999) generalizes on the laws to suggest three main criteria for an ethical military attack: noncombatant immunity during the attack, proportionality of the size and scope of the attack to the provocation (i.e., nonoverreaction), and that the attack does more good than harm. All are difficult to guarantee in cyberspace. Nearly all authorities agree that international law does apply to cyber warfare (Schmitt, 2002).

We examine here the application of these concepts to cyber war attacks (or "cyber attacks"), that is, attacks on the computer systems and computer networks of an adversary using "cyber weapons" built of software and data (Bayles, 2001; Lewis, 2002). A first problem is determining whether one is under cyber attack (or is a defender in "information warfare"), since it may not be obvious (Molander & Siang, 1998). Manion and Goodrum (2000) note that legitimate acts of civil disobedience, such as spamming oppressive governments or modifying their Web sites, can look like cyber attacks and need to be distinguished by their lack of violence. Michael, Wingfield, and Wijiksera (2003) proposed criteria for assessing whether one is under "armed attack" in cyberspace by implementing the approach of Schmitt (1998) with a weighted average of seven factors: severity, immediacy, directness, invasiveness, measurability, presumptive legitimacy, and responsibility. Effective cyber attacks are strong on immediacy and invasiveness (most subvert an adversary's own systems). But they can vary greatly on severity, directness, and measurability, depending on the methods. There is no presumption of legitimacy for cyber attacks; and responsibility is notoriously difficult to assign in cyberspace. These make it hard to justify counterattacks to cyber attacks.

PACIFISM AND CONDITIONAL PACIFISM

A significant number of the world's people believe that military attacks are unjustified regardless of the circumstances—the idea of "pacifism" (Miller, 1991). Pacifism can be duty-based (from the moral unacceptability of violence), pragmatics-based (from the rarity of net positive results from attacks), or some combination of these. Duty-based pacifists are most concerned about the violence and killing of warfare, and cyber attacks could be more acceptable to them than conventional attacks, if only data is damaged. But nonviolence may be hard to guarantee in a cyber attack, since, for instance, the nonviolent disabling of a power plant may result in catastrophic accidents, looting, or health threats. To pragmatics-based pacifists, war represents a waste of resources and ingenuity that could be better spent on constructive activities (Nardin, 1998), and this applies equally to cyber warfare. To them, cyber attacks are just as unethical as other attacks because both are aggressive antisocial behavior. Most psychologists do see types of aggression on a continuous spectrum (Leng, 1994).

More popular than pure pacifism are various kinds of "conditional pacifism," which hold that attacks are permissible under certain circumstances. The most commonly cited is counterattack in response to attack. The United Nations Charter prohibits attacks by nations unless attacked first (Gutman & Rieff, 1999), and the wording is sufficiently general to apply to cyber attacks. Counterattacks are only allowed in international law against nation-states, not groups within countries like "terrorists," however they may be defined. Arquilla 1999) points out, however, that cyber attacks are such a tempting form of first attack that they are likely to be popular for surprise attacks.

COLLATERAL DAMAGE IN CYBER ATTACKS

Cyber attacks exploit vulnerabilities of software, both operating systems and applications. Unfortunately, the increasing standardization of software means that military organizations often use the same software as civilians do, and much of this software has the same vulnerabilities. Many viruses and worms that could cripple a command-and-control network could just as easily cripple a civilian network. And the increasing interconnection of computers through networks means there are many routes by which an attack could spread from a military organization's computers to those of civilian "innocent bystanders" (Arquilla, 1999; Westwood, 1997). Military systems try to isolate themselves from civilian systems but are not very successful because access to the Internet simplifies many routine tasks. Furthermore, information flow from civilian to military systems is often less restricted than flow in the other direction, which actually encourages an adversary to first attack civilian sites.

Disproportionate damage to civilians is a key issue in the Geneva Conventions. Incomplete knowledge of an adversary's computer systems may worsen the spread of the attack to civilians: What may seem a precisely targeted disabling of a software module on a military computer may have profound consequences on civilian computers that happen, unknown to attackers, to use that same module. And even if attackers think they know the addresses of target military computers, the adversary may change their addresses in a crisis situation, or meanwhile have given their old addresses to civilian computers. Another problem is that it is easy to create disproportionately greater damage to civilian computers by a cyber attack, since there are usually more of them than military computers and their security is not as good. Cyber attacks are more feasible for small organizations, like terrorist ones, than conventional warfare is (Ericsson, 1999), but such organizations may lack the comprehensive intelligence necessary to target their adversary precisely. In addition, it can be tempting to attack civilian systems anyway for strategic reasons. Crippling a few sites in a country's power grid, telephone system, or banking system can be more damaging to its capacity to wage war than disabling a few command-and-control centers, considering the back-up sites and redundancy in most military command-and-control systems.

Another collateral-damage problem is that staging a cyber attack almost invariably requires manipulating a significant number of intermediate computers between the attacker and the victim, since such route finding has been deliberately made difficult. In fact, a route may even be impossible, since critical computers can be "air-gapped" or disconnected from all external networks. This means attackers need to do considerable exploratory trespassing, perhaps fruitlessly, to find a way to their target. Himma (2004) points out that cyber trespassing is poorly justified on ethical grounds. Even if it were in pursuit of a criminal, which is often not true for cyber attacks, police do not have to right to invade every house into which a criminal might have fled. Trespassing on computers also steals computation time from those computers without permission, slowing their legitimate activities.

Reducing Collateral Damage

Two factors can mitigate collateral damage from cyber attacks: targeting precision and repair mechanisms. Cyber attacks often can be designed to be selective in what systems they attack and what they attack in those systems. Systems can be defined by names and Internet protocol (IP) addresses, and attacks can be limited to a few mission-critical parts of the software. So an attack might disable "instant messaging," while permitting (slower) e-mail, or insert delays into key radar defense systems; but use of denial-of-service, which would swamp resources with requests, would be too broad in effects to justify ethically. Naturally an adversary will make it difficult to get accurate information about their computer systems, their "electronic order of battle." They could deliberately mislead attackers as to the addresses and natures of their sites, as with "honeynets" or fake computer networks (The Honeynet Project, 2004). Furthermore, Bissett (2004) points out that modern warfare rarely achieves its promise of precise "surgical strikes" for many reasons that apply to cyber attacks, including political pressures to use something new whether or not it is appropriate, the inevitable miscalculations in implementing new technology, lack of feeling of responsibility in the attacker due to the technological remoteness of the target, and the inevitable surprises in warfare that were not encountered during testing in controlled environments.

An intriguing possibility for ethical cyber attacks is to design their damage to be easily repairable. For instance, damage could be in the form of an encryption of critical data or programs using a secret key known only to the attacker, so performing a decryption could repair the damage. Or a virus could store the code it has replaced, enabling substitution of the original code later, but this is hard to do when viruses attack many kinds of software. Repair procedures could be designed to be triggerable by the attacker at a time that they choose or could be kept in escrow by a neutral party, such as the United Nations, until the termination of hostilities.

DAMAGE ASSESSMENT FOR CYBER ATTACKS

Damage assessment is difficult in cyberspace. When a computer system does not work, it could be due to problems in any number of features. For instance, code destruction caused by a virus can be scattered throughout the software. Unlike conventional weapons, determining how many places are damaged is difficult, since often damage is not apparent except under special tests. This encourages more massive attacks than necessary to be sure they cause sufficient damage. The difficulty of damage assessment also makes repair difficult. Damage may persist for a long time and its cumulative effect may be great even when it is subtle, so noncombatant victims of a cyber attack could continue to suffer long afterwards from attacks on military computers that accidentally spread to them, as with attacks by chemical weapons. Repair can be accomplished by just reinstalling software after an attack, but this is often unacceptable since it loses data. With "polymorphic," or shape-changing, viruses, for instance, it may be hard to tell which software is infected; if the infection spreads to back-up copies, then reinstalling just reinfects. Computer forensics (Mandia & Prosise, 2003) provides tools to analyze computer systems after cyber attacks, but their focus is determining the attack mechanism and constructing a legal case against the perpetrator, not repair of the system.

DETERMINING THE PERPETRATORS AND VICTIMS

Even if an attack minimizes collateral damage, it can be unethical, if it cannot be attributed. It can be difficult to determine the perpetrator of a cyber attack because most attacks must be launched through a long chain of jurisdictions enroute to the victim. Route-tracing information is not available on all sites, and even when it is available, stolen or guessed passwords may mean that users have been impersonated. So a clever attacker can make it appear that someone else has launched the attack, although this violates the prohibition in international law against ruses like combatants wearing the wrong uniforms. In addition, a cyberspace attacker may not be a nation but a small group of individuals or even a single individual acting alone. So just because you have traced an attack to a country does not mean that country is responsible. This makes counterattack difficult to justify in cyberspace as well as risking escalation even if it correctly guesses the attacker. Legally and ethically, people should be responsible for software agents acting on their behalf (Orwant, 1994), so unjustified indirect attacks and counterattacks are as unethical as direct attacks.

Intended victims of attacks also may be unclear, which makes it difficult to legitimize counterattacks. Suppose an attack targets a flaw in a Microsoft operating system on a computer used by an international terrorist organization based in Pakistan. Is this an attack on Pakistan, the terrorist organization, or Microsoft? Nations often think that attacks within their borders are attacks on the nation, but if the nation does not support the terrorist group, it would be unfair to interpret it as the target. Multinational corporations like Microsoft have attained the powers of nation-states in their degree of control of societies, so they can certainly be targets, too. But chaos can ensue, if entities other than nation-states think they can wage war.

REUSABILITY OF CYBER ATTACKS

Cyber attacks have a peculiar problem not shared by traditional attacks. They can generally be highly effective only once (Ranum, 2004). Analysis of an attack by the victim usually reveals the software that was exploited and the vulnerabilities in it. This software can be immediately disabled, and then fixed ("patched") to prevent a repeat of the attack (Lewis, 2002). News of the attack can be quickly disseminated through vulnerability clearinghouse Web sites, like www.kb.cert. org, cve.mitre.org, and www.securityfocus.com, so that other potential victims can be quickly protected, and automatic downloading of a security update for all installations can be initiated by the vendor. This can be accomplished nowadays within a few days. So if an attacker tries the same attack later, it is likely to be much less effective. Countermeasures also can be found, independent of attacks, by security professionals in testing and analyzing software, so a new attack may be foiled before it can ever be used.

On the other hand, cyber attacks are costly to develop. "Zero-day," or new, attacks are the most effective ones, but new weaknesses in software that no one has found are rare and difficult to find. Software engineers are getting better at analyzing and testing their software for security holes. Another problem is that at least part of a new attack ought to be pre-tested against an adversary to see if the adversary is vulnerable to it. Since there are many variables (like the version of software that the adversary is running) that may prevent the success of an attack, such initial testing can warn the adversary of the type of full attack to come. Thus, generally speaking, research and development of cyber attacks appears highly cost ineffective and a waste of resources, and thus ethically questionable.

SECRECY AND CYBER ATTACKS

A related problem with cyber attacks is the greater need for secrecy than with traditional attacks. With bombs one does not need to conceal the technology of the explosives from the adversary, because most of it is well known and bigger surprises are possible with the time and place for attacks. But knowledge about the nature of cyber attacks and the delivery mechanisms usually entails ability to stop them (Denning, 1999). Time and place do not provide much surprise, since everyone knows attacks can occur anytime at any place. Thus cyber attacks require secrecy of methods for a significant period of time from the discovery of the attack to its employment. Since many adversaries have intelligence resources determined to ferret out secrets, this secrecy can be very difficult to achieve. Bok (1986) points out other disadvantages of secrecy, including the encouragement of an elite that is out of touch with the changing needs of their society. Secrecy also promotes organizational inefficiency, since organizations easily may duplicate the same secret research and development. Thus cyber-attack secrecy can be argued to be questionable on ethical grounds.

POLICY FOR ETHICAL CYBER ATTACKS

Hauptman (1996) argues that computer technology is sufficiently advanced that we should have a full set of ethics for it, not just a set of guidelines. So cyber warfare should have ethics policies with associated justifications. Arquilla (1999) proposes some possible policies. One is a "no first use" pledge for cyber attacks analogous to pledges on other kinds of dangerous weapons. Another is that cyber attacks should only be in response to cyber attacks and should be proportionate to the attack. Another is a pledge simply to never use cyber weapons, since they can be weapons of mass destruction. When cyber weapons are used, additional policies could require that the attacks have distinctive nonrepudiable signatures that identify who is responsible and the intended target, or that attacks are easily reversible. Policy also is needed on the status of participants in cyber war, as to whether they are soldiers, spies, civilians, or something else (Nitzberg, 1998).

CONCLUSION

Cyber attacks raise many serious ethical questions for societies, since they can cause mass destruction. They raise so many questions that it is hard for a responsible country to consider them as a military option, so they are somewhat like chemical or biological weapons, although not as bad. Although cyber weapons can be less lethal than other weapons and can sometimes be designed to have reversible effects, their great expense, their lack of reusability, and the difficulty of targeting them precisely, usually makes them a poor choice of weapon. International law should prohibit them and institute serious punishments for their use.

REFERENCES

Arquilla, J. (1999). Ethics and information warfare. In Z. Khalilzad, J. White, & A. Marsall (Eds.), *Strategic appraisal: The changing role of information in warfare* (pp. 379-401). Santa Monica, CA: Rand Corporation.

Bayles, W. (2001). Network attack. *Parameters, US Army War College Quarterly, 31*, 44-58.

Bissett, A. (2004). High technology war and "surgical strikes." *Computers and Society (ACM SIGCAS), 32*(7), 4.

Bok, S. (1986). *Secrets.* Oxford, UK: Oxford University Press.

Denning, D. (1999). *Information warfare and security.* Boston: Addison-Wesley.

Ericsson, E. (1999). Information warfare: Hype or reality? *The Nonproliferation Review, 6*(3), 57-64.

Gutman, R., & Rieff, D. (1999). *Crimes of war: What the public should know.* New York: Norton.

Hauptman, R. (1996). Cyberethics and social stability. *Ethics and Behavior, 6*(2), 161-163.

Himma, K. (2004). The ethics of tracing hacker attacks through the machines of innocent persons. *International Journal of Information Ethics, 2*(11), 1-13.

The Honeynet Project. (2004) *Know your enemy* (2nd ed.). Boston: Addison-Wesley.

Leng, R. (1994). Interstate crisis escalation and war. In M. Portegal & J. Knutson (Eds.), *The dynamics of aggression* (pp. 307-332). Hillsdale, NJ: Lawrence Erlbaum.

Lewis, J. (2002). *Assessing the risks of cyber-terrorism, cyber war, and other cyber threats.* Washington, DC: Center for Strategic and International Studies. Retrieved November 23, 2005, from http://www.csis.org

Mandia, K., & Prosise, C. (2003). *Incident response and computer forensics.* New York: McGraw-Hill/Osborne.

Manion, M., & Goodrum, A. (2000). Terrorism or civil disobedience: toward a hacktivist ethic. *Computers and Society (ACM SIGCAS), 30*(2), 14-19.

Michael, J., Wingfield, T., & Wijiksera, D. (2003). Measured responses to cyber attacks using Schmitt analysis: a case study of attack scenarios for a software-intensive system. In *Proceedings of the 27th IEEE Computer Software and Applications Conference,* Dallas, TX.

Miller, R. (1991). *Interpretations of conflict: ethics, pacifism, and the just-war tradition.* Chicago, IL:: University of Chicago Press.

Molander, R., & Siang, S. (1998). The legitimization of strategic information warfare: Ethical considerations. *AAAS Professional Ethics Report, 11*(4). Retrieved November 23, 2005, from http://www.aaas.org/spp/sfrl/sfrl.htm

Nardin, T. (Ed.). (1998). *The ethics of war and peace.* Princeton, NJ: Princeton University Press.

Nitzberg, S. (1998). Conflict and the computer: Information warfare and related ethical issues. In *Proceed-*

ings of the 21st National Information Systems Security Conference, Arlington, VA (p. D7).

Orwant, C. (1994). EPER ethics. In *Proceedings of the Conference on Ethics in the Computer Age*, Gatlinburg, TN (pp. 105-108).

Ranum, M. (2004). *The myth of homeland security*. Indianapolis: Wiley.

Schmitt, M. (1998). Bellum Americanum: The U.S. view of twenty-first century war and its possible implications for the law of armed conflict. *Michigan Journal of International Law, 19*(4), 1051-1090.

Schmitt, M. (2002). Wired warfare: computer network attack and jus in bello. *International Review of the Red Cross, 84*(846), 365-399.

Westwood, C. (1997). *The future is not what it used to be: Conflict in the information age*. Fairbairn, Australia: Air Power Studies Center.

TERMS AND DEFINITIONS

Collateral Damage: This is damage from an attack to other than the intended targets.

Computer Forensics: This includes methods for analyzing computers and networks to determine what happened to them during a cyber attack, with the hope of repairing the damage and preventing future similar attacks.

Cyber Attack: This refers to offensive acts against computer systems or networks.

Cyber War: This is attacks on computer systems and networks by means of software and data.

Cyber Weapon: Software designed to attack computers and data.

Jus in Bello: These are international laws for conducting warfare.

Pacifism: An ethical position opposed to warfare and violence.

Patch: This means a modification of software to fix vulnerabilities that a cyber attack could exploit.

Zero-Day Attack: This is a type of cyber attack that has not been used before.

Chapter XV
International Outsourcing, Personal Data, and Cyber Terrorism:
Approaches for Oversight

Kirk St.Amant
Texas Tech University, USA

ABSTRACT

An individual's personal information can be a valuable commodity to terrorists. With such data, terrorists can engage in a variety of illicit activities including creating false bank accounts, procuring various official documents or even creating mass panic. Unfortunately, such personal data is generally easy to access, exchange, or collect via online media including Web sites, chat rooms, or e-mails. Moreover, certain common business practices, particularly those related to data processing in international outsourcing, can facilitate such activities by placing personal information into a legal grey area that makes it easy to misuse. For these reasons, organizations and individuals need to be aware of the potential for such data misuse as well as be informed of steps they can take to curtail such abuses. This essay examines the privacy/data abuse problems related to international outsourcing and presents approaches designed to prevent the misuse of personal information by cyber terrorists.

INTRODUCTION

An individual's personal information can be a valuable commodity to terrorists. With such data, terrorists can set up false addresses for receiving materials, establish unknown lines of credit, apply for visas, passports, or other documents, or siphon money from bank accounts (Lormel, 2002; Sullivan, 2004). On a large scale, terrorists can misuse personal data in ways that could cause mass panic; crash an organization's or a region's computer systems, or spread misinformation throughout a community (Lormel, 2002; Sullivan,

2004). For these reasons, the protection of personal information is of paramount importance to combating terrorism.

Unfortunately, such data is often freely exchanged and easily compiled via online media such as Web sites, chat rooms, or e-mails. As a result, personal information can be a prime and easy target for *cyber terrorists*—or individuals who use online media to engage in or enable terrorist activities. Moreover, certain business practices actually place large amounts of personal data into an environment where it can easily be abused by others.

One of the more problematic of these practices is international outsourcing. By moving personal data beyond the reach of certain authorities, international outsourcing activities can facilitate the uses of personal data for nefarious ends. This chapter examines privacy and data abuse problems related to international outsourcing. It also presents approaches organizations can use to prevent the misuse of personal data by cyber terrorists.

BACKGROUND

When organizations outsource, they allow other individuals or companies to perform work for them (Bendor-Samuel, 2004). The decision to outsource usually involves two factors: cost and efficiency. That is, client businesses outsource tasks to organizations that can perform them more cheaply and efficiently than the client business can. Such work, moreover, is often outsourced to persons or organizations located in other nations—a process known as *international outsourcing* or *offshoring.*

While companies have been sending manufacturing work overseas for some time, the nature of the work being outsourced now includes a wide range of knowledge-based tasks including information technology (IT) management, software and video game programming, accounting, and medical transcription. In many cases, companies based in North America and Western Europe export work to outsourcing providers located in developing nations such as India, China, and the Philippines.

The benefits associated with such offshoring practices have led to an explosion in this industry. Today, international outsourcing is worth some $10 billion and accounts for almost 500,000 jobs in India alone (Baily & Farrell, 2004; Rosenthal, 2004b). These situations might be the tip of a growing outsourcing iceberg, for certain observers claim the international outsourcing market will grow 20% a year through 2008 and account for three to five million knowledge-based jobs by the middle of the next decade (Baily & Farrell, 2004; Garten, 2004; Rosenthal, 2004b). This expansion will also mean outsourcing providers will arise in a wider range of developing nations as workers in Eastern Europe, Asia, South America, and Africa try to tap into this lucrative service market (Reuters, July 18, 2004; Rosenthal, 2004a; Rosenthal, 2004c).

This growth in outsourcing, moreover, will involve a wider range of knowledge-based work, particularly in the areas of financial processing and medial care. As a result, more sensitive information will move overseas to facilitate these activities. Such trends, however, create new legal situations related to data collection and distribution. By using more than one nation in a data processing activity, offshoring involves more than one legal system in the regulatory process.

The problem involves the legal concept of jurisdiction, or when a particular law can and cannot be enforced. According to this idea, the laws of one nation are often only enforceable within its borders. Thus, once individuals or materials move beyond those borders, they are generally beyond the legal protection of that nation.

Offshoring creates an interesting jurisdiction situation. If work is performed in another nation, then employees might be operating under a set of laws that is quite different from those that govern the company that provided the work. Therefore, a process that might be an illegal—or black market—activity in the nation of the outsourcing client could be a legal—or white market—one in the nation where the outsourcing employee resides. This situation is particularly problematic in relation to the protection of personal information, for the national laws dealing with this issue vary from the strict (e.g., European Union's Data Protection Directive) to almost non-existent (e.g., the

People's Republic of China) (Swire & Litan, 1998). Such contrasts create a gray area in international law—which laws should apply where and how (Rosenthal, 2005)? This gray area, in turn, leaves personal data open to misuse by terrorists through a process of *gray market informatics.*

MAIN THRUST OF THE CHAPTER

Four major factors can provide offshoring workers with the opportunity to engage in gray market informatics. First, and perhaps foremost, the outsourcing worker could be located in a nation where the collection and sale of personal information is completely legal. As a result, there is no legal mechanism to prevent (via punishment) or dissuade (via threat of sanctions) individuals from performing these activities. Second, such information has a relatively high market value if sold to the right individual or organization (e.g., terrorists) (Koerner, 2006; Lormel, 2002). Thus, there is incentive to misuse personal data for profit with no fear of punishment to temper this incentive. Third, as such sales might occur overseas, the client organizations that supplied personal data might never realize abuses are taking place. Such a condition further mitigates the threat (and thus the deterrence) of prospective punishment for abuses via sanctions (e.g., boycotts) imposed by clients. Fourth, outsourcing providers often use external subcontractors and do not make clients aware of these practices. Subcontractors, however, introduce a new degree of separation and make monitoring and accountability even more difficult for enforcement agencies and companies.

All of these situations provide terrorists with an excellent opportunity to acquire large amounts of personal data on individuals from a variety of nations. Factors of physical distance further contribute to such misuses, for they mean that such practices could go on for long periods of time before they are noticed—if they are noticed at all. Moreover, terrorists can easily insert themselves directly into overall processes—as employees or as subcontractors—and

cause damage not only to individuals, but to organizations, businesses, or even overall industries. Thus, for terrorists, the benefits of gray market informatics (easy access to data) are high while the risks (being captured) remain low.

Recent events have made organizations and individuals uncomfortably aware of how dangerous such misuses of personal data by terrorists are. The September 11 hijackers, for example, likely used illicitly obtained social security numbers and driver's license numbers to get the fake IDs needed to carry out their plot (Sieberg, 2001). Additionally, raids on terrorist camps in Afghanistan produced laptop computers which contained compiled personal data on a number of U.S. citizens (Bloys, 2006). Additionally, an Al-Queda terrorist cell in Spain was caught after using stolen credit information to purchase provisions for its activities and to transfer funds to other terrorists in Pakistan (Lormel, 2002).

More recently, known misuses of personal data have expanded to include abuses of medical information and have been more closely tied to offshoring activities. In one case, a Pakistan-based medical transcriptionist threatened to post patient records on the Internet unless her employer paid her $500 (Lazarus, March 28, 2004). She eventually received her payment, but there is no guarantee she did not share information with or sell information to other parties. In a second case, disgruntled outsourcing employees in India threatened to release patient information if a particular client failed to pay an unspecified sum of money (Lazarus, April 2, 2004). The perpetrators were eventually caught and the threat proved false. Both situations reveal the ease and the potential for abuses of personal data provided via offshoring activities. These situations also reveal that others recognize this potential.

In these more recent instances, outsourcing workers could have made money selling the same information to terrorists who could have then used that data for nefarious purposes. In fact, there is no way to know that such sales did not occur. Both of these cases also reveal that the outsourcing of personal data should be regulated or monitored in order to curtail abuses of such information. Such oversight, however, does not necessarily need to be governmental in nature. Rather, companies and organizations within overall industries can address such data abuse problems by adopting five relatively simple approaches in relation to international outsourcing:

- **Approach #1: Develop a sensitive data classification system and share this system with employees.** The key to avoiding data abuses is to determine which information is particularly "sensitive" and should remain within a company for protection. Nonsensitive data could then be sent abroad without worry. The processing of sensitive data, however, would remain "in-house" where both organizations and national laws could oversee its uses and protect it from abuses. Organizations should therefore allocate time and money to reviewing the kinds of data they have or they use and then develop categories for different kinds of sensitive data. Personal information could then be coded and distributed according to these categories.

  Organizations should simultaneously develop a plan for helping in-house employees understand the importance of data security related to international outsourcing. Such informed employees are more likely to take steps to treat the processing and the distribution of such data with care and thus reduce the potential for abuse (Goolsby, 2003; Peterson, 2002).

- **Approach #2: Create an intranet site that instructs employees and managers in how to recognize and address different data abuses they might encounter when working in outsourcing relationships.** To assist with preventing outsourcing oversights, organizations might create an intranet site that presents instructions for recognizing kinds of data abuses and provides a list of which corporate office or government agency to contact with concerns (Peterson, 2002). By increasing the number of individuals monitoring international outsourcing

activities, companies can decrease the chances that violations go unnoticed. Also, by helping employees feel like they are a part of such processes, organizations increase the chances that these employees will play a more active role in preventing outsourcing oversights (Goolsby, 2003; Peterson, 2002). Such intranet sites should include regular "outsourcing updates" which encourages regular use and provide "self test" scenarios employees can use to evaluate their understanding of outsourcing policies.

- **Approach #3: Work with outsourcing employees to develop data maps that catalog where information goes once it is sent to outsource workers.** Such a map should include the names and contact information for individuals working on each part of an outsourced processes. From a data security perspective, the single greatest problem is tracking where data goes once it is sent overseas. A map that clearly traces how such data moves once sent abroad could greatly help organizations locate where data abuses or data leaks might be taking place. Organizations could then use this information to address problems or devise alternative solutions (require the outsourcer to move or treat data in different ways) that would help avoid abuses (Atwood, 2004).

- **Approach #4: Raise management's awareness of outsourcers using subcontractors and develop policies for when to use subcontractors in outsourcing.** Include steps for registering subcontractors with the client or company so that clients can track the flow of information to these subcontractors (Peterson, 2002). As mentioned, a major problem with tracking violations is how subcontractors complicate dataflow situations. This problem is particularly important as many outsourcing providers use subcontractors but rarely notify the client of such uses.

- **Approach #5: Work with other companies to develop a network for sharing information on international outsourcing within specific industries and across different industries.**

Ideally, companies within an industry would work together to create an easy-access registry (e.g., a Web site) companies could use to enter the names and details of the outsourcing providers with which they worked. Companies could use this site to share information and opinions on the effectiveness with which they felt an outsourcing provider performed. Such a site would thus create a registry system, similar to the U.S. Better Business Bureau, that records if and how certain outsourcing providers engaged in personal data (or other) violations when working with a particular company. Registry listings could include who the violator is, what the nature of the violation was, what the client did in response to this violation, and what results came from this action. Such a registry could help companies avoid working with "disreputable" outsourcing providers and offer strategies for addressing misuses of personal information. Most important, this online resource would need to be updated regularly. Organizations that could oversee and update such a registry could include industry oversight bodies or the chamber of commerce or the Better Business Bureau in states where a large number of companies engage in international outsourcing.

While these approaches provide a means for overseeing international outsourcing, they are not definitive. Rather, these five strategies constitute a foundation upon which organizations can develop business- and industry-wide practices. Such practices, however, need to be examined soon, for new developments could create even more opportunities for cyber terrorists to abuse personal data.

FUTURE TRENDS

While reports of gray market informatics have been limited, certain trends could increase:

- The opportunities for terrorists to collect personal data
- The kinds of personal data available for misuse

A prime example of these trends can be seen in recent legislation in the United States. There, Section 404 of the Sarbanes-Oxley Act of 2002 requires chief executive officers and chief financial officers of public companies to review their internal controls over financial transactions ("404 tonnes," 2004). The costs and the staff needed for compliance are high, and the number of qualified, in-country employees (especially auditors) is limited ("404 tonnes," 2004; Byrnes, 2005).

Given the costs related to such activities and the fact that more complex accounting practices are being outsourced, it seems reasonable that some Statute 404 activities would be sent abroad for completion. It would also seem sensible that some auditing functions would become key service areas into which outsourcing providers would move—especially as demand has driven up pay for U.S. auditors by 1020% (Byrnes, 2005). Such outsourcing, however, would involve sending greater quantities and more kinds of sensitive financial data overseas. And this development is not unique to the United States. As more nations adopt more demanding and extensive accounting and reporting practices, businesses in several nations could increasingly turn to outsourcing to assist with various financial processes.

In a similar way, data related to personal medical records could create openings for cyber terrorists working in outsourcing situations. In the U.S., for example, health care legislation–the Health Insurance Portability and Accountability Act of 1996 (HIPAA)—is creating data processing situations that seem well suited for outsourcing. While HIPAA involves a mechanism for protecting patient information, it also mandates all of a patient's information be rendered into a digital format that can be easily shared (Goolsby, 2001b; Goolsby, 2001d). For health care organizations, converting all print medical records into a digital format introduces time consuming, costly, and monotonous tasks into their operations (Goolsby, 2001a; Goolsby, 2001d). Additionally, the time involved in converting information from one format to another creates delays that can affect the quality of patient health care and patient satisfaction. As a result, such HIPAA-related tasks (e.g., medical transcription and IT development) could be strong candidates for international outsourcing (Goolsby, 2001a; Salkever, 2004; "Sink or Schwinn," 2004). These situations, however, place a growing amount of personal information into contexts where it can be misused by terrorists as revealed by the recent cases of medical transcriptionists in Pakistan and India holding such data "hostage" (Salkever, 2004).

Trying to address such problem areas, however, is becoming increasingly complicated as more nations try to move into lucrative outsourcing markets. In China, for example, public and private sector programs are increasing the nation's online access in a way that would make it a good location for the outsourcing of knowledge work ("Wired China," 2000). Similarly, Malaysian companies are trying to present themselves as "outsourcing friendly" destinations, while the Philippines has developed a reputation for effectiveness in the outsourcing of English-language customer service calls and IT work (Gaudin, 2003; Reuters, September 2, 2004; Rosenthal, 2004c). Additionally, Russia and the Ukraine have established an outsourcing niche in the area of software programming (Goolsby, 2001c; Weir, 2004).

As more nations enter the outsourcing marketplace, the complexities of gray market informatics increase. Each new country brings with it different laws and customs related to the treatment of personal data. Each nation also becomes a prospective subcontractor or "middle person" though which data can be passed. As a result, tracking international data flows and isolating instances of abuse becomes even more difficult. These difficulties might actually become deterrents to enforcement, for the more time and money it takes to track data flows, the less likely organizations might be to pursue violators. Such situations create an ideal atmosphere in which cyber terrorists could collect large amounts of important information without attracting much attention. The convergence of these factors means now is the time for organizations to develop methods of ensuring the safe treatment of personal data in international outsourcing situations.

CONCLUSION

International outsourcing is radically affecting the distribution of personal data. While international outsourcing offers a range of benefits, it also creates certain problem areas that cyber terrorists can exploit for their own ends. Addressing these problems will not be easy. Organizations must, however, develop some form of outsourcing oversight if they are to protect information from terrorist abuses. The approaches presented in this chapter offer a first step toward addressing this situation. Yet public and private sector entities must act quickly and before changes in business practices and outsourcing destinations require more complex approaches to address this situation.

REFERENCES

404 tonnes. (2004, December 16). *The Economist.* Retrieved December 27, 2004, from http://www.economist.com/displaystory.cfm?story_id=3503931

Atwood, M. (2004). The art of governance. *Outsourcing Center.* Retrieved December 27, 2004, from http://www.outsourcing-requests.com/center/jsp/requests/print/story.jsp?id=4616

Baily, M. N. & Farrell, D. (2004, July). Exploding the myths of offshoring. *The McKinsey Quarterly.*

Retrieved November 11, 2004, from http://www.mckinseyquarterly.com/article_print.aspx?L2=7&L3=10&ar=1453

Bendor-Samuel, P. (2004). Lou Dobbs: Here's why you're wrong! *Outsourcing Center.* Retrieved December 20, 2004, from http://www.outsourcing-requests.com/center/jsp/requests/print/story.jsp?id=4565

Bloys, D. (2006, January 22). Online records linked to identity theft and worse. *News for Public Officials.* Retrieved August 25, 2006, from http://www.davick-services.com/Online_Records_Linked_To_Crime.htm

Byrnes, N. (2005, January 1). Green eyeshades never looked so sexy. *BusinessWeek Online.* Retrieved January 5, 2005, from http://www.businessweek.com/@@na*EhYQQxu80VAkA/magazine/content/05_02/b3915041_mz011.htm

Garten, J. E. (2004, June 21). Offshoring: You ain't seen nothin' yet. *BusinessWeek Online.* Retrieved December 30, 2004, from http://businessweek.com/print/magazine/content/04_25/b3888024_mz007.htm

Gaudin, S. (2003, November 19). Offshoring IT jobs expected to accelerate. *ClickZ.* Retrieved November 30, 2004, from http://www.clickz.com/stats/sectors/b2b/print.php/3111321

Goolsby, K. (2001a). Healthcare's biggest challenge. *Outsourcing Center.* Retrieved December 12, 2004, from http://www.outsourcing-requests.com/center/jsp/requests/print/story.jsp?id=1660

Goolsby, K. (2001b). How to get ready for HIPAA. *Outsourcing Center.* Retrieved December 12, 2004, from http://www.outsourcing-requests.com/center/jsp/requests/print/story.jsp?id=1686

Goolsby, K. (2001c). Nobody does it better. *Outsourcing Center.* Retrieved December 12, 2004, from http://www.outsourcing-requests.com/center/jsp/requests/print/story.jsp?id=1816

Goolsby, K. (2001d). *Perspectives on HIPAA.* Dallas, TX: Outsourcing Center.

Goolsby, K. (2003). *Governing attitudes: 12 best practices in managing outsourcing relationships.*

Dallas, TX: Outsourcing Center.

Koerner, B. (2006). Terrorist groups relying on identity theft for funding operations. *About.com.* Retrieved September 1, 2006, from http://idtheft.about.com/od/useofstolenidentity/p/IDTheftTerror.htm

Lazarus, D. (2004, March 28). Looking offshore: Outsourced UCSF notes highlight privacy risk. *San Francisco Chronicle.* Retrieved March 1, 2005, from http://www.sfgate.com/cgi-bin/article.cgi?file=/chronicle/archive/2004/03/28/MNGFS3080R264.DTL

Lazarus, D. (2004, April 2). Extortion threat to patients' records: Clients not informed of India staff's breach. *San Francisco Chronicle.* Retrieved March 1, 2005, from http://sfgate.com/cgi-bin/article.cgi?file=/c/a/2004/04/02/MNGI75VIEB1.DTL

Lormel, D. M. (2002, July 9). Testimony of Dennis M. Lormel, Chief, Terrorist Financial Review Group, FBI before the Senate Judiciary Committee Subcommittee on Technology, Terrorism and

Government Information July 9, 2002 Hearing On S. 2541, "The Identity Theft Penalty Enhancement Act". *Federal Bureau of Investigation.* Retrieved February 12, 2006, from http://www.fbi.gov/congress/congress02/idtheft.htm

Peterson, B. L. (2002). Information security in outsourcing agreements. *Outsourcing Center.* Retrieved December 27, 2004, from http://www.outsourcing-requests.com/center/jsp/requests/print/story.jsp?id=2355

Reuters. (2004, July 18). France outsources, Senegal calls. *Wired.* Retrieved September 20, 2004, from http://www.wired.com/news/print/0,1294,64262,00.html

Reuters. (2004, September 2). Outsourcing's next big thing—Malaysia? *News.Com.* Retrieved September 7, 2004, from http://news.com.com/2100-1011-5344618.html

Rosenthal, B. E. (2004a). How real estate choices affect offshoring decisions. *Outsourcing Center.* Retrieved December 12, 2004, from http://www.outsourcing-requests.com/center/jsp/requests/print/story.jsp?id=4718

Rosenthal, B. E. (2004b). META predicts offshoring will continue to grow at 20 percent clips through 2008. *Outsourcing Center.* Retrieved December 27, 2004, from http://www.outsourcing-requests.com/center/jsp/requests/print/story.jsp?id=4714

Rosenthal, B. E. (2004c). Why the US and UK are calling South African call centers. *Outsourcing Center.*

Retrieved December 12, 2004, from http://www.outsourcing-requests.com/center/jsp/requests/print/story.jsp?id=4717

Rosenthal, B. E. (2005). New outsourcing risks in 2005 and how to mitigate them. *Outsourcing Center.* Retrieved January 2, 2005, from http://www.outsourcing-requests.com/center/jsp/requests/print/story.jsp?id=4721

Salkever, A. (2004, July 7). Racing to cure sickly medical security. *BusinessWeek Online.* Retrieved December 30, 2004, from http://www.businessweek.com/print/technology/content/jul2004/tc2004077_9847_tc_171

Sieberg, D. (2001, September 21). Expert: Hijackers likely skilled with fake IDs. *CNN.com.* Retrieved August 28, 2006, from http://archives.cnn.com/2001/US/09/21/inv.id.theft/

Sink or Schwinn. (2004, November 11). *The Economist.* Retrieved December 6, 2004, from http://www.economist.com/printedition/PrinterFriendly.cfm?Story_ID=3351542

Sullivan, B. (2004, August 4). 9/11 report light on ID theft issues. *MSNBC.* Retrieved January 2, 2006, from http://www.msnbc.msn.com/id/5594385

Swire, P. P., & Litan, R. E. (1998). *None of your business: World data flows, electronic commerce, and the European privacy directive.* Washington DC: Brookings Institution Press.

Weir, L. (2004, August 24). Boring game? Outsource it. *Wired.* Retrieved September 20, 2004, from http://www.wired.com/news/print/0,1294,64638,00.html

Wired China. (2000, July 22). *The Economist*, pp. 24-28.

TERMS AND DEFINITIONS

Cyber Terrorist: Individuals who use online media to engage in or enable terrorist activities.

Gray Market Informatics: Processes in which differences in national privacy laws are used to compile and distribute personal data on individuals.

International Outsourcing: A production process in which different job tasks are assigned to overseas individuals who are responsible for completing these tasks. (Also referred to as "offshoring.")

Personal Data: Any information that can be associated with a specific individual.

Sensitive Data: Information, especially information on a particular individual, that requires special treatment and cannot be readily shared with individuals inside of or outside of an organization.

Chapter XVI
Network–Based Passive Information Gathering

Romuald Thion
University of Lyon, France

ABSTRACT

The information gathering process in cyber-warfare is as important as in real warfare. Once blackhats or cyber-ter-rorists aimed at an organization, they need to known as much as possible about its structure, its network organization, the people working in it, their addresses, hardware and software in use: the very first step of a cyber-battleplan is to know as much as possible about the battleground and the enemy. Though social engineering is a widely spread effective technique used for this purpose, other network-based techniques can be used in order to gather as much information as possible: from DNS query to infer network topology, NSLookUp to retrieve names and e-mails to intrusive techniques such as scanning tools. All this information correlated can produce very accurate results. Nowadays, the forthcoming Google Hacking is a new extremely powerful method to retrieve sensitive information anonymously. We present basic types of non-intrusive information retrieving tools, dedicated either to web server, software or hardware digging. We also describe interesting use of the Google Search engine involving advanced queries/techniques. A set of best individual and general practices are described in order to reduce the information disclosure risks.

INTRODUCTION

The rise of the Internet has been a blessing for computer science and the world of economy. It has redefined the word "information"; the Internet is the tip of the information revolution iceberg. The information revolution implies the rise of a mode of warfare in which neither mass nor mobility will decide outcomes; it is the new concept of "cyber war." It means trying to know everything about an adversary via network interconnections, while keeping the adversary from knowing much about him or herself. This tactical principle has already been exposed by Tzu in his *Art of War* (1910), but clearly it takes a new dimension in our interconnected world:

... what enables the wise sovereign and the good general to strike and conquer, and achieve things beyond the reach of ordinary men, is foreknowledge. Now this foreknowledge cannot be elicited from spirits; it cannot be obtained inductively from experience, nor by any deductive calculation. Knowledge of the enemy's dispositions can only be obtained from other men. (Chapter XIII, verses 4, 5 and 6)

In this topic, we are specifically interested in *passive* network-based information gathering techniques. In the context of networks, passive refers to techniques that do not connect to the targeted system or that would not be normally associated to an attack, whereas *active* refers to techniques that create network traffic and could be associated with suspicious or malicious behavior (e.g., port scanning).

BACKGROUND

Penetration testers, ethical hackers, and cyber criminals conduct cyber attacks in the same way. Whereas penetration testers are reliable people paid by an organization to conduct a security audit by "attacking" the target to find vulnerabilities and security weaknesses, cyber criminals and "nonethical" hackers conduct attacks without an organization's consent, to earn money, to undermine the credibility of the target, or for any other motive. In both cases, the techniques are identical. An attack can be roughly separated into five steps (FX et al., 2004).

1. **Information gathering:** By gathering as much information as possible about the target, in this step, the hacker is looking for potential vulnerabilities as well as software and hardware in use, network topology, and any information that will be useful for its attack (Grubb, 2004).
2. **Exploitation:** Using foreknowledge, a cyber criminal can focus on a specific vulnerability to take the initiative. In this step, the hacker is trying to find the most powerful and least difficult way to exploit vulnerability.

3. **Privileges elevation:** Often an exploited vulnerability does not award full control of the system. In this step, the hacker elevates his privileges to root around any means available.
4. **Cover tracks:** Once a system has been compromised, the hacker wants to cover his tracks as soon as possible, thus providing more time to act and lessen the possibility of being caught.
5. **Carry out his objective:** The hacker reaps the fruits of his or her efforts. He or she can gather any sensitive information wanted, use the compromised system to attack another one, delete data, and so forth. The hacker achieves the attack objectives.

This topic focuses on the very first step of any attack, information gathering, also known as preassessment information gathering. During this phase, the attacker is interested in obtaining preliminary information about the target—the foreknowledge.

Information gathering techniques can be roughly classified into the following:

*   **Social engineering:** These nonnetwork-based techniques are the practice of obtaining confidential information by manipulating users. A social engineer fools people (e.g., by phone, by e-mail) into revealing sensitive information or getting them to do something that is against typical policies, using their gullibility. Social engineering is made possible because "the weakest link of the security chain is the human factor." For instance, the famous hacker Kevin Mitnick has extensively used these techniques (Mitnick, Simon, & Wozniak, 2002).
*   **Active:** This includes intrusive reconnaissance that sends (specially crafted) packets to the targeted system, for example, port-scanning. Advanced network enumeration techniques avoid direct communication with the targeted host (e.g., Nmap (Fyodor, 2006)).
*   **Passive:** This includes reconnaissance that either does not communicate directly to the targeted system or that uses commonly available public

information, not normally identifiable from standard log analysis (Zalewski, 2005). This topic is focused on this category.

Every Internet-connected system unintentionally leaks internal information about its organization, making the passive information gathering process possible. Moreover, many organizations fail to identify potential threats from information leakage that could be used to build an attack.

Most information about an organization is publicly available using the Internet, or contained on systems unrelated to the target. This kind of information can be accessed anonymously by anyone without ever coming into direct contact with the organization's system; this is an important aspect of information leakage. Passive information gathering techniques could be applied to any public service available, for instance, job announcement services, public reports, or public directories.

PASSIVE TECHNIQUES

This section reviews traditional network-based passive information gathering techniques. All of these techniques use unsuspicious-looking connections. Most of them are based on collecting and harvesting publicly available information, such as:

- **"Real-life" information**, for example, physical locations, real names, telephone numbers, the internal structure of organizations, business processes, and so forth that could be later used in social engineering techniques (by endorsing an employee's identity, for example, Mitnick et al., 2004). This kind of information broadens an attacker's knowledge of the victim, making his attack well-targeted.
- **"Technical" information**, for example Internet protocol (IP) addresses, network topology, and software and hardware versions of both servers and clients. This kind of information helps the attacker to find the weakest link of the security

chain. An attacker's goal cannot be reached directly, most of the time, instead the attacker needs to breach the systems by using the most simple and effective way. Technical information can reveal easy to exploit vulnerabilities or interesting devices he or she needs to control to reach his goal.

Internet Service Registration

Every accessible host over the Internet must have a unique IP address (e.g., 207.46.20.60). To simplify host addressing and its usage by human beings, the domain name system (DNS) associates IP addresses to a unique domain name (e.g., microsoft.com).

International structures manage both IP addresses and domain names. Organizations must supply administrative information to these international instances, which is publicly available and may be accessed freely by anyone. Querying those international databases is the very first step in information gathering. The whois resource service provides a mechanism for querying these databases. Among the useful information provided are physical location, real names, and phone numbers. This information is particularly useful for social engineering (Ollman, 2004). The dNS addresses, the number of IP addresses attributed, Internet service provider (ISP) contact and registrar can reveal sensitive technical information. Table 1 is an extract of a whois query revealing phone numbers, physical addresses, and real names. A collection of tools related to domain name and IP registration can be found at http://www.dnsstuff.com/.

Domain Name Service

Most operating systems (OS) include the *name service look up* (nslookup) tool (Mockapetris, 1987). The Unix based OS includes the *dig* tool as well. These tools are made to query DNS records (on DNS service, such as BIND, TCP/UDP port 53). They can provide extensive valuable information to an attacker. They can be used to resolve names into IP addresses and vice versa. One of the most powerful functionalities

Table 1. A sample name service-based whois result: "whois -h whois.nic.fr univ-lyon1.fr"

```
domain:       univ-lyon1.fr
address:       Centre Informatique Scientifique et Medical de
l'Universite Claude Bernard Lyon 1
address:      batiment 101, 27 A 43 boulevard du 11 Novembre 1918
address:      69622 Villeurbanne Cedex
address:      FR
phone:        +33 4 72 44 83 60
fax-no:       +33 4 72 44 84 10
e-mail:       gilles.rech@univ-lyon1.fr
admin-c:      GR258-FRNIC
tech-c:       GR1378-FRNIC
zone-c:       NFC1-FRNIC
nserver:      dns.univ-lyon1.fr 134.214.100.6
nserver:      dns2.univ-lyon1.fr 134.214.100.245
nserver:      ccpntc3.in2p3.fr 134.158.69.191
nserver:      ccpnvx.in2p3.fr 134.158.69.104 …
```

Table 2. Sample reverse (from IP to name) DNS results

```
smtphost.example.com(192.168.0.4), mail server
dns.example.com(192.168.0.6), dns server
pop.example.com(192.168.0.7), mail server
routeur-ipv6-v100.example.com(192.168.0.45) , IPV6 router
dhcprov100-02.example.com(192.168.0.47), DHCP server
testmath.example.com(192.168.0.231), promising "unsecure" host
cisco-ls.example.com (192.168.4.9), cisco router
hpserv. example.com (192.168.4.10), Hewlett-Packard server
```

is the "zone transfer," where complete DNS records are transferred from one DNS server to another, but it can be manually executed using nslookup or dig, thus providing exhaustive information about the targeted organization (Barr, 1996). The interesting information includes e-mail servers names (and addresses), Web servers, routers and firewall addresses. Most of the time, sensitive information can be deduced from the organizational naming convention, such as software and hardware information (e.g., OS, constructor), services available, and so forth (Grubb, 2004). For instance, some illustrative results are shown in Table 2 for example.com, which is a registered domain name.

E-Mail Systems

If Web sites provide the shop front of business organizations, e-mail provides essential business communication systems. A lot of information can be collected through the analysis of mail systems. Simple mail transfer protocol (SMTP) (Postel, 1982) is the standard protocol for e-mails. The analysis of its header can provide internal server naming, topology of network, user accounts, a version of e-mail services, clients, patch level, type and version of content filter, and antispam or antivirus solutions. Table 3 shows a sample SMTP header. It can be seen that this e-mail was sent by "Sample User" whose address is user@example.com, using Microsoft Outlook on a laptop with the IP address 192.168.5.26. This sample does not

Table 3. Sample SMTP header

```
Return-Path: <user@example.com>
Received: from cri14.sample.fr
    by dsi02.sample.fr (Cyrus v2.2.12) with LMTPA;
    Wed, 22 Feb 2006 12:02:37 +0100
...
Received: from out4.example.fr
    by cismrelais. sample.fr (Postfix) with ESMTP id 8417E48104
    for <john.doe@dummy.com>; Wed, 22 Feb 2006 11:52:20 +0100
Received: from UserLaptop ([192.168.5.26]) by out4.example.fr
(Sun Java System Messaging Server 6.1 HotFix 0.11 (built Jan 28 05))
Date: Wed, 22 Feb 2006 12:51:58 +0200
From: Sample User < user@example.com >
Subject: Sample test, France
In-reply-to: <34f699a5f6e6a879072a609ea2b46d6d@example.com >
To: "'John DOE'" <john.doe@dummy.com >
X-MIMEOLE: Produced By Microsoft MimeOLE V6.00.2800.1106
X-Mailer: Microsoft Outlook CWS, Build 9.0.2416 (9.0.2910.0)
X-Virus-Scanned: by AMaViS snapshot-20020222
X-Virus-Scanned: amavisd-new
```

include the SMTP relay, but analyzing the chain also is very useful. It can reveal trusted relationships between e-mail servers and internal topology. According to this example in which Outlook 2000 (Microsoft Outlook Build 9) is used by Sample User, a cyber attacker may focus on Outlook vulnerabilities to break into example. com, or he may try to exploit Microsoft Office 2000, conjecturing that it is used by the company.

Web Site Analysis

The larger or more complex a Web site is, the higher the probability of it inadvertently leaking internal information, and the more information an attacker can obtain. Large sites can be managed by several administrators, built by dozens of developers, and filled in by hundreds of people; this may lead to information disclosure. A common technique for an attacker is to retrieve the whole targeted site and to analyze its content on his local image, thus avoiding multiple suspicious connections. The hackers will freely explore and harvest the site for sensitive information. The process of automatically retrieving a Web site and analyzing its content is commonly referred to as "Web crawling." Common tools for Web scraping are Sam Spade and Wget. Sam Spade crawls and discovers

linked Web pages on a site. This is an efficient tool that can quickly download a company's entire Web site. Another very powerful tool is Wget, a scriptable command-line browser. It can grab HTML pages, images, and forms as a "standard" browser.

Interesting findings include (Ollman, 2004):

- Real names and e-mail addresses
- Comments from internal developers can reveal technical information about technologies in use, maintenance operations, internal resources, or connectivity methods (e.g., database connector). Badly cleaned sources can even reveal pieces of server-side code or even default passwords.
- Comments can reveal debug, prototype, or test information, such as disabled pages or internal development hosts that would be normally inaccessible.
- Signature of tools (within metatags, for example) can give very precise information about version and development software.
- Logs and temporary files are very fruitful findings that can reveal very sensitive details, like user habits or links to external customer Web sites.

- Error pages, such as 404 (page not found) and 500(internal error), can be fruitfully exploited. They can reveal the existence (or absence) of files, coding errors, or dead URLs.
- Links to documents and binary data may suffer from great leakage. For example, Microsoft Word files usually include internal host names, real names, and even shared resource locations.

Thus, it is very important that all content be analyzed and cleaned for any unintentional leakage.

CURRENT ISSUES

Techniques discussed in the previous section are based on publicly available information; domain registration, DNS, mail headers. Web content, and binary data available over the Internet also were discussed. Whereas the first ones imply the use of dedicated (although very common) tools, such as dig, whois, or *traceroute*, there exists an extremely powerful tool that crawls the Internet with very accurate and efficient querying capabilities of Web content—the Google search engine (Long, Skoudis, & Van Eijkelenborg, 2001).

Google's cache system, advanced query operators, such as *site:*, *filetype:*, *intitle:*, or even translation services, makes it a major tool in the passive information gathering arsenal. We will describe a few techniques using Google that can be successfully applied to gather information without any direct connection to the target and to harvest Web content that should be kept private.

- **Using the cache system:** Google keeps snapshots of crawled pages in its own repository. You may have experienced it using the "cached" link appearing on search results pages. The advanced operator cache: is used to jump directly to the cached snapshot of a Web site without performing a query. This is a quite simple and effective way to browse Web pages without any direct connection to the target.

- **Using Google as a proxy server:** Google can be used as a transparent proxy server via its translation service. When you click on the "translate this page" link, you will be taken to a version of the page that has been automatically translated into your language. You can use this functionality to translate a page into the same language it is written in, thus, Google crawls the page, does nothing in the translation process (e.g., from English to English) and gives you back that page. This trick can be done by modifying the hl variable in Google search URL to match the native language of the page.

- **Discovering network resources:** Google can help with the network discovery phase. Google searches can be seen as an alternative to DNS queries, by combining the site: operator and logical NOT, a hacker can obtain a list of public servers. For example, "site:microsoft.com -www. microsoft.com" will reveal msdn.microsoft. com, directory.microsoft.com, partnerconnect. microsoft.com, officelive.microsoft.com, and so forth. Moreover the *link:* operator finds pages that link to the queried URL; it can be used to provide important clues about relationships between domains and organizations. The *intitle:* and *inurl:* operators can be used to detect the presence of Web-enabled network devices, such as routers. For example, *inurl:tech-support inurl: show Cisco OR intitle:"switch home page" site: example.com* searches Cisco's Web-enabled devices on the domain example.com.

- **Harvesting system files, configuration files, and interesting data using advanced specific queries:** Hundreds of Google searches can be found in Long et al. (2001). Their book describes in depth advanced operators and how to use them to find passwords (clear or hashed), user names, Web-enabled devices, and so on. Table 4 presents simple, but powerful, Google searches that can be processed to retrieve system files, configuration files, and specific data. The main idea is to combine operators, such as *intitle:*, *inurl:*, and *site:*, with specific sentences. For example "#

Table 4. Ten security queries that work from johnny.ihackstuff.com

```
1) "http://*:*@www" domainname (get inline passwords)
2) intitle:index.of.password (or passwd or passwd)
3) "access denied for user" "using password" (SQL error message, this message
can display the username, database, path names and partial SQL code)
4) "AutoCreate=TRUE password=*" (Searches the password for "website access.
Analyzer")
5) intitle:"Index of" _ vti _ inf.html ("vti _ " files are part of the FrontPage
communication system between a web site and the server)
6) "# -FrontPage-" ext:pwd inurl:(service | authors | administrators | users) "#
-FrontPage-" inurl:service.pwd (search for MD5 hashed FrontPage password)
7) inurl:passlist.txt
8) "A syntax error has occurred" filetype:ihtml (Informix error message,
this message can display path names, function names, filenames and partial
code)
9) allinurl:auth _ user _ file.txt (DCForum's password file. This file gives a
list of passwords, usernames and email addresses)
10) allinurl: admin mdb (administrator's access databases containing user-
names, passwords and other sensitive information)
```

-FrontPage-" is a banner from FrontPage files. The 10 queries in Table 4 are realistic sample queries that can be successfully processed to find passwords or configuration files.

CONCLUSION

Most organizations and system administrators are familiar with penetration-testing and intrusion-detection techniques. These techniques are cornerstones in security evaluation and focus mainly on the exploitation of vulnerabilities and suspicious/malicious behavior (e.g., log analysis). However, an organization relying mainly on these techniques may underestimate the huge amount of information that can be anonymously obtained from publicly available content over the Internet. This topic gives an overview of network-based passive information gathering techniques. Some can note that passive techniques are also very useful from an internal perspective; it reduces traffic within the internal network (e.g., passive OS fingerprinting to enumerate OSs in use (Treurniet, 2004)). To protect themselves, organizations should carefully check their publicly available information.

- Some information must be published (e.g., contact e-mail), but protection measures should be established to prevent automated crawlers from finding this information, if it can be misused (e.g., for spam). A common way to avoid sensitive information being crawled is to protect it by mechanisms simple for humans but complex for machines. For example, regular expressions cannot match "[at]" images within e-mail addresses (do not write e-mail clearly).

- The principle of the least privilege must be respected by publishing only a strict minimum, denying bots the ability to crawl public but sensitive information. This advice is legitimate for DNS; do not publish names of hosts or devices that should not be accessed from the outside Internet. It is also legitimate for configuration files. If a file is not meant to be public (e.g., _vti_ files for FrontPage, debug/test pages), keep it private.

- Conduct reviews of code and Web pages to keep them clean and avoid comments, prolix banners, version numbers, and so forth . A lot of information can be gathered from error pages, banners, and seemingly innocuous information. Comments can be incredibly information leaking; entire blocks of server side code within client's pages are not so uncommon.

To sum up, information gathering is the very first step of an attack and probably the most crucial in achieving the attacker's goal. Information collected in this phase is raw material that is used to build a firm attack. The attackers can obtain a global view of the target, can focus on the weakest link in security, and can obtain enough information to conduct social engineering. If conducted cleanly via passive techniques using publicly available information, this step is anonymous and practically undetectable. Thus, organizations should be very careful with content anonymously available over the Internet and should take simple, but effective, measures.

Your physical mail box should be accessible to anyone, at least your mailman. However, nobody will write his own Social Security number, birth date, or job on his or her mail box in the real world. Such information must be kept private from mailmen and passers-by; it should be the same in the cyber world.

REFERENCES

Barr, D. (1996). RFC 1912: Common DNS operational and configuration errors.

FX, Craig, P., Grand, J., Mullen, T., Fyodor, Russell, R., & Beale, J. (2004). *Stealing the network: How to own a continent.*

Fyodor. (2006). *Nmap (network mapper) documentation (including zombie scanning technique).* Retrieved from http://www.insecure.org/nmap/docs.html

Grubb, L. (2004). *Survey of network weapons: part 1: weapons for profiling.* Consortium for Computing Sciences in Colleges (CCSC).

Long, J., Skoudis, E., & Van Eijkelenborg, A. (Eds.). (2001). *Google hacking for penetration testers..*

Mitnick, K., Simon, W., & Wozniak S. (2002). *The art of deception: controlling the human element of security.*

Mockapetris, P. (1987). RFC 1035: Domain names—Implementation and specification.

Ollman, G. (2004). *Passive information gathering: The analysis of leaked network security information* (Tech. paper). Next Generation Security Software Ltd.

Postel, J. (1982). *RFC 821: Simple mail transfer protocol.*

Treurniet, J. (2004). *An overview of passive information gathering techniques for network security* (Tech. memo.). Defence R&D Canada.

Tzu, S. (1910). *Sun Tzu on the art of war, the oldest military treatise in the world.* (L. Giles, Trans.).

Zalewski, M. (2005). *Silence on the wire: A field guide to passive reconnaissance and indirect attacks.*

TERMS AND DEFINITIONS

Domain Name System or Domain Name Server or Domain Name Service (DNS): This is a system that stores information associated to domain names. The most important being the Internet protocol (IP) addresses associated with a domain name, but it also lists mail servers and administrative contacts. The domain name system makes it possible to attach a "hard-to-remember" IP address (e.g., 66.249.93.99) to an "easy-to-remember" domain name (e.g., google.com).

Proxy Server: This computer offers a computer network service, allowing clients to make indirect network connections to other network services. It acts as a relay of service, including filtering and caching capabilities (e.g., Web proxy that denies access to black-listed sites). A client connects to the proxy server and requests a connection; the proxy provides the resource either by connecting to the specified server or by serving it from a cache.

Simple Mail Transfer Protocol (SMTP): This is the de facto standard for e-mail transmission across the Internet. SMTP is a simple text-based protocol

(SMTP commands are commonly achieved by telnet for test purpose), using TCP port 25. To determine the SMTP server for a given domain name, the mail exchange (MX) DNS record is used.

Social Engineering: This is the practice of obtaining confidential information by manipulation of legitimate people. Social engineering is used by hackers (e.g., Kevin Mitnick, a famous social engineer) as an effective technique to achieve their goal. It is agreed that exploiting computer vulnerability is often more difficult than tricking people. In order to enhance his or her credibility against the target and to build up trust, a social engineer needs accurate, truthful, and convincing information.

Web Crawling: A Web crawler (or Web spider) is a program that browses Web pages in a automated manner. Crawling the Web enables the creation of a copy of all visited pages for later processing, via a search engine, for example. Web crawling permits gathering specific information, such as e-mail (usually for spam).

Whois: This is a query/response protocol that is used for determining owners of domain names and IP addresses or autonomous system information. This system originates as "white pages" for system administrators to contact their peers. Nowadays, it is used to find certificate authority of secured Web pages. Data returned from a query can be used by hackers to broaden their knowledge of a system or for spam (e.g., bot automatically processing whois records to build e-mail bases).

Zone Transfer: It is a type of DNS transaction used to replicate DNS databases across DNS servers. The opcodes (used in the "dig" tool, for example) associated with this type of transaction are AXFR (full transfer) and IXFD (incremental transfer). Zone transfer is a way for hackers to manually obtain content of a zone.

Chapter XVII
Electronic Money Management in Modern Online Businesses

Konstantinos Robotis
University of the Aegean, Greece

Theodoros Tzouramanis
University of the Aegean, Greece

ABSTRACT

This chapter discusses electronic money management via modern payment processing systems. The protocols and architectures of modern payment processing systems are reviewed and the way to identify and eliminate the threats of abuse of an electronic payment system by cyber fraud is discussed. The countermeasures necessary to combat possible depredations are detailed methodically. There is also a brief presentation of the payment processing system of PayPal and the payment gateway service that is provided by VeriSign. While this chapter shows that perceptions of the Web as a dangerous place to operate a business are justified, the main objective is to help e-commerce and online businesses understand the nature of possible threats for the safeguard of their customers' financial transactions against all risks.

INTRODUCTION

In today's global marketplace, the Internet is no longer just about e-mail and Web sites. The Internet has become the vital channel powering a growing list of revenue-generating e-business activities, from e-commerce and e-supply chain management to online marketplaces and collaboration.

E-commerce transactions management has become one of the most sensitive issues in the field of information security. This chapter discusses electronic money management via modern payment processing systems. The protocols and architectures of modern payment processing systems are reviewed and the way to identify and eliminate the threats of abuse of an electronic payment system by cyber fraud is discussed. The countermeasures necessary to combat possible depredations are detailed methodically. There is also a brief presentation of the payment processing system of PayPal and the payment gateway service that is provided by VeriSign. While this chapter shows that perceptions of the Web as a dangerous place to operate a business are justified, the main objective is to help e-commerce and online businesses understand the nature of possible threats for the safeguard of their customers' financial transactions against all risks.

BACKGROUND

Information security focuses on protecting valuable and sensitive enterprise data. To secure information assets, organizations must at the same time provide availability to legitimate users and bar unauthorized access.

To fully satisfy the security requirements of the electronic payment process, a system is necessary to provide certain security services that differ slightly from the common security ones. The most important payment transaction security requirements (Asokan, Janson, Steiner, & Waidner, 1997) are:

- **Authentication:** Authentication is critical to a payment system. It ensures that a message originates from the alleged source.
- **Confidentiality:** It safeguards the user's privacy and prevents the theft of enterprise information both stored and in transit.
- **Integrity:** Data integrity is achieved by preventing unauthorized or improper changes of data, ensuring internal and external consistency and ensuring that other data attributes (such as timeliness and completeness) are consistent with requirements.
- **Availability and reliability:** These two requirements ensure the uninterrupted service to authorized users. Service interruptions can be either accidental or maliciously caused by denial-of-service attacks.
- **Non-repudiation:** A requirement which ensures that neither the sender nor the recipient of a message can deny the transmission.

Additional payment security services (Hassler, 2001) include: user anonymity and privacy, which ensure protection against the disclosure of the buyer's identity (and the payer's, should they not be the same) and the disclosure of the buyer's network address or location. To provide these crucial protection features, information security must be an integral part of the electronic payment system, design, and implementation.

MAIN THRUST OF THE CHAPTER

E-commerce refers to the exchange of goods and services over the Internet. All major retail brands have an online presence and many brands have no associated bricks-and-mortar presence. In the online retail space, online payment has become an essential part of the e-commerce process. Electronic payment systems and e-commerce are highly linked given that online consumers must pay for products and services.

Payment System

An electronic payment system in general denotes any kind of network (e.g., Internet) services that includes the exchange of money for goods or services. The goods can be physical goods, such as books or CDs, or electronic goods, such as electronic documents, images or music. Similarly, there are "traditional" services such as hotel or flight booking, as well as electronic services, such as financial market analyses in electronic form (Hassler, 2001).

Electronic payment systems have evolved from traditional payment systems and, consequently, the two types of systems have much in common. Commerce always involves a payer (customer) and a payee (merchant)—who exchange money for goods or services—and at least one financial institution. The customer's bank is usually referred to as the issuer bank and the merchant's bank is referred to as the acquirer bank (Asokan et al., 1997). Electronic

Figure 1. Electronic payment system overview

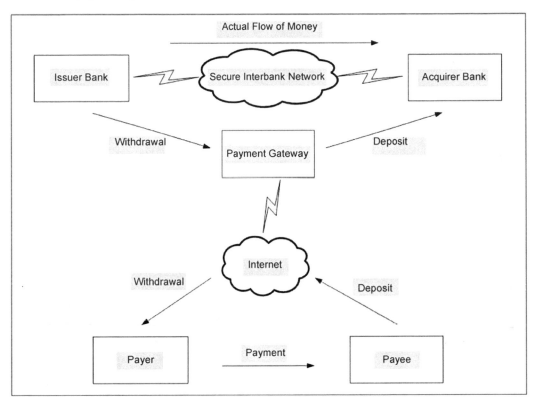

payment is implemented by a flow of money from the payer via the issuer and acquirer to the payee.

A typical payment electronic system is described in Figure 1, which shows some typical flows of money in the case of prepaid, cash-like payment systems. In these systems, a certain amount of money is withdrawn from the issuer bank and deposited in the acquirer bank through the payment gateway. The payment gateway serves as an intermediary between the traditional payment infrastructure and the electronic payment infrastructure (Hassler, 2001). It acts as the front-end to the existing financial network and, through this the card issuer can be contacted to explicitly authorize each and every transaction that takes place (O'Mahony, Peirce, & Tewari, 2001).

A financial institution operates the payment gateway. The institution provides the merchant with an interface to the gateway as a software component. For example, VeriSign's PayFlow Pro payment gateway provides a variety of PFPro components, including a Java object, a Microsoft COM DLL, and a UNIX shared module.

Electronic payment processing systems communicate with the payment gateway via the payment gateway interface to verify the authenticity of the customer's method of payment for the purchases (McClure, Shah, & Shah, 2002). In the case of credit cards, the payment gateway validates credit card numbers and expiration dates, verifies ownership, determines whether the credit balance covers the amount of the purchase, and so on.

The payment gateway interface component is invoked by the electronic storefront application (the merchant's application). This component transmits the payment information to the payment gateway system over an encrypted channel such as secure socket layer

Figure 2. Payment system: Technology perspective

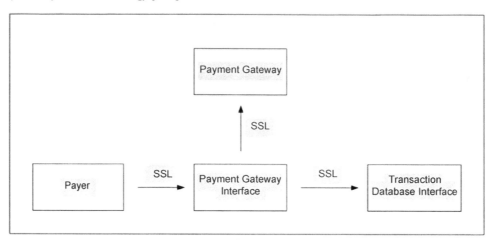

(SSL). This component also returns a response code to the electronic storefront application, indicating the status of the transaction. The response code indicates whether the transaction succeeded or failed and gives various other details about the transaction. Based on the response code, the electronic storefront application decides what to do with the order.

Once a transaction is passed to the payment gateway, the transaction details, along with the response code, are written into a backend transaction database for future use. The transaction database interface must be carefully designed so it does not allow attackers to retrieve or tamper with the transaction data.

At the electronic storefront site, the payment processing system keeps a detailed log of all transactions so that they can be reconciled when payments are settled with the financial institution. Maintaining transaction logs is mandatory in most cases and they should also be closely guarded. An attacker's gaining access to the transaction log database would pose a huge security risk involving customers' identities and payment instruments, which could then be used in fraudulent schemes.

Once the payment is processed successfully, the payment system application in the electronic storefront confirms the order acceptance and generates a receipt for the customer. Such applications have the ability to e-mail receipts to customers and notify them of the initiation of shipment, with a tracking number for use with the delivery agency so that the customers can track their shipments themselves.

Threats

All financial systems attract fraudsters and embezzlers. The problem typically ranges from individuals stealing small amounts to organized criminal activities involving large sums. Electronic financial systems connected to public networks multiply the opportunities for such criminal activity by allowing access from anywhere in the world, often with much scope for anonymity.

It is important to note that there are alternative (and very effective) methods that make it possible to threaten the legitimate operation of an electronic payment system besides the ones described. Some of the easiest and most profitable attacks are based on tricking an employee or user, also known as social engineering techniques (Garfinkel, 2001). Another modern form of social engineering attacks are phishing programs. For more information on phishing or its consequences refer to Litan (2005). Additional threats that are difficult to handle and rectify are physical threats (Platt, 2002). There exists finally the threat of "insider attacks," that is, the intentional attacks by employees either for revenge or money (Tippett, 2002).

Brute Force

Most commonly, brute force is applied to locate cryptographic keys and user passwords (Schneier, 1995). Of all the application layer protocol authentications, perhaps HTTP authentication is the easiest to crack by using brute force (McClure et al., 2002). Some famous tools for brute forcing HTTP authentication are Brutus and WebCracker, which can exhaust a long list of user names and passwords in a matter of hours or even minutes.

The success of this method depends on the attacker's processing power and the length of the cryptographic key in the case of a cryptosystem. Statistically, half of the potential keys have to be examined from the domain of the possible keys in order to successfully decrypt the message. Considering the present technology standards, a 128-bit length key would most probably suffice to deter the attacker from using this method.

Software Vulnerabilities

Every e-commerce application is composed of several parts, such as the database, Web server, a portal framework, or an application server. After identifying the precise versions running on a server, hackers exploit their vulnerabilities.

Software vulnerabilities exist in network services such as FTP, bind, and SMTP (Ghosh, 2002). A common target in Web security is the database, the Web server, the application server, and operating system vulnerabilities (Ghosh, 1998; McClure, Scambray, & Kurtz, 2005). Another form of common security vulnerability built into commercial software is buffer overflows (McClure et al., 2002).

Denial-of-Service

A denial-of-service (DoS) attack (Garfinkel, 2001) is aimed solely at making services unavailable. DoS attacks pose a serious threat not only to an electronic payment system but also to e-commerce generally. Successful defense against these attacks will come only when there is widespread cooperation among all Internet service providers (ISPs) and other Internet-connected systems worldwide.

Countermeasures

There are some important defenses against the various threats and attacks described previously. These defenses can be technical, nontechnical or physical. An example of nontechnical defense is user education. Extensive information on defensive countermeasures concerning the e-commerce playground generally can be found in Smith (2004) and McClure, et al. (2002).

In the recent past, several electronic credit card payment schemes have been designed, proposed, and implemented (O'Mahony et al., 2001). The iKP (where i = 1; 2; or 3) family of Internet-keyed payments protocol developed by IBM in the early 1990s (Bellare et al., 1995), the Secure Electronic Payment Protocol (SEPP) developed by a consortium chaired by MasterCard are some of the most typical examples. Additionally, CyberCash, Inc. defines a protocol to facilitate and protect credit card payment transactions over the Internet (Eastlake, Boesch, Crocker, & Yesil, 1996).

iKP, CyberCash and SEPP are no longer in use, however they serve as the foundation of secure electronic transactions (SET) protocol (SET, 1999). The SET protocol was heavily publicized in the late 1990s as the credit card approved standard, but failed to win the expected market share. It was commonly agreed and expected that SET would become the technology of choice for electronic credit card based payments over the Internet. This expectation has not become true and there never was strong support for SET in the commercial world. One reason for this is that the SET protocols are complex and difficult to implement.

Secure Sockets Layer (SSL)

SSL protocol was developed by Netscape for managing the security of a message transmission over the Internet (Freier, Karlton, & Kocher, 1996). It is not a payment technology per se, but has been proposed as a means to secure payment messages. SSL requires public key infrastructure (PKI) and provides authentication, confidentiality, and integrity mechanisms and it is the security cornerstone in the e-commerce industry.

The descendant of SSL is called transport layer security (TLS) protocol and was proposed by the Internet Engineering Task Force (IETF) in RFC 2246 (Dierks & Allen, 1999). There are slight differences between SSL 3.0 and TLS 1.0, but the protocol remains substantially the same.

Current Payment Processing Systems

Payment processing systems such as PayPal or VeriSign's PayFlow Pro have enabled individuals, businesses, and online merchants with an e-mail address to securely, instantly, and cost-effectively send and receive electronic payments over the Web.

PayPal

PayPal's service builds on the existing financial infrastructure of bank accounts and credit cards and aims to create a safe, global, real-time payment solution. According to Garfinkel (2001), it is this ease of account creation that is largely responsible for PayPal's success.

PayPal automatically encrypts a client's confidential information in transit from the client's computer to Paypal's server using the SSL protocol with an encryption key length of 128-bits (PayPal, n.d.). Before a customer even registers or logs onto the PayPal site, the server assesses whether the customer is using a browser that supports SSL v3.0 or higher.

PayPal stores credit card and bank account information in encrypted form on servers that are not connected to the Internet and sit behind a firewall (PayPal, n.d.). These servers are heavily guarded both physically and electronically. Additionally, access to the information is restricted to the employees who need to have that information in order to provide the customer with products or services.

VeriSign's Payment Gateway Service

A popular payment gateway service called PayFlow Pro is provided by VeriSign. PayFlow Pro's client-side component resides in the electronic storefront application. The client component interfaces with PayFlow Pro's servers owned by VeriSign using HTTP requests sent via SSL.

PayFlow Pro gives direct access to the PayFlow payment processing API via a "thin-client" network service. The API is provided by the PayFlow Pro SDK. The PayFlow Pro SDK, installed on a system, is a small (400k footprint) messaging agent that uses SSL and X.509 digital certificate technology to securely communicate with VeriSign's payment servers. Once installed, the PayFlow Pro API client software establishes an SSL connection between the merchant storefront application and VeriSign's transaction servers to securely exchange payment data between parties (VeriSign, n.d.).

VeriSign securely routes the transaction through the financial network to the appropriate bank, ensuring that the customers are authorized to make their purchases. When a customer makes a purchase, the transaction data is passed from the merchant's portal to the PayFlow Pro client, which then securely passes the payment transaction data to VeriSign's payment servers for processing.

The merchant and the customer automatically receive e-mail confirmation that the transaction is approved and then funds are transferred to the Internet merchant account. The PayFlow Pro client also sends an acknowledgment back to VeriSign after returning the payment results to the merchant, in order to protect the consumer against double billing due to

Internet latency or broken communication sessions. The PayFlow Pro client does not contain any payment-specific logic, allowing VeriSign to introduce additional services or transaction types at any time without requiring the merchant to upgrade their PayFlow Pro client software.

FUTURE TRENDS

E-commerce has experienced tremendous growth since its inception, which can be credited to the ease of use of this resource when it comes to performing business transactions. More and more online business transactions are taking place than ever before (Johnson & Tesch, 2005). There are also disadvantages in running an online business, of which fraud and identity thefts are among the most common. Regan (2005) and Litan (2005) support this view, reporting a significant increase within a year for e-commerce fraud losses; hence, online security is a big concern for most businesses and for people doing business online.

An interesting idea, which can be applied today, is reported in Tippett (2002). It states that the payment processing systems and the security services that support them are changing at an increasingly rapid rate and this fact has an analogous effect on the vulnerabilities of the corresponding system. The security products will improve but, meanwhile, new security requirements will surface; therefore forming a volatile environment that is hard to secure (Ritter & Money, 2002).

Taking into account the previous efforts of standardization such as iKP or SET that have failed to win a market share, it is not at all clear how the market for electronic credit card payments will evolve in the future.

CONCLUSION

In this growing age of e-commerce, plenty of organizations and merchants are excited about the benefits of e-commerce and are working readily on resolving the security issues. Online sales are increasing and Internet commerce is thriving despite consistent fears about privacy issues and safety concerns. If these problems can be solved or if improvements can be made, then e-commerce will eventually emerge in the business industry as an equal of traditional commerce.

The heart of an e-commerce application is the electronic payment system. The security infrastructure that partners it is essential to the overall success of the application. The security of the system must be analogous to the threats, so as to deal effectively with the system's vulnerabilities. The goal for the e-commerce industry is to take the necessary steps to ensure that adequate levels of security are in place so that the possibility of a security incident is insignificant and in order to reassure buyers and sellers that their transactions are secure.

REFERENCES

Asokan, N., Janson, P. A., Steiner, M., & Waidner, M. (1997). The state of the art in electronic payment systems. *IEEE Computer, 30*(9), 2835.

Bellare, M., Garay, J. A., Hauser, R., Herzberg, A., Krawczyk, H., Steiner, M., et al. (1995). iKP—A family of secure electronic payment protocols. *Usenix Electronic Commerce Workshop.*

Dierks, T., & Allen, C. (1999). *The TLS protocol version 1.0.* Internet Engineering Task Force, Request For Comments: 2246.

Eastlake, D., III, Boesch, B., Crocker, S., & Yesil, M. (1996). *Cybercash credit card protocol version 0.8.* RFC 1898.

Freier, A. O., Karlton, P., & Kocher, P. C. (1996). *The SSL protocol version 3.0.* Internet Engineering Task Force, Internet Draft.

Ghosh, A. K. (1998). *E-commerce security: Weak links, best defenses.* John Wiley & Sons.

Ghosh, A. K. (2002). E-commerce vulnerabilities. In S. Bosworth & M. E. Kabay (Eds.), *Computer security handbook* (4th ed., chap. 13, pp. 13-113-21). John Wiley & Sons.

Hassler, V. (2001). *Security fundamentals for e-commerce.* Artech House.

Johnson, A. C., & Tesch, B. (2005). *US e-commerce: 2005 to 2010: A five-year forecast and analysis of US online retail sales.* Forrester Research.

Litan, A. (2005). *Increased phishing and online attacks cause dip in consumer confidence.* Gartner Group.

McClure, S., Shah, S., & Shah, S. (2002). *Web hacking: Attacks and defense.* Addison-Wesley.

McClure, S., Scambray, J., & Kurtz, G. (2005). *Hacking exposed: Network security secrets & solutions* (5th ed.). McGraw-Hill Osborne Media.

O'Mahony, D., Peirce, A. M., & Tewari, H. (2001). *Electronic payment systems for e-commerce* (2nd ed.). Artech House.

PayPal Corporation. (n. d.). Retrieved from http://www.paypal.com

Platt, A. F. (2002). Physical threats to the information infrastructure. In S. Bosworth & M. E. Kabay (Eds.), *Computer security handbook* (4th ed., chap. 14, pp. 14-114-25). John Wiley & Sons.

Regan, K. (2005). *Fraud seen rising among large e-commerce companies.* http://www.ecommercetimes.com/story/47260.html

Ritter, J. B., & Money, M. (2002). E-commerce safeguards. In S. Bosworth & M. E. Kabay (Eds.), *Computer security handbook* (4th ed., chap. 19, pp. 19-119-31). John Wiley & Sons.

Schneier, B. (1995). *Applied cryptography: Protocols, algorithms and source code in C.* John Wiley & Sons.

SET—Secure Electronic Transaction LLC. (1999). *The SET™ specification.* Retrieved from http://www.setco.org/

Smith, G. (2004). *Control and security of e-commerce.* John Wiley & Sons.

Tippett, P. (2002). The future of information security. In S. Bosworth & M. E. Kabay (Eds.), *Computer security handbook* (4th ed., chap. 54, pp. 54-154-18). John Wiley & Sons.

VeriSign. (n. d.). *PayFlow Pro, how it works.* Retrieved from http://www.verisign.com/products-services/payment-processing/online-payment/payflow-pro/how-it-works.html

TERMS AND DEFINITIONS

Brute-Force Attack: Attempt to decrypt the message exhaustively, working through all possible keys. Most attempts will fail, but eventually one of the attempts will succeed and either allow the cracker into the system or permit the ciphertext (encrypted data) to be decrypted. Most commonly, brute force is applied to locate cryptographic keys and user passwords.

Denial-of-Service (DoS) Attack: An assault on a network that floods it with so many additional requests so that it leaves no resources and thereby "denies" service to other users. DoS attacks cause a loss of service to users, typically the loss of network connectivity and services by consuming the bandwidth of the target network or overloading the computational resources of the target system.

Public Key Infrastructure (PKI): A set consisting of policies, processes, hardware, and software used to administer certificates and public-private key pairs, including the ability to issue, maintain, and revoke public key certificates.

Secure Electronic Transaction (SET): Online payment protocol designed for securing credit card transactions over the Internet. The SET standard was jointly developed by MasterCard, Visa, and various computer companies including Netscape, IBM, Microsoft, and VeriSign. SET provides privacy and nonrepudiation for credit card transactions; and it prevents merchants from getting credit card numbers.

Social Engineering Attack: The practice of obtaining confidential information by manipulation of legitimate users. A social engineer will commonly use the telephone or Internet to trick a person into revealing sensitive information or will get them to do something that goes against official policy.

Threat: Any (deliberate or accidental) circumstance or event with the potential to adversely impact an information system through unauthorized access, destruction, disclosure, modification of data, and/or denial-of-service. A threat is exploiting a known vulnerability.

Transport Layer Security (TLS): A protocol intended to secure and authenticate communications across public networks using data encryption. TLS is derived from SSL v3 and is a proposed Internet standard (RFC 2246).

Vulnerability: A flaw or weakness in a system's design, implementation, or operation and management that could be exploited (by a threat) to violate the system's security policy.

Chapter XVIII
The Analysis of Money Laundering Techniques

Krzysztof Woda
European University Viadrina, Germany

ABSTRACT

There exist many connections between money laundering and terrorism financing concerning illicit practices for fundraising, transfer or withdrawal of funds. The characteristic multistage process of money laundering is also typical for the terrorism financing and often contains a series of transactions in order to conceal the origin or disposition of money. The purpose of this article is the analysis of the best suited techniques of money laundering for terrorism financing using electronic payment systems (like transfers, mobile payment systems or virtual gold currencies). Furthermore, the suitability of payment systems for conducting secret transactions for terrorism financing will be analyzed regarding the realization of a single phase of money laundering.

INTRODUCTION

Cyber terrorism is often defined as an attack against information systems, computer systems, and data, or, more generally, as disruption of critical infrastructures caused by information systems (Krasavin, 2000, as cited in *'Cyber terrorism' testimony*, 2000; Nisbet, 2003, as cited in Center for International Security and Co-operation). The definition of cyber terrorism can be limited to supporting activities for the purpose of preparing of terrorist acts (Krasavin, 2000). Such a narrow definition of cyber terrorism has many common characteristics with modern practices of money laundering (e.g., techniques for money transfers or disposition of money), which are mostly carried out by cyber systems.

The qualities of Internet communication, like anonymity, person-to-person payments, low communication and transaction cost, free transferability of assets between privates and banks internationally, and so forth, predispose the Internet for many illicit actions, like money laundering or fundraising for terrorism. Some techniques of money laundering used to conceal or disguise the origin, nature, source, location, disposition, or ownership of assets can be used to conduct terrorism financing.

There are many questions concerning connections between money laundering and terrorism financing. For example, what are the most suitable money laundering practices operated through telecommunication networks, electronic banks (e.g., offshore banks) or with electronic payment systems that could finance terrorism (fundraising, transfer and withdrawal of funds)? Are the traditional money laundering techniques, as with shell companies and nominees, through unofficial money transfer systems, structured payments, wire transfers, and so forth, useful for financing terrorism or preparing for terrorist acts (Financial Action Task Force on Money Laundering (FATF), 2005)? How do the money laundering techniques differ with regard to their suitability for a single money laundering phase (and, thereby, for financing terrorism)?

CYBER TERRORISM AND MONEY LAUNDERING: DEFINITIONS, DIFFERENTIATIONS, AND CONNECTIONS

The broad definition of cyber terrorism is any kind of computer attacks against critical infrastructures, which does not differ from the definition of computer crime. Hence, many authors tried to concretize the definition of cyber terrorism (Krasavin, 2000; Nisbet, 2003; Pollitt, 1997). Pollitt (1997) combines the definitions of cyberspace and terrorism obtaining the definition for cyber terrorism. As a result, he defines cyber terrorism as follows: "Cyber terrorism is the premeditated, politically motivated attack against information, computer systems, computer programs, and data which result in violence against non-combatant targets by sub national groups or clandestine agents" (Pollitt, 1997, p. 2).

Nevertheless, this definition also contains areas or activities in common with computer crime (e.g., hacking) and, therefore, positions computer terrorism as a

part of computer crime. Krasavin (2000, p. 2) defines computer terrorism as "use of information technology and means by terrorist groups and agents" and notes the motivation as a differentiation criterion from computer crime. The motivation of cyber terrorists is the use of computer systems and networks for the organization and execution of attacks; computer crime aims for the destruction of programs, infrastructures, or data (Krasavin, 2000). Institutions like the Center for International Security and Co-operation define computer terrorism narrowly as an attack against cyber systems (Nisbet, 2003, as cited in Center for International Security and Co-operation).

Money laundering is defined as an intentional committed offense that contains the conversion and transfer of properties of illicit origin (European Parliament and of the Council, 2001; U.S. Patriot Act, 2001). The purpose of money laundering is to conceal or to disguise the true origin, the nature, the disposition, or the controlling rights of properties that were acquired illegally (European Parliament and of the Council, 2001). Many assets are suited as potential properties for money laundering, such as cash, deposits, checks, and electronic currencies (e.g., prepaid payment instruments and virtual gold currencies), financial products, real estate, and services (e.g., in restaurants, casinos, or fictitious transactions in electronic commerce (e-commerce)). Operations like exchange, transfer, transport, acquisition, possession, or use of the properties for the purposes of the illicit money flows are typical of money laundering (European Parliament and of the Council, 2001;) U.S. Patriot, 2001). The new definition proposed by the Commission of the European Communities (2003) extends the present definition to terrorist financing (Article 1 of the Proposal for a Directive of the European Parliament and the Council, 2003, analogy in U.S. PATRIOT Act of 2001—Section 981 a(1)(G)).

Now supporting on the definitions of Krasavin (2000) and the Center for International Security and Co-operation, the connections between terrorism financing and money laundering will be searched. Krasavin (2000) refers to the preparing of terrorist acts (planning, logistics, and acquisition of objects for terrorism), which also includes financial support or financing. To keep terrorism preparations secret from authorities, such financing activities mostly must be carried out illegally. The origin and the disposition of money should be concealed. Besides, computers systems play no destructive role, but their use often prevents the detecting of illicit money flows (e.g., cryptography). Such activities cannot be carried out without cyber systems, because they are often a component of legal systems (e.g., bank transfers). The definition of the Center for International Security and Co-operation differs from the definition of Krasavin (2000), while they concentrated on attacks against cyber systems.

Both computer terrorism and money laundering emphasize the important role of cyber systems. While the modern practices of money laundering use above all the complicated electronic transfer methods, computer terrorism makes use primarily of communication technologies. Other common characteristics between cyber terrorism and money laundering exist in relation to missing legal authority as well as on potential damages (Nisbet, 2003, as cited in Center for International Security and Co-operation). Money laundering brings not only disproportionate profits to the intermediaries, but it could cause the liquidity risks for the involved companies and financial service providers and as a consequence it could precipitate a trust crisis for the whole payment and banking system (system risk) (Basel Committee on Banking Supervision (BCBS), 2003).

Between money laundering and terrorism financing, some differences also exist (U.S. Treasury—The Office of Terrorism and Financial Intelligence (TFI), 2003). Money laundering is carried out to conceal the nature or origin of money derived from a criminal activity. In the case of terrorism financing, the origin of money also can be legal. The purpose of the detecting of money laundering operations remains prosecution and forfeiture, while in case of terrorism financing, the prevention of payment flows is the most important (and urgent) task for authorities (U.S. Treasury—TFI, 2003).

ANALYSIS OF MONEY LAUNDERING TECHNIQUES AND METHODS AND THEIR SUITABILITY FOR TERRORISM FINANCING

Many money-laundering techniques have been identified by organizations like the Financial Action Task Force on Money Laundering (FATF) or the U.S. Department of the Treasury. FATF mentions the easy access to assets, the complexity of potential investments, and the international transfer capability as important factors for the suitability of systems or properties for money laundering (FATF, 2004a). The high complexity of products and their high spreading complicate the traceability of transfers. Also, the international character of transfers, often through countries that do not cooperate in combating money laundering, allows for concealing of the origin of money. The choice of a technique for money laundering and terrorism financing depends on many factors, for example, duration of a transaction, transaction volume, international or local character of transfers. However, it depends also on individual preferences of the money launderer or terrorist, for example, technology affinity, knowledge of new payment methods, and so forth.

Transfers

Transfers are financial transactions enabling money to flow from the payer to the payee through telecommunication networks (Europäische Zentralbank [EZB], 2003). There exist legal and illicit transfer systems. The illicit transfer systems often are called parallel bank transfer systems (U.S. Treasury—TFI, 2003). The legal transfer systems are present in the private customer area in electronic banking and internationally through special settlement and transfer systems, like SWIFT or TARGET (especially for companies with large value transfers). The illicit transfers are conducted through systems, such as Hawala, which is based on informal or trust contacts and effects monetary transfers without using official bank accounts (The Hawala representatives calculate demands and obligations often mutually to balance the difference.) (U.S. Treasury—TFI, 2003). The payments in the Hawala system are cash-based, while the communication and payment confirmations occur often electronically (e.g., e-mail, fax). Hence, the Hawala transfer system combines the advantages of traditional cash systems, like anonymity, no registration of the transactions, and transferability to other individuals with the high speed and cost efficiency of electronic communication.

In spite of the electronic tracks and identification duties (e.g., customer identification rogram in the United States), the transfers are an effective money transfer method for terrorism financing. The bank accounts of legal account holders are often open to the money launderers or terrorists by the disclosure of a personal identification number (PIN) or password (motives, as e.g., religious or national affiliation) (U.S. Treasury—TFI, 2003). A preserved method against the detecting of illicit money transfers are structured payments (smurfing), which divide large payments into smaller sums (e.g., under the legal threshold of $10,000 in the United States) (FATF, 2005). Such structured payments often are conducted through several channels (phone, online banking, smart cards, and mobile payment systems) and bank systems (from offshore countries). Other methods for the short-term collection of money for terrorism financing are intrusions by hackers into bank systems and in the following the transfer of stolen funds. The possible combination of legal banking transfers with the Hawala system as well as the use of Internet communication predispose the transfers as ideal instruments for short-term illicit activities like terrorism financial operations.

Shell Companies, Offshore Corporations, Nominees, and Charities

Companies or nonprofit organizations, like charities, can transfer far larger amounts also internationally than individuals and, thereby, could be very successful with the collection of money for terrorists. Charities often operate in crisis areas where the terrorists also are active. The collection of money for humanitarian purposes does not often distinguish of the collection for terrorist financing. Hence, the disposal of money plays a key role in detecting illicit financing activities. Informal charities also exist that operate above all in quite closed ethnic or religious groups and transfer money informally, for example, through a Hawala system (FATF, 2004b). The charities could take even the role of the informal transfer system if, for example, their employees from several countries (also from countries where terrorists operate) conduct transfers without transferring the money physically; rather internal accounts are balanced.

Other methods for large money transfers, for example, to the accounts of shell corporations (intermediaries for the transfer of capital, often with a pyramided owner structure, a nominee like an attorney or manager of the offshore corporation, having many bank accounts (Madinger & Zalopany, 1999)) or through manipulation of invoices (underinvoicing and overinvoicing) are typical due to long-term horizon and complexity (registration of companies, etc.), rather for money laundering than for terrorism financing.

FINANCIAL PRODUCTS

The financial products (insurance policies, unstandardized derivatives, for example, swaps, securities for the advanced loan-back schemes) are well suited due to the size of the market, easy access, and the availability, as well as the diversity, as ideal instruments for money laundering (FATF, 2004b). Nevertheless, these instruments are not suitable for terrorism financing, because they have, in general, a long planning horizon, are less liquid than currency, and require the intermediation of a licensed security broker.

Virtual Gold Currencies

Virtual gold currencies are account-based electronic payment systems whose value is protected by 100% of golden deposit in physical form (bullions, bars, or specie) (e-gold Ltd., n.d.). The user needs an Internet account at a system provider of virtual currency for the exchange or purchase of gold currencies and an e-mail account for a registration. The exchange of gold against a central bank currency occurs through an agent on the Internet. In spite of the registration and verification duties for customers (e.g., a copy of an ID, physical address, verification code, check of the transaction value on money laundering suspicion), such virtual gold currencies appear suitable for money laundering and also for short-term actions, like financing of terrorism. Several accounts can be opened at a system provider and, thereby, the structured payments could be carried out. The detecting of the illicit money flows also complicates the possibility of the person-to-person transfers between users of virtual gold currencies, also worldwide. Special anonymous payment cards for ATMs, based on virtual gold deposits, which are often issued by offshore banks (without name, addresses, or creditworthiness check), are suited for withdrawal of money (Gold-ATM). Some agents also accept money or postal transfer orders in exchange for virtual golden coins. Furthermore, the localization of many system providers of virtual gold currencies in offshore countries, which do not cooperate with organizations or countries combating money laundering, could be crucial for use of such payment systems for terrorist financing.

Prepaid Cards

Prepaid smart multipurpose cards can be used in stationary trade for person-to-person transfers as well as for e-commerce (using the special card readers). Most card products are only conditionally suited for money laundering and terrorism financing, due to loading limits (e.g., 200 Euro for the German GeldKarte), the account-based character (customer identification), the transaction protocol by system provider (serial number of value unities, card number, terminal number, etc.), and the low spreading of payment and loading terminals (Stickel & Woda, 2005). The projects with prepaid cards

have often only a national character. Nevertheless, some qualities, for example, the possibility of person-to-person transfers in the offline mode (e.g., Mondex wallet), anonymity (e.g., WhiteCard-GeldKarte), or interoperability (e.g., Proton Prisma systems), could be used by terrorists for money transfers or withdrawals (EURO Kartensysteme, 2006; MasterCard Int., 2006; STMicroelectronics, 2006). Nowadays such prepaid products are unsuited for present illicit money flows or money disposition because of very low spreading of prepaid cards. High number and volumes of transactions conducted with prepaid cards quickly would arouse the suspicion of illicit activities. However, such unaccounted products with a multicurrency character and free transferability between private parties can be for the preparing of terrorist actions of big importance in the future.

Mobile Payment Systems

Mobile payment systems characterize themselves, in general, by their high flexibility of applications possibilities (mobile commerce, e-commerce, in stationary trade, as well as for person-to-person transfers), high convenience (wallet function), and a high diversity with account methods, access methods, and so forth (McKitterick & Dowling, 2003). The mobile payment systems operating today are unsuitable for money laundering operations because of their server-based character with unequivocal identification duties and real-time customer authentication. However, many system qualities position mobile payment systems as important payment methods for the organization of terrorism actions in the future. The international character of payment systems, high flexibility of application possibilities, as well as the direct payment possibilities locally (often anonymous; using the special card readers, e.g., with dual-slot or dual-chip end devices) increase, in connection with huge mobility of the users, the suitability of mobile payment systems for terrorist transactions.

SUITABILITY FROM CYBER SYSTEMS CONCERNING DIFFERENT PHASES OF MONEY LAUNDERING

Money laundering is a complicated and multistage process that can consist of many single transactions. The model of the U.S. Customs Service distinguishes three phases of money laundering (Bongard, 2001, as cited in U.S. Customs Service, 1989; Madinger & Zalopany, 1999). Properties from illicit activities are converted in other form to allow investment in other legal properties during the placement phase. In the layering phase, a set of transfers occurs between accounts of different institutions and persons with the purpose to conceal the identity of the launderer. In the integration phase, the legal as well as the illicit assets are combined with each other and integrated into the business cycle. The transactions of money laundering are quasi legal in the integration phase, while transactions for terrorism financing remain strictly secret. On the other hand, the preparing of a terrorism action will be successful only if the money circulates through the (business) cycle (from collection to withdrawal) without disclosure of its illicit origin.

Payment systems are mostly suited for the realization of a single phase of money laundering. Most electronic payment systems (transfers, mobile payment systems) are suited merely for the layering phase, for a set of transfers among different accounts, countries, and persons. Prepaid cards (especially anonymous cards) are suited for the placement phase of money laundering. The important restrictions for the use of cyber systems for money laundering often present the registration or identification duties for customers and no possibility of person-to-person transfers. Nevertheless, the traditional payment methods can use other methods, for example, shell corporations, camouflage companies, charities, anonymous e-mail accounts, back-loan schemes, and over- and under-invoicing, to help reintegrate illicit money into the business cycle (with the purpose of spending money for terrorism financing).

Gold currencies seem to be an attractive payment system for money laundering and terrorism financing, because they could be used for the realization of every phase of money laundering (U.S. Treasury—TFI, 2003). In the placement phase, the funds can be deposited through an agent on the Internet, a shell corporation, a trustee, or a private transfer system (e.g., the Hawala) in the form of a postal order, checks, payments from charities, or from already existing anonymous users of gold currencies (person-to-person transfers). The network of numerous providers and agents on the Internet creates ideal conditions on the movements of money between physical persons and companies and from offshore countries (layering phase). The cash withdrawals with the so-called Gold ATM cards back exchange transactions with gold currencies and central bank currencies, or payoff of profits, for example, from the fictitious e-commerce activities, reintegrate the laundered money again in the legal transaction systems.

CONCLUSION

Gold currencies appear based on their qualities well suitable for money laundering as well as for terrorism financial transactions. Other electronic payment systems support only certain qualities and, thereby, are suitable only conditionally for a single phase of money laundering. However, the differences between money laundering and terrorism financing are also in relation on single methods. The banking transfers are not suited for money laundering, for instance, due to the electronic tracks in the system, but well suited for terrorism financial transactions combined with other techniques, like the Hawala, camouflage companies, or shell corporation. Money laundering as well as terrorism financing change constantly. Hence, the development of suitable countermeasures and detecting methods appears to be important. The suggestions, for example, of regulation of the maximum value for loading of prepaid cards, of no possibility of person-to-person transfers, or of restriction of the application possibilities on national level, are not innovative. Therefore, the research should concentrate on the development of suitable solutions (technical, cryptographic, monitoring systems, etc.) that consider new technologies and techniques.

REFERENCES

Basel Committee on Banking Supervision (BCBS). (2003). *Initiatives by the BCBS, IAIS and IOSCO to combat money laundering and the financing of terrorism.*. Retrieved February 15, 2006, from http://www.bis.org/publ/joint05.pdf

Bongard, K. (2001). *Wirtschaftsfaktor Geldwäsche.* Wiesbaden, Germany: Deutscher Universitäts-Verlag.

Center for International Security and Co-operation. *Proposal for an international convention on cyber crime and terrorism.* Retrieved February 3, 2006, from http://www.iwar.org.uk/cyberterror/#cyber

Commission of the European Communities. (2003). *Proposal for a directive of the European Parliament and of the council on measures and procedures to ensure the enforcement of intellectual property rights* (Brussels, 30.1.2003). Retrieved February 15, 2006, from http://europa.eu.int/eur-lex/en/com/pdf/2003/com2003_0046en01.pdf

'Cyberterrorism' testimony before the House Special Oversight Panel on Terrorism Committee on Armed Services. (2000). (testimony of D. E. Denning). Retrieved February 3, 2006, from http://www.cs.georgetown.edu/~denning/infosec/cyberterror.html

e-gold Ltd. (n.d.). *What is e-gold?* Retrieved February 3, 2006, from http://www.e-gold.com/unsecure/qanda.html

EURO Kartensysteme. (2006). *Kartenarten.* Retrieved February 15, 2006, from http://www.geldkarte.de/ww/de/pub/rund_um_die_geldkarte/hintergruende/karten_arten.htm

Europäische Zentralbank. (EZB). (2003). *Elektronisierung des Zahlungsverkehrs in Europa* (Monatsbericht, S. 65-78).

European Parliament and of the Council. (2001). *Directive 2001/97/EC.* Retrieved February 15, 2006, from http://europa.eu.int/eurlex/pri/en/oj/dat/2001/l_344/l_34420011228en00760081.pdf

Financial Action Task Force on Money Laundering (FATF). (2004a). *Report on money laundering typologies, 2003-2004.* Retrieved February 3, 2006, from http://www.fatf-gafi.org/dataoecd/19/11/33624379.pdf

Financial Action Task Force on Money Laundering (FATF). (2004b). *Report on money laundering and terrorist financing typologies, 2003-2004* (FATF-XV). Retrieved February 3, 2006, from http://www1.oecd.org/fatf/pdf/TY2004_en.PDF

Financial Action Task Force on Money Laundering (FATF). (2005). *Typologies report 2004-2005.* Retrieved February 15, 2006, from http://www.fatf-gafi.org/dataoecd/41/25/34988062.pdf

Gold-ATM. *Debit and prepaid cards for digital currencies users.* Retrieved February 13, 2006, from http://www.gold-atm.biz/cards.php

Krasavin, S. (2000). *What is cyber-terrorism?* Computer Crime Research Center. Retrieved February 3, 2006, from http://www.crime-research.org/library/Cyber-terrorism.htm

Madinger, J., & Zalopany, S. A. (1999). *Money laundering. A guide for criminal investigators.* Boca Raton, FL: CRC Press.

Mastercard Int. *Frequently asked questions.* Retrieved February 15, 2006, from http://www.mondex.com/faq.html#q07

McKitterick, D., & Dowling, J. (2003). *State of the art review of mobile payment technology* (Tech. Rep.). The University of Dublin, Trinity College. Retrieved February 15, 2006, from http://www.cs.tcd.ie/publications/tech-reports/reports.03/TCD-CS-2003-24.pdf

Nisbet, C. (2003). Cybercrime and cyber terrorism. In S. Paulus, N. Pohlmann, & H. Reimer (Eds.), *Securing electronic business processes—Highlights of the information security solutions conference 2003.* Vieweg. Retrieved February 3, 2006, from http://www.qinetiq.com/home_enterprise_security/conference_papers_index.Par.0001. File.pdf%5D

Pollitt, M. M. (1997). A cyberterrorism fact or fancy? In *Proceedings of the 20th National Information Systems Security Conference, 1997* (pp. 285-289). Retrieved February 3, 2006, from http://www.cs.georgetown.edu/~denning/infosec/pollitt.html

Stickel, E., & Woda, K. (2005): Electronic money. In E. Petzel (Ed.), *E-finance* (pp. 831-860). Gabler Verlag.

STMicroelectronics, Proton PRISMA. (n.d.). Retrieved February 15, 2006, from http://www.st.com/stonline/products/promlit/pdf/flprotongen-1003.pdf

U.S. Patriot Act of 2001. §§ 1956, 981.

U.S. Treasury—The Office of Terrorism and Financial Intelligence (TFI). (2003). *National money laundering strategy.* Retrieved February 3, 2006, from http://www.treas.gov/offices/enforcement/publications/ml2003.pdf

TERMS AND DEFINITIONS

Hawala: This is an informal value transfer system (also known as parallel remittance transfer system) for international money transfers. The payer deposits a sum of money at a Hawala broker in his country who communicates with another Hawala broker in the country of the payee (disposition to pay out of the money sum). Instead of moving the money, the brokers carry out a settlement of debts internally.

Integration: This refers to the legitimization of laundered assets.

Layering: In money laundering, this is a set of transfers of assets between accounts of companies, institutions, and other persons to conceal the origin of assets and the identity of money launderer.

Money Laundering: This term is defined as an intentional committed offense with the purpose of concealing or disguising of the true origin, the nature, the disposition, or of the controlling rights of properties, which were acquired illegally.

Placement: At the beginning of money laundering process, assets derived from criminal activities are converted into other forms of properties to allow their investment or movement in legal properties.

Shell Corp: This is a company with no real assets or operations, with a pyramided structure of owners, and with many bank accounts used often for fraudulent purposes.

Smurfing: Smurfing, or structured payments, are carried out to avoid reporting or scrutiny by law enforcement. The smurfing method refers to dividing of large payment sums into multiple deposits below a given limit.

Chapter XIX
Spam, Spim, and
Illegal Advertisement

Dionysios V. Politis
Aristotle University of Thessaloniki, Greece

Konstantinos P. Theodoridis
Centre of International & European Economic Law, Greece

ABSTRACT

Economists and regulators, along with the Internet community as a whole, are involved in confronting illegal promotional strategies that may deregulate the advertising sector. Apart from the quantitative research (ex ante and ex post) on policy changes, spam and illegal advertisement are actions that target after all the average Internet user, factually challenging the peer-to-peer nature of the Internet. Alarming is also the projection of this situation to mobile telephony, the so called spim. Having reached record levels the last couple of years, the phenomenon of unsolicited commercial communication raised consciousness that the Internet was endangered by an erosive threat similar to the uncontrollable, massive, free circulation of MP3s that devastated the musical industry some years ago. Recent combined advances in the software industry and in the legal front have reduced the phenomenon. The technical, social, financial and legal parameters of this issue are examined in this article, under the prism of networked economies.

INTRODUCTION

A significant problem of our times, accelerated by the advances in technology, is the plethora of commercial Internet messages usually referred to as *spam*, while the equivalent in classic television emission is the frequent and uncontrollable advertisement. Adver-

tisement, perceived as an expression and factor of the economy, is legitimate and desirable. However, abusive advertising practices can cause much damage, such as: invasion in to our private communication space, homogenisation of morals and customs leading to globalized overconsumption, and damage so much in the recipients as in the legal advertisers and suppliers of communication services due to deregulation.

Variations and cloning of spam and advertisement include *spim*, distributed instant messaging using bulk *short messaging services (SMSs)* over mobile telephone networks or the Web, wireless attacks and penetration, targeted unsolicited online harassment, and others.

Until now the rule was that anyone can send a message to anyone else with impunity, unless the content runs foul of some content-regulating law. The new initiatives seek to promote ways to restrict excessive electronic publicity so that the recipient or consumer is protected and the interests of good commercial communication are safeguarded.

DEFINITIONS AND PROVISIONS

Spam is usually defined as "unsolicited bulk e-mail." This is generally done for financial reasons, but the motive for spamming may be social or political. Unsolicited means that the recipient has not granted verifiable permission for the message to be sent. Bulk means that the message is sent as part of a larger collection of messages, all having mostly identical content (Cheng, 2004).

Rough estimates conclude that e-mails like "buy this product" or "participate in this campaign" are more than 60% of what is the normal daily load (Doyle, 2004). Generally, the longer an e-mail address has been in use, the more spam it will receive. Moreover, any e-mail address listed on a Web site or mentioned in newsgroups postings will be spammed disproportionally. Mailing lists are also a good target (Loia, 2004).

Recent figures show a dramatic increase in spam trafficking (Jung, 2004). Although not easily verifiable,[1] they are indicative of the extent:

- Spam trafficking has increased the last few years about 1,000% in comparison to what it was in 2002.
- The average user now gets six spams per day, or over 2,000 per year. Of these, 24% of spam

accounts were for scams and fraud, 23% were for product advertising, 14-19% were for pornography (91% of users find these the most annoying), 11% were for health remedies, and 1% were for politics.

- Up to 8% of Internet users have purchased spam promoted goods and services.
- Up to 28% of Internet users have replied to spam mail at some stage.
- Costs of spamming are so low that even a few replies in a million make the spammers' efforts profitable.

The evolution of the phenomenon is presented in Figure 1.

Although spam is readily conceived, confusion reigns over its phenotype (Robinson, 2003). More than two-thirds of e-mail account holders think that they can decipher an e-mail message when they see it, while 9% have to open the message to ascertain the infringement. The extent of intrusion is also variably conceived: 70% of e-mailers believe that spam has made being online "unpleasant or annoying," 27% think spam is a "big problem" for them. However, 14% think its impact is negligible (Fetterly, 2004; Grimes, 2004).

Spam has a serious impact on lost productivity. Hours spent deleting unwanted e-mail, reporting spam senders, or researching companies that send spam are lost.[2]

A variation of spam is *spim*. It is defined as unsolicited commercial messaging produced via an *instant messaging* (IM) system. It disperses messages to a predetermined set of screen names, which are generated randomly or are harvested off the Internet. Marketers have never seen a medium they did not want to exploit. So spam has evolved to IM yielding spim. It has been around a few years, but only in the past few months has it become a disruption.

Spam as a social phenomenon arising from an online social situation that technology created. First, it costs no more to send a million e-mail messages than to send one. Second, hits are a percentage of transmis-

Figure 1. The increase of spam trafficking

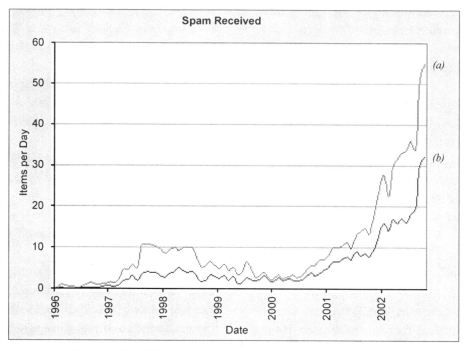

Note: Line (a) = spam sent to all accounts; Line (b) = spam sent to reference accounts

sions, so sending more spam means expecting more profit (Whitworth, 2004). So, from the advertising point of view, the important characteristic of spam is that it is practically free. It is not the best e-mail communication technique, it is not the most efficient, but it attracts people because it is free.

Another aspect of spam is its implementation on mobile telephony. The spam projection has the morphotype of an unsolicited SMS message or of a *scam*, that is, a fraudulent business of any kind. The impact of spam or scam on mobile phones may be more severe than that of a personal computer, since it may provoke recipient hidden charges, reduce battery charge, retrieve personal directory services, and provided that the mobile telephone is equipped with an operating system, it may be used in a manner that causes unpredictable behaviour (Leavitt, 2005).

If spam is seen now primarily as an annoyance—in its implementation to mobile telephony it can be costly.

Receiving and replying to SMSs costs time and money, and communication costs are by far more expensive than Internet access costs.

Apart from charges and tariffs, there are some differences in the techniques used, since *global system for mobile communication* (GSM) standards allow SMS messages to be up to 160 characters in length.

This is the reason that mobile spam trafficking is, as a mass communication expedition, follows slightly different practices to spam. Since there is a charge for sending an SMS message, spammers avoid using it. However, it is used by advertisers relying on: (a) that they can have special rates for mass communication, (b) it is a more interactive media, (c) it has a more wide spread circulation, reaching absolute penetration.

Already heavy SMS trafficking has been reported on special occasions, like the referendum on the accession of a former Eastern Country to the EU, in national elections, and so forth.

The existence of a significant cost on the senders side, compared to the sender's cost in spam practices differentiates the legal approach to spam. It is obvious that a significant cost, that of sending SMS messages nationwide, was undertaken by institutional organisations or advertisers.

THE LEGAL ASPECTS OF SPAM

Anti-Spam Legislation in the U.S. and the EU

The increasing intensity of the spam phenomenon caused the timely reaction of the legislator, who is exceedingly often asked to regulate Internet behaviour. This act involves, by necessary implication, the balancing of the interests of user protection, on the one hand, and the guarantee of fundamental freedoms of citizens and of netizens, on the other.

However, it should be noted that litigation based on spam forensic data evidence is sometimes problematic; laws are uneven over jurisdictions, and it is often hard to find the spammer. It is estimated that 70% of spam is sent via hijacked computers. Additionally, uniform application of national measures, that is, the degree of harmonisation, is questionable (Khong, 2001).

Currently, the number one spam mail recipient is U.S., followed by China (Chua, 2004; Yeh, 2004), and the EU on the whole.

United States

The U.S. is not only the homeland of the Internet, but also a basic spam source (almost 90% of the spam received in Europe is sent from the U.S.).[3] Since 1996 many cases[4] between Internet Service Providers (ISPs) and spammers found their way to court; however the problem has always remained the same: lack of specific legal regulation, which led to objectionable decisions (Frank, 2003; Kasprzycki, 2004). The need for an ad hoc federal law was obvious and after many rejected drafts, on January 1, 2004, the "CAN SPAM Act

2003"[5] was finally put into force. This Act includes a variety of measures (Clarke, 2005) for the prevention and the restriction of the problem and provides serious penalties for the spammers. More specifically, among others:

- Spammers face penalties of imprisonment up to 5 years and/or high fines.
- The falsification of the sender identity or header information, the harvesting of electronic addresses and the unauthorized manipulation of computers and servers is penalized (Sec. 4).
- Advertisers are obliged to include an "opt-out" option in each advertising e-mail (Sec. 5).
- E-mail advertisements must be labelled as such, with the addition of the abbreviation "ADV" in the subject line (Sec. 11).
- The formation of a "Do-Not-E-mail-Registry" is foreseen (Sec. 9),[6] where the Internet users can register themselves in order to avoid receiving advertising e-mails. Advertisers are, theoretically, to consult this list before launching a mass electronic advertising campaign.

According to the "CAN SPAM Act," the ISPs are granted the right of legal action against spammers (Sec. 7 (g)) and did not waste any time in putting it in use.[7] However, antispam activist organisations[8] criticise consistently the lack of a clause enabling individual users to take spammers to court.

European Union

The European Union has reacted promptly as far as the protection of European consumers is concerned, by publishing the Directive 1997/7/EC "on the protection of consumers in respect of distance" and preventing the use of certain means of distance communication (telephone, fax), without the prior consent of the consumer (Art. 10). Later on, the Directive 2000/31/EC "on electronic commerce" focused further on the unsolicited commercial electronic communication prescribing the formation of "opt-out" registers (Art. 7). Finally the Directive 2002/58/EC "on privacy and electronic communication,"[9] replacing the Directive 1997/66/EC, is providing a powerful legal tool against spamming. According to Article 13 of the new Directive:

- The communication for the purpose of direct marketing via telephone, fax, or e-mail requires the prior consent of the consumer-user ("opt-in") or is acceptable in the context of the sale of a product or a service ("soft opt-in").
- Each advertising e-mail must incorporate an easy and costless "opt-out" opportunity for the recipient in order to object to such use of electronic contact details.
- Disguising or concealing the sender identity and providing an invalid reply address for the "opt-out," shall be prohibited.

A careful reading of the Directive 2002/58/EC, reveals stricter antispam protection compared to the " CAN SPAM Act." Selecting the "opt-in" (or at least "soft opt-in") method, the EU Directive prevents *a priori* all the advertising e-mails, without the prior consent of the user, while the "CAN SPAM Act" permits the first sending of spam and tries to restrict it *ex post* using the "opt-out" way. However it depends on the will of the national legislator, to adjust the content of the directive to the internal legislation of each member-state. For example, the Netherlands have already adjusted the national legislation and have established regulatory authorities like OPTA,[10] that has issued its first fines (LeClaire, 2004).[11]

SPAM and the Protection of Personal Data

Apart from the fact that spam is a nuisance, there is definitely an aspect of violation in the sphere of personal communications and not only. Data protection authorities are involved in the spam issue as far as:

- *Harvesting* personal data a file is created containing personal data that has not been legally gathered. No prior consent of the subject has been given in collecting this personal data. As a result, electronic addresses and communication numbers are associated with distinctive persons. It should be noted that data originating from lists addressed to the general public or publicly accessible sources intended for the provision of information or personal data the subject has made public for relevant purposes such as distribution of promotional literature, inclusion in trade exhibitions, directories, Web sites, do not fall into this constraint.[12]
- Legal gathering of personal data definitely involves the prior consent of the subject, definitely not the tactics used in hacking. Hacking is by itself an illegal action.
- The exploitation of personal data files is unacceptable, especially when illegally gathered or formed e-mail address directories are used. Even if a file of personal data is formed legally, it should not be transferred, sold, or elsewhere marketed.

In this sense, for a third party, keeping a file with personal data like a directory of mobile telephone numbers and recipient data is illegal, if the controller has not given his prior consent. However, the use of an algorithm to find valid mobile telephone numbers and to send them a promotional e-mail en masse does not violate legislation.

Also, in some legal documents, natural persons are assimilated with legal entities. If spamming originates from an e-mail account that belongs to a company domain how is responsibility attributed?

Ultimately, the most challenging aspect of antispam legislation compliance will be technical. Companies, legal entities, institutions, Internet service providers are recommended to implement their own "Do-Not-E-mail" database of e-mail addresses of those individuals who have "opted-out." This may be either a single database for the entire company or separate databases for separate groups within the company. And, prior to sending each future commercial e-mail, the service provider will have to check the target e-mail address against its "Do-Not-E-mail" database.

CONCLUSION

The combined action of substantial legal countermeasures and advanced techniques of content filtering have limited the spread of spam. Recent statistics estimate spam prevalence at 67% of daily e-mail communication, on a worldwide scale.

The spam issue is part of a more complex phenomenon concerning the governance of the Internet, the economics of networked industries, technological advances, and software development (Shy, 2001).

The prospect of new technological initiatives like the launch of digital television, the convergence of the Internet with broadcasting networks, it has importance on major e-commerce practices like advertisement.

The spam issue does not merely threaten the future of a self-governed Internet; it tests the tolerances of many factors for networked economies.

REFERENCES

Cheng, T. (2004). Recent international attempts to can spam. *Computer Law & Security Report, 20*(6), 472-479.

Chua, C. E. H., & Wareham, J. (2004). Fighting internet auction fraud: An assessment and proposal. *IEEE Computer, 37*(10), 31-37.

Clarke, I., Flaherty, T., & Zugelder, M. (2005). The CAN-SPAM act: New rules for sending commercial e-mail messages and implications for the sales force. *Industrial Marketing Management, 34*(4), 399-405.

Doyle, E. (2004, November/December). Spam rules—And there's nothing you can do. *Elsevier Infosecurity Today*, pp. 24-28.

Fetterly, D., Manasse, M., & Najorket, M. (2004, June 17-18). Spam, damn spam, and statistics—Using statistical analysis to locate spam web pages. In *Proceedings of the 7th International Workshop on the Web and Databases (WebDB 2004)*, Paris (p. 16).

Frank, T. (2003). *Zur strafrechtlichen Bewältigung des Spamming, Würzburg , Diss.*, p. 177.

Funk, A., Zeifang, G., Johnson, D., & Spessard, R. (2003). Unsolicited commercial e-mails in the jurisdictions of Germany and the USA. *CRi* 5, p. 141.

Grimes, A., Hough, M., & Signorella, M. (in press). E-mail end users and spam: Relations of gender and age group to attitudes and actions. *Computers in Human Behavior.*

Jung, J., & Smit, E. (2004, October 25-27). An empirical study of spam traffic and the use of DNS black lists. *Proceedings of The Internet Measurement Conference (IMC'04)*, Taormina, Italy.

Kasprzycki, D. (2004). Trends in regulating unsolicited commercial communication. *CRi* 3, p. 77.

Khong, W. (2001). Spam law for the internet. *The Journal of Information, Law and Technology(JILT)*, (3). http://elj.warwick.ac.uk/jilt

Leavitt, N. (2005). Mobile phones: The next frontier for hackers? *IEEE Computer, 38*(4), 20-23.

LeClaire, J. (2004, December 29). Netherland issues its first fines against spammers. *E-commerce Times.*

Loia, V., Senatore, S., & Sessa, M. (2004). Combining agent technology and similarity-based reasoning for targeted e-mail services. *Fuzzy Sets and Systems, 145*(1), 29-56.

Robinson, G. (2003, January 3). Statistical appoach to the spam problem—Using Bayesian statistics to detect an e-mail's spamminess. *ACM Linux Journal.*

Shy, O. (2001). *The Economics of Network Industries.* Cambridge University Press.

Watel, J. (2001). Le problème du Spamming ou comment guérir le cancer de l' Internet, JurPC Web-Dok. 163/2001.

Whitworth, B., & Whitworth, E. (2004). Spam and the social-technical gap. *IEEE Computer, 37*(10), 38-45.

Yeh, A. (2004). China now world's number two spam recipient, after United States. *Privacy and Security Law Report, 3*(13), 361.

TERMS AND DEFINITIONS

Chat Room: An Internet relay chat (IRC) channel designated for the real-time exchange of text messages. Technically, a chat room is a communication channel, but the term room is used to promote the chat metaphor for an online place where a group of people can communicate about a particular subject or just chat. Usually users are asked to sign in and accordingly they are assigned a name. Voice and video channels may be established as well, enhancing typing communication. Some chat rooms allow users to talk to one individual without the others seeing the conversation. Most chat rooms allow users to see who else is participating in the conversation.

Data Protection Authority: Independent administrative authority supervising the implementation of acts and regulations pertaining to the protection of the individual with respect to the processing of their personal data.

Global System for Mobile Communication (GSM): This is a globally accepted standard for digital cellular communication.

ID Masquerading and ID Theft: Crimes where the stealing of personal data (like credit card numbers, social security number, or driver's license) is involved for personal and/or economic gains. Such crimes involve fraud, deception, and theft.

Instant Message (IM): A type of communications service that enables Internet users to create a kind of private chat room with another individual in order to communicate in real-time in text mode. IM is expected to promote IP-based telephony by allowing users to switch from typing to voice-based communication.

Internet Relay Chat (IRC): A computer network of Internet servers, using its own protocol through which individual users can hold real-time online conversations. It is mainly designed for group (many-to-many) communication in discussion forums called *channels*, but also allows one-to-one communication.

Opt-In and Opt-Out: Exercising this right means that the recipient declares to some kind of regulating authority that they do not want to receive direct or indirect marketing communication (e-mails, telephone calls, SMS's, turtle mail). A "Do-Not-Spam-List" is formed and marketers are not supposed to contact the person at the addresses included in that list. Under the CAN-SPAM Act, in the U.S. a national "Do-Not-E-mail-Registry" similar to the national "Do-Not-Call-Registry" that restricts telemarketing calls has been formed.

The "opt-out" approach operates complementarily to the "opt-in" one. If a recipient finds themselves in a situation where they receive unwanted communication, they can at any point break the communication channel by taking ancillary measures. These include sending a predescribed e-mail to the mailing list, clicking on a link, returning the message with the word "unsubscribe," call a toll-free phone numbers, return a turtle mail as unwanted, and so forth. The sender is obliged not only to stop further communication but to remove the requester's identity from their list.

Protection of Personal Data: The advances in information technology, the development of new technologies, the novel forms of advertising, and the concomitant electronic transactions as well as the need for e-organisation of the State result in an extensive trafficking of personal information from both the private and the public sector. Uncontrollable personal data filing and processing by companies, organisations, or institutions may create problems and jeopardize a citizen's privacy. Citizens should be in a position to know at every moment who, where, when, how, and why processes their personal data.

Short Messaging Service (SMS): It is a text message service offered by the GSM digital cellular telephone system. Short text messages are delivered to and from a mobile phone, fax machine, or IP address. Messages must be up to a maximum of 160 alphanumeric characters and contain no images or graphics. Even if the recipient's mobile phone is inactive, the message is buffered by the GSM network until the end user's terminal equipment becomes active.

ENDNOTES

[1] Figures are taken from various sources, mainly from antispam or antivirus Internet online sites and have some variance, depending on the source and the date they were cropped. Up-to-date figures can be seen at http://www.spamhaus.org

[2] "Junk e-mail costs Internet users 10 billion Euro worldwide," European Union Commission Study IP/01/154, Brussels, 2/2/2001.

[3] See http://www.spamhaus.org/statistics.lasso

[4] For example, America Online Inc. v. Cyber Promotions Inc. (E.D. Pa. 1996), CompuServe Inc. v. Cyber Promotions Inc. (S.D. Ohio 1997), Hotmail Corp. v. Van$ Money Pie Inc. (N.D. Cal. 1998), America Online Inc. v. LCGM Inc. (E.D. Va. 1998).

[5] Controlling the Assault of Non-Solicited Pornography and Marketing Act of 2003, 15 U.S.C.A. § 7701-7713.

[6] For further analysis see Funk (2004).

[7] See Macworld article of March 11, 2004 at http://www.macworld.co.uk/news/index.cfm?newsid=8137&page=1&pagepos=2

[8] About anti-spam organizations, see Watel (2001). http://spamcon.org and http://www.wired.com/news/business/0,1367,62020,00.html?tw=wn_story_related

[9] Directive 2002/58/EC of the European Parliament and of the Council of 12 July 2002 concerning the processing of personal data and the protection of privacy in the electronic communications sector (Directive on privacy and electronic communications). OJ L 201, 31.7.2002, pp. 37-47.

[10] OPTA, Netherland's Independent Post and Telecommunications Authority. http://www.opta.nl

[11] For example, $61,000 against an individual, who was involved in four spam campaigns, $34,000 against a company spamming about financial software, $27,000 against a company sending spam text messages on mobile phones.

[12] For example, see Data Protection Authority, Greece, Decision No. 050/20.01.2000: Terms for the lawful processing of personal data as regards the purposes of direct marketing/advertising and the ascertainment of creditworthiness. http://www.dpa.gr

Chapter XX
Malware:
Specialized Trojan Horse

Stefan Kiltz
Otto-von-Guericke University, Germany

Andreas Lang
Otto-von-Guericke University, Germany

Jana Dittmann
Otto-von-Guericke University, Germany

ABSTRACT

The Trojan horse can be used in cyber-warfare and cyber-terrorism, as recent attacks in the field of industrial espionage have shown. To coordinate methods of defence a categorisation of the threat posed by Trojan horses in the shape of a list of tuples is proposed. With it, a set (consisting of methods for the distribution, activation, storage, means of execution, communications, malicious functionality) can be defined, which describes the Trojan horse by its features. Each of these aspects can be accompanied by methods of self-defence (e.g., armouring or encryption) against detection and removal by protection software. The list of tuples and therefore the categorisation of the Trojan horse properties is a vital first step to develop and organise counter measures against this kind of threat. A new category of Trojan horses, the special and universal Trojan horse, is proposed. This type of malware is particularly well suited for cyber-warfare and cyber-terrorism, as it unlikely to be picked up by common protection software (e.g., virus scanner). To achieve this, a Trojan horse is tailor-made for one special attack of a particular computer system and can provide espionage or sabotage functionality. If it is not used on large-scale attacks, anti-malware software producers will have little or no chance to extract a signature for this code. Systems being spied upon without notice can deliver vital information for the attacker. In addition, the attacker can choose to permanently or temporarily disrupt IT-infrastructure (e.g., denial-of-service, destruction of hardware). The universal Trojan horse can be updated by the attacker to achieve an extended functionality which makes it universal. The above-proposed list of tuples can be a tool to describe such special and universal Trojan horses which will be introduced in the full item description.

INTRODUCTION

Trojan horses as a special kind of malware (malicious software) have been around for quite some time. The threat prosed by this sort of program should not be underestimated. Therefore, the manufacturers of antivirus software today offer means to detect and, if possible, to remove Trojan horses from a computer system. But they almost exclusively rely on signatures to detect this sort of program. If a carefully crafted Trojan horse is used only once or at least very rarely, chances are that this piece of malware will remain undetected, simply because no one could record a signature for this particular code and integrate that signature in antivirus databases. Such a Trojan horse can be used in cyber warfare and cyber terrorism, as recent attacks in the field of industrial espionage have shown (Neumann, 1997).

This chapter will show the threat posed by this subcategory of Trojan horses. It will then propose ways to systematically describe the characteristics of this type of malware. Such a classification can be the first step to finding suitable countermeasures against that type of malware.

BACKGROUND

Trojan horses as a special form of malware got their name from the tales of Greek mythology, where an entire army was hidden in an enormous wooden horse that was given as a present to the people of the city of Troy. The gift provided a means to bypass the heavily defended outer wall and attack the city from the inside (Trojan War, 2005).

Similarly, computer programs pretending to be useful to the user and also having hidden, undocumented and malicious features are called Trojan horses. Or as Matt Bishop (Trojan War, 2005, p. 614) defined: "A Trojan horse is a program, that has overt (documented and known) functions as well as covert (undocumented and unexpected) functions."

Trojan horses often use the techniques of social engineering. That means that the user is tricked into installing and running the program. All the automated defenses, such as firewalls, e-mail spam filters, and so forth, are of no use because the user insists on running the program.

MAIN THRUST OF THE CHAPTER

The Special and Universal Trojan Horse

With Trojan horses having been around for some time, the authors will now focus on a new and dangerous subcategory of Trojan horses, the special and universal Trojan horse (Dittman & Lang, 2004). This type of malware is particularly well suited for cyber warfare and cyber terrorism, as it unlikely to be picked up by common protection software (e.g., virus scanner). To achieve this, a Trojan horse is tailormade for one special attack on a particular computer system and can provide espionage or sabotage functionality. If it is not used on large-scale attacks, antimalware software producers will have little or no chance to extract a signature for this code. Systems being spied upon without notice can deliver vital information for the attacker. In addition, the attacker can choose to permanently or temporarily disrupt information technology (IT) infrastructure (e.g., denial-of-service, destruction of hardware).

The authors define a special and universal Trojan horse as follows: "A special and universal Trojan horse is a specialised piece of code that is purpose built to attack a particular computer system in such a way that it allows the attacker unauthorised and universal access to the victim computer system." What makes this Trojan horse *special* is the choice of properties of the code that is tailored to the demands of the system being attacked. Such a Trojan horse is also *universal* in that allows the attacker to reconfigure the functionality of the code at run time.

Although some protection mechanisms (e.g., firewalls) allow for blind blocking, that is, defense against a threat without prior detection, in order to detect Trojan horses, it is often necessary to detect their presence first. To defend against special and universal Trojan horses, it is particularly helpful to look at their properties in detail and look for attack patterns, based on those properties.

The authors propose to describe the properties of special and universal Trojan horses by using a tuple list. In the next section, this list will be introduced and described in detail.

Tuples to Describe the Properties of Special and Universal Trojan Horses

In order to describe the properties of such a piece of malicious code, several major categories of functionality have to be observed. In a special and universal Trojan horse, those categories proposed by the authors are:

- Distribution method V
- Activation method A
- Placement method U
- Communication method K
- Mode of operation W

- Payload function F
- Self-protection measures S

This categories form the tuple as follows:

T=(V|S, A|S, U|S, W|S, K|S, F|S).

It should be noted, that a special and universal Trojan horse can apply different self-protection measures to safeguard different categories, which is denoted by the | operator.

In the following, each of those categories will be introduced both with a description and exemplary tuple elements. The tuple elements $v_{i,j}$, ϵ, and V are constructed using the main method identified by the number (i) and an item number (j), which defines the exact association for the main method. Hence an example would take on the form $v_{i,j}$. The tables shown in the following represent work in progress. They are designed to be easily extended both in the direction of the category as well as the individual items.

In the category distribution method V, the means,

Table 1. Selected examples for distribution method V

$v_{i,j}$	i=1 **Executable files, download**	i=2 **Social engineering**	i=3 **Exploits**	i=4 **Malformed data objects**	i=5 **Physical access**
j=1	E-mail attachment				
j=2	Instant messaging				
j=3	File sharing networks (peer to peer)				

Table 2. Selected examples for activation method A

$a_{i,j}$	i=1 **Boot sequence of the operating system**	i=2 **Program call (unintended)**
j=1	Init scripts (e.g., win.ini with Windows or init.d scripts when using Linux)	Modified programs
j=2	Registry entry (about 50 possible locations)	Exploiting mix ups (Unix "cp" ←→ Windows "copy")
j=3	Kernel modules (dynamically added at runtime)	Using social engineering

Table 3. Selected examples for placement method U

$u_{i,j}$	i=1 As a file on mass storage devices	i=2 File system independent on the hard drive	i=3 Within modules/memory areas of any given hardware (RAM, Flash memory, USB sticks, etc.)	i=4 Distributed in separate files (puzzle Trojan horse)
j=1		Within clusters marked as defective		
j=2		Within slack space in occupied clusters		
j=3		Within partition slack space		

Table 4. Selected examples for mode of operation W

$w_{i,j}$	i=1 DLL injection	i=2 Process injection	i=3 Altering configurations	i=4 Protected stack bypassing	i=5 Loading/adding of modules
j=1					

Table 5. Selected examples for communication methods K

$k_{i,j}$	i=1 Active (direct) communication	i=2 Passive (indirect) communication	i=3 E-mail, IRC, ICQ, HTTP	i=4 Tunneling using other protocols (e.g., ICMP, DNS, HTTP)
j=1	Open port (server is polling for clients)			
j=2	Closed port (port knocking, opened after a request)			
j=3	Stealth mode (sniffer)			

by which the special and universal Trojan horse gets to the victims computer, is depicted. Depending on the particular way of distribution the user interaction required to install the Trojan horse can range from an absolute necessity up to not requiring any action at all. In Table 1, distribution methods are shown.

The category activation method A describes the means with which the attacker gets the code of the Trojan horse executed on the victim's computer. A couple of techniques are available, most of which depend on the operating system used on the attacked computer. Examples of the activation methods are proposed in Table 2.

Table 6. Selected examples for payload function F

$f_{i,j}$	i=1 **File manager**	i=2 **Process manager**	i=3 **Key logger**	i=4 **Update functionality**	i=5 **Registry**
j=1	File up/download	Reveal running processes	Offline key logger (storage of keystrokes)	Adding of modules	Jump to a particular key
j=2	Create/delete directory	Terminate/start processes	Online key logger (transmitting keystrokes)	Removal of modules (size reduction)	Delete/create key
j=3	Execute file		Search within stored keystrokes		Add/change a key value

Table 7. Selected examples for self-protection measures S

$s_{i,j}$	i=0 **None**	i=1 **Armoring**	i=2 **Polymorphy**	i=3 **Stealth**	i=4 **Steganograpy**	i=5 **Encryption**	i=6 **Manipulate protection software**
j=1							

It is often important for the attacker to permanently store both the program code of the Trojan horse and the results (e.g., gathered espionage information) on the victim's computer system. Hence, the placement method *U* describes where that data is located in the local computer system. Examples of those methods proposed are introduced in Table 3.

Sometimes Trojan horses use special techniques to "infect" the victim's computer. The category mode of operation *W* can be used to describe known methods. Examples are shown in Table 4.

In order to establish a communication between the attacker and his Trojan horse certain methods are available. The category communication method *K* describes those means. In general two different ways to establish such a communication exist, a passive and an active connection. The only difference thereby is the initiator. When the attacker waits for his malicious code to connect to his system, it is a passive communication. This method is usually stealthy and hard to detect. If the attacker is using an active communication method, he can send commands to his Trojan horse at a time

of his choosing. Examples of the communications methods proposed are shown in Table 5.

Almost any Trojan horse is sent to the victim's computer to fulfill a certain purpose. The method to achieve that purpose is the payload function *F*. This category has to have the most items in order to cover a wide range of possible functions. The payload function examples are shown in Table 6.

For a Trojan horse to remain undetected or to resist a deletion attempt it can employ several defense mechanisms denoted here as self-protection measures *S*. The protection mechanisms used are similar to those employed by computer viruses (these are covered in detail in Szor, 2005). As already stated, these defense mechanisms can be used individually to protect a particular category within the tuple. Possible self-protection measures are shown in Table 7.

With the proposed tuple list, it is now possible to describe the properties of a given Trojan horse. In the following section, two examples of abstract special and universal Trojan horses will be introduced to illustrate the usage of the proposed tuple list.

Examples of Special and Universal Trojan Horses

To illustrate the usage of the proposed tuple list, two abstract special and universal Trojan horses are to be defined. The first one is modelled around spying on the computer on which it was placed. Such a Trojan horse t_1 could have the following description:

$$t_1 = (\{v_{1.1},\ v_4\}|\{s_3\}, \{a_1, a_{2.1}\}|\{s_3\},\ \{u_{2.3}\}|\{s_3\},\ \{w_2\}|\{s_3\}, \{k_2, k_3, k_4\}|\{s_3\},\ \{f_{1.5},\ f_{3.1}\}|\{s_3\}).$$

This means that t_1 is sent to the victim computer via e-mail ($v_{1.1}$). Using an exploit within the e-mail program (v_4), it is started with the activation method $a_{2.1}$. By bringing malicious code into the operating system (using mode of operation w_3), it is from now on started with the activation method a_1, together with the manipulated kernel. This Trojan horse stores its results outside the normal file system on the systems hard disk ($u_{2.3}$). It is looking for particular files of interest, located on the victim's computer; it is using the look-up functionality ($f_{1.5}$). In order to communicate with the attacker, it uses existing communications channels (k_2) and manipulates them as well (k_3). The idea is to use a normal e-mail sent by the victim as a container for the results that have been gathered by the Trojan horse. In order to bypass any encryption mechanisms, the Trojan horse t_1 comes with a key logger to record any passwords typed in by the victim ($f_{3.1}$). So a manipulated e-mail is first sent to the attacker, who then extracts the gathered information only to send the remainder to the original address (k_4). Every aspect of t_1 is protected using the stealth mechanism (s_3), so for as long as the manipulated operating system kernel is booted; the chances of detecting t_1 are very slim indeed.

The second abstract Trojan horse t_2 is modelled to cause as much damage as possible on the victim's computer in as little time as possible. Therefore, t_2 could have the following description:

$$t_2 = (\{v_3\}|\{s_0\},\ \{a_2\}|\{s_0\},\ \{u_3\}|\{s_0\},\ \{w_2\}|\{s_0\},\ \{f_{1.2}, f_{11}\}|\{s_0\}).$$

This means that t_2 is employing a recent exploit (v_3) to distribute itself onto the victim's computer. By using a buffer overflow and injecting code into a running server process (a_2 and u_3), it is able to obtain administrator permissions. This Trojan horse t_2 is only present within the main memory (u_3). It tries to achieve maximal damage by erasing all file systems available and destroying the hardware by erasing flash-updatable firmware of the devices within its reach. No communication is needed and self-protection measures are not necessary because t_2 is doing its damage instantly after arriving on the victim's computer.

CONCLUSION

Trojan horses and special and universal Trojan horses, in particular, are a clear and present threat to computer systems. Although antivirus software vendors include a Trojan horse-scanning capability, it is possible that some Trojan horses escape detection. Other automated defenses, such as firewalls, can block standard means of malicious software getting onto a computer system but are of little help in the case of an attack using a special and universal Trojan horse. Intrusion-detection systems employing anomaly detection mechanisms are more capable of detecting certain attack patterns but are prone to deliver false positives.

The tuples list can be a first step in analyzing the threat posed by special and universal Trojan horses. Also by taking appropriate measures, certain properties of Trojan horses can be deflected and an attack can be foiled (e.g., not using file sharing networks, which are a constant source of malware).

With today's software, technical measures alone cannot provide guaranteed protection against special and universal Trojan horses. Employing certain organizational measures, such as the minimal permission concept or the exclusive use of certified software (for applications and the operating system), could reduce the threat. Personal measures, such as regular education, can help with combating social engineering techniques. It can be concluded that the three measures (technical, organizational, and personal) together can minimize the threat drastically.

REFERENCES

Bishop, M. (2005). *Introduction to computer security.*

Trojan War. (2005). In *Britannica.com*. Retrieved from http://www.britannica.com/ebc/article-9381198?query=trojan\%horse&ct=

Dittmann, J., & Lang, A. (2004). *Lecture selected aspects of IT-security (WS 04/05)* (Internal Rep.).

Neumann, P. G. (1997). Computer security in aviation: Vulnerabilities, threats, and risks. In *Proceedings of the International Conference in Aviation Safety and Security in the 21st Century, White House Commission on Safety and Security, and George Washington University.* Retrieved from http://www.csl.sri.com/neumann/air.html

Szor, P. (2005). *The art of computer virus research and defense.*

Chapter XXI
SQL Code Poisoning:
The Most Prevalent Technique for Attacking Web Powered Databases

Theodoros Tzouramanis
University of the Aegean, Greece

ABSTRACT

This chapter focuses on the SQL code poisoning attack. It presents various ways in which a Web database can be poisoned by malicious SQL code, which can result in the compromise of the system. Subsequently, techniques are described for the detection of SQL code poisoning and a number of lockdown issues that are related to this type of attack are discussed. This chapter also reviews security mechanisms and software tools that protect Web applications against unexpected data input by users; against alterations of the database structure; and against the corruption of data and the disclosure of private and confidential information, all of which are owed to the susceptibility of these applications to this form of attack.

INTRODUCTION

Web application attacks are continuously on the rise, posing new risks for any organization that have an "online presence." The *SQL code poisoning* or *SQL injection attack* (CERT, 2002) is one of the most serious threats faced by database security experts. Today it is the most common technique used for attacking, indirectly, Web powered databases and disassembling effectively the secrecy, integrity, and availability of

Web applications. The basic idea behind this insidious and pervasive attack is that predefined logical expressions within a predefined query can be altered by simply injecting operations which always result in true or false statements. With this simple technique, the attacker can run arbitrary SQL queries and thus they can extract sensitive customer and order information from e-commerce applications, or they can bypass strong security mechanisms and compromise the backend databases and the file system of the data server. Despite these threats, a surprisingly high number of systems on the Internet are totally vulnerable to this attack.

This chapter focuses on the SQL code poisoning attack. It presents various ways in which a Web database can be poisoned by malicious SQL code, which can result in the compromise of the system. Subsequently, techniques are described for the detection of SQL code poisoning and a number of lockdown issues that are related to this type of attack are discussed. This chapter also reviews security mechanisms and software tools that protect Web applications against unexpected data input by users; against alterations of the database structure; and against the corruption of data and the disclosure of private and confidential information, all of which are owed to the susceptibility of these applications to this form of attack.

BACKGROUND

Online businesses and organizations are protected these days by some kind of software or hardware firewall solution (Theriault & Newman, 2001). The purpose of the firewall is to filter network traffic that passes into and out of the organization's network, limiting the use of the network to permitted, "legitimate" users. One of the conceptual problems with relying on a firewall for security is that the firewall operates at the level of IP addresses and network ports. Consequently, a firewall does not understand the details of higher level protocols such as hypertext transfer protocol, that is, the protocol that runs the Web applications.

There is a whole class of attacks that operate at the application layer and that, by definition, pass straight through firewalls. SQL code poisoning is one of these attacks. It takes advantage of nonvalidated input vulnerabilities to pass SQL commands through a Web application for execution by a backend database, that is, the heart of most Web applications. Attackers take advantage of the fact that programmers often chain together SQL commands with user-provided parameters, and can therefore embed SQL commands inside these parameters. Therefore, the attacker can execute

malicious SQL queries on the backend database server through the Web application.

In order to be able to perform SQL code poisoning hacking, all an attacker needs is a Web browser and some guess work to find important table and field names. This is why SQL code poisoning is one of the most common application layer attacks currently being used on the Internet. The inventor of the attack is the Rain Forest Puppy, a former hacker and, today, a security advisor to international companies of software development.

THE SQL CODE POISONING ATTACK

SQL Code Poisoning Principles

SQL code poisoning is a particularly insidious attack since it transcends all of the good planning that goes into a secure database setup and allows malicious individuals to inject code directly into the database management system (DBMS) through a vulnerable application (Spett, 2002). The basic idea behind this attack is that the malicious user counterfeits the data that a Web application sends to the database aiming at the modification of the SQL query that will be executed

Figure 1. A typical user login form in a Web application

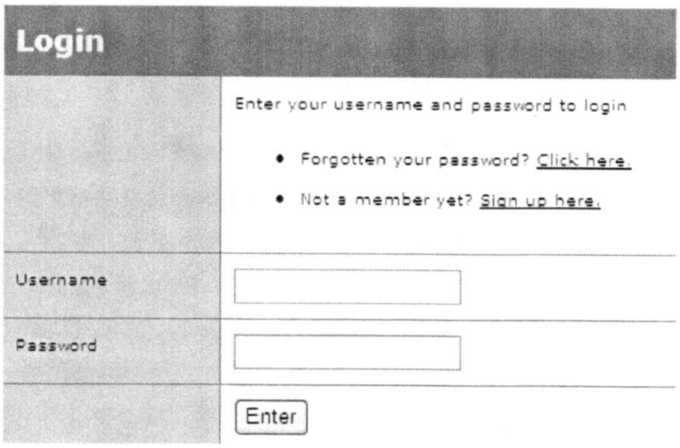

Figure 2. An ASP code example that manages the users' login requests in a database through a Web application

```
<%
dim username, password;
username = Request.form("text_username");
password = Request.form("text_password");

var con = Server.CreateObject(ADODB.Connention");
var rso = Server.CreateObject(ADODB.Recordset");

var str_query = "select * from USERS where username = ' " + text_username +
                " ' and password = ' " + text_password + " ';";

rso.open(str_query, con);
if (rso.eof) then
    response.write "Invalid login."
else
    response.write "Welcome to the database!";
%>
```

by the DBMS. This falsification seems harmless at first glance but it is actually exceptionally vicious. One of the most worrying aspects of the problem is that successful SQL code poisoning is very easy to accomplish, even if the developers of Web applications are aware of this type of attack.

Web programming languages vulnerable to SQL code poisoning attack are the dynamic script languages ASP, ASP.NET, PHP, JSP, CGI, and so forth (Anupam & Mayer, 1998). Imagine for example, the typical user and password entry form of a Web application that appears in Figure 1. When the user provides their credentials, an ASP (Active Server Page) code similar to the one that appears in Figure 2 might undertake the production of the SQL query that will certify the user's identity.

In practice, when the user types a combination of valid login name and password the application will confirm the elements by submitting a relative SQL query in some table *USERS* with two columns: the column *username* and the column *password*. The most important part of the code of Figure 2 is the line:

*str_query = "select * from USERS where username = "*
" + text_username +" ' and password = ' " + text_pass-
word + " ' ";

The query is sent for execution into the database. The values of the variables *text_username* and *text_password* are provided by the user. For example, if the user types:

username: *george*
password: *45dc&vg3*

the SQL query that is produced is the:

*select * from USERS where username = 'george' and password = '45dc&vg3';*

which means that if this pair of *username* and *password* is stored in the table *USERS*, the authentication is successful and the user is inserted in the private area of the Web application. If however the malicious user types in the entry form the following unexpected values:

username: *george*
password: *anything' or '1' = '1'*

then the dynamic SQL query is the:

*select * from USERS where username = 'george' and password = 'anything' or '1' = '1';*

The expression *"1"="1"* is always true for every row in the table, and a true expression connected with *"or"* to another expression will always return true. Therefore, the database returns all the tuples of the table *USERS*. Then, provided that the Web application received, for an answer, certain tuples, it concludes that the user's password is *"anything"* and permits their entry. In the worst case the Web application presents on the screen of the malicious user all the tuples of the table *USERS*, which is to say all the *usernames* with their *passwords*.

If the malicious user knows the whole or part of the login name of a user, they can log on without knowing their *password*, by entering a *username* like in the following form:

username: *' or username = 'admin'; --*
password:

The "--" sequence begins a single-line comment in transact-SQL, so in a Microsoft SQL server environment everything after that point in the query will be ignored. By similar expressions the malicious user can change a user's *password*, drop the *USERS* table, create a new database: they can effectively do anything they can express as an SQL query that the Web application has the privilege of doing, including running arbitrary commands, creating and running DLLs within the DBMS process, shutting down the database server, or sending all the data off to some server out on the Internet.

Poisoning the URL

An SQL code poisoning attack can also be performed by using URL parameters. When a user enters the URL *http://www.mywebapplication.com/products. asp?Pid=158*, an SQL query similar to the following is executed:

select Pname, Pdetails from PRODUCTS where PID = 158

An attacker may abuse the fact that the *PID* parameter is passed to the database without sufficient validation by manipulating the parameter's value to build malicious SQL statements. For example, setting the value *"158 or 1=1"* to the *PID* variable may result in the following URL:

http://www.mywebapplication.com/products. asp?Pid=158%20or%201=1

Each "%20" in the URL represents a URL-encoded space character, so the URL actually looks like this:

http://www.mywebapplication.com/products. asp?Pid=158 or 1=1

The corresponding SQL statement is:

select Pname, Pdetails from PRODUCTS where PID = 158 or 1=1

This condition would always be true and all *Pname* and *Pdetails* products' pairs are returned. The attacker can manipulate the application even further by inserting malicious commands. For example, in the case of Microsoft SQL server, an attacker can request the following URL, targeting the name of the products table:

http://www.mywebapplication.com/products.asp?Pid=15 8%20having%201=1

This would produce the following error in the Web browser:

Column 'PRODUCTS.PID' is invalid in the select list because it is not contained in an aggregate function and there is no GROUP BY clause.
/products.asp, line 22

Now that the attacker knows the name of the products table (*'PRODUCTS'*) they can modify its contents or drop the entire table by calling up the following URL in the browser:

http://www.mywebapplication.com/products.asp?Pid=15 8;%20drop%20table%20PRODUCTS

An attacker may use SQL code poisoning to retrieve data from other tables as well. This can be done using the SQL "*union select*" statement. This statement allows the chaining of the results of two separate SQL *select* queries. For example, an attacker can request the following URL:

http://www.mywebapplication.com/products.asp?Pid=15 8%20union%20select%20number,%20expires_end%20f rom%20CREDITCARDS%20where%20type='visa'

seeking for the execution of the following SQL query:

select Pname, Pdetails from PRODUCTS where PID = '158'
union
select number, expires_end from CREDITCARDS where type='visa';

The result of this query is a table with two columns, containing the results of the first and second queries, respectively.

Advanced SQL Code Poisoning Techniques

Amongst more advanced methods used to gain access to Web powered databases is the method of extracting information using time delays. The basic idea is that the attacker can make the SQL query that the database server is in the process of executing, pause for a measurable length of time in the middle of execution, on the basis of some criteria. The attacker can therefore issue multiple (simultaneous) queries via SQL code poison, through the Web application into the database server and extract information by observing which

queries pause, and which do not. This technique was used in a practical demonstration across the Internet and achieved with a satisfactory degree of reliability a bandwidth of about 1 byte per second (Andrews, Litchfield, Grindlay, & NGS Software, 2003). This technique is a real, practical, but low bandwidth method of extracting information out of the database.

Also, if SQL code poisoning vulnerability is present in a Web application, the attacker has a wealth of possibilities available to them in terms of system-level interaction. The extended stored functions and procedures provide a flexible mechanism for adding functionality to the DBMS. The various built-in extended functions and procedures allow the database server administrator (DBA) to create scripts that interact closely with the operating system. For example, the extended stored procedure *xp_cmdshell* executes operating system commands in the context of Microsoft SQL Server (Cerrudo, 2004; Peikary & Fogie, 2003). These functions can be used by an attacker to perform any administrative task on a machine, including administration of the operating system's active (users) directory, the registry, the Web and data server itself.

Protection from SQL Web Hacking

The great popularity and success of the SQL code poisoning attack is based on the fact that malicious users post the attack against the database by using legal entry forms of the Web application. The simplest solution to counter this attack is to check the user's entry for the existence of single quotes in the strings that they type. As was shown from the examples discussed, the majority of code poisoning attacks require the use of single quotes to terminate an expression. However, in many applications, the developer has to side step the potential use of the apostrophe as a way to get access to the system by performing a string replace on the input given by the user. This is useful for valid reasons, for example, for being able to enter surnames such as "O'Hara" or "M'Donalds." By using simple replace functions such as the ones appearing in Figure 3 which

Figure 3. A simple function that filters and removes all single quotes from the data which have been inserted by the user

```
function escape( input )
        input = replace(input, " ' ", "");
        escape = input;
end function;
```

remove all single quotes (or even convert all single quotes to two single quotes), the chance of an code poisoning attack succeeding is greatly reduced.

As shown earlier in this chapter, certain characters and character sequences such as "*select,*" "*where,*" "*from,*" "*insert,*" "*xp_,*" and "*;*" can be used to perform an SQL code poisoning attack. By removing these characters and character sequences from the user input before building a query (see for example the *validate_string()* function in Figure 4a, we can help reduce the chance of a code poisoning attack even further. So if the attacker runs the query:

select Pname from PRODUCTS where Pid=158; xp_cmd-shell 'format c: /q /yes '; drop database SYSTEM; --

and runs it through a Microsoft SQL Server environment, it would end up looking like this:

Pname PRODUCTS Pid=158 cmdshell "format c: /q /yes " database SYSTEM

which is basically useless, and will return no records from the SQL query. In this method some attention needs to be made to avoid false rejects and thus to reject strings that might seem dangerous but they appear in legitimate input, as for example the word "fromage" (cheese) whose first four characters form the harmful keyword "*from.*" Therefore an additional check whether an input has the correct format can be performed by using regular expressions.

However, while a few troublesome characters can be easily "disallowed," this approach is less than optimal for two reasons: First, a character that is useful to attackers might be missed, and second, there is often more than one way of representing a bad character. For example, an attacker may be able to escape a single quote so that the validation code misses it and passes the escaped quote to the database, which treats it the same way as a normal single quote character. Therefore, a better approach is depicted in Figure 4b where the *validate_password()* function identifies the

Figure 4. Functions that (a) identify and remove all known bad entry that can be inserted by the user or (b) identify the "permitted" characters of their input and gives permission to those characters only

```
function validate_string( input )
        known_bad =  a rray( " select", " insert",
        "update", " delete", " drop", " shutdown",
        "--", " ' " );
        validate_string = true;
        for i  =  l  bound( k  nown_bad )  to
        ubound( known_bad )
                if ( i nstr( 1, i nput, k nown_bad(i),
                vbtextcompare ) <> 0 ) then {
                        validate_string = false;
                        exit function;
                }
end function;
```

(a)

```
function validate_password( input )
        good_password_chars = "abcdefghijkl
        mnopqrstuvwxyzABCDEFGH
        IJKLMNOPQRSTUVWXYZ0123456789
        ~@#$%^*(){}[]<>,.?"
        validate_password = true;
        for i = 1 to len( input ) {
                c = mid( input, i, 1 )
                if ( InStr( good_password_chars, c ) = 0 )
                        then {
                                validate_password = false; }
                        exit function;
                };
end function;
```

(b)

"permitted" characters of the user's entry and gives permission to those characters only. This approach requires more work but ensures a much tighter control on input. A more secure solution would combine the two functions that appear in Figure 4 by investigating for dangerous strings after the filtering for allowable characters. Regardless of which approach will be followed, limiting the permitted length of the user's entry is essential because some SQL code poisoning attacks require a large number of characters.

Also if the Web application needs to accept a query string value for a product ID or the like, a function (such as the *IsNumeric*() function for ASP) is always needed, which checks whether the value is actually numeric. If the value is not numeric, then either an error or redirection of the user to another page is suggested, where they can choose a product. Yet again, always posting the forms with the method attribute set to POST is required, in order to prevent smart users from getting ideas—as they might, if they see form variables tacked onto the end of the URL.

Regarding the connection to the database, one of the practices that have to be avoided is the use of a database account with DBA's privileges. A user with DBA's privileges is allowed to do anything in the DBMS: creating logins and dropping databases are just two possibilities. It is sufficient to say that it is a very bad idea to use the DBA (or any high-privileged account) for application database access. It is much better to create a limited access account and use that instead. This account may run with permitted access to reading the tables of the database only (Breidenbach, 2002).

To further reduce the risk of an SQL code poisoning attack, all technical information from client-delivered error messages has to be removed. Error messages often reveal technical details that can enable an attacker to discover vulnerable entry points. It remains an open question whether the problem with SQL code poisoning attacks is the input or the output provided and one should therefore also filter the output. Also unused stored procedures or triggers or user-defined functions need to be removed.

Finally, the last but not least important security measure is the encryption of sensitive stored information. Even if the attacker somehow managed to break through the defense, the sensitive information in the database needs to remain secret, and thus, encrypted. Candidates for encryption include user personal information, user log-in details, financial information such as credit card details, and so forth.

Software Tool Solutions

One way of checking whether a Web application is vulnerable to SQL code poisoning attacks is with the use of specialized software, which is able to automatically scan the entire Web application for vulnerabilities to SQL code poisoning. This software will indicate which URLs or scripts are vulnerable to SQL code poisoning attack so that the developer can fix the vulnerability easily. Besides SQL code poisoning vulnerabilities, a Web application scanner may also check for cross-site scripting and other Web vulnerabilities.

In order to check if the SQL statement execution is authorized or not, a proxy server is needed to get the SQL statement that is being executed. To check if a SQL statement is allowed, the proxy driver will normalize the SQL statement, and search to determine whether this statement already exists in a ready-sorted

Figure 5. A semi-secure architecture for protection from SQL code poisoning attacks

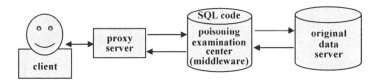

list. If the normalized SQL statement does exist, the SQL execution will be allowed only if the variables are within their expected values. If the normalized SQL statement is not in the permitted list, the system checks against another user supplied list of regular expressions. If the normalized SQL statement does not match any regular expression on this list, the SQL execution will be blocked. This semi-secure architecture is illustrated in Figure 5 and allows the system to handle exceptional cases that might not be compatible with current algorithm of variable normalization. Since system checks against the regular expression list after variable normalization, attackers should not be able to bypass the authorization process. And since most SQL statements do not need to be matched against the regular expression, performance impact should be minimal.

Finally, there are automatic tools that protect from SQL code poisoning by randomizing the SQL statement, creating instances of the language that are unpredictable to the attacker (Boyd & Keromytis, 2004). They also run as proxy servers.

FUTURE TRENDS

There are still a variety of problems to be solved in order to come up with a system that can support the full range of potential applications from SQL code poisoning attacks in a secure fashion. The most notable omission in the list of solutions was an answer to the question of how to support multi-threaded applications. We are not aware of any system tool that has addressed this problem.

Another important improvement is to provide network-based intrusion detection tools (Axelsson, 2000; Wagner & Dean, 2001) with the ability to detect all known types of SQL code poisoning attacks, both at HTTP protocol layer or database connection (Mookhey & Burghate, 2003).

CONCLUSION

SQL code poisoning attacks are a serious concern for Web application developers as they can be used to break into supposedly secure systems and steal, alter, or destroy sensitive data. Unfortunately, the security model used in many Web applications assumes that an SQL query is a trusted command. This enables attackers to exploit SQL queries to circumvent access controls, authentication, and authorization checks. In some instances, SQL queries may also allow access to host operating system level commands.

How to perform the SQL code poisoning attack by using Web applications' forms or URLs and how to prevent it by securing the input provided by the user have been shown. The best way to provide a defense against SQL code poisoning attack is to filter extensively any input that a user may type and "remove everything but the known good data." This will ensure that only what should be entered in the field will be submitted to the server. However, it is not always possible to guard against every type of SQL code poisoning attack. In any case, it is required that the developer be informed of the various types of attacks in order to be able to plan ways to fight them.

Sensitive to SQL code poisoning are the Oracle database, IBM DB2, Microsoft SQL server, MySQL, PostgreSQL to mention but a few database servers. In other words, SQL code poisoning is a real threat and no DBMS is safe from, or invulnerable to this attack.

REFERENCES

Andrews, C., Litchfield, D., Grindlay, B., & NGS Software. (2003). *SQL server security*. McGraw-Hill/Osborne.

Anupam, V., & Mayer, A. (1998). Security of web browser scripting languages: Vulnerabilities, attacks, and remedies. In *Proceedings of the 7th USENIX Security Symposium* (pp. 187-200).

Axelsson, S. (2000). *Intrusion detection systems: A survey and taxonomy* (Tech. Rep. No. 99-15). Chalmers University.

Boyd, S., & Keromytis, A. (2004, June 8-11). SQLrand: Preventing SQL injection attacks. In *Proceedings of the Second Applied Cryptography and Network Security (ACNS) Conference*, Yellow Mountain, China (LNCS 2121, pp. 292-302). Heidelberg, Germany: Springer-Verlag.

Breidenbach, B. (2002). *Guarding your website against SQL injection attacks* (e-book). Apress.

Cerrudo, C. (2004). *Manipulating Microsoft SQL server using SQL injection* (Tech. Rep.). Application Security, Inc.

CERT. (2002). *CERT vulnerability note VU#282403*. Retrieved from http://www.kb.cert.org/vuls/id/282403

Mookhey, K. K., & Burghate, N. (2003). *Detection of SQL injection and cross-site scripting attacks* (Tech. Rep.). Retrieved from http://www.securityfocus.com/infocus/1768

Peikary, C., & Fogie, S. (2003). *Guarding against SQL server attacks: Hacking, cracking and protection techniques* (Tech. Rep.). AirScanner.

Spett, K. (2002). *SQL injection: s your Web application vulnerable?* (Tech. Rep.). SPI Dynamics Inc.

Theriault, M., & Newman, A. (2001). Oracle security handbook. In *Firewalls and oracle*. Osborne/McGraw-Hill.

Wagner, D., & Dean, D. (2001). Intrusion detection via static analysis. In *Proceedings of the IEEE Symposium on Security and Privacy*, Washington, DC (pp. 156-169).

TERMS AND DEFINITIONS

Anomaly Detection: This is the process of using specialized software to examine computer log files and discover information or activity that are out of place, and thus suspicious. It usually seeks only to identify all "known good" behaviours and assumes that everything else is bad. It has the potential to detect attacks of all kinds—including "unknown" attacks on custom code.

Cookie Poisoning: Is the modification of a cookie (which is personal information in a Web user's computer) by an attacker to gain unauthorized information about the user. The attacker may use the information to open new accounts or to gain access to the user's existing Web accounts. To guard against cookie poisoning, Web applications that use them need to protect cookies (through encryption, for example) before they are sent to a user's computer.

CRLF Injection Attack: The term CRLF stands for Carriage Return (CR, ASCII 13 or '\r') Line Feed (LF, ASCII 10 or '\n'). These are ACSII characters which display nothing on screen but are very widely used in Windows to indicate the end of the line. On UNIX systems the end of a line is indicated by the use of the Line Feed only. A CRLF injection attack occurs when a hacker manages to inject CRLF commands into the system. This kind of attack is not a technological security hole in the operating system or server software, but rather it depends on the way that a Web application is developed. Some developers are unaware of this kind of attack and leave open doors when developing Web applications, allowing hackers to inject CRLF commands.

Cross-Site Scripting (or CSS) Attack: Cross-site scripting generally occurs when a dynamic Web page gathers malicious data from a user and displays the input on the page without it being properly validated. The data is usually formatted in the form of a hyperlink, which contains malicious content within it and is distributed over any possible means on the Internet.

Database Administrator (DBA): Is an individual responsible for the planning, implementation, configuration, and administration of DBMSs. The DBA has permission to run any command that may be executed by the DBMS and is ordinarily responsible for maintaining system security, including access by users to the DBMS itself and performing backup and restoration functions.

Database Management System (DBMS): Is a software package used to create and maintain databases. It provides a layer of transparency between the physical data and application programs.

Database Structured Query Language (SQL): Is the standardized query language for accessing, querying, updating, and managing data from a relational DBMS. The original version called SEQUEL (Structured English QUEry Language) was designed by an IBM research center in 1975.

Directory Traversal Attack: Is an HTTP exploit which allows attackers to access restricted directories and execute commands outside of the Web server's root directory. With a system vulnerable to directory traversal attack, an attacker can step out of the root directory and access other parts of the file system. This might give the attacker the ability to view restricted files, or even more dangerous, allow the attacker to execute powerful commands on the Web server which can lead to a full compromise of the system. Depending on how the Web site access is set up, the attacker will execute commands by impersonating themselves as the user which is associated with "the Web application."

Therefore it all depends on what the Web application user has been given access to in the system.

Google Hacking Attack: Google hacking is the term used when a hacker tries to find exploitable targets and sensitive data by using search engines. The Google Hacking Database (GHDB) is a database of queries that identify sensitive data. Although the Google search engine blocks some of the well known Google hacking queries, nothing stops a hacker from crawling a Web application and launching the Google Hacking Database queries directly onto the crawled content. The Google Hacking Database is located at http://johnny.ihackstuff.com/index.php?module=prodreviews

Secrecy; Integrity; and Availability: These are the three most important security services which ensure respectively that (a) sensitive stored information is kept hidden from others; (b) modifications to it are detectable; and, finally, (c) information is accessible and useable upon demand by an authorized person.

SQL Code Poisoning (or SQL Injection) Attack: Is a form of attack on a database-driven Web application that comes from user entry that has not been checked to see whether it is valid. The objective is to poison the database system by running malicious code that will reveal sensitive information or otherwise compromise the server.

Section III
Human Aspects of Cyber Warfare and Cyber Terrorism

All modern activities seem to blend the use of technology, organization and humans. This also applies to cyber warfare and cyber terrorism. Here, the human aspect of information technology is extremely important. Kevin Mitnik, quoted extensively by many of the authors included in this book, has said that the simplest method of breaking into a system is not to use a sophisticated computer application but instead influence the owner of a password to reveal it.

As a result of the proliferation of information technology, more and more information detailing the personal information and activities of individuals is stored in databases. These databases have grown both in the number and in the volume of information stored. It is estimated that the average person living in United States has a personal file in approximately 200 different databases, while in New Zealand this number is around 40. The proliferation of databases has some very serious consequences. As these databases are not often logically connected, there is not an easy means of keeping an individual's records up to date. An individual rarely has any significant influence on the content of information that is being accumulated about their person. In addition, there is also a legitimate concern related to the protection of privacy, as historically these systems have been breached and large amounts of records have been disclosed. The security of these databases and the contents within are rarely comprehensive and enforced. All of this means that privacy protection for electronic records have become illusionary. The views presented in this section cover these issues and include:

Chapter XXII
Electronic Surveillance and Civil Rights

Kevin Curran
University of Ulster, UK

Steven McIntyre
University of Ulster, UK

Hugo Meenan
University of Ulster, UK

Ciaran Heaney
University of Ulster, UK

ABSTRACT

Modern technology is providing unprecedented opportunities for surveillance. Employers can read e-mail, snoop on employee's computer files, and eavesdrop on their calls. Many companies also have cameras monitoring their employees all day. Since employees do not usually have access to their own electronically stored data, they cannot correct inaccurate information. Strangely, this type of information gathering is not illegal even if it is done unbeknownst to an employee. This is because there are no laws regulating electronic surveillance in the private sector workplace. This chapter presents an overview of electronic surveillance and civil liberties.

INTRODUCTION

Employers have a legitimate interest in monitoring work to ensure efficiency and productivity, however electronic surveillance often goes well beyond legitimate management concerns and becomes a tool for spying on employees. In 2002, postal workers in New York City were horrified to discover that management had installed video cameras in the restroom stalls.

Female workers at a large north eastern department store discovered a hidden video camera installed in an empty office that was commonly used as a changing room. Waiters in a large Boston hotel were secretly videotaped dressing and undressing in their locker room. Although in each of these instances the employer claimed it was concerned about theft, no illegal acts were ever uncovered. But the employees were robbed of their dignity and personal privacy (ACLU, 2004).

With the amount of information that is freely available on the Internet, people are becoming more informed of what governments, companies, or corporations are doing. The Internet also provides an open forum where citizens can voice concerns for civil liberties (Arterton, 1989). The Civil Liberties Monitoring Project (CLMP)[1] is an American based organisation whose mission statement is to monitor, document, advocate, and educate about civil rights and human rights abuses by law enforcement and other government agencies. The aim of CLMP, founded by local citizens of Southern Humboldt County, CA, is to encourage public awareness of constitutional rights and encourage involvement of the whole community in preserving and protecting these rights. The European equivalent is StateWatch[2] which monitors civil liberties, security, and intelligence issues.

Modern technologies are providing unprecedented opportunities for surveillance. Employers can read e-mail, look at workers computer files and eavesdrop on phone calls. Many companies also have cameras monitoring their employees all day. Since employees do not usually have access to their own electronically stored data, they can not correct inaccurate information. Although it is often done without an employee's knowledge, this kind of information gathering is almost always legal. This is because there are no laws regulating electronic surveillance in the private sector workplace. Employers have a legitimate interest in monitoring work to ensure efficiency and productivity, however it can be argued that electronic surveillance often goes well beyond legitimate management concerns and becomes a tool for spying on employees. Computer data banks help employers track employees' past employment records, financial status, and medical histories. Although there are laws that prevent an employer from sharing intimate employee information with individuals outside the company, there are few restrictions on an employer's right to share it with people on the inside (ACLU, 2004).

We are living in a digital world and surveillance is very much a part of that. It seems that we have to just get used to it. One of the more intrusive mechanisms at present are speed cameras which pick up and record the vehicle registration numbers of any vehicle traveling too fast along particular stretches of road (Simons & Spafford, 2003). They do however often serve another purpose, and that is to identify vehicles without "road tax." This is done by running the plates against a road tax database.

In a security-conscious world it seems that no activity is off limits to government inspection. Polls show that many people are willing to tolerate increased surveillance, higher encryption standards, and other measures for the sake of security (Ang & Nadarajan, 1996; Barquin, LaPorte, & Weitzner, 1995; Borland & Bowman, 2002). But civil libertarians worry that the increased investigative powers granted since the attacks, and people's eagerness to comply with them, have needlessly entangled innocent citizens and threaten to undermine constitutional rights to privacy and free speech. Even without explicit limitations, some say that fear of reprisal may have a chilling effect on public behaviour. Given the proliferation of log files and massive customer databases, combined with easy access to controversial sites and other information, the Internet has accelerated the debate over electronic information and terrorism (Borland & Bowman, 2002). In the United States, since September 11, an unnamed supermarket chain had given shopping club card records to federal investigators and Lexis/Nexis, (the large database containing news articles, legal filings, and public records of all kinds), says it is working more closely with law enforcement on several fronts since September 11, including "authentication" of individuals' identity (Borland & Bowman, 2002).

In early 2005, Google, to the dismay of many, announced that it had agreed to censor its results in China, adhering to the country's free-speech restrictions in return for better access in the Internet's fastest growing market (Liedtke, 2005). Because of government barriers set up to suppress information, Google's China users have been blocked from using the search engine due to barriers or when they can actually get through to the site—they experience long delays in response time. China already has more than 100 million Web surfers and the audience is expected to swell substantially (Liedtke, 2005).

COMPUTER MONITORING

The Canadian Judicial Council[3] states that:

Computer monitoring involves the use of software to track computer activities. Monitoring may include tracking of network activities and security threats, as well as Internet usage, data entry, e-mail and other computer use by individual users. Monitoring is done by someone other than the user, and may be made known to the user or may be surreptitious. In either case, the user has no control over the monitoring activities and the data that is generated.

Employers want to be sure their employees are doing a good job, but employees do not want intrusive monitoring techniques used throughout the work day. This is the essential conflict of workplace monitoring. New technologies make it possible for employers to monitor many aspects of their employees' jobs, especially on telephones, computer terminals, through electronic and voice mail, and when employees are using the Internet. Most people have some form of Internet access at work and a lot of them have some restrictions put on them. These may come in the form of Internet access control developed from packages that were used to restrict children using PCs at home but this has proved difficult to implement and administer, often preventing employees gaining access to legitimate sites; although they have developed new technology that enables greater administration capabilities to be incorporated into applications. Thus different levels of protection can be implemented for different employees. Even with these developments companies must trust their employees to use the resource properly. Sometimes this trust can be hard to understand. An employee's productivity, the company's security and liability are all affected by an Internet connection. Take for example, some of the figures banded about for the loss of productivity from employees using the Internet during company time. Companies are reported to be losing millions of pounds each year due to employees surfing on the Web during working hours. A recent Chartered Institute of Personnel Development (CIPD)[4] report found that UK companies are losing up to £2.5m each year due to non-work-related surfing. Another report claimed that employees posed more problems to businesses than hackers. Viruses can also be downloaded onto their system by the negligence of their employees. This can happen in a number of different ways. For example an employee may receive a file attachment on a personal e-mail and when they download it they may not realise that it contains a virus which could cost the company millions if it were to stop operations for any length of time depending on the size of the firm. An employee may take work home with them and work on their own PC at home and not realise that they have just brought back a virus that they did not even realise was on their home computer. These examples may be accidental but they still cost a lot of money. E-mail has also made it much easier for information to be passed from one company to another. This in turn makes it much easier for employees to pass information to rival companies since sending attachments by e-mail is easy to do. This kind of action can be catastrophic for a company such as the case of an employee who came across the plans for a new car design and passed them to a rival which lead to the car design being scraped, costing millions. With all these dangers faced by business today people claim that there is no other alternative but to monitor employee's use of computers (Introna, 2000).

Employees however, are given some protection from computer and other forms of electronic monitoring under certain circumstances. Union contracts, for example, may limit the employer's right to monitor. When using the Internet for electronic mail, the employee should assume that these activities are being monitored and are not private. Most people would assume correctly that the company's own e-mail system is being monitored because the employer owns it and is allowed to review it. However many employees wrongly believe that by using Web based e-mail accounts that these are not being monitored. Indeed, messages sent within the company as well as those that are sent from your terminal to another company or received from another company can be subject to monitoring by employers. Several workplace privacy court cases have been decided in the employer's favour for example, Bourke v. Nissan,[5] Smyth v. Pillsbury,[6] and Shoars v. Epson.[7] Technologies to monitor workplaces have become unavoidable facts of life. A survey by the American Management Association in New York found that 77% of major U.S. firms in 2001 recorded and reviewed employee communications and activities on the job—a figure that had doubled in just four years (Immen, 2004). More than one-third of companies surveyed said they do video security surveillance and 15% said they keep tape or digital recordings for review of employee performance. Most of the firms reported they both review and record telephone conversations, voicemail and e-mail messages, and monitor what Web sites employees go to. Many said they also routinely record the time logged onto a computer and the number of keystrokes people make in a day (Immen, 2004).

MONITORING SOFTWARE AND HARDWARE

Keystroke recording software has existed almost since the arrival of the first computers. These programs create a log of all keystrokes typed and store the log file on the computer hard drive. These programs are generally interrupt-driven (from the keyboard interrupt). Thus, it consumes computer time while it reads the keystrokes and writes them to the computer hard drive. Further, the file on the hard drive may be discovered and erased or modified. *WinWhatWhere*[8] was one of the first professional monitoring programs available, and has continued to evolve. It can even be set up to automatically uninstall itself at a predetermined date, possibly preventing detection. Users also have the option of being e-mailed the log files and/or storing them locally on the hard drive. Spectorsoft[9] can record screen images, and play them back similar to a VCR. Some programs can e-mail the keystroke logs to a remote computer.

Antispy programs can detect and remove software keystroke recorders. SpyCop[10] can detect over 300 available keystroke recording programs. SpectorSoft

acknowledges that it is detected by the SpyGuard antispy software. Some antivirus programs are also beginning to attack the software keystroke recorders as well. McAfee antivirus detects some of the popular keystroke recording software. Erasers attempt to cover the tracks of the computer user. Surfsecret Privacy Protector will erase all Internet history, and history from over 30 third-party applications. SpyGuard combines the antispy functions with the eraser functions by both detecting monitoring software and erasing Internet history.

Hardware keystroke recorders contain two main components: a simple microprocessor and nonvolatile memory. The microprocessor handles tasks such as: interpreting keystrokes, checking for the access password, and displaying menu options. The nonvolatile memory is a fairly large sized memory which is used to store the keystrokes. Nonvolatile memory retains data even during a power loss. Hardware keystroke recorders come in two different physical forms. Devices such as 4spycameras[11] keystroke recorders are about the size of an AA battery, and plug in to the back of the computer between the keyboard port and the keyboard cable. The InstaGuard[12] computer security keyboard has the hardware keystroke recorder physically built-in to the keyboard case. In both of these cases, the power to the device is supplied by the keyboard port, so that no additional wiring is necessary. Hardware keystroke recorders require no specialized software on the computer system. They are accessed through a "host program," which can be any word processor or text editor. Hardware keystroke recorders are constantly examining the keystroke stream looking for the access password. As soon the device sees the access password, it temporarily shuts down the keyboard and "types" a menu on the screen. This is perhaps the most novel aspect of the hardware keystroke recorder. This technology allows hardware keystroke recorders to be used without installing any software on the computer system, and allows recording to take place without consuming any CPU cycles. Another technology which has governments scared is Pretty Good Privacy (PGP).[13] PGP allows the encryption of information—including electronic mail—with an encryption algorithm that has, to date, proven to be unbreakable. This software is so strong that the U.S. Department of Defense has formally declared PGP to be a "munition," and has banned PGP's export outside North America. Some believe that a legitimate use for these systems might be when a parent or guardian has a serious worry about what or who their child is viewing or communicating with through the Internet.

GOVERNMENTAL SURVEILLANCE TECHNIQUES

The European Council has taken steps to establish a Europe-wide arrest warrant and a common definition of "terrorist crime." Germany's government has loosened restrictions on phone tapping and the monitoring of e-mail and bank records and freed up once-proscribed communication between the police and the secret services. In June 2002, the UK attempted to introduce regulations under the pretext of antiterrorism that would have mandated almost all local and national government agencies to gain access without warrant to communications traffic data. Australia introduced a terrorist law to intercept e-mail (giving powers to the nation's chief domestic spy agency, the Australian Security Intelligence Organization), creating an offense related to preparing for or planning terrorist acts, and will allow terrorist property to be frozen and seized. New Zealand commenced similar legislation in keeping with the bilateral legal harmonization agreements of the two countries. India also passed its Prevention of Terrorism Ordinance allowing authorities to detain suspects without trial, impose capital punishment in some cases, conduct wiretapping, and seize cash and property from terrorist suspects—despite concerns it would be used to suppress political opponents.

The introduction of compulsory identity cards[14] in Britain has moved a step closer with a plan for "entitlement cards." It is suggested they would be used to clamp down on fraud by checking rights to receive NHS treatment, education, and state benefits. The computerized cards could store a photograph, fin-

gerprints, and personal information including names and addresses. David Blunkett has stated that the main use of the cards would be to demonstrate what entitlement people have to state services and not to identify them. David Blunkett states that "We're not interested in just having another form of ID because people already have a passport or driving licence" (BBC, 2002). It is thought the system could also make it easier for banks to cut down on identity fraud, such as credit card crime or bogus benefit claims, however, Liberty's (a civil liberties organisation) campaigns director Mark Littlewood called on the government to look at alternative ways of tackling identity fraud. Rejecting the idea that people would not be forced into carrying the cards, he said: "If it's going to be necessary to have one to access all types of service it is, for all intents and purposes, compulsory" (BBC, 2002).

Since September 11, 2001, some people it seems have become more prepared to give up civil liberties in order to increase security. Not everyone is convinced that limiting privacy is a good thing. In 2004, U.S. scuba divers found out just how far the long arm of the law can reach since September 11. Federal agents concerned about scuba-related terrorist plans requested the entire database of the Professional Association of Diving Instructors (Borland & Bowman, 2002). Unknown to most of its members, the organisation voluntarily handed over a list of more than 100,000 certified divers worldwide, explaining later that it wanted to avoid an FBI subpoena that would have required far more information to be disclosed.[15] Of late, private databases have found their way into the hands of federal investigators hungry for any scraps of data that might serve as leads in terrorism investigations. Grocery shopping lists, travel records, and information from other public databases have all been caught in the government's antiterrorism net (Borland & Bowman, 2002).

The Federal Bureau of Investigation (FBI) runs an Internet surveillance tool called Carnivore,[16] (or DCS1000) which allows law enforcement agents to intercept and collect e-mail and other electronic communications authorized by a court order. Due to the nature of packet networks it is a lot harder to identify particular target information compared with traditional telephone systems. FBI personnel only receive and see the specified communications address-ing information associated with a particular criminal subject's service, concerned which a particular court order that has been authorized. Recently, according to an FBI press release, the FBI uncovered a plot to break into National Guard armoires and to steal the armaments and explosives necessary to simultane-ously destroy multiple power transmission facilities in the southern U.S. "After introducing a cooperating witness into the inner circle of this domestic terrorist group, it became clear that many of the communica-tions of the group were occurring via e-mail. As the investigation closed, computer evidence disclosed that the group was downloading information about Ricin, the third most deadly toxin in the world. It is easy to understand why people feel uneasy about Carnivore. The installation of Carnivore at ISP facilities is carried out only by FBI technicians and all the traffic on the ISP goes through the surveillance system which can leave it open to unauthorized surveillance. The system is reportedly able to track a lot more information than it needs which anyone with the correct passwords can access. Compared with traditional wire tapping systems were the provider of the service gathers the information that is required by a court order and hands it over to the agency that requests it, the FBI system can by-pass this. This leaves them open to the claim that they break one of the American amendments that prohibits law enforcement agencies from gathering more information than is required although the bureau says that future systems will have audit trails and features to guard against abuse.

PRIVACY RIGHTS ORGANISATIONS

There are those who oppose the invasion of privacy and fight for the rights of victims of Internet abusers. Two of these organisations who oppose privacy invasion are the Privacy Rights Clearinghouse and the Electronic Privacy Information Center (EPIC).

Privacy Rights Clearinghouse[17]

The Privacy Rights Clearinghouse is a nonprofit con-sumer education and research program which educates on controlling personal information by providing practical tips on privacy protection. The majority of people on a daily basis give away information. "Junk mail" is among the top five consumer complaint top-ics each year.

Wireless phones have become very popular in the last few years and the number of people who use them is steadily growing. Although wireless devices have many advantages, privacy is not one of them. Depending on the type of phone being used, other people can listen into conversations. Scanners can zoom in on devices as diverse as baby monitors and walkie-talkies, and can intercept any transmission from emergency and police calls, aircraft, weather reports, and user maintenance reports, among others. Wireless phones that operate on a higher frequency (900MHz to 5.8GHz) are more secure but not im-mune to monitoring. Pager messages are also not immune to monitoring, as networks are generally not encrypted. They transmit in lower frequencies than radio scanners and baby monitors, and so forth, operate on, although messages cannot be deciphered without special equipment attached to the scanner. It is still unclear on whether text messages, or short message services (SMS) from mobile phones can be intercepted (Kamien, 2006).

A person's chance of landing a job or getting promoted may depend on the information revealed in a background check. Background checks can be random as current employees may be asked to submit a check, but they are often asked of a job applicant. For certain areas of employment, screening is com-pulsory, for example, au pairs and teachers need to have a clean record to stand any chance of a job and employers will scour through their employment history to ensure they have no previous history of ill-treatment of children. In short, employers are being cautious, although applicants and current employees may fear that employers will dig through their history for other reasons than the job. The things an employer needs to know about the applicant can vary with the nature of the job. Negligent hiring lawsuits are rising, and if there is an accident the employer can be liable, which is a good reason to be cautious about potential employees (Thuraisingham, 2002).

Electronic Privacy Information Centre

EPIC is a public interest research centre, which focuses public attention on emerging civil liberties issues. In January 2004, their Alert newsletter[18] mentioned an agreement between the U.S. and the EU concerning the disclosure of passenger name records of Europeans travelling to the U.S. The European Parliament criticised this agreement, and urged the European Commission to broker another agreement, which offered genuine privacy guarantees for air passengers. Pending conclusion of this new agreement, the European Parliament's resolution asked European countries to immediately comply with European and domestic data protection laws. The Spanish government put forward a proposal suggesting airlines which operate within Europe would be required to provide passenger data to governments in the EU country of arrival.

In regards to spam, EPIC supports the creation of a Do-Not-E-mail-Registry to prevent spam, which supports enrolment at the domain-level, so that individuals can enjoy whatever benefit it gives without revealing the individuals e-mail address. EPIC also encouraged antispam principles endorsed by a coalition of privacy groups, which urged regulators to adopt a clear definition of spam as unsolicited, bulk, commercial mail, to establish opt-in protections, to establish private rights of action for individuals, to enable technical solutions for spam, to support international antispam co-operation, and to oppose pre-emption of state efforts to curb spam (Danchev, 2005).

EPIC and a coalition of privacy and consumer groups have put pressure on Google to suspend its plans to deploy G-mail,[19] a Web mail system that will scan user's communications in order to target advertisements. This is regarded as an unprecedented invasion into the privacy of communications. The system keeps communications for an extended period of time, causing users to have less privacy protection in their communications. EPIC launched a page on its site on the privacy of diplomats in the aftermath of United Nations Secretary Kofi Annan and other UN officials personal conversations' and telephone communications being bugged by the U.S. National Security Agency and the British Government Communication Headquarters (BBC, 2004).

In January 2003, European governments forced Microsoft to modify Passport—an online authentication system which identifies Internet users and enables the transfer of personal information between various Web sites around the world—in order to protect the privacy rights of computer users in the European Union. It was found that Passport violated several EU data protection rules. In stating this rule meant Microsoft had to make more clear privacy rights under European laws and to collect and process personal data fairer. It also gives users the right to indicate on a site-by-site basis which personal information they wish to disclose. This rule has waited almost 18 months since EPIC and a coalition of privacy and consumer groups initiated a complaint against Microsoft at the Federal Trade Commission in July 2001, which alleged that Passport violated a section of the Federal Trade Commission Act and constituted an "unfair and deceptive trade practice." EPIC provides an extensive range of secure communications tools on its site[20] such as CryptoAnywhere, Ensuredmail, Hushmail, and Mutemail. These tools all basically allow secure e-mail traffic through encrypted connections (Gordon & Loeb, 2005, p. 22).

CONCLUSION

Governments are seeking to control the Internet and monitor computers because of the current threat of terrorism. In the U.S., the Patriot Act[21] has been introduced. This brings into question civil liberties of privacy versus security for a government, employer, or indeed, another individual (McClure, Scambray, & Jurtz, 2003; MOR, 1996).

Indeed, the current trend of information gathering is growing and without proper restrictions, leaving it open to abuses and mishandling. The Freedom of Information Act entitles us to know exactly what information is being held on us by businesses and even the police. There is a very small amount of people who actually know this or who take of advantage of this opportunity. There is always a chance that incorrect information gathered about us is being used in decisions that could affect us adversely in the future. Simon Davies (Davies, 2002) sums this topic up and splits the beliefs of citizens into just two groups. "A sceptic would call this censorship; a patriot would call it cooperation." This is true to a certain extent but it is in everyone's interest to ask the difficult questions of our governments and to preserve our civil liberties today, and for future generations.

REFERENCES

ACLU. (2004). *Privacy in America: Electronic monitoring*. Retrieved 14 May, 2005 from http://archive.aclu.org/library/pbr2.html

Ang, P., & Nadarajan, B. (1996, June). Censorship and the internet: A Singapore perspective. *Communications of the ACM, 39*(6), 7278.

Arterton, C. (1989). Teledemocracy: Can technology protect democracy? In T. Forester (Ed.), *Computers in the human context* (pp. 438450). Cambridge, MA: MIT Press.

Barquin, R., LaPorte, T., & Weitzner, D. (1995, April 28). Democracy in cyberspace. *Presented at the 4th National Computer Ethics Institute Conference*, Washington, DC.

BBC. (2002, February 5). Move towards compulsory ID cards. *BBC News Online*. Retrieved May 25, 2004, from http://news.bbc.co.uk/1/hi/uk_politics/1802847.stm

BBC. (2004, February 27). UN bugging scandal widens. *BBC News*. http://news.bbc.co.uk/2/hi/asia-pacific/3492146.stm

Borland, J., & Bowman, L. (2002, August 27). E-terrorism: Liberty vs. security. *ZDNet.com*. Retrieved 22 May, 2005 from http://zdnet.com.com/2100-1105-955493.html

Danchev, D. (2005, December 19). Cyberterrorism—don't stereotype and it's there! *Mind Streams of Information Security Knowledge blog*. Retrieved 12 May, 2005 from http://ddanchev.blogspot.com/2005/12/cyberterrorism-dont-stereotype-and-its.html

Davies, S. (2002). A year after 9/11: Where are we now? *Communications of the ACM, 45*(9), 35-39.

Gordon, L., & Loeb, M. (2005). *Managing aging cybersecurity resources: A cost-benefit analysis* (1st ed.). McGraw-Hill.

Immen, W. (2004, April 28). Workplace privacy gets day in court. *The Globe and Mail*. Retrieved 12 May, 2005 from http://www.theglobeandmail.com

Introna, L. (2000, December). Workplace surveillance, privacy and Distributive justice. *ACM SIGCAS Computers and Society, CEPE 2000, 30*(4), 33-39.

Kamien, D. (2006). *The McGraw-Hill homeland security handbook*. McGraw-Hill.

Liedtke, M. (2005, January 24). Google agrees to censor results in China. *BREITBART.COM*. Retrieved 12 May, 2005 from http://www.breitbart.com/article.php?id=2006-01-25_D8FBONMG7&show_article=1&cat=breaking

McClure, S., Scambray, J., & Jurtz, G. (2003). *Hacking exposed: Network security secrets and solutions* (4th ed.). Osbourne McGraw-Hill.

MOR. (1996). Ministry of Research. *The global short-circuit and the explosion of information*. Retrieved 15 May, 2005 from http://www.fsk.dk/fsk/publ/info2000-uk/chap01.html

Simons, B., & Spafford, E. H. (2003, March). Inside risks 153. *Communications of the ACM, 46*(3).

Thuraisingham, B. (2002, December). Data mining, national security, privacy and civil liberties. *ACM SIGKDD Explorations Newsletter, 4*(2), 1-5.

TERMS AND DEFINITIONS

Civil Liberties: Civil liberties is the name given to freedoms that completely protect the individual from government. Civil liberties set limits for government so that it cannot abuse its power and interfere with the lives of its citizens.

Eavesdropping: Eavesdropping can also be done over telephone lines (wiretapping), e-mail, instant messaging, and any other method of communication considered private. Messages can be protected against eavesdropping by employing a security service of privacy. This privacy service is implemented by encryption.

Electronic Privacy Information Centre (EPIC): EPIC is a public interest research centre, which focuses public attention on emerging civil liberties issues.

Electronic Surveillance: Electronic Surveillance involves the use of electronic equipment to track an individual's activities.

Keystroke Recording: Programs that create a log of all key presses and store the log file on the computer hard drive. These programs are generally interrupt-driven (from the keyboard interrupt). Thus, it consumes computer time while it reads the keystrokes and writes them to the computer hard drive.

ENDNOTES

1. http://www.civilliberties.org
2. http://www.statewatch.org
3. http://www.cjc-ccm.gc.ca/english/publications/ComputerMonitoringGuidelines.htm
4. http://www.cipd.co.uk/default.cipd
5. http://www.loundy.com/CASES/Bourke_v_Nissan.html
6. http://www.loundy.com/CASES/Smyth_v_Pillsbury.html
7. http://www.law.seattleu.edu/fachome/chonm/Cases/shoars.html
8. http://www.winwhatwhere.com
9. http://www.spectorsoft.com
10. http://www.spycop.com
11. http://www.4spycameras.com
12. http://www.instaguard.com/
13. http://www.pgp.com/
14. http://www.homeoffice.gov.uk/comrace/identitycards/
15. http://www.civilliberties.com
16. http://stopcarnivore.org/
17. http://www.privacyrights.org/
18. http://www.epic.org/alert/
19. https://gmail.google.com
20. http://www.epic.org/privacy/tools.html
21. http://www.lifeandliberty.gov/

Chapter XXIII
Social Engineering

B. Bhagyavati
DeSales University, USA

ABSTRACT

This chapter will present a detailed view of social engineering and why it is important for users to beware of hackers using this technique. What social engineering is, what techniques can be employed by social engineers and what kinds of information can be gathered by these techniques will form the core of the chapter. We will also present case studies of notorious social engineers such as Kevin Mitnick. Different modes of social engineering attacks will be described. Such attacks could occur in person, via the telephone, or via the Internet. An in-depth presentation of the consequences of a successful social engineering attack will be presented. A series of steps users can take in order to avoid becoming a victim of the social engineer are explored, along with examples. We will also present strategies for training employees and users so that there is minimal risk of a successful social engineering attack. Finally, we caution against ignoring the training and awareness program for front-line employees such as secretaries. Since social engineers often try to bypass front-line employees, there is a critical need to train front-liners to recognize and repel such attacks.

INTRODUCTION

Social engineering is the process by which one gets others to do one's wishes. It is the term used to describe techniques and methods used by people who wish to indirectly obtain sensitive information (usually) without having legal access to the information. These people are referred to as social engineers, and they typically induce other people with legitimate access to information to divulge it to them. In political science, the term social engineering refers to a concept that involves methods used by governments or individuals to manage the social behavior of people on a large scale, as in a society (*Wikipedia,* 2006a).

In the realm of computer security, the term social engineering is used to describe the malicious intent of people who are trying to gain access to sensitive data and information through illegal means. The process of obtaining information through social engineering techniques implies a lack of technical skills but places a strong emphasis on social skills. However, a skilled social engineer can spend a lot of time gathering publicly available information about the targeted data and talking to eventual victims before directly requesting access to the desired information.

Harl (1997) says of social engineering: "Like hacking, most of the work is in the preparation, rather than the attempt itself". For example, a social engineer may gain knowledge of an organization's chain of command and hierarchical structure by studying internal documents of the organization through dumpster diving or other means. By means of a telephone call, the social engineer may then determine that the employee's supervisor is out of town and not easily reachable. Finally, the social engineer may pose as a guest of the supervisor and ask a particular employee for sensitive information, knowing that the employee's supervisor is currently not reachable for verification of the social engineer's identity.

BACKGROUND

Human beings manage computers and information systems, and they are vulnerable to social engineering attack techniques. People can be persuaded by skilled social engineers to divulge confidential information even against their better judgment. This weakness is universal among human beings and does not depend on the platform, operating system, hardware, software, or type of equipment that the information system uses. Social engineering is, therefore, a powerful tool in the cyber terrorist's arsenal, and defenders would do well to consider countermeasures against social engineering attacks.

According to Harl (1997), even people who are not considered as part of the security policy may unknowingly contribute to increasing a social engineer's knowledge of the overall organization's policies and procedures; a skilled social engineer can then cause

a security breach and losses to the organization by exploiting such sources that are traditionally outside the security-policy loop. Therefore, training and awareness must be addressed as critical challenges in defending against social engineering attacks. Any human being who has knowledge of the physical and/or electronic set up of the information system should be considered as an attractive target for potential social engineers.

The techniques used by social engineers can vary depending on several factors, such as the response time required, preparation time needed, the circumstances of the attack, the awareness (or lack thereof) among the people who manage the data, and the sensitivity of the information. Social engineering attacks typically use a combination of methods, such as the desire to trust and the helpfulness of the victims; use of publicly available information; informed guesses about or actual knowledge of internal processes; and the use of authority or any other ruse to gain the reluctant victims' cooperation. If social engineers are skilled, they often have the technical knowledge to gain access to part of the system and need other people's knowledge and access for the remainder of the system.

Generally, social engineers use several miniattacks and integrate knowledge gained from these seemingly innocuous requests for information into a large pool of sensitive data and reach their goal of compromising the organization. As Dolan (2004) states, "Social engineering is all about taking advantage of others to gather information and infiltrate an attack". In today's post-Sept. 11, 2001, world, social engineering can be part of a well-orchestrated cyber attack that is timed to cause panic in conjunction with a physical attack on critical infrastructure and facilities, such as utilities, water supplies, and energy systems. The need to be aware of and guard against social engineering tactics is compelling in light of the interconnectivity between current systems.

The *Wikipedia* (2006) encyclopedia defines social engineering as "the practice of obtaining confidential information by manipulation of legitimate users".

Commonly used modes of social engineering are via the telephone or through the Internet, although face-to-face conversations also form part of the social engineer's repertoire of techniques. Social engineering attacks rely on the victim's natural human tendency to trust rather than rigidly following security policies. In general, security professionals agree that human beings are the weakest link in computer and network security; social engineers confirm this fact through their exploits.

EXAMPLES AND CONSEQUENCES OF SOCIAL ENGINEERING ATTACKS

Since the basic goal of social engineering is to gain unauthorized access to systems or sensitive information, it is similar to the goal of hackers, in general. After gaining access or information, the social engineer either uses it in other attacks or disrupts the system to cause damage. Highly organized social engineers may even attack for profit; a cyber terrorist may pay them for access to internal systems and confidential information, or the organization may pay them to educate and train their users on countermeasures. Typically, social engineers target large organizations that collect and store sensitive data. These may include telephone service providers, multinational corporations, financial entities, hospitals, and the military.

Actual examples of successful social engineering exploits are not easy to determine because of the embarrassment and loss of reputation to the organization. It is difficult for a company to detect that a security breach has occurred, due, in part, to a successful social engineering attack. Even if the company detects that an attack has occurred, the potential damage and loss to its reputation hinders public acknowledgment of the breach (Granger, 2001). Beyond embarrassment and damaged reputations, organizations may find that a successful social engineering attack, coupled with another cyber attack, causes substantial financial loss. The loss may be due to stricter enforcement policies in the future, mandated government regulations,

employee training costs, or lawsuits from people whose confidential data may have been breached due to the attack.

In order to trick potential victims, successful social engineers possess excellent communication skills and are resourceful enough to change strategies midstream. They may pose as help desk staff or callers to a help desk, executive-level officials or colleagues in another business unit, network administrators or the chief financial officer of an organization to gain access to sensitive information. They also may induce artificial panic or an emergency situation so that victims do not stop to think about their actions. Social engineers also take advantage of circumstances. For example, if a friendly employee holds the door open, they will walk through; they will pretend to be maintenance technicians or janitors; they will chat up front-line personnel, such as receptionists and secretaries, to gain information about hierarchies; and so on. Kevin Mitnick is generally quoted as a successful example of a social engineer (Mitnick, 2002). He has broken into systems at Motorola, DEC, Sun Microsystems, and Novell.

THE SOCIAL ENGINEER'S METHODOLOGY

Social engineers exploit people's natural tendency to trust other people and cooperate with reasonable-sounding requests for information (*SearchSecurity. com's Definitions: Social Engineering,* 2005). They ask for information or access to data by the most simple and direct methods. Sometimes, they also work to establish trust with small talk, a sympathetic demeanor, and a pleasant manner of speech. Other techniques include gaining little tidbits of information, one at a time, from several people. Successful social engineers have good communication skills and often pick up on hesitation or reluctance on the victim's part; in these cases, they move on and ask someone else, to avoid arousing suspicion. According to Granger (2001), the different methods by which social engineers persuade their victims to part with information are "impersonation, ingratiation, conformity, diffusion of responsibility, and plain old friendliness."

In his book about his exploits, Mitnick outlines how social engineering exploits are almost always easier and far less time-consuming than technical exploits to gain sensitive data. In many cases, he simply asked for the information over the phone by using a plausible tale and identity, and people complied (Mitnick, 2002). Another technique he used was posing as an employee of the same organization as that of the victim and calling to "help" the victim by passing on information about a (fictitious) virus; when the victim was grateful for the "helpful" information, he asked him or her to reset the password and thus obtained control over the information accessible by the victim's organizational profile.

Preparation and research about an organization before contacting an employee often works to the social engineer's advantage, by helping him or her to obtain a list of potential victims who have access to the desired information. Such preparation and research may be performed via dumpster diving or other means. For example, if the social engineer knows, through advance research, that the conference room in the organization has network connectivity to the enterprise network, then gaining physical access to the conference room is all that is needed to secure sensitive information on the organization. Gaining physical access to the conference room can be obtained by requesting e-mail access from the front desk staff person, who is usually unaware of the ease of connecting a wireless sniffer to eavesdrop on the company's network traffic.

To be effective, a social engineer must allay suspicion on the part of victims by displaying familiarity with the company's processes, so the victims let down their guard and believe the social engineer to be who he or she pretends to be. For example, if a social engineer calls an employee and pretends to be one of the help desk staff involved in assisting with password resets, the employee is more likely to cooperate without suspicion, if the social engineer uses organizationally unique jargon during the conversation. If the social engineer is a disgruntled employee, then malicious software installed by this employee before leaving

the company can be activated by an unsuspecting victim through similar means (Kratt, 2004). Some social engineers pose as high-ranking officials in the company, so the victim, intimidated by authority, gives out sensitive information.

Although a successful social engineer does not need advanced technical knowledge to carry out the attack, such knowledge can be used in conjunction with social engineering techniques to amplify the consequences of the attack. For example, a virus can be sent as an e-mail attachment to a victim after gaining trust; then a malicious patch can be installed; user keystrokes can be captured by a key logging device attached surreptitiously to the keyboard; and a fake window can overlay the log in window, so the user's log in credentials can be stolen by the social engineer. Detailed technical knowledge about the organizational infrastructure also may be a goal of the social engineering exploits. For instance, a social engineer may gain valuable chain-of-command information by soliciting the cooperation of different employees. A social engineer may send a virus or Trojan horse as an e-mail attachment so that the employees install them as "patches."

MODES OF ATTACK

A social engineer may employ one or more of the following modes of attack: (1) in person, (2) over the telephone, and (3) via e-mail. Each mode of attack has advantages and limitations, and a successful social engineer may use different modes in the same overall attack. Social engineers also switch modes if they feel that their victims are growing suspicious of their questioning and approach. For example, an employee may be suspicious of strange requests via e-mail, but may be cooperative if the same request was made over the telephone by an authoritative-sounding official high up in the organizational hierarchy. Strangers asking questions of the receptionist may be looked upon with suspicion, but the same receptionist may provide information unsuspectingly when a "network administrator" calls over the telephone and sounds the alarm about a possible virus attack, hence the need to reset the password.

There are pros and cons to an in-person social engineering attack. The victim may suspect that an attack is taking place; the social engineer may not be able to cover tracks as easily as in other modes; and the chances of alerting a higher authority may be greater. On the other hand, a friendly social engineer may be able to persuade a reluctant employee better in person than over the telephone. The most widespread mode of social engineering attack is over the telephone (Granger, 2001). Voice and facts can be disguised easily and caller ID can be spoofed. Help desk personnel are particularly susceptible to this form of attack because they may not suspect a social engineering attack, because they help legitimate employees with their computing problems. E-mail attacks have the advantage of being used to convey malicious code as attachments but may suffer from suspicion by the potential victim because of the impersonal nature of the medium. After having established trust in person or over the telephone, a social engineer may use e-mail advantageously to get employees to install malware.

ANATOMY OF A SOCIAL ENGINEERING EXPLOIT

There are four major phases of a social engineering attack:

1. Preparation phase
2. Pre-attack phase
3. Attack phase
4. Postattack phase

The preparation phase is concerned with gathering information about the organization and determining potential victims. In the pre-attack phase, the social engineer determines the mode of attack and objectives to be achieved. The attack phase consists of the actual interaction with the victim(s) and accomplishing the objectives. The postattack phase is dedicated to controlling the aftermath of the attack and integrating the

objectives into other attacks, which collectively can cause substantial damage to the organization.

In the preparation phase, the social engineer targets an organization and spends some time preparing for the exploit by gathering information about the target. This step can be performed through passive monitoring of the network traffic; reconnaissance of the organization's buildings and people's work schedules; collecting information from publicly available sources, such as the library and the Internet; and tactics, such as dumpster diving. Information about the potential employees to be contacted, their backgrounds, their vacation schedules, their position in the organizational hierarchy, and the likelihood of their cooperation are all components of interest to the social engineer.

The pre-attack phase addresses the mode of the attack and the objectives to be achieved. Gaining physical access to a section of the building (e.g., the server room) or connecting a device to the company's network to observe all traffic remotely in the future (e.g., through a sniffer) are two such objectives.

The next major phase is the actual attack. During this phase, the social engineer may have to revise strategy, depending on circumstances and behavior of the chosen victims. The goal of this phase is to achieve the goals determined in the preparatory phase. If the goal is to achieve physical access to a room, then the social engineer may try different strategies before achieving success. If the goal is to install malicious software, the social engineer may use various approaches, for example, posing as information technology (IT) staff and asking the employee to install the patch, being "helpful" and installing the patch on the employee's machine, and so forth.

The social engineer tries to control the aftermath of the exploit in the postattack phase. This phase involves covering tracks and integrating the information gained with other information. After this phase, the social engineering exploit has been completed, and the attacker can then coordinate with others to mount a combined strategy that will cause severe consequences for the organization. For example, gaining an employee's log in and password information may result in accessing sensitive data behind protected firewalls because the firewalls recognize the legitimacy of the trusted user's credentials. Various types of malware can now be placed deep within the organization's systems to be activated on demand.

SAFEGUARDS AGAINST SOCIAL ENGINEERING ATTACKS

A starting point to defend against social engineering and any other attacks is to have an organization-wide security policy that specifically mentions all forms of common attacks and describes countermeasures. Well-planned security policies and procedures provide a guide for existing and new employees to familiarize themselves with attacks and defenses. Countermeasures should address the physical and human aspects of social engineering attacks. For example, cautioning security guards to not allow access to anyone without employee IDs safeguards against physical access. Training employees on telephone-based social engineering tactics safeguards against the human element inherent in such attacks. Providing a strong rationale for security measures is a sound motivator for employees to practice safe computing policies. Publicizing and enforcing penalties for violations will ensure compliance.

All employees, including full-time and part-time personnel, staff, and contractors, front-line office workers and janitors, security people and others, need to be trained and periodically retrained on awareness and policy issues. Personnel who habitually deal with telephone and e-mail requests from visitors must be made aware of the potential for social engineering attacks targeted toward them. Successful social engineers target these employees because they are nontechnical and have little understanding of all the issues involved. The front-line personnel are also the least invested in the integrity of the data and access to company networks. Other measures include shredding sensitive information and keeping passwords secret, even from purported network administrators over the telephone or via e-mail.

The training program must include information on how social engineers mine publicly available details about an organization from seemingly harmless sources, such as the internal telephone directory, meeting memos, scheduling calendars of executives, unsecured magnetic media, and dumpsters. The training must address common office practices, such as sharing passwords and writing passwords in easily accessible places (e.g., taping them to the monitor, underneath desk drawers, etc.). All employees need to be aware of the potential hazards of trying to be helpful and answering "network administrators'" questions about passwords (U.S. Computer Emergency Response Team (US-CERT), 2004). Frequent refresher courses, in addition to initial orientation to new employees, go a long way in mitigating social engineering attacks. Organizations need to incorporate the signs of a social engineering attack into their training. For instance, intimidation, name-dropping, requesting sensitive information, simulation of an emergency situation, instigation of panic, escalation of circumstances, and so forth are signs of a potential attack.

In addition to education, technical safeguards must be maintained. Sound security principles must be deployed, such as the need-to-know principle, two- or three-factor authentication for critical assets, the principle of least privilege, and nondisclosure of passwords over the telephone or via e-mail (Granger, 2002). Strict password creation and replacement policies, aging and lockout policies, and restrictive administrative and supervisory password standards are critical (Wilson, 2002). Password resets can be done after verifying the identity of the individual by a variety of means, such as the challenge-response mechanisms. Identity confirmation and verification policies at the front desk may help eliminate the social engineer walking in by capitalizing on the door that was opened by some other employee. Periodic vulnerability assessments by external, independent auditors can help an organization maintain the security of its internal systems.

The security and threat implications of ease-of-use application software, such as single sign-on systems and discrete system design approaches, must be considered thoroughly before deciding to deploy such systems. In the interests of usability and user friendliness, these systems might indirectly and unintentionally render assistance to the social engineer (Clear, 2002). Although inconvenient, multiple layers of authentication and a level of paranoia among employees in an organization will help in countering social engineering attacks and hindering the success of the approaches made by social engineers. Also, other components of information, such as maintaining data integrity, are critical to organizations, and these components tend to take priority over social engineering awareness programs.

FUTURE TRENDS AND CONCLUSION

As social engineers work around safeguards, organizations need to continually upgrade their security and employee training so as to minimize the harm and damage caused by such attacks. In the future, as blended threats become common, social engineering should be addressed as part of a larger threat scenario (Gaudin, 2003). Successful social engineers use social engineering exploits to minimize the time needed for other attacks (Barnes, 2004). Another trend in the future is likely to be organized cyber-crime groups that target specific organizations for profit. For example, exhorting money from an organization for withholding a denial of service attack during a high-visibility event could yield handsome profits for organized cyber criminals. Such groups are likely to use a combination of attacks, ranging from social engineering to denial of service attacks and Web site defacement.

Yet another frightening trend is that social engineering attacks will be blended with other cyber and physical attacks. In his book *Black Ice*, Verton (2003) paints a scenario of targeted social engineering attacks against members of a certain organization or government occurring simultaneously with physical attacks, such as bombing utility companies. He highlights the interdependence of such diverse applications as banking, utilities, finance, health care, and entertainment on computer systems and networks. Since digital and physical security will become increasingly intertwined in the future, organizations need to address social engineering threats as part of the overall threat scenario in the digital world that may have serious repercussions in the physical world. In addition, trade offs between security and collaboration, which fosters productivity, seem to be tilted heavily in favor of the latter. Although a level of paranoia helps in minimizing social engineering threats, organizations function well on the basis of mutual trust and minimal restrictions on the free flow of information. Any program tailored to counter social engineering must carefully weigh the benefits associated with awareness against the risks inherent in a trustworthy collaborative environment.

People are the weakest link in organizational security, and social engineers target people's friendliness, trust, sense of cooperation, and willingness to help others. An organization with strict technical security is still vulnerable if employees are not educated about social engineering attacks and how to safeguard against them. It is also easier to secure an organization's systems against social engineering threats than other sophisticated attacks. Granger (2002) provides a table of the areas of common risk within an organization, how social engineers try to exploit those areas, and what strategies work to counteract the social engineers' attacks. All employees, including front-line staff and personnel, such as secretaries, should be trained to recognize a social engineering attack and how to prevent it. Education, awareness, implementation, and enforcement of carefully planned policies provide the best methods of minimizing social engineering attacks. These methods may not eliminate all attacks, but aware employees can become the first line of defense against the tactics of social engineers.

REFERENCES

Barnes, V. (2004). *An hour with Kevin Mitnick, Part 2*. Retrieved May 23, 2007, http://www.enterpriseit-planet.com/security/features/article.php/3337141

Clear, T. (2002). Design and usability in security systems: Daily life as a context of use? *Inroads SIGCSE Bulletin, 34*(4).

Dolan, A. (2004). *Social engineering* (GSEC Option 1 version 1.4b). Retrieved March 1, 2006, from http://sans.org/rr

Gaudin, S. (2003). *Smarter 'blended threats' replacing simple viruses.* Retrieved March 2, 2006, from http://www.winplanet.com/article/2310-.htm

Granger, S. (2001). *Social engineering fundamentals, part I: Hacker tactics.* Retrieved May 23, 2007 from http://www.securityfocus.com/infocus/1527

Granger, S. (2002). *Social engineering fundamentals, part II: Combat strategies.* Retrieved May 23, 2007 from http://www.securityfocus.com/infocus/1533

Harl. (1997). *People hacking: The psychology of social engineering* (text of Harl's talk at Access All Areas III). Retrieved May 23, 2007 from http://packetstormsecurity.nl/docs/social-engineering/aaatalk.html

Kratt, H. (2004). *The inside story: A disgruntled employee gets his revenge.* Retrieved May 23, 2007, from http://sans.org/rr

Mitnick, K. D., Simon, W. L., & Wozniak, S. (2002). *The art of deception: Controlling the human element of security.* John Wiley & Sons.

Ross, S. (2005). *A guide to social engineering* (vol. 1 and 2). Astalavista.

SearchSecurity.com's definitions: Social engineering. (2005). Retrieved May 23, 2007 from http://searchsecurity.techtarget.com/sDefinition/0,290660,sid14_gci531120,00.html

Symantec Internet sescurity threat report, volume IX: March 2006 (Highlights). (2006). Retrieved March 5, 2006, from http://www.symantec.com/enterprise/threatreport/index.jsp

U.S. Computer Emergency Response Team (US-CERT). (2004). Cyber security tip ST04-014: Avoiding social engineering and phishing attacks. Carnegie Mellon University, U.S. Computer Emergency Readiness Team National Cyber Alert System. Retrieved May 23, 2007 from http://www.us-cert.gov/cas/tips/ST04-014.html

Verton, D. (2003). *Black ice: The invisible threat of cyber-terrorism.* McGraw-Hill Osborne.

Webopedia: Trojan horse. (2006). Retrieved May 23, 2007 from http://www.webopedia.com/TERM/T/Trojan_horse.html

Wikipedia. (2007). Social engineering (political science). Retrieved March 6, 2006, from http://en.wikipedia.org/wiki/Social_engineering_(political_science)

Wikipedia. (2007). Social engineering (computer security). Retrieved March 6, 2006, from http://en.wikipedia.org/wiki/Social_engineering_%28computer_security

Wilson, S. (2002). *Combating the lazy user: An examination of various password policies and guidelines.* Retrieved March 1, 2006, http://sans.org/rr

TERMS AND DEFINITIONS

Authentication: This is the act of verifying the identity of a person.

Blended Threat: This attack aims to maximize the gravity of the consequences by combining attack techniques, for example, social engineering combined with a Trojan horse.

Dumpster Diving: A technique adopted by social engineers that involves physically searching through trash in dumpsters in an attempt to retrieve useful information prior to launching a social engineering attack.

Key Logging: A technique of monitoring the keystrokes of a person by using a hardware device to capture the keyboard movements or software to record keystrokes. The hardware or software is pre-programmed to provide a periodic log of user activities to the hacker who installed it.

Malware: Refers to malicious software, such as Trojan horses, sniffers, viruses, and worms, that causes damage to computer systems by eavesdropping, infection, replication, propagation, congestion, and slowdown of the entire network.

Social Engineering: The process and techniques involved in getting people to comply with one's wishes and requests such that one is able to access unauthorized (usually sensitive) information.

Trojan Horse: A malicious program that disguises itself as a safe application. Trojan horses do not replicate themselves, but they are as damaging to a computer system as viruses, which replicate themselves.

Chapter XXIV
Social Engineering

Michael Aiello
Polytechnic University, USA

ABSTRACT

Traditionally, "social engineering" is a term describing "efforts to systematically manage popular attitudes and social behavior on a large scale" (Wikipedia, 2006). In this context, the practice of social engineering is the application of perception management techniques to a large populous. As it relates to terrorism, social engineering is a tool used by terrorists whose actions are intended to cause the loss of confidence in a social institution's ability to protect the security of its citizens and assets.

INTRODUCTION

Traditionally, "social engineering" is a term describing "efforts to systematically manage popular attitudes and social behavior on a large scale" (Wikipedia, 2006). In this context, the practice of social engineering is the application of perception management techniques to a large populous. As it relates to terrorism, social engineering is a tool used by terrorists whose actions are intended to cause the loss of confidence in a social institution's ability to protect the security of its citizens and assets.

In the context of cyber security, social engineering is the process of manipulating individuals to perform actions or reveal privileged information that benefits the engineering party. This is usually accomplished by forming a trust with a victim and later transitioning their psychological state to one which renders them more vulnerable to the attacker's instruction. In the simplest case, an attacker may call an employee of an organization, claim to be a help-desk technician, and ask the user to reveal password information for maintenance purposes. However, social engineering attacks take place over many mediums and are not limited to persuasive phone calls.

SOCIAL ENGINEERING

The practice of social engineering as a method to exploit computer systems was popularized by Mitnick, a cracker turned security professional, describes his techniques in *The Art of Deception* (Mitnick, 2002). Mitnick used these techniques to successfully convince several technology organizations to release proprietary source code, which he then used to exploit systems.

On a large scale, it is difficult to describe the threat of social engineering attacks. This is due to its broad definition, the complexity of the attacks in which social engineering is used, and the general difficulty of producing statistics on "hacking events." However, examples of social engineering vulnerabilities and attacks on government systems have been made public.

1. In a March 15, 2005, U.S. Treasury report, it was shown that out of 100 employees auditors were "able to convince 35 managers and employees to provide their username and to change their password." This figure is "about a 50 percent improvement over the previous test conducted in 2001" (United States Department of Treasury, 2005).

2. In early 2006, after a recent image-handling exploit was released for the Microsoft Windows operating system, attackers attempted to send UK government e-mail addresses malicious software that would enable them "to see classified government passwords." "The attack occurred on the morning of 2 January, before Microsoft's official patch was available. The hackers tried to send e-mails that used a social-engineering technique to lure users into opening an attachment containing the WMF/Setabortproc Trojan" (Espiner, 2006).

Furthermore, Mitnick (2002) claims that "companies that conduct security penetration tests report that their attempts to break into client company computer systems by social engineering methods are nearly 100 percent successful" (p. 245).

TYPES OF SOCIAL ENGINEERING

In *A Proactive Defense to Social Engineering*, Arthurs (2001) breaks social engineering down into two main attack avenues: human based and computer based. In human-based attacks, attackers directly interact with their victims (in person, by phone, via e-mail, snail mail, etc.) and persuade them to comply with their requests. In computer-based attacks, computer systems persuade victims to reveal information or perform actions. E-mail phishing, for example, is a computer-based social engineering attack, where attackers send e-mail messages to victims, claiming to be another trusted entity and direct them to submit their authorization credentials or install software.

THE SOCIAL ENGINEERING PROCESS

Social engineering attacks tend to follow a simple process that contains three broad steps: information gathering, relationship establishment, and social exploitation.

In the information gathering step, the social engineer will mine public intelligence sources for information. This includes organization Web sites, quarterly reports, newsgroup postings, publicly available legal documents, vendor advertisements, and other public descriptions of the people, operations, and systems that the organization houses. The goal of the information gathering step is to heighten the attacker's ability to be able to give the impression that the he or she is part of the victim organization. The successfulness of this step is directly proportional to the amount of publicly availability information pertaining to the victim organization (i.e., acronyms, organizational charts, and other organization specific information).

In the relationship establishment step, social engineers feign a relationship with the victim. The depth and nature of this attempted relationship is dependent on the type of attack. This step can vary from a simple statement in which the attacker claims to be a technician or supervisor, to a complex, long-term guise where the victim feels personally connected to the attacker. The goal of the relationship establishment step is to build a trust with the victim in order to exploit it.

In the social exploitation step, attackers attempt to heighten or minimize one of the victim's psychological arousal in an attempt to progress the victim to react in a premeditated manner. In a phishing e-mail, for example, the attacker may heighten a victim's excitement by claiming that the victim has won a large sum of money. The attacker hopes that the large sum of money will overwhelm the victim and result in compliance with the attacker's demands. In an interactive scenario, once the attacker determines that the victim has altered his or her state, the attacker will ask the victim to perform an action or reveal information that is beneficial to the attacker. If the victim's social state has changed significantly (the victim feels extremely obliged, apathetic, fearful, angered, etc.) the victim will be more likely to comply with the attacker.

PSYCHOLOGICAL TRIGGERS EMPLOYED BY SOCIAL ENGINEERS

In *A Multi-Level Defense against Social Engineering*, Gragg (2003) describes the primary psychological triggers that enable social engineers to "exhibit some kind of power to influence or persuade people." These psychological factors include the following.

Strong Affect

Strong affect is a "heightened emotional state." The notion Gragg (2003) presents is that attackers who are able to elevate the emotional state (anger, joy, anticipation, etc.) of their victims beyond what is generally reasonable, have a better chance of controlling their responses to requests. This is possible because the victims are "less likely to think through the arguments that are being presented" in such heightened emotional states (Gragg, 2003).

In an attack situation, a social engineer may employ this psychological trigger by claiming to be from the human resources department of the organization and by telling the victim that he or she has been terminated for inappropriate computer usage. This will likely bring about strong emotions (strong affect) that may overwhelm the victim's ability to internally validate requests as potentially dangerous or inappropriate. The attacker, upon realizing the victim has transitioned to such a state, may then ask the victim for his or her password for maintenance purposes.

Overloading

Burtner (1991) claims that when an individual is presented with a large amount of information quickly, he or she may transition into a "mentally passive" social state and "absorb information rather than evaluate it" (Burtner, 1991, p. 2). Social engineers may attempt to overload their victims, and, upon realizing that they are overwhelmed, may ask them to perform actions to resolve the fabricated situation. In reality, these actions benefit the social engineer.

As an example, a social engineer may claim to work for a tax auditing service, explain an elaborately complicated tax refund scenario to a victim, and then ask for the victim's social security and bank account information to verify that they have the correct routing information for a large wire transfer. The victim may be overwhelmed trying to interpret the tax benefit they are supposedly entitled to and will give their personal information without attempting to validate the caller's identity.

Reciprocation

"There is a well-recognized rule in social interactions that if someone gives us something or promises us something, we should return the favor" (Gragg, 2003). Social engineers use this reaction to generosity or assistance in order to deceive victims into revealing information or performing actions that benefit the attacker.

Mitnick (2002) outlines a ploy where the attacker disables a victim's Ethernet port. The attacker then calls the victim, explains that he is a help-desk technician who has noticed that the victim has lost Internet connectivity. While on the phone, the attacker restores the victim's connectivity. The attacker then asks the victim to download a "patch" to prevent this problem in the future. In reality, the patch is a Trojan horse prepared by the attacker. The victim feels obliged to assist the technician because the technician, without being asked, assisted the victim.

Deceptive Relationships

In the context of social engineering, a deceptive relationship is a relationship established by an attacker with the purpose of exploiting the victim's developed trust in the attacker. This is usually accomplished by sharing personal information, discussing a common enemy, or pretending to have similar characteristics or interests.

As an example, an attacker may target a local bar near the headquarters of a major defense contractor. The attacker may be able to establish an emotional relationship with one of the employees of the contractor. Once established, the attacker may attempt to elicit proprietary information about research being conducted by the victim or the organization.

Diffusion of Responsibility

"Diffusion of responsibility is when the target is made to feel that he or she will not be held solely responsible for his or her actions" (Gragg, 2003). Attackers use this psychological trigger to coerce victims to carry out actions they would not generally perform under normal circumstances. In an organization, there are often surveys or forms that all employees fill out. Employees do not feel responsible for information revealed in such a manner, particularly if they are convinced that all of their colleagues are releasing this information as well.

Attackers may successfully diffuse responsibility to entities outside of the organization being attacked.

An attacker may send a single employee within an organization a survey promising a cash reward for its completion. The victim believes that many individuals across the industry have received such a survey. The information requested may be proprietary or the URL provided to complete the survey online could contain malware. The victim does not consider the security implications because the victim does not feel uniquely responsible for his or her actions.

Integrity and Consistency

In the context of social engineering, integrity and consistency can be described as social forces that push individuals away from states of chaos and into states where they perceive that their environment is tending towards stability. If a social engineer can give the impression that the victim's environment is deteriorating, then the victim will be more likely to perform actions that bring their environment back to "normal."

A consistency attack may prey on a victim's willingness to help others. In *The Art of Deception* Mitnick (2001) describes an attack where a social engineer learns when a specific employee goes out to lunch and then asks for information from another branch of the organization on behalf of that individual. The attacker claims that this information is critical to that day's business and needs to be handled immediately. The victim is unable to validate the identity of the office mate who the attacker is "assisting," and performs actions believing that he or she is significantly impacting the operation of the organization in a positive way. In reality, these actions have only benefited the attacker.

Authority

"People are conditioned to respond to authority" (Graag, 2003). This is particularly true in military organizations where the integrity of command and control structure is based on the notion of orders being followed. If a social engineer is able to convince a victim that he or she is in an authoritative position or is performing actions on behalf of an individual of authority, then the victim is more likely to comply with the attacker's request.

As an example, a social engineer, impersonating an enraged vice president, may call a new administrative assistant demanding that a specific customer's file be faxed to a certain number. The assistant feels as though he or she is obliged to comply with the request because of its urgency and perceived importance.

DETERMINING SOCIAL ENGINEERING VULNERABILITY

An organization's vulnerability to social engineering can be described in terms of how accessible employees are to external contacts and their awareness to these types of attacks. Occasionally, the goal of a social engineering attack is to simply obtain a list of employee names, positions, and phone numbers. Later this information may be leveraged to perform more attacks. It is, therefore, easier for an attacker to socially engineer an organization that publicly displays its organizational structure, than it is to compromise one where this information is considered proprietary and is kept confidential.

Organizations often perform assessments to determine their susceptibility to social engineering. A commonly accepted assessment is described in the *Open Source Testing Methodology Manual*, which has published a set of personnel testing guidelines and templates (Herzog, 2006). Assessment methods generally involve randomly calling a determined number of individuals from a select demographic within an organization and then attempting a common ruse. Using this method, it may be possible to determine which sections of the organization need additional training exercises in social engineering prevention.

Large organizations are particularly vulnerable to social engineering attacks because the probability of interacting with an unknown person is generally higher. This decreases the likelihood of a victim recognizing an obscure sounding communication as a social engineering attack. Attackers leverage the organization's intended dissociation between personnel during impersonation attacks to achieve their goals. Also, organizations where personnel have been trained to strictly follow commands passed down from higher-ranked personnel may be more vulnerable to authority attacks. This is because individuals may be less likely to question commands and orders coming from those of a higher rank or position.

PREVENTION

A successful social engineering prevention program should be integrated with the overall information security program. This includes creating and enforcing an appropriate communication and computing policy, maintaining a need-to-know environment, orientation training specific to social engineering, and maintaining an active security awareness program. Most prevention frameworks categorize these activities and describe best practices for implementing each.

As an example, Gragg's (2003) model proposes a multilevel approach with security policy at the foundation. This policy should be supplemented by awareness training, resistance training for highly vulnerable personnel, a reminder program, and a defined incident response plan. In addition to these standard information assurance practices applied to social engineering threats, Gragg (2003) describes a "gotcha level" of prevention.

The "gotcha level" is a set of techniques employees should be aware of that assist in the identification of an individual over the phone when they are suspicious of that individual's identity. The first suggested technique is a call-back policy, where individuals request a call-back number before releasing any sensitive information over the phone. The "three question rule" is a set of personal questions previously answered by those with access to private information, which the help desk has access to in order to assist in the validation of an individual. The individual must answer three random questions successfully to achieve access. The "bogus question" is a method anyone in the organization can use to attempt to determine if the caller is being deceiving. A bogus question attempts to elicit a fabricated response from attackers. One example would be to ask a suspicious caller how the brake job went on their vehicle. A normal caller would simply state that he or she did not have a brake job recently or do not own a car at all. However if the caller answers in a casual manner, he or she is clearly attempting to be deceiving. Finally, personnel should be trained to put callers on hold if they feel they are becoming overwhelmed or overly emotional. This will allow them to regroup their thoughts and potentially recognize attacks that may occur.

SOCIAL ENGINEERING AND CYBER WARFARE

In Sun Tzu's classic *The Art of War*, he states, "All warfare is based on deception." It follows, that an understanding of social engineering, the premier deceptive attack method used to attack cyber resources, is critical to engaging in cyber war. Often, it is simpler for an attacker to overtake a cyber resource by convincing a user to open an unscrupulous e-mail attachment entitled "I love you," than it is to defeat firewalls, intrusion detection systems, and other cyber-only defensive tactics. By deceiving users, aggressors are able to trump these sophisticated notification and detection systems to achieve their goal. Examples of these attacks, which can be considered acts of cyber war, include:

1. The 2004 Myfip worm "assumes[d] the guise of an email from a webmaster at eBay. The email asks the recipient to take part in a 'Multiple Item Auction' with the chance of winning a prize" (McArdle, 2004). The worm then gathered and compressed all Adobe portable document, Microsoft Word, Microsoft database and AutoCAD files on the compromised host and sent them to an address in China's Tianjin province. This is an example of a basic phishing attack that deceives the user into believing a trusted entity (in this case eBay) is potentially giving away a free prize. This type of attack is designed to excite or intrigue the victim into executing the attachment.

2. In a 2005 string of targeted phishing attacks against critical British government computer networks, attackers download publicly available government documents off the Internet, load[ed] them with the Trojan horse, and then e-mail[ed] them to carefully selected employees who would be likely to open such a file. To make the notes even more realistic, the e-mail appear[ed] to come from a coworker. (Swartz, 2005)

    In this case, attackers targeted specific groups working on projects of interest to the attacker. The perceived credibility of the e-mail is enhanced by describing and providing documents about a project the victim is familiar with, but the general public is not, and by forging the origin of the e-mail to that of a colleague's address.

3. In 2005, sales employees at Choicepoint, a customer data broker, were socially engineered into selling 145,000 customer records to attackers "posing as businesses seeking information on potential employees and customers. They paid fees of $100 to $200, and provided fake documentation, gaining access to a trove of personal data including addresses, phone numbers, and social security numbers"(Perez, 2005).

FUTURE TRENDS AND CONCLUSION

The significance of this attack method will intensify as technological countermeasures become more sophisticated and are able to successfully thwart cyber-only intrusions. Social engineering is becoming a key component of blended attacks, where attackers employ nontechnical methods to defeat the "outer shell" of an organization and use traditional technical methods once inside.

There are systems in infancy that are being developed that attempt to use prosodic voice features combined with emotional state identification to detect social engineering during phone calls (Haddad, Walter, Ratley, & Smith, 2002). However, their potential is currently limited to assisting a robust social engineering prevention program detect and respond to incidents. In order to successfully thwart social engineering, organizations must develop a secure and aware environment from the ground up.

Social engineering has existed in many forms from the time organizations grew beyond the ability to have each individual in the organization personally know all of the entities that the organization interacted with. These techniques have been and are currently used by terrorists, spies, head hunters, and curious hackers, who attempt to elicit private information from both technological and nontechnological targets. In situations where individuals in an organization have been thoroughly trained to heed to authoritative direction, for example, military institutions, social engineering attacks may be especially effective. Military institutions engaged in a war where cyber resources are at risk should prepare for attacks using this vulnerability. Ultimately, the success of a social engineering endeavor is inversely proportional to the awareness of the personnel in the organization that is being attacked.

REFERENCES

A proactive defense to social engineering. (2001). Wendy Arthurs. Retrieved January 30, 2006, from http://www.sans.org/rr/whitepapers/engineering/511. php

Burtner, W. (1991). Hidden pressures. *Notre Dame Magazine,* 29-32.

Hackers attacked parliament using WMF exploit. (2006). Tom Espiner. Retrieved January 30, 2006, from http://news.zdnet.co.uk/internet/security/0,39020375,39248387,00.htm

A multi-level defense against social engineering. (2003). David Gragg. Retrieved January 30, 2006, from http://www.sans.org/rr/whitepapers/engineering/920.php

Haddad, D., Walter, S., Ratley R., & Smith, M. (2002). *Investigation and evaluation of voice stress analysis technology* (NIJ 193832). Washington, DC: Office of Justice Programs, National Institute of Justice, Department of Justice.

OSSTMM: Open source security testing methodology manual. (2006). Pete Herzog. Retrieved January 30, 2005, from http://www.isecom.org/osstmm/

McArdle, D. (2004). Myfip packing trait worries virus experts. *Electricnews,* Retrieved July 15, 2006, from http://www.electricnews.net/news. html?code=9561560

Mitnick, K. (2002). *The art of deception: Controlling the human element of security.* New York: John Wiley & Sons.

Perez, E. (2005, February 18). Identity theft puts pressure on data sellers. *Wall Street Journal.*

Social engineering. (2006). In *Wikipedia: The free encyclopedia.* Retrieved December 18, 2005, from http://en.wikipedia.org/wiki/Social_engineering

Swartz, N. (2005). Britain warns of Trojan horse computer attacks. *Information Management Journal,* Retrieved July 15, 2006, from http://www.findarticles. com/p/articles/mi_qa3937/is_200509/ai_n15350562

While progress has been made, managers and employees are still susceptible to social engineering techniques (2005). U.S. Department of Treasury. Retrieved December 15, 2005, from http://www.treas.gov/tigta/auditreports/2005reports/200520042fr.html

TERMS AND DEFINITIONS

Deceptive Relationship: This relationship is established by a social engineer with the purpose of exploiting a victim's developed trust in the attacker.

Diffusion of Responsibility: This is a social condition where social engineering victims feel that they will not be held solely responsible for their actions.

Overloading: This refers to a social engineering attack where the attacker quickly presents the victim with a large amount of information in an attempt to overwhelm the victim into a mentally passive state.

Phishing: In this computer-based social engineering attack, attackers send e-mail messages to victims and claim to be a trusted entity. The e-mails attempt to deceive victims into submit their private information to malicious Web sites or install malware.

Reciprocation: This is an instinctual bias towards returning favors, which is leveraged by social engineers to elicit information from victims.

Social Engineering: This is the process of manipulating individuals to perform actions or reveal privileged information that benefits the engineering party.

Social Exploitation: This is the act of heightening or minimizing a social engineering victim's psychological arousal level in an attempt to progress the victim to react in a premeditated manner.

Strong Affect: This means a heightened emotional state.

Chapter XXV
Behavioral Information Security

Isabelle J. Fagnot
Syracuse University, USA

ABSTRACT

The effectiveness of information security can be substantially limited by inappropriate and destructive human behaviors within an organization. As recent critical security incidents have shown, successful insider intrusions induce a fear of repeated disruptive behaviors within organizations, and can be more costly and damaging than outsider threats. Today, employees compose the majority of end-users. The wide variety of information that they handle in a multitude of work and non-work settings brings new challenges to organizations and drives technological and managerial change. Several areas of studies such as behavioral information security, information security governance and social engineering to name a few, have emerged in an attempt to understand the phenomena and suggest countermeasures and responses. This paper starts by defining behavioral information security and provides examples of security behaviors that have an impact on the overall security of an organization. Threats' mitigations are then depicted followed by future trends.

INTRODUCTION

Behavioral information security refers to the study of the human aspect of information security. This aspect of information security has been taken into account only recently. Beforehand, information security referred principally to its mechanical elements–the security status of an organization was only characterized by the quality and accountability of the technical aspect of its information systems. Accordingly, one critical security attribute that organizations tend to neglect is the consequence of human behaviors on the organization's overall information security and assurance. This omission becomes disturbing when an organization needs to collect an increasing amount of customers, clients, patients, and coworkers' sensitive information to operate. The organization is then responsible to insure the sensitive information's security and privacy.

In today's information society, information technology (IT) end user communities mostly consist of employees. This fact increases the amount of human mistakes within organizations. Yet employees' behaviors are still being misguidedly neglected by managers and security analysts. The human factor of information security plays an important role in corporate security status. Today, a vigilant organization should pay close attention to both aspects of security: highly secure technical information systems and well-developed information security policies. If employees have not received proper security training and are unaware of the safeguarding policies and procedures–and if corporate governance is not reinforced–then the security of the information flowing into the organization will be jeopardized (David, 2002). Assuring up-to-date security awareness of employees is essential for optimizing security against threats to an organization. The media coverage of several recent vital security incidents, that caused in some cases the organization at stake to close down, has brought more attention to insider threats (Keeney, Kowalski, Cappelli, Moore, Shimeall, and Rogers, 2005). The cost of such encounters for the victim organizations has been tremendous. Consequently, a new area of corporate governance emerged: information security governance (Conner, Noonan, & Holleyman, 2003) which stresses the fact that security policies and procedures in organizations must be well articulated, adhered to by employees, and regularly reinforced by management.

The purpose of this chapter is twofold: To define behavioral information security illustrated by specific employees' behaviors that might enhance or hinder information security and to examine what countermeasures could help heighten the security status within organizations and mitigate the threat.

BACKGROUND

Information security, particularly its human aspect, is a fairly recent phenomenon of general research interest, and it has been intensifying as information technologies keep developing and corporations routinely depend upon it for their success. The capability of information security, however, is faced with a growing preponderance of vulnerabilities, becoming a source of apprehension in organizations as attacks—whether coming from the outside or the inside—gain in sophistication, incidence, and cause financial loss.

On the one hand, computers' technical security has expanded with computers' growth. On the other hand, it is only for the past decade—coinciding with the exponential growth of the Internet, thus more information circulating and more human beings involved in its flow—that more attention has been devoted to the human factor and to behavioral information security. As more cases of hacking, outside intrusions, data loss, insider threats, time loss, costs, and so forth occur and are made public, research is being undertaken to uncover, explain, and find solutions to counter such harmful behaviors.

At present insider threats are receiving better consideration (Keeney et al., 2005) due to recent acknowledgments that attacks on organizations are more successful when perpetrated from the inside rather than from the outside (Schultz, 2002). The fact that some insider attacks were successful has made organizations more aware of possible recurrences in the same vein. Insider threats may not only be extremely monetarily costly, but also harm an organizations reputation (Ernst & Young, 2002). Consequently, the effectiveness of information security can be substantially limited by inappropriate and destructive human behaviors within the organization. Behavioral information security, then, begins to develop coherent concepts, theory, and research germane to how humans behave in organizations and how that behavior affects information security.

MAIN THRUST OF THE CHAPTER

Behavioral Information Security: Significant Behaviors

Recognizing the human factor of information security, a team of researchers at Syracuse University School of Information Studies conducted, for over three years, a seminal project on the politics, motivation, and ethics of information security in organizations.[1] This research study exemplifies the topic of behavioral information security: excerpts of the analysis are presented in this section corroborating with the literature on information security.

Table 1. Two factor taxonomy of security behaviors (Adapted from Stanton et al., 2005)

Expertise	Intentions	Title	Description
High	Malicious	Intentional destruction	Behavior requires: -Technical expertise -Intention to do harm
Low	Malicious	Detrimental misuse	Behavior requires: -Minimal technical expertise -Intention to do harm
High	Neutral	Dangerous tinkering	Behavior requires: -Technical expertise -No clear intention to do harm
Low	Neutral	Naïve mistakes	Behavior requires: -Minimal technical expertise -No clear intention to do harm
High	Beneficial	Aware assurance	Behavior requires: -Technical expertise -Strong intention to do good
Low	Beneficial	Basic hygiene	Behavior requires: -No technical expertise -Clear intention to protect

Nguyen, Reiher, and Kuenning (2003, p. 1) argued that "while attacks on computers by outside intruders are more publicized, attacks perpetrated by insiders are very common and often more damaging", as well as very costly (D'Arcy, 2005). Being able to identify employees' behaviors that might enhance or hinder organizational security is essential given that today employees tend to be regarded as the weakest link of organizational security (Mitnick & Simon, 2002).

In order to capture some of the behaviors normally exhibited by employees, and to determine if those behaviors were malicious or beneficial, intentional or unintentional, researchers needed to catalogue, characterize, organize, and analyze end user actions. To do so, Stanton, Stam, Mastrangelo, and Jolton (2005) developed "a taxonomy of information security end user behaviors" that summarizes the behaviors that may affect security in an organization.

To enhance understanding of employees' behaviors, the Syracuse Information Systems Evaluation (SISE) project team conducted sociotechnical security assessments in small- and medium-sized organizations of various sectors. The data collected consisted mainly of one-on-one interviews (N = 75) with the aim of capturing employees' perceptions of information security. These interviews were analyzed focusing on two main issues: uncovering employees' behaviors affecting information security and articulating which countermeasures were present or not, which needed revision and/or reinforcement.

Based on its analyses, the SISE team identified factors (such as naïve mistakes) that affect organizational security. One of their findings is that a security threat can occur by lax information security policies, for instance, allowing employees to disable antivirus software thinking it is what slows their computer down. Further, when an organization functions on a trust basis work environment, employees do often share passwords or stick it on their desks (Sasse, Brostoff, & Weirich, 2001; Stam, Guzman, Fagnot, & Stanton, 2005).

From aspects identified through such taxonomy, researchers were able to demonstrate statistically significant differences among categories, and to begin pointing towards clearer understanding of security threats.

Behavioral Information Security: Threats' Mitigation

In order to be able to mitigate threats, one must have the means to identify threats. Schultz (2002, p. 527) provided "a framework for understanding and predicting insider attacks." The author suggested a list of potential indicators of insider threats that are critical to take into account when reflecting on information security. These indicators are as follows: personality traits, verbal behavior, correlated usage patterns, preparatory behavior, meaningful errors, and deliberate markers.

Researchers interested in the human aspect of information security have identified countermeasures to insider threats. Sushma and Dhillon (2006) in their work on information systems security governance reviewed the literature and classified these countermeasures in five categories: proactive security culture, internal control assessment, security policy implementation, individual values and beliefs, and security training. Similarly, Stanton, Yamodo-Fagnot and Stam (2005) claimed that "training and security awareness are key factors in improving the security within organizations." If it is critical to train employees about the technical aspect of their work, it is also crucial to increase their awareness about threats such as social engineering (Mitnick & Simon, 2002): being able, for example, to quickly be wary of a malevolent phone call was an important behavior to categorize with a potential correlative security outcome. In organizations that can allocate a high budget to security,

they can hire an IT security officer to make sure the organizational security status of their organization is up-to-date. Such countermeasures would help to verify policies and procedures related to security, as well as their compliance. Effective security organization, positive security leadership, monitoring of employees' behaviors (D'Arcy, 2005) and a clear designation of user roles and behaviors become beneficial countermeasures to improve security status.

As innovative research gets better at organizing and analyzing effective and ineffective end user behaviors across enterprise types, performance of information security systems may improve by implementing strategic countermeasures sufficiently detailed for real world problems.

In order to capture employees' behaviors a qualitative approach contains richer data than a quantitative approach. However, conducting qualitative sociotechnical security assessments is subject to two factors: Qualitative assessments are more time consuming and costly than quantitative ones. Organizations are often reluctant to revealing too much about their security status. This might be a reason why as Kotulic and Clark (2004) advocated there are few exciting research studies pertaining to the issue.

FUTURE TRENDS

Given the expanding use of technologies and information systems in organizations, it is important to acknowledge more fully the human aspect of information security and to gain insight about employees' behaviors. Doing so will ensure that an optimal level of security is maintained within an organization and that confidentiality of sensitive information is well-managed and assured. The increasing interest among researchers about human behavior surrounding security issues promises that future studies examining these trends will continue.

Investigating employees' behaviors is commonly performed through security assessments. Such assessments usually consist of measuring and interpreting qualitative data often gathered in the form of questions and interviews. Stanton and Fagnot (2006, p. 2) argued that:

Through in depth questioning of the organization's information security professionals, the assessors learn about the organization's information systems architecture, formal security policies, typical security practices, weaknesses in policies and practices, as well as the preparedness of the staff, the supportiveness of management, and the competence of outsource providers.

As new studies are launched, evolving methods of qualitative data analysis will be investigated with a corresponding aim of reducing time and cost to organizations. Also, a recent innovative methodology currently explores an in-depth analysis of the language used by employees to describe their work environment and habits (Fagnot & Stanton, 2006; Stanton & Fagnot, 2006). So a new trend has started inquiring how linguistics may be playing an increasing role in such behavior analyses (Chand & Orgun, 2006; Symonenko, Liddy, Yilmazel, Del Soppo, Brown, & Downey, 2004). Rendering the analysis of security assessments more systematic would help organizations save a significant amount of time and money. Organizations could take necessary measures to improve their overall security status sooner and at a lesser cost.

CONCLUSION

There are two major components necessary to ensure the wellbeing and security of any organization: the excellence of its information technologies and appropriate employees' behaviors. Managers play a vital role in exploiting these components. They need to be even more cognizant of behavioral issues relevant to information security and pay closer attention to the critical role every employee plays in the protection of information.

Human behaviors are complex, thus necessitate constant and ever deeper understanding on how these behaviors may impact the information security within an organization. Behavioral information security can help organizations have a clearer grasp of employees' behaviors and decrease threats (both internal and external) that a company is subject to nowadays. There exist measures whose implementation would assist managers push the development of specific training and awareness programs to augment information security in organizations. If managers are provided with the means to optimize behavior information principles so that security policies are reinforced, then the security status of an organization may indeed become more secure.

REFERENCES

Chand, V., & Orgun, C. O. (2006). Exploiting linguistic features in lexical steganography: Design and proof-of-concept implementation. *Proceedings of the 39th Annual Hawaii International Conference on System Sciences (HICSS)*.

Conner, B., Noonan, T. & Holleyman, R.W., II. (2003). *Information security governance: Toward a framework for action.* Business Software Alliance.

D'Arcy, J. (2005). *Improving IS security through procedural and technical countermeasures: An analysis of organizational security measures* (Research report). Temple University, Irwin L. Gross e-business Institute.

David, J. (2002). Policy enforcement in the workplace. *Computers and Security, 21*(6), 506513.

Ernst and Young LLP. (2002). *Global information security survey.* Presentation Services.

Fagnot, I. J., & Stanton, J. M. (2006). Using security assessment interviews to predict organizational security status. *The Security Conference,* Las Vegas, NV.

Keeney, M.M., Kowalski, E.F., Cappelli, D.M., Moore, A.P., Shimeall, T.J., and Rogers, S.N. (2005). Insider hreat study: Computer system sabotage in critical infrastructure sectors. *National Threat Assessment Center, United States Secret Service; CERT® Pro-*

gram, Software Engineering Institute, Carnegie-Mellon University.

Kotulic, A. G., & Clark, G. J. (2004). Why there aren't more information security research studies. *Information & Management, 41,* 597-607.

Mitnick, K. D.,& Simon, W. L. (2002). *The art of deception: Controlling the human element of security.* Indianapolis, IN: Wiley

Nguyen, N., Reiher, P., & Kuenning, G. H. (2003). Detecting insider threats by monitoring system call activity. *Proceedings of the 2003 IEEE Workshop on Information Assurance.*

Sasse, M. A., Brostoff, S., & Weirich, D. (2001). Transforming the "weakest link": A human/computer interaction approach to usable and effective security. *BT Technology Journal, 19*(3), 122-131.

Schultz, E. E. (2002). A framework for understanding and predicting insider attacks. *Computers and Security, 21*(6), 526-531.

Stam, K., Guzman, I., Fagnot, I., & Stanton, J. (2005). *What's your password? The experience of fieldworkers using ethnographic methods to study information technology in work organizations.* Paper presented at the 2005 American Anthropological Association Annual Meetings, Washington, DC.

Stanton, J. & Fagnot, I. (2006). Extracting useful information from security assessment interviews. *Proceedings of the 39th Annual Hawaii International Conference on System Sciences (HICSS).*

Stanton, J. M., Stam, K. R., Mastrangelo, P., & Jolton, J. (2005). An analysis of end user security behaviors. *Computers and Security, 24,* 124-133.

Stanton, J. M., Yamodo-Fagnot, I., & Stam, K. R. (2005). The madness of crowds: Employees beliefs about information security in relation to security outcomes. *The Security Conference,* Las Vegas, NV.

Sushma, M., & Dhillon, G. (2006). information systems security governance research: A behavioral perspective. *NYS Cyber Security Conference (NYS CSIS),* Albany, NY.

Symonenko, S., Liddy, E. D., Yilmazel, O., Del Soppo, R., Brown, E., & Downey, M. (2004). *Semantic analysis for monitoring insider threats.* Presented at The Second NSF/NIJ Symposium on Intelligence and Security Informatics (ISI). Tucson, AZ.

TERMS AND DEFINITIONS

Behavioral Information Security: An aspect of information security dealing with the human behaviors that affect overall organization security.

Human Factor: The mere fact that human beings can potentially make mistakes that might affect a given situation.

Information Security: Term that refers to the assurance of the security of not only information systems but of all aspects of protection for all kinds of information.

Information Security Governance: Aspect of corporate governance which stresses the fact that security policies and procedures in organizations must be well articulated, adhered to by employees, and regularly reinforced by management.

Information Technology Security Officer: A person responsible in an organization to verify policies and procedures related to security as well as the organization's compliance of information technologies security.

Insider Threat: Intentionally disruptive, unethical, or illegal behavior enacted by individuals who possess substantial internal access to the organization's information assets (Stanton et al., 2005, p. 2)

Organizational Security: Term that encompasses all the aspects of security an organization must be aware of: technical and behavioral security.

Security Policy: Term that includes all the rules, laws, procedures, and practices that an organization is subject to in order to maintain confidentiality and security of information.

Sensitive Information: A term that refers in the security context to private information such as social security number, date of birth, medical and financial information, and any other kind of personal information that should remain confidential.

Social engineering: The act of manipulating IT ends users to obtain sensitive information. It is usually conducted over the phone and involves several end users so that none of them suspect the malicious intent.

ENDNOTE

[1]   Syracuse Information Systems Evaluation (SISE) project: http://sise.syr.edu Director: J. M. Stanton, Associate Director: K. R. Stam and Assistant Director: I. J. Fagnot.

Chapter XXVI
Toward a Deeper Understanding of Personnel Anomaly Detection

Shuyuan Mary Ho
Syracuse University, USA

ABSTRACT

Recent threats to prominent organizations have greatly increased social awareness of the need for information security. Many measures have been designed and developed to guard against threats from outsider attacks. Technologies are commonly implemented to actively prohibit unauthorized connection and/or limit access to corporate internal resources; however, threats from insiders are even more subtle and complex. Personnel whom are inherently trusted have valuable internal corporate knowledge that could impact profits or organizational integrity. They are often a source of potential threat within the corporation, through leaking or damaging confidential and sensitive information—whether intentionally or unintentionally. Identifying and detecting anomalous personnel behavior and potential threats are concomitantly important. It can be done by observation and evaluation of communicated intentions and behavioral outcomes of the employee over time. While human observations are subject to fallibility and systems statistics are subject to false positives, personnel anomaly detection correlates observations on the change of personnel trustworthiness to provide for both corporate security and individual privacy. In this paper, insider threats are identified as one of the significant problems to corporate security. Some insightful discussions of personnel anomaly detection are provided, from both a social and a systems perspective.

ABSTRACT

Recent threats to prominent organizations have greatly increased social awareness of information security. Many countermeasures have been designed and developed to guard against threats from outsider attacks.

Technologies are commonly implemented that will actively prohibit rogue connections or limit access to corporate internal resources; however, threats from insiders are even more subtle and complex. Personnel who also are trusted corporate assets generally have valuable internal corporate knowledge that could impact profits. They are often the source of potential threats within the corporation, through leaking or damaging confidential and sensitive information—whether intentionally or unintentionally. Identifying and detecting anomalous personnel behavior and potential threats are concomitantly important. In this chapter, insider threats are identified as one of the significant problems in corporate security. Some insightful discussions of personnel anomaly detection are provided, from both a social and a systems perspective.

INTRODUCTION

The concept of information security and privacy have been discussed and researched in many disciplines. In the realm of political science, corporate ethics, secrecy, and sensitive information like the trade secrets, market competitive intelligence, and intellectual property are rigorously discussed. Corporate security policy that governs the principles of protecting corporate assets is therefore in place (Stevenson, 1980; Swann & Gill, 1993). Government surveillance of citizens for the sake of the national security has been a critical issue discussed throughout decades. George Orwell identified this issue in the book *Nineteen Eighty-Four*:

In the past, no government had the power to keep its citizens under constant surveillance. The invention of print, however, made it easier to manipulate public opinion, and the film and the radio carried the process further. With the development of television, and the technical advance which made it possible to receive and transmit simultaneously on the same instrument, private life came to an end. (Orwell, 1949, pp. 206-207)

Events surrounding the domestic surveillance scandal by the Bush administration (Associated Press, 2005) evolved as a result of expanding surveillance of terrorism activities into the lives of American citizens. The need for national security has begun to overshadow citizen's right to privacy. This principle applies to corporate governance as well. While gov-

ernment or corporate surveillance has terminated the freedom of personal privacy, the emphasis on personal privacy, however, would lead to a black box of human interactions within a corporate domain and, as a result, would threaten corporate, government, and national security. It becomes vitally important to balance individual privacy with surveillance interests governed by corporate security. How much security is necessary to protect corporate security interests, and how does this impact individual privacy? These questions are indeed a challenge today.

BACKGROUND

There have been ongoing discussions on the protection of business intelligence in order to remain competitive. Solutions in the social context can be found in business strategy, policy decisions, management processes, and in operational production. Social scientists have offered different aspects and findings in providing information assurance and security. Critical theory has been discussed and extensively applied in assessing management communication and interaction, accounting and information systems, as well as marketing and strategic management (Alvesson & Willmott, 1996). Social cognition has discussed the role of affect in cognitive-dissonance processes (Forgas, 2001). Whether a disgruntled employee could cause significant harm to corporate information security, how early such a negative impact could be detected, and how much change there would be on the trust level of an employee, and so forth are all critical issues to be studied. Furthermore, whether "the dark side of man" (Ghiglieri, 1999) would betray and change a person's trustworthiness after she or he has obtained high security clearance remains an issue. Incidents of such have been found on many occasions. Jonathan Pollard, for example, who had high-level security clearance, was arrested in 1985 for passing classified U.S. information, such as satellite photographs and weapon systems data, to Israelis (Noe, 2007; Haydon, 1999).

Not only do security incidents occurring in the last decade provide social context, many of them are systematic and technical. They range from physical facility break down, illegal network/system penetration and Internet transaction counterfeiting activity, to unauthorized modification or divulgence of confidential information. These incidents have raised the awareness of researchers and scientists to further investigate technical and systematic solutions for providing layered defense (Park & Ho, 2004). Such awareness prompts us not only to identify vulnerabilities and threats in existing physical infrastructure, policy, operational procedure, personnel trustworthiness, and technology, but also to investigate countermeasures and defense strategy in safeguarding both tangible and intangible assets. Many threats from malicious external hackers/crackers can be detected and prevented by both active and passive instruments[1], however, threats from malicious personnel are generally subtle and complex (Keeney et al., 2005). The complexity and difficulty of identifying internal threats lies in the question of how much information and how much authority to entrust to those handling top secrets. The more knowledge a particular person has about internal resources, the greater the potential threat from that person. Because being able to verify the trustworthiness of specific personnel becomes increasingly critical, an extensible research dimension has been created in the area of personnel security.

Since critical information can be misused and the network can be spoofed by either outsiders or insiders, digital security[2] is implemented to prevent, detect, and protect corporate information assets. The systematic research perspective normally focuses on aggregating audit logs from selected resources (such as database, applications, and network devices) and builds individual uses behavioral profiles through natural language processing (DelZoppo et al., 2004; Symonenko et al., 2004), text mining, and information extraction techniques. The goal is to identify anomalies when compared to normalized behavior patterns. In addition to digital security, cognitive mapping techniques can be adopted to study personnel trustworthiness, construct normal behavior profiles in the social context, as well as define and apply security policy and identify anomalies against the normal behavioral patterns. Correlations of the findings from both the social and systematic aspects of the normal behavior profile and discovering the monitoring mechanisms for anomaly detection[3] is a critical research area in personnel security. The personnel activities between social and digital levels can be analyzed and correlated to discover anomalous activities initiated by malicious insiders.

PERSONNEL PROBLEMS IN CORPORATE SECURITY

Information convenience/availability and information security are fundamentally two different user needs that contradict one another. Before we can say that the information security for a Web site is sustainable, it is necessary to submit to an attack/defense mechanism (such as the penetration test). In fact, this is the same for personnel management. For example, individuals sometimes do not follow security instructions well. What is more, personnel policies generally do not highlight information security; and employees' concepts of information security might be outdated. In a case of implementation, senior officers sometimes add their personal (and nontechnical) opinions to the info-sec solutions implemented at a site, which may endanger overall security. This is one of the most critical issues we face today. As a result, how to make a site truly secure is really a difficult question. The "penetration practice" tests security by having security professionals ("white hats") try to penetrate and test the site while assuring accessibility to the site. If the site is able to sustain the penetration test of attack/defend practices, the security mechanism for the site would fall within the tolerance scope. It is appropriate to state that the site is secured from outside threats.

When dedicated personnel are in charge of managing information security issues for defense, security can be considered intact. But many times, incidents are caused by personnel who work on administrative computers. For example, specific procedures need to be conveyed to remote personnel on correct access procedures, so that they understand the security access requirements. Even when access procedures are as simple as "common sense," it is still necessary to convey these "common sense" procedures to personnel who live abroad to secure their remote access. While end users, including data entry administrators, always want the convenience of easy access, they might accidentally enable Internet availability on a computer that connects directly to the internal network. Not having a reinforced physical separation in the network will make it vulnerable to threats and risks to the internal information assets and the network. While the invention of the Internet has brought much more convenience to our lives, such as the "digital library" provided through the Internet infrastructure, the convenience of the Internet has actually created a greater threat to our internal networks. What we need to have is layered security that examines all the layered devices involved.

"Rank" is a problem sometimes in the military settings. Highly ranked officers might be exempt from the tedious administrative checking, or may not follow the administrative procedures that the security policy requires. The issue of highly ranked privileges in the military is much more difficult to deal with than issues of corporate security in organizations because of different cultures and disciplines. The "ranking" and "self-awareness" go hand-in-hand when considering security mechanisms.

The ranking issue can add to the potential for insider threats. A common practice in the military is that rank should not get in the way, if there is a security concern. However, there might be incidents where a higher authority would refuse and bounce back regular inspection and security auditing with excuses of classified information. This causes some difficulties for investigation and gathering evidence. Some mobile devices used for convenience (such as the floppy drives, memory sticks, or mp3 devices) can be used as tools for transferring sensitive information. The policy of restricting mobile devices within corporate or defense settings for outside visitors are not generally applied to employees and internal personnel across different departments. From the inspection perspective of a building's information security mechanism, the proper way is to treat everyone equally; no individuals with higher ranks or elevated position should have privileges or exemption from security inspection.

A higher authority may often request classified information without proper authorization. Access control of who accesses what resources and authentication of proper personnel to process classified information are very important mechanisms. In addition to proper authorization, the increase in administrative work often causes the application for obtaining information to be opted out of regular access control mechanisms.

SOCIAL ASPECTS OF TRUSTWORTHINESS ASSESSMENT

Personnel trustworthiness can be considered at two levels: current status and also through a background check. Both include investigation into physical access, circles of friends, and personal and private life, at present time and in the past. Those who might want to steal and/or sell critical information are generally those who want to make a personal profit.

Although personnel security auditing is currently in practice, it is still difficult for either the auditor or the superior to understand personnel trustworthiness through interviewing or conversation. Bound by the culture, it may not be a common practice to report your peers or colleagues for little incidents. However, it is generally believed that "one would know what colleagues at neighboring desks are doing."

A person's financial, disciplinary, and job-related incidents also can serve as indicators in measuring trust level. Most importantly, a person's financial stability and statement, revenue fluctuation over time, and property report and property declaration from a bank can say a lot. However, debt needs to be specifically investigated, and generally most banks will not disclose a person's private debt information.

Physical monitoring through access control system logs can identify physical access activities when a person uses a personal identification card (PID) to access a physical facility. The same identification card that is used to trace physical access logs also could be use to log access activities on files, information, or the database. A critical vulnerability occurs when all the events are monitored and logged, but not analyzed. The camera monitor, for example, requires a person sitting behind the monitor to analyze observed activities. Likewise, a network infrastructure based on host-based intruder alerts that has logged massive events is highly vulnerable without an effective mechanism to analyze aggregated events. If suspicious activity is not immediately identified, it might be ignored. Activities that appear to be normal, but might intrinsically serve as possible forensic evidence in the future, might be deleted after a short period of time. The files in the database or on the videotapes might have been deleted, if such activities did not raise suspicions in the first place.

Since management structure tends to be flat and simplified in a computerized environment, layoffs may cause an insufficient number of personnel to scrutinize log files or to monitor telecommunication/information security. Although it may not involve physical acts, the possibility of information warfare exists in every wired and wireless environment. Keeping sufficient staff to manage information security is critical to the integrity of the system.

It is "rarely possible" to detect changes in a person's trust level. From the security standpoint, it is appropriate to be suspicious of everyone in the organization. From the administration decision-making perspective, the trust in those who handle top-secret information has to be set high—with absolute trust. His or her loyalty to the company and trust level should be without question. However, in the event of investigating those who handle top secrets, the investigation process should be executed and conducted without mercy.

Do people really pay close attention to the loyalty of those who handle sensitive, confidential, or even top-secret files and information? Although supervisory authority usually takes the time to check to see if business negotiations have been adequately reported by subordinates, they often neglect to understand other significant aspects about subordinate activity. It is difficult to detect changes in a person's trust level. To detect changes in a person's trust level would require direct and close supervision and also indirect monitoring through the security auditor. Regular security "auditing" and emergency-response "investigation" ought to be designed into management operational procedures.

Whether monitoring personnel activities is appropriate or not is still under debate. Monitoring personal information will always conflict with personal privacy. Auditing and investigating a person's social circles of friends and their financial stability through personal honest declaration does not violate privacy boundaries, since this is a regular part of a background check. However, to monitor and log individual's online transactions, such as stock purchasing and so forth, is a very sensitive issue that relates to personal privacy. The law declares that it protects all citizens' right of privacy. It is possible to monitor a person's financial activities through the current technology, such as the network infrastructure, satellite system, and a sensor chip built in a person's physics or belongings, but it may seriously violate the citizen's right to privacy. This is especially true in national security defense interests. How to find a balance in between these two requirements is an ongoing debate. It might be necessary to wait until an incident happens for the "law" to permit investigation and gathering of evidence through advanced science and technology.

The background check can be conducted through filing forms; however, the honesty and integrity check of such filings is another question. The concepts of prolonged observation can give a more appropriate understanding of a person's life transitions, from school life and career change, to special events. The longer a person is observed, the more accurate observation and understanding is possible for that person. In addition, requesting a recommendation letter is a demonstration of a person's past social relationships and offers a good way to understand a person's background.

DIGITAL ASPECTS OF TRUSTWORTHINESS ASSESSMENT

Smart identification (ID) card usage is a practical identification mechanism that logs access activities of all personnel in a facility. However, one drawback is that the employees can interchange their personal ID cards. This practice of using only one's own identification must be mandated and controlled by security policy at the personnel level. In addition, fingerprint, palm-reading, pulse measuring, or body-heat sensing technology can be used as effective (though expensive) identity authentication mechanisms. Moreover, it is an appropriate practice that photos/images are required for access to a facility or a system. Such identity-based image processing could work simultaneously with an access control mechanism, and access logs can be generated for the purpose of forensics.

While access activities can be logged, the content and purpose of the activities may still not be detected or cannot be analyzed. While it is not impossible to analyze the content of the access objects, it is not extensively practiced. Many content analysis techniques, such as data mining and natural language processing, can be utilized to analyze the content of access activities. Communication content of e-mails and instant messages also can be analyzed by social network analysis technique (Natarajan & Hossain, 2004).

It is normally hard to detect malicious intent when a person regularly accesses certain files. It is possible that this person might take the opportunity to obtain other files of the same or higher level, and transfer them out to the hands of others. These personnel would hide malicious intent behind regular assignments. In Gilad's competitive early warning (CEW) triangle, he identified three interlocking steps that would help an organization in refining corporate strategies and countermeasures to respond to early warnings of risk. In the framework of CEW, risks are first identified, which become indicators for intelligence monitoring. After monitoring, alerts may be generated for the corporate management to take action. The feedback of the actions is sent to the risk identifier to form further

detection decision (Gilad, 2004). To detect abnormal behavior, a computer system generally would set a baseline, profile normal behavior, and detect outliers. However, this would be a hard practice if the function and nature of a personnel's job fluctuates too much. It sometimes is hard to "patternize" the behaviors of someone like a salesperson or a researcher who have irregular access to databases or systems.

CONTENT-BASED PERSONNEL ANOMALY DETECTION

Generally, intrusion detection system (IDS) technologies are classified into misuse detection and anomaly detection (Lee & Stolfo, 2000; Michael & Ghosh, 2002); however, most of the recent studies have been focused on program- and system-based IDS (Burgess et al., 2002; Michael & Ghosh, 2002), and network-based IDS (Huang & Lee, 2003; Lee & Stolfo 2000; Zhang & Lee, 2000; Zhang, Lee, & Huang, 2003). Content-based semantic anomaly detection (Berger, Della Pietra, & Della Pietra, 1996; DelZoppo et al., 2004; Raz, Koopman, & Shaw, 2002b; Symonenko et al., 2004) would adopt either a natural language processing or a data mining technique (Teoh, Zhang, Tseng, Ma, & Wu, 2004) to semantically detect anomalies from data sources, such as e-mail or a database. The correlation mechanism between digital and social activities in the context of personnel anomaly detection in an organization is significant for personnel security. In order to detect personnel anomalous activities, personnel social activities, such as financial activities and physical facility access logs, are believed to be important sources of data for pattern identification and detection evaluation. Digital activities, such as database and application access by personnel, are also important sources of data for pattern identification and detection evaluation.

In the research of personnel anomaly detection, identifying criteria of personnel security in social and systematic context as well as how anomalies can be effectively analyzed and detected from aggregative atomic events is critical. Specifically, it can be subcategorized into two angles when looking at the personnel trustworthiness assessment.

1. **Social context:** Some indications, such as personnel physical building access activities, financial stability, emotional stability, and disciplinary and incident-based measures, must be taken into account in the social context of the assessment.
2. **Systematic context:** In the systematic context, audit trail, system logs, e-mail and instant messages, corporate scheduling, and so forth are point-based data that we can gather to analyze the electronic communication interactions among employees.

Further content analysis and social network analysis can be done digitally to further identify clues of the anomalous behavior. Employee behavior profiles and patterns can be identified through various available technologies. After normal profiles have been generalized, abnormal behavior or outliers can be identified through correlation analysis.

CONCLUSION

Personnel anomaly detection involves a strategic understanding of interactions among people, technology, policy, and organizations through the lens of corporate security. It establishes a baseline model, and profiles normal user behavior for individuals who have authorized access to an organization's internal and external resources, including accessibility to systems, networks, applications, and facilities. Personnel anomaly detection seeks to identify the communication and coordination patterns among employees in organizations, to detect behavior that is peculiar, while suggesting that a possible insider threat could come from specific perpetrator(s), as a result of a series of suspicious or eccentric events.

Both social- and system-related assessments of employee trustworthiness are important factors in the mechanisms of personnel anomaly detection. With

consistent utilization, these factors can definitely provide an indication of when a person's activities are suspicious and worth further investigation. Technology convergence and correlation analysis research will continue to clarify the parameters necessary to help detect personnel anomalies and to identify potential insider threats before they become serious breaches to organizations.

ACKNOWLEDGMENT

The author currently conducts research on personnel anomaly detection for countering insider threats and coordinated defense at School of Information Studies, Syracuse University. In 2004, the author participated in a SRC-SU joint research project called Countering Insider Threat, which was researched by the joint effort of Liddy at Center of Natural Language Processing (CNLP), D'Eredita et al. at Syracuse University, and DelZoppo et al. at Syracuse Research Corporation. This research was supported by the Information Assurance for the Intelligence Community (IAIC) program of the Advanced Research and Development Activity (ARDA). The author also graciously thanks Conrad Metcalfe for editing assistance.

REFERENCES

Alvesson, M., & Willmott, H. (1996). *Making sense of management: A critical introduction.* SAGE Publications.

Associated Press. (2005, December 18). *Bush says domestic surveillance a 'vital tool'.* Retrieved May 18, 2007 from http://www.msnbc.msn.com/id/10505574/

Berger, A. L., Della Pietra, S. A., & Della Pietra, V. J. (1996). A maximum entropy approach to natural language processing. *1996 Association for Computational Linguistics, 22*(1), 1-36.

Burgess, G., Clark, T. D., Hauser, R. D. Jr., & Zmud, R. W. (1992). The application of causal maps to develop a collective understanding of complex organizational contexts in requirements analysis. *Accounting, Management and Information Technology, 2*(3), 143-164.

DelZoppo, R., Browns, E., Downey, M., Liddy, E. D., Symonenko, S., Park, J. S., et al. (2004). A multidisciplinary approach for countering insider threats. *Workshop on Secure Knowledge Management (SKM)*, Amherst, NY.

Forgas, J. P. (Ed.). (2001). *Handbook of affect and social cognition.* Lawrence Erlbaum Associates.

Ghiglieri, M. P. (1999). *The dark side of man: Tracing the origins of male violence.* Perseus Books.

Gilad, B. (2004). *Early warning: Using competitive intelligence to anticipate market shifts, control risk, and create powerful strategies.* AMACOM.

Haydon, M. V. (1999). *The insider threat to U.S. government information systems* [INFOSEC 1-99]. National Security Telecommunications and Information Systems Security Committee. Retrieved June 4, 2006 from http://www.nstissc.gov/Assets/pdf/NSTIS-SAM_INFOSEC1-99.pdf

Huang, Y. A., & Lee, W. (2003). A cooperative intrusion detection system for ad hoc Networks. *Proceedings of the 1st ACM Workshop Security of Ad Hoc and Sensor Networks* (pp. 135-147).

Keeney, M., Kowalski, E., Cappelli, D., Moore, A., Shimeall, T., & Rogers, S. (2005). *Insider threat study: Computer system sabotage in critical infrastructure sectors.* National Threat Assessment Center, U.S. Secret Service, and CERT® Coordination Center/Software Engineering Institute, Carnegie Mellon. Retrieved from http://www.cert.org/archive/pdf/insidercross051105.pdf

Lee, W., & Stolfo, S. (2000). A framework for constructing features and models for intrusion detection systems. *ACM Transactions on Information and System Security, 3*(4), 227-261.

Michael, C. C., & Ghosh, A. (2002). Simple, state-based approaches to program-based anomaly detection. *ACM Transactions on Information and System Security, 5*(3), 203-237.

Natarajan, A., & Hossain, L. (2004). Towards a social network approach for monitoring insider threats to information security. *Proceedings of the Second NSF/NIJ Symposium on Intelligence and Security Informatics,* Tucson, AZ.

Noe, D (2007). *The near escape: The Jonathan Jay Pollard spy case.* Retrieved May 18, 2007 from http://www.crimelibrary.com/terrorists_spies/spies/pollard/1.html

Orwell, G. (1949). *Nineteen eighty-four.* New York: Harcourt Brace Javanovich.

Park, J. S., & Ho, S. M. (2004). Composite role-based monitoring (CRBM) for countering insider threats. *Proceedings of Second Symposium on Intelligence and Security Informatics (ISI),* Tucson, Arizona.

Raz, O., Koopman, P., & Shaw, M. (2002). Enabling automatic adaptation in systems with under-specified elements. *WOSS'02.*

Raz, O., Koopman, P., & Shaw, M. (2002b). Semantic anomaly detection in online data sources. In Proceedings of the *ICSE'02* (pp. 302-312).

Stevenson, Jr. R. B. (1980). *Corporations and information: Secrecy, access, and disclosure.* The John Hopkins University Press.

Swann, P., & Gill, J. (1993). *Corporate vision and rapid technology change: The revolution of market structure.* New York: Routledge.

Symonenko, S., Liddy, E. D., Yilmazel, O., Del Zoppo, R., Brown, E., & Downey, M. (2004). Semantic analysis for monitoring insider threats. The *2nd NSF/NIJ Symposium on Intelligence and Security Informatics (ISI 2004).*

Teoh, S. T., Zhang, K., Tseng, S. M., Ma, K. L., & Wu, S. F. (2004). Combining visual and automated data mining for rear-real-time anomaly detection and analysis in BGP. *VizSEC/DMSEC'04.*

Zhang, Y., & Lee, W. (2000) Intrusion detection in wireless ad-hoc networks. *MOBICOM 2000.*

Zhang, Y., Lee, W., & Huang, Y. A. (2003). *Intrusion detection techniques for mobile wireless networks.* The Netherlands: Kluwer Academic Publishers.

TERMS AND DEFINITIONS

Anomaly: A deviation or departure from normal or common order, form, or rule that is peculiar, irregular, and/or abnormal to an extent that includes both good and bad trends.

Anomaly Detection: An act or a perception that deconstructs a hidden, disguised or deviational act or state of a person from the norm, including both good and bad trends, and flags irregular behaviors as an early warning indicator in the context of organizations.

Detection: An act or a perception that demodulates a hidden or disguised act of a person, a series of events that have occurred, and/or a state that exists.

Integrity Check: Inspection or analysis of a person whose personal inner sense of "wholeness" deriving form honesty and consistent uprightness of character.

Natural Language Processing (NLP): It is a subfield of artificial intelligence and linguistics, which studies the science of human language, speech, and the mechanism of converting information from computer databases into normal-sounding human language.

Penetration Test: A method of evaluating the security of a computer system or network by simulating an attack from a malicious cracker. The process involves an active analysis of the system for any vulnerabilities and technical flaws. Any security vulnerability that is found is presented to the system owner with an assessment of their impact and often with a proposal for mitigation or a technical solution.

Personnel: Individuals whom are employed by or active in an organization or a corporate entity, and whom have authorized access to organizational internal and external resources which include systems, networks, applications, and facilities.

Personnel Anomaly Detection: An approach or a mechanism that deconstructs a disguised act / state from the norm of a person with authorized access to organizational internal and external resources, and flags such a deviational behavior that comes in observable patterns, in which a person acts in response to a set of conditions or a particular situation / stimulus, and distinguishes or suggests that a possible insider threat could come from specific perpetrator(s), a series of suspicious events or eccentric states.

Trustworthiness: The degree of correspondence between communicated intentions and behavioral outcomes that are observed and evaluated over time. One important implication of this definition is that there must be an individual, group, or some system that observes and evaluates communication and behavior of the employee over time.

White Hat: A hacker who focuses on securing information systems and is ethically opposed to the abuse of information systems.

ENDNOTES

[1]   Active and passive instruments are classified by the essence of design, usage, and control. Active instruments are identified as access control policy, security architecture and management, and advanced security-driven technology; passive instruments are identified as detection and monitoring mechanisms.

[2]   Digital security is defined by the author as the aggregation of information systems security and network security.

[3]   The author participated in and extracted ideas from a SRC-SU joint research called Insider Threat, which had been researched by the joint

effort of Liddy at Center of Natural Language Processing (CNLP), D'Eredita et al. at Syracuse University, and DelZoppo et al. at Syracuse Research Corporation. This research was supported by the Information Assurance for the Intelligence Community (IAIC) program of the Advanced Research and Development Activity (ARDA).

Chapter XXVII
Cyber Stalking:
A Challenge for Web Security

Alok Mishra
Atilim University, Turkey

Deepti Mishra
Atilim University, Turkey

ABSTRACT

Cyber stalking is a relatively new kind of cyber terrorism crime. Although it often receives a lower priority then cyber terrorism it is an important global issue. Due to new technologies, it is striking in different forms. Due to the Internets provision of anonymity and security it is proliferating quickly. Technology and tools available to curb it have many limitations and are not easy to implement. Legal acts to protect people from cyber stalking are geographically limited to the concerned state or country. This chapter reviews cyber stalking, its approaches, impacts, provision of legal acts, and measures to be taken to prevent it. There is an immediate need for research in the various dimensions of cyber stalking to assess this social problem.

INTRODUCTION

A survey of Fortune 1000 companies found an annual 64% growth rate in cyber attacks being carried out through the Internet (Bagchi & Udo, 2003). The New York state police cyber terrorism unit takes into account cyber stalking as a part of their cyber crime investigation. The behaviour of stalking has been reported since the 19th-century (Lewis, Fremouw, Ben, & Farr, 2001). The Internet has provided users with new opportunities (Miller, 1999) yet, many users are unaware that the same qualities found off-line exist online (Lancaster, 1998). Cyber stalking is when a person is

followed and pursued online. Their privacy is invaded, their every move watched. It is a form of harassment, and can disrupt the life of the victim and leave them feeling very afraid and threatened. Many authors, have defined cyber stalking, as the use of electronic communication including, pagers, cell phones, e-mails and the Internet, to bully, threaten, harass, and intimidate a victim (CyberAngels, 1999; Dean, 2000; Ellison & Akdeniz, 1998; Laughren, 2000; Ogilvie, 2000). Thus it is a kind of cyber attack which may lead to cyber terrorism. With the growing economic dependency on information technology (IT), civilian infrastructures are increasingly the primary targets of cyber attacks.

This growing reliance on IT has increased exposure to diverse sources of cyber war threats. Cyber stalking is an important global issue and an increasing social problem (CyberAngels, 1999; Ellison, 1999; Ellison & Akdeniz, 1998; Report on Cyberstalking, 1999) creating new offenders' and victims' (Wallace, 2000). For instance, in *Stalking and Harassment,* one of a series of Research Notes published on behalf of The Scottish Parliament in August 2000, stated: "Stalking, including cyberstalking, is a much bigger problem than previously assumed and should be treated as a major criminal justice problem and public health concern." (Bocij, 2004). Another detailed definition of cyber stalking that includes organisations by Bocij and McFarlane (2002) is:

A group of behaviours in which an individual, group of individuals or organisation, uses information and communications technology (ICT) to harass one or more individuals. Such behaviours may include, but are not limited to, the transmission of threats and false accusations, identity theft, data theft, damage to data or equipment, computer monitoring, the solicitation of minors for intimidation purposes and confrontation. Harassment is defined as a course of action that a reasonable person, in possession of the same information, would think causes another reasonable person to suffer emotional distress.

This definition shows cyber stalking may sometimes involve harassment carried out by an organisation also. Such behaviour is often termed corporate cyber stalking. This may lead to cyber warfare within the corporate world.

Typically, the cyber stalker's victim is new on the Web, and inexperienced with the rules of netiquette and Internet safety. Their targets are mostly females, children, emotionally weak, or unstable persons. It is believed that over 75% of the victims are female, but sometimes men are also stalked. These figures are assumed and the actual figures may never be known since most crimes of this nature go unreported ("Cyber Crime," 2004). To date, there is no empirical

research to determine the incidence of cyber stalking (Ogilvie, 2000).

However depending on the use of the internet, there are three primary ways of cyber stalking (Ogilvie, 2000):

- **E-mail stalking:** This is direct communication through e-mail. Which is the most easily available form for harassment. It is almost similar to traditional stalking in some aspects. One may send e-mail of a threatening, hateful, or obscene nature, or even send spam or viruses to harass others. For example, in India in 2004 two MBA students sent e-mails to their female classmate to intimidate her. The free availability of anonymisers and anonymous remailers (which shield the sender's identity and allow the e-mail content to be concealed) provide a high degree of protection for stalkers seeking to cover their tracks more effectively.

- **Internet stalking:** There is global communication through the Internet. Here the domain is more wide and public in comparison to e-mail stalking. Here stalkers can use a wide range of activities to harass their victims. For example, a woman was stalked for a period of six months. Her harasser posted notes in a chat room that threatened to intimidate and kill her, and posted doctored pornographic pictures of her on the net together with personal details (Dean, 2000).

- **Computer stalking:** This is unauthorised control of another person's computer. In this type of stalking, the stalker exploits the working of the Internet and the Windows operating system in order to to assume control over the computer of the targeted victim. Here the cyber stalker can communicate directly with their target as soon as the target computer connects in any way to the Internet. The stalker can assume control of the victim's computer and the only defensive option for the victim is to disconnect and relinquish their current Internet "address." In this way, an individuals Windows-based computer connected to the Internet can be identified, and connected to, by another computer connected to the Internet. This "connection" is not the link via a third party characterising typical Internet interactions; rather, it is a computer-to-computer connection allowing the interloper to exercise control over the computer of the target. At present, a reasonably high degree of computer savvy is required to undertake this form of explotiation of the Internet and the Windows operating system. However, instructions on how to use technology in this way are available on the Internet. It is likely that in the future easier scripts will be made freely available for anyone inclined to download them.

Furthermore cyber stalkers can be categorized into three types:

- **The common obsessional cyber stalker:** These stalkers refuses to believe that their relationship is over.
- **The delusional cyber stalker:** They may be suffering from some mental illness like schizophrenia, and so forth,. and have a false belief that keeps them tied to their victims. They assume that the victim loves them even though they have never met. A delusional stalker is usually a loner and most often chooses victims such as a married woman, a celebrity, a doctor, a teacher, and so forth. Those in the noble and helping professions like doctors, teachers, and so forth, are often at risk for attracting a delusional stalker. They are very difficult to shake off.
- **The vengeful stalker:** These cyber stalkers are angry at their victim due to some minor reason—either real or imagined. Typical example are disgruntled employee or ex-spouse, and so forth.

Cyber stalking can take many forms. However, Ellison (1999) suggests, cyber stalking can be classified by the type of electronic communication used to stalk the victim and the extent to which the communication is private or public. Ellison (1999) has classified cyber stalking as either "direct" or "indirect." For example, direct cyber stalking includes the use of pagers, cell phones and e-mail to send messages of hate, obscenities, and threats to intimidate a victim. Direct cyber stalking has been reported to be the most common form of cyber stalking with a close resemblance to off-line stalking (Wallace, 2000). Direct cyber stalking is claimed to be the most common way in which stalking begins. For instance, Working to Halt Online Abuse (2003) show the majority of online harassment or cyber stalking begins with e-mail.

While indirect cyber stalking includes the use of the Internet to display messages of hate, and threats or used to spread false rumours about a victim (Ellison & Akdeniz, 1998). Messages can be posted on Web pages, within chat groups, or bulletin boards. Working to Halt Online Abuse (2003) statistics show chat rooms, instant messages, message boards, and newsgroups to be the most common way that indirect cyber stalking begins. Ogilvie (2000) claims indirect cyber stalking has the greatest potential to transfer into real-world stalking. Messages placed within the public space of the Internet can encourage third parties to contribute in their assault (Report on Cyberstalking, 1999). Therefore, indirect cyber stalking can increase the risk for victims by limiting the geographical boundaries of potential threats. Consequently, indirect cyber stalking can have a greater potential than direct cyber stalking to transfer into the real world as it increases the potential for third parties to become involved (Maxwell, 2001). According to Halt Online Abuse (2003) in the year 2000, 19.5% of online harrassment or cyber stalking cases became off-line stalking. Cyber stalking can vary in range and severity and often reflects off-line stalking behaviour. It can be seen as an extension to off-line stalking however, cyber stalking is not limited by geographic boundaries.

OFFENDERS AND THEIR BEHAVIOUR

What motivates a cyber stalker? Most studies have focused on the off-line stalking offender. Studies, (Farnham, James, & Cantrell, 2000; Meloy, 1996; Meloy & Gothard, 1995; Mullen, Pathe, Purcell, & Stuart, 1999) of off-line stalking offenders have placed offenders into three main groups. Zona, Sharma, and Lone (1993) grouped off-line stalkers into either the "simple obsessional," the "love obsessional," or the "erotomanic" group. The majority of stalkers are simple obsessional they have had a prior relationship with the victim and are motivated to stalk with the aim to reestablish the relationship or gain revenge once the relationship has been dissolved. Mullen, et al. (1999) claims the majority of simple obsessional stalkers have some form of personality disorder and as a group have the greatest potential to become violent. The love obsessional stalkers are those who have never met their victim. The erotomanic group is the smallest among stalkers and is motivated by the belief that the victim is in love with them, as a result of active delusions (Zona et al., 1993). Studies show that irrespective of the groups, male offenders account for the majority of off-line stalking (Meloy & Gothard, 1995; Mullen et al., 1999). Furthermore, according to Working to Halt Online Abuse (2003) statistics show that in the year 2000, 68% of the online harassers or cyber stalkers were male. But now that trend is reversing and male harassers have decreased (52% in 2003) while female harassers have increased (from 27% in 2000 to 38% in 2003). Another interesting factor which has been found in common with off-line stalking offenders is that social factors such as the diversity in socioeconomic backgrounds and either underemployment or unemployment are significant (Meloy, 1996). While Kamphuis and Emmelkamp (2000) investigated psychological factors and found social isolation, maladjustment and emotional immaturity, along with an inability to cope with failed relationships common with off-line stalking groups.

Furthermore, off-line stalkers were above intelligence and older in comparison to other criminal offenders (McCann, 2000). According to (Maxwell, 2001) studies of off-line stalking offenders can present insights to cyber stalkers with some limitations. As earlier observed, only 50% of stalkers are reported to authorities, furthermore, only 25% will result in the offenders being arrested and only 12% will be prosecuted (Kamphuis & Emmelkamp, 2000). Researchers have claimed that cyber stalkers have similar characteristics to the off-line stalkers and most of them are motivated to control the victim (Jenson, 1996; Ogilvie, 2000; Report on Cyberstalking, 1999).

VICTIMS AND THEIR CHARACTERISTICS

Studies have shown that the majority of victims are females of average socioeconomic status, and off-line stalking is primarily a crime against young people, with most victims between the ages of 18 and 29 (Brownstein, 2000). Stalking as a crime against young people may account for the high prevalence of cyber stalking within universities. For example, the University of Cincinnati study showed 25% of college women had been cyber stalked (Tjaden & Thoennes, 1997). Also according to Working to Halt Online Abuse (2003) the majority of victims of online harassment or cyber stalking are between 18 and 30 years of age. Studies that have investigated offenders of off-line stalking found some common symptoms regarding victims, for instance, most are regular people rather than the rich and famous (Brownstein, 2000; McCann, 2000; Sinwelski & Vinton, 2001). Goode (1995) also supports that up to 80% of off-line stalking victims are from average socioeconomic backgrounds. Another important observation by Hitchcock (2000) is that 90% of off-line stalking victims are female. While Halt Online Abuse (2003) reports it to 78% as gender of victim's cumulative figure between 2000 and 2003. Zona, et al. (1993) reported, 65% of off-line victims had a previous relationship with their stalker. However according to Working to Halt Online Abuse (2003) statistics it is 51% but not enough to support this reason as a significant risk factor for cyber stalking.

SOCIAL AND PSYCHOLOGICAL EFFECTS

The studies, which have looked at off-line stalking and its effects on victims by and large, are of the university populations (Maxwell, 2001). For instance, the Fremauw, Westrup, and Pennypacker (1997) study explored coping styles of university off-line stalking victims. They found that the most common way of coping with a stalker was to ignore the stalker and the second most common way, was to confront the stalker. According to them, victims were least likely to report the off-line stalker to the authorities. Many victims felt ashamed or were of the belief that the stalking was their fault (Sheridan, Davies, & Boon, 2001). Working to Halt Online Abuse (2003) reports that the majority of online cyber stalking was handled by contacting the Internet service provider (ISP), which accounted for 49% of cases, followed by, 16% contacting the police. Furthermore, 12% coped by other means including ignoring messages, taking civil action, or not returning to the forum in which the cyber stalking took place. The Report on Cyberstalking (1999) mentions that many victims of cyber stalking claimed they did not think that they would be listened to if they reported the cyber stalking to authorities. Mostly victims of cyber stalking were unaware that a crime had been committed. Currently there are only a few studies on the psychological impact on victims (Maxwell, 2001). Westrup, Fremouw, Thompson, and Lewis (1999) studied the psychological effects of 232 female off-line stalking victims and found the majority of victims had symptoms of depression, anxiety, and experienced panic attacks. In another study by Mullen and Pathe (1997) found that 20% of victims showed increased alcohol consumption and 74% of victims suffered sleep disturbances. However social and psychological effects are interrelated. In a separate study, David, Coker, and Sanderson (2002) found that the physical and mental health effects of being stalked were not gender-related. Both male and female victims experienced impaired health, depression, injury, and were more likely to engage in substance abuse than their nonstalked peers.

TECHNICAL APPROACHES FOR AVOIDANCE

Although tools and techniques are available to protect users, their implementation is not easy and there are number of limitations. For example, answering machines and caller identification are two technologies that help to protect against telephone harassment, although these are of limited effectiveness. In contrast, the potential exists online to completely block contact from unwanted mailers with tools for different online media (Spertus, 1996):

- Programs to read Usenet news support *kill files*, used to automatically bypass messages listed as being from a certain individual or meeting other criteria specified by the user. This allows an individual to choose not to see further messages in a given discussion "thread" or posted from a specified user account or machine. People can choose to share their kill files with others in order to warn them about offensive individuals.
- Real-time discussion forums, such as MUDs and Internet relay chat (IRC), allow a user to block receiving messages from a specified user. Similar technology could be used to allow blocking messages containing words that the user considers unwelcome. Individuals can also be banned from forums at the operators' discretion.
- Programs have existed for years to automatically discard (file, or forward) e-mail based on its contents or sender and are now coming into widespread use. The second generation of filtering tools is being developed. The LISTSERV list maintenance software (Lsoft 96) contains heuristics to detect impermissible advertisements, and an experimental system, Smokey, recognizes "flames" (insulting e-mail).
- Numerous tools exist to selectively prevent access to World Wide Web sites. While the simplest ones, such as SurfWatch, maintain a central database of pages that they deem unsuitable for children, others are more sophisticated.

SafeSurf rates pages on several different criteria. Net Nanny provides a starting dictionary of offensive sites, which the user can edit. The user can also specify that pages containing certain words or phrases should not be downloaded.

One of the biggest limitations to the above techniques is the computer's difficulty in determining whether a message is offensive. Many of the above tools use string matching and will not recognize a phrase as offensive if it is misspelled or restated in other words. Few systems use more sophisticated techniques. Smokey recognizes that "you" followed by a noun phrase is usually insulting, but such heuristics have limited accuracy, especially if they are publicly known.

LEGAL ACTS PROVISIONS AND PROTECTION

Law enforcement agencies now know that cyber stalking is a very real issue that needs to be dealt with, from local police departments to state police, the FBI, and the U.S. postal inspection service, among others. Many are asking their officers to learn how to use the Internet and work with online victim groups such as WHOA (Women Halting Online Abuse), SafetyED, and CyberAngels. Others are attending seminars and workshops to learn how to track down cyber stalkers and how to handle victims (Hitchcock, 2000).

Legal acts aimed to protect other from off-line stalking are relatively new. Only in the past ten years have off-line antistalking laws been developed (Goode, 1995). The first "Antistalking" law was legislated in California, in 1990 and in 1998 the antistalking law, specified cyber stalking as a criminal act. However, less than a third of the states in the U.S. have antistalking laws that encompass cyber stalking (Miller, 1999). According to Hitchcock (2000) in the U.S. almost 20 states with cyber stalking or related laws, a federal cyber stalking law is waiting for senate approval. Several other states with laws pending, cyber stalking is finally getting noticed, not only by law enforcement, but by media too. To protect against off-line stalking or cyber stalking the UK has the "Protections Against Harassment Act 1997" and the "Malicious Communication Act 1998" (ISE, n.d.). In New Zealand the "Harassment Act 1997," the "Crimes Act 1961," the "Domestic Violence Act 1995," and the "Telecommunication Act 1987" can apply to online harassment or cyber stalking (Computers and Crime, 2000). While in Australia, Victoria and Queensland are the only states to include sending electronic messages to, or otherwise contacting, the victim, as elements of the offence for most states cover activities which "could" include stalking.

These activities are the following (Ogilive, 2000):

- Keeping a person under surveillance
- Interfering with property in the possession of the other person, giving or sending offensive material
- Telephoning or otherwise contacting a person
- Acting in a manner that could reasonably be expected to arouse apprehension or fear in the other person
- Engaging in conduct amounting to intimidation, harassment, or molestation of the other person

Two possible exceptions here are New South Wales and Western Australia, which have far narrower definitions of what constitutes stalking. Hence, both states identify specific locations such as following or watching places of residence, business, or work, which may not include cyber space. While cyber stalking could be included within "any place that a person frequents for the purposes of any social or leisure activity," the prosecution possibilities seem limited. Other difficulties may occur in South Australia and the Australian Capital Territory, where there is a requirement that offenders intend to cause "serious" apprehension and fear. Thus, the magistrates may dismiss cases of cyber stalking, given the lack of physical proximity between many offenders and victims (Ogilive, 2000).

There is a significant growth in cyber stalking cases in India, primarily because people still use the

Internet to hide their identities and indulge in online harassment. It is important to note that though cyber stalking has increased, the number of cases reported is on the decline. This could be because of the failure of the law in dealing with this crime. The Information Technology Act 2000 does not cover cyber stalking and the Indian Penal Code 1860 does not have a specific provision that could help victims of cyber stalking. The government has now thought it fit to enact a distinct provision relating to cyber squatting. The provision is mentioned in the proposed Communications Convergence Bill 2001 which has been laid before Parliament, and the Parliamentary Standing Committee on Information Technology has already given its detailed report and recommendations on the proposed law to the government. The relevant provision relating to cyber stalking in the convergence bill is as follows:

Punishment for sending obscene or offensive messages:

Any person who sends, by means of a communication service or a network infrastructure facility:

a.   any content that is grossly offensive or of an indecent obscene or menacing character;
b.   for the purpose of causing annoyance, inconvenience, danger, obstruction, insult, injury, criminal intimidation, enmity, hatred or ill-well, any content that he knows to be false or persistently makes use for that purpose of a communication service or a network infrastructure facility, shall be punishable with imprisonment which may be extended upto three years or with fine which may be extended to approximate USD 4,25000 or with both. This is one of the heaviest fines known in criminal jurisprudence in India.

It is hoped that when it does come into effect, victims of cyber stalking can breathe a sigh of relief ("No Law," 2004).

Currently, there is no global legal protection against cyber stalking (Ellison & Akdeniz, 1998). Within the cyber world the lack of global legal protection further adds to an increasing problem. This is even true in the case of cyber warfare and cyber terrorism. Unlike offline stalking there are no geographical limitations to cyber stalking. Although some countries and/or states have responded to the increase of cyber stalking by the modification of current antistalking laws, laws criminalizing cyber stalking by and large are limited to the country and/or state and are ineffective within the cyber world. Furthermore according to Ogilvie (2000) while the criminalisation of threatening e-mails would be a reasonably easy fix, it does not overcome the primary difficulties in legislating against cyber stalking, which are the inter-jurisdictional difficulties. While in many ways cyber stalking can be considered analogous to physical world stalking, at other times the Internet needs to be recognised as a completely new medium of communication. It is at this point that legislating against cyber stalking becomes difficult. For example, according to Ogilvie (2000) if a stalker in California uses an international service provider in Nevada to connect to an anonymiser in Latvia to target a victim in Australia, which jurisdiction has responsibility for regulating the cyber stalking? This is a major constraint to be taken into consideration while formulating laws to curb cyber stalking. Nevertheless, the implementation of legal acts to protect from off-line stalking or cyber stalking remains dependent on victims to report the offence and the concerned authorities ability to gain adequate evidence (Maxwell, 2001).

PREVENTION STRATEGIES

As we know, prevention is always better than the cure and just a little care makes accidents rare. The best way to avoid being stalked is to always maintain a high level of safety awareness. The suggestions regarding staying safe online by Hitchcock (2000) are as follows:

1.   Use your primary e-mail account only for messages to and from people you know and trust.

2. Get a free e-mail account from someplace like Hotmail, Juno, or Excite, and so forth, and use that for all of your other online activities.

3. When you select an e-mail username or chat nickname, create something gender-neutral and like nothing you have elsewhere or have had before. Try not to use your name.

4. Do not fill out profiles for your e-mail account, chat rooms, IM (instant messaging), and so forth.

5. Do set your options in chat or IM to block all users except for those on your buddy list.

6. Do learn how to use filtering to keep unwanted e-mail messages from coming to your e-mail-box.

7. If you are being harassed online, try not to fight back. This is what the harasser wants—a reaction from you. If you do and the harassment escalates, do the following:

   a. Contact the harasser and politely ask them to leave you alone

   b. Contact their ISP and forward the harassing messages

   c. If harassment escalates, contact your local police

   d. If they can not help, try the State Police, District Attorney's office and/or State Attorney General

   e. Contact a victims group, such as WHOA, SafetyED or CyberAngels

CONCLUSION

It is estimated that there are about 200,000 real-life stalkers in the U.S. today. Roughly 1 in 1,250 persons is a stalker—and that is a large ratio. Out of the estimated 79 million population worldwide on the Internet at any given time, we could find 63,000 Internet stalkers travelling the information superhighway, stalking approximately 474,000 victims (Cyber Crime in India, 2004; Hitchcock, 2000). It is a great concern for all Internet users. Cyber stalking may lend support to cyber warfare and cyber terrorism. Present laws to tackle cyber stalking are geographically limited to the concerned state or country. Therefore, there is an urgent need to make global legislation for handling cyber warfare and cyber terrorism. Organizations like the UN and Interpol should initiate this. In addressing cyber stalking, new and innovative legislations, technologies, and investigative countermeasures will almost certainly be mandatory. We hope that information system security professionals will move in this direction. Researchers will also put their efforts for empirical studies in various aspects of cyber stalking to know more about it, which will help technologist, lawmakers and others to make a real assessment.

REFERENCES

Brownstein, A. (2000). In the campus shadows, women are stalkers as well as the stalked. *The Chronicle of Higher Education, 47*(15), 4042.

Bagchi, K., & Udo, G. (2003). An analysis of the growth of computer and internet security breaches. *Communications of the Association for Information Systems, 12*(46), 129.

Bocij, P. (2004). *Corporate cyberstalking: An invitation to build theory.* http://www.firstmonday.dk/issues/issues7_11/bocij/

Bocij, P., & McFarlane, L. (2002, February). Online harassment: Towards a definition of cyberstalking. [HM Prison Service, London]. *Prison Service Journal, 139*, 31-38.

Computers and Crime. (2000). IT law lecture notes (Rev. ed.). http://www.law.auckland.ac.nz/itlaw/itlawhome.htm

Cyber Crime in India. (2004). *Cyber stalking—online harassment.* http://www.indianchild.com/cyberstalking.htm

CyberAngels. (1999). http://cyberangels.org

Davis, K. E., Coker, L., & Sanderson, M. (2002, August). Physical and mental health effects of being stalked for men and women. *Violence Vict 2002,* *17*(4), 429-43.

Dean, K. (2000). The epidemic of cyberstalking. *Wired News* http://www.wired.com/news/politics/0,1283,35728,00.html

Ellison, L. (1999). Cyberspace 1999: Criminal, criminal justice and the internet. *Fourteenth BILETA Conference,* York, UK. http ://www.bileta. ac.uk/99papers/ellison.html

Ellison, L., & Akdeniz, Y. (1998). Cyber-stalking: The regulation of harassment on the internet (Special Edition: Crime, Criminal Justice and the Internet). *Criminal Law Review,* 2948. http://www.cyber-rights. org/documents/stalking

Farnham, F. R., James, D. V., & Cantrell, P. (2000). Association between violence, psychosis, and relationship to victim in stalkers. *The Lancet, 355*(9199), 199.

Fremauw, W. J., Westrup, D., & Pennypacker, J. (1997). Stalking on campus: The prevalence and strategies for coping with stalking. *Journal of Forensic Sciences, 42*(4), 666-669.

Goode, M. (1995). Stalking: Crime of the nineties? *Criminal Law Journal, 19,* 21-31.

Hitchcock, J. A. (2000). Cyberstalking. *Link-Up, 17*(4). http://www.infotoday.com/lu/ju100/hitchcock.htm

ISE. (n.d.). *The internet no1 close protection resource.* http://www.intel-sec.demon.co.uk

Jenson, B. (1996). *Cyberstalking: Crime, enforcement and personal responsibility of the on-line world.* S.G.R. MacMillan. http://www.sgrm.com/art-8.htm

Kamphuis, J. H., & Emmelkamp, P. M. G. (2000). Stalking—A contemporary challenge for forensic and clinical psychiatry. *British Journal of Psychiatry, 176,* 206-209.

Lancaster, J. (1998, June). Cyber-stalkers: The scariest growth crime of the 90's is now rife on the net. *The Weekend Australian,* 20-21.

Laughren, J. (2000). *Cyberstalking awareness and education.* http://www.acs.ucalgary.ca/~dabrent/380/webproj/jessica.html

Lewis, S. F., Fremouw, W. J., Ben, K. D., & Farr, C. (2001). An investigation of the psychological characteristics of stalkers: Empathy, problem-solving, attachment and borderline personality features. *Journal of Forensic Sciences, 46*(1), 8084.

Maxwell, A. (2001). *Cyberstalking.* Masters' thesis, http://www.netsafe.org.nz/ie/downloads/cyberstalking.pdf

McCann, J. T. (2000). A descriptive study of child and adolescent obsessional followers. *Journal of Forensic Sciences, 45*(1), 195-199.

Meloy, J. R. (1996). Stalking (obsessional following): A review of some preliminary studies. *Aggressive and Violent Behaviour, 1*(2), 147-162.

Meloy, J. R., & Gothard, S. (1995). Demographic and clinical comparison of obsessional followers and offenders with mental disorders. *American Journal of Psychiatry, 152*(2), 25826.

Miller, G. (1999). Gore to release cyberstalking report, call for tougher laws. *Latimes.com.* http://www. latimes.com/news/ploitics/elect2000/pres/gore

Mullen, P. E., & Pathe, M. (1997). The impact of stalkers on their victims. *British Journal of Psychiatry, 170,* 12-17.

Mullen, P. E., Pathe, M., Purcell, R., & Stuart, G. W. (1999). Study of stalkers. *The American Journal of Psychiatry, 156*(8), 1244-1249.

No Law to Tackle Cyberstalking. (2004). *The Economic Times.* http://ecoonomictimes.indiatimes. com/articleshow/43871804.cms

Ogilvie, E. (2000). *Cyberstalking, trends and issues in crime and criminal justice.* 166. http://www.aic. gov.au

Report on Cyberstalking. (1999, August). *Cyberstalking: A new challenge for law enforcement and industry*. A Report from the Attorney General to The Vice President.http://www.usdoj.gov/criminal/cybercrime/cyberstalking.htm

Sheridan, L., Davies, G. M., & Boon, J. C. W. (2001). Stalking: Perceptions and prevalence. *Journal of Interpersonal Violence, 16*(2), 151-167.

Sinwelski, S., & Vinton, L. (2001). Stalking: The constant threat of violence. *Affilia, 16*, 46-65.

Spertus, E. (1996). *Social and technical means for fighting on-line harassment.* http://ai.mit.edu./people/ellens/Gender/glc

Tjaden, P., & Thoennes, N. (1997). Stalking in America: Findings from the National Violence. Retrieved May 25, 2007 from http://www.ncjrs.gov/txtfiles/169592.txt

Wallace, B. (2000, July 10). Stalkers find a new tool—The Internet e-mail is increasingly used to threaten and harass, authorities say. *SF Gate News.* http://sfgate.com/cgi-bin/article_cgi?file=/chronicle/archive/2000/07/10/MN39633.DTL

Westrup, D., Fremouw, W. J., Thompson, R. N., & Lewis, S. F. (1999). The psychological impact of stalking on female undergraduates. *Journal of Forensic Sciences, 44*, 554-557.

Working to Halt Online Abuse. (WHO). (2003). *On-line harrassment statistics.* Retrieved May 25, 2007 from http://www.haltabuse.org/resources/stats/index.shtml

Zona, M. A., Sharma, K. K., & Lone, J. (1993). A comparative study of erotomanic and obsessional subjects in a forensic sample. *Journal of Forensic Sciences, 38*, 894-903.

TERMS AND DEFINITIONS

Netiquette: The etiquette of computer networks, especially the Internet.

SPAM: Unsolicited e-mail, often advertising a product or service. Spam can occasional "flood" an individual or ISP to the point that it significantly slows down the data flow.

Stalking: To follow or observe (a person) persistently, especially out of obsession or derangement.

Viruses: A malicious code added to an e-mail program or other downloadable file that is loaded onto a computer without the users knowledge and which runs often without their consent. Computer viruses can often copy themselves and spread themselves to a users e-mail address book or other computers on a network.

Section IV
Technical Aspects of Handling Cyber Attacks

The security measures used for handling cyber attacks are divided into three broad categories: technical, human and organizational. We must stress the importance of the application of each of these to any measures when using a system approach. This means that the evaluation of any possible use of a given measure must be governed by an effective means to secure any system. Unfortunately, such an approach is not used very often. The piecemeal approach to handling these issues is dominant in most organizations. Piecemeal means that the implementation of a given security measure is examined only from the perspective of a particular issue, and does not consider a holistic approach to comprehensive security.

In this section, the following opinions and views on the organizational and technical aspects of handling cyber warfare and cyber terrorist attacks are presented:

Chapter XXVIII
Cyber Security Models

Norman F. Schneidewind
Naval Postgraduate School, USA

ABSTRACT

Predictive models for estimating the occurrence of cyber attacks are desperately needed to counteract the grow-ing threat of cyber terrorism. Unfortunately, except to a limited degree, there is no genuine database of attacks, vulnerabilities, consequences, and risks to employ for model development and validation. However, it is still useful to provide definitions, equations, plots, and analyses to answer the "what if" questions concerning potentials at-tacks. We do this by reasoning about the elements of predictive models and their relationships, which are needed to mirror objects and events in the real world of cyberspace. The application of these models is to provide the user with a vehicle for testing hypotheses about how to respond to a cyber attack before it occurs, using risk, vulner-abilities, time between attacks, and intrusion (number and duration) concepts.

INTRODUCTION

Motivation

We are interested in developing *cyber security predic-tion models* to serve as a frame work for researchers to develop models of cyber threats and for practitioners to use for input in their decision-making process when responding to cyber terror. We are motivated to de-velop the models because of the severity of the cyber security problem and the havoc that cyber attacks are wreaking on the world's information infrastructure. The criticality of the cyber threat problem is expressed in excerpts from the following report:

The Nation's information technology (IT) infrastruc-ture, still evolving from U.S. technological innovations such as the personal computer and the Internet, today is a vast fabric of computers—from supercomputers to handheld devices—and interconnected networks enabling high-speed communications, information access, advanced computation, transactions, and automated processes relied upon in every sector of society. Because much of this infrastructure connects to the Internet, it embodies the Internet's original at-tributes of openness, inventiveness, and the assumption of good will. ("Cyber Security," 2005)

These attributes have made the United States information technology (IT) infrastructure an irresistible target for vandals and criminals worldwide. Members of the President's Information Technology Advisory Committee (PITAC) believe that terrorists will inevitably follow suit, taking advantage of vulnerabilities, including some that the nation has not yet clearly recognized or addressed. The computers that manage critical U.S. facilities, infrastructures, and essential services can be targeted to set off system-wide failures, and these computers frequently are accessible from virtually anywhere in the world via the Internet ("Cyber Security," 2005).

Computing systems control the management of power plants, dams, the North American power grid, air traffic control systems, food and energy distribution, and the financial system, to name only some. The reliance of these sensitive physical installations and processes on the IT infrastructure makes that infrastructure itself critical and in the national interest to safeguard ("Cyber Security," 2005).

Evidence of this problem is contained in the following excerpt from an article in *The Washington Post* (Graham, 2005):

Web sites in China are being used heavily to target computer networks in the Defense Department and other U.S. agencies, successfully breaching hundreds of unclassified networks, according to several U.S. officials. Classified systems have not been compromised, the officials added. But U.S. authorities remain concerned because, as one official said, even seemingly innocuous information, when pulled together from various sources, can yield useful intelligence to an adversary.

It's not just the Defense Department but a wide variety of networks that have been hit,' including the departments of State, Energy and Homeland Security as well as defense contractors, the official said. 'This is an ongoing, organized attempt to siphon off information from our unclassified systems.'

'With the threat of computer intrusions on the rise generally among Internet users, U.S. government officials have made no secret that their systems, like commercial and household ones, are subject to attack. Because the Pentagon has more computers than any other agency—about 5 million worldwide—it is the most exposed to foreign as well as domestic hackers,' the officials said. (p. A1)

It is evident that the potential for cyber attacks is not limited to sources in the United States. For example, Yurcik and Doss (2001) report in their paper *Internet Attacks: A Policy Framework for Rules of Engagement* that there also is concern about foreign sources as well, as articulated in the following testimony:

We are detecting, with increasing frequency, the appearance of doctrine and dedicated offensive cyberwarfare programs in other countries. We have identified several (countries), based on all-source intelligence information that are pursuing government-sponsored offensive cyberprograms. Information Warfare is becoming a strategic alternative for countries that realize that, in conventional military confrontation with the United States, they will not prevail. These countries perceive that cyberattacks launched within or outside of the U.S. represent the kind of asymmetric option they will need to level the playing field during an armed crisis against the U.S. The very same means that the cybervandals used a few weeks ago could also be used on a much more massive scale at the nation-state level to generate truly damaging interruptions to the national economy and infrastructure. (John Serabian, the CIA's information operations issue manager, in testimony before the Joint Economic Committee of Congress 3/4/00)

In the commercial arena, Microsoft, heretofore not noted for the security of its systems, has done an about face and has instituted the following policy: "With the implementation of Trustworthy Computing, security has become the number one priority. Default installations aimed at ease of use are now not always sufficiently secure, but, going forward, security in Microsoft's products will take precedence over ease of-use." Given Microsoft's influence in the software industry, it is interesting that they have endorsed the idea of cyber security modeling in that threat modeling is a key part of its Trustworthy Computing program (Schoonover, 2005).

Research Questions

In response to the *cyber security crisis,* we suggest that the research questions that are important to address are: (1) Can various representations and models of cyber security be developed that would provide a framework for researchers and practitioners to advance the field? (2) Can theoretical prediction models be developed to assess the risk of various types of cyber attacks?

Models are important in developing and understanding the theory of cyber security. These models support our objective of predicting cyber security risks. One type of model, the *risk* model, predicts the risk of attack, given the vulnerabilities and consequences of a specified cyber security situation.

The second model, the *exponential model,* is time based and predicts the *time between attacks* as a function of probability of attack for a given risk priority. *Time between attacks* is a surrogate measure of risk because the shorter the time between attacks, the greater the risk for the user, due to the consequences of an increased frequency of attack.

It is important to note that these models cannot be validated against real-world attack events because the nature of future attacks is unknown. The best we can do is to *illustrate* for researchers and cyber security officials the important parameters and variables in the cyber security environment and the likely outcome of cyber security scenarios under specified "what if" conditions.

RELATED RESEARCH

Availability is a system attribute that is not ordinarily associated with security. The *IEEE Standard Glossary of Software Engineering Terminology* defines *availability* as follows: "The degree to which a system or component is operational and accessible when required for use. Often expressed as a probability" (*IEEE Standard Glossary*). However, in the paper, *End-to-End Availability Policies and Noninterference,* Zheng and Myers (2005) relate *availability* to security. Although this approach does not comport with the standard definition cited above, it is a valuable idea because if a system is attacked and compromised, its availability has been decreased. Thus, it would make sense to include *unavailability* as one of the consequences of a cyber attack. Unfortunately, this attribute is not included in cyber security databases.

Additional data is required to support model validation. In this regard, Yurcik, Loomis, and Korzyk, Sr. (2000) in their paper, *Predicting Internet Attacks: On Developing an Effective Measurement Methodology,* one of the first articles to call for measurement in cyber security, state that:

available metrics that could be collected to develop an Internet attack prediction methodology include:

1 *Type of Internet attack based on a common taxonomy*
2 *Number/percentage of Internet attack frequency growth*
3 *Number/percentage of detected/undetected Internet attacks*
4 *Number/percentage of successful/unsuccessful Internet attacks*
5 *Number/percentage of reported/unreported Internet attacks*
6 *Number/percentage of automated Internet attacks*
7 *Types of automated Internet attacks—tools used/ports probed*
8 *Stationarity of Internet attacks over time (day/ day of week/month/year/season)*
9 *Duration of Internet attacks (day/month/year)*
10 *Number of hosts involved in Internet attacks*
11 *Damage Cost estimate for distinct Internet attacks*
12 *Geographical location (physical and virtual mapping) of Internet attacks*

13 Targeted systems (location/organization/vendor/operating system)

We suggest that 3, 4, 5, 6, and 7 are infeasible to collect because much of these data are only known to the attacker, and he is not going to tell anyone. Although data in 11 would be useful to have, it is unlikely that it could be obtained in quantity because a business is not going to publicize information that would put it at a competitive disadvantage. In addition, the above list does not include information about vulnerabilities, risks, and consequences—the pillars of cyber security analysis.

Tinnel, Saydjari, and Farrell (2002) in their paper, *An Analysis of Cyber Goals, Strategies, Tactics, and Techniques,* advocate the interesting approach to cyber warfare of gathering intelligence information to proactively monitor the activities of would-be attackers. Although this facet of cyber security protection is beyond the scope of this paper, it is an excellent area for all researchers to consider. Briefly, the method could be implemented by using, for example, intrusion detection devices not only on the user organization's premises, but at strategic points in the Internet, as well.

RISK MODEL

Definitions

- R_i: *Risk of priority* i. Risk priority is the consequences of a given type of attack (e.g., denial of service) relative to the consequences of other types of attacks (e.g., virus).
- P_{ai}: *Relative probability of attack of risk priority* i
- P_{vi}: *Probability of vulnerability of risk priority* i. Since we know little about organizations' vulnerabilities (they are not going to admit to any), we must randomize this probability in the analysis so that there will be no bias in the computations.

- C_i: *Consequence associated with risk priority* i. Examples are destruction of cyber infrastructure and the number of network objects affected (e.g., routers, Internet service providers (ISPs), servers, hosts, Web sites, links).
- $T_L(i)$: *Relative threat level of attack of risk priority* i
- **n:** Total number of attacks

Model Structure

This model relates *relative* probability of attack, probability of vulnerability, and consequence of an attack, as shown in Figure 1. While it is not feasible to include probability of attack per se because the data that would allow us to estimate this quantity is not available, it is possible to use a surrogate measure—*relative* probability of attack—that is computed from evaluations of the *relative* threat level of various types of attacks, as shown in equation (5).

We assume that risk can be accurately computed using equation (1). The justification is that intuitively risk would increase as all three quantities comprising equation (1) increase.

Risk = Relative Probability of Attack * Probability of Vulnerability * Consequence   (1)

$$R_i = P_{ai} * P_{vi} * C_i: (2)$$

Examples of equation (2) include:

$R_1 = P_{a1}$ (Denial of Service) * P_{v1} (No Firewall) * C_1 (Consequence of Risk Priority 1)   (3)

$R_2 = P_{a2}$ (Virus) * P_{v2} (Telnet Access) * C_2 (Consequence of Risk Priority 2)   (4)

The surrogate measure for probability of attack, Relative Probability of Attack, is estimated using equation (5).

$$P_{ai} = \frac{T_L(i)}{\sum_{i=1}^{n} T_L(i)}   (5)$$

Figure 1. Cyber security in the critical infrastructure

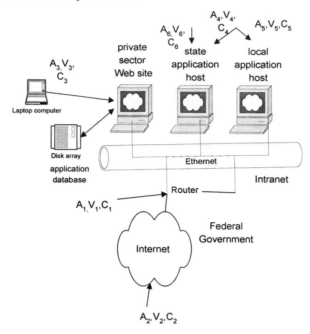

A_i:	Attack, Risk Priority i (Order of Priority)	Vulnerability V_i		Consequence C_i	
A_1:	Denial of Service: Flood Router	V_1:	Firewall	C_1:	Loss of Connectivity Between Internet and
A_2:	Packet Sniffer: Capture Passwords	V_2:	No Password Capture Protection		Intranet
A_3:	Probe: Obtain Web Server Account Informa-	V_3:	No Web Server Firewall	C_2:	Intranet Passwords Compromised
	tion	V_4:	No Anti Worm Software	C_3:	Web Server Programs Hijacked
A_4:	Worm: Replicates Itself	V_5:	No Anti Virus Software	C_4:	Intranet Brought Down
A_5:	Virus: Corrupt Operating System	V_6:	No Software to Detect Trojan Horse	C_5:	Operating System Rendered Inoperatble
A_6:	Trojan Horse: Hide in Host and Corrupt			C_6:	Application Programs Corrupted
	Applications				

Example Calculations for Risk Model

Next we show example calculations and plots that illustrate risk model outputs. The data in the Table 1 were developed as follows.

The top part of the table shows 11 types of attacks, starting with *denial of service* (DoS)—the most severe—and ending with *corruption of database*—the least severe.

$T_L(i)$ represents a subjective assessment of the relative threat level of various types of attacks, starting with *DoS* = 100, and ending with *corruption of database* = 3. Note that the purpose of the example is illustrative; a different assignment of relative threat levels to types of attack would lead to different results.

P_{ai} is computed from equation (5). As stated previously, data is not available for P_{vi}. Thus it is necessary to randomize this quantity as $0,...,1$. C_i is assigned linearly to the types of attacks, assigning 11 to DoS, 10 to virus, and so forth.

The desired output risk = R_i is computed from equation (2). The bolded values in the table highlight the significant results. Figure 2 shows how risk varies with probability of attack. The plot is annotated with the attack types associated with the major risk vales. As a practical matter, the plot indicates that risk would rise rapidly at a value of $P_{ai} \cong 0.15$. This could be considered a significant risk and that the user should prepare, in particular, against *DoS* and *Probe* attacks. However, we note in Table 1 that R_i

Table 1.

Relative Threat Level = Relative Probability of Attack = P_{ai}	
Denial of Service	Prevent legitimate users of a service from using it
Virus	Self-replicating programs
Probe	Discover information about the system
Scan	Large number of probes using an automated tool
Account Compromise	Unauthorized use of user account
Packet Sniffer	Captures data from information packets
Root Compromise	Account compromised has privileges
Trojan Horse	Hidden in legitimate programs or files
Worm	Spread with no human intervention
Spyware	Permits unauthorized access to a computer
Corruption of Database	Data is rendered unrecognizable

$T_L(i)$:	P_{ai}	P_{vi}	C_i	R_i
100	**0.2288**	0.4384	**11**	1.1034
100	0.2288	0.1355	10	0.3101
70	**0.1625**	0.7639	**9**	1.1170
45	0.1030	0.7190	8	0.5923
33	0.0755	0.1741	7	0.0921
26	0.0595	0.4932	6	0.1761
13	0.0595	0.0213	5	0.0064
12	0.0297	0.6479	4	0.0771
8	0.0275	0.2946	3	0.0243
3	0.0183	0.8708	2	0.0319
437	0.0069	0.1832	1	0.0013
$\sum_{i=1}^{n} T_L(i)$	$\dfrac{T_L(i)}{\sum_{i=1}^{n} T_L(i)}$	RAND		
				$R_i = P_{ai} * P_{vi} * C_i$

is significantly a function of *consequences* C_i. Thus, a sensitivity analysis of the assignment of C_i to the relative threat levels could be performed.

Figure 3 shows that risk increases with consequences, as we would expect, and again the diagram is annotated with the major risk attacks of *DoS* and *Probe*. The reason for Figures 1 and 2 is that the relationships among risk, probability of tack, and consequences are not obvious *a priori*. It is important to have more than one view of the relationships so that one view can confirm the other (i.e., Figure 3 confirms the Figure 2

result of *DoS* and *Probe* attacks being the major risks). Figure 4 shows key information about the nature of attacks, as a function of probability of attack.

EXPONENTIAL MODEL

The basis of this model is that the time between attacks, t_a, is a key variable in counteracting attacks. Since, as mentioned, data on probability of attack, P_{ai}, is not available, we are forced to use the surrogate

Figure 2. Risk R$_i$ *vs. probability of attack* P$_{ai}$

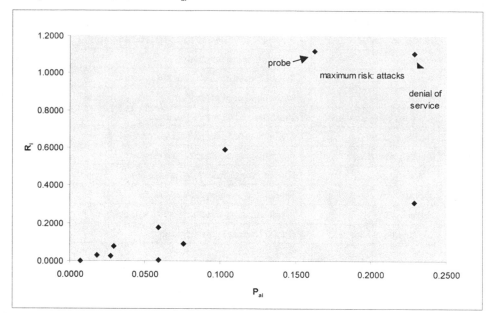

Figure 3. Risk R$_i$ *vs. consequence* C$_i$

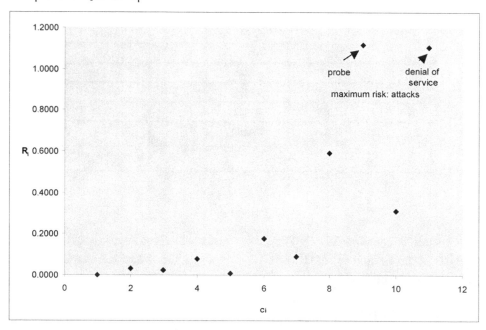

measure relative threat level, T$_L$, in order to estimate P$_{ai}$. Additionally, t_a can be interpreted as a surrogate measure of risk (i.e., the smaller the value of t_a, and, hence, the higher the *frequency* of attack, the higher the risk). Note that this model, as opposed to the risk model, accounts for risk priority, i, and specific types of attacks.

Figure 4. Expected number of attacks vs. probability of attack, $P_a(t)$, *at Time* t

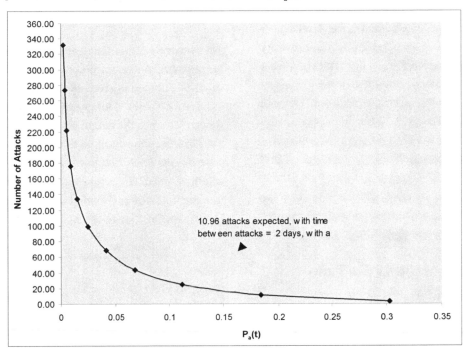

To develop the model, we formulate probability of attack as a function of *relative threat level* in equation (7).

$P_{ai} = f(T_L)$ = relative probability of attack of type *a* of risk priority *i*   (7)

where T_L = relative threat level; t_a = time between attacks of type *a* (e.g., days between attacks); N (T) = number of attacks in Time T; and T = specified attack time period (e.g., in 365 days).

$\lambda = \dfrac{N(T)}{T}$ = mean rate of attacks (e.g., attacks per day)   (8)

Equation (9) is the probability density function for the exponential distribution, assumed for P_{ai}.

$P_{ai} = \lambda e^{-\lambda t_a}$ (9)

In order to solve for the time between attacks, t_a, we operate on equation (9) to produce equations (10) and (11).

$\log(P_{ai}) = \log \lambda - \lambda t_a$ (10)

$\lambda t_a = \log \lambda - \log(P_{ai})$ (11)

Solving equation (11) for t_a, we obtain equation (12).

$t_a = \dfrac{1}{\lambda} \log\left(\dfrac{\lambda}{P_{ai}}\right)$ (12)

Time Between Attacks

Using equation (12), the plot of *time between attacks,* t_a, vs. *probability of attack,* P_{ai}, is shown in Figure 5, where we demark the region to the *right* of the objective of $t_a > 24$ hours as the region to avoid because low values of t_a imply high frequency of attack and, hence, high risk. This policy would exclude all attacks except *DoS*. This decision is illustrative; another user may find this policy unacceptable due to the severity of *DoS* attacks. However, the penalty of the significant effort and cost involved in implementing a countermeasure against *DoS* should be considered. This plot shows how trade offs can be made between security and cost. In Table 2, the 24-hour point corresponds to $P_{ai} = 0.0183$, whereas a policy to protect against *DoS* corresponds to the 52-hour point, with a $P_{ai} = 0.0069$. The user would have to weigh whether it is worth the effort and cost to employ increased countermeasures in the face of a very low probability of attack.

Example Calculations for Time Between Attacks

Table 2 shows sample calculations for time between attacks. The first column, N(T), is an assumed set of number of attacks per year; T = 365 days; N(T) / T = λ, the attack rate; P_{ai} is obtained from equation (7); the fourth column computes the time between attacks, t_a, in days; and fifth column provides t_a in hours, which is plotted in Figure 5.

Rate of Change of Time Between Attacks

The rate of change of time between attacks relative to the probability of attack is obtained by differentiating equation (12) and is given by equation (13), which is tabulated in Table 2. This quantity is of interest because we can see when the rate of change of t_a—a surrogate for risk—becomes so small that the threat is virtually nonexistent. This situation is portrayed in Figure 6, where $P_{ai} = 0.0275$ corresponds to a *Probe* attack At this point, the rate of change is miniscule, meaning that the rate of change of *risk* is very small.

$$\frac{d(t_a)}{d(P_{ai})} = -\frac{1}{\lambda}(\frac{1}{P^2_{ai}})(\frac{P_{ai}}{\lambda}) = -(\frac{1}{\lambda^2})(\frac{1}{P_{ai}}) \text{ (e.g., days per}$$

probability) (13)

Expected Number of Attacks

Using λt = number of attacks in time interval t, we produce Figure 7, which shows that we can expect 10.96 attacks, with time between attacks = 2 days, with a probability = 0.18. Subjectively, we could say that a probability of 0.18 is relatively small. Thus, if

Table 2. Time between attacks

N(T)	$\frac{N(T)}{T}$	P_{ai}	$\frac{1}{\lambda}\log(\frac{\lambda}{P_{ai}})$	$t_a * 24$	$\frac{d(t_a)}{d(P_{ai})}$
1000	2.74	0.0069	2.19	52.47	-19.4064
2000	5.48	0.0183	1.04	24.97	-1.8194
3000	8.22	0.0275	0.69	16.65	-0.5391
4000	10.96	0.0297	0.54	12.94	-0.2799
5000	13.70	0.0595	0.40	9.53	-0.0896
6000	16.44	0.0595	0.34	8.21	-0.0622
7000	19.18	0.0755	0.29	6.93	-0.0360
8000	21.92	0.1030	0.24	5.87	-0.0202
9000	24.66	0.1625	0.20	4.89	-0.0101
10000	27.40	0.2288	0.17	4.19	-0.0058
11000	30.14	0.2288	0.16	3.89	-0.0048
	λ		t_a	hours between attacks	
365	attacks per day		days between attacks		

attacks do occur, we would expect 11 of them, each of which would be spread two days apart.

CORRESPONDENCE BETWEEN RISK AND EXPONENTIAL MODELS

Having stated that time between attacks, t_a, is a surrogate for risk, R_i, we wanted to investigate this hypothesis by plotting the former against the latter. The result is shown in Figure 8, which shows a fairly good correspondence. The importance of this result is that, since the exponential model is easier to implement than the risk model, the former could be the user's prediction model of choice.

CONCLUSION

In the "Introduction" section, we suggested the following questions be answered by this research: (1) Can various representations and models of cyber security be developed that would provide a framework for researchers and practitioners to advance the field? We suggest that based on our cyber security research approach, definition, equations, plots, and tables, which comprise a frame work, the answer is "yes." (2) Can theoretical prediction models be developed to assess the risk of various types of cyber attacks? In answering this question in the affirmative, we cite as evidence pertinent plots. For example, the *Risk Model* in Figure 2 identifies the maximum risk attacks,

Figure 5. Expected number of attacks vs. probability of attack, $P_a(t)$, at time = t

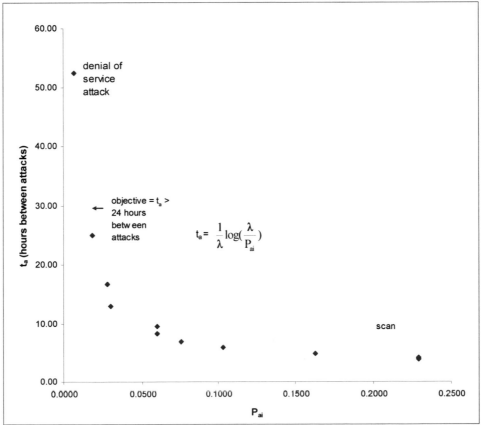

Figure 6. Rate of change of time between attacks, $d(t_a)/d(P_{ai})$ *vs. probability of attack,* P_{ai}

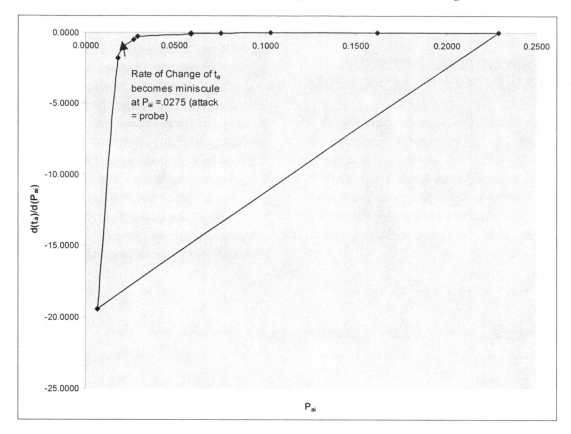

Figure 7. Rate of change of time between attacks, $d(t_a)/d(P_{ai})$ *vs. probability of attack,* P_{ai}

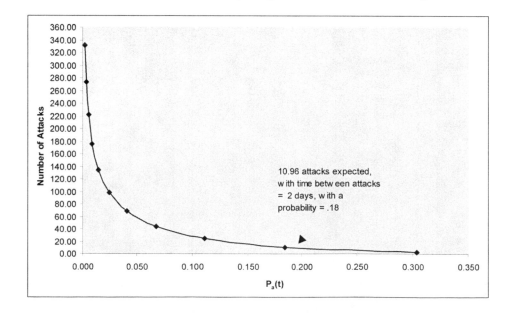

Figure 8. Time between attacks, t_a, *vs. risk* R_i

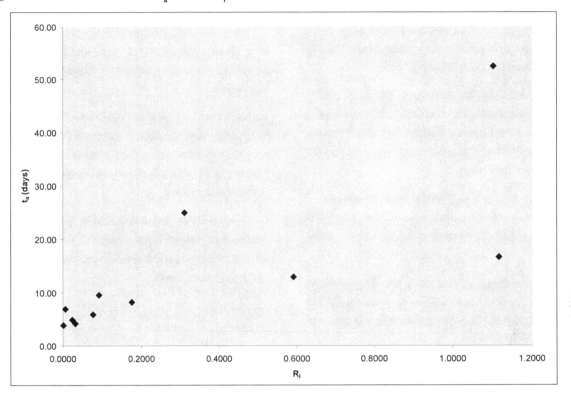

Probe, and *DoS.* Furthermore, with respect to the *Risk Model,* Figure 4 portrays the relationship among cyber security variables. Additionally, Figure 5, related to the *Exponential Model,* provides us with the *Probability of Attack* vs. *Time between Attacks* threshold.

However, in reaching these conclusions, we must be mindful of the fact that the models will only be as good for prediction purposes as the underlying assumptions. For example, regarding Figure 2, since we do not have empirical information about the probability of vulnerability of attack, P_{vi}, we had to randomize this quantity. Thus, the identification of risk depends, in part, on the output of a random number routine. The way that such probabilistic information could be used is to pose "what if" questions. For example, we would be curious about the implication for risk, if P_{vi} had a distribution different from the one shown in Table 1. A second example is posed by Figure 4. What if there is a different distribution of the probability of

attack P_{ai}? What could we then say about the expected number of attacks?

REFERENCES

Cyber Security: A Crisis of Prioritization. (2005, February). President's Information Technology Advisory Committee.

Graham, B. (2005, August 25). Hackers attack via Chinese Web sites, U.S. agencies' networks are among targets. *The Washington Post,* p. A1.

IEEE standard glossary of software—Engineering-terminology [Standard 610.12-1990]. (n.d.).

Schoonover, G. (2005). Enhancing customer security: Built-in versus bolt-on. *DoD Software Tech News, Secure Software Engineering, 8*(2).

Tinnel, L. S., Sami Saydjari, O., & Farrell, D. (2002, June). An analysis of cyber goals, strategies, tactics, and techniques. In *Proceedings of the 2002 IEEE Workshop on Information Assurance*, United States Military Academy, West Point, NY.

Yurcik, W., Loomis, D., & Korzyk, Sr., A. D. (2000, September). Predicting Internet attacks: On developing an effective measurement methodology. In *Proceedings of the 18th Annual International Communications Forecasting Conference*.

Yurcik, W., & Doss, D. (2001). *Internet attacks: A policy framework for rules of engagement*. Department of Applied Computer Science, Illinois State University.

Zheng, L., & Myers, A. C. (2005). *End-to-end availability policies and noninterference*. Presented at the 18th IEEE Computer Security Foundations Workshop, Aix-en-Provence, France.

TERMS AND DEFINITIONS

Risk Priority: Risk priority is the consequences of a given type of attack (e.g., denial of service) relative to the consequences of other types of attacks (e.g., virus).

Vulnerability of Risk Priority: Since we know little about organizations' vulnerabilities (they are not going to admit to any!), we must randomize this probability in the analysis so that there will be no bias in the computations.

Consequence Associated with Risk: Example: Destruction of cyber infrastructure. Example: Number of network objects affected (e.g., routers, ISPs, servers, hosts, web sites, links)

Chapter XXIX
Cyber War Defense:
Systems Development with Integrated Security

Murray E. Jennex
San Diego State University, USA

ABSTRACT

Cyber war is real and is being waged. Cyber terrorists and cyber warriors are attacking systems, but fortunately, they are attacking systems in much the same way hackers attack systems. This is good for system security designers as the security controls installed to protect against hacking will work to protect against cyber terrorists and warriors. However, while there are several tools that can be used to identify security requirements including checklists, threat and risk analysis, and security policies, these methods are not integrated into an overall design methodology that can be used to ensure that security requirements are identified and then implemented. This chapter proposes using barrier analysis and the concept of defense in depth to modify Siponen and Baskerville's (2001) integrated design paradigm that is more graphical and easier to understand and use methodology that is expected to improve security to be built into systems and improve defenses against cyber warfare.

INTRODUCTION

Cyber terrorists and cyber warriors attack systems much the same way as hackers and über hackers (the best hackers) attack systems. This is good for system security designers as the same protections used to defend against hacking will work against cyber terrorists/warriors. However, while there are numerous modeling methods and design methodologies for aiding system analysts in identifying information systems (IS) user requirements, the tools that can be used to identify security requirements are not integrated into an overall design methodology that can be used to ensure that security requirements are identified and then implemented when building a system or application. The result is that oftentimes systems and applications are built to meet end-user needs and then security is added or "bolted on" as an afterthought. Alternately, many system analysts/designers do not consider it their job to include security in the design of a system or application, leaving or trusting security to the network technicians. This leads to an over reliance on firewalls and antivirus as the foundation of security with little use of robust programming, administrative controls, interface and database design, and back up and recovery to enhance security. Siponen and Baskerville (2001) attempted to resolve this by proposing a security design paradigm that relied on metanotation to abstract and document integrated security requirements into IS development methods. However, this paradigm has not been widely adopted.

This chapter proposes using barrier analysis and a defense-in-depth approach to modify Siponen and Baskerville's (2001) and Lee, Lee, and Lee's (2002) integrated design methodologies that are more graphical and easier to understand and use methodology. In addition to the metanotation proposed by Siponen and Baskerville (2001), this chapter proposes the use of barrier diagrams in conjunction with barrier analysis to provide a visual and integrative approach to adding security into systems analysis and design, and to ensure that adequate levels or layers of security are in place at all stages of the software development life cycle (SDLC). Barrier analysis is a concept developed by Haddon, Jr. (1973). Barrier analysis is most widely known in the nuclear energy arena and has been improved upon by the System Safety Development Center, a training division of the Department of Energy (Clemens, 2002). Barrier analysis is a method of identifying hazards or threats, and determining the effectiveness of the preventative/mitigating factors that are constructed to prevent the occurrence of the hazard/threat. Barrier analysis also can be used after an event has occurred to determine the root cause and to help develop barriers to prevent repeat occurrences (Crowe, 1990).

To document the validity and usefulness of the proposed methodology, barrier analysis and defense in depth was tested by a group of graduate students as part of their systems design project. The goal was to determine if the concept of barrier analysis and barrier diagrams could be effectively used in IS design, and whether or not this methodology was useful in discovering and implementing security requirements.

The pilot study was done to determine if further studies and research should be performed to demonstrate that this is a useful methodology that should be adopted as an industry standard practice for ensuring that security requirements are thoroughly discovered, documented, followed, and tracked throughout the systems development life cycle.

BACKGROUND

Information and systems security is a continuing problem. According to a survey performed by the Computer Security Institute (CSI) and the FBI, more than 50% of respondents of large corporations and U.S. government agencies reported security breaches during 2004, with reported financial losses due to these violations of more $141 billion (Computer Security Institute (CSI), 2005). The losses included lost revenue and costs relating to clean up, data loss, liability issues, and, most importantly, loss of customer trust (Allen, Mikoaki, Jr., Nixon, & Skillman, 2002). While this is a declining trend seen since 2001, these figures coupled with the research finding from Jennex and Walters (2003) that current hacking tools require decreased intruder technical knowledge to effectively hack/penetrate security, suggests that there are greater numbers of potential hackers (Allen et al., 2002). It also suggests that despite the overwhelming efforts made on the part of organizations by means of security policies, practices, risk management, technology, security architecture, and design, security for information and systems is still a serious concern.

IS Security Design Paradigms

There are two main paradigms for designing security solutions in IS as defined by Baskerville (1993). The mainstream paradigm is based on the use of checklists, while the integrative paradigm uses engineering processes or logical abstractions and transformational models to combine viewpoints and functions into a single security model. These paradigms are discussed further.

Mainstream Paradigm

The mainstream paradigm is focused on risk identification, analysis, and assessment to identify security needs and then uses checklists, best practices, and/or cookbook approaches to select known solutions to mitigate the identified risks. According to Siponen and Baskerville (2001) these approaches have three underlying flaws:

1. By design, the checklist approach is like a template in nature and does not address the unique and individual security needs of an organization. Furthermore, when developers encounter a situation that requires a decision on the part of management, the checklist approach cannot offer a solution.
2. Developmental duality, the conflict created by the disparate requirements of creating security and IS development, is a problem with the use of checklists, risk management, and formal development.
3. The social nature of the organization is ignored with the "mechanistic and functionalistic" characteristics of checklists and formal method development.

Many current security management textbooks and guidelines from professional organizations, such as ones from the National Institute of Standards and Technology (NIST), the Computer Security Resource Center (CSRC), Computer Emergency Readiness Team (CERT), and SysAdmin, Audit, Network, Security (SANS) Institute, are based on providing templates, checklists, and best practices.

Integrative Paradigm

Given the limitations of mainstream approaches for security design, the need for more integrative approaches has produced integrative paradigms, such as information and database modeling approaches, responsibility approaches, business process approaches, and the security-modified IS development approach. There are four basic weaknesses with the existing integrative approaches, pushing the need for further development in the integrative approach arena (Siponen & Baskerville, 2001):

1. The current integrative approaches lack comprehensive modeling support for security for the three levels of modeling, which are organizational, conceptual, and technical.
2. Most of the existing approaches are difficult or sometimes impossible to integrate into the IS development process, leading to the problem of developmental duality (developing the system and system security utilizing separate groups and efforts).
3. These approaches stifle the creativity and autonomy of the developer, sometimes limiting the developmental approach the developer normally would choose to use.
4. Emerging IS methods create an ongoing gap between IS development and the implementation of the necessary security, since the methodology is not always implemented the same way in practice.

The National Security Agency, (NSA) National Security Telecommunications and Information Systems Security Committee, (NSTISSC) security model (Whitman & Mattord, 2004) and CERT's operationally critical threat, asset, and vulnerability evaluation (OCTAVE) method (Alberts & Dorofee, 2001) are current examples of integrated methodologies that combine technical, organizational, personal, and educational issues into the same method. However, neither method incorporates system development methodologies or usable graphical representations.

Siponen and Baskerville (2001) integrate security design into system development by adding metanotation to the development process. Metamethodology seeks to provide a means for rapidly developing computer-aided systems analysis and software engineering. Metanotation is considered to be a key feature of most methods and metamethods. The metanotation includes five areas: security subjects, security objects, security constraints, security classifications, and security policy. By addressing each of these five dimensions in the development process, security is addressed in IS development in an integrative approach (Siponen & Baskerville, 2001). In a typical use case, the actor becomes the security object, and the security classification is added to the use case (Siponen & Baskerville, 2001). Additionally, the security policy and preconditions are included in the use case to show the application of security in the use case model. This insures that security is addressed for each actor, that the appropriate policy is in place and addressed appropriately as part of the IS design.

Lee et al. (2002) also has proposed an integrative approach. Their approach integrates mainstream security approaches with standard software engineering approaches and the software development life cycle. This approach provides a road map between life cycle processes, security engineering, and life cycle data for the supply, development, and operations and maintenance processes. However, this is still using standard, checklist and is only successful in limiting the development duality issue discussed above with the other issues still being valid concerns.

Ultimately, this chapter is proposing using the defense-in-depth approach as the developmental paradigm, while using the Lee et al. (2002) methodology with some aspects of Siponen and Baskerville (2001).

Threat Analysis

A threat is defined as a set of circumstances that has the potential to cause loss or harm (Pfleeger & Pfleeger, 2003). These circumstances may be caused intentionally, unintentionally, or even by natural events. Another perspective incorporating cyber warfare concerns comes from Jennex (2003) where threats are the capabilities and intentions of adversaries to exploit an IS; or any natural or unintentional event with the potential to cause harm to an IS, resulting in a degradation of an organization's ability to fully perform its mission. Risk analysis is the identification, categorization, and assessment of threats.

There are many methods for identifying threats including the use of Courtney's (1997) exposure groups, Fisher's (1984) exposure-identification structure, and Hutter's (2002) tree diagramming process. The most classical of these are Courtney's (1997) exposure groups where six groups of threats are identified: accidental disclosure, accidental modification, accidental destruction, intentional disclosure, intentional modification, and intentional destruction. Jennex (2003) identifies risks based on location and intention and offers five basic threat groups that are somewhat consistent with Courtney (1997): external accidental, external intentional, internal accidental, internal intentional, and acts of God (large scale events, such as equipment failures, fires, earthquakes, etc.). Each of these five threat groups has three degrees of risk, destruction of data, unplanned modification of data, and unapproved disclosure of data, that respectively relate to the availability, integrity, and confidentiality aspects of the CIA triangle model from the NSTISSC model (Whitman & Mattord, 2004). This paper uses the Jennex (2003) threat groups. These threat groups are complete for penetration type attacks; however, they do not account for attacks designed to prevent legitimate external users from accessing the system. Denial of service attacks is a class of attacks that are external to the system and which need to be protected against with the Internet service provider. Additionally, it is recommended that risk analysis be used to determine which threats and risks need to be protected against. The second step of a threat analysis is to conduct research to identify specific vulnerabilities for each threat.

Risk Analysis

In addition to threat analysis, organizations conduct a risk analysis to determine the financial impact of threats. The likelihood or probability of a threat is determined by summing the probabilities of the component vulnerabilities. The probability of a vulnerability occurring is determined via testing and/or use of operational and industry data. This multiplied by the consequence (in dollars) should the attack succeed to generate a cost for each risk. Risk analysis is used to determine the priority of risks and how much to spend on controls. Risk analysis also is used to determine an organization's approach to managing risk and serves as inputs into the security plan.

Barrier Analysis

Barrier analysis is a method of identifying hazards or threats and determining the effectiveness of the mitigating factors currently in place. Barrier analysis also can be used after an event has occurred to determine the cause and to help develop barriers to prevent repeat occurrences by determining future preventive action (Crowe, 1990).

Barriers and barrier systems can be classified as material or physical, functional, symbolic, and immaterial (Hollnagel, 1999). For example, material or physical could be containment, such as walls, doors, or restriction of physical access. By functional, we mean preventing or hindering, such as with passwords, preconditions, or delays. Symbolic refers to countering, regulating, indicating, permission, or communication, such as coding of functions, procedures, signs, work permit, or clearance. Finally, by immaterial, we mean monitoring or prescribing, such as with visual inspection, checklists, rules, or restrictions (Hollnagel, 1999).

Barrier analysis, when used for cyber security, is for the analysis, design, placement, maintenance, and evaluation of cyber controls for mitigating risks or threats to a system or application. A goal of barrier analysis is to place more barriers/controls on the higher risk threats (Jennex, 2003) and then to use barrier analysis to assess effectiveness should a penetration occur.

Ultimately, the advantages of using barrier analysis are that it helps to identify and place controls prior to an attack and then determines the causal factors and the actions needed to correct the problems after an attack has occurred (Crowe, 1990). The disadvantage of barrier analysis is that the method does not ensure that all appropriate controls have been identified, that failed barriers are recognized, and that the ef-

fects of the risks or threats that are applied in barrier analysis are properly identified (Crowe, 1990). These disadvantages are mitigated by using barrier analysis in an integrated design paradigm.

BARRIER ANALYSIS AND DEFENSE IN DEPTH AS A DESIGN PARADIGM

Barrier Diagrams

In terms of the original design or purpose of barrier analysis and barrier design, barrier diagrams show the necessary ingredients for an accident, including the environmental condition that causes the harm; vulnerable people or objects that can be hurt by the condition; failure/lack of controls that are designed to keep them apart; and events that lead into the final accident (Trost and Nertney, 1995). Crowe (1990) uses a simpler approach that utilizes the threat: the chain of barriers designed to prevent the threat and the asset being protected. Barrier analysis is then used to assess the overall effectiveness of the barrier system and of each individual barrier in preventing the event. Figure 1 illustrates a barrier diagram. This is the format chosen for use as a proposed method for modeling IS security.

Defense in Depth

Hartman (2001) suggests that any IS security design that relies on a single point of protection will probably be defeated. It is also reasonable to assume that in an evolving threat world, it is not possible to foresee and plan for all future threats or for all the different possible attack methods. To counter this, it is suggested that the defense in depth, also called multilayered, approach be used. Defense in depth is a concept that utilizes multiple compensating controls in layers to prevent or mitigate a threat (Bass & Robichaux, 2002). The use of multiple, independent controls increases the effort required to attack an asset. By being independent, it is not likely that a single attack could compromise

Figure 1. Sample barrier diagram (Crowe, 1990)

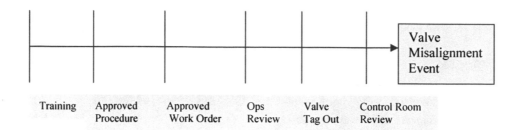

all the controls; and, should one or even several of the controls be circumvented or corrupted, there are other controls still providing protection (Hartman, 2001; McGuiness, 2001; Straub, 2003). To ensure independence, designers use a variety of technical, administrative, and operational controls to protect the asset (Anderson, 2001). Placing the controls in layers allows designers to establish a series of defensive perimeters that support each other and allow for the penetration of some layers, while still protecting the critical asset. Potential threats could be intentional or unintentional, internal or external, or any combination of these options. The number of controls and layers and the intensity of each are contingent on the type of the threat and the importance of the asset. There must be a balance between the risk/threat and the cost or overhead in protecting the system (Allen et al., 2002; Jennex, 2003). When used in barrier analysis, a barrier is defined as the combination of the layer with its controls.

PROPOSED METHODOLOGY

This chapter proposes modifying the integrated approach of Lee et al. (2002) and Siponen and Baskerville (2001) with the use of barrier analysis and defense in depth to create a security requirement identification and design methodology that is incorporated into traditional systems analysis and design methodol-

ogy. The methodology encourages using Siponen and Baskervilles's (2001) metanotation to add security detail to existing system development diagrams, such as use cases and/or data flow diagrams (DFDs). The methodology also uses barrier analysis diagrams as a graphical method of identifying and documenting security requirements. Barrier diagrams are used to identify the necessary barriers, that is, controls and layers, to prevent events caused by credible threats identified through risk analysis. The defense-in-depth paradigm is used to ensure that there are multiple, independent security barriers (controls and layers) between threats and events. Additionally, it is intended that the process follow the approach of integrating security design into the software development lifecycle as proposed by Lee et al. (2002).

Security barrier (layer and control) requirements are identified in the analysis phase of system development by applying the security plan (in particular, security policies) and best practices, conducting risk assessments, and generating barrier diagrams. Risk assessments are used to determine credible threats and key assets. Barrier diagrams are used to document those threats that need to be guarded against, those assets needing to be protected, key processes where threats could intervene, and key actors involved in those processes. Each barrier is a layer with specific controls and is identified based on stakeholder input, existing security policies, existing barriers in support and infrastructure systems, and using the defense-in-depth philosophy. Layers are labeled across the top of the barrier diagram, and controls are listed at the bottom of the barrier. Stakeholders for this phase include system analysts, users, management, and any existing security team or group. Entity relation diagrams (ERDs), DFDs, and use cases should be used to assist in asset, critical process and key actor identification. The final use of the barrier diagrams will be to gain concurrence from the users and other stakeholders that all threats and assets have been identified and that adequate security requirements have been identified. The systems requirements document should include security requirements identified by the barrier diagrams and the actual barrier diagrams as a security model. Additionally, the organization should initiate any needed security policies to support the identified security requirements.

Required barriers are specified with appropriate control design specifications during the design phase of system development. Analysts, developers, and security experts identify technologies and methods for implementing the identified barriers. Design specifications are determined using the security plan, policies, and procedures; the existing security and technical infrastructure; and standard data integrity and fault tolerant design practices.

Developers and security experts use the barrier diagrams and security design specifications during the development phase to build security into the system. Barrier construction is determined using security policies, processes, and procedures; security infrastructure; checklists/best practices; and data integrity and fault tolerant construction practices. Implementation details are added to the diagrams as metanotations.

Testing of the security barriers occurs during the system testing and implementation phases. The barrier diagrams should be used to generate test scripts and success criteria, user training requirements and the implementation plan. Details of these plans and scripts should be linked by document reference to the barrier diagram metanotation.

Integrity of the security barriers is maintained during the maintenance phase. The barrier diagrams are used to track continued implementation of security requirements and to verify that enhancements and fixes do not reduce the effectiveness of security barriers either individually or within the context of defense in depth.

Finally, barrier diagrams and analysis can be used in all phases to analyze security events. The analysis uses the diagrams to determine which barriers failed and what corrective actions or design implementations need to be taken to prevent recurrence of the event.

BARRIER DIAGRAM EXAMPLE

A knowledge management system (KMS) will be used to illustrate how barrier diagrams and the defense-in-depth paradigm can be used. For this example, it is assumed the KMS is Internet based to allow both internal and external access by employees, and the knowledge base is located in a single database on a single server. The KMS is for tracking and documenting maintenance lessons learned in maintaining F18 Hornet aircraft. This is a system that could be targeted by cyber terrorists/warriors as disclosure of the knowledge base contents could allow adversaries to discover weaknesses in the aircraft that could be exploited in aerial combat; or modification or destruction of the knowledge base could adversely impact maintenance activities causing slower, less effective maintenance, which could be critical in time of war.

The requirements phase involved the systems analyst, key knowledge users, management, and the security group. There is consensus that all knowledge in the knowledge base needs to be protected and that project experience related to the core business area is critical. There is also consensus that all five threat groups; external accidental, external intentional, internal accidental, internal intentional, and acts of God for all three degrees (except acts of God, which only has inappropriate destruction), inappropriate disclosure, modification, and destruction, and need to be protected against. Identification of key knowledge base assets is accomplished through metanotation in the form of comments added to the entity relation diagram or data dictionary. The barrier diagram for the external intentional and accidental threats with inappropriate disclosure, modification, or destruction is shown in Figure 2 and is a roll up of diagrams created for each level of damage and each degree of external threat. Space considerations prevent showing all these diagrams. but they are summarized for external intentional threats as follows:

- External intentional with inappropriate disclosure uses the layers (controls) of network access, spyware checking, system access, interface design (user views), and database (DB) design (encryption, no global create, read, update, delete [CRUD], user groups).
- External intentional with modification uses the layers (controls) of network access, virus checking, system access, interface design (controlled update process), database design (no global CRUD, user groups, value checking), and back up and recovery (transaction logs).
- External intentional with destruction uses the layers (controls) of network access control, vi-

rus checking, system access control, interface design, database design (no global CRUD, user groups), and back up (B/U) and recovery.

Combining the barriers into one diagram results in virus checking and spyware checking being combined into simply malware checking. Functional requirements come from the identified controls and are added to the system requirements specification (SRS) (example discussed later) with the threat table and barrier diagrams as supporting documentation. Finally, the current security plan and policies are reviewed to ensure policies exist for the identified security requirements.

Figure 3 is the diagram for the internal intentional and accidental threats with inappropriate disclosure, modification, and destruction. Figure 4 is the diagram for the acts of God threats with destruction.

Boxes represent the threat entity (left end) (this can also be specific vulnerabilities) and the asset to be protected (right end). The line connecting the boxes represents the path the threat takes to get to the protected asset. The lines perpendicular to the threat

Figure 2. External intentional and accidental threats requirements and design barrier diagram

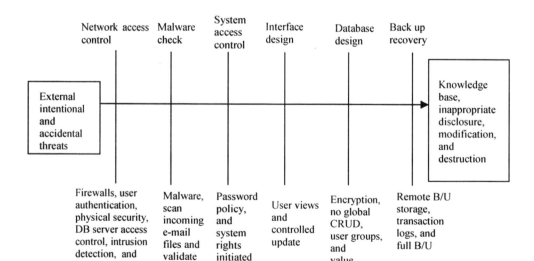

Figure 3. Internal intentional and accidental threats requirements phase barrier diagram Minnesota Multiphasic Personality Inventory (MMPI)

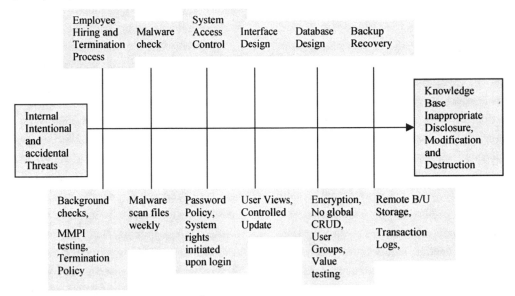

Figure 4. Acts of God threats requirements phase

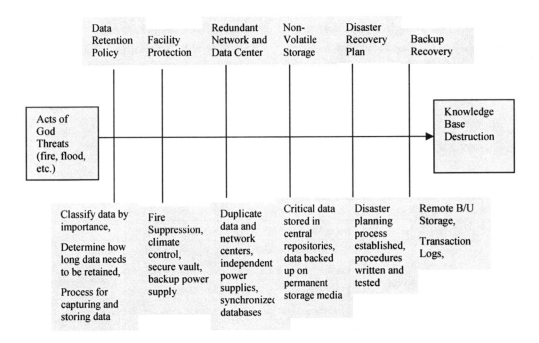

path are the barriers erected to prevent the threat from reaching the protected asset. Top text lists the layer, while the lower text lists the controls. Security requirements are generated from the identified and needed controls. Barriers and requirements vary based on the threat group with some overlap expected, since security strategies may be applied to multiple threats.

These barrier diagrams illustrate defense in depth by showing that there are six barriers that integrate multiple, independent, security technologies and approaches with existing security policies and infrastructure for each set of threats. Figure 2 illustrates this approach. Firewalls are used to screen for authorized users; passwords are used to authenticate user identities; user rights groups and user views are used to limit user access to what is needed; data entry testing is used to validate data before it is stored to prevent potentially incorrect data from being stored; encryption is used to prevent unauthorized data disclosure; and back up and recovery is used in case all the barriers fail and the threat entity destroys or modifies the data.

Analysts can use Figures 2, 3, and 4 as is or can combine the diagrams into a single master diagram. Either way, the security requirements from each of the barrier diagrams are combined to generate the final requirements specification. Additionally, the barrier diagrams are useful for communicating these requirements to the stakeholders and security specialists and in gaining their concurrence and approval.

Once the security requirements are approved, the analyst uses them to generate security design specifications. The analyst can continue to develop the metanotation on the barrier diagram to include more layers of detail, specifically design specifications. Alternately, this detail can be added by supplementing the barrier diagram with tables of design specifications tied to requirements. Table 1 illustrates the table approach to documenting design specifications for the database design barrier in Figures 2 and 3. The table approach is recommended to keep the barrier diagrams readable. This detail is generated during the design phase of system development and could be extracted or generated using the logical data model and physical table design chart. Design detail is expressed as design specifications for each of the functional requirement specifications.

During the coding and testing phase, unit and functional test scripts are generated using the design specifications. The barrier diagrams are used to generate integrated system test plans that establish

Table 1. Sample barrier diagram requirements (taken from Figure 2)

Functional requirement	Design requirement
Encrypt critical knowledge	Encrypt Project_Report.Lessons_Learned attribute
No global CRUD rights	Instantiate database rights upon log in to system
Establish CRUD rights via user groups (user groups)	Establish administrative user group with administrative rights
	Establish management user group with partial read, update (RU) rights
	Establish update user group with full CRUD rights
	Establish project manager user group with partial CRUD rights
	Establish knowledge user group with partial CRUD rights
Check data input before writing to DB (value checking)	Use choice lists for attributes with finite selections
	Range check numeric and currency attributes
	Format attribute input for those with set formats

initial conditions, expected system responses, and allow for a series of monitored attacks by a variety of attacker profiles. Attacker profiles are designed to fit the expected attacker profiles of the analyzed vulnerabilities. The barrier diagrams show how the security system is supposed to work and provides a basis for analyzing failures in individual barriers. Testers need to develop scenarios that test the ability of total security system, that is, of all the barriers working together, to protect the assets. Testing is completed when scenarios cannot be generated that successfully penetrate the asset. If scenarios are found that result in penetration, then designers need to revise the security system to counter it. Scenarios that result in some barriers being defeated need to be reviewed to determine if there are vulnerabilities in the barrier design. Testing can be performed by using "white-hat" hackers to attempt penetration. These testers would use their skills to attempt penetration and to identify vulnerabilities in the overall security plan should they penetrate the outer network security. Additionally, automated network security scans can be used to identify vulnerabilities in network security. Ultimately, it should be assumed that network security will be penetrated and the other barriers need to be tested to determine their effectiveness in protecting or minimizing damage to the assets.

The barrier diagrams and vulnerability assessment are used during the maintenance phase to assess system changes for impact to the security design. As new knowledge bases are added, they are assessed for criticality and the need for encryption. As the organization expands to new locations the diagrams provide a blueprint for designing local facility and network security. As employees change jobs, are hired, or quit, the diagrams provide guidance to what user groups need to be modified. Finally, as new threats are identified, the diagrams are used to assess any needed changes to the security system.

The final use of the diagrams is in assessing the impact of attempted penetrations, events, or internal acts that defeat some or all of the barriers designed to prevent the penetration, event, or internal act. Security specialists can use the diagrams to identify security implementations that failed and what caused the failure. The goal is to identify user behaviors, policy issues, or weak technologies that need changing or improving.

EXPERIENCE USING BARRIER DIAGRAMS AND DEFENSE IN DEPTH

Barrier diagrams and defense in depth was pilot tested by a team of graduate students, designing a Web site for the International Student Center. The Web application is for potential students to contact the university as well as for existing international students to participate in the International Students Association. Functions included databases, Web forms, a schedule of events and meetings, and supports the use of online chat for members and potential students. Security requirements were determined through a threat analysis and the generation of barrier diagrams. The diagrams were generated based on discussions with the chair of the university's IS security committee and were validated as correct. Design specifications were generated, documented in tables, and discussed with the chair of the university's IS security committee for approval. The specifications were approved and the final design documented in a system design specification. Interviews with the project team found that the diagrams were very effective and useful in identifying the full set of security requirements needed for the system and in generating the system security design specifications. The diagrams also were found to be effective in conveying security requirements. The team also stated that the diagrams helped them discover weaknesses that they would have otherwise missed.

FUTURE TRENDS

System analysis and design is moving towards automation. Computer aided software engineering (CASE) tools are being developed and implemented to support all phases and activities in the system development life cycle. It is expected that for the proposed methodology to be accepted, CASE tools that automate barrier diagram generation, barrier analysis, and defense-in-depth analysis will need to be developed. Additionally, existing CASE tools will need to be modified to incorporate adding metanotation to system analysis models.

CONCLUSION

Barrier diagrams provide a graphical tool for identifying and determining security requirements. Graphical tools enhance understanding and communications between stakeholders. This tool is expected to enhance understanding of and compliance with security requirements.

The defense-in-depth paradigm enhances security by providing multiple barriers to prevent threats from causing damaging events. When coupled with barrier diagrams, it provides a tool for all stakeholders to integrate security needs and efforts and provides a process for ensuring security measures work together and not against each other.

Combining these tools provides a means for integrating security design and implementation across the SDLC. While the traditional lifecycle was discussed, these tools can be applied to any life-cycle approach. Integrating security design and implementation into the life cycle should improve overall system quality.

Finally, barrier diagrams and analysis can be used much as it is used in the United States nuclear industry, as a tool for determining root cause. This tool provides an analysis tool for determining what failed and how preventative actions can be taken to prevent future security breaches.

REFERENCES

Alberts, C. J., & Dorofee, A. J. (2001). *OCTAVE method implementation guide version 2.0*. Retrieved February 27, 2006, from Carnegie Mellon Software Engineering Institute Web site: http://www.cert.org/octave/download/intro.html

Allen, J. H., Mikoski Jr., E. F., Nixon, K. M., & Skillman, D. L. (2002). *Common sense guide for senior managers: Top ten recommended information security practices.* Arlington, VA: Internet Security Alliance.

Anderson, P. (2001). *Deception: A healthy part of any defense in-depth strategy.* Retrieved February 25, 2006, from SANS Institute Web site: www.sans.org/rr/whitepapers/policyissues/506.php

Baskerville, R. (1993). Information systems security design methods: Implications for information systems development. *ACM Computing Surveys, 25*(4), 375-414.

Bass, T., & Robichaux, R. (2002). *Defense in depth revisited: Qualitative risk analysis methodology for complex network-centric operations.* Retrieved February 26, 2006, from http://www.silkroad.com/papers/pdf/archives/defense-in-depth-revisited-original.pdf

Clemens, P. L. (2002). *Energy flow/barrier analysis* (3rd ed.). Retrieved February 26, 2006, from http://www.sverdrup.com/safety/energy.pdf

Computer Security Institute. (2005). 2005 CSI/FBI computer crime and security survey. *Computer Security Issues and Trends.* Retrieved February 26, 2006, from http://www.gocsi.com

Courtney, R. (1997). Security risk assessment in electronic data processing. *AFIPS Proceedings of the National Computer Conference, 46* (pp. 97-104).

Crowe, D. (1990). *Root cause training course for Catawba nuclear station.* General Physics Corporation.

Fisher, R. (1984). *Information systems security.* Englewood Cliffs, NJ: Prentice-Hall.

Haddon Jr., W. (1973). Energy damage and the ten countermeasure strategies. *Human Factors Journal, 15,* 355-365.

Hartman, S. (2001). *Securing e-commerce: An overview of defense in-depth.* Retrieved February 26, 2006, from http://www.giac.org/certified_professionals/practicals/gsec/0592.php

Hollnagel, E. (1999). *Accident analysis and barrier functions.* Retrieved July 3, 2005, from http://www.hai.uu.se/projects/train/papers/accidentanalysis.pdf

Hutter, D. (2002). *Security engineering.* Retrieved July 3, 2005, from http://www.dfki.de/~hutter/lehre/sicherheit/securityengineering.ppt

Jennex, M. E. (2003). *Security design.* Unpublished system design lecture [IDS 697]: San Diego State University.

Jennex, M. E., & Walters, A. (2003). A comparison of knowledge requirements for operating hacker and security tools. *The Security Conference,* Information Institute.

Lee, Y., Lee, Z., & Lee, C. K. (2002). A study of integrating the security engineering process into the software lifecycle process standard [IEEE/EIA 12207]. *6th Americas conference on information systems, AMCIS* (pp. 451-457).

McGuiness, T. (2001). *Defense in depth.* Retrieved February 25, 2006, from SANS Institute Web site: http://www.sans.org/rr/whitepapers/basics/525.php

Pfleeger, C. P., & Pfleeger, S. L. (2003). *Security in computing* (3rd ed.). Upper Saddle River, NJ: Prentice-Hall.

Siponen, M., Baskerville, R. (2001). A new paradigm for adding security into IS development methods. *8th Annual Working Conference on Information Security Management and Small Systems Security.*

Straub, K. R. (2003). *Managing risk with defense in depth.* Retrieved February 25, 2006, from SANS Institute Web site: http://www.sans.org/rr/whitepapers/infosec/1224.php

Trost, W. A., & Nertney, R. J. (1995). *Barrier analysis.* Retrieved July 3, 2005, from http://ryker.eh.doe.gov/analysis/trac/29/trac29.html

Whitman, M. E., & Mattord, H. J. (2004). *Management of information security.* Boston: Thomson Course Technology.

TERMS AND DEFINITIONS

Barrier: The combination of controls implemented within a security layer.

Barrier analysis (also barrier diagrams): A tool used in root cause analysis that utilizes barrier diagrams. Barrier analysis is the process of identifying organizational, procedural, managerial, and so forth barriers that exist to prevent a specific action from occurring.

Control: This security mechanism, policy, or procedure can counter system attack, reduce risks, limit losses, and mitigate vulnerabilities (Whitman & Mattord, 2004).

Defense in depth (also multilayered design): This is an approach to security that relies on multiple technologies and multiple approaches to mitigate risk.

Layer: This defensive perimeter/boundary consisting of a set of controls is established to protect a specified asset or set of assets.

Root cause analysis: A process used to identify the base cause of an event.

System development life cycle (SDLC) (also software development life cycle): An approach to system development based on identifying requirements early in the development process, building to the requirements, then maintaining the requirements over the life of the system. SDLC processes usually rely on a series of phases, such as feasibility analysis, requirements analysis, design, construction, implementation, and maintenance.

Chapter XXX
Antispam Approaches Against Information Warfare

Hsin-Yang Lu
Technology Marketing Corporation, USA

Chia-Jung Tsui
Syracuse University, USA

Joon S. Park
Syracuse University, USA

ABSTRACT

The term "spam" refers to unsolicited bulk e-mail that people do not want to receive. Today it is gradually becoming a serious problem that results in significant cost both to e-mail receivers and to ISPs (Internet Service Providers). More and more people have become concerned about the issue and are making efforts to develop various anti-spam approaches, some of which are in-process proposals, while others are currently in use. In this chapter, key anti-spam approaches that include filtering, remailers, e-postage, hashcash, and sender authentication, are analyzed and discussed how these antispam approaches can be used against information warfare and cyber terrorism. Furthermore, we analyze vulnerabilities in each approach and recommend possible countermeasures. Technical details and comparisons of each antispam approach are not discussed in this chapter because of space limitations.

BACKGROUND

According to the Federal Bureau of Investigation (FBI), cyber terrorism is "the premeditated, politically motivated attack against information, computer systems, computer programs, and data which results in violence against noncombatant targets by sub-national groups or clandestine agents" (Pollitt, 1997). While the FBI focuses cyber terrorism more on political aspects, some people define it as "any occurrence that can compromise the integrity of an electronic business operation" (Gustin, 2004).

Today, cyber terrorists' major weapons include Trojan horses, viruses, worms, denial-of-service (DoS) programs, password/ID theft tools, and other malicious software. The term "spam" refers to unsolicited and inappropriate bulk e-mail that recipients do not want to receive (Cerf, 2005; Denning, 1992; Neumann & Weinstein, 1997). A cyber terrorist can exploit spam techniques as complementary ways to use their weapons in information warfare.

The e-mail system is one of the most common communication platforms these days, and there are always some people who lack security awareness, no matter how much antiterrorism programs or knowledge is disseminated. Therefore, from a cyber terrorist's point of view, spamming millions of people with malicious codes or links to false Web sites is one of the most effective ways to reach as many gullible people as possible to compromise security. In this chapter, we analyze key antispam approaches, including filtering, remailers, e-postage, hashcash, and sender authentication, and we discuss how antispam approaches can be used against information warfare and cyber terrorism. Furthermore, we analyze vulnerabilities in each approach and recommend possible countermeasures.

SPAM FILTERING

Typically, there are two categories of spam filtering: rule-based (heuristic) and Bayesian-based (statistical) approaches.

The rule-based filtering approach was the most used until 2002. It checks predefined lists and patterns that indicate spam is present (Park & Deshpande, 2005). In essence, e-mail from senders defined in the black lists is considered to be spam and, consequently, are filtered out, whereas e-mail from those senders defined in the white lists are considered to be legitimate messages. For effective usage, these lists should be kept up to date constantly. As for the patterns, they include, but are not limited to, specific words and phrases, many uppercase letters and exclamation points, malformed e-mail headers, dates in the future or the past, improbable return addresses, strange symbols, embedded graphics, and much fraudulent routing information (Androutsopoulos, Koutsias, Chandrinos, & Spyropoulos, 2000; Cournane and Hunt, 2004; Cranor & LaMacchia, 1998; Hidalgo,

Opez, & Sanz, 2000; Ioannidis, 2003). The filter scores each message scanned. Those whose scores exceed a threshold value will be regarded as spam. The main drawback of a rule-based filter is that e-mail headers can be easily manipulated with the very real possibility that a spammer has falsified the header information, including the fields for domain name service (DNS) names, senders' e-mail addresses, and delivery paths, so the e-mail appears to be from a legitimate source. Since the rules are static, spammers can usually find ways to tune e-mails in order to circumvent the filter, once new rules are set. If the filter is available to the public, then spammers can even test their spam on the filter before sending it out.

On the contrary, the Bayesian-based (Androutsopoulos et al., 2000; Sahami, Dumais, Heckerman, & Horovitz, 1998; Schneider, 2003) filtering approach is more dynamic, since it learns over time what each user considers spam to be. Basically, it uses the knowledge of prior events to predict future events. If a user marks messages as spam, the Bayesian filter will learn to automatically put messages from the same source or with the same kind of patterns into a spam folder the next time such messages are delivered. If the user does not mark those messages as spam, the filter will learn to consider them legitimate. Because Bayesian filters can be trained, their effectiveness improves continually. On the other hand, since they need to be trained, a user has to rectify them every time they misclassify an e-mail. Fortunately, the more examples or patterns that are learned by the filter, the less additional work will be required of a user.

One major role that spam plays in cyber terrorism is "phishing," an emerging criminal technique that solicites users for their personal or financial information. For example, spammers can make spam almost identical to official bank e-mails, requesting customers' financial information, assuming some recipients happen to be targets. In that case, the rule-based filtering approach described above checks predefined lists and patterns that indicate spam. In order to pass the list-based filtering, namely black lists and white lists, phishing e-mail can simply use a bank's official outgoing e-mail address since spammers do not expect replies by e-mail but lead recipients to a fake bank Web site into which they are to enter account information. The e-mail may look like official e-mail to the recipient. For instance, to trick recipients, the displayed Web site address in the phishing e-mail could be correct, but links to a false address, usually in the form of an Internet protocol (IP) address.

Therefore, the principal way to fight phishing is to ascertain whether senders are actually who they claim to be or to verify the e-mail routing path from the originator to the recipient. A simple filtering technique cannot do much to avoid phishing attacks because phishing makes its e-mail almost the same as the official e-mail, except for some routing information and links to a false Web site. We recommend combining filtering with sender authentication solutions and to not only to check spam for specific patterns, but also to verify the source of e-mail.

REMAILER

Gburzynski and Maitan (2004) proposed the remailer approach for limiting spam. The main idea of this approach is to set a program called "remailer" between senders and recipients to forward each other's e-mail. A user is allowed to set up an unlimited number of aliases of his or her permanent e-mail address to be protected. The aliases are handed out to other users willing to communicate with the owner of the aliases. A user is able to set up the validity of his or her alias based on a specific time period, number of received messages, population of senders, or in other ways. By processing and transforming the e-mail through the remailer, the true and permanent e-mail address of the remailer user is hidden, and the users only communicate with other people via aliases. Since the use of aliases is compatible with the existing e-mail infrastructure, it can be easily integrated with other antispam techniques.

There are several major elements of the remailer approach. The first is aliasing. It is possible for a user to create one alias for each person or small group he or she contacts. By restricting each alias to specific

senders (people who want to communicate with the owner of the alias), the chance of these aliases being used for spamming is greatly reduced. Another technique used in the remailer approach is the use of a master alias for the public e-mail address and a challenge question. The challenge question is usually an image with randomly distorted texts that can be easily interpreted by a human, but difficult for computers to interpret. Spammers will fail to do this task because it is impossible for them to answer a challenge question manually for each of the thousands of e-mails they send.

By using the remailer technique, not only will spam decrease, but most spam-related cyberterrorism can be prevented. Regular spam sent by cyber terrorists can no longer reach the targeted people because millions of e-mails sent by robots will not be able to pass the challenging questions that are necessary to initiate communication. Attackers could still make successful attacks by sending e-mails manually (i.e., answering challenging questions for each e-mail), but the attackers would then lose the ability to fake the sender's e-mail address. For example, in a phishing attack, terrorists can send their e-mail to the master alias manually, answer the challenge question, and get a specific alias valid for their own e-mail address, say "Bob@cyber. com," in order to communicate with the permanent e-mail address connected to the master alias. Then in the following attacks, if they want to pretend to be real staff in a legitimate company, say Citibank, by using this alias they cannot make recipients fall into the scam by faking a sending e-mail address, such as "services@citibank.com," because they can only send e-mail to this alias from the e-mail address they have used to answer the challenge question at the very beginning, namely, Bob@cyber.com here. They will never be able to get an alias personalized to services@ citibank.com because in the challenge-response procedure, only the e-mail initiating the request to communicate will get the question to answer, and the attackers have no access to read and reply to e-mail in services@citibank.com.

However, this does not mean that there is no way for terrorists to send phishing e-mail. For example, the terrorists can still make a phishing attack as long as they have a large number of aliases and all of the sender addresses to which each of those aliases is personalized. The e-mail sent to those aliases with the corresponding sender address will be delivered, since the remailer will consider that those senders have answered the questions before. It is not impossible for attackers to steal address books from users' computers by using some malicious program, such as a Trojan horse. To prevent such attacks in information warfare, sender authentication can be integrated with the remailer to check the links between aliases and senders' identities.

E-POSTAGE

E-postage has been proposed and discussed as a solution for spam prevention (Fahlman, 2002). As the name "e-postage" hints at, the solution is inspired by the mechanism of post services in the real world. Different versions of an e-postage system have been proposed by different researchers, but generally the idea is to introduce a cash payment for every e-mail sent. The difference is that in the digital world, a "stamp" represents a piece of code sent along with e-mail. For ensuring the validity of an e-stamp and for preventing fraud, an e-stamp needs to be certified by a third party, using some authentication technology, such as public key infrastructure (PKI) (FIPS PUB 186, 1994; Rivest, Shamir, & Adleman, 1978)). The third party works like a post office in the real world. They issue senders e-stamps and guarantee that the e-stamp can be recognized and admitted by all mail servers in the world.

Unlike the physical postage service, e-postage is mostly paid to the ultimate recipient or to the recipient's Internet service provider (ISP), instead of to third parties who issue e-stamps, although there may be a cut taken by them. The reason for this is that the major cost resulting from spam is to the recipients and their ISPs who handle e-mail, so their loss should be reimbursed with e-postage. In addition, the amount of e-postage is decided by the recipients, since everyone has a different price in mind for receiving a spam e-mail. A recipient can choose to receive only e-mail with e-postage over a certain amount that he or she has decided on in advance or simply accept e-mail without e-postage from people on the white list.

The e-postage approach is generally effective in preventing spam-related activities. However, some terrorists can still choose to spam a group of people by paying for the e-stamps, as long as they think the attack is economically feasible or politically worthwhile. Moreover, terrorists also can compromise e-postage by using skillful techniques. For instance, terrorists can steal address books from users' computers by sending malicious programs. Once they get the address books, they can send e-mail to those addresses, with the sender identities of the books' owners. Then the attackers will have a good chance of not having to pay e-postage for that e-mail because the sender address they fake is probably in the recipients' white lists.

To prevent such attacks, the e-postage system needs to be improved. One way would be to increase the e-stamp rate and, if possible, provide certain ways to track people who actually bought e-stamps. Since e-stamps are issued by a third-party authority and cannot be duplicated, it is technically possible to give each e-stamp or a group of e-stamps a unique identification number. Each e-stamp would need to be purchased before being issued, so that the identification number would somehow be associated with the identity of the buyers for tracking purposes, or at least serve to narrow down the search for suspected terrorist groups.

HASHCASH

Hashcash is another solution to spam that was proposed in early 1990 (Dwork & Naor, 1992). The idea is similar to e-postage—attaching an e-stamp to every e-mail sent. The difference is that e-stamps are not obtained by a cash payment in advance, but by a consumption of computing power. Hashcash requires each e-mail be sent with an e-stamp that represents an answer to a certain computing question, such as finding an input of a hash function (Rivest, 1992) for a specific result. These computing questions usually take a computer with normal capability a few seconds to answer. This performance loss is not a significant delay to regular end users but is not feasible for spammers who send thousands or millions of e-mail messages at a time. Like e-postage, hashcash employs the white list mechanism. Users can put their friends and the mailing list or newsletter they subscribe to on the white list. Then e-mail from addresses on the white list will require no e-stamps of hashcash. There is already some commercial antispam software implementing hashcash that is installed on ISP mail servers, including SpamAssassin, Tagged Message Delivery Agent (TMDA), and Camram.

For preventing cyber terrorism attacks, hashcash has similar strengths and drawbacks as e-postage, since they work on the same principle–getting money from senders. Terrorists will not be able to send spam if they cannot afford the computing cost for sending a large amount of unsolicited e-mail, and the inability to send e-mail in bulk will hinder their attacks, given that the success rate for each e-mail attack is low. However, hashcash may be a little easier to compromise than e-postage because, generally speaking, processing power is more widely available and easier to obtain than real money for e-postage. Besides, if attackers use malicious codes to send less spam at a time from their "zombie" computers using hashcash , it is harder for users to feel that their computers have become slower due to the attack. As for improving the technique against information warfare or cyber terrorism, it is more difficult to put any kind of tracking mechanism on hashcash than on e-postage. Once the computing power is consumed, the entire process passes without leaving much identifying information or a usage log. This makes it difficult to identify terrorists. Hashcash might be employed along with other techniques, such as sender authentication, to further enhance the security of the system.

SENDER AUTHENTICATION

Unlike antispam proposals, such as remailer, e-postage, and hashcash, sender authentication is more practical and has already been adopted by some major players, such as Yahoo!, AOL, and Microsoft. The principle of sender authentication is to add a layer of responsibility to the e-mail system, which has been notorious for its anonymous action in the spam war. There are no certifiable ways for senders to prove their identities when sending e-mail. Therefore, it is easy and free for senders to claim to be someone else, given the assumption that they do not mind not getting replies. Although the recognition of a sender's identity is not sufficient to make a decision as to whether a message is spam or not, such information is still very useful, since, from now on, the sender's reputation can be tracked and used to determine the possibility of it being the source of spam. As a result, it becomes more and more important for sending domains to publish authentication records for their outbound e-mail in order to distinguish their e-mail from spam. Below, domain-basis and per-user sender authentication is discussed.

Domain-Basis Sender Authentication

There are two categories of domain-basis sender authentication. One is IP-based authentication, which verifies the address of sending domains; the other is crypto-based authentication, which verifies a digital signature extracted from a message header. Both depend on publishing some information in the sending domain's domain name system's (DNS) records and on verifying the messages received with published information at the receiving domain. It is clever to take advantage of the DNS as an authority to publish public keys in cryptographic schemes or sender policy framework (SPF) (Wong, 2006) records in IP-based schemes. DNS plays a fine distributed authority, and each domain runs its own DNS. This attribute assures availability by helping the domain-basis sender authentication avoid DoS attacks, since there is no central authority in that case. Once the domain-basis sender authentication approach becomes popular, sending domains will be correctly recognized. Thus, the past behavior or reputation of sending domains will be an important factor in dealing with incoming messages to decide whether to accept them unconditionally, filter for future review, or reject directly. Each sending domain, on the other hand, would have to take more responsibility for its outbound e-mail, by monitoring any abnormal traffic to prevent potential spammers from abusing its service.

For phishing attacks to compromise domain-basis sender authentication in cyber terrorism, it would be quite simple for spammers to register a confusing domain name, similar to the official and well-known one, and send "legitimate" e-mail. They could follow the procedures to publish some information in the domain's DNS and then send spam through those "authorized" outbound e-mail servers for the new domain. Since e-mail is either from a registered list of IP addresses or correctly signed by the claimed IP-based domain, phishing e-mail will pass the verification test on the receiving side, while the new domain has not yet accumulated any reputation for sending e-mail. As for the e-mail body, it could be made as similar as possible to the official one but with a link to the false Web site that entices recipients to disclose critical personal information for phishing attacks. For example, spammers could register citibanking.com to masquerade as citibank.com, for financial information or fbi.org to masquerade as fbi.gov for social security numbers. This presents a major threat, especially when the first impression on the spammer's domain name directly connects recipients to the company the domain name intends to suggest. The threat would continue until some security is breached or the new domain name accumulates a bad enough reputation.

Despite the vulnerabilities described above, domain-basis sender authentication can still be a reliable solution to cyber terrorism, since the idea of authenticating that senders are who they claim to be is still a principal way to fight phishing attacks or other social-engineering spam. Educating end users

is necessary for domain-basis sender authentication. For example, end users must be careful anytime they enter critical information requested by e-mail, even if the e-mail is actually from the claimed domain, since it is sometimes uncertain that the domain belongs to the company it names.

Per-User Sender Authentication

Today some e-mail-sending servers require the sender's account information after registration to use their services (e.g., Yahoo!, Hotmail, and many other credible organizations that provide e-mail accounts and services on Web sites). Those servers authenticate senders prior to providing access to their services. The sender's identity will be included in the e-mail header by the email-sending server, in which case the spammer cannot forge the "From" field or the email-sending server's DNS name in the "Received" lines. Since spam includes the spammer's identity, it can simply be filtered out in the future by adding the sender to the black list. However, if a spammer uses a fake registered e-mail account for sender-authentication in the server, such spam will be successfully delivered to the recipients. Although the senders have to be registered and authenticated with the accounts in the servers before sending e-mail, they can create fake accounts whenever needed and use them for sending spam. Later, the accounts are used for sending spam, but the real identity of the spammer cannot be traced via the fake account. Furthermore, the spammer can use another fake account another time. To prevent from this kind of problem, we need a strong mechanism to bind the sender's real identity and e-mail accounts. However, this introduces an argument regarding anonymous e-mail services that are needed in some cases.

If per-user sender authentication works on a worldwide basis, recipients can make sure that the sender is actually whom he claims to be, not just from the claimed domain in the domain-basis sender authentication. However, verification of a sender's identity cannot guarantee that the sender has sent the e-mail himself. For example, this kind of attack could be achieved by worms. Worms are computer programs capable of self-replicating throughout the network. In the world of cyber terrorism, worms are mostly used to obstruct e-mail servers. Therefore, one might get an e-mail from a friend whose computer is compromised by the worm. The e-mail subject could begin with "Fw:," which suggests that the e-mail, usually with some malicious attachments, is some kind of "goody" for him to check out. Since the source is sure to be from one of his acquaintances, according to per-user sender authentication, one might execute the attachments for fun and with confidence. This way, worms can be spread further with the "support" of the per-user sender authentication. Like domain-basis sender authentication, it is still necessary to educate end users and keep them alert to cyber terrorism, even if e-mail passes the sender authentication.

CONCLUSION

In this chapter, we have analyzed key antispam approaches, including filtering, remailers, e-postage, hashcash, and sender authentication, and discussed how these antispam approaches can be used against information warfare and cyber terrorism. Furthermore, we analyzed vulnerabilities in each approach and recommended possible countermeasures. Technical details and comparisons of each antispam approach are not discussed in this chapter because of space limitations.

REFERENCES

Androutsopoulos, I., Koutsias, J., Chandrinos, K., & Spyropoulos, D. (2000). An experimental comparison of naive Bayesian and keyword-based anti-spam filtering with personal email messages. In *Proceedings of the 23rd ACM SIGIR Annual Conference* (pp. 160-167). Athens, Greece.

Cerf, V. G. (2005). Spam, spim, and spit. *Communications of the ACM, 48*(4), 39-43.

Cournane, A., & Hunt, R. (2004). An analysis of the tools used for the generation and prevention of spam. *IEEE Computers & Security, 23*(2), 154-166.

Cranor, I., & LaMacchia, B. (1998). Spam! *Communications of the ACM, 41*(11), 74-84.

Cyber terrorism and critical infrastructure protection. (2002) (testimony of Ronald L. Dick). Retrieved from www.fbi.gov/congress/congress02/nipc072402.htm

Denning, P. J. (1992). Electronic junk. *Communications of the ACM, 25*(3), 163-165.

Dwork, C., & Naor, M. (1992). Pricing via processing or combating junk mail. In *Proceedings of the 12th Annual International Cryptology Conference on Advances in Cryptology* (pp. 139-147). Santa Barbara, CA.

Fahlman, S. E. (2002). Selling interrupt rights: A way to control unwanted e-mail and telephone calls. *IBM Systems Journal, 41*(4), 759-766.

FIPS PUB 186. (1994). FIPS 186: Federal Information Processing Standard: Digital Signature Standard (DSS). National Institute of Standards and Technology (NIST). Retrieved from http://www.taugh.com/epostage.pdf

Gburzynski, P., & Maitan, J. (2004). Fighting the spam wars: A remailer approach with restrictive aliasing. *ACM Transactions on Internet Technology, 4*(1), 1-30.

Gustin, J. F. (2004). *Cyber terrorism: A guide for facility managers.* Fairmont Press.

Hidalgo, J., Opez, M., & Sanz, E. (2000). Combining text and heuristics for cost-sensitive spam filtering. In *Proceedings of the 4th Computational Natural Language Learning Workshop (CoNLL)* (pp. 99-102). Lisbon, Portugal.

Ioannidis, J. (2003). Fighting spam by encapsulating policy in email addresses. In *Proceedings of the 10th*

Annual Network and Distributed System Security Symposium (NDSS). San Diego, CA.

Neumann, P., & Weinstein, L. (1997). Inside risks: Spam, spam, spam! *Communications of the ACM, 40*(6), 112.

Park, J. S., & Deshpande, A. (2005). Spam detection: Increasing accuracy with a hybrid solution. *Journal of Information Systems Management (ISM), 23*(1), 57-67.

Rivest, R. L. (1992). *The MD5 message-digest algorithm.* MIT LCS and RSA Data Security, Inc. RFC 1321. Retrieved from http://www.faqs.org/rfcs/rfc1321.html

Rivest, R. L., Shamir, A., & Adleman, L. M. (1978). A method for obtaining digital signatures and public-key cryptosystems. *Communications of the ACM, 21*(2), 120-126.

Sahami, M., Dumais, S., Heckerman, D., & Horovitz, E. (1998). A Bayesian approach to filtering junk email. In *AAAI Workshop on Learning for Text Categorization* (pp. 26-27). Madison, WI.

Schneider, K.-M. (2003). A comparison of event models for naive Bayes anti-spam e-mail filtering. In *Proceedings of the 10th Conference of the European Chapter of the Association for Computational Linguistics (EACL)* (pp. 307-314). Budapest, Hungary.

Wong, M. (2006). *Sender policy framework (SPF) for authorizing use of domains in e-mail.* Network Working Group. RFC 4408. Retrieved from http://tools.ietf.org/html/4408

TERMS AND DEFINITIONS

E-Postage: This is a piece of code sent along with e-mail that ensures a cash payment for each e-mail message sent. Unlike the physical postage service, e-postage is mostly paid to the ultimate recipient or to the recipient's Internet service provider (ISP) instead of to third parties who issue e-stamps.

Hashcash: This refers to a piece of code sent along with e-mail that proves the sender has consumed a modest amount of computing power to send the e-mail.

Spam: This is unsolicited and inappropriate bulk e-mail that recipients do not want to receive.

Remailer: This refers to a software program between e-mail senders and recipients to forward each other's e-mail using aliases.

Trojan Horse: This rogue software program is installed on the victim's machine and can run secretly with the user's privileges.

Virus: This program attaches itself to other programs, propagating itself in this way, and unexpectedly does something, usually malicious.

Worm: This program makes copies of itself and propagates the copies to other computers throughout the network. A worm can run by itself and cause denial of service (DoS) attacks.

Chapter XXXI
Denial-of-Service (DoS) Attacks:
Prevention, Intrusion Detection, and Mitigation

Georg Disterer
University of Applied Sciences and Arts, Germany

Ame Alles
University of Applied Sciences and Arts, Germany

Axel Hervatin
University of Applied Sciences and Arts, Germany

ABSTRACT

Since denial-of-service (DoS) attacks are a major threat to e-commerce, waves of DoS attacks against prominent Web pages gained wide publicity. Typically DoS attacks target Web sites with bogus requests for data in order to slow or block legitimate users from accessing services. In recent years, distributed denial-of-service (DDoS) attacks have been used, which expand the vulnerability of Web sites. Attackers use hundreds or thousands of compromised systems in order to harm commercial Web sites. Attackers use different ways to harm their victims. They manipulate the target networks or target server servers directly by using lacks of protocols and standards to force failures and shut-downs. Or, they try to deplete resources like bandwidth, memory, or processing capacities. Attackers try to hinder or interfere with legitimate users with both strategies. Damages from DDoS attacks can range from inconvenience for legitimate users and customers to a lack of reliability for the site and—finally—to a shutdown of the server and some delay until web services are continued. This is a severe threat for all companies involved in e-commerce, and managing that risk is important to offer secure and reliable services. Therefore, management must take actions of prevention, detection and mitigation in order to protect their Web services.

INTRODUCTION

Denial-of-service (DoS) attacks are a major threat to electronic commerce (e-commerce). In 2000 and 2004, waves of DoS attacks against prominent web pages like Yahoo, Google, Double-click, Alta Vista, and others gained publicity. While early attacks on computer networks in the 1980s and 1990s were imputed to experts with a high level of technical expertise, today nearly anyone can use tools and scripts available on the Internet to attack Web sites. Attackers are no longer experts with high technical or ideological ambitions only, but also script kids using available tools and techniques just for fun or by order of criminals, who try to blackmail companies and threaten them with DoS attacks.

In recent years distributed denial-of-service (DDoS) attacks are used, which expand the vulnerability of Web sites. Attackers use hundreds or thousands of compromised systems in order to harm commercial Web sites. In an empirical study by Ernst & Young (Ernst & Young, 2004) 23% of the respondents indicated that DDoS attacks resulted in an unexpected outage of critical systems in 2003. Scotland Yard got some evidence about trends towards the monetization of Internet crime in the way that criminals offer activities like these under the slogan "rent a botnet" (Reuters, 2004).

Attackers use different ways to harm their victims. They manipulate the target networks or target servers directly by using a lack of protocols and standards to force failures and shutdowns. Or they try to deplete resources like bandwidth, memory, or processing capacities. With both strategies, attackers try to hinder or interfere with legitimate users of the Web site. Damages from DoS and DDoS attacks against a Web site can range from inconvenience for legitimate users and customers, to a lack of reliability of the site and finally to a shutdown of the server and some delay until Web services are continued. This is a severe threat for all companies involved in e-commerce, managing that risk is important to offering secure and reliable services. Therefore, management must take action to prevent, detect, and mitigate, in order to protect Web services. This chapter gives an overview of the risks and threats and a classification of possible countermeasures.

The outage of Web services is a particular threat to companies that rely strongly on the Web to generate revenue, like Internet service providers, online payment services, news providers, online stock brokers,

online betting services, and so forth. In addition, attacks damage the image of the effected companies; surveys show a decline in stock price between 1 and 4% shortly after ad hoc disclosures about DoS attacks have been published (Garg, Curtis, & Halper, 2003). In general, these attacks are considered to be one of the most dangerous threats to e-commerce.

CHARACTERISTICS OF DoS AND DDoS ATTACKS

In e-commerce, customers use the Internet to request information about products and services or to settle business transactions. Such requests are usually made by legitimate users who have honest intentions. As providers are interested in fulfilling requests quickly and reliably, the availability of servers is mission critical.

DoS and DDoS attacks try to address this dependency. Typically the attacks are targeted against servers with bogus requests for data in order to slow or block legitimate users from accessing services. Some other types of attacks try to manipulate servers directly in order to cause system outages. With improved security systems, the latter type of attacks today is classified as controllable. However, attacks that try to take up transaction and processing capacities in a way that legitimate users are hindered remain a severe threat to e-commerce.

In the basic form of DoS attacks, attackers try to interfere directly with target servers. An attack method called "ping-flooding" tries to flood a server by sending a high volume of simple requests. Today this type of attack is rarely successful as the resources of the target usually significantly exceed those of the attacker. Only mailbombing is still considered to be a threat in this regard. Once the storage of a mail server has been exceeded, electronic messages of legitimate users cannot be processed until unsolicited messages have been deleted.

About the year 2000, attackers started bundling the resources of multiple systems coordinated in networks

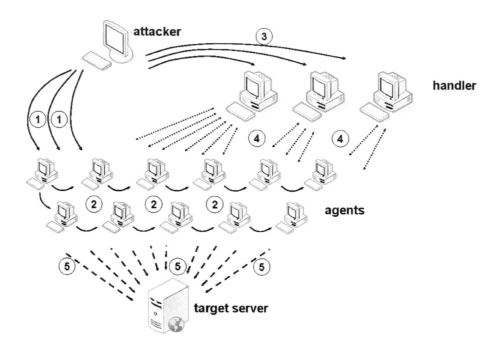

Figure 1. Setup of a DDoS network, including the attacker, handlers, and agents

("botnets") for DDoS attacks. Normally users do not realize that their systems are infected and misused for DDoS attacks. Using infected systems, attackers recruit new agents for their networks (Figure 1). Without users noticing, they transfer executable code to the agent systems and invoke malicious procedures.

At its core, the Internet transfer protocol TCP/IP allows spoofing by sending packets with faked source IP addresses. Thus, attackers makes their agents spoof the real addresses to restrict traceback options significantly. This technique is used for all types of DDoS attacks today, which makes it difficult to identify attackers and call them to account.

In order to prepare and execute an attack, possible agents are scanned for known security holes that are then exploited by malicious code. This code may contain several attack techniques. The attack will be initiated either by hard-coded date and time or dynamically. To send commands to their agents, attackers use different protocols like user datagram

protocol (UDP), TCP, and higher-level protocols, such as Telnet and IRC. When executing an attack against a target server at a definite point in time, the number of agents involved is limited to those that are currently online.

Scanning and infecting computers is usually automated by script programs. These programs scan systems connected to the Internet for known security holes. Another way of recruiting agents for a DDoS network is the use of malicious programs called worms, which are sent via e-mail attachments (depicted in (1) Figure 1). After infecting a target with malicious code, a worm sends copies of itself to further recipients. To increase the credibility of such harmful and unsolicited messages, worms use sender addresses and entries of electronic address books of already infected systems for their activities (depicted in (2) Figure 1).

A group of handlers may be established as intermediaries to avoid direct and traceable connections between the attacker and its agents (depicted in (3)

Figure 1). Typically, attackers consider those systems for the role of handlers that can be utilized inwardly. In the described setup, agents subscribe to the commands of handlers who give the starting signal for the attack at a later point (depicted in (4) Figure 1). Finally, the agents execute the attack against the target server (depicted in (5) Figure 1).

Patches to known security holes help to prevent DDoS networks from growing. However, once a network has gained critical size, patches can no longer prevent the actual attack. For example, on June 16, 2001, the company eEye discovered a security hole in the Internet information server (IIS) software. eEye reported the issue to Microsoft, the manufacturer, which provided a patch only 10 days after the issue had been revealed. However, as many system administrators missed installing this patch in time, the worm Code Red spread rapidly in July 2001. At peak times, the worm infected more than 359,000 systems within 14 hours. Hence, many systems were infected even after the security hole had been disclosed and the patch was released. The attacks caused by Code Red targeted the Web site of the White House in Washington, DC. The total damage caused for all systems involved is estimated to be US$2.6 billion (Moore, Shannon, & Brown, 2002).

CLASSIFICATION OF ATTACKS

DoS and DDoS attacks can be classified by the flaws of the Internet protocol family on which the attacks are based.

Flood attacks. This type of attack tries to overload the target server by sending a high volume of data packets, which are sent via UDP. These packets consume bandwidth and processing capacities restricting the availability of services for legitimate users.

Alternatively, high volumes of Internet control message protocol (ICMP) messages are sent using spoofed source addresses, pretending there is an existing session between server and client. The target server is forced to continue the faked session. Because the peer address is faked, the server will give up on re-establishing the session only after a fair number of unsuccessful attempts. This repeating consumes resources not available to legitimate users.

Amplification attacks. These attacks—also known as "smurf" or "fraggle" attacks—exploit certain security holes of systems and protocols. Until recently, routers accepted packets targeted at broadcast addresses and distributed them automatically to all computers of a specified range. Thus, not only a single but many target systems process packets received. If attackers spoof their source using a broadcast address within the target network, fatal chain reactions consuming additional bandwidth and processing capacities are caused. As the target systems respond to the broadcast address, reply messages will be distributed again to all computers amplifying the traffic volume.

Attacks exploiting TCP handshake. Another way of burdening processing capacities is to exploit a flaw of the TCP protocol. When executing TCP SYN attacks, agents undermine the rules of the TCP standard, which specifies that connections are established by a three-way handshake between client and server. First, the client sends a request to the server in the form of a SYN packet. Next, the server accepts the request by responding with a SYN ACK packet. Finally, the client confirms by sending an ACK packet to the server. Both sides can now consider the session to be established.

During a TCP SYN attack, agents send many SYN requests to the target server, which stores them in a buffer until responding with SYN ACK packets. Due to the high volume of SYN packets sent by agents and limitations of the buffer, the server is forced to reject further SYN requests including those of legitimate users. Moreover, agents enforce the negative effect by spoofing their source addresses. This forces the server to send SYN ACK packets to faked addresses several times without receiving any ACK confirmations (Figure 2). Until timeout, the buffer is used up

Figure 2. Failed handshake caused by spoofing

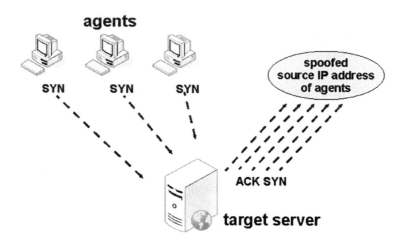

by SYN packets of the agents occupying the target server.

Attacks using malformed packets. According to the TCP/IP protocol, servers check received packets for syntactic errors. However, some semantic errors created intentionally by agents are not detected by the normal checking procedures. This can cause processing failures, which are generally prevented by service packs released in the recent years. However, such exploits may reappear. Additionally older systems like Windows 95 and NT do not reject malformed packets with identical source and recipient addresses ("land attack"), which cause system outages. Another reason for outages are "teardrop attacks," which prevent reassembling of IP fragments through manipulated header information. In addition, some older operating systems are limited to process packets up to 65,536 bytes. "Ping of death" attacks exploit this limitation by sending larger packets and causing server outages.

The threat of DDoS attacks is increased by scripts and programs that help to combine and automate the techniques described. Most of the tools are Linux/Unix based and have graphical user interfaces that provide ready-to-use kits for attackers. Thus, attackers are no longer required to have sophisticated technological know how. In fact, the entry barrier for potential attackers drops to a level of so-called "script kids" (Brustoloni 2002), who are said to be driven by schadenfreude and vandalism instead of technical ambition.

The oldest of these programs is Trin00 released in 1999. Trin00 uses UDP attacks and encrypts the communication between the attacker, handlers, and agents. The program Tribe Flood Network (TFN) supports various techniques, such as TCP SYN, ICMP flood, smurf, and spoofing. Like Trin00 the programs, TFN2K and Stacheldraht, a relatively widespread tool, encrypt the communication within a DDoS network. Statistics about the DDoS network and the current progress of the attack are provided by Shaft. The program Trinity uses IRC and encrypts the communication within the DDoS network, an improved version is known as Plague. The latest development of DDoS programs show that since network administrators are monitoring their networks for DDoS-specific traffic (like known character strings, known passwords, default ports), attackers implemented many small variations to prevent detection.

COUNTERMEASURES AGAINST DDoS ATTACKS

Prevention

As DDoS attacks severely threaten e-commerce, systematic and continuous measures have to be established to prevent attacks or at least mitigate the damage caused. Information technology (IT) managers have to plan, establish, and control sufficient procedures in order to prevent DDoS attacks. First of all, users should be instructed about proper handling of passwords and e-mail attachments. In addition, all users should be aware of policies and procedures established in the case of an attack. Moreover, for prevention the following best practices have been proven to be effective.

Configure systems conservatively. System and application software should only be installed to the required extent. Software that is no longer used should be uninstalled. In general, ports of workstations should only be opened for registered applications (white-list approach) to prevent unauthorized usage of services like FTP or Telnet. In addition, access privileges to data and application software should only be granted as necessary.

Install updates instantly. By installing security updates and patches, system administrators reduce the threat of DDoS attacks significantly. Usually, software manufacturers provide security updates at no charge, shortly after information about a security hole has been disclosed. Administrators are required to check for new updates frequently as potential attackers might be inspired by these announcements as well. Scanning of corporate networks for security holes is supported by a number of software products like Retina by eEye, NetRecon by Symantec, and Internet Scanner by ISS.

The previously mentioned Code Red example shows that attacks exploit system vulnerabilities for which patches already have been released. In fact, the time between the disclosure of a security hole and attacks that exploit the vulnerability averages 5.8 days (Symantec, 2004). This leads to the assumption that solely the disclosure of information about flaws inspires attackers.

Encrypt communication. Data transmitted via SMTP, Telnet, or FTP can be read by unauthorized third parties, since the information is sent as clear text. Attackers can spy out passwords by using tools called *sniffers* and use these passwords to install malicious code. This can be prevented by switching communication to newer standards, such as Secure FTP and SSH.

Control configuration of routers. Routers connecting corporate networks to the Internet should be enabled to check packets for spoofed addresses. Agents of DDoS networks often spoof source addresses to pretend an origin within the corporate network. *Ingress* filters installed on routers discard external packets that show this pattern. If computers of corporate networks are misused as agents or handlers, they will spoof their source addresses as well. In such cases, *egress* filters installed on routers discard outgoing packets from invalid addresses. Moreover, broadcasting should be switched off to prevent smurf and fraggle attacks.

Separate services. In order to mitigate the impact of DDoS attacks, services like Web and e-mail should be separated on different server systems. Otherwise, an attack targeted at one service might also affect all others.

Establish assessments and certificates. IT assessments should be based on the Common Criteria, which were developed by various nations and became ISO standard 15408 in 1999. The British standards authority published a security management policy (BS 7799) for corporations. In addition, trainings for IT management staff should be considered. Public authorities like the Bundesamt für Sicherheit in der Informationstechnik in Germany certify corporations and systems after assessing their compliance with established standards.

Prepare emergency plans. Corporations should arrange detailed emergency plans including organizational measures, like installing task forces (computer emergency response reams (CERTs)) that coordinate the most important jobs in the case of an attack. Contact persons, information policies, and first actions should be documented.

INTRUSION DETECTION AND RESPONSE

Detecting attacks early can minimize loss and provide sufficient time for countermeasures. Corporations should monitor their systems continuously to allow prompt reactions. Such measures of *intrusion detection* can be distinguished by the following criteria.

On the one hand, resource consumption, such as network traffic, is constantly scanned for signatures of known DDoS attack types and exploits. Updates of signatures can be obtained from security service providers. However, this strategy is limited to detect attack types and exploits already known.

On the other hand, host-based and network intrusion detection scans traffic on and between hosts for anomalies (Innella, 2001). Heuristics to uncover attacks and exploits are based on recorded data of resource consumption. Host-based intrusion detection is mainly based on the analysis of system log files. To secure systems, packet sniffer software should be installed on all major network devices, such as routers, firewalls, load balancers, and Web servers.

Mitigation and Quality of Service Guarantee

When a DDoS attack occurs, further actions must be taken besides early measures to guarantee quality of service (QoS) for legitimate users. The following approaches should be considered for Web servers, routers, and work stations. All concepts require significant preparation to mitigate the impact of attacks. They should be due to IT security reviews.

Configure servers and routers explicitly. Web servers and routers should be configured to discard SYN requests received the first time. Only if a request is retransmitted will it be processed. Thus, agents' requests sent with changing source addresses are filtered out. To identify repeated requests sent by legitimate users, this configuration requires servers and routers to store source addresses temporarily. With this approach, processing of all incoming requests is slowed down, including service requests of legitimate users who have to wait for retransmitted SYN requests. Moreover, attackers can bypass this protection by sending agents' requests twice (Kargl, Maier, Weber, 2001).

Dedicate resources to services. "Class based queuing" reserves traffic capacities for requests of certain types, recognized by a special segment of the IP header ("type-of-service byte"). Unmarked packets are limited to consuming only a certain quota. Thus, attack packets can only consume limited resources and sufficient traffic capacities remain for legitimate users, indicated by type-of-service entries. However, attackers may randomly switch type-of-service entries in order to bypass this protection.

Load balancing. In case of a DDoS attack, devices that load-balance traffic and processing capacities manage to delay interference of legitimate requests. In the meantime additional capacities can be allocated. When processing capacities are short, throttling of router capacity can prevent bottlenecks. These measures help to delay the impact of DDoS attacks and gain time needed to take action.

History-based IP filtering. This approach mitigates the impact of a DDoS attack by accepting requests of known users only. Thus, attack packets with randomly spoofed source addresses are discarded. To identify legitimate users, in case of an attack, providers need to store source addresses of known users (Peng, Leckie, & Ramamohanarao, 2003).

Server pools. To protect Internet-based services against attacks, several replicated servers can be pooled, whereas one of them is active at a time. The active server is switched periodically so that the IP address of this active server alternates. This ensures that attackers cannot block services by targeting a single IP address because a moving target is created (Khattab & Sangpachatanaruk, 2003).

Further to server configuration, the following changes of router set ups may be considered. However, these changes require the availability of additional services and the cooperation of Internet service providers (ISPs).

VIP services. ISPs who offer so called VIP services give requests of privileged users top priority by allocating dedicated resources that attackers cannot absorb. Therefore, requests of legitimate users are protected against interference caused by DDoS attacks. Corporations involved in e-commerce register customers with their source addresses for a charge at an ISP providing a VIP service (Brustoloni, 2002). Packets of unregistered users are limited to consuming only a certain quota of resources.

Coordinate routers. Requests of all users are sent via routers to target servers. Routers should check packets against suspicious patterns caused by potential agents and discard affected traffic. Having rejected packets, routers should push back the source address of discarded packets to preceding routers. This prevents potential attackers from reaching their target over an alternative transmission path (Ioannidis & Bellovin, 2002). If all routers on the transmission path from agents to target servers follow this procedure, suspicious packets will be rejected early.

Other concepts subject to further research affect computers of legitimate user in addition to Web servers.

Micropayments. Recruiting agents and initiating DDoS attacks is principally free of charge for attackers.

To discourage attackers micropayment systems can be used to charge for the consumption of traffic and processing capacities. According to the "market-based service quality differentiation" concept (Mankins, Krishnan, Boyd, Zao, & Frentz, 2001) users should be charged based on their resource consumption. Users whose systems are occupied to execute DDoS attacks may realize the misuse due to increased costs charged to them.

Puzzles. Usually agents involved in DDoS networks require few resources while inducing target servers with heavy traffic and processing load. In evidence of a DDoS attack, a target server requires clients to solve computing-intensive puzzles before requests are processed by the server (Juels & Brainhard, 1999).

Traceback the Source of Attacks

To ensure acceptable QoS for legitimate users in evidence of a DDoS attack detection and mitigation should be made top priority. Then corporations should try to trace the attacker and uncover the DDoS network to prevent further threats. If sufficient evidence has been collected about damages and the amount of proven loss, attackers should be prosecuted to the full extent of civil or criminal laws to deter other potential attackers.

To uncover agents and handlers, corporations need to traceback the transmission path from the target server to the attacker (Figure 1). As attackers usually spoof their IP source address, at first, transmission paths can only be reconstructed backwards to the last router that processed packets. To continue the traceback, all ISPs along the transmission path are required to collaborate. Without cooperation between the administrators of all involved routers from the target server to the DDoS network, traceback is impossible. As yet, no proven and tested procedures are known to automate this time-consuming task (Douligeris & Mitrokotsa 2004), although refining the ability to traceback sources of attacks has been on the agenda for years.

Some approaches suggest including traceback information in transmitted packets. However, this requires cooperation of all Internet routers. To traceback, ICMP messages could be used (*ICMP traceback*) in such way that every router involved in the transmission path sends an ICMP message as a receipt to the target server. Thus, the target server is able to reconstruct the transmission path to the DDoS attack network. To reduce traffic, it is sufficient that routers only generate such receipts for randomly chosen packets. Due to the high volume of packets sent during a DDoS attack, the target server will still be able to reconstruct the path (Douligeris & Mitrokotsa, 2004).

Alternatively, traceback information could be included in IP packets directly (Savage, Wetherall, Karlin, & Anderson, 2001). Each router signs processed packets by attaching its address. Thus, the target server can reconstruct the transmission path easily. Due to high volumes, routers only sign randomly chosen packets to reduce overhead (*probabilistic packet marking*).

Another approach suggests routers temporarily store a 32-bit digest for all processed packets. In case of an attack, the target server checks with routers to see if DDoS traffic has been transmitted by them (Snoeren et al., 2001) in order to do a stepwise traceback.

All these approaches uncover only agents and handlers of DDoS attack networks; it remains unlikely that the location of the actual attacker would be revealed. To accomplish this, malicious code running on agent and handler systems has to be analyzed.

CONCLUSION

Measures of prevention, intrusion detection, and mitigation cannot provide sufficient protection against DDoS attacks unless flaws in the TCP/IP protocol have been addressed. Thus, the approaches mentioned above can provide only limited protection. Others approaches require reconfiguring or replacing all systems of the Internet transport infrastructure, which seems to be unrealistic for the near future. In fact, corporations

should anticipate a further increase in DDoS attacks. For the first half of 2005, Symantec recorded nearly 1,000 attacks daily and a strong increase in DDoS network activities (Symantec, 2005).

Attackers often exploit insufficiently protected systems of private users. The BSI, a German IT security authority, reported in January 2005 that only every fourth privately used system is protected by antivirus software and only every second uses a firewall. Symantec estimates in the first half of 2005 the percentage of infected systems to be highest in United Kingdom with 32% and United States with 19%, while other countries have significantly lower numbers (Symantec, 2005). The fact is that attackers can easily acquire a large number of systems to misuse for DDoS attack networks, some of which are reported to have several thousand compromised systems.

Due to unlimited or traffic-based rates, privately used systems often stay connected to the Internet for a long time. Thus, many unprotected systems are constantly exposed to exploits. Compromised with malicious code, such systems can be misused anytime to start DDoS attacks.

In addition, authorities report an increase in cybercrime using DDoS networks. Companies that rely strongly on e-commerce need secure and reliable Web servers. Criminals using this dependency start some form of online extortion to blackmail companies with DDoS attacks. Businessmen try to disrupt key Web services of competitors (McAfee, 2005). Additionally, connections to mafia organizations have been assumed. Parts of an East European syndicate are said to offer DDoS networks under the slogan "rent a botnet." Furthermore, the U.S. justice department notes a trend in terrorist organizations like Al-Qaida trying to hire attackers to penetrate government systems (NN, 2005).

REFERENCES

Brustoloni, J. C. (2002). Protecting electronic commerce from distributed denial-of-service attacks.

Current Information

The following Web sites provide current information. Additionally, software manufacturers' Web sites could be visited for product news:

- CERT Coordination Center, Research Center at Carnegie Mellon University: www.cert.org.
- Symantec, a commercial provider of security software and a source for information, securityresponse.symantec.com/avcenter/vinfodb.html.
- HackerWatch is an online community where users can share information about security threats and unwanted traffic: hackerwatch.org.
- DFN-CERT Computer Emergency Response Team of Deutsches Forschungsnetz DFN: www.cert.dfn.de
- SecurityFocus, Security Professionals Community, sponsored by Symantec: www.securityfocus.com.
- SANS SysAdmin, Audit, Network, Security Institute: www.sans.org.
- US-CERT United States Computer Emergency Readiness Team: www.us-cert.gov.
- CIAC Computer Incident Advisory Capability, U.S. Department of Energy: www.ciac.org/ciac.
- CSRC Computer Security Resource Center, National Institute of Standards and Technology (NIST): www.csrc.nist.gov.
- ICAT Metabase, Computer Vulnerability Search Engine, National Institute of Standards and Technology (NIST): icat.nist.gov.

Proc. 11th International WWW Conference, Honolulu. Retrieved from http://wwwconf.ecs.soton.ac.uk/archive/00000333/01

BSI Bundesamt für Sicherheit in der Informationstechnik BSI. Erkennung und Behandlung von Angriffen aus dem Internet. Retrieved from http://www.bsi.bund.de/fachthem/sinet/webserv/angriff.htm

Douligeris, C., & Mitrokotsa, A. (2004). DDoS attacks and defense mechanisms: Classification and state-of-the-art. *Computer Networks: The International Journal of Computer and Telecommunications Networking Archive, 44*(5), 643-666.

Ernst & Young. (2004). *Global information security survey.* Retrieved from http://www.ey.com

Garg, A., Curtis, J., & Halper, H. (2003). Quantifying the financial impact of IT security breaches. *Information Management and Computer Security, 11*(2), 74-83.

Innella, P. (2001). *The evolution of intrusion detection systems.* Retrieved from http://www.securityfocus.com/printable/infocus/1514

Ioannidis, J., & Bellovin, S. M. (2002). *Implementing pushback: Router-based defense against DDoS attacks.* Retrieved from http://www.isoc.org/isoc/conferences/ndss/02/proceedings/papers/ioanni.pdf

Juels, A., & Brainhard, J. (1999). Client puzzles: A cryptographic countermeasure against connection depletion attacks. In *Proceedings of the Conference Networks and Distributed Security Systems* (pp. 151-165). San Diego, CA. Retrieved from http://www.isoc.org/isoc/conferences/ndss/99/proceedings/papers/juels.pdf

Kargl, F., Maier, J., & Weber, M. (2001). Protecting Web servers from distributed denial of service attacks. In *Proceedings 10th International WWW Conference* (pp. 514-524). Hong Kong. Retrieved from http://www.www10.org/cdrom/papers/p409.pdf

Khattab, S. M., & Sangpachatanaruk, C. (2003). Melhem, R.; Mosse, D.; Znati, T.: Proactive server roaming for mitigating denial-of-service attacks. In *Proceedings 1st Int. Conference on International Technology: Research and Education ITRE* (pp. 500-504). Newark, NJ. Retrieved from http://www.cs.pitt.edu/NETSEC/publications_files/itre03.pdf

Mankins, D., Krishnan, R., Boyd, C., Zao, J., & Frentz, M. (2004). *Mitigating distributed denial of service attacks with dynamic resource pricing.* Retrieved from http://www.ir.bbn.com/~krash/pubs/mankins_acsac01.pdf

McAfee. (2005). *Virtual criminology report: North American study into organized crime and the Internet.* Santa Clara, CA.

Moore, D., Shannon, C., & Brown, J. (2002). *Code-Red: A case study on the spread and victims of an Internet worm.* Retrieved from http://www.caida.org/outreach/papers/2002/codered/codered.pdf

NN. (2004). Attracting hackers. *Communications of the ACM, 48*(11), 9.

Peng, T., Leckie, C., & Ramamohanarao, K. (2003). Protection from distributed denial of service attack using history-based IP filtering. *Proc. of IEEE Int. Conference of Communication ICC*, Anchorage. Retrieved from http://www.ee.mu.oz.au/staff/caleckie/icc2003.pdf

Reuters. (2004, July 7). Scotland Yard and the case of the Rent-A-Zombies. *Online News.* Retrieved 16 May, 2007 from http://news.zdnet.com/2100-1009_22-5260154.html

Savage, S., Wetherall, D., Karlin, A., & Anderson, T. (2001). Network support for IP traceback. *Transactions on Networking, 9*(3), 226-237.

Snoeren, A. C., Partridge, C., Sanchez, L. A., Jones, C. E., Tchakountio, F., Kent, S. T.; & Strayer, W. T. (2001). Hash-based IP traceback. In *Proceedings of the ACM SIGCOMM 2001 Conference on Applications, Technologies, Architectures, and Protocols for Computer Communication* (pp. 3-14). New York.

Symantec. (2004). Internet security threat report Vol. VI, Cupertino. Retrieved from http://www.enterprise-security.symantec.com

Symantec. (2005). Internet security threat report Vol. VIII, Cupertino. Retrieved from http://www.enterprisesecurity.symantec.com

TERMS AND DEFINITIONS

Agent: In distributed denial-of-service (DDoS) networks agents execute attacks against target servers. Without users noticing, their systems are occupied by handlers and attackers who transfer executable code to systems and invoke malicious procedures.

Attacker: Attackers play the role of an initiator and coordinator in denial-of-service (DoS) attacks. They exploit security holes of TCP/IP and common operating systems. In distributed denial-of-service (DDoS) networks, attackers misuse systems as handlers and agents to harm the business of electronic commerce providers.

Denial-of-Service (DoS) Attack: DoS attacks are targeted against servers with bogus requests for data, in order to slow or block legitimate users from accessing services. In the basic form of DoS attacks, attackers try to interfere directly with target servers.

Distributed Denial-of-Service (DDoS) Attack: DDoS attacks are advanced types of denial-of-service (DoS) attacks. By bundling the resources of multiple coordinated systems attack network are created, consisting of attackers, handlers and agents. DDoS networks are difficult to detect and can cause severe damages on target servers and financial loss for corporations.

Handler: Handlers act as intermediaries between attackers and agents in distributed denial-of-service (DDoS) networks in order to avoid direct and traceable connections between attackers and their agents.

Malicious Code: Attackers in distributed denial-of-service (DDoS) networks exploit security holes and infect other systems with malicious code. With this, code systems are forced to act as handlers or agents in attack networks. The code may contain several attack techniques.

Spoofing: Spoofing means sending packets via TCP/IP with faked source IP addresses. Spoofing is used for all types of denial-of-service (DoS) attacks to restrict traceback options and prevent identification of agents, handlers, and attackers.

Chapter XXXII
Large-Scale Monitoring of Critical Digital Infrastructures

André Årnes
Norwegian University of Science and Technology, Norway

ABSTRACT

Network monitoring is becoming increasingly important, both as a security measure for corporations and organizations, and in an infrastructure protection perspective for nation-states. Governments are not only increasing their monitoring efforts, but also introducing requirements for data retention in order to be able to access traffic data for the investigation of serious crimes, including terrorism. In Europe, a resolution on data retention was passed in December 2005 (The European Parliament, 2005). However, as the level of complexity and connectivity in information systems increases, effective monitoring of computer networks is getting harder. Systems for efficient threat identification and assessment are needed in order to handle high-speed traffic and monitor data in an appropriate manner. We discuss attacks relating to critical infrastructure, specifically on the Internet. The term critical infrastructure refers to both systems in the digital domain and systems that interface with critical infrastructure in the physical world. Examples of a digital critical infrastructure are the DNS (domain name service) and the routing infrastructure on the Internet. Examples of systems that interface with the physical world are control systems for power grids and telecommunications systems. In 1988, the first Internet worm (called the Morris worm) disabled thousands of hosts and made the Internet almost unusable. In 2002, the DNS root servers were attacked by a distributed denial-of-service (DDoS) attack specifically directed at these servers, threatening to disrupt the entire Internet.[1] As our critical infrastructure, including telecommunication systems and power grids, becomes more connected and dependent on digital systems, we risk the same types of attacks being used as weapons in information warfare or cyber terrorism. Any digital system or infrastructure has a number of vulnerabilities with corresponding threats. These threats can potentially exploit vulnerabilities, causing unwanted incidents. In the case of critical infrastructures, the consequences of such vulnerabilities being exploited can become catastrophic. In this chapter, we discuss methods relating to the monitoring, detection, and identification of such attacks through the use of monitoring systems. We refer to the data-capturing device or software as a sensor. The main threats considered in this chapter are information warfare and cyber terrorism. These threats can lead to several different scenarios, such as coordinated computer attacks, worm attacks, DDoS attacks, and large scale scanning and mapping efforts. In this context, the primary task of network monitoring is to detect and identify unwanted incidents associated with threats in order to initiate appropriate precautionary measures and responses.

NETWORK MONITORING AND INTRUSION DETECTION

In this chapter, we will look at different aspects of network monitoring. Network monitoring is the field of capturing traffic data on a network in order to perform corresponding analysis. We consider the areas of threat monitoring, intrusion detection, and security monitoring to be covered by the term network monitoring. Threat monitoring is a term currently used by, for example, the Internet Storm Center. The term was used by NIST in a publication regarding the monitoring of internal and external threats to a computer system (Anderson, 1980). Intrusion detection is the specialized field of detecting attempts to attack and compromise computer systems. Early work on intrusion detection systems (IDS) was published by D. E. Denning (1987). The practice of intrusion detection is discussed in several books, such as *Network Intrusion Detection* (Northcutt, 2002). Stefan Axelsson published a survey and taxonomy for IDS in 2000 (Axelsson, 2000). The term security monitoring was used by Bishop (1989), which provided a formal description of a security monitoring system with logging and auditing as its main components. Richard Bejtlichs book *Network Security Monitoring Beyond Intrusion Detection* (Bejtlich, 2004) defines the term network security monitoring as a process consisting of the collection, analysis, and escalation of indications and warnings to detect and respond to intrusions.

There are currently several organizations on the Internet that monitor and publish security relevant trends and events. Most notably, the Computer Emergency Response Team (CERT)[1], established in 1988, alerts users to potential threats on the Internet, and the Internet Storm Center[2], established in 2001, provides trend reports and warnings for its users. The Cooperative Association for Internet Data Analysis (Caida)[3] is another organization that provides tools for and publishes analysis results based on Internet monitoring. The European Union is currently funding a specific support project, Lobster for large-scale monitoring of the backbone Internet infrastructure. The project is currently in its implementation phase,

and it is intended to provide a network monitoring platform for performance and security measurements in research and operational use.

Recent research on intrusion detection has, to a high degree, focused on scalability and performance for large-scale and high-speed monitoring. To address larger networks and increased scalability requirements, distributed intrusion detection has been discussed in several research papers (Snapp et al., 1991; Staniford-Chen et al., 1996). A variation on this is the agent-based IDS (Balasubramaniyan, Garcia-Fernandez, Isacoff, Spafford, & Zamboni, 1998; Carver, Hill, Surdu, & Pooch, 2000; Helmer, Wong, Honavar, Miller, & Wang, 2003). IDMEF is a recent standard for an intrusion detection message exchange proposed to facilitate standardized messaging between sensors and analysis systems (Debar, Curry, & Feinstein, 2005). It is used in distributed intrusion detection systems such as Prelude and STAT.

Threat and intrusion detection is generally on data analysis, being either a type of signature or pattern detection, or a statistical analysis. In intrusion detection, these are referred to as misuse detection and anomaly detection respectively. Misuse detection generates alerts based on known signatures of suspected security incidents, whereas anomaly detection generates alerts based on deviations from known or assumed normal traffic or use pattern. Another type of statistical analysis is data mining, as discussed in Jesus Menas book *Investigative Data Mining for Security and Criminal Detection* (Mena, 2003). Data mining can also be combined with intrusion detection (Barbara, 2002; Lee & Stolfo, 1998). See Marchette (2001) for a discussion on statistical analysis in computer intrusion detection and network monitoring.

Two central research topics in network monitoring and intrusion detection are detection of DDoS and worm detection. Such attacks can be efficient weapons in an information warfare or cyber terrorism scenario. The detection of zero-day worms is a problem that has provided inspiration for several research projects (Akritidis, Anagnostakis, & Markatos, 2005; Zou, Gong, Towsley, & Gao, 2005), and the Wormblog[4] is a resource for sharing updated information about worms and worm research. Similarly, DDoS detection has received much attention and its predecessor in studies of the prevalence of DDoS attacks on the Internet, based on monitoring data from sample corporations (Moore, Shannon, Brown, Voelker, & Savage, 2006; Moore, Voelker, & Savage, 2001).

SENSOR TECHNOLOGIES

The basic component of any monitoring system is the sensor. A sensor is a device or program that records and reacts to specific events, in our case network traffic on a computer network. Different types of network monitoring systems exist, with functionalities like data recording, collection, filtering, and alarm generation. The correct placement of sensors is essential; ideally one should have full monitoring coverage, without overlapping. Without full coverage, one may experience false negatives, that is, some incidents may go undetected. Next we will provide an overview of sensor technologies that may provide security relevant data.

Network Sniffers

A network sniffer is the most basic sensor type in most network monitoring applications. It is capable of intercepting and storing data from a network connection. The amount of network traffic processed and stored can be limited by applying a filter based on certain attributes in the network packet headers, by preserving only parts of the data (such as the packet header), or by employing sampling. Specialized hardware for reliable high bandwidth sniffing was developed as part of the EU Scampi project (Coppens et al., 2004), and it is also available commercially. Standards for logging network flows are, for example, IPFIX (Claise, 2005) and its predecessor NetFlow (a Cisco standard). In the context of lawful interception of network traffic, a sniffer is usually referred to as a wiretap.

Intrusion Detection Sensors

IDS technology has become widespread, available both as off-the-shelf products, and as outsourced solutions from security vendors. An IDS is intended to detect and report possible attacks and malicious network activity. Intrusion detection systems are classified according to several criteria. Based on the functionality of the IDS sensors, they can be classified as either host IDS (HIDS) or network IDS (NIDS). A HIDS sensor monitors the integrity of a host, whereas a NIDS monitors network traffic based on data from a network sniffer. The detection algorithm of an IDS is either signature based (based on recognition of attributes that are associated with possible attacks) or anomaly based (using statistical methods to detect anomalies). An IDS may be either centralized or distributed based on whether the data and alarms are processed and stored centrally or locally.

System and Network Logging

Most computer systems implement a degree of logging to record events related to the operating system, user activity, applications, and security specific events. Logs usually contain timestamps and addresses regarding transactions, and they can be vital in incident handling and criminal investigations. Logs can be found on any computer system, including Internet servers, as well as in network components such as firewalls and routers. Logs may be stored locally on each host, or there may be an infrastructure for centralized logging, using a standard protocol such as syslog. Note that the accuracy of local log data is questionable, as the data can be tampered with by a privileged user of the system.

Virus Detection

Virus detection systems are getting increasingly widespread, both as a security measure for workstations and laptops, and as part of network filtering mechanisms. Virus detection systems have the capability to detect and report malicious code (e.g., virus and worms), and in some cases to quarantine or remove the malicious code. Virus detection software may be managed by central management systems for larger networks, and it can be integrated into more general network management systems.

Production Honeypots

Honeypot technology is a data collection tool suitable for both computer security research and operational network monitoring. Lance Spitzner has published several books on the issue (Spitzner, 2001, 2002, 2004) and defined a honeypot as a "security resource whose value is in being probed, attacked or compromised." Note that, in this context, production honeypots have two main functions; as a sensor and as a means of deception. Simple honeypots may not convince a competent attacker in the long run, but the use of production honeypots may force an attacker to use time and resources on mapping and identifying honeypots, thereby allowing the honeypots to gather information about the tools and methods being used. Honeypots can also be used as tools for detection and analysis of zero-day worms (Dagon et al., 2004; Riordan, Wespi, & Zamboni, 2005).

CHALLENGES IN NETWORK MONITORING

There are many challenges associated with the practice of network monitoring. Some of the challenges related to intrusion detection in particular are discussed in Ranum (2002).

The most significant issue is that of information overload, which is both a technical and an organizational issue. Information is gathered from large high-speed networks for processing, but the high volume of data generated is difficult for human analysts to manage. In order to support the analysts in making efficient and correct decisions, it is necessary to organize and prioritize the monitoring data. However, this processing necessarily introduces false positives, where an alert is issued despite the absence of an

incident, and false negatives, where no alert is issued despite the occurrence of an incident. Data reduction through correlation, fusion, and visualization tools can be helpful in addressing this problem. Alert correlation or alert fusion is a research topic that provides a higher level view of security incidents in a network based on several sensors (Kruegel, Valeur, & Vigna, 2005; Valeur, Vigna, Kruegel, & Kemmerer, 2004). Such systems may significantly reduce the volume of data to be considered, but they can also introduce additional false negatives, depending on the correlation algorithms in use. More intelligent assessment applications, capable of identifying and assessing threats and risks in a real-time environment, can further aid efficient and correct decision making. For this purpose, assessment systems based on quantitative methods have been proposed to aid the decision-making process. An example of a host-based risk assessment system was published by Gehani and Kedem (2004), and a network-oriented system for quantitatively assessing risk based on input from intrusion detection systems has been proposed by Årnes et al. (2005).

Current high-speed Internet backbone infrastructures require that monitoring systems are able to handle extremely high bandwidths. Current sensor technologies allow monitoring up to 10Gb/s with limited on-board processing. At this rate, every operation, such as pattern analysis, protocol reassembly, distributed analysis, and data storage becomes difficult, and it is often necessary to sample or filter data even before analysis. Such approaches necessarily lead to the loss of information and false negatives.

Depending on the analysis performed, encryption and anonymity can reduce the possibility of detecting threats through the use of network monitoring systems. Content-based analysis may not be possible when commonly used encryption protocols such as SSL, SSH, PGP, and IPSEC are employed. On the other hand, even traffic-based analysis becomes difficult if anonymity systems, as introduced by Chaum (1981, 1988) and implemented in Onion routing (Dingledine, Mathewson, & Syverson, 2004; Goldschlag, Reed, & Syverson, 1999), are in use.

Network monitoring places a great responsibility on the operator for the confidentiality and privacy of the data that is recorded and processed. The contents of network traffic can obviously be private or confidential, but even traffic data alone can compromise a user's privacy. This is particularly important in the cases where monitoring data is shared between multiple parties. It is important that the data is protected in such away that only the minimum amount of data necessary for analysis is provided. Current solutions for protecting IP addresses in monitoring data, such as prefix-preserving pseudonymization (Xu, Fan, Ammar, & Moon, 2002) fail to provide protection against simple cryptographic attacks (Brekne & Årnes, 2005; Brekne, Årnes, & Øslebø, 2005). More secure solutions have to be considered.

CONCLUSION

We have seen that there are many aspects of network monitoring, both in terms of sensors, methods of analysis, and architectures. Each technology has its advantages and disadvantages, so that a sound approach has to take into consideration multiple technologies. In particular, a monitoring system should depend on a comprehensive set of sensors and analysis algorithms. We have also considered some specific challenges in network monitoring and made the case for employing privacy-preserving measures and for performing real-time quantitative assessment of threats and risks to facilitate efficient and correct response to security incidents.

ACKNOWLEDGMENT

Thanks to Professor Svein J. Knapskog for helpful feedback. This work was in part supported by the U.S. – Norway Fulbright Foundation for Educational Exchange. The "Centre for Quantifiable Quality of Service in Communication Systems, Centre of Excellence" is appointed by The Research Council of Norway, and funded by the Research Council, NTNU, and UNINETT. The author is also associated with the High-Tech Crime Division of the Norwegian National Criminal Investigation Service (Kripos).

REFERENCES

Akritidis, P., Anagnostakis, K., & Markatos, E. (2005). Efficient content-based fingerprinting of zero-day worms. *Proceedings of the International Conference on Communications (ICC 2005)*.

Anderson, J. P. (1980). *Computer security threat monitoring and surveillance* (Technical Report). Fort Washington, PA.

Årnes, A., Sallhammar, K., Haslum, K., Brekne, T., Moe, M. E. G., & Knapskog, S. J. (2005). Real-time risk assessment with network sensors and intrusion detection systems. *Proceedings of the International Conference on Computational Intelligence and Security (CIS 2005)*.

Axelsson, S. (2000). *Intrusion detection systems: A survey and taxonomy* (Tech. Rep. No. 9915). Chalmers University, Sweden.

Balasubramaniyan, J. S., Garcia-Fernandez, J. O., Isacoff, D., Spafford, E., & Zamboni, D. (1998). An architecture for intrusion detection using autonomous agents. *Proceedings of the 14th Annual Computer Security Applications Conference,* IEEE Computer Society, p. 13.

Barbara, D. (2002). *Applications of data mining in computer security* (S. Jajodia, Ed.). Norwell, MA: Kluwer Academic Publishers.

Bejtlich, R. (2004). *The tao of network security monitoring: Beyond intrusion detection.* Addison Wesley Professional.

Bishop, M. (1989, December). A model of security monitoring. *Proceedings of the Fifth Annual Computer Security Applications Conference,* Tucson, AZ.

Brekne, T., & Årnes, A. (2005). Circumventing IP-address pseudonymization in O(n2) time. *Proceedings of IASTED Communication and Computer Networks (CCN 2005).*

Brekne, T., Årnes, A., & Øslebø, A. (2005). Anonymization of IP traffic monitoring data: Attacks on two prefix-preserving anonymization schemes and some proposed remedies. *Proceedings of the Privacy Enhancing Technologies Workshop (PET 2005).*

Carver, C. A., Jr., Hill, J. M., Surdu, J. R., & Pooch, U. W. (2000, June 6-7). A methodology for using intelligent agents to provide automated intrusion response. *Proceedings of the IEEE Systems, Man, and Cybernetics Information Assurance and Security Workshop,* West Point, NY.

Chaum, D. (1981). Untraceable electronic mail, return addresses, and digital pseudonyms. *Communications of the ACM, 24*(2), 8488.

Chaum, D. (1988). The dining cryptographers problem: Unconditional sender and recipient untraceability. *Journal of Cryptology, 1*(1), 6575.

Claise, B. (2005). IPFIX protocol specification. *IETF Internet Draft.*

Coppens, J., Markatos, E., Novotny, J., Polychronakis, M., Smotlacha, V., & Ubik, S. (2004). Scampi: A scaleable monitoring platform for the internet. *Proceedings of the 2nd International Workshop on Inter-domain Performance and Simulation (IPS 2004).*

Dagon, D., Qin, X., Gu, G., Lee, W., Grizzard, J. B., Levine, J. G., et al. (2004). Honeystat: Local worm detection using honeypots. *Proceedings of the Seventh International Symposium on Recent Advances in Intrusion Detection (RAID 2004).*

Debar, H., Curry, D., & Feinstein, B. (2005). Intrusion detection message exchange format (IDMEF). *IETF Internet-Draft.*

Denning, D. E. (1987, February). An intrusion-detection model. *IEEE Transactions on Software Engineering, 3*(2), 222-232.

Dingledine, R., Mathewson, N., & Syverson, P. (2004). Tor: The second-generation onion router. *Proceedings of the 13th USENIX Security Symposium.*

European Parliament, The. (2005). Electronic communications: Personal data protection rules and availability of traffic data for anti-terrorism purposes (amend. direct. 2002/58/EC).

Gehani, A., & Kedem, G. (2004). Rheostat: Real-time risk management. *Proceedings of the 7th International Symposium on Recent Advances in Intrusion Detection (RAID 2004).*

Goldschlag, D., Reed, M., & Syverson, P. (1999). Onion routing. *Communications of the ACM, 42*(2), 3941.

Helmer, G., Wong, J. S. K., Honavar, V. G., Miller, L., & Wang, Y. (2003). Lightweight agents for intrusion detection. *Journal of Systems and Software, 67*(2), 109122. Internet Society, The. (2005). 20 DNS root name servers—frequently asked questions. *ISOC Member Briefing #20.* Retrieved July 31, 2006, from http://www.isoc.org/briefings/020/

Kruegel, C., Valeur, F., & Vigna, G. (2005). *Intrusion detection and correlation: challenges and solutions* (Vol. 14). Springer.

Lee, W., & Stolfo, S. (1998). Data mining approaches for intrusion detection. *Proceedings of the 7th USENIX Security Symposium.* San Antonio, TX, 2004.

Marchette, D. J. (2001). *Computer intrusion detection and network monitoring: A statistical viewpoint.* Springer-Verlag.

Mena, J. (2003). *Investigative data mining for security and criminal detection.* Butterworth Heinemann.

Moore, D., Shannon, C., Brown, D., Voelker, G. M., & Savage, S. (2006). Inferring internet denial-of-service activity. *ACM Transactions on Computer Science, 24*(2), 115-139.

Moore, D., Voelker, G. M., & Savage, S. (2001). Inferring internet denial-of-service activity. *Proceedings of the 2001 USENIX Security Symposium.*

Northcutt, S. J. N. (2002). *Network intrusion detection* (3rd ed.). Sams.

Ranum, M. (2002). Intrusion detection: Challenges and myths. *Network Flight Recorder, Inc.* Retrieved July 31, 2006, from http://www.windowsecurity.com/whitepapers/

Riordan, J., Wespi, A., & Zamboni, D. (2005). How to hook worms. *IEEE Spectrum.*

Snapp, S. R., Brentano, J., Dias, G. V., Goan, T. L., Heberlein, L. T., Ho, C.lin, et al. (1991). DIDS (distributed intrusion detection system) motivation, architecture, and an early prototype. *Proceedings of the 14th National Computer Security Conference.* Washington, DC.

Spitzner, L. (2001). *Know your enemy: Revealing the security tools, tactics, and motives of the blackhat community.* Addison Wesley.

Spitzner, L. (2002). *Honeypots: Tracking hackers.* Addison Wesley.

Spitzner, L. (2004). *Know your enemy: Learning about security threats* (2nd ed.). Addison Wesley.

Staniford-Chen, S., Cheung, S., Crawford, R., Dilger, M., Frank, J., Hoagland, J., et al. (1996). GrIDS: A graph-based intrusion detection system for large networks. *Proceedings of the 19th National Information Systems Security Conference.*

Valeur, F., Vigna, G., Kruegel, C., & Kemmerer, R. A. (2004). A comprehensive approach to intrusion detection alert correlation. *IEEE Transactions on Dependable and Secure Computing, 1*(3), 146169.

Xu, J., Fan, J., Ammar, M., & Moon, S. B. (2002). Prefix-preserving IP address anonymization: Measurement-based security evaluation and a new cryptography-based scheme. *Proceedings of the 10th IEEE International Conference on Network Protocols (ICNP 2002).*

Zou, C. C., Gong, W., Towsley, D., & Gao, L. (2005, October). The monitoring and early detection of internet worms. *IEEE/ACM Transactions on Networking, 13*(5).

TERMS AND DEFINITIONS

Data Retention: Data retention refers to the capture and storage of telecommunications and network traffic by service providers and governments. The purpose of this practice is to perform analysis on the data or to facilitate accountability of transactions.

False Negative: The term false negative is a statistical term used to describe the failure to detect an attack. In statistics, a false negative refers to a type II error in hypothesis testing, where a test fails to reject a null hypothesis when it is false.

False Positive: The term false positive is a statistical term used to describe a false alert from intrusion detection systems. In statistics, a false positive refers to a type I error in hypothesis testing, where a null hypothesis is incorrectly rejected.

Intrusion Detection Systems: Intrusion detection systems (IDS) are used to monitor network traffic and computer systems in order to detect potential threats. Misuse IDS refers to systems that detect potential attacks by comparing monitored data to known attack signatures. Anomaly IDS employs statistical methods to detect anomalous events based on a model of normal traffic or user patterns. As opposed to misuse IDS, anomaly IDS is capable of detecting unknown attacks.

Lawful Interception: Lawful interception refers to the interception of telecommunications and network traffic by law enforcement and national security agencies. The interception has to be authorized by a competent authority according to applicable national laws. Lawful interception is also referred to as wiretapping.

Network Flow: There is no authoritative definition of the term network flow, but it usually refers to a set of packets sharing a common property. A common flow definition is defined as a 5-tuple, where all packets have the same protocol number (typically IP) source and destination addresses and port numbers.

Network Monitoring: Network monitoring refers to the practice of monitoring computer networks in order to identify traffic trends, failing systems, and anomalous behavior. Network monitoring is used in network management to collect necessary data in order to make informed decisions.

Chapter XXXIII
Public Key Infrastructures as a Means for Increasing Network Security

Ioannis P. Chochliouros
Hellenic Telecommunications Organization S.A.
and University of Peloponnese, Greece

Stergios P. Chochliouros
Independent Consultant, Greece

Anastasia S. Spiliopoulou
Hellenic Telecommunications Organization S.A.,
General Directorate for Regulatory Affairs, Greece

Evita Lampadari
Hellenic Telecommunications Organization S.A.,
General Directorate for Regulatory Affairs, Greece

ABSTRACT

The work investigates some "core" features of public key infrastructures (PKI), including fundamental technologies and infrastructures, within the context of recent market demands for increased network security applications. To this aim, we explain the basic features of public key cryptography, in parallel with a variety of other major PKI functional operations, all able to affect network development and growth. Then, we discuss some among the relevant basic and PKI-derived services, in order to comply with current needs and security requirements, thus supporting both usage and deployment of such infrastructures in competitive markets. In addition, we focus on several recent advances of information and communication convergence, and the effect those advances have on the notion of PKI, especially if considering future challenges. PKI have now become a central part of securing today's networked world and it should be expected that it will continue to have a huge impact on businesses. Furthermore, we correlate the above activities to recent European regulatory initiatives and similar commonly applied policies, to promote the appliance of digital signatures in a fully converged and liberalized market environment.

INTRODUCTION

After a period of fast growth from 1998-2000, the electronic communications sector is currently undergoing a "severe" adjustment process. Its implications and possible outcomes raise extremely important issues for the future and for economic growth worldwide (European Commission, 2003). In any case, the importance of the electronic communications sector lies in its impact on all other sectors of the economy. It offers the potential and the dynamism for organizations to make best use of their investment in information society technology (IST) and to realize productivity gains, improvements in quality, and opportunities for greater social inclusion (Chochliouros & Spiliopoulou, 2003).

The rollout of innovative technologies (such as broadband and 3G) as well as the development of new content, applications, and/or (public and private) services (European Commission, 2004) result in new security challenges (Kaufman, 2002). Addressing security issues is also crucial to stimulating demand for new electronic communications services and to develop, further, the digital worldwide economy (Chochliouros & Spiliopoulou, 2005). Networks and information systems are now supporting services and carrying data of great value, which can be vital to other applications. Increased protection against the various types of attacks on infrastructures, therefore, is necessary to maintain their availability, authenticity, integrity, and confidentiality. In the current European markets, the use of encryption technologies and electronic signatures towards providing enhanced security is becoming indispensable (Brands, 2000; European Parliament and Council of the European Union, 1999), while an increasing variety of authentication mechanisms is required to meet different needs in converged environments (European Commission, 2002).

Within such a generalized context, public key infrastructures (PKI) are becoming a central part of securing today's networked world; they can provide a focal point for many aspects of security management, while, at the same time, they can serve as an "enabler" for a growing number of various security applications, both in private and public organizations (International Organization for Standardization (ISO), 2005). Most standard protocols for secure e-mail, Web access, virtual private networks (VPNs) and single sign-on user authentication systems make use of some form of public-key certificates and for that reason require some specific form of PKI. The security of transactions and data has become essential for the supply of electronic services, including electronic commerce (e-commerce) and online public services, and low confidence in security could slow down the widespread introduction of such services. Given the rapid evolution of today's computer and network technology, our work intends to examine the impact of this evolution on the notion of PKI and the supporting business and legal framework in the context of relevant policies, mainly promoted through the European Union (EU).

BACKGROUND: PKI FUNDAMENTAL TECHNOLOGIES AND BASIC INFRASTRUCTURES

In general, a PKI is a combination of hardware and software products, policies, and procedures that offer enhanced security, required to carry out e-commerce activity in order that various users can communicate securely through a "chain of trust." Its basis is digital identifications known as "digital certificates" (Brands, 2000). These act like an electronic passport and bind the user's "digital signature" to his or her public key. In the following sections, we discuss some basic notations relevant to public key cryptography processes, and then we analyze some essential features of PKI. In fact, PKI is an authentication technology, a technical means for identifying entities in an environment.

PUBLIC KEY CRYPTOGRAPHY

Public key cryptography is used (Feghhi, Williams, & Feghhi, 1998) in conjunction with the following options to create a technology for identifying entities: (i) a mechanism for establishing trust according to a (pre-)defined trust model; (ii) a mechanism for uniquely naming entities; and (iii) a mechanism for distributing information regarding the validity of the binding between a particular key pair and a name. Under appropriate conditions (Kaufman, 2002), the use of public key cryptography can be considered as a modern technological basis for securing electronic business processes. Security requirements, such as data integrity, nonrepudiation of signing, data authentication, confidentiality, and authentication for access control, can be implemented by using cryptographic tools, providing digital signature and encryption facilities.

Public key cryptography was invented in 1976 (Diffie & Hellmann, 1976). Unlike symmetric cryptography (such as, the data encryption standard (DES)), in which the same cryptographic key is shared between all parties (i.e., senders and receivers), pairs of corresponding public and private keys for each party allow the realization of the necessary cryptographic operations (Coppersmith, 1994). The process of public key cryptography involves creating a public and private key simultaneously, using the same algorithm provided by an appropriate certificate authority (CA). The private key is given only to the requesting party, while the public key is made publicly available in a directory that can be accessed by all potential parties, aiming to realize electronic transactions. The private key is kept secret by the appropriate authority; it is never given to anyone other that the original requester and is never sent across the Internet. The private key is then used to decrypt data that has been encrypted by a third entity, by using the corresponding public key.

Public key cryptography is a critically important technology, since it realizes the concept of the *digital certificate*. The idea of the key-pair (one private, one publicly available) enables a variety of different services and protocols, including confidentiality, data integrity, secure (pseudo-)random generation, and zero-knowledge proofs of knowledge.

The concepts of public key cryptography (with various implementation algorithms) have, nowadays, reached a state of high maturity. However, in order to create conditions for further expansion to end users (corporate or private), it is necessary to make the related technologies available to an extensive variety of applications and environments in a uniform way.

PKIS: FUNCTIONAL OPERATIONS

PKI assumes the use of public key cryptography, which is a common method on the Internet for authenticating a message's sender or encrypting (and/or decrypting) a message. PKI allows users to exchange data securely over any kind of network; it involves the use of a public and private cryptographic key pair, which is obtained through a *trusted authority*. PKI provides for digital certificates (Feghhi et al., 1998) that can identify individuals or organizations and directory services that can store and revoke them, if necessary.

A *digital signature* is an electronic signature allowing for the authentication of the sender of a message (or signer of a document). It also can be used to ensure that the contents of a received message have remained unchanged while in transit. Digital signatures can be used with encrypted (or decrypted) messages, allowing the receiver to decide about the claimed "nature" of the sender, and to ensure that a message arrives in its "original" format. A digital signature also is encapsulated within a digital certificate to identify the authority responsible for issuing the certificate. Additional benefits to its use are that it is straightforwardly transportable, cannot easily be repudiated, cannot be imitated by another party, and can be automatically time stamped. (Time stamping is the mechanism to provide the existence of a time source that the population of the PKI environment users will trust.)

The seed idea is to consider that "the PKI is the basis of a security infrastructure whose services are implemented and delivered using public key concepts and techniques" (Adams & Lloyd, 2002). On its own, public key technology only supports asymmetric, mathematical operations on data (such as encrypting or signing a message), while it does not provide a connection to applications (or environments), such as e-mail, electronic business (e-business), or electronic government (e-government). A fully functional PKI, as the basis of the security infrastructure providing such a connection, encompasses several additional components and services (Housley, Ford, Polk & Solo, 1999).

As previously mentioned, in order to verify the sender's online identity, it is necessary to create a separate entity, known as the CA. The latter acts as a trusted party for the function of binding a cryptographic key pair to an entity, verifying the sender's identity and issuing both public and private keys. A CA certifies the binding by digitally signing a data structure (which is called a *public-key certificate*) that contains some representation of the identity and the correspondent public key, for a specific time period. A certificate repository is the particular location where any entity can retrieve an issued public key certificate. The private key is forwarded securely to the sender and the CA signs the latter's public key with its own private key, known as the *root key*. The combination of these two keys composes the sender's digital certificate. The root key is seen as a *watermark* that validates the sender's certificate and proves that the sender is indeed who he or she claims to be (Brands, 2000).

Meanwhile various functions can occasionally take place, like: (a) the key update, which is the (ideally automatic) mechanism to force the expiration of a given certificate and the replacement with a new certificate prior to the end of its lifetime or (b) the key back-up and recovery, which is a specific function that, when properly implemented, offers the possibility of avoiding the loss of encrypted data protected by inaccessible private cryptographic keys, ideally without the user's knowledge.

In general, the following steps must be followed to incorporate PKI as an appropriate method of purchasing goods electronically.

- A trusted third party (i.e., the CA) issues a private key to an individual user and a validated public key, accessible to the wider public.
- A customer expresses his or her wish to purchase an item from a vendor's Web site. The vendor requests that the customer proves his or her identity to ensure the purchase order is genuine.

- The customer "signs" the order with the private key, earlier issued by the CA.
- PKI software uses the private key and a complex mathematical formula to generate a digital signature that is unique to the purchase order.
- The encrypted signed purchase order is forwarded to the vendor.
- The vendor uses the customer's public key, which must be validated by the CA, to decrypt the purchase order and validate the relevant "signature."
- The PKI software uses the public key to run a similar mathematical formula on the order to generate a matching computation.
- If the original and subsequent computations match, then customer's identity is confirmed and the order is processed normally.

This method conducts a public and private key exchange, with the backing of a trusted CA. It provides a secure way of conducting business across public and private networks. PKI technology means that business transactions (such as credit card transactions) can be performed with the knowledge that the details: (1) are sent by the right sender; (2) can be read only by the intended recipient; and (3) arrive at their destination in the form originally intended by the sender.

Under appropriate terms public key cryptography (and the PKI) can become a preferred approach on the Internet, as they can avoid unwanted decryption and/or malicious changes of informative data transferred over modern networks, especially when keys are discovered (or intercepted) by unauthorized parties.

PKI BASIC SERVICES: SECURITY REQUIREMENTS

The deployment of PKI technology has a substantial impact on business entities, andthe technical aspects as well as the organizational and legal ones have to be taken into account. The management of PKI depends on a detailed control framework for certificate issuance and for the use of certificates (Adams & Lloyd,

2002). There is a range of services/applications to be exploited that can bring excellent new business opportunities for telecommunication operators (and other market players as well). In the near future, digital certificates will rapidly become a widely used means for user authentication; inevitably, they will play a crucial role for providing services over network infrastructures.

A great variety of key applications can benefit from an effective PKI integration (European Institute for Research and Strategic Studies in Telecommunications (Eurescom) GmbH, 2000). These can comprise document exchange (such as electronic document interchange (EDI), XML, secure e-mail, registered mail, secure workflow), e-commerce, mobile commerce, home banking, health care services, single sign-on services, Internet service provider (ISP) roaming, distance learning, secure networking (virtual private networking), remote work. A PKI is generally considered to be associated with three main security requirements, which in turn, can be considered as the basic (core) services such an environment offers. These are: authentication, integrity, and confidentiality.

Authentication is the assurance provided to an entity that a second one is really "who" it claims to be. Authentication finds application in two primary contexts: entity identification and data origin identification (Boyd & Mathuria, 2003). Rapid technological development and the global character of the Internet necessitate particular approaches that are open to various technologies and services capable of authenticating data electronically. In electronic communications, the concept of digital signatures is linked to the use of a kind of "electronic seal," affixed to the data and allowing the recipient to verify the data origin or, more accurately, to the use of a key assigned to a certain sender. However, authentication of the data source does not necessarily prove the identity of the key owner. The recipient of the message cannot be sure whether the sender is really the "original" one, as the "public" key may be published under another name. A method for the recipient to obtain reliable information on the identity of the sender is confirmation by a third party, that is a person (or institution) mutually trusted by both parties.

Integrity is the assurance offered to an entity that data (either in transit or in storage) has not been altered (with or without intention) between two communication points or a given time gap (Merkle, 1978). The challenge for ensuring communications' integrity is a very important one (especially for e-commerce activities), and proper technical solutions have to be applied (European Commission, 2002). The response to this problem again lies in the use of a digital signature, involving not encryption of the "message text" itself, but solely encryption of the signature, which is attached to the normal readable "text" and enables the receiver to check whether the data has been changed. As previously mentioned, from the technical point of view, the most effective digital signatures have consisted of two keys: a published public key and a confidential private key. The relevant public key is used to check whether the signature has, in fact, been created using the private key. The recipient also can use it to check whether data has been changed, thus enabling him or her to check whether the sender's public and private keys form a complementary pair and whether data has been remained unchanged during transmission. A CA need not be involved at this stage.

Confidentiality is the assurance given to an entity that nobody can "read" a particular piece of data, except the intended recipient (Treasury Board of Canada Secretariat, 1999). PKI support is an important component for key-agreement procedures in confidentiality services, where public key algorithms (and certificates) are used to securely negotiate/establish symmetric encryption keys. In any case, e-commerce and many other innovative applications will only develop if confidentiality can be guaranteed in a user-friendly and cost-efficient way.

It is obvious that when consumers use services, such as teleshopping or telebanking, they have to be sure that personal data (such as credit card numbers) remain secret. In commercial contacts performed on open networks, firms have to be able to protect themselves against industrial espionage relating to their business plans, invitations to tender, and research results. On the other hand, law enforcement authorities and national security agencies fear that more widespread use of encrypted communication may hinder them in the fight against crime. All the above challenge entities to "prove" their identities, to be assured that important data has not been altered in any way, and to be convinced that data sent to another recipient can be understood only by the latter.

In order to realize the provision of the above fundamental features, various implementation mechanisms (Adams & Lloyd, 2002) can be considered:

- A PKI service of authentication (as opposed to the nonPKI operation to the authentication in a local environment, which may include single- or multifactor authentication, also providing password or biometric devices) employs the cryptographic technique of a digital signature. The signature may be computed over the hash value of one of the following three factors: (1) data to be authenticated; (2) submission of a request for data to be sent to a remote server; and (3) creation of a *random* challenge, issued by a remote party. The first issue supports the PKI service of data origin authentication, while the other two support the PKI services of entity authentication.

- The PKI service of integrity may employ one of two specific techniques. The first is a digital signature. Although it serves the purpose of authentication, it simultaneously provides integrity over the signed data, due to the necessary property of the related (hash and signature) algorithms. Consequently, any possible change in the input data may lead to a large unpredictable change in the output data. The second technique that can be deployed is the message authentication code. It uses a symmetric block cipher (or a hash function). Although these two alternatives are symmetric solutions, it is important to point out that both are *keyed mechanisms*, as they strongly depend on a key, which has to be shared between the sender and receiver. The shared key can be derived, if considering the key establishing functions of a PKI.

- The PKI service for confidentiality uses a mechanism similar to one of the alternatives of the integrity.

PKI: CERTAIN BASIC EXAMPLES

Over the last 10 years, several PKI solutions have been proposed and implemented. These can be categorized into three general sectors.

The *X.509 standard* and its exhaustive Internet profile (Housley et al., 1999) represent quite satisfactorily the PKI components. In most cases, implementations differ based upon the rigor with which they implement the suite of appropriate standards (Chokhani & Ford, 1999). The commercial market for X.509 CAs continues to evolve in terms of product sophistication and also in terms of awareness of how PKI can secure applications. (In particular, more than 90% of first-generation production PKIs integrate with only "Internet-centric" applications.) X.509 digital certificates actually integrate relatively easily with applications like e-mail clients and Web browsers; however, their integration with packaged mainframe and with legacy applications is more problematic. Currently, there is a trend of *application Webification*, with the aim to replace customized clients with browsers as universal clients running over TCP/IP, as this is expected to reduce maintenance costs. Nevertheless, digitally signing and encrypting transactions become more critical due to the increased security risks derived from the elimination of proprietary client software and the reduced protection of proprietary network protocols.

Pretty good privacy (PGP) is a program used to encrypt and decrypt e-mail for transmission over the Internet, but it can also be used to send an encrypted digital signature, enabling the receiver to verify the sender's identity and be sure that the message was not changed whilst in transit (Zimmermann, 1995). Other users also can use PGP to encrypt files a user may wish to store, thus rendering these unreadable. When used in conjunction with e-mail, PGP allows encryption and transmission of a message to the possessor of a public key. The receiver's public key is used by the sender to encrypt the message and is decrypted on receipt with the receiver's private key. PGP users share a directory of public keys that is called as "key ring." To enable a recipient reading a message, he must have access to this key ring. PGP also enables senders to sign their mail with digital signatures, using their own private keys. In more recent times, PGP has highlighted its ability to support features similar to X.509. Traditionally, however, PGP has been distinguished by its distributed approach to key management. PGP certificates are formed of one or more certifications, which bind keys to user's information with a digital signature. There is great flexibility in the key and user information that can be conveyed in a single certificate. Thus, a PGP PKI has "avoided" the need for any form of authority.

Simple public key infrastructure (SPKI) was developed in response to several methods for further analysis of X.509 (Ellison, 1999). The major philosophical objection to X.509 surrounds its relation to X.500 naming. SPKI, more correctly an authorization infrastructure, relies upon the uniqueness of the combination of a pseudonym and a public key.

PKI: CURRENT EUROPEAN REGULATORY ISSUES

In the light of the increasingly important role played by electronic services in the economy, the security of networks and services is of growing public interest (European Commission, 2001). There is a growing potential for information security issues in Europe, which is a direct result of the rapid development of the Internet, e-commerce, and business-to-business (B2B) transactions (Chochliouros & Spiliopoulou, 2003). Consequently, the security of network infrastructures has been improved significantly and will continue to improve in the next few years. This has increased the demand for a variety of PKI solutions.

It is a prerequisite for individuals, businesses, administrations, and other organizations to protect their own data and information by deploying effective security technologies, where appropriate. In particular, various market players acting in a competitive market environment, and through their capacity to innovate, offer a variety of solutions adapted to real market needs. In the European context, there are legal requirements imposed on providers of telecommunications services to take appropriate technical and organizational measures to safeguard the security of their services. Towards fulfilling this aim, the "core" principles (European Commission, 2001, 2003, 2004) are about: (1) ensuring the availability of services and data; (2) preventing the disruption and unauthorized interception of communications; (3) providing appropriate confirmation that data that has been sent, received, or stored are complete and unchanged; (4) securing the confidentiality of data; (5) protecting information systems against unauthorized access (and against malicious attacks); and (6) securing dependable authentication.

The EU has addressed these issues in a pragmatic way, establishing a distinction between authentication and confidentiality, even though they both rely on the same cryptographic technologies. For authentication, a proper European directive has been enabled on electronic signatures, to secure the internal market for certificates and certification services (European Parliament and Council of the European Union, 1999). Moreover, things get more sensitive when referring to confidentiality. The scrambling of electronic communications has raised some legitimate public security concerns, for which various research projects have been developed in the field of cryptography. The most challenging short-term goal is to bring existing security and privacy solutions into the large-scale mass market, for the benefit of the end user. Modern electronic communication and commerce necessitate electronic signatures and related services, allowing data authentication; divergent rules with respect to legal recognition of electronic signatures and the accreditation of certification-service providers in the European Member States, may create a significant barrier to the use of these electronic facilities. On the other hand, a clear European framework regarding the conditions applying to electronic signatures will strengthen confidence in, and general acceptance of, the new technologies.

Moreover, legislation in the EU Member States should not hinder the free movement of goods and services in the internal market, enabling certification-service providers to develop their cross-border activities with a view to increasing their competitiveness, thus offering consumers and businesses new opportunities to exchange information and trade electronically, in a secure way, regardless of frontiers. However, it is always important to strike a balance between consumer and business needs.

CONCLUSION AND PROJECTION TO THE FUTURE

Since the early introduction of asymmetric key algorithms with the further development of high-speed digital electronic communications (Chochliouros & Spiliopoulou, 2005), a need became evident for ways in which users could securely communicate with each other and, as a consequence of that, for ways in which users could be sure with whom they were actually interacting. The idea of cryptographically protected certificates binding user identities to public keys was eagerly developed. With the deployment of the World Wide Web and its rapid spread, the need for authentication and secure communication became still more acute. The result was the effective creation of a PKI structure for Web users/sites wishing secure (or more secure) communications. The deployment of PKI technology had a substantial impact on multiple business entities.

The use of PKI is having, and will continue to have, a huge impact on the European (and the global) telecommunications business. Corporate and personal e-banking is currently a major application for PKI, while other applications (such as the e-government) are expected to develop in the future, especially in the context of recent business initiatives like those promoted in the EU context (Lalopoulos, Chochliouros, & Spiliopoulou, 2004). Trusted third-party services

generate different kinds of business opportunities. One large class is generic PKI services, providing public key certificates and their management.

Another application-independent service area is the support of electronic signatures, where the provision of time stamps constitutes a fundamental component. While certificates are issued once and can be used many times, time stamps are to be invoked for every transaction, in some cases (as in contract negotiations) repeatedly, during the process. This is generally valid for all nonrepudiation services. In the area of PKI-based electronic signatures, it is estimated, in the future, to see many products based on recent technological developments (such as mobile signatures and signature servers). It is of great importance, therefore, that supervision bodies, regulators, the industrial sector, and, of course, all market players involved in the development of PKI-integration look at these technologies with an open mind to promote appropriate and applicable solutions and to enhance network security.

ACKNOWLEDGMENT

All authors would like to dedicate the present work to the memory of Panagiotis Chochliouros, who was, and will always be, an active inspiration.

REFERENCES

Adams, C., & Lloyd, S. (2002). *Understanding PKI: Concepts, standards, and deployment Considerations.* Addison-Wesley Professional.

Brands, S. A. (2000). *Rethinking public key infrastructures and digital certificates: Building in privacy.* MIT Press.

Boyd, C., & Mathuria, A. (2003). *Protocols for key establishment and authentication.* Germany: Springer-Verlag, Berlin and Heidelberg GmbH & Co.

Chochliouros, I. P., & Spiliopoulou, A. S. (2003). Perspectives for achieving competition and development in the European information and communications technologies (ICT) markets. *The Journal of the Communications Network, 2*(3), 42-50.

Chochliouros, I. P., & Spiliopoulou, A. S. (2005). Broadband access in the European Union: An enabler for technical progress, business renewal and social development. *The International Journal of Infonomics, 1,* 5-21.

Chokhani, S., & Ford, W. (1999). *Internet X.509 public key infrastructure: Certificate policy and certification practices framework, RFC 2527.* Sterling, VA: Internet Engineering Task Force (IETF).

Coppersmith, D. (1994). The data encryption standard (DES) and its strength against attacks. *IBM Journal of Research and Development, 38*(3), 243-250.

Diffie, W., & Hellman, M. (1976). New directions in cryptography. *IEEE Transactions on Information Theory, 22*(6), 644-654.

Ellison, C. (1999). *SPKI requirement, RFC2692.* Sterling, VA: Internet Engineering Task Force (IETF).

European Commission. (2001). *Communication on network and information security: Proposal for a European policy approach* [COM (2001) 298 final, 06.06.2001]. Brussels, Belgium: European Commission.

European Commission. (2002). *Communication on eEurope 2005: An information society for all: An action plan* [COM(2002)263 final, 28.05.2002]. Brussels, Belgium: European Commission.

European Commission. (2003). *Communication on electronic communications: The road to the knowledge economy* [COM(2003) 65 final, 11.02.2003]. Brussels, Belgium: European Commission.

European Commission. (2004). *Communication on connecting Europe at high speed: Recent developments in the sector of electronic communications* [COM(2004) 61 final, 03.02.2004]. Brussels, Belgium: European Commission.

European Institute for Research and Strategic Studies in Telecommunications (Eurescom) GmbH. (2000). *EURESCOM Project P944: Impact of PKI on the European telecommunications business. deliverable* [1, Main Rep.]. Heidelberg, Germany: Eurescom GmbH.

European Parliament and Council of the European Union. (1999). *Directive 1999/93/EC of 13 December 1999, on a community framework for electronic signatures* [Official Journal (OJ) L13, 19.01.2000, pp. 12-20]. Brussels, Belgium: European Parliament and Council of the European Union.

Feghhi, J., Williams, P., & Feghhi J. (1998). *Digital certificates: Applied Internet security.* MA: Addison-Wesley.

Housley, R., Ford, W., Polk, W., & Solo, D. (1999). *Internet X.509 public key infrastructure. Certificate and CRL profile, request for comments (RFC) 2459.* Sterling, VA: Internet Engineering Task Force (IETF).

International Organization for Standardization (ISO). (2005). *ISO/IEC 17799: Information technology—Security techniques: Code of practice for information security management.* Geneva, Switzerland: ISO.

Kaufman, C. (2002). *Network security: Private communication in a public world* (2nd ed.). Prentice Hall.

Lalopoulos, G. K., Chochliouros, I.P., & Spiliopoulou, A. S. (2004). Challenges and perspectives for Web-based applications in organizations. In M. Pagani (Ed.), *The encyclopedia of multimedia technology and networking* (pp. 82-88). Hershey, PA: IRM Press.

Merkle, R. C. (1978). Secure communications over insecure channels. *Communications of the ACM, 21*(4), 294-299.

Treasury Board of Canada Secretariat. (1999). *Digital signature and confidentiality—Certificate policies for the government of Canada public key infrastructure* [Government of Canada (GOC), PKI Certificate Policies version 3.02].

Zimmermann, P. R. (1995). *The official PGP user's guide.* Cambridge, MA: MIT Press.

TERMS AND DEFINITIONS

Authentication: A process of verifying an identity claimed by or for a system entity. An authentication process consists of two steps: (1) identification step, which presents an identifier to the security system and (2) verification step, which presents or generates authentication information that corroborates the binding between the entity and the identifier.

Certification Authority (CA): An entity that issues digital certificates (especially X.509 certificates) and vouches for the binding between the data items in a certificate. Consequently, it is an authority trusted by one or more users to create, assign, and manage certificates. Optionally, the CA may create the user's keys. As certificate users depend on the validity of information provided, a CA usually holds an official position created and granted power by a government, a corporation, or some other organization.

Cryptographic Key: A parameter (e.g., a secret 64-bit number for data encryption system (DES)) used by a cryptographic process that makes the process completely defined and usable only by those having that key.

Encryption: The process of transforming data to an unintelligible form in such a way that the original data either cannot be obtained (one-way encryption) or cannot be obtained without using the inverse decryption process (two-way encryption). It is a cryptographic transformation of data (called "plaintext") into a form (called "ciphertext") that conceals the data's original meaning to prevent it from being known or used.

Certification: This is the process in which a CA issues a certificate for a user's public key, and returns that certificate to the user's client system and/or posts that certificate in a repository.

Public-Key Infrastructure (PKI): A system of certification authorities (and, optionally, registration authorities and other supporting servers and agents) that perform some set of certificate management, archive management, key management, and token management functions for a community of users in an application of asymmetric cryptography.

Security Management: This means system activities that support security policy by monitoring and controlling security services, elements, and mechanisms; distributing security information; and reporting security events. The associated functions comprise: (1) controlling (granting or restricting) access to system resources; (2) retrieving (gathering) and archiving (storing) security information; and (3) managing and controlling the encryption process.

Chapter XXXIV
Use of Geographic Information Systems in Cyber Warfare and Cyber Counterterrorism

Mark R. Leipnik
Sam Houston State University, USA

ABSTRACT

Geographic information systems (GIS) are defined and discussed both in general and specifically with reference to their applications in three distinct modalities. These are, firstly, the application of computer mapping and spatial analysis technologies encompassed by the term GIS in counter terrorism. Secondly, the potential for misuse of GIS technologies in both terrorism in general and more specifically the unique vulnerabilities of these suites of complex programs and the huge and sophisticated datasets that are managed by GIS programs to exploitation and damage by cyber terrorists. Lastly the ways in which these terrorist threats to geo-spatial infrastructure can be detected, avoided and minimized will be discussed.

BACKGROUND

Definition and Structure of GIS: Geographic information systems (GIS) are a rapidly evolving suite of computer programs and related geospatial data sets that provide for the input, storage, manipulation, spatial analysis, query and generation of cartographic and other output related to features existing on the earth. GIS contain data stored in specialized topological data structures with multiple co-registered layers that have coordinate systems and map projections. Features portrayed in each layer including topogra-phy, infrastructure data such as streets portrayed as lines, jurisdictional boundaries portrayed as polygonal shapes and incident locations portrayed as points all have corresponding descriptive data linked to them in a series of attribute database tables. The topology and coordinate system(s) built into GIS allows the location of features to be precisely determined in real world coordinates and features existing over considerable portions of the curved surface of the earth to be portrayed in the two dimensional space of computer monitors and potentially on printed cartographic output (Burroughs, 1986).

Generic Applications of GIS: GIS was invented in the middle 1960s in Canada to manage large natural resources related data sets (Foresman, 1998). By the 1980s, the typical application areas for GIS had expanded to include such fields as public utility and infrastructure management, land records mapping and management (cadastral applications), business and marketing applications; such as site selection and logistics and in a range of social science and physical science applications (Steinberg & Steinberg 2006). The 1990s saw additional applications develop in such areas as interactive Web-based mapping, vehicle navigation and integration with global positioning systems technology, computer aided design and image processing for remotely sensed data and digital aerial photography (Longley, McGuire, Goodchild, & Rhind, 1999).

GIS Programs and Requirements: GIS programs include the ArcGIS and related software such as AR-CVIEW and ArcIMS and the older Arc/Info software from the Environmental Systems Research Institute (ESRI) in Redlands, California (www.ESRI.com), GIS software and related CAD and design tools from Intergraph Corporation in Huntsville, Alabama (www. Intergraph.com) and the less powerful, but less costly, desktop mapping software from MapInfo Corporation in Troy, New York (www.Mapinfo.com). These are also related software for many specific applications such as serving maps interactively over the Internet, interfacing with relational database management systems and various types of modeling and analysis. In some organizations, software from three or more vendors may be employed; thus at the Federal Emergency Management Agency (FEMA), ArcGIS is used to create GIS data, but the simpler MapInfo software is used on laptop computers in the field (URISA, 2003). GIS programs and their associated topologically structured vector and high-resolution raster data sets have substantial system requirements. Specifically, current generations of GIS software run best on machines with at least 1 gigabyte of RAM and featuring high power graphics cards that are a necessary investment. In addition, large high resolution displays, large format

plotters, large format scanners, tape backup devices for low cost, high capacity storage and global positioning systems units capable of displaying GIS data and running "mini" GIS programs such as ARCPAD are a frequent component of GIS installations (GIS, 2005).

APPLICATIONS IN COUNTERTERRORISM

One of the very first GIS applications was a national defense application by the Canadian Navy to map and study attributes of coastal areas, but this mid-1960s application of GIS was actually predated by a decade, by a defense application of computerized maps developed for the RAND Corporation by Dr. Waldo Tobler. This featured the use of computers (without linked databases and therefore not a true GIS) to display radar data from the defense early warning (DEW) line (Monmonier, 1982). Interestingly, with the end of the cold war, defense applications of GIS fell temporarily into decline. An indication of this decline was the consolidation of the mapping functions of the Defense Mapping Agency and the map making functions at the CIA into the National Imagery and Mapping Agency. The attacks on 9/11 had a major impact on this decline, leading to a huge infusion of funds and staff into what has now been dubbed geospatial intelligence and the creation of the National Geospatial-Intelligence Agency (NGA) within the U.S. Defense Department (Greene, 2003). The intention of this agency is to convey often largely paper maps and largely sterile aerial imagery into "advanced" geospatial intelligence; where not merely high resolution images are available in near real-time, but fully descriptive attribute data and current "ground truthed" intelligence is added to enhance the imagery. Increasingly advanced geospatial intelligence is being made available over computer networks and wirelessly to field operations personnel, intelligence analysts, and other widely distributed users.

GIS is featured ever more frequently in both military and law enforcement applications (Leipnik & Albert, 2003). Specifically, with reference to the convergence of military and law enforcement responsibilities surrounding counterterrorism, GIS is being utilized in five specific ways. These modes include: (1) As a tool to aid assessment of the spatial extent of past terrorist attacks and the assessment of vulnerabilities. (2) In the simulation of specific terrorist attacks and in conducting planning exercises using scenarios played out using geospatial data. (3) For the coordination of actual incident response in the short-term to attacks of various sorts including those on computer networks. (4) To coordinate recovery efforts and conduct assessments of the actual impact of terrorists attacks. (5) To provide for the planning of and management during counterstrikes against terrorist groups and facilities such as training camps. This last approach is the most directly military in character, while coordinating critical incident response is largely a law enforcement and civil emergency response agency responsibility. Both actual and hypothetical (but realistic) examples of use of these technologies in each application will be discussed further.

1. Mapping the spatial extent of terrorist attacks can be accomplished by using an appropriate set of digital data such as, the Digital Chart of the World or the ESRI world data set, which includes over 175,000 attributed features. Examples of mapping and analysis of attacks includes GIS generated maps of terrorist truck bombings, terrorist kidnappings, and air and marine piracy. Consultants to the U.S. Defense Department have mapped all attacks on U.S. forces in Iraq (U.S. Navy, 2004). Part and parcel of such mapping is that many locational data are not suitable for accurate mapping. Thus an attack in a town in Iraq may be digitally mapped at a scale appropriate to a world map or even a nation-wide map of Iraq, but cannot be mapped to a street or region of a town. Other problems include linguistic difficulties particularly in places like Afghanistan with many dialects and dated or incomplete data.

2. Simulations of attacks can be carried out using a GIS to portray the spatial interactions between multiple factors. Data used might include: aerial photography, street network (portrayed by street centerlines or curbs, with street names and address ranges), building foot-prints perhaps linked to engineering drawings "as builts" and other thematic layers of data. Simulations can include scenarios for attacks, simulations of vapor clouds or explosion zones, and access and deployment of critical incident response resources. Some of this training is taking place in simulated command centers using plasma screens and virtual reality technologies (NGIF, 2005).

3. Coordination of resources can be accomplished with data links between responders in the field, dispatching, and emergency coordination centers. For more extended events, mobile command centers situated in specially equipped vehicles can be used. Increasingly, data is being wirelessly sent to PDA and even cell phones with GPS that have camera and display screens capable of displaying and manipulating maps (Peng & Tsou, 2003). One key aspect of coordination of response is using GIS to determine proximity to emergency resources such as fire, police, and hospital facilities and avoiding interjurisdictional overlap such as the muddled response of two dozen Colorado law enforcement agencies to the Columbine High School incident, with the subsequent confusion as to which agency had lead responsibility (Wang, 2005).

4. The assessment of the long-term impact is the area where the typical strength of GIS in comprehensive planning and environmental assessment comes most strongly to the fore. This is perhaps best illustrated by the use of GIS in the recovery efforts after 9/11 where a large range of technologies were employed to assess the immediate hazards, assist in evacuations and the logistics of personnel and equipment deployment and as an aid in relocation and especially in combination with GPS and laser total station surveying in the recovery and identification of victims. In the 9/11 response, the existence of an accurate multilayer GIS, assistance from professionals in

municipal government at FEMA, in academia, and later help from GIS vendors was critical. Also important was the use of light detection and ranging (LIDAR) technology which along with pictometry (high resolution oblique aerial photography) will find even more important uses in a wide range of GIS applications (Kwan & Lee, 2005).

5. The area of planning counterstrikes utilizing GIS is one application where much of the material remains highly classified. Nevertheless, it is a well established fact that aerial reconnaissance imagery is being processed by remote sensing image processing software and GIS to extract coordinates that are reentered into guidance systems for cruise missiles used in counter terrorist strikes. Similarly, digital cameras, GPS, and other sensors on Global Hawk and Predator unmanned airborne vehicle (drone) aircraft are transmitted to control centers outfitted with customized GIS programs that coordinate observation and occasionally direct attacks with Hell Fire missiles. A great deal of intelligence gathered from special operation troops, by CIA, and other intelligence operatives is being built into GIS data sets, so GPS coordinates of suspected targets can be combined with aerial imagery and other layers to analyze, coordinate, and assess the effectiveness of attacks often carried by stand-off aircraft which are themselves guided using GPS and GIS related technologies (Monmonier, 2002).

POTENTIAL OR ACTUAL USE BY TERRORISTS

Another set of considerations involves the issue of use of geospatial data and GIS programs by terrorists and cyber criminals and the appropriate limitations on access to geospatial data that needs to be implemented to safeguard this often critical data from access by potentially dangerous individuals and groups. Increasingly, geospatial data including topographic, infrastructure

and geodemographic data is available over the Internet for download from sites like the Geography Network or from ESRI or for use in Web-based interactive mapping programs maintained by local, regional, and national governments, and certain private companies. A more recent variation uses software such as ESRI's Map Publisher and Map Reader to serve and publish maps over the Internet, which can then be further manipulated with freely available software on the user's computer. This means that geospatial data can be downloaded and manipulated without the need to be connected to the Internet after the data and Map Reader programs have been downloaded. This ease of access makes the potential for misuse of geospatial data greater and appropriate restrictions more vital.

COUNTERMEASURES AND FUTURE TRENDS

Countermeasures: The most important countermeasure is to limit access to critical geospatial infrastructure data to those with appropriate permissions and to allow users to obtain and use geospatial data, but not to alter the underlying data sets without a careful vetting of the users credentials, training, and backgrounds. This is not really feasible when geospatial data is being served over the Internet on either interactive mapping Web sites or software such as ESRI's Map Publisher and Map Reader software. In that situation the integrity of the data may not be compromised on the server, but the data itself may be misused without the knowledge of the organization creating the data. A paramount example of dissemination of data where the danger of misuse of the data exceeded any potential benefits from dissemination of the data over the Internet involved the Office of Surface Water Quality of the U.S. Environmental Protection Agency (EPA). As part of the agency's mandate to regulate drinking water quality under the auspices of the Safe Drinking Water Act, the EPA placed on a Web site using interactive Wweb-based maps showing the location of roads, hydrographic features, and the fairly exact location of the intakes for upwards of 25,000 domestic water supply systems in the United States. Many of these sites were not huge water treatment plants processing millions of gallons per day with appropriate fences, security, or procedures in place to protect the water system intake from unauthorized attack. Instead, many were simply an open pipe and grating at the end of an obscure county road with hardly a fence separating visitors from the intake (and generally no protection on the reservoir or stream side of the intake). The EPA promptly removed this material from the Internet following 9/11 (EPA, 2003). Likewise engineering drawings of commercial nuclear power plants were belatedly removed from Nuclear Regulatory Commission Web sites after 9/11 (NRC, 2003). One way to protect content being served over the Web is to realize that more than one site might be employed by a potential terrorist. Thus a site that provides coordinates for a water system intake might be used in conjunction with a site providing driving directions and .25 meter color aerial photography and another site that allows mapping of the population density of a town being served by the system and another showing critical holes in emergency room capacity or distances to law enforcement facilities might all be used in conjunction with each other. Likewise, an engineering drawing of a nuclear plant, when combined with high resolution aerial photography, driving directions, data on prevailing winds, population density, and possible evacuation routes (or lack there of) has a synergistic potential for misuse. Since it is clear that the content of geospatial data available over the Internet for many areas of the world and in particular for the United States is vast and detailed, it is especially important to remove the critical last links in a chain of terrorist planning.

FUTURE TRENDS

GIS and related technologies continue to rapidly proliferate. This proliferation takes several directions. One is the continued expansion into new application areas, such as consumer decision making, trip planning, and tourism. This increasing availability of geospatial data

to largely anonymous users over the Internet does pose potential security risks. Likewise, GIS is migrating to ever more portable devices such as laptops, personal digital assistants, vehicle navigation systems, and now cell phones. Also, there is an ever greater availability of geospatial data for new areas of the world and covering new themes of information. So for example, eastern European countries, some Middle Eastern, and south Asian countries long plagued by terrorism are starting to develop geospatial data. Thus aging topographic maps are being supplanted in Turkey, Tunisia, Thailand, and Taiwan with geospatial data readily available over the Internet. Malaysia currently has a very good set of geospatial data as does Qatar and Kuwait. Egypt has excellent data for major cities, while Israel has long had superior geospatial data (Ralston, 2004). Security precautions are being considered with respect to release of critical infrastructure data in countries like Israel long affected by terrorism, but some of these other countries with rapidly evolving geospatial data also may have evolving terrorist movements.

CONCLUSION

GIS are an important form of digital data with a myriad of valuable uses, including many directly relevant to counterterrorism. However, GIS data sets can be misused and since GIS data sets are unusually large and complex and often of critical importance to the functioning of organizations, such as emergency responders and public utilities, the data sets are vulnerable to corruption and alteration. The tendency to use distributed networks to share and update geospatial data and the likelihood that data sets for multiple sources will be combined together in a multilayer GIS, make it essential that appropriate security precautions be taken with the increasing volume of geospatial data now available over the Internet. In particular, the advent of Web-based interactive mapping has given many new users access to powerful spatial analysis techniques and monumental data sets. These numerous new users of GIS include: some that are skilled, some that are just causal users, and some who are no doubt bent on using the data for nefarious and sometimes terroristic purposes. All this, behooves those in positions to regulate the release and content of geospatial data to take due care, least the desire to facilitate ease of use of this valuable resource inadvertently assist destructive use of the same set of powerful tools and digital information.

REFERENCES

Burroughs, P. A. (1986). *Principles of geographic information systems for land resources assessment.* Oxford: Claredon Press.

EPA. (2003). *Information management branch update.* http://www.epa.gov/OGWDW/imb_update/february2003.htm

Foresman, T. (Ed.). (1998*). The history of geographic information systems: Perspectives from the pioneers.* Prentice Hall.

GIS. (2005). *Discussion of GIS system requirements.* www.gis.com/implementing_gis/sysrequirements.html

Greene, R. W. (2002). *Confronting catastrophe: A GIS handbook.* Redlands, CA: ESRI Press.

Kennedy, H. (2001). *Dictionary of GIS terminology.* Redlands, CA: ESRI Press.

Kwan, M.-P., & Lee, J. (2005). Emergency response after 9/11. *Computers, Environment and Urban Systems, 29*(2).

Leipnik, M. R., & Albert, D. (Eds.). (2003). *GIS in law enforcement.* London: Taylor and Francis

Longley, P. A., McGuire, D. J., Goodchild, M. F., & Rhind, D. (Eds.). (1999*). GIS principles and applications.* London: Longmans.

Monmonier, M. (1982). *Computer assisted cartography, principles and prospects.* Eaglewood Cliffs, NJ: Prentice-Hall.

Monmonier, M. (2002). *Spying with maps.* New York: University of Chicago Press.

NGIF. (2005). National geospatial intelligence foundation. *Proceedings of the Technologies for Critical Incident Response Conference and Exposition,* San Diego, CA.

NRC. (2003). *NRC initiates additional security review of publicly available records.* Nuclear Regulatory Commission News, No. 04-135, Office of Public Affairs. www.nrc.gov

Peng, Z.-R., & Tsou, M.-H. (2003). *Internet GIS: Distributed GIS for the internet and wireless networks.* Hoboken, NJ: John Wiley & Sons.

Ralston, B. (2004). *GIS and public data.* Clifton Park, NY: Thompson/Delmar Press.

Stienberg, S., & Stienberg, S. (2006). *GIS for the social sciences.* Thousand Oaks, CA: Sage Publications.

URISA. (2003). Initial response and recovery at the World Trade Center. *Urban and Regional Information Systems Association Journal, January-February 2003.* www.URISA.org

U.S. Navy. (2004). *Patterns of global yerrorism.* Monterey, CA: Naval Postgraduate School. http://library.nps.navy.mil/home/terrorism.htm

Wang, F. (2005). *GIS and crime analysis.* IGI Global.

TERMS AND DEFINITIONS

Critical Incident Response: Coordination of the response of emergency services and/or law enforcement agencies using various tools including mobile communications, global positioning systems, GIS-based mapping, and spatial analysis.

Geographic Information Systems (GIS): A collection of computer hardware, software, and geographic data for capturing, storing, updating, manipulation, analyzing, and displaying all forms of geographically referenced data. (Kennedy, 2001, p. 42)

Geospatial Data: Digital data with a spatial reference such as a coordinate system and a link to descriptive attribute data for use in a geographic information system. Examples include Vector format: Shape files, Arc/Info Coverages, TIGER data and design files and geodatabase data sets, also raster format GEOTIFS, DRG's, Mr SID data sets, GRID files, TIN's.

Geospatial Intelligence: The use of geospatial data and programs such as GIS and image processing software in military and counterterrorism applications.

Global Positioning Systems (GPS): A constellation of 24 satellites developed by the U.S. Defense Department that orbit the earth at an altitude of 20,000 kilometers. These satellites transmit signals that allow a GPS receiver anywhere on earth to calculate its own location. The global positioning system is used in navigation, mapping, surveying, and other applications where precise positioning is necessary. (Kennedy, 2001, p. 44)

Interactive Web-Based Mapping: Use of the Internet to provide customized maps and a limited array of spatial analysis tools and view and query capabilities to access geospatial data stored on a server. Examples of software capable of serving maps over the Internet in an interactive fashion include ESRI's Arc Internet Map Server and Map Info MapXreme.

Spatial Analysis: Studying the locations and shapes of geographic features and the relationships between them. It traditionally includes map overlay, spatial joins, buffer-zone determination, surface analysis, network and linear analysis, and raster and analysis. (Kennedy, 2001, p. 93)

Chapter XXXV
Use of Remotely Sensed Imagery in Cyber Warfare and Cyber Counterterrorism

Gang Gong
Sam Houston State University, USA

Mark R. Leipnik
Sam Houston State University, USA

ABSTRACT

Remote sensing refers to the acquisition of information at a distance. More specifically, it has come to mean using aerial photographs or sensors on satellites to gather data about features on the surface of the earth. In this article, remote sensing and related concepts are defined and the methods used in gathering and processing remotely sensed imagery are discussed. The evolution of remote sensing, generic applications and major sources of remotely sensed imagery and programs used in processing and analyzing remotely sensed imagery are presented. Then the application of remote sensing in warfare and counterterrorism is discussed in general terms with a number of specific examples of successes and failures in this particular area. Next, the potential for misuse of the increasing amount of high resolution imagery available over the Internet is discussed along with prudent countermeasures to potential abuses of this data. Finally, future trends with respect to this rapidly evolving technology are included.

INTRODUCTION: DEFINITION AND HISTORY

Numerous definitions of remote sensing have been proposed. For example: "Remote sensing is the acquiring of data about an object without touching it" (Fussell et al., 1986), and "Remote sensing is the collection and interpretation of information about an object without being in physical contact with the object" (Weissel, 1990). Other definitions are more focused and precise:

Remote sensing is the non-contact recording of information from the ultraviolet, visible, infrared, and microwave regions of the electromagnetic spectrum by means of instruments such as cameras, scanners, lasers, linear arrays, and/or area arrays locates on platforms such as aircraft or spacecraft, and the analysis of acquired information by means of visual and digital image processing. (Jensen, 2000, p. 4)

Remote sensing is formally defined by the American Society for Photogrammetry and Remote Sensing (ASPRS) as: "The measurement or acquisition of information of some property of an object or phenomenon, by a recording device that is not in physical or intimate contact with the object or phenomenon under study" (Colwell, 1983, p. 23). Then in 1988, ASPRS adopted a combined definition of photogrammetry and remote sensing:

Photogrammetry and remote sensing are the art, science, and technology of obtaining reliable information about physical objects and the environment, through the process of recording, measuring and interpreting imagery and digital representations of energy patterns derived from non-contact sensor systems. (Colwell, 1997, pp. 33-48)

The history of remote sensing has extended back to the early days of photography, but the field received a major impetus during both world wars, when very extensive use was made of aerial photography taken from aircraft for reconnaissance. The science of aerial photography interpretation developed to systematize the detection of features from high-altitude aerial photography. Remote sensing received another boost during the Cold War, as instruments were developed to obtain digital high resolution images from satellites flying above the earth's atmosphere (Goodchild, Pratt, & Watts, 2000). It was then that the term *remote sensing* was coined by the Office of Naval Research, Geography Branch (Pruitt, 1979). Instruments other than cameras (e.g., scanners, radiometers), are now often deployed and imagery has expanded into the regions of the electromagnetic spectrum beyond the visible and near-infrared regions (e.g., thermal infrared, microwave). In the 1990s the field was further fuelled by launch of a series of satellite-borne remote sensing systems by NASA, the Earth Observing System (EOS),

the French SPOT series of satellites and of commercial high resolution earth-orbiting systems like IKONOS and QUICKBIRD (www.earth.nasa.gov).

STRUCTURE OF REMOTE SENSING

Modern remote sensing uses digital instruments attached to satellites or aircraft. Passive remote sensing systems record electromagnetic energy that is reflected from the surface of the earth, while active systems generate their own electromagnetic energy and measure the proportion reflected. Light Detection and Ranging (LIDAR) is one widely used active remote sensing system, it uses lasers to measure distances to reflecting surfaces, usually the ground. The radiation detected in a small area known as the instantaneous field of view (IFOV) is integrated, and recorded. A complete image is assembled as a two-dimensional array of pixels. Scientists have made significant advances in digital image processing of remotely sensed data for scientific visualization and hypothesis testing (Jensen, 2000). The major digital image processing techniques include image enhancement and correction, image classification, pattern recognition, and hyperspectral data analysis.

GENERIC APPLICATIONS OF REMOTE SENSING

There are two broad types of applications; some systems are designed to provide data that can be treated as measurements of some variable which is then analyzed such as the "Ozone Hole" over Antarctica. More often, systems are used primarily for mapping, in which case the image is used to identify and locate various types of features on the earth's surface, such as vegetation, crops, roads, buildings, or geological features (Goodchild, Pratt, & Watts, 2000). Remote sensing systems are widely used today in many areas including intelligence gathering, weather forecasting, crop yield estimation, land use and land cover change detection, hazard monitoring, and occasionally, for law enforcement surveillance (particularly in drug interdiction and eradication efforts). Recently there is increased use of unmanned airborne vehicles for both civilian and military applications.

REMOTE SENSING IMAGE PROCESSING PROGRAMS AND REQUIREMENTS

Remote sensing programs include ERDAS from Leica Geosystems Geospatial Imaging, LLC (http://gis.leica-geosystems.com), ER MAPPER from Earth Resource Mapping (http://www.ermapper.com) in California, ENVI from Research Systems Inc. (http://www.rsinc.com), PCI (http://www.pcigeomatics.com) from Canada, and also much less costly IDRISI from Clark Labs (http://www.clarklabs.org) in Massachusetts. (Kruse, Lefkoff, Boardman, Heidebrecht, Shapiro, & Barloon, et al., 1992; Landgrebe, 1999).

Remote sensing programs usually have substantial system requirements due to high resolution and large-scale data sets (Jensen, 2005). They often require multiple gigabytes disc space (e.g., 2.7 gigabytes for ERDAS) and at least 512 megabytes RAM, and a high power graphics card is a necessity. In addition, the peripherals such as large format plotter, large format scanners, and Geographic Information Systems (GIS) are often required for a complete remote sensing system.

REMOTE SENSING IN WARFARE

It is no exaggeration to state that all of the significant advances in remote sensing both with respect to aerial photography and satellite based imaging have arisen from military and national security programs and considerations. From its earliest years, the advantage of being able to see the full scope of a battlefield or enemy country was recognized. Aerial photography was first taken from balloons in the U.S. Civil War (Haydon, 2000). Even before the advent of the airplane and zeppelin, pigeons were fitted with time-activated

cameras by the German general staff to photograph French border fortifications. The real growth of aerial photography came not with the Wright Brothers, but with the First World War. The interwar years saw further refinement of aerial photography and the German rocket program introduced the capability of taking high altitude photographs (Estes, 1999). Once artificial satellites began to be placed in orbit then spy satellites soon began to be used. These earliest satellites were similar to aerial photography in that they used film which was then parachuted back to earth. Soon however, electronic sensors and radio frequency broadcast of data were developed. Early satellite imagery was often at a low resolution on the order of 100 foot resolution (or approximately 1/10,000th the resolution of current imagery). Programs such as the Corona satellite effort of the U.S. Defense Department (Ruffner, 2005) are an example. At the same time, high level aerial photography platforms capable of obtaining much higher resolution images were in use by the U.S. and its allies. Notable in these efforts were the photographs of Cuban missile sites which triggered the Cuban missile crisis of 1961 and the downing of Francis Gary Powers U2 spy plane on a covert mission over the Soviet Union (Gentry & Powers, 2003).

In many ways, the technology developed for Cold War programs like the ongoing Keyhole spy satellite program, has found new and more or less successful applications in the war on terrorism (Geospatial Solutions, 2003). Specifically, imagery of such things as terrorist training camps in Afghanistan has been acquired and used in targeting. The success of such efforts is debatable, with the main problem being that merely photographing a suspected training camp at a resolution sufficient to identify vehicles or tents may help target cruise missiles or GPS guided JDAM (Joint Direct Attack Munitions) bombs, but the imagery cannot determine intentions nor identify individuals (Boeing, 2006).

The main advance in spy satellites has been even higher resolution and the deployment of various active sensors such as synthetic aperture radar (SAR). But we are still a long way from being able to reliably track an individual terrorist suspect from a platform passing hundreds of miles overhead at speeds of thousands of miles per hour. In fact, countermeasures to satellite observation are numerous and often far cheaper and more effective than the difficult adjustments in procedures needed for the satellites to over come them (Moniz, 2002). For example, countermeasures to observation include conducting activities when tracked satellites are absent, by night, under tree canopy, underground, or in dense urban centers where the shear number and complexity of potential targets of observation overwhelms even the most sophisticated image processing techniques. The Indian government took advantage of many of these techniques as well as using blowing dust to obscure and prevent the detection of nuclear bomb testing preparations from the prying eyes in the sky of the National Reconnaissance Office and other defense and intelligence agencies (Ladeen, 2000). Furthermore, it has frequently proved very difficult in operational situations such as in Afghanistan to tell the difference between, for example, a wedding party and a group of terrorists (Shroder, 2005). Depending on the critical parameter of the resolution of the imagery, it has also proved impossible for analysts at various U.S. intelligence agencies to differentiate scud missile launchers from chicken coops in Saddam Hussein's Iraq. In this case, the coops were made from discarded large diameter pipes that had similar size and reflective properties as scud launchers. This highlights the great limitation of all imagery in that it is essentially missing attribute data. Attribute data is the descriptive information that if developed from other sources such as *ground truthing* tells users what they are looking at not merely where it is located. Addition of this attribute data into a GIS along with the remotely sensed imagery is essential, but is also problematic as indicated by the accidental attack on the Chinese embassy in Belgrade. This building had been inadvertently labeled by the National Imagery and Mapping Agency's data base as a Yugoslavian government logistics center (Gertz, 2000). Frequently, satellites are used to identify potential areas of interest, while manned reconnaissance aircraft are used to

obtain higher resolution imagery of them, but there is a great fear that flying manned aircraft over terrorist or hostile areas will result in capture of pilots. The track record indicates that pilots prefer to parachute and be captured than take their own lives (as it was hoped that Francis Gary Powers would…) (Gentry & Powers, 2003).

Recently a very effective enhancement to the traditional dichotomy between low resolution spy satellite imagery and the higher resolution, but more dangerous, airborne imagery from fixed wing aircraft has developed, this is the drone or unmanned aerial vehicle. Credit must be given to the inventive German general staff of the First World War for the development of the first drone aircraft designed to fly over trench lines and capture air photographs without risk to a shrinking cadre of pilots in the face of ever more effective antiaircraft measures (Nuke, 2002). Similar considerations, along with the advent of far more sophisticated tracking, control, and communications capabilities, have led to the deployment of the Global Hawk and Predator UAV aircraft. These have been used in monitoring and, occasionally, in attacking suspected terrorists in places like Yemen and Pakistan (Moniz, 2002).

POTENTIAL TERRORIST USE OF REMOTELY SENSED IMAGERY

Terrorists groups do not generally have access to spy satellites, but they have almost unlimited access over the Internet to high resolution imagery of many areas. It is noteworthy that while the U.S. and other governments have tried (usually unsuccessfully) to suppress imagery of sensitive military facilities such as the Groom Lake Proving Ground (Area 51) in Nevada or the radar antenna array outside Moscow used for early warning purposes, they have not typically made an effort to remove from sites like Google Earth or Terraserver images of potential terrorist targets. Thus, one can obtain 1 meter and sometimes .25 meter resolution of images of nuclear power plants, refineries, port facilities, skyscrapers or synagogues in the U.S. Outside the U.S. high resolution data exists online for the United Kingdom and Sweden and lower resolution of data from 1 meter to 79 meters exists for features like the Golden Temple of Amritsar, Mosques in Samara, railway systems in Spain or night club zones in Bali that have actually been targets of terrorism. It seems likely that well coordinated terrorist groups have been and are using all available public online resources including sites like Teraserver and Google Earth to plan attacks in the past and to execute future attacks. The issue of just what should be suppressed in the interests of national security seems however to be locked in to a Cold War perspective of limiting access only to imagery of "sensitive facilities" like missile bases, while allowing easy access to high resolution imagery of much more likely targets. But of course, those more likely targets such as, for example, the National Mall in Washington, D.C., are also of general interest and have long had readily available images, first from the National Aerial Photography Program, then in digital format from sources such as the Earth Data Center (http://edcwww.cr.usgs.gov/) and now from Web sites like Terrasever (http://terraserver.microsoft.com/) and Google Earth (http://earth.google.com/).

Another interesting aspect of the movement of large image files over the Internet is that such images can be used to cover transmission of coded messages. This is sometimes referred to as steganography, although the hidden messages can also be encoded further. It has been alleged that by replacing the values for hue, saturation, and chroma in a predetermined row and column of pixels in a raster image, it is possible to transmit coded messages. Any reasonably high resolution image could potentially be used in this manner producing an area of what would appear composed of random or blurred pixels. In a ordinary photography of say 3 megabyte size such manipulation could perhaps be more easily detected than in a relatively smaller portion of a much larger raster format file say for example a 750 megabyte Landsat scene. Also many patterns in remotely sensed imagery appear to be rather random, so the apparent randomization induced by using imagery to transmit coded messages is less evident. This advantage is probably offset by the much more suspicious character of e-mail transmissions with attached geospatial imagery, rather than the apparently less suspicious digital camera pictures of daily events, ordinary persons, run-of-the-mill marketing, and pornographic images that are saturating international cyber space transmissions at present (Wayner, 2006).

FUTURE TRENDS

Several trends with respect to remotely sensed imagery are important. One is the coming disappearance of film-based aerial photography in favor of digital cameras in aircraft. This will make aerial photography and satellite remotely sensed imagery very similar in many ways. Another trend is the development of smaller and smaller remotely controlled imaging platforms, so small remotely controlled helicopters and aircraft and eventually bird sized and even insect sized remote sensing devices may evolve. Thus to be "bugged" might mean to be observed by a small device the size and shape of a house-fly or bumble bee. Today, such a device that could hover over a battlefield is more likely to be the size of a pterodactyl, a condor, or albatross, but smaller devices with longer duration in the air are rapidly evolving (Nuke, 2002). Last but not least, there is a proliferation of imagery at ever higher resolutions over the Internet. Google Earth is just the latest incarnation of this trend, and it may well be superseded by sites that have an interactive Web-based mapping component which serves intelligent imagery coupled with spatial analysis and view and query tools which will allow users not only to search for street addresses but to generate buffer zones and recover attributes of features portrayed in the imagery. Sites designed to show high resolution oblique imagery (pictometry) linked to addresses of businesses and a search engine that can locate firms and services geospatially or home values along with high resolution aerial photography are already up and running in the U.S. and their popularity is immense.

CONCLUSION

From its outset, remotely sensed imagery has been a vital part of warfare, much of the development of this technology both in terms of aircraft-based aerial photography and satellite remotely sensed image acquisition and subsequent processing have been driven by national security imperatives. While much spy satellite and reconnaissance aircraft imagery is highly classified, commercial satellite companies such as Ikonos, Digital Globe, or SPOT and some governmental data such as NASA's EOS program, the SPIN program of the Russian Defense Ministry, and Indian Research Satellite have made available an ever growing mountain of remotely sensed imagery. This imagery is now accessible for view, quarry, download, and/or purchase over the Internet. Most potential and actual users of this imagery have peaceful intent; however as with any technology of great utility, those with destructive intent will also find a powerful tool to support their nefarious plans. Ultimately, limitation of assess to imagery useful in planning and executing terrorist activities is problematic and perhaps impossible, but it is nevertheless important that those involved in safeguarding security and combating terrorism are aware of and on the look out for, such misuse of this tremendous geospatial asset.

REFERENCES

Boeing Company. (2006). *JDAM information.* www.boeing.com/defence-space/missiles/jadam/news/index.html

Colwell, R. N. (Ed.). (1983). *Manual of remote sensing* (2nd ed.). Falls Church, VA: American Society of Photogrammetry.

Colwell, R. N. (1997). History and place of photogrammetric interpretation. In W. R. Philipson (Ed.), *Manual of photographic interpretation* (2nd ed., pp. 3348). Bethesda: American Society for Photogrammery and Remote Sensing.

Estes, J. (1999). *History of remote sensing.* Santa Barbara, CA: National Center for Geographic Information and Analysis.

Fussell, J., Rundquist, D.C., & Harrington, J. A., Jr. (1986). On defining remote sensing. *Photogrammetric Engineering and Remote Sensing, 52*(9), 15071511.

Geospatial Solutions. (2003, February). Satellite imagery: History through the keyhole. *Geospatial Solutions Magazine,* (Feb), 19.

Gentry, C., & Powers, F. G. (2003). *A memoir of the U@ incident.* Potomac Books, Inc.

Gertz, B. (2000). *The China threat* (1st ed.). Regnery Publishing.

Goodchild, M. (2000). Remote sensing. In R. J. Johnston et al. (Eds.), *The dictionary of human geography* (4th ed., pp. 699701). Oxford, UK: Blackwell.

Haydon, F. (2000). *Military ballooning during the Civil War.* Johns Hopkins University Press.

Jensen, J. (2000). *Remote sensing of the environment.* Upper Saddle River, NJ: Prentice-Hall.

Jensen, J. (2005). *Introductory digital image processing.* Prentice Hall.

Kruse, F. A., Lefkoff, A. B., Boardman, J. W., Heidebrecht, K. B., Shapiro, A. T., & Barloon, P. J. et al. (1992). The spectral image processing system (SIPS): Interactive visualization and analysis of imaging spectrometer data. In *Proceedings of the International Space Year Conference,* Pasadena, CA.

Ledeen, M. (2000). Blame the United States for India's Nukes: Indian nuclear testing program and CIA intelligence failure. *Journal of the American Enterprise Institute.* http://www.aei.org/publications/pubID.9068/pub_detail.asp

Landgrebe, D. (1999). *An introduction to MULTISPEC.* West Lafayette, IN: Purdue University.

Moniz, D. (2002). U.S. fine tunes its air war capabilities. *USA Today* 12/06/2002.

Nuke, L. (2002). *A brief history of unmanned aerial vehicles.* American Institute of Aeronautics and Astronautics.

Pruitt, E. L. (1979). The office of naval research and geography. *Annals, Association of American Geographers, 69*(1), 106.

Ruffner, K. (2005). *Corona: Americas first satellite program.* Morgan James Publishing, LLC.

Shroder, J. (2005). Remote sensing and GIS as counterterrorism tools in the Afghanistan war: Reality, plus the results of media hyperbole. *The Professional Geographer, 57*(4).

Wayner, P. (2006). *Disappearing cryptography: Information hiding, steganography and water marking.* Morgan Kaufman.

Weissel, J. (1990). Remote sensing entry. *Remote sensing Glossary.* Retrieved from http://rst.gsfc.nasa.gov/AppD/glossary.html

TERMS AND DEFINITIONS

Aerial Photography: Photography from airborne platforms (3).

Classification: Process of assigning individual pixels of an image to categories, generally on the basis of spectral reflectance characteristics (3).

False Color Image: A color image where parts of the non-visible EM spectrum are expressed as one or more of the red, green, and blue components, so that the colors produced by the earth's surface do not correspond to normal visual experience. Also called a false-color composite (FCC). The most commonly seen false-color images display the very-near infrared as red, red as green, and green as blue (2).

Image Processing: Encompasses all the various operations which can be applied to photographic or image data. These include, but are not limited to image compression, image restoration, image enhancement, preprocessing, quantization, spatial filtering, and other image pattern recognition techniques (2).

Oblique Hotograph: Photograph acquired with the camera intentionally directed at some angle between horizontal and vertical orientations (1).

Platform: The vehicle which carries a sensor. For example; satellite, aircraft, balloon, and so forth (2).

Polar Orbit: An orbit that passes close to the poles, thereby enabling a satellite to pass over most of the surface, except the immediate vicinity of the poles themselves (1).

Remote Sensing: The science, technology, and art of obtaining information about objects or phenomena from a distance (i.e., without being in physical contact with them) (3).

Resolution: Ability to separate closely spaced objects on an image or photograph. Resolution is commonly expressed as the most closely spaced line-pairs per unit distance that can be distinguished. Also called spatial resolution (1). **Satellite:** A vehicle put into orbit around the earth or other body in space and used as a platform for data collection and transmission (2).

Definitions are taken from the following sources (1) National Aeronautics and Space Administration 2006, http://rst.gsfc.nasa.gov/AppD/glossary.html, (2) Natural Resources Canada, 2006, #3) University of California at Santa Barbara, Remote Sensing Lab 2006, http://www.sdc.ucsb.edu/services/rsgloss_v2.htm

Section V
Identification, Authorization, and Access Control

Access control occupies a special role in securing systems. The first stage of a significant number of cyber attacks begins with an attacker obtaining unauthorized access to a system.

Gaining unauthorized access can be accomplished in many ways. In this section, we are providing discussions covering the technical methods of gaining such an access or preventing its occurrence. These include "traditional hacking" (i.e., using system vulnerabilities to defend system protection mechanisms), access methods based on correlations between the owner of the record and it content, search of internet identities using data mining, and the properties and taxonomies of the access control methods. In this section, the following opinions and views are being presented:

Chapter XXXVI
Hacking and Eavesdropping

Kevin Curran
University of Ulster, UK

Peter Breslin
University of Ulster, UK

Kevin McLaughlin
University of Ulster, UK

Gary Tracey
University of Ulster, UK

ABSTRACT

Many self-proclaimed hackers would actually consider themselves to be performing a service to businesses as they claim they are simply showing businesses the flaws within their systems so that they can implement ways to prevent future attacks. They state that if it was not for hacking, then security software would not be where it is today. An ethical hacker will tell you that someone who hacks into a system for purposes of self benefit would be best known as a cracker, rather than a hacker, for it is the latter that gives cause for security software in the first place. This chapter reviews the tools, methods, and rationale of hackers.

INTRODUCTION

"Access" is defined in Section 2(1)(a) of the Information Technology Act[1] as "gaining entry into, instructing or communicating with the logical, arithmetical, or memory function resources of a computer, computer system or computer network." Unauthorized access, therefore, would mean any kind of access without the permission of either the rightful owner or the person in charge of a computer, computer system, or computer network. Thus not only would accessing a server by cracking its password authentication system be unauthorized access, switching on a computer system without the permission of the person in charge of such a computer system would also be unauthorized access. Raymond (1996), compiler of *The New Hacker's Dictionary*, defines a hacker as a clever programmer. According to Raymond, a *good hack* is a clever solution to a programming problem and *hacking* is the act of doing it. Raymond lists five possible characteristics that qualify one as a hacker:

1. A person who enjoys learning details of a programming language or system
2. A person who enjoys actually doing the programming, rather than just theorizing about it
3. A person capable of appreciating someone else's hacking
4. A person who picks up programming quickly
5. A person who is an expert at a particular programming language or system, as in "Unix hacker"

Raymond, like a lot of hackers, condemns someone who attempts to crack someone else's system or otherwise uses programming or expert knowledge to act maliciously. This type of person, according to most hackers would better be described as a *cracker.* A cracker is someone who illegally breaks into someone else's computer or network by bypassing passwords, licences, and so forth. A cracker could be doing this for purposes of maliciously making a profit. On the other hand, a hacker (according to a hacker) would break into a system to supposedly point out the site's security problems. Therefore, we must carefully distinguish between a hacker and a cracker. Although hacking, according to a lot of hackers themselves is beneficial to the development of systems security, it is still known as a crime under the Computer Misuse Act. Categories of misuse under this act, include: computer fraud—unauthorized access to information; computer hacking; eavesdropping; unauthorized use for personal benefit; unauthorized alteration or destruction of data; denying access to authorized user; and unauthorized removal of data (Harris, Harper, Eagle, Ness, & Lester, 2005).

The law does not distinguish between a hacker and a cracker. In relation to this, reformed hacker John Draper states that:

Hackers are very important for the Internet community as a whole because they are the ones who will be buttoning up the holes in the system. Governments should be a little more tolerant of what is going on and hackers should be willing to contact a company and say "I found bugs in your system." (Machlis, 2000)

He believes that without hackers, security would not be where it is today. He believes that hackers are playing a valuable part in the development of highly effective security systems, and that the government and the law should recognize this. They should try to distinguish more carefully between a hacker with intent of displaying security flaws for the company and a cracker whose intent is truly malicious.

Crackers use various methods to maliciously attack a computer system's security, one such method is a "virus." A virus is defined as a piece of programming code usually disguised as something else that causes some unexpected and usually undesirable event. A *computer virus* attaches itself to a program or file, so it can spread from one computer to another, leaving infections as it travels. The severity and effects of a computer virus can range much the same as a human virus. Some viruses have only mild affects simply annoying the host, but more severe viruses can cause serious damage to both hardware and software. Almost all viruses are attached to an executable file, which means the virus may exist on your computer, but it cannot infect your computer unless you run or open the malicious program. It is important to note that a virus cannot be spread without a human action (such as running an infected program) to keep it going. People continue the spread of a computer virus, mostly unknowingly, by sharing infecting files or sending e-mails with viruses as attachments in the e-mail.

Another method is to use a "worm." A worm is similar to a virus in both design and in the damage it can cause. Like a virus, worms spread from system to system, but unlike a virus, it has the ability to travel without any help from the user. It does this by taking advantage of the files and information already present on the computer. The biggest danger with a worm is its ability to replicate itself on your system, so rather than your computer sending out a single worm, it could send out hundreds or thousands of copies of itself, creating a huge devastating effect. For example, it is common for a worm to be sent through e-mail. If you receive a worm via e-mail, it is possible for the worm to use the information in your e-mail address book to send duplicates of itself to your contacts, their contacts, and so forth. Due to the copying nature of a worm and its ability to travel across networks, the end result in most cases is that the worm consumes too much system memory (or network bandwidth), causing Web servers, network servers, and individual computers to stop responding. In more recent worm attacks, such as the much talked about Ms.Blaster Worm, the worm had been designed to tunnel into the system and allow malicious users to control the computer remotely (Imai, 2005).

To combat viruses and worms, there are a lot of measures that can be taken. Measures include antivirus software and firewalls. The firewall is software that will prevent the attacks from entering your system, and if a virus or worm manages to get through, then the anti-virus software (a utility that searches a hard disk for viruses and removes any that are found.) can scan your system to remove the pest. Most antivirus software has an auto update feature that can automatically update the programs virus definitions and so forth for greater security (Vines, 2002).

EAVESDROPPING

Eavesdropping can be thought of as another form of hacking. In a lot of cases, it involves unlawfully accessing a computer system in order to listen (gather) to information. This is an invasion of privacy. Eavesdropping can be used by a hacker to gain information on the victim, such as passwords and bank account details, although not all forms of eavesdropping are used for malicious purposes. Some governments use computer eavesdropping as a way of surveillance. They use it to catch pedophiles and other people who could be holding illegal information on their computers. More and more employers are investing in surveillance software (eavesdropping software) that allows them to monitor or eavesdrop on everything their employees type on their computers, be it e-mail, Web site surfing, or even word processing. Therefore, not all forms of eavesdropping may be illegal. More and more eavesdropping software is being developed.

The FBI is developing eavesdropping software called "Magic Lantern." The Magic Lantern technology, part of a broad FBI project called "Cyber Knight," would allow investigators to secretly install over the Internet powerful eavesdropping software that records every keystroke on a person's computer. Magic Lantern could be installed over the Internet by tricking a person into double-clicking an e-mail attachment or by exploiting some of the same weaknesses in popular commercial software that allow hackers to break into computers. It's uncertain whether or not Magic Lantern software would transmit keystrokes it records back to the FBI over the Internet or if it would store the information that later could be seized in a raid. The reality of Magic Lantern was first disclosed by MSNBC.

This kind of surveillance (eavesdropping) software is very similar to so-called Trojan software, which is already used illegally by some hackers and corporate spies. Trojan software is a very common hacking and eavesdropping tool used by a lot of hackers. Trojan horse software allows the hacker to enter your system and even take control of it. It gives the hacker remote access to your computer. The Trojan horse, at first glance, will appear to be useful software but will actually do damage once installed or run on your computer. Those who are at the receiving end of the Trojan will have to activate it (by opening it) for the hacker to gain access; the users are normally tricked into doing so, because they appear to be receiving legitimate software or files from a legitimate source. Once the Trojan is activated on your computer, the hacker can then gain access. The effects of the Trojan can vary much like a virus; sometimes the effects can be more annoying than malicious (like changing your desktop, adding silly active desktop icons) and sometimes the effects can be severe with Trojans causing serious damage by deleting files and destroying information on your system. The Trojan opens a "back door" on your system, which allows the Trojan user to view personal and confidential files. This kind of information can then be used for purposes, such as blackmail.

Electronic eavesdropping is perhaps the most sinister type of data piracy. Even with modest equipment, an eavesdropper can make a complete transcript of a victim's actions—every keystroke and every piece of information viewed on a screen or sent to a printer. The victim, meanwhile, usually knows nothing of the attacker's presence, and blithely goes about his or her work, revealing not only sensitive information, but the passwords and procedures necessary for obtaining even more. In many cases, you cannot possibly know that you are being monitored. Sometimes you learn of an eavesdropper's presence when the attacker attempts to make use of the information obtained: often, by then, you cannot prevent significant damage. There are different methods to eavesdropping I have listed a few below and described what they are.

Electrical wires are prime candidates for eavesdropping (hence the name wiretapping). An attacker can follow an entire conversation over a pair of wires with a simple splice. Sometimes he does not even have to touch the wires physically; a simple induction loop coiled around a terminal wire is enough to pick up most voice and RS-232 communications. Ethernet and other local area networks are also susceptible to eavesdropping; unused offices should not have live ethernet or twisted-pair ports inside them. You may wish to scan periodically all of the Internet numbers that have been allocated to your subnet to make sure that no unauthorized Internet hosts are operating on your network. You also can run local area network (LAN) monitoring software and have alarms sound each time a packet is detected with a previously unknown ethernet address. Some 10Base-T hubs can be set to monitor the Internet protocol (IP) numbers of incoming packets. If a packet comes in from a computer connected to the hub that does not match what the hub has been told is correct, it can raise an alarm or shut down the link. This capability helps prevent various forms of ethernet spoofing (McClure, Scrambray, & Kurtz, 2003).

Key Loggers

Another method of computer systems eavesdropping is to use what is know as a key logger. A key logger is a program that runs in the background, recording all of the keystrokes. Once keystrokes are logged, they are hidden in the machine for later retrieval or sent automatically back to the attacker. The attacker can use the information gained by the key logger to find passwords and information like bank account details.

It is important to remember that a key logger is not just used as a hacking tool. Many home users and parents use key logger, such as invisible key loggers, to record computer and Internet activities. These key loggers are helpful in collecting information that will be useful when determining if your child is talking to the wrong person online or if your child is surfing inappropriate Web site content; and again it can be used by businesses to monitor employees' work ethics. Normally there may be many files to key loggers and this means that it can be difficult to manually remove them. It is best to use antivirus software or try to use methods such as firewalls to prevent them form getting onto the system in the first place.

On Thursday March 17, 2005, it was revealed that one of the largest bank robberies in Britain was foiled by police in London. The target was the London branch of the Japanese bank Sumitomo Mitsui. The bank robbers planned to steal an estimated £220 million. The stolen money was to be wired electronically from the bank into 10 different off-shore bank accounts. This planned robbery was unlike any traditional bank robbery in Britain's history. It did not involve running into the bank with handguns, taking hostages, and leaving in a getaway car. This bank robbery was much more high tech.[2] The bank robbers uploaded a program onto the bank's network that recorded every keystroke made on a keyboard. This type of program is known as key logging software. The program recorded the Web sites that were visited on the network, the passwords, bank account numbers, and personal identification numbers (PINs) that were entered on these Web sites and saved them to a file. This file was accessed by the robbers, and when they visited the same sites as the people in the bank, they could use their log in information to log on. The site would not have any reason to think that the person logging on was not authorized to do so.

Key logging software can record all sorts of computer operations not just keystrokes. It also can record e-mails received and sent, chats and instant messages, Web sites, programs accessed, peer-to-peer file sharing, and take screen snapshots. Key logging can occur in two ways. A specially coded program can be uploaded onto a network from anywhere in the world. The other is a piece of hardware that is about the size of a battery. This piece of hardware is plugged into the computer from the keyboard and records the keystrokes made. This has to be physically installed onto the machine by a person; and, in order to retrieve the information gathered by the minihard drive, the person also has to physically remove the hardware.[3] The key logging software was uploaded to the network more than six months prior to the planned robbery. It was first noticed that the key logging software was on the network in October 2004. It was then that the National Hi-Tech Crime Unit (NHTCU) kept a close eye on the situation. This was the biggest and most high-profile coup in the unit's short history (Vines, 2002).

Password grabbers however are useful to the owners of systems as well as the crackers as it provides them with the capabilities of monitoring transactions carried out by the users for security auditing purposes. There are several types of password grabbers available, such as Keycopy, which copies all the keystrokes to a file using time stamp; Keytrap, which copies all the keyboard scan codes for later conversion to ASCII; and Phantom, which logs keys and writes them to file every 32 keystrokes (Wright, 2003).

Spyware

The most common form of computer eavesdropping is adware and spyware software. Spyware can be defined as software that covertly gathers user information through the user's Internet connection without his or her knowledge, usually for advertising purposes. Spyware applications are typically bundled as a hidden component of freeware or shareware programs that can be downloaded from the Internet; however, it should be noted that the majority of shareware and freeware applications do not come with spyware. Once installed, the spyware monitors user activity on the Internet and transmits that information in the background to someone else. Spyware can also gather information about e-mail addresses and even passwords and credit card numbers (CMC, 2005).

Spyware software is quite similar to a Trojan horse in that the user will install unknowingly the software. The software also can cause a decrease in bandwidth as it runs in the system's background sending and receiving information from the software's home base. The most common way in which spyware software is installed on a machine is when the user has downloaded certain freeware peer-to-peer file swapping software, such as WarezP2p or Kazaa. Spyware software can be used by companies for advertising purposes as well as being used by hackers to gain incriminating information. Adware is extremely similar to spyware. It affects your computer in much the same way; the main difference is that adware is used more for advertising purposes. Adware can cause a lot of pop ups to appear once you have connected to the Internet; also it can allow icons to be added to your desktop and add Web sites to your Internet favorites. Both adware and spyware can be tricky to remove, as they will attach themselves to various parts of your system's registry. Adware and spyware can be removed by downloading various software tools from the Internet, although the best advice is prevention through a firewall.

The law looks down upon unauthorized computer access and computer eavesdropping, but in actual fact in a lot of cases, eavesdropping is not used for incriminating purposes. It can simply just be a set of parents logging on to their child's computer in order to view the Web history and the content of the sites in which the child has visited. It could also be that an employer is using certain eavesdropping software to simply check that an employee is working and is doing his or her job. Although again there are also those who would use eavesdropping and unauthorized access for the purposes of self benefit.

Packet Sniffing

Packet sniffing is a technology used by crackers and forensics experts alike. Data travels in the form of packets on networks. These packets, also referred to as data-grams, are of various sizes, depending on the network bandwidth as well as amount in bytes of data being carried in the packet. Each packet has an identification label also called a header. The header carries information of the source, destination, protocol, size of packet, total number of packets in a sequence, and the unique number of the packet. The data carried by the packet is in an encrypted format, not as much for the sake of security as for the sake of convenience in transmitting the data. This cipher text (encrypted form) is also known as the hex of the data. When a person, say A, sends a file to B, the data in the file gets converted into hex and gets broken into lots of packets. Finally headers are attached to all packets and the data is ready for transmission.

When being transmitted, the packets travel through a number of layers (open systems interconnection (OSI) model). Amongst theses layers, the network layer is responsible for preparing the packet for transmission. This is the level where most hackers and adversaries like to attack, knowing that the packets are usually not secured and are prone to spoofing and sniffing attacks. Now, when an adversary (a person trying to hack into a system) to the whole process—C wishes to intercept the transmission between A and B, he or she would have intercept the data packets and then translate them back from hex to the actual data. For doing this, he would normally use a technology called "packet sniffing." When he uses this technology, he is able to intercept all or some of the packets leaving the victim (sender) computer. The same deception also can be practiced at the point of the intended recipient of the message, before it can actually receive the packets. To use the sniffing technology, the adversary only needs to know the IP address (e.g., 202.13.174.171) of either of the parties involved in the communication. He would then instruct the sniffer to apply itself to the network layer of the victim's IP address. From then on, all packets leaving the IP address will be "sniffed" by the sniffer and the data that is being carried will be reported to the adversary in the form of logs. The sniffed data would still be in the hex format; however, nowadays, most sniffers can convert the stolen hex into actual human readable data, with varying success.

Tempest Attack

Tempest is the ability to monitor electromagnetic emissions from computers in order to reconstruct the data. This allows remote monitoring of network cables or remotely viewing monitors. The word tempest is usually understood to stand for transient electromagnetic pulse emanation standard. There are some fonts that remove the high-frequency information, and thus severely reduce the ability to remotely view text on the screen. PGP also provides the option of using tempest-resistant fonts. An appropriately equipped car can park near the target premises and remotely pick up all the keystrokes and messages displayed on the computer's video screen. This would compromise all the passwords, messages, and so on. This attack can be thwarted by properly shielding computer equipment and network cabling so that they do not emit these signals.

HACKING

More experienced, professional hackers will choose targets that have significant rewards and appeal to them. They will be willing to work persistently for a long period of time to achieve their goal, and it is almost certain that the hacker will gain access to the system at some stage. If a cracker is embarking on a long-term attack within a system, he or she will avoid any unusual patterns appearing on the logs. This is achieved by spreading the attacks throughout different remote sites and time patterns, to ensure that any system administrator will be unable to detect an intrusion (Dr-K, 2000).

System back doors are used to gain access. Here an attacker will significantly increase the chance of gaining access by learning the IP network protocols, and odd switches on user and system commands. In addition, knowledge of underlying design features is essential. Access is achieved by researching the best way to secure a site. This is done by reading through different security manuals to establish the recommendations they offer, and why these are necessary. When hackers gain access to a system, they gain administrative privileges which make the attack worthwhile. This also gives them the freedom that a basic user will not experience. For example, when it comes to privileges, the system administrator is at the top of the hierarchy, so access to such capabilities give the attacker major advantages, such as access to all types of files. The basic user with set basic privileges, on the other hand, can only access the files associated with the work that the particular employee carries out. The attacker is also capable of editing the computer logs of the system in order to cover up his or her tracks. These capabilities could be used to set up bogus user accounts, allowing the attacker to gain easy access to the system upon re-entry (Raymond, 1996).

An important aspect of hacking into a system is the ability to cover up any trace of the intrusion. This is possible via a variety of methods; the most important of course being that the cracker approaches the attack cautiously. However there are "rootkits" to aid the cracker in doing this. This is the hacker's toolkit and is essential for covering tracks. Within this toolkit is a piece of software that when compiled in the targets systems will perform many of the routine tasks needed to hide a hacker's actions. However, it is important that the attacker understands the software, making sure to run it in the right locations on the system, that is, the log files (Dr-K, 2000). Other tools available include password grabbers and key loggers, which are tools that assist crackers' activities by intercepting and storing keystrokes of a legitimate system user into a file from which the attacker acquires valid log in details to gain entry.

Web Server Hacking

Web server hacking is when a hacker detects and takes full advantage of the vulnerabilities of Web server software or add-on components. An example of this occurred when worms Nimba and Code Red exploited the vulnerabilities of Microsoft's ISS Web server software. Source code disclosure allows the cracker to view the source code of application files on a vulnerable Web server and together with other techniques gives the attacker the capabilities of accessing protected files containing information such as passwords (McClure et al., 2003).

Computer and network resources can often be addressed by two representations. Canonicalization resolves resource names into a standard form. Applications that make their security decisions based on the resource name can be extremely vulnerable to executing unexpected actions known as canonicalization attacks. Web distributed authoring and versioning is an extension of the http protocol that enables distributed Web authoring through a set of http headers and methods, which allows such capabilities as creating, copying, deleting, and searching for resources as well as set and search for resource properties. This ability would cause a major threat to a company if it was available to an attacker. Web field overflow is where an attacker through the use of a Web browser can bring down a Web server. This vulnerability exists because the web developer often prefers to concentrate on functionality rather than security. A solution would be for developers to employ an input sanitization routine in every program. The developer could move the administration page to a separate directory. There are Web server vulnerability scanners available to scan through a system to find vulnerabilities and detect a wide range of well-known vulnerabilities (McClure et al., 2003).

Password Cracking

To crack a password means to decrypt a password or to bypass a protection scheme. When the UNIX operating system was first developed, passwords were stored in the file "/etc/passwd." This file was readable by everyone, but the passwords were encrypted so that a user could not figure out what a another person's password was. The passwords were encrypted in such a manner that a person could test a password to see if it was valid, but could not decrypt the entry. However, a program called "crack" was developed that would simply test all the words in the dictionary against the passwords in "/etc/passwd". This would find all user accounts whose passwords where chosen from the dictionary. Typical dictionaries also included people's names, since a common practice is to choose a spouse or child's name. Password crackers are utilities that try to "guess" passwords. One way, also known as a dictionary attack, involves trying out all the words contained in a predefined dictionary of words. Ready-made dictionaries of millions of commonly used passwords can be freely downloaded from the Internet. Another form of password cracking attack is the "brute force" attack. In this form of attack, all possible combinations of letters, numbers, and symbols are tried out one by one until the password is found. Brute force attacks take much longer than dictionary attacks (Nakhjiri, 2005).

Viruses

A virus provides hackers with the ability to cause damage to a computer system by being destructive. It is initially a program that copies itself within the operating system of a computer. Hackers who develop viruses to plant in their targets' systems must write the viruses in assembly code, specifying them around their potential target's operating system, forming protection for themselves, while the virus spreads through the system. Protection from viruses comes in the form of antivirus software that will detect and remove any suspected viruses. It does this by looking out for "viral signatures" embedded in programs and also "viral behavior," which can detect any potential attacks before they occur. This software has the sophistication of being aware of the behavior adopted by the virus that proves invaluable. The types of destruction caused from these viruses range from nondestructive behavior,

like pop ups and banners, which basically only cause a general nuisance, to random destruction that carries out such actions as altering the users keystrokes, to heavy destruction, which affects files through such activities as removing data (Dr-K, 2000).

Wireless Hacking

Wireless networks broadcast signals throughout an area, which allows hackers to easily connect to their network by simply being physically within range. Hackers can access the network by war-driving, provided that they are within range and have the use of hardware, such as a large antenna, a small laptop, a wireless card, and other palm-sized computing devices, such as iPAQ. This can be done by simply walking through the hall of an office block or driving through a business center (McClure et al., 2003). A hacker will initially locate the wireless device, using either the passive method of listening for access points and broadcast beacons, or the aggressive method of transmitting client beacons in search of a response. Through the use of GPS systems, the wireless hacker then has the ability to pinpoint the precise location of the network. Wire-based network hacking requires the hacker to have an in-depth knowledge, so that they can apply the most appropriate tools, know what to look for, and how to cover their tracks (Briere, 2005). In contrast to other systems, however, wireless networks are easily located and poorly protected.[4]

One method of security that is applied widely is the wireless encryption protocol (WEP) (AirDefense, 2003). By using a key, it encrypts the data shared by all users of the network; however, with the correct software, WEP can be easily bypassed.[5] Another method involves MAC address filtering, which allows only specific wireless network adaptors to connect to the network. This is facilitated by using a unique identifier; however, this method is both time consuming and requires greater networking knowledge (Hardjono & Lakshminath, 2005). To overcome this type of obstacle, hackers have been known to monitor the traffic of packets within the network to capture an approved MAC address. This is then imitated to gain access.[6] Wireless routers commonly come with firewalls to control access to the computer from the outside. However, anyone with the ability to access the wireless portion of the network will be able to bypass the firewall (Wright, 2003).

FUTURE TRENDS

Currently, an enormous number of new vulnerabilities are discovered every week. Vulnerabilities are widely publicized; despite the long duration it takes for many software vendors to release fixes. It usually takes even longer for companies to deploy effective countermeasures and patches. Additionally, crackers have teamed up around the globe to share information and coordinate attacks. It is the golden age of hacking (Cole, 2003). We can expect to see an increase in Web-based malware-type exploits, such as the Santy. a worm, which targeted vulnerabilities in some versions of the phpBB bulletin board system application to damage content on Web sites. This was done by simply creating an automated search in a Google query string. Google was able to stop the worm quickly by blocking any searches used for malicious purposes, once the company figured out what was going on. The most common Google hacks involve queries that call up user names and passwords on unsecured servers. Log files for these particular users were put in jeopardy by not placing security measures and access privileges on important documentation. Google is not to blame for this information; it is just the tool provider, but we can expect to see more copycat versions to follow (Gilmer, 2006).

We also can expect to see more use of advanced hiding techniques in steganography tools. The word steganography means "covered or hidden writing." The object of steganography is to send a message through some innocuous carrier (to a receiver while preventing anyone else from knowing that a message is being sent at all). Computer-based stenography allows changes to be made to what are known as digital carriers, such as images or sounds. The changes represent the hidden message but result, if successful, in no discernible change to the carrier (Bailey, Curran, & Condell, 2004). Unfortunately, it can be used by terrorists to communicate with one another without anyone else's knowledge. Other trends include mobile malware being successfully monetized; the anonymous and illegal hosting of (copyrighted) data; the rise in encryption and packers; and hijacking botnets and infected PCs (Danchev, 2006).

CONCLUSION

Computer eavesdropping and hacking can both be considered forms of the general term unauthorized computer access. Unauthorized access can be described as an action in which a person accesses a computer system without the consent of the owner. This may include using sophisticated hacking/cracking software tools to gain illegal access to a system, or it could simply be a case of a person guessing a password and gaining access. There are a lot of methods that can be taken in an attempt to prevent unauthorized computer access, such as regularly changing your password, ensuring antivirus software is up to date, and ensuring that an up-to-date firewall exists on each system.

REFERENCES

AirDefense. (2003). *Wireless LAN security: What hackers know that you don't.* Retrieved from http://ssl.salesforce.com/servlet.Email/AttachmentDownload?q=00m0000000003Pr00D00000000hiyd00500000005k8d5

Bailey, K., Curran, K., & Condell, J. (2004). An evaluation of pixel based steganography and stego-detection methods. *The Imaging Science Journal, 52*(3), 131-150.

Briere, D. (2005). *Wireless network hacks and mods for dummies* [For Dummies S.]. Hungry Minds Inc.

CMC (2005) *Watch Your Identity: Tips for reducing the risk of identity theft.* Retrieved May 17, 2007 from http://www.cmcweb.ca/epic/site/cmc-cmc.nsf/en/fe00040e.html

Cole, E. (2003). *Hacking: What the future holds. Computer and hacker exploits.* SANS Publishers.

Danchev, D. (2006, January 9). Malware: Future trends. *Mindstreams of information security knowledge blog.* Retrieved May 17, 2007 from http://ddanchev.blogspot.com/2006_02_01_archive.html

Dr-K. (2000). *Complete hacker's handbook.* London: Carlton Book Limited.

Gilmer, C. (2006, February 15). Worms prey on Google for victims. *The unofficial Google weblog.* retrieved on May 17, 2007 from http://google.weblogsinc.com/2006/02/15/worms-prey-on-google-for-victims/

Hardjono, T., & Lakshminath R. D. (2005). *Security in wireless LANs and MANs.* Artech House Books.

Harris, S., Harper, A., Eagle, C., Ness, J., & Lester, M. (2005). *Gray hat hacking: The ethical hacker's handbook.* McGraw-Hill Publishing Co.

Imai, H. (Ed.). (2005). *Wireless communications security.* Artech House Books.

Machlis, A. (2000, April 21). *Protecting the net.* Retrieved May 17, 2007 from http://www.jewishjournal.com/old/hackers.4.21.0.htm

McClure, S., Scrambray, J., & Kurtz, G. (2003). *Hacking exposed: Network security secrets & solutions* (4th ed.). McGraw-Hill/Osborne.

Nakhjiri, M. (2005). *AAA and network security for mobile access: Radius, diameter, EAP, PKI and IP mobility.* John Wiley & Sons.

Raymond, E. (1996). *The new Hacker's dictionary* (3rd ed.). The MIT Press.

Vines, R. D. (2002). *Wireless security essentials, defending mobile systems from data piracy.* IN: Wiley Publishing.

Wright, J. (2003). *Detecting wireless LAN MAC address spoofing.* Retrieved from http://home.jwu.edu/jwright/papers/wlan-mac-spoof.pdf

TERMS AND DEFINITIONS

Back Door: In the security of a system, this is a hole deliberately left in place by designers or maintainers. It may be intended for use by service technicians. However, now it is more commonly used to refer to software that has been maliciously loaded by persons remotely in order to allow them to enter the system through a "back door" at an opportune time.

Brute Force: A hacking method used to find passwords or encryption keys by trying every possible combination of characters until the code is broken. Common names and words are tried first and then a sequential run through combinations of letters and numbers.

Cracker: This was coined by hackers in defense against journalistic misuse of the term "hacker." The term "cracker" reflects a strong revulsion at the theft and vandalism perpetrated by cracking rings.

Firewall: This is a program or piece of hardware that filters out unwanted incoming packets from the Internet. They can be configured to allow only certain traffic, thereby making it harder for hackers to gain access to a computer or network.

Hacking: Hacking is commonly used today to refer to unauthorized access to a computer network. Breaking into a computer system or network is simply one of many forms of hacking.

Honeypot: A honeypot is a system whose value comes from being probed, attacked, or compromised, usually for the purpose of detection or alerting of black-hat activity. Typically, honeypots have been systems that emulate other systems or known vulnerabilities or create jailed environments. A honeynet is different from most honeypots as it is a tool for research.

Rootkit: The primary purposes of a rootkit are to allow an attacker to maintain undetected access to a compromised system. The main technique used is to replace standard versions of system software with hacked version and install back-door process by replacing one or more of the files, such as ls, ps, netstat, and who.

Trojan: A Trojan (a.k.a. Trojan horse) is a software program in which harmful or malicious code is contained within another program. When this program executes, the Trojan performs a specific set of actions, usually working toward the goal of allowing itself to persist on the target system.

ENDNOTES

[1]   http://www.stpi.soft.net/itbill2000_1.html

[2]   http://news.bbc.co.uk/2/hi/technology/4357307.stm

[3]   http://searchsecurity.techtarget.com/sDefinition/0,,sid14_gci962518,00.html

[4]   http://news.bbc.co.uk/1/hi/sci/tech/1639661.stm

[5]   http://www.pcstats.com/articleview.cfm?articleID=1489

[6]   http://www.pcstats.com/articleview.cfm?articleid=1489&page=2

Chapter XXXVII
Access Control Models

Romuald Thion
University of Lyon, France

ABSTRACT

Access control, or authorization, is arguably the most fundamental and most pervasive security mechanism in use today in computer systems. In computer systems, to grant authorization is to determine whether a subject can access resources. Informally speaking it is to decide "who can do what." Access control is critical to enforce confidentiality (only authorized users can read information) and integrity (only authorized users can alter information) in computer systems, preventing hackers and cyber-terrorists from reading and modifying sensitive files. Several access control models have been proposed since 1960 up today: from simple access matrix to task based access control through military models. Each one providing a different way to organize and express users' privileges. For example, the role based access control model aggregate privileges thanks to the concept of role: all users receive permissions only through the roles to which they are assigned. We first introduce the purpose of access control, then we describe models in use today, their specificities and the mechanisms which they rely on. The end of the this chapter is dedicated to current issues on access control.

INTRODUCTION

Information knowledge has been acknowledged for a long time in warfare. For example, Tzu's section III. Attack by Stratagem (1910) describes the importance of knowledge:

If you know the enemy and know yourself, you need not fear the result of a hundred battles. If you know yourself but not the enemy, for every victory gained you will also suffer a defeat. If you know neither the enemy nor yourself, you will succumb in every battle. (Verse 18)

This quotation points out that information knowledge is among the most important factors in winning a war, this quotation is a 2,500 year old introduction to information warfare. Information warfare means a

strategy for acquiring an enemy's information, while defending one's own. It is a kind of warfare where information and attacks on information and its system are used as a tool of warfare.

Common mechanisms enhancing security and protecting one's own information are cryptography, *authentification,* or *authorization.* This topic focuses on a particular aspect of security mechanisms: authorization, also known as access control. This concept, in its broadest sense, came about prior to computer science; chests, locks, fences, and guards have always been used to protect valuable information from foes.

Access control has been used since the very beginning of distributed systems in which multiple users can share common resources. With the increased dependence of defense on computer systems, the U.S. Department of Defense (DoD) investigated the vulnerability of government systems in the late 1960s, leading to the first definitions of access control principles. Researchers also considered the problem. For example, Lampson's (1974) access control matrix is the first formal mathematical description of what access control is. The DoD investigation led to a definition of multilevel access control, relating to classified documents, such as unclassified, confidential, secret, and top-secret, identifying clearly the separation between authorization and authentification. From then on, access control has been abundantly studied, extended, and commercialized to fill the security gap of computer systems, and is a major tool for preventing cyber terrorists from accessing sensitive data.

THE PURPOSE OF ACCESS CONTROL

In computer systems, access control denotes whether a *subject* (e.g., process, computer, human user, etc.) is able to perform an *operation* (e.g., read, write, execute, delete, search, etc.) on an *object* (e.g., a tuple in a database, a table, a file, a service, and, more generally, any resource of the system) according to a *policy.* These concepts are commonly encountered in most access control and computer security literature. The right to carry out an operation on an object is called permission. *Access control policies* define the subjects' permissions in a computer system, in order to enforce the security of an organization. One of the fundamental best practices in security is developing, deploying, reviewing, and enforcing security policies.. These policies are organized according to an access control model. The model may add intermediate concepts between subjects and permission to organize policies. Intermediate concepts are chosen among tasks, groups, roles, or confidentiality labels, for example. They aim at making policies, management, and definition easier, fitting in as best as possible with the internal structure and needs of the protected system (Ferraiolo, Kuhn, & Chandramouli, 2003).

Informally speaking access control means to decide "who can do what." Access control is arguably the most fundamental and most pervasive security mechanism in use in computer systems.

Information security risks are commonly categorized into:

- **Confidentiality:** Information must be kept private; only authorized users can read the information.
- **Integrity:** Information must be protected from being altered; only authorized users can write the information.
- **Availability:** Information must be available for use.

The purpose of access control is to preserve the confidentiality and integrity of information and, to a lesser extent, availability. Access control aims at providing only useful permissions to subjects, thus avoiding improper writing (mainly related to integrity) and reading (mainly related to confidentiality) operations. Access control is not as obviously related to availability, but it has an important role. A cyber terrorist who is granted unauthorized access is likely to bring the system down (Ferraiolo et al., 2003). Moreover, access control provides protection against internal attacks and information disclosure. With an authorization mechanism, a sleeping agent, who is member of an organization, a renegade, or a cyber spy, is not able to access the most valuable information. Information leakage is a major threat for private industry, whose intellectual property, business processes, and methodology are targeted by cyber terrorists.

ACCESS CONTROL MODELS

An access control model defines relationships among *permissions*, *operations*, *objects,* and *subjects.* We distinguish here the difference between *users,* the people who use the computer system, and *subjects,* computer processes acting on behalf of users. Several intermediate concepts have been introduced over the past decades to organize these relationships. This section surveys three widespread access control models: mandatory, discretionary, and role-based.

Lampson's Matrix and Discretionary Access Control

Access control terminology was established in the late 1960s by Lampson (1974), when he introduced the formal notions of subjects, objects, and access control *matrix.* An access control matrix is a simple representation in which each entry [i,j] of the matrix specifies the operations granted to subject *i* on resource *j.* An example from the medical field is shown in Table 1. For example, user *Charly* (more precisely processes

invoked by user Charly) is allowed to write and read/access both *administrative* and *medical records* objects and read/access to *prescriptions*.

Such a matrix can be read either:

- **By rows:** Thus the matrix is interpreted as *capabilities list,* defining what is allowed for each user, for example, "David: **read** access on *medical* and *administrative* records";
- **By columns:** Thus the matrix is interpreted as a*ccess control list* (ACLs), defining which permissions are granted to each object, for example, "prescriptions: **read** access by *Alice* and *Charly.*"

Nowadays, an access control matrix tends is rarely used with the increasing number of resources and users; this model is not adequate for large organizations. The main goal of new models (e.g., role-based access control) is to overcome these limitations by proposing organizational grouping of subjects or resources.

Discretionary access control (DAC) (Department of Defense (DoD) National Computer Security Center, 1985) is one of the most widespread access control models. It can be seen as an access control matrix including an *ownership* relation, allowing subjects to settle policies for their own objects. This principle is implemented in the Unix/Linux operating systems to control access to files (e.g., a chown command that changes the owner of a file). This mechanism permits granting and revocations of permissions to the discretion of users, bypassing system administrator control.

Table 1. A sample access control matrix

	Medical record	Administrative record	Prescriptions
Alice	**W,R**	**R**	**R**
Bob		**R**	
Charly	**W,R**	**W,R**	**R**
David	**R**	**R**	

Even though DAC mechanisms are in widespread commercial use, they suffer from several difficulties among which are the following:

- Users can settle insecure rights, for example, the classical "chmod 777," which allows any permission to anybody in Unix/Linux system
- Transitive read access, for example, if Bob is allowed to read Charly's file, he can copy its content into a new file (of which Bob is the owner) and allow other users to read its content

Thus, safety has been shown to be undecidable (Harrison, Ruzzo, & Ullman, 1976) in access control matrix. It is impossible to prove whether an initial set of access rights that is considered safe would remain safe. The system may grant "unsafe" rights because the system has no control over permissions passed from one user to another. Thus, the use of this access control should be limited to noncritical structures. This model provides security, but as the risks of serious damages or leakage are really high once the system is compromised, it should not be used by potential targets of cyber terrorism (e.g., governmental organizations, large companies, and chemical, biological, or war industries).

Bell-LaPadula, Lattice-Based and Mandatory Access Control

In many organizations, end users do not "own" the information to which they are granted access. Information is the property of organizations, and no user should be able to settle its own permission. To overcome the difficulties of DAC in confidentiality critical environments, mandatory access control (MAC) has been developed (Bell & LaPadula, 1973). MAC was designed to deal with classified documents in computer systems (e.g., military ones). The basic principle of MAC is to control access according to the user's clearance and the object's classification. These classifications are divided into security levels (one can refer to MAC as a multilevel access control); the higher the level is, the more confidential the information is. For example, the common government classifications are *unclassified, confidential, secret,* and *top-secret.*

The principles shown in Table 2 have been formalized by Bell-LaPadula into a mathematical model suitable for defining and evaluating security in computer systems, making it possible to analyze their properties. We note that security levels are related to an organization's information flow; they represent the hierarchical structure of the organization. Users are able to write to a higher classification in order to transmit documents within their hierarchy.

Table 2. MAC control principles

- Only administrators, not data owners, make changes to an object's security label.
- All data is assigned a security level that reflects its relative sensitivity, confidentiality, and protection value.
- All users can read from classifications lower than the one they are granted.
- All users can write to a higher classification.
- All users are given read/write access to objects only of the same classification.
- Access is authorized or restricted to objects, depending on the labeling on the resource and the user's credentials.

Figure 1. A product of lattices

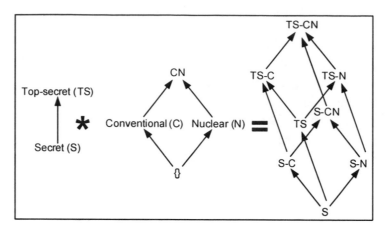

Fully ordered levels are quite restrictive. The basic MAC principles of Table 2 can be applied to partially ordered levels by combining several classifications; these are called lattice-based access control models (a product of a lattice is a lattice). Figure 1 illustrates these combinations.

This access control model is arguably the most effective in maintaining confidentiality. However, it suffers from a rigidity that commercial companies cannot accept. Thus, this model should be used either by highly hierarchical organizations (e.g., banks or armies) or for critical parts of information systems of organizations in which several access control models cohabit. This model and the simple, but effective, classification of data it imposes has to be taken into account in any security planning, particularly for organizations threatened by cyber terrorism. Historically, this model originated from investigations on information warfare.

Role-Based Access Control

Role-based access control (RBAC) models constitute a family in which permissions are associated with roles (the intermediate concept of *roles* can be seen as collections of permissions), and users are made members of appropriate roles. Permissions are not directly assigned to users (Figure 2). The definition of role is quoted from Sandhu, Coyne, Feinstein, and Youman (1996): "A role is a job function or job title within the organization with some associated semantics regarding the authority and responsibility conferred on a member of the role" (p. 5)

RBAC was developed to overcome administration difficulties encountered in large commercial organizations for which DAC was impracticable and MAC much was too restrictive. As the major part of access control decisions is based on the subjects' function or job, introducing roles greatly simplifies the management of the system. Since roles in an organization are relatively consistent with respect to user turnover and task reassignment, RBAC provides a powerful mechanism for reducing the complexity, cost, and potential for error in assigning permissions to users within the organization (Ferraiolo et al., 2003). RBAC was found to be among the most attractive solutions for providing access control in electronic commerce (e-commerce), electronic government (e-government), or electronic health (e-health) and is also a very active research field.

An important feature of the RBAC model is that roles are hierarchical; roles inherit permissions from their parents. Thus, roles are not flat collections of groups of permissions. Hierarchy aims at increasing

Figure 2. RBAC model (without constraints)

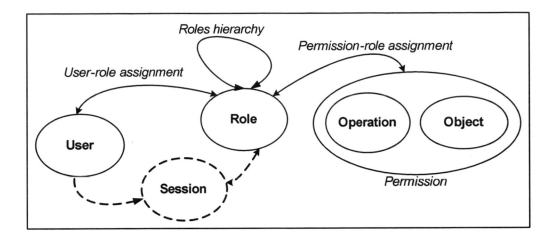

Figure 3. A sample role hierarchy

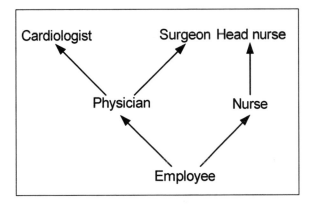

system administrator productivity by simplifying distribution, review, and revocation of permissions. A sample role hierarchy is shown in Figure 3. In this example, Physician and Nurse inherit Employee, thus every permission assigned to the role Employee is also assigned to both Physician and Nurse roles. By transitivity, Cardiologist and Surgeon roles inherit all the permissions granted to both Physician and Employee.

RBAC constitute a family of four conceptual models, readers may encounter these specific acronyms:

- $RBAC_0$ contains the core concepts of the model;

- $RBAC_1$ adds role hierarchy to $RBAC_0$;
- $RBAC_2$ adds static (not related to sessions) and dynamic (related to sessions) constraints between core concepts; and
- $RBAC_3$ includes all aspects of $RBAC_1$ and $RBAC_2$.

Nowadays, an international consensus has been established (National Institute of Standards and Technology (NIST), 2004) It describes the requirements and functionalities of RBAC implementations. RBAC's evolution from concept to commercial implementation (IBM Corporation, 2002) and deployment was quite rapid. For example, the U.S. Health Insurance

Portability and Accountability Act of 1996 explicitly defines RBAC requirements. The introduction of RBAC in a large organization like Siemens, for example, was developed in Roeckle, Schimpf, and Weidinger (2000).

Clearly, this access control model is attractive for large organizations, where many different users' profiles are involved. It is arguably the most cost effective model. From a cyber terrorism perspective, it is interesting to point out that this model is considered as "neutral policy." It can coexist with other policies. Thus, it can be thought of as the main access control model (for day-to-day operations) of an organization. A more restrictive one, a mandatory model, for example, should be reserved for sensitive services or information. Such architecture will protect against insiders (e.g., angry users), but also against external attackers (e.g., cyber spies, cyber terrorists) targeting valuable, sensitive, or critical information.

Other Access Control Models

DAC, MAC, and RBAC are among the most widely used access control models, but several others exist. This subsection surveys Biba's integrity model, the Chinese-Wall policy and Clark-Wilson model.

Biba's (1977) integrity model was introduced as an alternative to the Bell-LaPadula (1973) model to enforce integrity in military-oriented policies, focusing mainly on confidentiality. In Biba's model, security levels are integrity-oriented, for example, the levels are *critical*, *important*, and *ordinary*. The properties of the Biba model are similar to Bell-LaPadula's, except that read and write permissions are reversed. A subject is permitted read (respectively write) access to an object, if the object's (resp. subject's) security level dominates subject's (resp. object's) level.

Clark and Wilson (1987) have compared commercial security policies and military-oriented policies, pointing out their differences. They proposed two general security principles: *separation of duties* (SoD) and *well-formed transaction* to ensure information integrity. The Clark-Wilson model is commercially oriented; it ensures that information is modified only in authorized ways, by trusted people. Whereas military models can be defined in terms of low-level operations, such as read and write, Clark-Wilson's is application-level oriented. It defines a higher abstract notion of transaction.

Chinese-wall policies (Brewer & Nash, 1989) are for business transaction what Bell-LaPadula's policies are to the military. Brewer and Nash identified the notion of *conflict of interest* (COI). The objective of Chinese-wall policies is to avoid such conflicts. The basis of the policies is that subjects are only allowed access to information that does not conflict with any that they already possess (i.e., held on the computer and that has been previously accessed). Informally speaking, "users cannot go through the wall between conflicting classes of interest."

CURRENT ISSUES

Research into access control models aims at providing more expressive models that are able to take into account emerging trends on geographical, temporal, context-aware, and pervasive computer systems. Nowadays, nomadic computing devices and wireless communications force inclusion of geographical and context awareness in access control models. RBAC models have received particular attention, mainly because RBAC is now a de facto standard. For example, the geographical-RBAC model (Bertino, Catania, Damiani, & Perlasca, 2005) is a spatially aware access control model for location-based services and mobile applications. This research tends to be a major concern for the security of wireless information systems. These new proposals may protect against roaming attackers who are looking for wireless access points to target. A practice called war-driving. With the development of ubiquitous mobile computing, its introduction into cyber terrorism, and targeted fields, such as health (e.g., emergency units equipped with PDA and wireless communication devices) or oil companies (e.g., sensor infrastructures with query capabilities that are used by workers' laptops), dealing with geographical and temporal aspects is one of the major trends in access control.

Researchers also have focused on policy administration (Sandhu, Bhamidipati & Munawer, 1999; Ferraiolo, Chandramouli, Ahn & Gavrila, 2003) and common security description in XML (Organization for the Advancement of Structured Information Standards (OASIS), 2005). In fact, policies can be huge in international structures, and can involve thousands of users and hundreds of security administrators. For example, constraints have been introduced to reflect specificities of organizations, such as mutually exclusive roles or prerequisites. Unfortunately, these constraints may obfuscate the meaning of policies and can lead to inconsistencies; this is especially true in distributed systems where policies from different suborganizations must cohabit. Recent research tries to fill this gap, proposing methods for distributed policies and tools facilitating design and maintenance of access control policies. This aspect of the research is of great importance because most security flaws are due to misconfigurations or administrative mistakes. An organization protecting itself against cyber terrorism must define a security policy and enforce it via access control mechanisms. However, it has to verify the implementation of the policies and be sure that no flaws have been introduced, from either inattention or malevolence.

CONCLUSION

Access control is a fundamental aspect of security and is paramount to protecting private and confidential information from cyber attackers. Understanding the basics of access control is fundamental to understanding how to manage information security. Several models have been developed over the decades to enhance confidentiality, integrity, availability, or administration flexibility. Being sometimes clearly military or commercially oriented, they share common criteria:

- Being built on formal mathematical models (matrix; lattice, entity-relation, etc.)

- Guaranteeing a set of properties (confidentiality of information, integrity of transactions, absence of conflicts of interest, etc.)

However, access control itself is not a panacea; it is a cornerstone of security, but is useless without rigorous security management or if built over insecure authentification mechanisms. It may be a lot easier for cyber criminals to endorse someone else's identity, than to gain unauthorized access inside a computer system that uses access control mechanisms.

The rising threat of cyber terrorism has been taken into account by researchers in access control. The authors Belokosztolszki and Eyers (2003) have highlighted several threats related to cyber terrorism against distributed access control policies. Such aspects of access control have to be investigated more deeply in order for us to protect ourselves against cyber terrorists.

REFERENCES

Bell, D. E., & LaPadula, L. J. (1973). *Secure computer systems: Mathematical foundations and model.* The Mitre Corporation.

Belokosztolszki, A., & Eyers, D. (2003). Shielding the OASIS RBAC infrastructure from cyber-terrorism. In *Research Directions in Data and Applications Security: Proceedings of the Sixteenth Annual IFIP WG 11.3 Conference on Data and Application Security,* (pp. 3-14).

Bertino, E., Catania, B., Damiani, M. L., & Perlasca, P. (2005). GEO-RBAC: A spatially aware RBAC. *10th Symposium on Access Control Models and Technologies,* 29-37.

Biba, K. J. (1977). *Integrity considerations for secure computer systems.* The Mitre Corporation.

Brewer, D., & Nash, M. (1989). The Chinese wall security policy. *Proceedings of the IEEE Computer Society Symposium on Research in Security and Privacy* (pp. 215-228).

Clark, D. D., & Wilson, D. R. (1987). A comparison of commercial and military computer security policies. *IEEE Symposium of Security and Privacy,* 184-194.

Department of Defense (DoD) National Computer Security Center. (1985). *Department of Defense trusted computer systems evaluation criteria* (DoD 5200.28-STD).

Ferraiolo, D. F., Chandramouli, R., Ahn, G. J., & Gavrila, S. I. (2003). The role control center: Features and case studies. *8th Symposium on Access Control Models and Technologies,* 12-20.

Ferraiolo, D. F., Kuhn, R., & Chandramouli, R. (2003). *Role-based access controls.* Artech House.

Harrison, M., Ruzzo, W., & Ullman, J. (1976). Protection in operating systems. *Communication of the ACM, 19*(8), 461-471.

IBM Corporation. (2002). *Enterprise security architecture using IBM Tivoli security solutions.*

Lampson, B. (1974). Protection. *ACM Operating System Reviews, 8*(1), 18-24.

National Institute of Standards and Technology (NIST). (2004) *Role-based access control* (NIST Standard 359-2004).Retrieved from http://csrc.nist.gov/rbac

Organization for the Advancement of Structured Information Standards (OASIS). (2005). *eXtensible access control markup language* (XACML 2.0).

Roeckle, H., Schimpf, G., & Weidinger, R. (2000). Process-oriented approach for role-finding to implement role-based security administration in a large industrial organization. *Proceedings of the Fifth ACM Workshop on Role-Based Access Control,* 103-110.

Sandhu, R. S., Bhamidipati, V., & Munawer, Q. (1999). The ARBAC97 model for role-based administration of roles. *ACM Transactions on Information System Security, 2*(1), 105-135.

Sandhu, R. S., Coyne, E. J., Feinstein, H. L., & Youman C. E. (1996). Role-based access control models. *Computer, IEEE Computer Society Press, 29*(2), 38-47.

Tzu, S. (1910). *Sun Tzu on the art of war, the oldest military treatise in the world* (L. Giles, Trans.). Retrieved from http://classics.mit.edu/Tzu/artwar.html

U.S. Health Insurance Portability and Accountability Act (HIPAA). (1996). Retrieved from http://cms.hhs.gov/hipaa

TERMS AND DEFINITIONS

Access Control (or Authorization): The process of determining whether a subject (e.g., process, computer) is able to perform an operation (e.g., read, write) on an object (e.g., a file, a resource in the system).

Access Control Model: This is the underlying model upon which security policies are built. The access control model defines concepts and relations between them to organize access control.

Access Control Policy: This is the set of rules built on an access control model that defines the subjects, objects, permissions, and other concepts within the computer system. Authorization decisions are based upon access control policies settled in the system.

Discretionary Access Control (DAC): This is an access control model in which it is the owner of the object that controls other users' access to the object.

Mandatory Access Control (MAC): This refers to an access control model in which decisions must not be decided upon by the object owner. The system itself must enforce the protection decisions (i.e., the security policy).

Role-Based Access Control (RBAC): This is an access control model in which access decisions are based on the roles that individual users have as part of an organization.

Chapter XXXVIII
An Overview of IDS Using Anomaly Detection

Lior Rokach
Ben-Gurion University of the Negev, Israel

Yuval Elovici
Ben-Gurion University of the Negev, Israel

ABSTRACT

Intrusion detection is the process of monitoring and analyzing the events occurring in a computer system in order to detect signs of security problems. The problem of intrusion detection can be solved using anomaly detection techniques. For instance, one is given a set of connection data belonging to different classes (normal activity, different attacks) and the aim is to construct a classifier that accurately classifies new unlabeled connections data. Clustering methods can be used to detect anomaly in data which might implies intrusion of a new type. This chapter gives a critical summary of anomaly detection research for intrusion detection. This chapter surveys a list of research projects that apply anomaly detection techniques to intrusion detection. Finally some directions for research are given.

INTRODUCTION

One of the most practical forms of cyber warfare is penetrating a mission-critical information system or any other critical infrastructure, and maliciously affecting its availability, confidentiality, or integrity. While the popularity of the Internet increases, more organizations are becoming vulnerable to a wide variety of cyber attacks. Thus, organizations employ various computer and network security solutions to make their information systems tolerant of such threats. One of the solutions is intrusion detection and prevention systems. Intrusion detection is the process of monitoring and analyzing the events occurring in a computer system and communication networks in order to detect signs of security breaches.

A complete *intrusion detection system* (IDS) might monitor network traffic, server and operating system events, and file system integrity, using both signature detection and *anomaly detection* at each level. Mahoney and Chan (2002) distinguish between a host based IDS, which monitors the state of the host and a network IDS, which monitors traffic to and from the host. These systems differ in the types of attacks they can detect. A network IDS can monitor multiple hosts on a local network. On the other hand, a host based system must be installed on the system it monitors. A host based system may, for example, detect user-to-root (U2R) attacks, where a certain user gains the privileges of another user (usually root). A network IDS detects probes (such as port scans), denial-of-service (DOS) attacks (such as server floods), and remote-to-local (R2L) attacks in which an attacker without user level access gains the ability to execute commands locally. Also, because a network IDS monitors input (and output) rather than state, it can detect failed attacks (e.g., probes).

There are two different approaches to intrusion detection: misuse detection and anomaly detection. Misuse detection is the ability to identify intrusions based on a known pattern for the malicious activity. These known patterns are referred to as signatures. These attack signatures encompass specific traffic or activity that is based on known intrusive activity. The reader is referred to the work of Axelsson (2000), for detailed taxonomy about IDSs.

The second approach, anomaly detection, is the attempt to identify malicious activity based on deviations from established normal activity patterns. Usually anomaly detection is performed by creating a profile for each user group. These profiles are used as a baseline to define normal user activity. If any monitored activity deviates too far from this baseline, then the activity generates an alarm.

Classic implementations of IDS are rule based (see Roesch, 1999). The system administrator is responsible to write a set of rules, for example, to reject any packet addressed to a nonexistent host, or to restrict services to a range of trusted addresses. However, keeping the rules updated by monitoring the traffic to determine normal behavior is challenging. Both types of intrusion detection systems can be benefit from using *data mining* techniques as will be shown later in the chapter.

BACKGROUND

Data mining is a term coined to describe the process of sifting through large and complex databases for identifying valid, novel, useful, and understandable patterns and relationships. Data mining involves the inferring of algorithms that explore the data, develop the model, and discover previously unknown patterns. The model is used for understanding phenomena from the data, analysis, and prediction. The accessibility and abundance of data today makes knowledge discovery and data mining a matter of considerable importance and necessity. Given the recent growth of the field, it is not surprising that a wide variety of methods is now available to researchers and practitioners.

Phung (2000) indicates that there are four shortfalls in classic IDS that data mining can be used to solve:

1. **Variants:** It is not uncommon for an exploit tool to be released and then have its code changed shortly thereafter by the hacker community. An example might be a Remote Procedure Call (RPC) buffer overflow exploit whose code has been modified slightly to evade an IDS using signatures. Since data mining is not based on predefined signatures the concern with variants in the code of an exploit are not as great.

2. **False positives:** A common complaint is the amount of false positives an IDS generates (i.e., alerting on non-attack events). A difficult problem that arises from this is how much can be filtered out without potentially missing an attack. With data mining it is easy to correlate data related to alarms with mined audit data, thereby considerably reducing the rate of false alarms (Manganaris, Christensen, Zerkle, & Hermiz, 2000) Moreover data mining can be used to tune the system and by that consistently reducing the number of false alarms.

3. **False negatives:** The dual problem of the false positive is the false negative in which an IDS does not generate an alarm when an intrusion is

actually taking place. Simply put, if a signature has not been written for a particular exploit there is an extremely good chance that the IDS will not detect it. In data mining by attempting to establish patterns for normal activity and identifying that activity which lies outside identified bounds, attacks for which signatures have not been developed might be detected.

4. **Data overload:** Another aspect is how much data can an analyst effectively and efficiently analyze. Depending on the intrusion detection tools employed by an organization and its size there is the possibility for logs to reach millions of records per day. Data mining techniques, such as feature selection or feature extraction, are capable of identifying or extracting data which is most relevant and provide analysts with different "views" of the data to aid in their analysis. Doak (1992) tested several feature selection techniques on simulated computer attack data to explore the possibility of using feature selection to improve intrusion detection techniques. Frank (1994) studied how feature selection can improve classification of network traffic. He compared three feature selection algorithms for selecting the best subset of features to classify connections using decision trees.

The process of knowledge discovery in databases consists of the following steps (Maimon & Rokach, 2005):

1. Developing an understanding of the application domain.
2. Selecting and creating a data set on which discovery will be performed. Having defined the goals, the data that will be used for the knowledge discovery should be determined. This includes finding out what data is available, obtaining additional necessary data, and then integrating all the data for the knowledge discovery into one data set, including the attributes that will be considered for the process.
3. Preprocessing and cleansing. In this stage, data

reliability is enhanced. It includes data clearing, such as handling missing values and removal of noise or outliers.

4. Data transformation. In this stage, the generation of better data for data mining is prepared and developed. Methods here include dimensionality reduction (such as feature selection, extraction, and record sampling), and attribute transformation (such as discretization of numerical attributes and functional transformation).
5. Choosing the appropriate data mining task. We are now ready to decide on which type of data mining to use, for example, classification, regression, or clustering. This mostly depends on the goals, and also on the previous steps. There are two major goals in data mining: prediction and description. Prediction is often referred to as supervised data mining, while descriptive data mining includes the unsupervised and visualization aspects of data mining. Most data mining techniques are based on inductive learning, where a model is constructed explicitly or implicitly by generalizing from a sufficient number of training examples. The underlying assumption of the inductive approach is that the trained model is applicable to future cases. The strategy also takes into account the level of metalearning for the particular set of available data.
6. Choosing the data mining algorithm. Having the strategy, we now decide on the tactics. This stage includes selecting the specific method to be used for searching patterns (including multiple inducers). For example, in considering precision versus understandability, the former is better with neural networks, while the latter is better with decision trees.
7. Employing the data mining algorithm. Finally the implementation of the data mining algorithm is reached. In this step we might need to employ the algorithm several times until a satisfactory result is obtained, for instance by tuning the algorithm's control parameters, such as the minimum number of instances in a single leaf

of a decision tree.

8. Evaluation. In this stage we evaluate and interpret the mined patterns (rules, reliability, etc.), with respect to the goals defined in the first step. Here we consider the preprocessing steps with respect to their effect on the data mining algorithm results (for example, adding features in Step 4, and repeating from there). This step focuses on the comprehensibility and usefulness of the induced model. In this step the discovered knowledge is also documented for further usage.

9. Using the discovered knowledge. We are now ready to incorporate the knowledge into another system for further action. The knowledge becomes active in the sense that we may make changes to the system and measure the effects. Actually the success of this step determines the effectiveness of the entire process. There are many challenges in this step, such as loosing the"laboratory conditions" under which we have operated. For instance, the knowledge was discovered from a certain static snapshot (usually a sample) of the data, but now the data becomes dynamic. Data structures may change (certain attributes become unavailable), and the data domain may be modified (such as an attribute that may have a value that was not assumed before).

MAIN THRUST OF THE CHAPTER

We will next explain how different data mining techniques help in improving the performance of IDSs that are based on anomaly detection.

Classification Based Techniques

The main challenge of intrusion detection can be solved by using data mining classification techniques. These techniques attempt to discover a relationship between the input attributes and the target attribute. The re-

lationship discovered is represented in a structure referred to as a classifier. Classifiers can then be used for classifying a new unseen instance based on knowing the values of its input attributes. In the intrusion detection problem a suitable set of classes is "normal," "worm attack," "Trojan attack," and so forth.

In a typical scenario, a training set is given and the goal is to form a description that can be used to predict previously unseen examples. An induction algorithm, or more concisely an inducer (also known as learner), is an entity that obtains a training set and forms a model that generalizes the relationship between the input attributes and the target attribute. For example, an inducer may take as an input, specific training tuples with the corresponding class label, and produce a classifier.

Given the long history and recent growth of the field, it is not surprising that several mature approaches to induction are now available to the practitioner.

Classifiers may be represented differently from one inducer to another. For example, C4.5 (Quinlan, 1993) represents a model as a decision tree while Naive Bayes (Duda & Hart, 1973) represents a model in the form of probabilistic summaries. Furthermore, inducers can be deterministic (as in the case of C4.5) or stochastic (as in the case of back propagation). The classifier generated by the inducer can be used to classify an unseen instance either by explicitly assigning it to a certain class

(crisp classifier) or by providing a vector of probabilities representing the conditional probability of the given instance to belong to each class (probabilistic classifier).

Frank (1994) illustrates the usefulness of decision trees in classifying network connections records as intrusion attacks. Early and Brodley (2003) examined the use of decision trees for server flow authentication. The trees are built from traffic described using a set of features that have been designed to capture stream behavior. They have shown that due to the fact the classification of the traffic type is independent of port label, it provides a more accurate classification in the presence of malicious activity.

Liepens and Vacaro (1989) examined a rule based induction algorithm for IDS. The rules specify legal values of features conditioned on the values of other features. Legality is determined from the history of data for each feature. Rules can overlap in specificity due to incomplete information in the history. Rule pruning occurs if there are too many legal values for a feature, too few historical values, the rule is too deep, if rules overlap, or a rule is conditioned on a previously determined anomalous value.

Bala, Baik, Hadjarian, Gogia, and Manthorne (2002) suggest building a global network profile by applying distributed data mining methods. This idea is useful when the collection of data from distributed hosts for its subsequent use to generate an intrusion detection profile may not be technically feasible (e.g., due to data size or network security transfer protocols). In the proposed method a classifier is learned via a top-down induction decision tree algorithm. Agents generate partial trees and communicate the temporary results among them in the form of indices to the data records. The process is terminated when a final tree is induced.

Manganaris et al. (2000) suggest a methodology for reducing false alarm by analyzing RTID (real-time intrusion detection) reports. As opposed to many existing approaches, they suggest that the decision to filter an alarm out should take into consideration the context in which it occurred and the historical behavior of the sensor it came from. Moreover based on alert history, they concluded that there are several different types of clients, with different alert behaviors and thus different monitoring needs.

Debar, Becker, and Siboni (1992) present a filtering system based on a neural network which acts to filter data which does not fit an observed trend. They assume that user activity contains notable trends that can be detected, and that there are correlations among the collected audit data. Regularity ensures that the network will pick up the regular trends exhibited, and automatically account for correlations in the input data. Using a type of neural network called a recurrent

network ensures that behavior trends can be accurately recalled. The network "forgets" behavior over time, and can thus adjust to new trends. Thus the network acts as a filter to determine whether or not an audit record fits the regular trends.

Clustering Based Techniques

Classification techniques need a labeled training set in order to induce the classifier. Thus someone is required to label each instance in the training set to either "normal" or to "worm attack," and so forth. Creating such a training set is not an easy task. One approach to overcome this disadvantage is to look for outliers in the unlabeled training set. For instance NIDES builds a model of long-term behavior over a period, which is assumed to contain few or no attacks (Anderson, Lunt, Javitz, Tamaru, & Valdes, 1995). If short-term behavior (seconds, or a single packets) differs significantly, then an alarm is raised.

Assuming that normal behavior is much more common than malicious behaviors and that the malicious behavior is different from the normal one, we just have to look for outliers in the data (Portnoy, Eskin, & Stolfo, 2001). One possible way to discover these kinds of outliers is to use clustering methods. Clustering methods group data instances into subsets in such a manner that similar instances are grouped together, while different instances belong to different groups. The instances are thereby organized into an efficient representation that characterizes the population being sampled. Based on the previous two assumptions, intrusive instances should be grouped together into small clusters while the normal instances should be grouped into different and larger clusters. At run time, new instances are set as either "normal" or "intrusive" by measuring the distance from the center of all normal and intrusive clusters. The closest center will determine to which class the new instance belongs.

Clustering can also be used as a reduction technique by storing the characteristics of the clusters instead of the actual data. Lankewicz and Benard (1991) suggest using k nearest neighbor (knn) clustering to reduce IDS data. Liepens and Vacaro (1989) partitioned the history of audit data into clusters which correspond to high density regions followed by low density regions; the historical data is then represented by clusters which represent each density region.

Julisch (2003) argues that each alarm occurs for a reason, which is referred to as the alarm's root causes. His research provides a few dozen main root causes that generally account for most of the alarms that an intrusion detection system triggers (it is shown that a few dozen of the rather persistent root causes generally account for over 90% of the alarms that an intrusion detection system triggers). Based on this observation Julisch (2003) suggests an alarm-clustering method that supports the human analyst in identifying root causes. Moreover he argues that alarms should be handled by identifying and removing the most predominant and persistent root causes. He shows that the alarm load decreases quite substantially if the identified root causes are eliminated so that they can no longer trigger alarms in the future.

The MINDS (Minnesota Intrusion Detection System) uses an anomaly detection technique to assign a score to each connection to determine how anomalous the connection is compared to normal network traffic (Ertoz et al., 2003; Kumar, Lazarevic, Ertoz, Ozgur, & Srivastava, 2003). MINDS has two unique components: (a) an unsupervised anomaly detection technique that assigns a score to each network connection that reflects how anomalous the connection is, and (b) an association pattern analysis based module that summarizes those network connections that are ranked highly anomalous by the anomaly detection module. The first step in MINDS derives new features from existing features by using a time-window and connection-window. The second step in MINDS employ an outlier detection algorithm to assign an anomaly score to each network connection. The network administrator then looks at the most suspicious connections to determine if they are real attacks or false alarms. Experimental results on live network traffic show that MINDS anomaly detection techniques are very promising and are successful in automatically detecting several novel intrusions that could not be identified using popular signature-based tools such as SNORT.

Association Rules Based Techniques

The original motivation for searching association rules came from the need to analyze so called supermarket transaction data, that is, to examine customer behavior in terms of the purchased products (Agrawal, Imielinski,& Swami, 1993). Thus association rules are rules of the kind "90% of the customers who buy bread and cheese also buy butter."' Association algorithms usually find all associations that satisfy criteria for minimum support (at least a specified fraction of the instances must satisfy both sides of the rule) and minimum confidence (at least a specified fraction of instances satisfying the left hand side, or antecedent, must satisfy the right hand side, or consequent). While the traditional field of application is market basket analysis, association rule mining has been applied in IDS.

The MADAM ID system (Lee, Stolfo and Kwok, 1998), which has been developed at Columbia University, has learned classifiers that distinguish between intrusions and normal activities. First all network traffic is preprocessed to create connection records. The attributes of connection records are intrinsic connection characteristics that will be referred to here as raw attributes. These attributes include the source host, the destination host, the start time, the duration, and so forth.

Then all connection records are classified in advance into "normal" or some kind of intrusions. MADAM ID proceeds in two steps. In the first step it does feature extraction in which some additional features are constructed that are considered useful for doing the analysis. The reason for that is that classifiers can perform really poorly when they have to rely solely on raw attributes that are not predictive of the target concept. One example of this step is to calculate the number of connections that have been initiated during the last two seconds to the same destination host as the current host.

The feature extraction is followed by the classifier induction. For this purpose the training set is split into two subsets: normal subset and intrusion subset. Association rules and frequent episode rules are inferred separately from the normal connection records and from the intrusion connection records. The resulting patterns from the normal subset that are also found in the intrusion subset are removed from the intrusion subset and the remaining patterns in the intrusion subset form the exclusive intrusion patterns. The exclusive intrusion patterns are then used to derive additional attributes. Finally a classifier is learned that distinguishes normal from intrusion connection.

Correlation Techniques

Usually IDSs focus on low level attacks or anomalies, and raise alerts independently, although there may be logical connections between them. In situations where there are intensive intrusions, not only will actual alerts be mixed with false alerts, but the amount of alerts will also become unmanageable. Several alert correlation methods have been proposed to address this problem. Ning, Cui, and Reeves (2002) suggest categorizing these methods into three classes. The first class correlates alerts based on the similarities between alert attributes (Staniford, Hoagland, & McAlerney, 2002). The second class bases alert correlation on attack scenarios specified by human users or learned through training datasets (Dain & Cunningham, 2001). The third class is based on the preconditions and consequences of individual attacks; it correlates alerts if the precondition of some later alerts are satisfied by the consequences of some earlier alerts. Ning and Xu (2003) examined the third class. Intuitively, the prerequisite of an intrusion is the necessary condition for the intrusion to be successful, while the consequence of an intrusion is the possible outcome of the intrusion. Based on the prerequisites and consequences of different types of attacks, the proposed approach correlates alerts by (partially) matching the consequence of some previous alerts and the prerequisite of some later ones. To evaluate the effectiveness of the method in constructing attack

scenarios and its ability to differentiate true and false alerts, Ning and Xu (2003) performed a series of experiments using the 2000 DARPA intrusion detection scenario specific data sets (for example, the ability to differentiate true and false alerts for LLDOS 1.0 DMZ data set was false alert rate—5.26%).

Hybridization of Techniques

Many of the data mining-based IDSs are using various techniques together. ADAM (Audit Data and Mining) is a combination anomaly detector and classifier trained on both attack-free traffic and traffic with labeled attacks. The ADAM system was developed at George Mason University (Barbara, Wu, & Jajodia, 2001). The system infers from nonmalicious network traffic the characteristics of normal behavior. This profile is represented as a set of association rules. For this purpose the ADAM system monitors port numbers, IP addresses and subnets, and TCP state. The system learns rules such as "if the source IP address is X, then the destination port is Y with probability p." It also aggregates packets over a time window. ADAM uses a naive Bayes classifier, which means that if a packet belongs to some class (normal, known attack, or unknown), then the probabilities for each condition are assumed to be independent. ADAM has separate training modes and detection modes. At run time, the connection records of past delta seconds are continuously mined for new association rules that are not contained in the profile. Moreover the online association rules mining algorithm is used to process a window of current connections. Suspicious connections are flagged and sent along with their feature vectors to the trained classifier, where they are labeled as attacks, normal, or unknown. When, the classifier labels connections as normal, it is filtering them out of the attacks set and avoiding passing these alerts to the system administrator. The unknown label is reserved for the events whose exact nature cannot be confirmed by the classifier. These events are also considered as attacks and they are included in the set of alerts that are passed to the system administrator.

Lee, Stolfo, and Kwok (1999) suggest a data mining

framework for adaptively building intrusion detection models. This framework consists of the following data mining programs: classification, metalearning, association rules, and frequent episodes. Metaclassification is used for combining evidence from multiple models. Combining multiple models can be used to avoid an IDS becoming an easy target of "subversion," because it is easier to overcome a single approach than overcoming an ensemble of approaches. Moreover combining the outputs of multiple classifiers improves the identification accuracy, mainly due to the phenomenon that various types of classifiers have different "inductive biases" and the ensemble employs such diversity to reduce the misidentification rate. Frequent episodes are used for discovering what timebased sequence of audit events are frequently occurring together. These methods can be used for creating and adding temporal statistical measures into intrusion detection models. For example, patterns from audit data containing networkbased DOS attacks suggest that several perhost and perservice measures should be included.

The IDS was evaluated using the DARPA IDS evaluation set and TP and FP of misuse detection models was 93% and 8% respectively.

Mahoney and Chan (2002) developed an IDS that is capable of detecting new attacks which do not have known signatures. The proposed IDS has two unique nonstationary components The first component is a packet header anomaly detector (PHAD) which monitors the entire data link, network, and transport layer, without any preconceptions about which fields might be useful. The second component is an application layer anomaly detector (ALAD) which combines a traditional user model based on TCP connections with a model of text-based protocols such as HTTP, FTP, and SMTP. Both systems learn which attributes are useful for anomaly detection, and then use a nonstationary model, in which events receive higher scores if no novel values have been seen for a long time. The IDS was evaluated using the 1999 DARPA IDS evaluation set and was able to detect 70 of 180 attacks (with 100 false alarms).

FUTURE TRENDS

There are several trends in the field of using data mining in IDS systems including:

1. The creation of a unified knowledge discovery framework for IDS.
2. Development of systems that can identify new types of attacks (Singhal & Sushil, 2005)
3. Developing a meta-data mining approach for IDS, in which knowledge about the organization will be used to improve the effectiveness of data mining methods.
4. Developing a distributed data mining framework for improving the capability of IDS systems by sharing patterns among organizations while preserving privacy.
5. Developing alarm correlation systems. More work needs to be done on alert correlation techniques that can construct "attack strategies" and facilitate intrusion analysis (Singhal & Sushil, 2005).
6. Effectively integrate data mining methods with knowledge-based methods to create an IDS which will allow the system administrator to more accurately and quickly identify an intrusion on the system.

CONCLUSION

In this chapter, we surveyed data mining methods and their applications in developing IDSs' that are based on anomaly detection. We presented various types of IDSs' and portrayed their main shortfalls. The general process of knowledge discovery in databases was presented. Then it has been illustrated how various research projects employed data mining techniques to perform intrusion detection. We have seen that data mining can improve the performance of current IDSs' and automate some of the tasks that are now performed by the system administrator. Finally future trends in this field have been presented.

REFERENCES

Agrawal, R., Imielinski, T., & Swami, A. (1993). Mining association rules between sets of items in large databases. In P. Buneman & S. Jajodia (Eds.), *Proceedings of the 1993 International Conference on Management of Data, (ACM SIGMOND), 22*(2), 207-216.

Anderson, D., Lunt, T. F., Javitz, H., Tamaru, A., & Valdes, A. (1995). Detecting unusual program behavior using the statistical component of the next generation intrusion detection expert system (NIDES). *Computer Science Laboratory SRI-CSL 95-06.*

Axelsson, S. (2000, March). *Intrusion detection systems: A survey and taxonomy* (Technical Report 99-15). Department of Computer Engineering, Chalmers University.

Bala, J. W., Baik, S., Hadjarian, A., Gogia, B. K., & Manthorne, C. (2002). Application of a distributed data mining approach to network intrusion detection. In *Proceedings of the first international joint conference on autonomous agents and multiagent systems: part 3* (pp. 1419-1420.)

Barbara, D., Wu, N., & Jajodia, S. (2001, April). Detecting novel network intrusions using bayes estimators. *Proceedings of the First SIAM Conference on Data Mining,* Chicago.

Dain, O., & Cunningham, R. (2001). Fusing a heterogeneous alert stream into scenarios. *Proceedings of the 2001 ACM Workshop on Data Mining for Security Applications, 113, 1-13.*

Debar, H., Becker, M., & Siboni, D. (1992). A neural network component for an intrusion detection system. *Proceedings, IEEE Symposium on Research in Computer Security and Privacy* (pp. 240-250).

Doak, J. (1992). *Intrusion detection: The application of feature selection, a comparison of algorithms, and the application of a wide area network analyzer.* PhD thesis, University of California, Davis.

Duda, R., & Hart, P. (1973) *Pattern Classification and Scene Analysis.* Wiley: New-York.

Early, J. P., & Brodley, C. E. (2003, September 24-26). Decision trees for server flow authentication. *Workshop on Statistical and Machine Learning Techniques in Computer Intrusion Detection,* George Mason University.

Ertoz, L., Eilertson, E., Lazarevic, A., Tan, P., Dokes, P., Kumar, V., et al. (2003, November). Detection of novel attacks using data mining. *Proceedings of the IEEE Workshop on Data Mining and Computer Security.*

Frank, J. (1994). Artificial intelligence and intrusion detection: Current and future directions. *Proceedings of the 17th National Computer Security Conference,* Baltimore (pp. 22-33).

Julisch, K. (2003, November). Clustering intrusion detection alarms to support root cause analysis. *ACM Transactions on Information and System Security (TISSEC), 6*(4), 443-471.

Kumar, V., Lazarevic, A., Ertoz, L., Ozgur, A., & Srivastava, J. (2003, May). A comparative study of anomaly detection schemes in network intrusion detection. *Proceedings of the Third SIAM International Conference on Data Mining,* San Francisco.

Lankewicz, L., & Benard, M. (1991). Realtime anomaly detection using a nonparametric pattern recognition approach. *Proceedings of the 7th Annual Computer Security Applications Conference* (pp. 80-89).

Lee, W., Stolfo, S. J., & Kwok, K. W. (1999, May). A data mining framework for building intrusion detection models. *IEEE Symposium on Security and Privacy,* Berkeley, CA, 120-132.

Lee, W., & Stolfo, S. J. (1998a). Data mining approaches for intrusion detection. *Proceedings of the Seventh USENIX Security Symposium,* San Antonio, TX.

Lee, W., Stolfo, S. J., & Kwok, K. W. (1998b). Mining

audit data to build intrusion detection models. *Proceedings of the Fourth International Conference on Knowledge Discovery and Data Mining*, NY.

Liepens, G., & Vacaro, H. (1989). Anomaly detection: purpose and framework. *Proceedings of the 12th National Computer Security Conference* (pp. 495-504).

Mahoney, M., & Chan, P. (2002). Learning nonstationary models of normal network traffic for detecting novel attacks. *Proceedings of the SIGKDD,* Edmonton, Alberta (pp. 376-385).

Maimon, O., & Rokach, L. (2005). *Introduction to knowledge discovery in databases.* In *The data mining and knowledge discovery handbook 2005* (pp. 1-17).

Manganaris, S., Christensen, M., Zerkle, D., & Hermiz, K. (2000). A data mining analysis of RTID alarms. *Computer Networks, 34,* 571-577.

Ning, P., Cui, Y., & Reeves, D. S. (2002). Constructing attack scenarios through correlation of intrusion alerts. *Proceedings of the ACM Computer and Communications Security Conference* (pp. 245-254).

Ning, P., & Xu, D. (2003). Learning attack strategies from intrusion alerts. *Proceedings of the ACM Computer and Communications Security Conference* (pp. 200 - 209).

Phung, M. (2000, October 24). *Data mining in intrusion detection.* http://www.sans.org/resources/idfaq/data_mining.php

Portnoy, L., Eskin, E., & Stolfo, S. J. (2001). Intrusion detection with unlabeled data using clustering. *Proceedings of ACM Workshop on Data Mining Applied to Security.*

Quinlan, J. R. (1993). *C4.5: Programs for machine learning,* Morgan Kaufmann: Los Altos.

Roesch, M. (1999, November). Snort-lightweight intrusion detection for networks. *Proceedings of the. USENIX Lisa '99,* Seattle, WA.

Singhal, A., & Jajodia, S. (2005). *Data mining for intrusion detection.* In *The data mining and knowl-edge discovery handbook 2005* (pp. 1225-1237). Springer.

Staniford, S., Hoagland, J. A., & McAlerney, J. M. (2002). Practical automated detection of stealthy portscans. *J. Comput. Secur., 10*(12), 105-136.

TERMS AND DEFINITIONS

Association Rules: Techniques that find in a database conjunctive implication rules of the form "X and Y implies A and B."

Attribute: A quantity describing an instance. An attribute has a domain defined by the attribute type, which denotes the values that can be taken by an attribute. In IDSs' usually this refers to attributes of systems, events, or connections (such as source IP).

Classifier: A structured model that maps unlabeled instances to finite set of classes.

Clustering: The process of grouping data instances into subsets in such a manner that similar instances are grouped together into the same cluster, while different instances belong to different clusters.

Data Mining: The core of the KDD process, involving the inferring of algorithms that explore the data, develop the model, and discover previously unknown patterns.

Feature Selection: A process to identify the important attributes in a given database and discard any other feature as irrelevant and redundant information.

Induction Algorithm: An algorithm that takes as input a certain set of instances and produces a model that generalizes these instances.

Instance: A single object of the world from which a model will be learned, or on which a model will be used. In IDSs' instance usually refers to systems, events, or connections.

Intrusion Detection System (IDS): A system that monitors and analyzes all events occurring in a computer system in order to detect signs of unwanted ativities. This includes network attacks against vulnerable services, data driven attacks on applications, host based attacks such as privilege escalation, unauthorized logins and access to sensitive files, and malware (viruses, trojan horses, and worms).

Knowledge Discovery in Databases (KDD): A nontrivial exploratory process of identifying valid, novel, useful, and understandable patterns from large and complex data repositories.

Outlier: An instance that deviates so much from other instances as to arouse suspicion that it was generated by a different mechanism.

Outlier Detection: A process for identifying outliers.

Chapter XXXIX
Bio–Cyber Machine Gun:
A New Mode of Authentication Access Using Visual Evoked Potentials

Andrews Samraj
Multimedia University, Malaysia

ABSTRACT

The bio-cyber machine gun (BCMG) is a defensive tool used to protect misuse of authentication, access control, and aid cryptography and information hiding by means of password shooting. BCMG is developed to be a ray of hope for the disabled community who live in the dark expanses of life, by providing all possible technical support to the disabled by increasing their ability by means of creating innovative software and hardware that helps them to live independently in a stress free environment and to enjoy the desired choice, control and freedom as others. The brain wave P300 component is used for this purpose. This chapter describes that how the P300 components are created, identified, extracted, and classified for the use in the BCMG.

INTRODUCTION

The *bio-cyber nachine gun* (BCMG) is a defensive tool used to protect misuse of *authentication*, and access control. It also aids cryptography and information hiding by means of biological password shooting. Use of biometrics as a tool for authentication is a popular means nowadays (Pankanti, 2001). Among various types of *biometrics* like fingerprints, palm prints, iris recognition, face recognition, voice recognition, and others using bio-signals for authentication purposes is novel and unique. The need for this tool amidst various existing authentication protection methods is to have an easy, cost effective, and reliable way. The conventional password, pin number, smart card, barcodes or biometric fingerprints, palm prints, iris pattern, and face recognition are only used for a specific purpose of authentication or access control on a one time basis. The amount of information we can pass through these methods is also very limited. The ever-growing demand for integration of services and higher level security needs, calls for an efficient and reliable system, which can do multiple tasks in a highly secured way. This kind of sensitive and complex system can be made effective and robust, but at the same time be simple to implement, when we use them from a very close mode like biometrics of a person. This has to be carried out exclusive of the major drawbacks of biometrics. More over this may be the only possible authentication and access control method for patients, the elderly, and the disabled who may not be able to adapt to conventional methods.

BACKGROUND

Biometrics is a technique which uses the unique features of the human body as an identification tool to recognize a person. The biometrics function works on a simple principle that everyone in the world is unique, and this inherent uniqueness can be used for identity verification. The face is a good example of what helps to identify each individual. Along with the face, height, skin, voice, and hair styles are also useful. Similarly the centuries old method of using fingerprints to identify people is still being used as a signature as well as in forensic science (Pankanti, 2001). The major disadvantage of using biometrics is that it is extremely sensitive. The biometric components are complex starting from access, deployment, and securing them for further use. It is prone to misuse if stolen and needs complex retrieval methods and expensive devises. In addition it involves ethical issues. Cancelable biometrics solves this problem to a certain extent (Vaughan, Wolpaw, & Donchin, 1996) and it still needs to be improved in terms of flexibility and reliance. The proposed method of using bio-signals for this purpose solves the problem innovatively and simply. The human body generates many kinds of signals known as, in general, bio-signals, which include signals from the heart beat (ECG), from the brain (EEG) and others. Using EEG signals for communication is an emerging technology in the rehabilitation field (Vaughan et al., 1996). Most of the bio-signals are independent from human activities and they are automatic, so these signals cannot be composed to a fixed rhythm by others.

On the other hand, some of the signals generated by muscle activities can be controlled by the person and can be made rhythmical. But the generation of these signals are not secured and protected. The *visual evoked potential* (VEP) signals for this purpose are found to be feasible and appropriate for sensitive multipurpose security systems since it is securely produced and can be made rhythmic.

The VEP that is generated using an oddball paradigm that gives a visual stimulus (Andrews, Palaniappan, & Kamel, 2005) normally buried in the ongoing background EEG. We can divert the function of the oddball paradigm and the signals produced can be made rhythmic to symbolize a particular meaning. It is faster than the mental prosthesis method (Donchin, Spencer, & Wijesinghe, 2000) used to generate brain activity signals. A conventional light machine gun (LMG) can fire at the rate of 300 to 500 rounds per minute in its rapid-fire mode (R) using a belt supply. We use this model of rapid-fire mode to randomly activate the paradigm to evoke the VEP from brain to coin the currently required password at any moment. So we could call this a brain computer machine gun.

METHODS AND BENEFITS

This BCMG tool that we designed for this purpose uses two major components, one is the signal capture unit and the second is an interface unit. Using the first unit the raw EEG recordings are taken from the scalp as shown in Figure 3. These signals are always contaminated with noise and artifacts which will be eliminated by filtering (Andrews, Kamel, & Palaniappan, 2005; Kriss, 1993).

The state of the art, cutting edge technology that BCMG utilizes is the simplest physiological behavior activity of viewing the paradigm that evokes brain potentials. Using the electrodes fixed on the parietal area of the scalp (Kriss, 1993) EEG signals for one second immediately after the visual stimulus is recorded. Using the interface unit, these recordings are band pass filtered to remove artifacts (Andrews et al., 2005; Kriss, 1993), using a low pass filter with the combination of a 9th order forward and 9th order reverse Butterworth digital filter with a cutoff frequency at 8 Hz. A minimum attenuation of 30 dB was achieved in the stop band. The intentions denoted by the subject in the form of signals were translated into rhythmic control codes after separating the VEP using the latest methods of principal component analysis (PCA) (Andrews & Palaniappan, 2004; Andrews, Palaniappan, & Asirvadam, 2004; Andrews et al., 2005; Palaniappan, Anandan, & Raveendran, 2002). This is achieved using the spelling or picture paradigm, which are used to evoke the VEP. These VEP signals are compared to find the target alphabet or picture that will form the code that is used as the bullets of the BCMG. Whenever the signal peak at P300 (Polich, 1991) goes high, the corresponding row or column of the spelling paradigm (Andrews et al., 2005) is considered for its characters and the intersecting character is selected as the target letter for coining the pass code being the criteria in controlling devices.

This spelling paradigm is shown in Figure 1(a). In the testing phase the translated and coined pass codes like "CAT" are stored and labeled. The experiment is repeated to reproduce the codes and are compared with the first set of control codes that are available in the database using a matching and non-matching routine. The average accuracy of reproducing 40 codes having three to five characters each is 90.24%. Similar procedures are followed to capture signals by changing the character paradigm to a picture paradigm shown in Figure 1(b) and the accuracy of finding 10 pictures is 100%

The signals shown in Figure 2 show three nontarget representations of the spelling paradigm and the one is the target representation which produces significant amplitude around 300 millisecond. The difference in amplitude heights from different channels of VEP for target as well as nontarget responses is tabulated in Table 1. By observing Figure 2, it is understood that it is impossible to be acquainted, fake, or reproduce such signals by a bare human eye and understand the meaning of each signal for the purpose of forging. Hence these signals are considered worthy to form rhythmic bullets that are emitted by the human brain at a rapid speed when there is a visual stimulus. These rhythmic bullets can be synchronized with any application for any individuals to use as a guarding weapon, to protect their electronic equipment, systems, files, and so forth.

The advantage of using this tool is its ability and efficiency in multitier password protected environments. Basically producing various combinations of these bullets involves no cost. The hardware device used to capture these signals is a few electrodes engraved on a cap or helmet as shown in Figure 3. This may aid the protection in generating the signals since no one can see or recognize the signal generated in the human brain. It is safer than generating signals using finger movements or any other muscle movements. It is easy and faster than generating biometric pass codes that need scanning and comparisons.

Using this weapon we gain more technical advantages such as, multiple levels of authentication. This is possible through BCMG since we use different bullets

Figure 1(a). Spelling paradigm

Figure 1(b). Picture paradigm

Table 1. P300 Amplitude peaks example

Channels	P300 Amplitude Peaks Example			
	Target Signal		Non Target Signal	
Of e-cap	Amplitude	Latency	Amplitude	Latency
Cz	2.0763	312	-0.3372	425.1
Pz	1.9526	312	-0.2380	429
Fz	2.0211	315.9	0.0090	429
FCz	2.0015	315.9	-0.0484	425.1
C1	2.0244	315.9	-0.0076	432.9
CP1	1.9217	315.9	-0.2292	432.9
CPz	1.9413	312	-0.0061	432.9
C2	1.9464	315.9	-0.3277	432.9

to hit different target authentication, which will make it difficult for the hacker to access the system by password sniffing, and so forth. This is just like using different kinds of locks and keys for every door in the house. A wide variety of signals provides a huge bandwidth of usage so there is no need to worry about limitations. These bullets can be changed from time to time for the same level of authentication so that we can arrive at a highly secured and reliable system at every time of use and is better than the cancelable biometrics

(Connie, Teoh, Goh, & Ngo, 2004) since no need to use more than one factor for authentication. Another advantage here is that there is no need for a media to store and carry this ever-changing authentication. Hence it is safer than any form of biometrics.

LIMITATIONS OF BCMG

BCMG requires some primary instruments that read brain signals like EEG. As it is, BCMG is not a mobile device; and it has to be incorporated with RFID technology to do so. Devices that can respond to the BCMG bullets need to be developed exclusively for this application. It may seem difficult but developing exceptional devices in rehabilitation engineering is the norm. The BCMG requires repeated training to shoot the target words as accurately as sharpshooters with conventional rifles.

Figure 2.

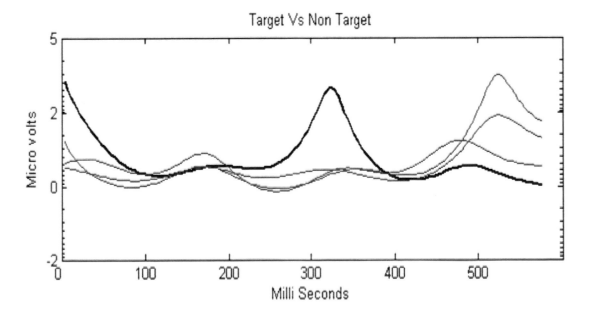

Figure 3. Taking raw EEG recordings from scalp

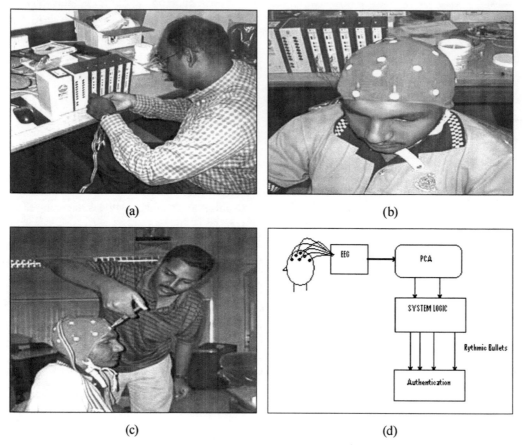

(a)   (b)

(c)   (d)

FUTURE TRENDS

Physically disabled people with locked-in syndrome often face stress related problems because of their inability to do some activities independently. They usually need assistance from others to conduct even simple activities like switching on the television, answering calls, using a computer, or even switching on lights and fans. If a physically disabled person can be more independent this will reduce their stress level which will lead to a healthier and more independent lifestyle. With this in mind, the BCMG was created to make use of the simplest brain activities. New devices could be attached to this system by expanding the usage BCMG to control various devices as well as for authentication purposes.

The future trend of this system will lead to multitier combination access codes, which will serve as a multipurpose smart card for the elderly and disabled. These systems can be embedded on any kind of device such as wheelchairs and will help the users to program their activities, including their secured operations, well in advance of going to work.

CONCLUSION

In the future, there will arise the need for multiple pass codes and pin numbers for access control and authentication. It is very difficult to possess or remember more numbers for such pins or codes for different or the same media which is dangerous too. The BMCG will be the suitable, safe, and cost effective solution for this purpose. It is not only safe and cheap but also user friendly and suitable for the elderly and the disabled who cannot handle other authentication tools easily. BCMG was developed out of the mission to be a ray of hope for the disabled community by providing possible information technology solutions to make their lives healthier and happier.

REFERENCES

Andrews, S., Kamel, N., & Palaniappan, R. (2005). Overcoming accuracy deficiency of filtrations in source separation of visual evoked potentials by adopting principal component analysis. *Proceedings of International Science Congress (ISC),* Malaysia (p. 344).

Andrews, S., & Palaniappan, R. (2004). Extracting single trial evoked potential signals using spectral power ratio principal components. *Proceedings of Annual Fall Meeting BMES 2004 (Biomedical Engineering Society),* Philadelphia.

Andrews, S., Palaniappan, R., & Asirvadam, V. S. (2004). Single trial source separation of VEP signals using selective principal components. *Proceedings of IEE MEDSIP 2004, International Conference on Advances in Medical Signal Processing,* Malta G.C, EU (pp. 51-57).

Andrews, S., Palaniappan, R., & Kamel, N. (2005). Single trial VEP source separation by selective eigen rate principal components. *Transactions on Engineering, Computing and Technology, Enformatika, 7, 330-333.*

Donchin, E., Spencer, K. M., & Wijesinghe R. (2000). The mental prosthesis: Assessing the speed of a P300-based brain-computer interface. *IEEE Trans. Rehabil. Eng., 8,* 174-179.

Kriss, A. (1993). Recording technique. In A. M. Halliday (Ed.), *Evoked potentials in clinical testing* (2nd edition) (pp. 1-56). New York: Churchill Livingstone.

Palaniappan, R., Anandan, S., & Raveendran, P. (2002, December 25). Two level PCA to reduce noise and EEG from evoked potential signals. *Proceedings of 7th International Conference on Control, Automation, Robotics and Vision,* Singapore (pp. 1688-1693).

Pankanti, P. J. (2001, December). On the individuality of fingerprints. *Proceedings of the IEEE Conference on Computer Vision and Pattern Recognition.*

Polich, J. (1991). P300 in clinical applications: Meaning, method and measurement. *American Journal of EEG Technology, 31,* 201-231.

Tee, C., Teoh, A., Goh, M., & Ngo, D. (2004). Palm hashing: A novel approach to cancelable biometrics. *Information Processing Letter, 93*(1), 15.

Vaughan, T. M., Wolpaw, J. R., & Donchin, E. (1996). EEG based communications: Prospects and problems, *IEEE Transactions on Rehabilitation Engineering, 4*(4), 425-430.

TERMS AND DEFINITIONS

P300 (Potential at 300 Millisecond): This positive peak is a late component of the event related potential which can be any one of the auditory, visual, or somatosensory.

Bio-Signals: The signals that are released and can be extracted from any biological source of any living organism are known as bBio-signals.

Biometrics: Biometrics is the automated method to recognize a person based on any one or more physiological or behavioral characteristic using the features like face, fingerprints, hand geometry, handwriting, iris, retinal, vein, and voice.

Electroencephalogram (EEG): An EEG or electroencephalogram is a test to detect the ongoing functions in the electrical activity of the brain.

Multitier Authentication: The multiple authentication system which requires varying password or pin numbers every time when accessing from one level to the next higher level.

Principal Component Analysis (PCA): Principal component analysis is a mathematical function that transforms a number of possibly correlated variables into a smaller number of uncorrelated variables called principal components.

Visual Evoked Potentials (VEP): The event related potentials with a short latency period that represents the immediate response of the brain to a swift visual stimulus.

Chapter XL
Content–Based Policy Specification for Multimedia Authorization and Access Control Model

Bechara Al Bouna
Bourgogne University, France

Richard Chbeir
Bourgogne University, France

ABSTRACT

Cyber terrorism is one of the emergent issues to handle in the domain of security and access control models. Cyber Terrorist attacks on information systems are growing further and becoming significantly effective. Multimedia object retrieval systems are considered one of many targets tolerable for such attacks due to the fact that they are being increasingly used in governmental departments. For these reasons, the need for an access control system is considered an unavoidable matter to be taken at a high priority. Several textual-oriented authorization models have been provided in the literature. However, multimedia objects are more complex in structure and content than textual ones, and thus require models to provide full multimedia-oriented components specification. In this paper, we point out some of the related work addressing multimedia objects authorization and access control models where objects such as documents, images, videos, sounds, etc., are being protected from unauthorized access. We describe also our model defined to handle multimedia content access control and security breaches that might occur due to users' relations.

INTRODUCTION

The war on terrorism as declared by the United States has emerged recently to cover new battlefields of different types. Terrorist groups become more and more aware of the damage they can cause by attacking information systems especially when governments depend on such information. The indispensable nature of information technology makes the process of blocking cyber terrorism a complex issue. The complexity resides in defining access control models for handling different types of data objects such as video scenes, images, sound clips, texts, and so forth, referred to as multimedia objects becoming abundant in several information systems. In essence, an access control is the process of managing requests upon sets of data. The increasing advances in information systems make the process of securing their data a serious issue to effectively consider. For instance, any breach or abuse of information in a CIA department may lead to undesired consequences for the agents who work in it. For this reason, almost every system integrates a component for security and access control management in which access managers specify rules and policies to be fulfilled when a request is generated. Several models have been considered in the literature for the purpose of providing safe information disclosure and denying unauthorized access. Models such Discretionary Access Control (DAC) (Landwehr, 1981), Mandatory Access Control (MAC) (Landwehr, 1981) and Role Based Access Control (RBAC) (Ferraiolo, Barkley, & Kuhn, 1999) have been widely used for information security in textual databases and traditional applications. Thus, the progressive use of multimedia objects on the Internet and intranets has brought dynamicity and complexity for such networks. Several *authorization and access control* problems have emerged and are related to the complex structure of these objects. Unlike textual information, these objects are of a complex nature and have several properties that form their structure and content. Properties such as low-level features (texture, color, shape, etc.), metadata (author name, key words, etc.), and relations between sub-objects (temporal, semantic, spatial, etc.), make the process of protecting multimedia objects a real complex task. The access to a multimedia database containing confidential pictures, interviews with secret agents, and presidential information should be restricted from unauthorized users. Such restriction can be applied for instance by covering agents' faces to maintain confidentiality.

In this chapter, we present the existing access control approaches in which these issues are addressed and we try to point out their limits when addressing

multimedia data. We also present our approach that addresses two main facets in the domain of multimedia authorization and access control:

Content-based policies: Since the last decade, multimedia applications allow users to write multicriteria queries able to address the content of multimedia objects (color, texture, shape, etc.) and are not limited anymore to textual characteristics. For these reasons, it is becoming difficult for authorization managers to protect multimedia objects with no textual description (scenes and images with no annotation) such as in real-time multimedia applications. For example, hiding the face of a secret agent next to the U.S. president with no related textual description remains a difficult task if current authorization models are used. In essence, these models (Aref & Elmagarmid, 2000; Bertino, Ferrari, & Perego, 2002; Bertino, Hammad, Aref, & Elmagarmid, 2000; PICS, n.d.) are successful when applying access policies upon multimedia objects with prior known objects' content description (e.g., video with annotated scenes, an image with textual description describing its content, etc.). This is why a new content-based access and authorization control model is required to define policies on the basis of any multimedia objects properties and not only on textual description.

Context-based role specification: Roles have been widely used in the literature to facilitate associating authorization and access policies to users (officer, manager, etc.). RBAC (Ferraiolo et al., 1999) is one of the most used role-based models where hierarchical links are defined between roles. As most of current models do not allow considering user properties and relations, the use of roles may conduct the authorization manager to give indirect access to an unauthorized user. Similarly, authorizations may depend on user device capabilities (e.g., users who use Cisco firewalls may download Video X), software properties (users who use Linux can not edit Video X), network description (connection between the client and the server is VPN), user interests (users interested in the army are allowed to view Video X), and so forth. Such constraints should be used to enforce the policies definition and management when a high security level is a must. For this reason, we do believe that the authorization and access control model must consider additional information related to the user context so that the authorization manager can be alerted about possible security breaches and guided when defining policies.

The rest of the chapter is organized as follows. We will discuss the motivation behind the specification of an authorization and access control model for multimedia objects. Then we describe the related work in this area. We will give an overview of our proposal by presenting the different components of an appropriate authorization and access control model for multimedia data. Finally, we conclude this work and discuss future trends.

MOTIVATION EXAMPLE

Let us consider a database containing recordings (images, videos, and sounds) of secret agents and confidential activities in a government center. This database is content unaware and annotations emptied (except the dates). For security and confidentiality reasons, the identity of some agents appearing in these recordings is highly classified and should be hidden from unauthorized viewers (e.g., monitoring staff). Solving such issues using current access control models is very hard as the content is not already defined. In reality, the authorization manager should be able to specify authorization rules and policies by stating the features of such agents or even providing their photos. For this reason, the authorization control core should be able to take the photo seized, extract its features, get similar target multimedia objects (identifying the faces of the agents in videos), and apply the restrictions upon them. Furthermore, due to the highly classified information to protect, the specification of roles based on user characteristics (e.g., job position = "major") is not sufficient all alone. Thus, devices, network characteristics, and particularly links between

agents are an equally important issue to consider for the specification of roles. For instance, let u be an agent in the governmental center. On the basis of his characteristics, u is assigned to the role officer 2 in the role hierarchy specified by the authorization manager. Due to the highly classified recording existing in the database, if u has accessed the database from unsecured connection, he should be granted less access than while accessing the database using a secured connection. In addition, u is married to a user s (assigned to the role officer 1) who works in the same department. In fact, officer 2 role is hierarchically linked to the role officer 1 thereafter inherits all its assigned permissions. Using his role officer 2, u is granted permission to view and save images showing secret agents. However, such permission is denied to the role officer 1 (for national security reasons) and thus users assigned to this role are not allowed to view these images. As we mentioned earlier, u is married to s and they live together in the same apartment. While working at home, s can benefit from the marital link existing with u and view some unauthorized images. This leads effectively to a breach of security in the role hierarchy set by the authorization manager. Therefore, the authorization and access model should grant the authorization manger the possibility to handle such situations and enforce policies while describing users based on their related information.

BACKGROUND

In this section, we will detail some of the work already done in the area of authorization and access control while revealing the need for a new full-fledged multimedia-oriented approach. In reality, authorization control models contain several common components to be addressed:

- **Subjects:** To whom the access is granted or denied. In fact, in the literature, subjects where referred to using different descriptions. They were defined as user identities, locations, credentials, roles, and so forth.

Figure 1. Restricted objects removed

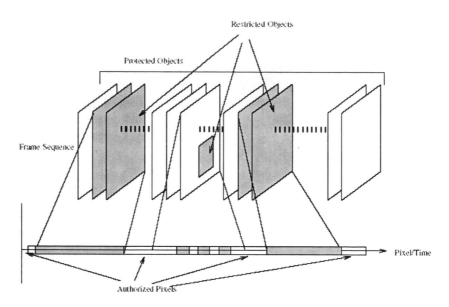

- **Objects:** Constitute elements to be protected against unauthorized access; they are related to the application domain in which the access control is applied.
- **Policies:** Defined for subjects upon objects, considered as a plan of action for controlling issues.
- **Actions:** To be performed (play, edit, etc.).
- **Conditions:** To be fulfilled based on contextual data (time > 19h:00, location = Paris, etc.).

In this chapter, we focus on presenting several research works already done in the area of objects, subjects, and action description. The other components are domain oriented and out of the scope of this chapter.

OBJECTS DESCRIPTION

In the literature, several approaches attempted to study object description in authorization and access control models (Adam et al., 2002; Bertino et al., 2002; Bertion et al., 2000; PICS, n.d.). In Bertino, et al. (2000), the authorization control model is designed to protect video objects based on user credentials and a textual content description of the video content. The designed model handles multimedia objects' protection on the basis of their textual annotations. In fact, the authors considered the fact that each video object (e.g., human face, car, building, etc.) and a video object occurrence have textual annotation that describe their semantic. For example, (x.annot contain "Charles De Gaulle") DURING (y.annot contain "World War II") which address all video objects x containing an annotation "Charles De Gaulle" and temporally fall during the video objects containing the annotation "World War II." The model was implemented on a school digital library where student and teacher access was to be controlled.

Similarly in Adam et al. (2002), object concept description was grouped into hierarchies along with the credentials to facilitate the management of rules and resolving conflicts. In fact, concepts determined are considered a set of key words describing the content of the multimedia object itself. In this work, the content of multimedia objects is controlled on the basis of the concepts determined. They have implemented their approach on the digital libraries environment of an international project for information interaction.

Whereas in MaX (Bertino et al., 2002), the proposed model integrated PICS (n.d.) in order to label the content of the digital libraries and addressed access and authorization control upon them based on these labels.

An interesting approach has been provided in Joshi, Li, Fahmi, Shafiq, and Ghafoor (2002) where a model based on military classifications (MAC) (Landwehr, 1981) has been designed to secure and protect a generalized OCPN [18] which is a synchronization graph for multimedia objects description. The authors used levels of classifications to label the target objects to be protected. Despite the fact that this approach looks interesting, MAC models are considered relevant and efficient when addressing textual objects but weak when addressing multimedia objects for polyinstantiation problem purposes (Abrams, Jajodia, & Podell, n.d.).

In Kodali, Farkas, and Wijesekera (2004a, 2004b), the authors addressed multimedia authorization and

access control by defining a secure platform for SMIL documents. In fact, they provided a normal form for these documents and annotated them with RDF metadata. These metadata served to describe the known security models such as MAC, RBAC, and DAC (Landwehr, 1981). However, the fact that multimedia objects can be broken down into several complex objects with unknown contents, such a model cannot effectively address their content protection.

On the other hand, standards such as XACML (n.d.) have been specified to address policy description issues. In fact, XACML provided the ability to describe complex policies. However, it is restrictive for multimedia objects. This is why another interesting approach described in Damiani, De Capitani di Vimercati, Fugazza, and Samarati (2004) has extended XACML to grant it the possibility to handle complex objects while specifying access policies. The approach proposed handles multimedia object protection using RDF ontology specification (see Figure 2), but considers the content of the multimedia objects as known. Thus, they have stated authorization rules based on the textual metadata that describe the objects in the concerned ontology.

As we can see in all these approaches and in others not mentioned here, the content of target objects

Figure 2. RDF metadata describing a video

```
<rdf:RDF
xmlns:rdf="http://www.w3.org/TR/WD-rdf-syntax#"
xmlns:md="http://ourdomain.it/MD/Schema/md-syntax#"
xmlns:ms="http://ourdomain.it/MS/Schema/ms-syntax#">
        <rdf:Description
        rdf:about="http://ourdomain.it/MD/Video/video010234.avi">
                <rdf:type rdf:resource="http://ourdomain.it/MD/
                Schema/md-syntax#Video" />
                <md:title>Treatment of Diseases</md:title>
                <md:duration>1054067</md:duration>
                <md:format>avi</md:format>
                <md:shows how rdf:nodeID="content"/>
        </rdf:Description>
        <rdf:Description rdf:nodeID="content">
                <ms:surgeon>Sam</ms:surgeon>
                <ms:operates on>Patient</ms:operates on>
        </rdf:Description>
</rdf:RDF>
```

has been widely considered as already known by the authorization manager. In fact, such models do not migrate well to fully address the protection of multimedia objects content because they allow specifying rules based on content's textual description which is restrictive when handling multimedia objects with unknown content description.

SUBJECT DESCRIPTION

Subjects have also been widely studied in access control models (Bertino, Castano, & Ferrari, 2001; Bertino, Ferrari, et al., 2002; Bertino, Hammad, et al.,2000; Damiani, De Capitani di Vimercati, Fernandez-Medina, & Samarati, 2002; Damiani, De Capitani di Vimercati, Paraboschi, & Samarati, 2000, 2002; Gabillon & Bruno, 2001; Joshi, Bhatti, Bertino, & Ghafoor, 2004; Joshi et al., 2002). To facilitate policy definition and management, they were replaced and represented by credentials (Adam et al.,

2002; Bertino et al., 2001; Bertino et al., 2000), user profiles (Damiani, De Capitani di Vimercati, Fugazza & Samarati, 2004), device description (Damiani, De Capitani di Vimercati, Paraboschi & Samarati 2000), and mainly by roles (Ferraiolo et al., 1999; Wang & Osborn, 2004).

In Adam et al. (2002), the authors have focused on describing subjects based on user's credentials representing a set of properties related to users and relevant for security systems (e.g., job function, age, etc.) To make policy management easier, the authors have defined a credential hierarchy (see Figure 3).

In Damiani, De Capitani di Vimercati, Fernández-Medina & Samarati (2002), subjects are identified on the basis of user's profiles in which they considered user characteristics as the basis for user specification. Thus, the authors did not detail the user profile description but only talked about user characteristics, which is considered limited when addressing high level security issues. Furthermore, their model lacks the ability of representing a subjects' hierarchy to facilitate

Figure 3. Credential hierarchy definition in [20]

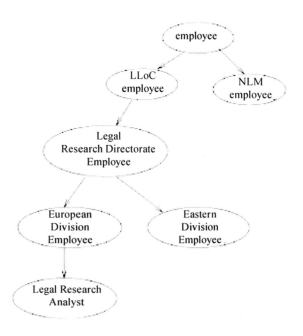

the administration to the authorization manager. In fact, user profile usually refers to a set of preferences or characteristics representing the user in question. On the basis of such characteristics, systems will be able to consider users' related information (e.g., device characteristics, network properties, interests, etc.) when performing several tasks (e.g., multimedia presentation and browsing, information protection, intrusion detection, etc.). Profiles reflect users and their environments where for each situation a user may have an instance of his profile. Profile instances may be effectively related when certain common information remains intact in each of these instances (e.g., user with several devices). Several researchers proposed to study a user's profile. Standardized norms such as CC/PP (n.d.) and CSCP (Buchholz, Hamann, & Hübsch, 2004), have been defined for the representation of profiles and the ease of identification process. Languages such as RDF have been used to ease the description of the different components in a profile. Our main concern in user profiling is when addressing information security. In fact, we consider that when more information about users is available a larger number of security constraints could be stated.

Several role-based access control (RBAC) approaches have also been provided in the literature to cover and facilitate subjects' management (Joshi et al., 2004; Wang & Osborn, 2004). With RBAC, access decision is based on the roles that users occupy in an organization. These users are assigned to roles on the basis of their job function in the organization. Operations that a user is permitted to perform are limited to their assigned roles, whereas the defined concept of user-role association gives the user the minimum privilege required to perform their job. Due to the highly classified information to protect in several multimedia domains, current role descriptions, subjects' credentials, and characteristics are restrictive to fully cover the policy specification for subjects' management. In essence, data authorization and access purposes in several multimedia applications need to handle subjects' management with higher precision, particularly the user should be represented on the basis of their contextual information and not only on their identity, credentials, or job function.

Actions

Actions in an access control model represent the tasks to be performed and managed in order to guarantee an authorized manipulation of existing information. In the literature, actions were defined differently on the basis of the application domain in which an access control model is applied. In essence, access control models (Bertino et al., 2001; Damiani et al., 2000; Damiani et al., 2002; Gabillon & Bruno, 2001; Wang & Osborn, 2004) define the set of actions that might be included in the access request:

- Read is defined when subjects need to view a set of textual objects and their content
- Write is defined when subjects need to update a set of textual objects
- And so forth

Thus, when addressing multimedia objects, new actions are introduced such as play, synchronize, resume, pause, modify, and so forth. Each handled and processed differently:

- Play is defined when subjects need to browse or activate a certain multimedia objects such as an image, sound file, or a video scene
- Synchronize is the action where a set of multimedia objects are played in a special order (e.g., two video scenes played in parallel, etc.)
- And so forth

PROPOSAL

Our approach consists of designing new components able to fully consider the rich content of multimedia objects. It particularly allows designing policies on the basis of object features. Furthermore, it extends the widely used RBAC model (Ferraiolo et al., 1999) to address role specification according to user context. In the following, we will describe the main component of our approach by revealing user concepts such as user model, role model, rule model, policy model, and link model.

User Model

As mentioned earlier, additional user related-information must be considered when defining authorization and access policies. Various methods and techniques are provided in the literature in different areas and by various scientific communities to represent user-related information commonly named user model or user profile (CCPP [n.d.], CSCP [Buchholz, Hamann, & Hübsch, 2004], MPEG-21 [Burnett, Van de Walle, Hill, Bormans, & Pereira, 2003], etc.). In our approach, the User Model (UM) is formally defined as:

$$UM: (id_{UM}, Cred^{*}, Int^{*}, S_M^{*}, id_D)$$

where:

- id_{UM}: is the identifier of the user.
- *Cred*: is the credential component containing a user attribute related to the application domain (e.g., age, profession, studies, etc.). It can be written as: $(a_1:v_1, a_2:v_2...)$ where a_i and v_i represent an attribute and its corresponding value (e.g., age: 18, profession: student, etc.)
- *Int*: describes a user interest. It can be written as: $(a_1:(v_1,w_1)^{*}, a_2:(v_2,w_2)^{*} ...)$ where a_i represents an attribute such as subjectsOfInterests and $(v_i,w_i)^{*}$ represent the set of values and their weights[1] which determine the degree of importance of its corresponding value for the specified attribute, such as (Football,0.5), (NBA,0.4), and so forth.
- S_M: contains a device feature such as the device name, its operating system, its manufacturer, IP address, and so forth. It can also be written as $(a_1:v_1, a_2:v_2...)$. For instance, Operating_System: Linux, firewall:Cisco, and so forth.
- id_D: is the identifier of the duration component during which the user model has been created. We formalize the *duration* as follows:

$$Duration: (id_D, type, [t_1 t_2], desc, id_{ev}^{*})$$

where:

- id_D: is the identifier of the duration.
- *type*: is the type to be described (e.g., time, date, etc.).
- $[t_1,t_2]$: represents the start and the end values related to the type specified (e.g., In case of a type ="Time" the interval will be [12:00 04:00]).
- *desc*: is a textual description of the duration.
- id_{ev}: represents the identifier of the event defined in the interval specified. In fact, the event component is formalized as follows:

$$Event: (id_{ev}, name, desc)$$

where:

- id_{ev}: is the identifier of the event.
- *name*: represents the name of the event.
- *desc*: represents the textual description of the event.

This model allows representing into the same structure the contents of current user-related information models. In essence, this component is important for subjects' specification due to the rich information description provided. Attributes and values of such components can serve as a basis for role designing and description.

Rule Model

A rule is the basic element of our authorization and access control model. A rule is considered as a 5-tuple of the following form:

$$(Id_{RU}, F_i^{*}, Action^{*}, Condition^{*}, Effect)$$

where:

- Id_{RU}: is the identifier of the rule.
- F_i: is an object feature. To describe it, we used some components (O, A, V) of the metamodel

M² provided in Chalhoub, Saad, Chbeir, and Yetongnon (2004). We briefly detail them here below:

- o   O: represents the raw data of the object (image, video, or audio) stored as a BLOB file or URI.
- o   A: represents the metadata describing the multimedia objects. It integrates:
    - ➢ Data directly associated with the objects such as the compression format (mpeg, mp3, jpg, etc.), size, and so forth.
    - ➢ Data independent of the objects content such as the name of the object owner, date, and so forth.
    - ➢ Data describing the semantic content of a multimedia object such as annotations, scene descriptions, keywords, and so forth.
- o   V: describes the physical content of a multimedia object (such as color histogram, color distribution, texture histogram, shapes, duration, audio frequency, amplitude, band no., etc.).
- •   *Action:* is the action to be performed upon the objects.
- •   *Condition*[2]*:* is a condition to be satisfied (e.g., time > 8 PM). Here, the condition can also be based on testing the existence of different types of links between our models components. This will help in avoiding security breaches in several cases.
- •   *Effect*: is the status of the rule. It is usually described as grant or deny.

This representation of a rule model allows for protecting multimedia objects according to a set of features (e.g., image of the agent, shape, etc.) provided manually or automatically by the authorization manager. In particular, our rule model provides protection when handling multimedia objects with no annotations. Due to such representation, it is possible to apply similarity functions to determine the objects to be protected in the target multimedia database.

Policy Model

Policies are considered one of the important issues to handle in the domain of authorization control models. Several researchers have worked in this area (Damiani et al., 2004; De Capitani di Vimercati & Samarati, 2005) to cover the related issues on policies, their evolution, and the way they should be manipulated. In our approach, a policy is considered as a set of rules assigned to a specified role. It is formally written as:

$$Policy: (Id_p, Id_{Rule}{}^*, status, desc)$$

where:

- • Id_p: is the identifier of the policy.
- • Id_{Rule}: is the identifier of the rule represented by the policy.
- •   *status*: specifies the status of the policy such as open policy or a closed one. In fact, in case of an open policy, we consider that the default effect specified in the set of rules is deny and grant for none specified, while it is the contrary for the closed policies.
- •   *desc*: is the textual description of the specified policy.

Our policy model considers all requirements of current methods and thus is able to represent most of them.

Link Model

In our approach, typed links can be defined between either Id_u, Id_R, or Id_p where Id_u is the user model identifier, the Id_R is the role identifier, and Id_p is the policy identifier. Link values can be computed automatically regarding other node components, or given manually by the authorization manager. It can formally be written as:

$$Link = (Id_L, Type, Desc, Weight, St_{Node}{}^*, End_{Node}{}^*)$$

where:

- *Id_L:* is the identifier of the link.
- *Type:* represents the type of the link such as hierarchical, parental, friendship, marital, similarity, and so forth. This will allow, for instance, creating a taxonomy between nodes when using hierarchical links, or creating clusters of similar nodes (to group user, roles or even policies) when using similarity links.
- *Desc:* is a textual representation of the link.
- *Weight:* is a value in [0, 1] describing the importance of the link in security breaches. For instance, the links of inheritance, conflict, and assignment types might have a weight of value 0, while a parental link has to be more weighted than friendship.
- *St_{Node}:* represents the start node which belongs either to *Id_u*, *Id_R*, or *Id_p*.
- *End_{Node}:* represents the end node which also belongs either to *Id_u*, *Id_R*, or *Id_p*.

Our link model allows for representing various types of links and thus tracking several security breaches. It provides, for instance, the possibility to represent authorization abuse in hierarchical linked roles while considering the different links that might exist between users of these roles. Whereas, the authorization manager has the possibility to enforce authorization system decisions with regards to the degree of authorization breach that might be caused due to such links. In Figure 4, we give an example of different links that might exist between roles. We can observe that an authorization breach can be identified due to the marital link of positive weight α established between a user of the role officer 1 and a user of the role officer 2. This representation of links will also allow easy resolving of security conflicts. However, this issue is out of the scope of this chapter.

CONCLUSION

In this chapter, we described some of the existing approaches that handle access and authorization control becoming indispensable with the increasing danger of cyber terrorism attacks on information systems. We presented the main components of access and authorization control models such as subjects, objects, actions, and so forth. We pointed out the different forms that define subjects in the literature (user id, location, credentials, profiles, etc.) and the importance of using user profiles for a full-fledged subject representation in information security. We showed how object definition has been addressed and highlighted the fact that only textual based policy specification can be handled in

Figure 4. Links between different components of our authorization model

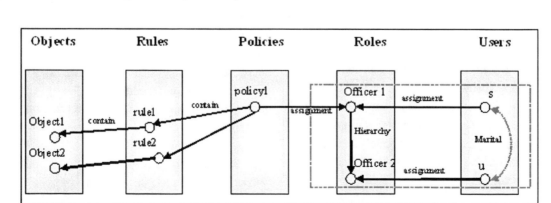

current approaches. In essence, almost all approaches proposed in the literature do not migrate well to handle full multimedia oriented access control and authorization issues where multimedia object protection should be based on the object content (shape, color, texture, etc.) and not only on their textual description. We also presented our model to handle full multimedia oriented access control and authorization issues where multimedia object protection is based on the object content (shape, color, relations, etc.) and not only on their textual description. Our approach is required for the protection of multimedia objects in applications where unknown content description and real-time data stream flow. Furthermore, it extends the RBAC model by providing further concepts and possibilities enabling the authorization manager to easily define policy and detect a breach of security when it occurs.

We are currently working on a prototype to provide a fine-grained access control to multimedia objects in which we implement the models described in this chapter.

In the near future, we plan to add to our model the possibility to handle security issues in a distributed environment where policy management becomes complex due to the several physical domains on which the objects are stored. We also plan to add a real-time conflict resolution unit to handle policy specification and a link detection unit to handle the link detection for weights greater than 0 and thereafter eliminate security breaches.

REFERENCES

Abrams, M. D., & Jajodia, S., & Podell, H. J. (1995, February). *Information security: An integrated collection of essays* (Essay 21, p. 768). Los Alamitos, CA: IEEE Computer Society Press.

Adam, N. R., Atluri, V., Bertino, E., & Ferrari, E. (2002). A content-based authorization model for digital libraries. *IEEE Transactions Knowledge and Data Engineering, 14*(2), 296-315.

Bertino, E., Castano, S., & Ferrari, E. (2001). Securing XML documents with author-X. *IEEE Internet Computing, 5*(3), 21.

Bertino, E., Ferrari, E., & Perego, A. (2002). MaX: An access control system for digital libraries and the web. *COMPSAC 2002,* 945-950.

Bertino, E., Hammad, M., Aref, W. G., & Elmagarmid, A. K.(2000). Access control model for video database systems. *Proceedings of the 9th International Conference on Information Knowledge Management, CIKM* (pp. 336-343).

Buchholz, S., Hamann, Th. & Hübsch, G. (2004). Comprehensive Structured Context Profiles (CSCP): Design and Experiences. In *Proceedings of PerCom Workshops* (pp. 43-47).

Burnett, I., Van de Walle, R., Hill, K., Bormans, J., & Pereira, F. (2003). MPEG-21: Goals and achievements. *IEEE MultiMedia, 10*(4), 6070.

CC/PP. (n.d.). *Composite capability/preference profiles.* http://www.w3.org/Mobile/CCPP

Chalhoub, G., Saad, S., Chbeir, R., & Yétongnon, K. (2004). Towards fully functional distributed multimedia DBMS. *Journal of Digital Information Management (JDIM), 2*(3), 116-121.

Damiani, E., De Capitani di Vimercati, S., Fernández-Medina, E., & Samarati, P. (2002). Access control of SVG documents. *DBSec 2002,* 219-230.

Damiani, E., De Capitani di Vimercati, S., Fugazza, C., & Samarati, P. (2004). Extending policy languages to the Semantic Web. *ICWE 2004,* 330-343.

Damiani, E., De Capitani di Vimercati, S., Paraboschi, S., & Samarati, P. (2000). Securing XML documents. *EDBT 2000,* 121-135.

Damiani, E., De Capitani di Vimercati, S., Paraboschi, S., & Samarati, P. (2002). A fine-grained access control system for XML documents. *ACM Transactions on Information and System Security (TISSEC), 5*(2), 169-202.

De Capitani di Vimercati, S., & Samarati, P. (2005). *New directions in access control, in cyberspace security and defense: Research issues.* Kluwer Academic Publisher.

Ferraiolo, D. F., Barkley, J. F., & Kuhn, D. R. (1999). A role-based access control model and reference implementation within a corporate intranet. *ACM Transactions on Information and System Security, 2*(1), 34-64.

Gabillon, A., & Bruno, E. (2001). *Regulating access to XML documents. Proceedings of the 15th Annual IFIP WG 11.3 Working Conference on Database and Application Security,* Niagara on the Lake, Ontario, Canada (pp. 299-314).

Joshi, J., Bhatti, R., Bertino, E., & Ghafoor, A. (2004). Access-control language for multidomain environments. *IEEE Internet Computing, 8*(6), 40-50.

Joshi, J., Li, K., Fahmi, H., Shafiq, C., & Ghafoor, A. (2002). A model for secure multimedia document database system in a distributed environment. *IEEE Transactions on Multimedia: Special Issue of on Multimedia Datbases, 4*(2), 215-234.

Kodali, N. B., Farkas, C., & Wijesekera, D. (2004a). An authorization model for multimedia digital libraries (Special Issue on Security). *Journal of Digital Libraries, 4*(3), 139-155.

Kodali, N. B., Farkas, C., & Wijesekera, D. (2004b). Specifying multimedia access control using RDF (Special Issue on Trends in XML Technology). *International Journal of Computer Systems, Science and Engineering, 19*(3), 129-141.

Landwehr, C. E. (1981). Formal models of computer security. *ACM Comput. Surv., 13*(3), 247-278.

PICS. (n.d.). *Platform for internet content selection.* http://www.w3.org/pics/

Wang, J., & Osborn, S. L. (2004). A role-based approach to access control for XML databases. *SACMAT 2004*, 70-77.

XACML. (n.d.). *eXtensible access control markup language.* http://www.oasis-open.org/committees/tc_home.php?wg_abbrev=xacml

TERMS AND DEFINITIONS

Authorization: Represents the process to decide whether a subject (as defined in the literature) is allowed to access certain information.

Composite Capabilities/Preference Profiles (CC/PP): A set of devices, characteristics, and user preferences designed with RDF language and able to support devices when addressing multimedia adaptation.

Comprehensive Structured Context Profiles (CSCP): A representation language for context information in which a dynamic profile is created in order to describe relatively complex information. CSCP overcomes the deficits of CC/PP by providing support for a full flexibility RDF to express natural structures of context information. (Buchholz, Hamann, & Hübsch, 2004)

Discretionary Access Control (DAC): Represents the basic access control for objects in information systems where objects are addressed based on their identities and the users need-to-know . For example granting *read* and *alter* operations to user *x* upon the table *employee* in a relational database.

Mandatory Access Control (MAC): A technique for information protection and classification replacing the DAC model. Information and users are labeled based on defined levels of security (public, classified, secret, top secret, etc.). Based on these labels, users are granted access.

Platform for Internet Content Selection (PICS): A platform created by W3C and used for content labeling and annotation of Web pages. It associates labels with Internet content.

Resource Description Framework (RDF): Language for resource description of the form subject-predicate-object expression, called a triple in RDF terminology. It was proposed by the W3C where software can store, exchange, and manipulate the metadata described for the different resources of the Web.

Role Based Access Control (RBAC): An approach to restricting system access to authorized users. In fact, users and policies are assigned to a set of hierarchically linked roles (job function they occupy). Role-based approach is considered effective due to the possibility of managing both MAC and DAC.

Synchronized Multimedia Integration Language (SMIL): Used to describe and synchronize multimedia representations. It is based on the well known Extensible Markup Language and is basically similar to an HTML file from the structure side.

ENDNOTES

[1]   *means a set of.

[2]   Weight is a value $\in [0, 1]$.

[3]   As described in the role model section

Chapter XLI
Data Mining

Mark Last
Ben-Gurion University of the Negev, Israel

ABSTRACT

Data mining is a growing collection of computational techniques for automatic analysis of structured, semi-structured, and unstructured data with the purpose of identifying important trends and previously unknown behavioral patterns. Data mining is widely recognized as the most important and central technology for homeland security in general and for cyber warfare in particular. This chapter covers the following relevant areas of data mining:

- *Web mining is the application of data mining techniques to web-based data. While Web usage mining is already used by many intrusion detection systems, Web content mining can lead to automated identification of terrorist-related content on the Web.*
- *Web information agents are responsible for filtering and organizing unrelated and scattered data in large amounts of web documents. Agents represent a key technology to cyber warfare due to their capability to monitor multiple diverse locations, communicate their findings asynchronously, collaborate with each other, and profile possible threats.*
- *Anomaly detection and activity monitoring. Real-time monitoring of continuous data streams can lead to timely identification of abnormal, potentially criminal activities. Anomalous behavior can be automatically detected by a variety of data mining methods.*

INTRODUCTION

Data mining (DM) is a rapidly growing collection of computational techniques for automatic analysis of structured, semi-structured, and unstructured data with the purpose of identifying various kinds of previously unknown behavioral patterns. According to Mena (2004), data mining is widely recognized as the most important and central technology for homeland security in general and for cyber warfare in particular. This relatively new field emerged in the beginning of the 1990s as a combination of methods and algorithms from statistics, pattern recognition, and machine learning. The difference between data mining and knowledge discovery in databases (KDD) is defined by as follows: data mining refers to the application of pattern extraction algorithms to data, while KDD is the overall process of "identifying valid, novel, potentially useful, and ultimately understandable patterns in data" (Fayyad, Piatetsky-Shapiro & Smyth, 1996, p. 6). The complete KDD process includes such stages as data selection; data cleaning and pre-processing; data reduction and transformation; choosing data mining tasks, methods and tools; data mining (searching for patterns of ultimate interest); interpretation of data mining results; and action upon discovered knowledge.

BACKGROUND

Tens of computational techniques related to various data mining tasks emerged over the last 15 years. Selected examples of some common data mining tasks and algorithms will be briefly described.

Association rules: Association rule mining is aimed at finding interesting association or correlation relationships among a large set of data items (Han & Kamber, 2001). The extracted patterns (association rules) usually have the form "if event X occurs, then event Y is likely." Events X and Y may represent items bought in a purchase transaction, documents viewed in a user session, medical symptoms of a given patient, and many other phenomena recorded in a database over time. Extracted rules are evaluated by two main parameters: *support*, which is the probability that a transaction contains both X and Y and *confidence*, which is the conditional probability that a transaction having X also contains Y. Scalable algorithms, such as *Apriori* (Srikant & Agrawal, 1996), have been developed for mining association rules in large databases containing millions of multi-item transactions.

Cluster analysis: A *cluster* is a collection of data objects (e.g., Web documents) that are similar to each other within the same cluster, while being dissimilar to the objects in any other cluster (Han & Kamber, 2001). One of the most important goals of cluster analysis is to discover *hidden patterns*, which characterize groups of seemingly unrelated objects (transactions, individuals, documents, etc.). Clustering of "normal walks of life" can also serve as a basis for the task of *anomaly detection*: an outlier, which does not belong to any normal cluster, may be an indication of abnormal, potentially malicious behavior (Last & Kandel, 2005, chap. 4 & 6). A survey of leading clustering methods is presented in *Data Clustering: A Reveiw* (Jain, Murty, & Flynn, 1999).

Predictive modeling: The task of *predictive modeling* is to predict (anticipate) future outcomes of some complex, hardly understandable processes based on automated analysis of historic data. Predicting future behaviors (especially attacks) of terrorist and other malicious groups is an example of such task. Han and Kamber (2001) refer to prediction of continuous values as *prediction*, while prediction of nominal class labels (e.g., terrorist vs. non-terrorist documents) is regarded by them as *classification*. Common classification models include ANN—Artificial Neural Networks (Mitchell, 1997), decision trees (Quinlan, 1993), Bayesian networks (Mitchell, 1997), IFN—Info-Fuzzy Networks (Last & Maimon, 2004), and so forth.

Visual data mining: *Visual data mining* is the process of discovering implicit but useful knowledge from large data sets using visualization techniques. Since "a picture is worth a thousand words," the human eye can identify patterns, trends, structure, irregularities, and relationships among data much faster in a representative landscape than in a spreadsheet. Scatter plots, boxplots, and frequency histograms are examples of techniques used by descriptive data mining. Last and Kandel (1999) use the concepts of fuzzy set theory to automate the process of human perception based on pre-defined objective parameters.

This chapter will cover in depth several application areas of data mining in the cyber warfare and cyber terrorism domain, namely: Web mining, Web information agents, and anomaly detection (closely related to activity monitoring).

WEB MINING

The military pressure put on the al-Qaeda leadership in Afganistan after 9/11 has dramatically increased the role of the Internet in the infrastructure of global terrorist organizations (Corera, 2004). In terrorism expert Peter Bergen's words:

They lost their base in Afghanistan, they lost their training camps, they lost a government that allowed them do what they want within a country. Now they're surviving on internet to a large degree. It is really their new base (ibid).

Beyond propaganda and ideology, jihadist sites seem to be heavily used for practical training in kidnapping, explosive preparation, and other "core" terrorist activities, which were once taught in Afghan training camps. The former U.S. Deputy Defense Secretary Paul D. Wolfowitz, in a testimony before the House Armed Services Committee, called such Web sites "cyber sanctuaries" (Lipton & Lichtblau, 2004). Of course, al-Qaeda is not the sole source of terror-related Web sites. According to a recent estimate, the total number of such Web sites has increased from only 12 in 1997 to around 4,300 in 2005 (Talbot, 2005).

Due to the extent of Internet usage by terrorist organizations, cyber space has become a valuable source of information on terrorists current activities and intentions (Last & Kandel, 2005, chap. 1 & 2). In this new kind of war, frequently called the "cyber war" or the "web war," homeland security agencies face a variety of extremely difficult challenges (Mena, 2004). Terrorist organizations can post their information on the Web at any location (Web server), in any form (Web page, Internet forum posting, chat room communication, e-mail message, etc.), and in any language. Moreover, they can take that information off-line within hours or even minutes. Accurate and timely identification of such material in the midst of massive Web traffic is by far the most challenging task currently faced by the intelligence community.

Furthermore, homeland security analysts are interested in identifying who is behind the posted material, what links they might have to active terror groups, and what threat, if any, they might pose. They would also like to identify temporal trends in terrorist-related content and track down the "target audience" of individual and public online messages. The current number of known terrorist sites is so large that a continuous manual analysis of their multilingual content is definitely out of the question. This is why the automated *Web mining* approach is so important for the cyber war against international terror.

Most common Web mining tasks can be divided into three different categories: *Web usage, Web structure*, and *Web content mining*. The main goal of Web usage mining is to gather information about Web system users and to examine the relationships between Web pages from the user point of view. Web usage mining methods include mining access logs to find common usage patterns of Web pages, calculating page ratings, and so forth. Many intrusion detection systems are routinely using Web usage mining techniques to spot potential intruders among normal Web users. In Web structure mining, the usual aim is to extract some useful information about a document by examining its hyperlinks to other documents. More sophisticated *link analysis* techniques, combined with information extraction (IE) tools, can discover other types of links between unstructured documents such as links between locations, organizations, and individuals (Mena, 2004). As shown by Ben-Dov, Wu, Feldman, and Cairns (2004), these techniques can reveal complex terrorist networks.

Applying data mining algorithms to the content of Web documents in order to generate an efficient representation of content patterns (such as patterns of terror-related pages) is a typical application of Web content mining. Traditional information retrieval and Web mining methods represent textual documents with a *vector-space model*, which utilizes a series of numeric values associated with each document. Each value is associated with a specific key word or key phrase that may appear in a document. However, this popular method of document representation does not capture important structural information, such as the order and proximity of term occurrence or the location of a term within the document. This structural information may be critical for a text categorization system, which is required to make an accurate distinction between terrorist pages (such as guidelines for preparing future terrorist attacks) and normal pages (which may be news reports about terrorist attacks in the past). Both types of pages may include nearly the same set of key words, though their structure could be radically different.

Last, Markov, and Kandel (2006) describe an advanced graph-based methodology for multilingual detection of terrorist documents. The proposed approach is evaluated on a collection of 648 Web documents in Arabic. The results demonstrate that documents downloaded from several known terrorist sites can be reliably discriminated from the content of Arabic news reports using a simple decision tree.

Most Web content mining techniques assume a static nature of the Web content. This approach is inadequate for long-term monitoring of Web traffic, since both the users interests and the content of most Web sites are subject to continuous changes over time. Timely detection of an ongoing trend in certain Web content may trigger periodic retraining of the data-mining algorithm. In addition, the characteristics of the trend itself (e.g., an increased occurrence of certain key phrases) may indicate some important changes in the online behavior of the monitored Web site and its users. Chang, Healey, McHugh, and Wang (2001) have proposed several methods for change and trend detection in dynamic Web content, where a trend is recognized by a change in frequency of certain *topics* over a period of time. Another trend discovery system for mining dynamic content of news Web sites is presented by Mendez-Torreblanca, Montes-y-Gomez, and Lopez-Lopez (2002). A novel, fuzzy-based method for identifying short-term and long-term trends in dynamic Web content is proposed by Last (2005).

WEB INFORMATION AGENTS

An *intelligent software agent* is an autonomous program designed to perform a human-like function over a network or the Internet. Specifically, information agents are responsible for filtering and organizing unrelated and scattered data such as large amounts of unstructured Web documents. Agents represent a key technology to homeland security due to their capability to monitor multiple diverse locations, communicate their findings asynchronously, collaborate with each other, analyze conditions, issue real-time alerts, and profile possible threats (Mena, 2004).

Autonomous information agents is the evolving solution to the problem of inaccurate and incomplete search indexes (Cesarano, d'Acierno, & Picariello, 2003; Klusch, 2001; Pant, Srinivasan, & Menczer (2004; Yu, Koo, & Liddy (2000). The basic idea of the search agent technology is to imitate the behavior of an expert user by submitting a query to several search engines in parallel, determining automatically the relevancy of retrieved pages, and then following the most promising links from those pages. The process goes on using the links on the new pages until the agent resources are exhausted, there are no more pages to browse, or the system objectives are reached (Pant et al., 2004).

Intelligent information agents can be classified in several ways (Klusch, 2001). They can be either *cooperative* or *non-cooperative* with each other. Agent functionality is usually based on a set of information processing rules that may be explicitly specified by the user, acquired by a knowledge engineer, or induced by data mining algorithms. Most popular data mining techniques used by information agent systems include artificial neural networks, genetic algorithms, reinforcement learning, and case-based reasoning. Agents can also be *adaptive*, that is, continue to learn from the environment and change their behavior accordingly. According to Klusch (2001), any information agent should possess the following key capabilities: access to heterogeneous sites and resources on the Web (from static pages to Web-based applications), retrieving and filtering data from any kind of digital medium (including documents written in any language and multimedia information), processing of ontological knowledge (e.g., expressed by semantic networks), and information visualization.

ANOMALY DETECTION AND ACTIVITY MONITORING

In *activity monitoring*, analysis of data streams is applied in order to detect the interesting behavior occurring which are referred to as a "positive activity." Positive activities should be different from each other and should be different from the non-positive monitored activities. Indication of a positive activity is called an alarm (Fawcett & Provost, 1999). There exist many applications that use activity monitoring such as computer intrusion detection, fraud detection, crisis monitoring, network performance monitoring, and news story monitoring. The representation of the input in these applications might be completely different from each other. The input data can be, for example, a feature vector, a collection of documents, and a stream of numbers. In activity monitoring the goal is to issue an accurate alarm on time. In order to address this goal, data mining techniques like classification regression and time series analysis are applied.

Anomaly detection relies on models of the intended behavior of users and applications and interprets deviations from this "normal" behavior as evidence of malicious (e.g., terrorist-related) activity (Kruegel & Vigna, 2003). This approach is complementary with respect to signature-based detection, where a number of attack descriptions (usually in the form of signatures) are matched against the stream of input data, looking for evidence that one of the expected attacks (e.g., a known computer virus) is taking place. The basic assumption underlying anomaly detection is that attack patterns differ from normal behavior.

There are two main stages in anomaly detection. In the first stage, a representation of the "normal" behavior is obtained by applying some data mining algorithms to examples of normal behavior. In the second stage, events different from the "normal" behavior are detected and classified as suspected to be malicious. Most intrusion detection systems that use anomaly detection (Sequeira & Zaki, 2002) monitor user actions and operations rather than content accessed by the users as an audit source.

In Elovici, Kandel et al. (2004) and Elovici, Shapira et al. (2005), a Terrorist Detection System (TDS) is presented aimed at tracking down suspected terrorists by analyzing the content of information they access on the Web. The system operates in two modes: the training mode is activated off-line, and the detection mode is operated in real-time. In the training mode, TDS is provided with Web pages of normal users from which it derives their normal behavior profile by applying data mining (clustering) algorithms to the training data. In the detection mode, TDS performs real-time monitoring of the traffic emanating from the monitored group of users, analyzes the content of the Web pages they access, and generates an alarm if a user accesses abnormal information, that is, the content of the information accessed is "very" dissimilar to the typical content in the monitored environment.

CONCLUSION

This chapter has briefly covered the wide potential of employing data mining and Web mining techniques as cyber warfare tools in the global campaign against terrorists who are using cyber space for their malicious interests. It is important to understand that applications of data mining technology to cyber warfare are in no way limited to the methods covered in this chapter. We believe that as computers become more powerful and Web users become better connected to each other we will see more information technologies aiding in the war on terror, along with a higher level of technological sophistication exposed by cyber terrorists. Examples of promising directions in the future of cyber warfare research include cross-lingual Web content mining, real-time data and Web mining, distributed data mining, and many others.

REFERENCES

Ben-Dov, M., Wu, W., Feldman, R., & Cairns, P. A. (2004). Improving knowledge discovery by combining text-mining and link analysis techniques. *Workshop on Link Analysis, Counter-Terrorism, and Privacy, in Conjunction with SIAM International Conference on Data Mining.*

Cesarano, C., d'Acierno, A., & Picariello, A. (2003, November 7-8). An intelligent search agent system for semantic information retrieval on the internet. *Proceedings of the Fifth ACM International Workshop on Web Information and Data Management,* New Orleans, LA (pp. 111-117).

Chang, G., Healey, M. J., McHugh, J. A. M., & Wang, J. T. L. (2001). *Mining the World Wide Web: An information search approach.* Norwell, MA: Kluwer Academic Publishers.

Corera, G. (2004, October 6). Web wise terror network. *BBC NEWS.* Retrieved October 9, 2004, from http://news.bbc.co.uk/go/pr/fr/-/1/hi/world/3716908.stm

Elovici, Y., Kandel, A., Last, M., Shapira, B., Zaafrany, O., Schneider, M., & Friedman, M. (2004). Terrorist detection system. *Proceedings of the 8th European Conference on Principles and Practice of Knowledge Discovery in Databases (PKDD 2004),* Pisa, Italy (LN in Artificial Intelligence 3202, pp. 540-542). Springer-Verlag.

Elovici, Y., Shapira, B., Last, M., Zaafrany, O., Friedman, M., Schneider, M., & Kandel, A. (2005, May 19-20). Content-based detection of terrorists browsing the web using an advanced terror detection system (ATDS). *Proceedings of the IEEE International Conference on Intelligence and Security Informatics (IEEE ISI-2005),* Atlanta, GA (pp. 244-255).

Fawcett, T. & Provost, F. (1999). Activity monitoring: Noticing interesting changes in behavior. *Proceedings of the Fifth ACM SIGKDD International Conference on Knowledge Discovery and Data Mining,* San Diego, CA (pp. 53-62).

Fayyad, U., Piatetsky-Shapiro, G., & Smyth, P. (1996). From data mining to knowledge discovery: An overview. In U. Fayyad, G. Piatetsky-Shapiro, P. Smyth, & R. Uthurusamy (Eds.), *Advances in knowledge discovery and data mining* (pp. 134). Menlo Park, CA: AAAI/MIT Press.

Han, J., & Kamber, M. (2001). *Data mining: Concepts and techniques.* Morgan Kaufmann.

Jain, A. K., Murty, M. N., & Flynn, P. J. (1999). Data clustering: A review. *ACM Computing Surveys, 31*(3), 264-323.

Klusch, M. (2001). Information agent technology for the internet: A survey [Special Issue on Intelligent Information Integration. D. Fensel (Ed.)]. *Journal on Data and Knowledge Engineering, 36*(3), 337-372.

Kruegel, C., & Vigna, G. (2003, October 27-31). Anomaly detection of web-based attacks. *Proceedings of the 10th ACM Conference on Computer and Communications Security (CCS'03),* Washington, DC (pp. 251-261).

Last, M. (2005). Computing temporal trends in web documents. *Proceedings of the Fourth Conference of the European Society for Fuzzy Logic and Technology (EUSFLAT 2005)* (pp. 615-620).

Last, M., & Kandel, A. (1999). Automated perceptions in data mining. *Proceedings of the 1999 IEEE International Fuzzy Systems Conference, Part I* (pp. 190-197).

Last, M., & Kandel, A. (2005). Fighting terror in cyberspace. *Singapore: World Scientific, Series in Machine Perception and Artificial Intelligence, Vol. 65.*

Last, M., & Maimon, O. (2004). A compact and accurate model for classification. *IEEE Transactions on Knowledge and Data Engineering, 16*(2), 203215.

Last, M., Markov, A., & Kandel, A. (2006, April 9). Multi-lingual detection of terrorist content on the web. *Proceedings of the PAKDD'06 Workshop on Intelligence and Security Informatics (WISI'06),* Singapore (LN in Computer Science, Vol. 3917) (pp. 16-30). Springer

Lipton, E., & Lichtblau, E. (2004, September 23). Even near home, a new front is opening in the terror battle. *The New York Times.*

Mena, J. (2004). *Homeland security techniques and technologies.* Charles River Media.

Mendez-Torreblanca, A., Montes-y-Gomez, M., & Lopez-Lopez, A. (2002). A trend discovery system for dynamic web content mining. *Proceedings of CIC-2002.*

Mitchell, T. M. (1997). *Machine learning.* McGraw-Hill.

Pant, G., Srinivasan, P., & Menczer, F. (2004). Crawling the web. In M. Levene & A. Poulovassilis (Eds.), *Web dynamics.* Springer.

Quinlan, J. R. (1993). *C4.5: Programs for machine learning.* Morgan Kaufmann.

Sequeira, K. & Zaki, M. (2002). ADMIT: Anomaly-based data mining for intrusions. *Proceedings of the Eighth ACM SIGKDD International Conference on Knowledge Discovery and Data Mining* (pp. 386-395).

Srikant, R. & Agrawal, R. (1996). Mining quantitative association rules in large relational tables. *Proceedings of the 1996 ACM SIGMOD International Conference on Management of Data,* Montreal, Quebec, Canada (pp. 1-12).

Talbot, D. (2005, February). Terror's server. *Technology Review.* Retrieved March 17, 2005, from http://www.technologyreview.com/articles/05/02/issue/feature_terror.asp

Yu, E. S., Koo, P. C., & Liddy, E. D. (2000). Evolving intelligent text-based agents. *Proceedings of the Fourth International Conference on Autonomous agents,* Barcelona, Spain (pp. 388-395).

KEY TERMS

Activity Monitoring: The process of monitoring the behavior of a large population of entities for interesting events requiring action (Fawcett & Provost, 1999).

Anomaly Detection: The process of detecting anomalies (irregularities that cannot be explained by existing domain models and knowledge) by monitoring system activity and classifying it as either normal or anomalous.

Data Mining: The process of applying pattern extraction algorithms to data. Data mining is considered the core stage of knowledge discovery in databases (KDD).

Intelligent Software Agent: An autonomous software program designed to perform a human-like function (e.g., information search). Basic capabilities of intelligent agents include adaptation and learning.

Knowledge Discovery in Databases (KDD): The overall process of "identifying valid, novel, potentially useful, and ultimately understandable patterns in data" (Fayyad et al., 1996).

Web Mining: The application of data mining algorithms to discover useful patterns from the Web. Three main categories of Web mining include Web usage mining, Web structure mining, and Web content mining.

Chapter XLII
Identification and Localization of Digital Addresses on the Internet

André Årnes
Norwegian University of Science and Technology, Norway

ABSTRACT

A central issue in assessing and responding to an attack on the Internet is the identification and localization of the attackers. In information warfare and cyber terrorism, an attack can be launched using a large number of hosts, in which case fast and accurate identification and tracing is crucial for handling and responding to the attack. In the digital world of the Internet, however, there are many cases where a successful trace is difficult or impossible. The design of the Internet, as well as services that hide the origin of communication and provide anonymity, complicate tracing and create a need for a wide range of tools for tracing. In this chapter, we provide a survey of different tools and services available for tracing the geographic location of hosts and users on the Internet. We consider both active and passive methods of identification and tracing. A passive trace uses information that is available through public sources, in log data, or through commercially available databases. Active methods involve the use of tools for probing the attacking party directly, for example, through scanning and pinging. Some of the methods for locating addresses on the Internet have been developed for use in electronic commerce and marketing applications, but the basic principles are equally applicable to digital investigations and information warfare. We consider only tracing of addresses on the Internet. Consequently, this chapter only considers the Internet Protocol (IPv4 and IPv6), as well as higher level protocols using IP (such as TCP, UDP, and HTTP). We refer to the host that we try to identify as the target host and its address as the target address. The system used to execute the tracing is referred to as the trace host.

AN INTERNET PRIMER

The Internet is the descendant of the U.S. Defense Advanced Research Projects Agency (DARPA) project ARPANET, whose first node was connected in 1969. The core protocol suite, TCP/IP, was introduced when the National Science Foundation (NSF) established a university network backbone in 1983. In 1991 Tim Berners-Lee at CERN in Switzerland publicized the basic protocols for the World Wide Web (WWW). The Internet was publicly known by the mid-nineties, and it is now an integral part of our society. As we have grown more dependent on Internet technologies, our society has also become more vulnerable to attacks; both on the digital infrastructure itself and on critical infrastructure connected to the Internet.

The Internet is a network of networks communicating according to a suite of standardized protocols. The physical network consists of a wide range of physical media, including optical fiber, copper cable, and wireless networks. The communication on the networks is governed by layered protocols, according to the applications in use. Most applications on the Internet rely on the Internet Protocol (IP) and the transport protocols TCP and UDP. IP is a packet-based, connectionless protocol, designed to transmit packets of data between a source address and a target address. It provides no reliability in itself, but the ability to use different routes between hosts makes the protocol very resilient to changes and disruptions on the network. An IP packet is routed between two hosts by intermediate routers. Each router makes a decision of how to route its packets based on its routing policy.

We refer to a digital address as any address that identifies a user, host, or service on the Internet. Examples of digital addresses are Ethernet MAC addresses, IP addresses, AS numbers, DNS domain names, URLs, and e-mail addresses. IANA (Internet Assigned Numbers Authority) is the highest authority for the allocation of IP addresses and AS numbers. A host on the Internet is associated with multiple registration databases. In particular, its IP address is registered in an IP WHOIS database, its domain name is registered in a DNS WHOIS database, and information about its location on the Internet is provided by the routing tables. All of this information can be used to obtain information about the location and identity of addresses and users on the Internet.

In order to perform a successful trace on the Internet, it is necessary to understand the interaction between different protocols. Each protocol may have its own addressing scheme, but it may be necessary to uncover the lowest level addresses, that is, the hardware address on the physical network, in order to associate an address with a physical user or location. There are several published accounts of computer attacks that have been traced successfully. Cheswick (1990) shows us how a hacker is studied in order to learn his intent and identity, and in a book by Stoll (1989) an attack is successfully traced to an espionage agent operating in West Germany.

PASSIVE TRACING

There are multiple sources of information that can be used for passive tracing on the Internet. The most important sources are the structured databases for DNS and IP registration, as well as the routing policies of the network operators. In addition, valuable information exists in unstructured sources, such as on the WWW and on Usenet. Network operators often provide information about their network and routing policies through Looking Glass services. A passive trace implies that there is no communication with the target system.

DNS binds domain names to their respective IP addresses (Mockapetris, 1987). A DNS lookup provides the IP address of a given domain name, whereas a reverse DNS lookup provides the domain name(s) associated with a given IP address. An important tool for identifying the contact persons of a domain name is the DNS WHOIS service. DNS WHOIS is a set of publicly available databases with contact information for DNS addresses. However, there is no authoritative DNS database; many top level domains have their own DNS WHOIS service. Some top level domains also provide anonymity for their customers and will not disclose a user's identity.

The IP WHOIS protocol, defined by Daigle (2004), is a system for finding contact and registration information for an IP address. The current IP WHOIS databases are RIPE (Europe), ARIN (North America), APNIC (Asia and Australia), LATNIC (South America), and AfriNIC (Africa). An IP WHOIS lookup can determine the names, addresses, and phone numbers of contacts, as well as the AS numbers associated with the address.

The most frequently used Border Gateway Protocol (BGP) is the routing protocol of the Internet (Lougheed & Rekhter, 1991; Rekhter, Li, & Hares, 2006). Routers maintain routing tables based on routing policies, make routing decisions based on network reachability, and may communicate with other routers using BGP. The protocols operate on the level of Autonomous Systems (AS), which is a collection of IP addresses with an assigned, unique AS number (Hawkinson & Bates, 1996).

There are also commercially available databases (such as IP2location and GeoIP) that attempt to keep up-to-date information about the regional location of IP addresses. Such databases may be able to indicate the country or city where an IP address is located, but the accuracy of the information is not guaranteed. Such databases are primarily developed for use in commercial applications, but they can also be useful for digital investigations.

Search engines such as Google, Yahoo, and Alltheweb may contain valuable information pertaining to the identification and localization of users on the Internet. Some of these can also provide historical information in temporary cache. Historical data is also available from the Internet Archive[1], a service providing access to copies of old versions of web sites. In some cases, search engines may reveal information about past and present IP addresses, DNS addresses, AS numbers, as well as information about specific users. Note, however, that the accuracy of such information is questionable, as there is no editorial control of the World Wide Web. Note also that a person in an investigation scenario may have to take care not to follow search results leading directly to the attacker host. This leads to the use of active methods, which can compromise an investigation.

ACTIVE TRACING

The use of active tracing methods implies probing the target host or network directly in order to obtain further information about its address, geographical location, or identity. Active tracing can, in some cases, reveal far more information about a target host than the passive methods. However, active methods can warn an attacker about an ongoing trace, possibly causing evidence to be compromised or destroyed. Also, active tracing methods may be illegal in some countries (Fossen, 2005; Padmanabhan & Subramanian, 2001).

Protocols such as ICMP (Rekhter et al., 2006) and SNMP (Harrington, Presuhn, & Wijnen, 2002) are designed for network management and diagnostics, and they are also suitable for active tracing applications. ICMP is used as a building block in several of the methods outlined. SNMP can also be used to get extensive information about network components and services.

The basic tool for identifying the route to a particular host on the Internet is known as *traceroute*. Traceroute identifies each host on the route to a target host by taking advantage of the time-to-live (TTL) field of an IP packet. Traceroute starts by setting the TTL field to 1 and increases it by 1 for each trace. Each router on the route to the target is revealed as it returns a packet when the TTL is decremented to zero. In some cases, traceroute is blocked by a firewall or NAT gateway, in which case a method called firewalking (Goldsmith & Schiffman, 1998) can be used instead. Firewalking takes advantage of the TTL field in the IP header in the same manner as traceroute, but firewalking is able to perform the same type of trace using an available TCP or UDP service as its target.

Ping is a tool for determining whether a particular IP address on the Internet is online and reachable. It can be used to determine the status of a particular host or of a number of hosts, for example in the same subnet. The latter case is usually referred to as a *pingsweep*. The ping tool is available on most TCP/IP compatible systems.

A *portscan* offers a higher level of detail by scanning a number of ports on the target system. Portscan tools, such as nmap, are capable of determining whether a port is open (i.e., a service is running), closed, or not reachable. Variations of the standard scan may be capable of circumventing security measures or determining information about the operating system and services of the target host. This is usually referred to as fingerprinting.

The round-trip time (RTT) of packets on the Internet can give an indication of the distance between hosts. The speed of light in fiber is approximately two-thirds the speed of light in vacuum (Midwinter, 1979). Fossen (2005) and Fossen and Årnes (2005) document a forensic application of the constraint based geolocation method proposed by Gueye, Ziviani, Crovella, and Fdida (2004). In this approach, the RTT from several known landmarks is determined using traceroute, and a technique called multilateration is used to estimate the region in which the target host is most likely located. The technique is dependent on the network topology between the source and target hosts, but it provides valuable information about the likely geographical location of the target host.

It is also possible to log in to and use services on the target system to find additional information, such as names, e-mail addresses, and phone numbers. Typical examples of such services are Web servers (often with forums or blogs), FTP-servers with anonymous access, and SNMP. Technically, it is also possible to gain access to other services by circumventing or breaching the system's security, but this is generally illegal in most jurisdictions.

UNCERTAINTIES IN TRACING

Each of the methods outlined have their limitations. There are several factors that can complicate the identification and localization of a user on the Internet, either because of the design and international aspect of the Internet, or because a malicious user employs methods to obfuscate their real location. We have to expect that sophisticated attackers involved in information warfare or cyberterrorism will take precautionary measures and employ the methods available to make tracing more difficult.

Lipson (2002) considers a number of challenges related to Internet tracing and discusses a number of policy and design changes that would better facilitate tracing on the Internet. Some of these challenges are being addressed by the IP traceback schemes, as discussed by Kuznetsov, Sandstrom, and Simkin (2002) and Lipson (2002). Such schemes enforce a degree of accountability on the Internet, for example, by querying routers about the traffic they forward, by creating an overlay network, or through marking packets along its path. Such schemes would, however, also be a threat to the privacy of legitimate users on the Internet, forcing them to take additional steps to protect their identity.

Another development that may improve the traceability of transactions on the Internet is the move towards data retention. Governments are currently imposing directives and laws to enforce network monitoring in order to give investigators of serious crimes access to traffic data. A resolution on data retention was passed in the European Union in 2005 (The European Parliament, 2005).

Technical Issues

Certain infrastructure configurations can make tracing difficult or impossible. The geographic distance between hosts provides a lower bound for the RTT, but routing topology and geographic properties significantly impact the RTT, as shown by Fossen and Årnes (2005). The route to a target host between two traces can differ, as IP is a packet-based protocol. Tracing is also affected by other network architectural issues. Firewalls and network address translation (NAT) can hide local addresses and prevent traces behind a router or firewall. Port address translation (PAT) is similar to NAT, but allows the forwarding of traffic to a certain port or service. In this case, a successful method must be able to trace the forwarded traffic itself. Finally, tunneled network traffic hides the route between the tunnel end-points. Also, hosts on the Internet may be multihomed, that is, they have multiple IP addresses.

Anonymity networks such as those proposed by Chaum (1981, 1988) and the more recent Onion routing (Goldschlag, Reed, & Syverson, 1999) and Tor systems (Dingledine, Mathewson, & Syverson, 2004) impose a serious difficulty when performing a trace. Such systems are designed to conceal the identity of the users of the network, and it may be impossible to perform a trace based on an anonymized IP address alone. Anonymous services are also provided by anonymous remailers and anonymous P2P networks such as Freenet. Anonymity can also be achieved through network access from publicly available systems (such as in libraries) or through unauthorized access to open or insecure systems, such as wireless LANs.

Services on the Internet can be attacked and subverted. This imposes significant difficulties in performing a successful trace. This may occur if an attacker, for example, compromises routing tables, or performs address spoofing (assumes the address of other hosts), man-in-the-middle attacks (hijacks a connection and assumes a role in communication), or bouncing and island hopping attacks (uses a number of compromised hosts to hide identity and location). Although some of these attacks may be difficult to detect, there are systems that can be employed to indicate whether the network has been manipulated. A system for detecting malicious inter-domain router messages was proposed by Kruegel, Mutz, Robertson, and Valeur (2003). Li, Dou, Wu, Kim, and Agarwal (2005) propose a system for categorizing BGP messages as normal, blackout, worm, or misconfiguration related, and Kim, Massey, and Ray (2005) provide a method for validating the correctness of routes using ICMP traceback.

Finally, a trace often depends on the availability of log data with information about the activities of a particular host. In some cases, log data may not be available, either because logging is disabled or because logs have been deleted.

Registration Issues

The Internet is glued together by registrations in DNS and IP registers, and the routing policies of the Internet operators dictate the traffic flow in the networks. The registrars and operators of the systems are distributed, and there are many examples of falsified or erroneous registrations. In IP and DNS hijacking, a malicious party changes the registration information for an IP address or DNS address without authorization from the original registrant. In the case of IP hijacking, this may result in an AS number being rerouted to another organization or country, and in the case of DNS hijacking (also referred to as domain hijacking and domain theft), a DNS address may resolve to an IP address controlled by the attacker. The Completewhois Project provides a database of known hijacked IP addresses with corresponding statistics (The Completewhois Project, 2004).

Political and Legal Issues

Finally, there are political or legal complications. This is particularly relevant for tracing the user name associated with an IP address at a particular time. In most jurisdictions, this can only be done by law enforcement or for national security purposes. If the tracing leads to addresses abroad this gets increasingly complicated, as several jurisdictions may be involved.

CONCLUSION

A trace on the Internet can rarely be concluded with absolute certainty; the number of uncertainties dictated by the many network technologies, as well as those controlled by malicious entities is too large. There are, however, multiple sources of identity and location information. Although results from these sources may be inconsistent, results from several data sources significantly improves the chance of a successful trace.

As of today, a physical investigation may be necessary to conclude a trace, or in the worst case scenario, a trace may end up a dead end. Technologies for increased accountability through IP traceback, data retention, and authentication schemes have been suggested to remedy this. However, they cannot guarantee a successful trace, as many of the uncertainties discussed in this chapter still apply.

ACKNOWLEDGMENT

Thanks to Professor Svein J. Knapskog for helpful feedback, and to the Master students Espen André Fossen, Christian Larsen, and Øystein E. Thorvaldsen, who have worked on the field of Internet Investigations as part of his Master thesis at NTNU. This work was in part supported by the U.S. – Norway Fulbright Foundation for Educational Exchange. The "Centre for Quantifiable Quality of Service in Communication Systems, Centre of Excellence" is appointed by The Research Council of Norway, and funded by the Research Council, NTNU, and UNINETT. The author is also associated with the High-Tech Crime Division of the Norwegian National Criminal Investigation Service (Kripos).

REFERENCES

Chaum, D. (1981). Untraceable electronic mail, return addresses, and digital pseudonyms. *Communications of the ACM, 24*(2), 8488.

Chaum, D. (1988). The dining cryptographers problem: Unconditional sender and recipient untraceability. *Journal of Cryptology, 1*(1), 6575.

Cheswick, B. (1990). An evening with Berferd in which a cracker is lured, endured, and studied. *Proceedings of USENIX* (pp. 163174).

Completewhois Project, The. (2004). Questions and answers on IP hijacking. Retrieved on July 31, from www.completewhois.com/hijacked/hijacked_qa.htm

Daigle, L. (2004). WHOIS protocol specification, RFC 3912. IETF.

Dingledine, R., Mathewson, N., & Syverson, P. (2004). Tor: The second-generation onion router. *Proceedings of the 13th USENIX Security Symposium, 2004.*

European Parliament, The. (2005). Electronic communications: Personal data protection rules and availability of traffic data for anti-terrorism purposes (amend. direct. 2002/58/EC).

Fossen, E. A. (2005). *Principles of internet investigation: Basic reconnaissance, geopositioning, and public information sources.* Unpublished master's thesis, Norwegian University of Science and Technology.

Fossen, E. A., & Årnes, A. (2005). Forensic geolocation of internet addresses using network measurements. *Proceedings of the Nordic Workshop on IT-Security (NORDSEC 2005).*

Goldschlag, D., Reed, M., & Syverson, P. (1999). Onion routing. *Communications of the ACM, 42*(2), 3941.

Goldsmith, D., & Schiffman, M. (1998). *Firewalking: A traceroute-like analysis of IP packet responses to determine gateway access control lists.* Retrieved July 31, 2006, from http://packetstormsecurity.org/UNIX/audit/firewalk/

Gueye, B., Ziviani, A., Crovella, M., & Fdida, S. (2004). Constraint-based geolocation of internet hosts. *Proceedings of ACM/SIGCOMM Internet Measurement Conference (IMC 2004).*

Harrington, D., Presuhn, R., & Wijnen, B. (2002, December). An architecture for describing simple network management protocol (SNMP) management frameworks, RFC 3411. IETF.

Hawkinson, J., & Bates, T. (1996, March). Guidelines for creation, selection, and registration of an autonomous system (AS). RFC1930. IETF.

Kim, E., Massey, D., & Ray, I. (2005). Global internet routing forensics: Validation of BGP paths using ICMP traceback. *Proceedings of IFIP International. Conference on Digital Forensics.*

Kruegel, C., Mutz, D., Robertson, W., & Valeur, F. (2003). Topology-based detection of anomalous BGP messages. *Proceedings of the International Symposium on Recent Advances in Intrusion Detection (RAID 2003).*

Kuznetsov, V., Sandstrom, H., & Simkin, A. (2002). An evaluation of different IP traceback approaches. *In ICICS '02: Proceedings of the 4th International Conference on Information and Communications Security (ICICS 2002).*

Li, J., Dou, D., Wu, Z., Kim, S., & Agarwal, V. (2005). An internet routing forensics framework for discovering rules of abnormal BGP events. *SIGCOMM Computer Communication Review, 35*(5), 5566.

Lipson, H. F. (2002). Tracking and tracing cyber-attacks: Technical challenges and global policy (Technical Report). CERT Coordination Center.

Lougheed, K., & Rekhter, Y. (1991). Border gateway protocol 3 (BGP-3). RFC 1267 (Historic), IETF.

Midwinter, J. E. (1979). *Optical fibres for transmission.* John Wiley & Sons.

Mockapetris, P. (1987). Domain names concepts and facilities. RFC 1034 (Standard). IETF. (Updated by RFCs 1101, 1183, 1348, 1876, 1982, 2065, 2181, 2308, 2535, 4033, 4034, 4035, 4343)

Padmanabhan, V. N., & Subramanian, L. (2001). An investigation of geographic mapping techniques for internet hosts. *Proceedings of the 2001 conference on Applications, technologies, architectures, and protocols for computer communications (SIGCOMM 2001).*

Rekhter, Y., Li, T., & Hares, S. (2006). A border gateway protocol 4 (BGP-4). RFC 4271 (Draft Standard). IETF.

Stoll, C. (1989). *The cuckoo's egg: Tracking a spy through the maze of computer espionage.* New York: Doubleday.

TERMS AND DEFINITIONS

Geolocation: Geolocation refers to techniques for determining the geographical location of a host based on a digital address, typically an IP address.

Internet Protocol: Internet protocol (IP) is the core protocol of the Internet. The protocol is used to transmit packets of data between hosts across a packet-switched network. IP depends on link-layer protocols such as Ethernet to transmit data on physical media, and higher-layer transport protocols such as TCP are used to facilitate a reliable connection between parties on the Internet.

IP Traceback: IP traceback refers to technical mechanisms that implements accountability on the Internet by making it possible to determine the origin of an IP packet.

Looking Glass Service: The Looking Glass Service is a service for accessing publicly available information about network infrastructures and address registrations on the Internet. Looking Glass is usually provided by telecommunication and network operators.

Portscan: Portscanning is a technique for scanning and identifying active and accessible services on a network. Portscanning is typically used in network management and vulnerability assessments, but it can also be employed as part of investigations on the Internet.

Routing: Routing refers to the method used to pass data from source to destination in a packet-switched network. On the Internet, routing is performed by routers that are responsible for forwarding IP packets according to routing policies.

Traceroute: The most common tool for identifying the route to a particular host on the Internet is known as traceroute. Traceroute identifies each host on the route to a target host by taking advantage of the time-to-live (TTL) field of a packet. Traceroute starts by setting the TTL field to 1 and increases it by 1 for each trace. Each router on the route to the target is revealed as it returns a packet when the TTL is decremented to zero.

WHOIS Services: WHOIS is a protocol for querying databases for registration information related to domain names, IP addresses, and autonomous system (AS) numbers on the Internet.

ENDNOTE

[1]   http://www.archive.org

Chapter XLIII
Identification Through Data Mining

Diego Liberati
Italian National Research Council, Italy

ABSTRACT

Four main general purpose approaches inferring knowledge from data are presented as a useful pool of at least partially complementary techniques also in the cyber intrusion identification context. In order to reduce the dimensionality of the problem, the most salient variables can be selected by cascading to a K-means a Divisive Partitioning of data orthogonal to the Principal Directions. A rule induction method based on logical circuits synthesis after proper binarization of the original variables proves to be also able to further prune redundant variables, besides identifying logical relationships among them in an understandable "if .. then .." form. Adaptive Bayesian networks are used to build a decision tree over the hierarchy of variables ordered by Minimum Description Length. Finally, Piece-Wise Affine Identification also provides a model of the dynamics of the process underlying the data, by detecting possible switches and changes of trends on the time course of the monitoring.

INTRODUCTION

In trying to detect cyber intrusions, it often turns out that one has to face a huge amount of data, which is often not completely homogeneous, and often without an immediate grasp of an underlying simple structure. Many records (i.e., logs from both authorized users and possible intruders) each instantiating many variables (like time, duration, Internet protocol (IP) address, and so on) are usually collected with the help of tracing tools.

Given the opportunity to have many logs on several possible intruders, one of the typical goals one has in mind is to classify subjects on the basis of a hopefully reduced meaningful subset of the measured variables.

The complexity of the problem makes it worthwhile to use automatic classification procedures.

Then, the question arises of reconstructing a synthetic mathematical model, capturing the most important relationships among variables, in order to both discriminate intruders from allowed users and possibly also infer rules of behavior that could help in identifying habits of some classes of intruders.

Such interrelated aspects will be the focus of the present contribution.

Four main general purpose approaches, also useful in the cyber intrusion identification context, will be briefly discussed in the present chapter as well as the underlying cost effectiveness of each one.

In order to reduce the dimensionality of the problem, thus simplifying both the computation and the subsequent understanding of the solution, the critical problems of selecting the most salient variables must be solved.

A very simple approach is to resort to cascading a divisive partitioning of data orthogonal to the principal directions divisive partitioning (PDDP) (Boley, 1998) already proven to be successful in the same context of analyzing the logs of an important telecommunications provider (Garatti, Savaresi, & Bittanti, 2004)

A possible approach that is more sophisticated is to resort to a rule induction method, like the one described in Muselli and Liberati (2000). Such a strategy also offers the advantage of extracting the underlying rules, implying conjunctions and/or disjunctions between the identified salient variables. Thus, a first guess of their even nonlinear relations is provided as a first step in designing a representative model, whose variables will be the selected ones. Such an approach has been shown (Muselli & Liberati, 2002) to be not less powerful over several benchmarks, than the popular decision tree developed by Quinlan (1994).

An alternative in this sense can be represented by adaptive Bayesian networks (Yarmus, 2003), whose advantage is that it is also available on a widespread commercial database tool like Oracle.

A possible approach to blindly build a simple linear approximating model is to resort to piece-wise affine (PWA) identification (Ferrari-Trecate, Muselli, Liberati, & Morari, 2003).

The joint use of (some of) these four approaches is described briefly in the present contribution, starting from data without known priors about their relationships, thus will allow reduction in dimensionality without significant loss in information, then to infer logical relationships, and, finally, to identify a simple input-output model of the involved process that also could be used for controlling purposes even in a critical field like cyber warfare.

BACKGROUND

The introduced tasks of selecting salient variables, identifying their relationships from data, and classifying possible intruders may be sequentially accomplished with various degrees of success in a variety of ways.

Principal components order the variables from the most salient to the least, but only under a linear framework.

Partial least squares do allow nonlinear models, provided that one has prior information on the structure of the involved nonlinearity; in fact, the regression equation needs to be written before identifying its parameters.

Clustering may operate even in an unsupervised way without the a priori correct classification of a training set (Boley, 1998).

Neural networks are known to learn the embedded rules with the indirect possibility (Taha & Ghosh, 1999) to make rules explicit or to underline the salient variables.

Decision trees (Quinlan, 1994) are a popular framework providing a satisfactory answer to the recalled needs.

MAIN THRUST OF THE CHAPTER

Unsupervised Clustering

In this chapter, we will firstly resort to a quite recently developed unsupervised clustering approach, the PDDP algorithm as proposed by Boley (1998).

According to the analysis provided in Savaresi and Boley (2004), PDDP is able to provide a significant improvement over the performances of a classical *k-means* approach (Hand, Mannila, & Smyth, 2001; MacQueen, 1967), when PDDP is used to initialize the k-means clustering procedure.

The approach taken herein may be summarized in the following three steps:

1. A principal component analysis (Hand et al., 2001; O'Connel, 1974) defines a hierarchy in the transformed orthogonal variables, according to the principal directions of the dataset.

2. The unsupervised clustering is performed by cascading a noniterative technique—PDDP (Boley, 1998), based upon singular value decomposition (Golub & van Loan, 1996) and the iterative centroid-based divisive algorithm k-means (MacQueen, 1967). Such a cascade, with the clusters obtained via PDDP used to initialize k-means centroids, is shown to achieve its best performance in terms of both quality of the partition and computational effort (Savaresi & Boley, 2004). The whole dataset, thus, is bisected into two clusters, with the objective of maximizing the distance between the two clusters and, at the same time, minimizing the distance among the data points lying in the same clusters. The classification is achieved without using a priori information on the user (unsupervised learning), thus automatically highlighting his or her belonging to a (possibly unknown) user class (Garatti et al., 2004). If he or she clusters with the group of the surely certified users, it could be assumed that he or she probably belongs to the authorized group; but it could be safe to deep the analysis, for instance, with the other methods described in the following. If not, a bigger warning flag should be taken into account in the present context of feared cyber intrusion.

3. By analyzing the obtained results, the number of variables needed for the clustering may be reduced by pruning all the original variables that are not needed in order to define the final partitioning hyperplane, so that the classification eventually is based on a few variables only, in order to reduce to number of original variables one would better need to monitor in the peculiar application.

Binary Rule Inference and Variable Selection while Mining Data via Logical Networks

Recently, an approach has been suggested—Hamming clustering—related to the classical theory exploited in minimizing the size of electronic circuits, with additional care to obtain a final function able to generalize from the training dataset to the most likely framework describing the actual properties of the data. In fact, the Hamming metric tends to cluster samples whose code is less distant (Muselli & Liberati, 2000).

The Hamming clustering approach enjoys the following remarkable properties:

- It is fast, exploiting (after the mentioned binary coding) just logical operations instead of floating point multiplications.
- It directly provides a logical understandable expression (Muselli & Liberati, 2002), which is the final synthesized function directly expressed as the OR of ANDs of the salient variables, possibly negated.

Adaptive Bayesian Networks

A learning strategy that looks for a trade off between a high predictive accuracy of the classifier and a low cardinality of the selected feature subset may be derived according to the central hypothesis that a good feature subset contains features that are highly correlated with the class to be predicted, yet uncorrelated with each other.

Based on information theory, the minimum description length (MDL) principle (Barron & Rissanen, 1998) states that the best theory to infer from training data is the one that minimizes the length (i.e., the complexity) of the theory itself together with the length of the data encoded with respect to it. In particular, MDL can be employed as criteria to judge the quality of a classification model (Friedman, Geiger, & Goldszmidt, 1997).

This approach can be applied to address the problem of feature selection, by considering each feature as a simple predictive model of the target class. As described in Kononenko (1995), each feature can be ranked according to its description length, which reflects the strength of its correlation with the target. In this context, the MDL measure is given by Yarmus (2003), again weighting the encoding length, where one has one submodel for each value of the feature, with the number of bits needed to describe the data, based on the probability distribution of the target value associated to each submodel.

However, when all features have been ordered by rank, no a priori criterion is available to choose the cut-off point beyond which features can be discarded. To circumvent this drawback, one can start with building a classifier on the set of the n-top ranked features. Then, a new feature is sequentially added to this set, and a new classifier is built until no improvement in accuracy is achieved.

Two different classifiers derived from Bayesian networks are considered of interest, that is, the naïve Bayes (NB) and the adaptive Bayesian network (ABN).

NB is a very simple Bayesian network consisting of a special node that is the parent of all other nodes that are assumed to be conditionally independent, given the value of the class. The NB network can be quantified against a training dataset of preclassified instances, that is, one can compute the probability associated to a specific value of each attribute, given the value of the class label. Then, any new instance can be easily classified making use of the Bayes rule. Despite its strong independence assumption, it is clearly unrealistic in several application domains. NB has been shown to be competitive with more complex state-of-the-art classifiers (Cheng & Greiner, 1999; Friedman et al., 1997; Keogh & Pazzani, 2002).

Over the last few years, a lot of research has focused on improving NB classifiers by relaxing their full independence assumption. One of the most interesting approaches is based on the idea of adding correlation arcs between the attributes of a NB classifier.

Specific structural constraints are imposed on these "augmenting arcs" (Friedman et al., 1997; Keogh & Pazzani, 2002), in order to maintain computational simplicity of learning. The algorithm proposed as ABN by Yarmus (2003) is a greedy variant, based on MDL, the approach proposed in Keogh & Pazzani (2002).

In brief, the steps needed to build an ABN classifier are the following. First, the attributes (predictors) are ranked according to their MDL importance. Then, the network is initialized to NB on the top k ranked predictors, which are treated as conditionally independent. Next, the algorithm attempts to extend NB by constructing a set of tree-like multidimensional features.

Feature construction proceeds as follows. The top-ranked predictor is stated as a seed feature, and the predictor that most improves feature predictive accuracy, if any, is added to the seed. Further predictors are added in such a way as to form a tree structure, until the accuracy does not improve.

Using the next available top-ranked predictor as a seed, the algorithm attempts to construct additional features in the same manner. The process is interrupted when the overall predictive accuracy cannot be further improved or after some preselected number of steps.

The resulting network structure consists of a set of conditionally independent multiattribute features, and the target class probabilities are estimated by the product of feature probabilities. Interestingly, each multidimensional feature can be expressed in terms of a set of if-then rules, enabling users to easily understand the basis of model predictions.

PWA Identification Through a Clustering Technique

Once the salient variables have been selected, it may be of interest to capture a model of their dynamical interaction. A first hypothesis of linearity may be investigated, usually being only a very rough approximation, when the values of the variables are not close to the functioning point around which the linear approximations are computed.

On the other hand, to build a nonlinear model is far from easy; the structure of nonlinearity needs to be a priori known, which is not usually the case. A typical approach consists of exploiting a priori knowledge, when available, to define a tentative structure, then refining and modifying it on the training subset of data, and finally retaining the structure that best fits cross-validation on the testing subset of data. The problem is even more complex when the collected data exhibit hybrid dynamics (i.e., their evolution in time is a sequence of smooth behaviors and abrupt changes).

An alternative approach is to infer the model directly from the data without a priori knowledge via an identification algorithm capable of reconstructing a very general class of PWA model (Ferrari-Trecate et al., 2003). This method also can be exploited for the data-driven modelling of hybrid dynamical systems, where logic phenomena interact with the evolution of continuously valued variables. Such an approach will be described concisely in the following.

PWA identification exploits k-means clustering that associates data points in multivariable space in such a way as to jointly determine a sequence of linear submodels and their respective regions of operation, without imposing continuity at each change in the derivative.

FUTURE TRENDS

The proposed approaches are now under application in other similar contexts. In the specific context of cyber terrorism and warfare the results described in Garatti et al. (2004) also do grant a powerful application to intrusion detection, while the other more sophisticated recalled approaches are still under analysis. The fact that a combination of different approaches, taken from partially complementary disciplines, proves to be effective may indicate a fruitful direction in com-

bining in different ways classical and new approaches in order to improve classification even in the critical field of cyber warfare.

CONCLUSION

The proposed approaches are very powerful tools for quite a wide spectrum of applications in and beyond data mining, providing an up-to-date answer to the quest of formally extracting knowledge from data and sketching a model of the underlying process.

In cyber warfare and protection against cyber terrorism such tools may be quite useful in order to complement other approaches in identifying possible intruders and classifying them on the basis of their identified, even nonlinear profile, as shown at least via the simplest among the approaches in Garatti et al. (2004).

REFERENCES

Barron, A., Rissanen, J., & Yu, B. (1998). The minimum description length principle in coding and modelling. *IEEE Transactions on Information Theory, 44,* 2743-2760.

Boley, D. L. (1998). Principal direction divisive partitioning. *Data Mining and Knowledge Discovery, 2*(4), 325-344.

Cheng, G., & Greiner, R. (1999). Comparing Bayesian network classifiers. *Proceedings of the Fifteenth Conference on Uncertainty in Artificial Intelligence.* San Francisco: Morgan Kaufmann Publishers.

Duda, R. O., & Hart, P. E. (1973). *Pattern classification and scene analysis.* New York: Wiley.

Ferrari-Trecate, G., Muselli, M., Liberati, D., & Morari, M. (2003). A clustering technique for the identification of piecewise affine systems. *Automatica, 39,* 205-217.

Friedman, N., Geiger, D., & Goldszmidt, M. (1997). Bayesian network classifiers. *Machine Learning, 29,* 131-161.

Garatti, S., Savaresi, S., & Bittanti, S. (2004). On the relationships between user profiles and navigation sessions in virtual communities: A data-mining approach. *Intelligent Data Analysis, 8*(6), 576-600.

Golub, G. H., & van Loan, C. F. (1996). *Matrix computations.* Johns Hopkins University Press.

Hand, D., Mannila, H., & Smyth, P. (2001). *Principles of data-mining.* Cambridge, MA: MIT Press.

Keogh, E., & Pazzani, M. J. (2002). Learning the structure of augmented Bayesian classifiers. *International Journal on Artificial Intelligence Tools, 11*(4), 587-601.

Kononenko, I. (1995). On biases in estimating multi-valued attributes. In *Proceedings of the International Joint Conference on Artificial Intelligence* (IJCAI 95)(pp. 1034-1040).

MacQueen, J. (1967). Some methods for classification and analysis of multivariate observations. *Proceedings of the Fifth Berkeley Symposium on Mathematical Statistics and Probability* (pp. 291-297).

Muselli, M., & Liberati, D. (2000). Training digital circuits with Hamming clustering. *IEEE Transactions on Circuits and Systems – I: Fundamental Theory and Applications, 47,* 513-527.

Muselli, M., & Liberati, D. (2002). Binary rule generation via Hamming clustering. *IEEE Transactions on Knowledge and Data Engineering, 14,* 1258-1268.

O'Connel, M. J. (1974). Search program for significant variables. *Computational Physic Commumications, 8,* 49.

Quinlan, J. R. (1994). *C4.5: Programs for machine learning.* San Francisco: Morgan Kaufmann.

Savaresi, S. M., & Boley, D. L. (2004). A comparative analysis on the bisecting K-means and the PDDP clustering algorithms. *International Journal on Intelligent Data Analysis, 8*(4), 345-363

Taha, I., & Ghosh, J. (1999). Symbolic interpretation of artificial neural networks. *IEEE Tranactions on Knowledge and Data Engineering., 11,* 448-463.

Yarmus, J. S. (2003). *ABN: A fast, greedy Bayesian network classifier.* Retrieved from http://otn.oracle.com/products/bi/pdf/adaptive_bayes_net.pdf

TERMS AND DEFINITIONS

Hamming Clustering: This is a fast binary rule generator and variable selector able to build understandable logical expressions by analyzing the Hamming distance between samples.

Hybrid Systems: Their evolution in time is composed by both smooth dynamics and sudden jumps.

K-Means: This is an iterative clustering technique that subdivides the data in such a way to maximize the distance among centroids of different clusters, while minimizing the distance among data within each cluster. It is sensitive to initialization.

Model Identification: This means the definition of the structure and computation of its parameters best suited to mathematically describe the process underlying the data.

Principal Component Analysis: This means rearrangement of the data matrix in new orthogonal transformed variables, ordered in decreasing order of variance.

Principal Direction Divisive Partitioning (PDDP): This one-shot clustering technique is based on principal component analysis and singular value decomposition of data, thus partitioning the dataset according to the direction of maximum variance of the data. It is used here in order to initialize K-means.

Rule Inference: This is the extraction from the data of the embedded synthetic logical description of their relationships.

Salient Variables: These are the real players among the many apparently involved in the true core of a complex business.

Singular Value Decomposition: This is an algorithm able to compute the eigenvalues and eigenvectors of a matrix; it is also used to make principal components analysis.

Unsupervised Clustering: This means an automatic classification of a dataset in two or more subsets on the basis of the intrinsic properties of the data, without taking into account further contextual information.

Section VI
Business Continuity

Every organization using information technology, large or small, operating in one location or spread around a country, must develop and implement a system of protection against cyber-based attacks. Such systems are designed to stop many attacks, but as everyone knows, it is impossible to attain a 100% security. Hence, protection mechanisms should include contingency plans aimed at handling any potential disaster.

These plans must cover the following overlapping activities:

- There must be plans on how to handle every emergency situation, which could occur. This is based on the fact that when a disaster strikes there is not enough time for a discussion of what must be done. Instead, everyone must recognize quickly the seriousness of a situation and act accordingly to limit the range of losses.
- There must be plans for how, after handling a particular accident, the organization will restore its operations to normal as soon as possible.
- During and after a disaster, the staff must know how the secure any evidence pertinent to a given incident. It is not only important from a law enforcement investigation's point of view but it may allow the identification of the true nature of the problem and launch an effective set of actions to rectify it. Knowledge in computer forensics is critical to such activities.
- Finally, all the above activities must be a part of a Business Continuity System that is aimed at the development and maintenance of all the above plans. For instance, regular fire drills must be part of this system. This means that every organization should evaluate how their information systems would survive a possible disaster, and test the plans developed to mitigate these risks. In the other words, they need to perform a detailed risk analysis of not only trying to establish a set of possible calamities and the methods of handling them, but also determine the extent of damage that could result and plan how to mitigate these in the future.

All of these activities are part of business continuity, and is the main theme of the chapters and views presented in this section.

Chapter XLIV
A Model for Emergency Response Systems

Murray E. Jennex
San Diego State University, USA

ABSTRACT

Cyber war and cyber terrorism is real and is being waged. Cyber terrorists and cyber warriors are attacking systems and succeeding in their attacks. This requires management to prepare for the worst case, the loss and destruction of critical data and systems. This chapter helps management prepare for this worst case by discussing how to design and build emergency response systems. These systems are used to respond to worst case attacks. Additionally, these systems are useful for responding to other disasters that can cause the loss of systems and data. This chapter presents research into emergency response systems and concludes with a model of what an emergency response system should consist of.

INTRODUCTION

It is clear from the 9/11 terrorist attacks, the anthrax events, the Slammer worm attack on the Internet, the London subway bombings, the 2004 Tsunami, and now Hurricane Katrina, that terrorist and cyber terrorist attacks and/or disasters (henceforth referred to generically as emergencies) are increasingly involving the necessity to coordinate activities and responses by a much broader host of organizations involving the private sector, nonprofits, and volunteer organizations.

While some of these organizations are always involved in emergency response; the total span of organizations depends very much on the type of emergency, its location, and scale of impact. As a result one can not completely predict where and who are the people and units that will be gathering and supplying information as well as who will be responding and contributing resources. The most likely way this will be done effectively is by utilizing a centrally organized but fully distributed command and control center that can add functional nodes and linkages as needed and is triggered by the occurring events (Turoff, Chumer, Van de Walle, & Yao, 2004). Additionally, while we have intrusion detection systems, IDS, for monitoring for cyber attacks, we need to become aware that these attacks also need emergency response systems that guide responders in the correct response and recovery actions and which facilitate communications between the various responding groups and managers.

The goal of this chapter is to provide a reference for managers needing to prepare, should their defenses fail and their organization is severely damaged. The chapter is primarily focused on providing a model for creating an emergency or crisis response system (henceforth referred to generically as Emergency Response System, ERS). An emergency response system is good for any emergency, be it cyber attack or natural. The chapter presents research conducted on emergency response systems and presents a model that reflects current thought for them.

EMERGENCY RESPONSE SYSTEM RESEARCH

Emergency response systems are used by organizations to assist in responding to an emergency situation. These systems support communications, data gathering and analysis, and decision-making. Emergency response systems are rarely used but when needed, must function well and without fail. Designing and building these systems requires designers to anticipate what will be needed, what resources will be available, and how conditions will differ from normal. A standard model for an ERS is from Bellardo, Karwan and Wallace (1984) and identifies the components as including a database, data analysis capability, normative models, and an interface. This model is only somewhat useful as it fails to address issues such as how the ERS fits into the overall emergency response plan, ERS infrastructure, multiple organization spanning, knowledge from past emergencies, and integrating multiple systems. Additionally, many organizations do not address the need for an ERS until an emergency happens, and then, only for a few months until something more pressing comes up (Jennex, 2003).

The result is that many organizations have an ERS that may not be adequate.

Emergencies are high stress situations that require organizations to respond in a manner that is different from their normal operating procedures (Turoff, 2002). Patton and Flin (1999) discuss these stresses on emergency managers and how to reduce them. Emergency stressors, in addition to fatigue, include dealing with a complex, unpredictable and dynamic response, time pressure, and communications, dealing with the media, and operating within an integrated emergency management context. To reduce these stresses, emergency response plans should be based on operational demands, tested regularly, and have resources allocated. These plans should not be based on implicit and untested assumptions that reflect routine operational requirements and conditions as plans based on assumed capabilities are less effective than anticipated and will increase ad hoc demands on managers. Working in teams is required during emergencies and having a well trained, experienced team will reduce the impact of team dynamic stressors. Additionally, emergencies may require interagency coordination and dealing with interagency conflict and terminology increases stress. These stresses can be reduced if these agencies are integrated in their response and participants train together so that they are familiar with each other and comfortable with the integrated emergency response plan. Finally, communication systems are necessary for getting the right information to the right people, but they will not reduce stress unless participants are trained and practiced in their use. In addition to the stresses identified by Patton and Flin (1999), Bellardo et al. (1984) identify the stress of decision-making during emergency response and recommend the creation of an ERS to assist decision makers. The components of the ERS, as suggested by Bellardo et al. (1984), were previously mentioned but several researchers have looked at decision stress and address methods for decreasing this stress. Turoff (2002) expands the discussion on stressors by discussing the philosophy of the United States Office of Emergency Preparedness (OEP) (Note: The OEP was disbanded in 1973 in the same executive order that also eliminated the

Office of Science and Technology from the executive offices of the president. OEP was divided up and sent in pieces to different agencies. The disaster response function was sent to the General Services Administration [GSA]). Key points of this philosophy are:

- An ERS not used regularly will not be used in an actual emergency.
- People in emergencies do not have time to deal with issues not related to the emergency.
- Learning what actually happened is extremely important to improving emergency response performance.
- It is difficult to predict exactly who will do what during an emergency.
- The crucial problem of the moment drives the allocation of resources.
- Roles can be planned but whoever steps into a role at any given moment defies the attempt to prescribe behavior.
- The need to have confidence in the currency and accuracy of the information provided to those making decisions greatly influences the generation of timely and effective decision making.
- Exceptions to the planned behavior are crucial factors in determining minute to minute operations.
- Severe emergency situations require large numbers of individuals to share information without causing information overload.
- Exact actions and responsibilities of individuals cannot be predetermined due to unforeseen events occurring during the crisis.

To improve the ERS Turoff (2002) suggests having multiple templates for a variety of actions that can be modified as needed. These templates should be able to be used by individuals initiating notifications using personal data assistants (PDAs). Additionally, these notifications should be self-organizing and all entered data tagged with the name or ID and time entered of the person entering the data. Finally, online communities of experts should be utilized to assist with the emergency.

Lee and Bui (2000) studied the Kobe, Japan earthquake disaster response and also propose using a template-based ERS. However, they observed that:

- The urgency in a disaster require that as much relevant information for resolving the disaster be gathered and stored prior to the disaster.
- Disaster information processing should be case based with lessons learned from previous disasters used to build new cases.
- To minimize stress the response processes and workflows should be as automated as possible.

Andersen, Garde, and Andersen (1998) investigated the use of Lotus Notes as a form or template-driven ERS and identified several potential communication problems:

- A sequence of messages from one organizational unit to another is misunderstood due to the initial message not being opened or lost.
- A command is misinterpreted as information (and not recognized as a command) by the receiver due to grammar issues.
- Decision makers and other personnel at emergency response centers are overwhelmed by bookkeeping while keeping track of responses to commands and messages.
- The meaning of a message is misunderstood when the message is not seen in the context of other messages to which it is related.
- Even though the emergency plan is well known there are still delays in communicating alarms and commands to relevant organizations and getting responses.

Fischer (1998) discussed the application of new technologies to emergency mitigation, response, and recovery and observed some issues associated with the technology used in an ERS. These issues include information overload, loss of information, retention of outdated information, the greater likelihood of the diffusion of inappropriate information, further diminution of nonverbal communication, and the inevitability of computer failures.

To improve the effectiveness of an ERS and the emergency response team several researchers recommend training (Andersen et al., 1998; Fischer, 1998; Lee & Bui, 2000; Patton & Flin, 1999; Renaud & Phillips, 2003; Turoff, 2002). Patton and Flin (1999) found that training exercises and simulations must test assumptions and examine procedural and conceptual issues to ensure the ERS and emergency response processes will work when needed. Fischer (1998) proposes the use of distance learning technologies to ensure distributed emergency response teams are trained. Turoff (2002) discusses how an ERS that is not normally used will not be used in an emergency.

Others suggest modifications and/or additions to the ERS. Fischer (1998) advocates using technologies such as CD/DVD-based storage media, Web sites as a common infrastructure providing access for disaster response teams distributed across multiple locations and organizations, and e-mail for improving communications. Gheorghe and Vamanu (2001) suggest adding Geographical Information System (GIS) and satellite capabilities to the ERS. Nisha de Silva (2001) expands on using GIS to aid decision-making during emergencies but warns of integration difficulties with other technologies. Gadomski, Bologna, Costanzo, Perini, and Schaerf (2001) discuss using case-based reasoning, artificial intelligence, and intelligent agents to aid decision makers during an emergency. They advocate the need for real-time operational data as decision makers need data from operational systems, and a user-friendly interface.

Finally, as a response to possible loss of the ERS infrastructure, Renaud and Phillips (2003) discuss the creation of infrastructure continuity plans for infrastructure continuity units (usually buildings). These were created for Y2K and incorporated detailed equipment information, data on failures, and detailed response procedures. This effort was coordinated across the Public Works and Government Services of Canada and is being evaluated for application by commercial organizations.

The real demonstration of the 9/11 event is the strategic and technical fallacy of making the integration of communications between incompatible systems (fire, police, medical, etc.) dependent upon a single physical command and control center. Such centers are vulnerable to a planned act of sabotage. If there is any strong technical conclusion from the events of 9/11 it is the requirement to develop an integrated communications capability that can react as a distributed virtual system with no required need for the humans involved to be in a single location (Smith & Hayne, 1991). A virtual command center can be created when the authorities, decision and reporting responsibilities, the accountability tracking, and the oversight monitoring functions are explicitly represented and present in the supporting communications software for the operation of such a human network. In fact, those involved should be able to operate from wherever they happen to be at the start of the crisis: their home, office, or in transit.

Very little has been published recently on specific functional requirements for the first responders to an emergency based situation. It is also noted that a great deal of the literature on emergency response prior to 9/11 focuses on the response of commercial firms to emergencies or crises largely restricted to the corporate environment (Barton & Hardigree, 1995; Braverman, 2003; Kim, 1998; Lukaszewski, 1987; Massey, 2001; Mork, 2002; Pearson, Misra, Clair, & Mitroff, 1997; Smart, Thompson, & Vertinsky, 1978; Smart & Vertinsky, 1977, 1984) or focused on the public relations aspects of a crisis (Coombs, 2000; Dyer, 1995). When an organizational emergency has macrosocial effects and causes potential or actual physical harm to people or facilities, it usually leaves the jurisdiction of the single organization and can evolve to be the concern of local, state, and federal agencies depending on the scope and nature of the emergency (e.g., Bhopal, Three Mile Island, Tylenol, and Exxon Valdez). However, there are a number of significant observations that apply to crisis situations regardless of the organizations involved. An important source for requirements will be the past operation and extensive experience of the Office of Emergency Preparedness (OEP) which existed for over 25 years until 1973 and was the only civil agency, prior to the new Department of Homeland Security, which could assume total control of a crisis or disaster situation via executive order of the president and execute the command and control function over all other federal agencies including the military. To address this need Turoff, et al. (2004) propose using a distributed command and control emergency information/crisis response system and identified design requirements that expand ERS capabilities in group communication, data, information, and knowledge management.

EXPANDED EMERGENCY RESPONSE SYSTEM MODEL

Jennex (2004) summarized these findings into an expanded emergency information response system model. These systems are more than the basic components of database, data analysis, normative models, and interface outlined by Bellardo, et al. (1984). A more complete ERS model includes these basic components plus trained users (where users are personnel using the system to respond to or communicate about the emergency), dynamic and integrated (yet possibly physically distributed) methods to communicate between users and between users and data sources, protocols to facilitate communication, and processes and procedures used to guide the response to and improve decision-making during the emergency. The goals of the emergency information response system are to facilitate clear communications, improve the efficiency and effectiveness of decision-making, and manage data to prevent or at least mitigate information overload. Designers use technology and work flow analysis to improve system performance in achieving these goals.

KNOWLEDGE MANAGEMENT AND EMERGENCY RESPONSE SYSTEMS

Jennex (2005) defines knowledge management (KM), as the practice of selectively applying knowledge from previous experiences of decision-making to current and future decision-making activities with the express purpose of improving the organization's effectiveness. KM is an action discipline; knowledge needs to be used and applied for KM to have an impact. Emergency response relies on the use of knowledge from past situations to generate current and future response procedures. Lessons learned and the understanding of what works best in given situations (both examples of knowledge) enables emergency managers to prepare planned responses as a counter to the stress of the emergency. Integration of KM into ERS is a recent development as will discussed.

The large number of groups that may respond to an emergency all need access to a wide range of real-time information and knowledge that requires coordination. Groups have proposed and created KM enhanced ERS that allow for more efficient use of data and faster response. One example that has been proposed is the Information Management System for Hurricane disasters (IMASH) (Iakovou & Douligeris, 2001). IMASH is an information management system based on an object-oriented database design, able to provide data for response to hurricanes. IMASH was designed with the premise that the World Wide Web is the medium of choice for presenting textual and graphical information to a distributed community of users. This design is much more effective in the fast-changing environment of a natural disaster than the historical use of static tools which, out of necessity, have been the tools used in disaster response. Kitamato (2005) describes the design of an information management system, Digital Typhoon, designed to provide a hub of information on the Internet during a typhoon disaster. The Digital Typhoon provides access to information from official sources (news, satellite imagery) as well as a forum for individuals to provide information (local, personal). It effectively became a hub of information, but created questions about organization, filtering, and editing. Systems used for Hurricane Katrina response realized the benefits and difficulties of these systems. Like IMASH, the systems described used the Internet to distribute data to a community of users, and like Digital Typhoon, the KM systems described for Hurricane Katrina response became hubs of information that required data management to reduce repetition and allow for editing. Murphy and Jennex (2006) added KM to the expanded ERS model proposed by Jennex (2004) and showed how it was used in open source developed systems used to aid in the response to Katrina through the implementation of the Peoplefinder and Shelterfinder systems. These systems were unique in that they were developed independent of government support or resources. Development was through volunteers and the systems used a Web interface tied to a knowledge base to gather information and knowledge on survival stories and sources of shelter. Experience with these systems showed the value of using open source, commercial tools, and wikis to build ERSs'. Success of these systems was dependent upon the interface and the quality of the knowledge stored and retrieved from the systems.

In summary, there is a fusion of ERSs' with KM. This is because decision makers, when under stress, need systems that do more than just provide data, they need systems that can quickly find and display knowledge relevant to the situation in a format that facilitates the decision maker in making decisions. It is expected that ERS evolution will continue to utilize KM concepts and approaches as experience in responding to disasters is showing that these systems are more effective than traditional ERSs'. Examples of how KM aids in emergency or crisis response includes using knowledge of past disasters to design communication, data, and information capture protocols and templates; capturing emergency response knowledge in procedures and protocols; incorporating lessons learned into response team training; interface and display design; the generation of heuristics guiding decision-making; and using knowledge to guide the creation of experience knowledge bases that responders can use to generate emergency response actions.

FUTURE TRENDS

Wide spread emergencies such as Hurricane Katrina and the 2004 Tsunami have shown the difficulty of building stand alone ERSs' (systems whose sole purpose is to respond to emergencies). These systems are expensive and it is difficult to not use them for routine activities when resources are low. Exercises preparing for a possible avian flu pandemic and for a pandemic coupled with a terrorist attack on critical infrastructure (Operation Chimera and Strong Angel III) are focusing on training large numbers of people in emergency response while using and developing open source ERSs' (Jennex, 2006). Strong Angel III in particular focused on creating and using an ERS based on open source development and commercial off-the-shelf components. The goal is to reduce the cost, time, and effort involved in building and implementing an ERS while maintaining system security, especially when using the Internet and other commercial, civilian communication networks. Additionally, Raman, Ryan, and Olfman (2006) discuss the use of wiki technology to facilitate KM for emergency response systems. It is expected that open source technologies such as wiki technology will be used to improve connectivity and communications between diverse groups needing to communicate during an emergency. It is expected that increased use of knowledge based systems and KM will continue for emergency response. Improved KM technologies for storing, searching, and retrieving knowledge will be used to integrate KM into emergency decision-making (Murphy & Jennex, 2006).

Finally, worms like Slammer which infected 90% of all vulnerable systems connected to the Internet within 10 minutes of its release in 2003 (Panko, 2003) show the vulnerability of cyber emergency response. Currently organizations rely on intrusion detections systems, IDS, which have some alarm functions, to detect such attacks and on firewalls to protect their networks. Emergency response under these conditions is still primitive with most organizations relying on emergencies being recognized and then responded to via sets of incident response procedures. It is expected that new, fast acting ERSs' will have to be developed that will rely on knowledge-based analysis and decision support to improve emergency response times to fit emergencies such as Slammer.

CONCLUSION

Preparing for cyber war or cyber terrorist attacks is more than constructing good defenses. Organizations need to be prepared to respond should the defenses fail and the organization's critical infrastructure such as networks, telephony, critical systems, and databases are destroyed or badly damaged. This chapter has presented a model for an emergency response system that should it be used, will assist managers in preparing their organizations to respond to disaster. Also, use of this model should be done as part of an integrated emergency response plan. Whitman and Mattord (2004) provide a good overview and direction on doing this planning. Performing this planning and having an ERS is important should the organization be attacked and is critical should society as a whole be attacked.

Large scale (multiple organizations, a city or state, etc.) emergency response in the U.S., is evolving from something that was locally handled to something that is standardized under federal control. The U.S. implemented the National Incident Management System, NIMS, in 2004. NIMS established standardized incident management protocols and procedures that all responders are to use to conduct and coordinate response actions (Townsend, 2006). Townsend (2006) discusses lessons learned from Katrina that include communications infrastructure, knowledge about emergency response plans, integration of civilian and military response activities, and critical infrastructure and impact assessment issues. Review of these issues suggests there were failings in the ERSs' that the expanded model with KM would have prevented.

What is certain is that ERSs' will rely on communications, training, integration of knowledge, dynamic infrastructure, and all the other components of the expanded ERS model with KM. Knowledge management will be a key contributor to building ERSs' that can react quickly to emergencies. Open source and commercial off-the-shelf components will be increasing used for ERS infrastructures to support cost cutting and simplifying system complexity and setup.

REFERENCES

Andersen, H. B., Garde, H., & Andersen, V. (1998). MMS: An electronic message management system for emergency response. *IEEE Transactions on Engineering Management, 45*(2), 132-140.

Barton, L., & Hardigree, D. (1995). Risk and crisis management in facilities: Emerging paradigms in assessing critical incidents. *Facilities Journal, 13*(9), 10-11.

Bellardo, S., Karwan, K. R., & Wallace, W. A. (1984). Managing the response to disasters using microcomputers. *Interfaces, 14*(2), 29-39.

Braverman, M. (2003). Managing the human impact of crisis. *Risk Management, 50*(5), 10-19.

Coombs, W. T. (2000). Designing post crisis messages: Lesson for crisis response strategies. *Review of Business, 21*(3/4), 37-41.

Cunningham, W. (2005). *Wikihistory*. Retrieved October 29, 2005, from http://c2.com/cgi/wiki?WikiHistory

Dyer, S. C. (1995). Getting people into the crisis communication plan. *Public Relations Quarterly, 40*(3), 38-41.

Fischer, H. W. (1998). The role of the new information technologies in emergency mitigation, planning, response, and recovery. *Disaster Prevention and Management, 7*(1), 28-37.

Gadomski, A. M., Bologna, S., Costanzo, G. D., Perini, A., & Schaerf, M. (2001). Towards intelligent decision support systems for emergency managers: The IDS approach. *International Journal of Risk Assessment and Management, 2*(3/4), 224-242.

Gheorghe, A. V., & Vamanu, D. V. (2001). Adapting to new challenges: IDSS for emergency preparedness and management. *International Journal of Risk Assessment and Management, 2*(3/4), 211-223.

Iakovou, E. & Douligeris, C. (2001). An information management system for the emergency management of hurricane disasters. *International Journal of Risk Assessment and Management, 2*(3/4), 243-262.

Jennex, M. E. (2003). Information security in the era of terrorist attacks. *Information Resource Management Association International Conference Panel.*

Jennex, M. E. (2004). Emergency response systems: The utility Y2K experience. *Journal of IT Theory and Application (JITTA), 6*(3), 85-102.

Jennex, M. E. (2005). What is knowledge management? *International Journal of Knowledge Management, 1*(4), iiv.

Jennex, M. E. (2006). Open source knowledge management. *International Journal of Knowledge Management, 2*(4), iiv.

Kim, L. (1998). Crisis construction and organizational learning: Capability building in catching-up at Hyundai Motor. *Organization Science, 9*(4), 506-521.

Kitamato, A. (2005). Digital typhoon: Near real-time aggregation, recombination and delivery of typhoon-related information. *Proceeding of the 4th International Symposium on Digital Earth.* Retrieved October 26, 2005, from http://www.cse.iitb.ac.in/~neela/MTP/Stage1-Report.pdf

Lee, J., & Bui, T. (2000). A template-based methodology for disaster management information systems. *Proceedings of the 33rd Hawaii International Conference on System Sciences.*

Lukaszewski, J. E. (1987). Anatomy of a crisis response: A checklist. *Public Relations Journal, 43*(11), 45-47.

Massey, J. E. (2001). Managing organizational legitimacy: Communication strategies for organizations in crisis. *Journal of Business Communications, 38*(2), 153-182.

Mattison, D. (2003). Quickwiki, swiki, twiki, zwiki and the plone wars: Wiki as PIM and collaborative content tool, searcher. *The Magazine for Database Professionals, 11*(4), 32.

Mork, L. (2002). Technology tools for crisis response. *Risk Management, 49*(10), 44-50.

Murphy, T., & Jennex, M. E. (2006). Knowledge management systems developed for Hurricane Katrina response. *International Journal of Intelligent Control Systems, 11*(4), 199-208.

Nisha de Silva, F. (2001). Providing spatial decision support for evacuation planning: a challenge in integrating technologies. *Disaster Prevention and Management, 10*(1), 11-20.

Panko, R. R. (2003). SLAMMER: The first blitz worm. *Communications of the AIS, CAIS, 11*(12).

Parlament of Victoria. (2005). *Victorian electronic democracy—Final report.* Retrieved October 29, 2005, from http://www.parliament.vic.gov.au/sarc/E-Democracy/Final_Report/Glossary.htm

Patton, D., & Flin, R. (1999). Disaster stress: An emergency management perspective. *Disaster Prevention and Management, 8*(4), 261-267.

Pearson, C. M., Misra, S. K., Clair, J. A., & Mitroff, I. I. (1997). Managing the unthinkable. *Organizational Dynamics, 26*, 51-64.

Raman, M., Ryan, T., & Olfman, L. (2006). Knowledge management systems for emergency preparedness: The Claremont University Consortium experience. *International Journal of Knowledge Management, 2*(3), 33-50.

Renaud, R., & Phillips, S. (2003). Developing an integrated emergency response programme for facilities: The experience of public works and government services Canada. *Journal of Facilities Management, 1*(4), 347-364.

Smart, C. F., Thompson, W., & Vertinsky, I. (1978). diagnosing corporate effectiveness and susceptibility to crises. *Journal of Business Administration, 9*(2), 57-96.

Smart, C. F., & Vertinsky, I. (1977). Designs for crisis decision units. *Administrative Science Quarterly, 22*, 639-657.

Smart, C. F., & Vertinsky, I. (1984). Strategy and environment: A study of corporate response to crises. *Strategic Management Journal, 5*, 199-213.

Smith, C. A. P., & Hayne, S. (1991). A distributed system for crisis management. *Proceedings of the 24th Hawaii International Conference on System Sciences, HICSS, 3*, 72-81.

Townsend, F. F. (2006). *The federal response to Hurricane Katrina, lessons learned.* Department of Homeland Security, United States of America.

Turoff, M. (2002). Past and future emergency response information systems. *Communications of the ACM, 45*(4), 29-32.

Turoff, M., Chumer, M., Van de Walle, B., & Yao, X. (2004). The design of a dynamic emergency response management information system (DERMIS). *The Journal of Information Technology Theory and Application (JITTA), 5*(4), 135.

Whitman, M. E., & Mattord, H. J. (2004). *Management of information security.* Boston: Thomson Course Technology.

Wikipedia. (2006). *Wiki.* Retrieved March 30, 2006, from http://en.wikipedia.org/wiki/Wiki

TERMS AND DEFINITIONS

Emergencies: High stress situations that require organizations to respond in a manner that is different from their normal operating procedures (Turoff, 2002).

Emergency Response System: The system used by organizations to assist in responding to an emergency situation. These systems support communications, data gathering and analysis, and decision-making. The components of an emergency response system include databases, knowledge bases, data analysis support, normative models, interface, trained users (where users are personnel using the system to respond to or communicate about the emergency), dynamic and integrated (yet possibly physically distributed) methods to communicate between users and between users and data sources, protocols to facilitate communication, and processes and procedures used to guide the response to and improve decision-making during the emergency. The goals of the emergency information response system are to facilitate clear communications, improve the efficiency and effectiveness of decision-making, and manage data to prevent or at least mitigate information overload (Murphy & Jennex, 2006).

Knowledge Management: The practice of selectively applying knowledge from previous experiences of decision-making to current and future decision-making activities with the express purpose of improving the organization's effectiveness (Jennex, 2005).

Wiki: A Web site or similar online resource which allows users to add and edit content collectively and/or collaboratively (Parlament of Victoria, 2005; Wikipedia, 2006). The wiki originated in 1994/1995 (Cunningham, 2005), but has only recently come become popular as a content management system (Mattison, 2003). Very recent research has found that wikis are useful for KM as they provide content management combined with knowledge exchange, communication and collaboration capabilities.

Chapter XLV
Bouncing Techniques

Stéphane Coulondre
University of Lyon, France

ABSTRACT

Police investigation methods and tools are very efficient today in tracking down a cyber-attack. As a consequence, skilled cyber-terrorists now use some particular techniques in order to hide their real electronic identity. They can even mislead the investigators by showing another identity. Unfortunately, these techniques increasingly become widespread. We present several of these techniques and show how they can either help or betray attackers. An important conclusion of this paper is that unfortunately nowadays anonymity is practically attainable. The solution can not only rely on technology. International collaboration and information sharing is a key to this problem.

INTRODUCTION

In order to make it difficult to track them down, cyber terrorists do not directly use their own computer to attack a target, especially if the target is in the same country as they are. Indeed, it is very often technically possible nowadays to gather enough information on the attacker to know where the attack has come from. For these reasons, they commonly use bouncing techniques. These techniques aim at hiding their real identity or, more precisely, at using another real cyber identity. In this case, the police are first confronted with

a wrong suspect, thus they have to find the previous computer in the attack chain, and so on. This can be a very difficult task, legally and technically.

We present basic types of bouncing techniques, their pros and cons, and discuss their efficiency and anonymity. We explain how and why these bounces are made possible. We also illustrate why international collaboration is essential. We finally show that it is very hard, if at all possible, to reconstruct the attack chain in order to find its origin.

BACKGROUND

Every computer on the Internet has an address that is either public or private. This address can reveal the identity of the owner, either by means of the *whois* protocol, which is a protocol widely used for querying the addresses and domain name registration databases, or with the help of Internet service providers (ISPs). When an attacker is using the Internet, every visited Web site and every attacked computer can virtually know where he or she is. This is indeed a huge drawback for cyber terrorists, who aim at keeping this information secret.

However, not every activity on the Internet is logged, because it would represent, if ever possible, a huge amount of information. Therefore, some techniques, namely forensic techniques (Jones, Bejtlich, & RoseReal, 2005), which have been greatly developed in these last years, aim at gathering traces whenever an attack has been performed. These techniques generally give some good results and the origin of the attack can often be traced back. Therefore, skilled cyber terrorists now rely on new sophisticated techniques to cover their tracks, based on bouncing techniques. These bouncing techniques aim at replacing the final origin of the attack with another address.

Bouncing techniques can be divided in two types:

- Those using the Internet identity of someone who is unaware of it
- Those using the Internet identity of someone who is aware of it (Notice that it does not mean that this person is aware of the corresponding kind of activity.)

BOUNCING TECHNIQUES

There are essentially two popular ways of getting access to the Internet using someone else's name. The first one relies on the poor security design of the first Wi-Fi networks, particularly those conforming to the 802.11b norm (Edney & Arbaugh, 2003). The second one relies on public proxies that can be found in the Internet. Each of them has advantages and drawbacks for a cyber terrorist.

The 802.11b access points have a well-known design flaw. In no more than five minutes, it is possible for a skilled hacker to break the cryptographic shared key (Fluhrer, Mantin, & Shamir, 2001), allowing a connection to this access point, thus to the Internet. This connection, including attacks, is realized in the name of the access point owner, who is not aware of it (unless using a specific intrusion detection system, which is very rare for individuals). One the favorite games of some hackers is to drive in an urban area with a laptop that can automatically detect 802.11b waves, which often overlap the streets, and construct a geographical map of encrypted (and unencrypted) 802.11b networks. Whenever an encrypted key has been detected, the hacker can break it from his or her car without being detected. Databases of broken keys and geographical 802.11b network positions are then published on the Internet.

Proxies are computers that agree to act in their name for a client (Luotonen, 1997). There are different types of proxies; the most used being *http* and *socks* proxies. Http proxies allow for Internet browsing, and socks proxies allow for almost all major Internet protocols. Public proxies can be roughly divided into three types:

- Misconfigured proxies, which allow everybody to use it without the owner being aware of it
- Free proxies, working with some organizations, which are then aware of it, but that could be used to gather personal information
- Nonfree commercial proxies, which aim at providing anonymous services, but nobody can truly verify this
- Hacked proxies, which are, by definition, made anonymous by the attackers

At the present time, very few public proxies can guarantee to be really anonymous, because there is no general way of knowing if the proxy is really free, misconfigured, or hacked, or if it keeps logs of activity, including who is connecting to it, visited sites, information sent, and so forth.

Cyber terrorists know that they cannot be sure of their anonymity and, therefore, can act in two different ways. The first one is to hack themselves into a nonpublic proxy, or to install a new one on an attacked computer, ensuring no eavesdropping has been planned. The second one is to perform a huge number of bounces, in various countries, thus complicating the identification task. Another way, reserved for skilled attackers, is to hack into other computers, in order to bounce through them. This is not as complicated as it may first appear. Indeed, there is no need to really attack a given computer to do this, but only to use *Trojans* (Erbschloe, 2004). Amongst them are special programs that allow a cyber terrorist to bounce through it. These programs then take their attack orders either directly from the attacker's address, or sometimes, to increase anonymity, by means of specific public discussion channels like *irc*, dedicated mailboxes, and so forth.

This leads to other kinds of bouncing techniques, based on a mix of the various protocols. For example, a popular service on the Internet is remailers, which allow for sending e-mails with another identity without the real e-mail address being revealed. Therefore, recipients cannot know who really sent it. Nevertheless, the remailer administrator can technically recognize this correspondence. On the other hand, some protocol conversion services also are offered on the Internet; these allow access to Web sites, file transfer protocol (ftp) sites, newsgroups, and so forth only by e-mail. Therefore, by mixing remailers, protocol conversion services, and Trojans, it is possible to launch an attack only by sending an e-mail. Again, by sending this e-mail by means of a public proxy, a supplemental layer of anonymity is added.

As strange as it may appear, most recent (and practical) bouncing techniques are based on a network of people letting their computer act as a bounce point and being aware of it. This is called onion routing (Dingledine, Matthewson, & Syverson, 2004). The

Figure 1. An example of an attack chain using several bouncing techniques

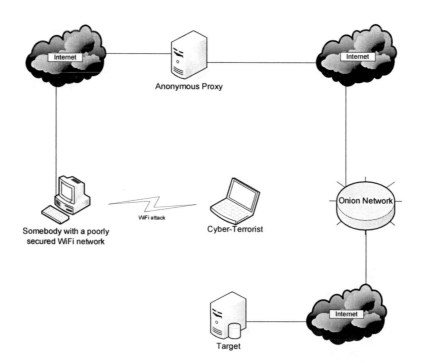

principle is based on public proxies, which are specially tailored for anonymity. For example, information flow is encrypted, a given number of proxies (up to 20) can be used as a chain (chosen by the sender), and each of them does not know the real origin, nor the real destination of the flow. Each proxy only knows the previous bouncing point, the encrypted flow, and dynamically only discovers the next bouncing point. This principle has led to the analogy of an onion, which is made of successive layers. This paradigm is actually a bit slower but can guarantee a high level of anonymity, because chasing back the attacker necessitates logging features on every proxy without exception, which is left to each owner's decision.

All these methods are infinitely combinable, and real anonymity is practically attainable. For example, Figure 1 shows a chain starting from a cyber terrorist using war driving to locate an 802.11b network. After breaking the encryption features, he or she connects to an anonymous proxy, and then to an onion network to finally attack the final target. This chain can involve more than 25 machines, in as many different countries. Tracing back this attack, which has taken minutes, could take several years but, in practice, will become impossible for many reasons: no logs, no inquiry duration, inefficient international cooperation, and finally because the terrorist car is not parked in the street anymore.

CONCLUSION AND PERSPECTIVES

Bouncing techniques are really a problem and the current situation is largely embroiled. Cyber terrorists can use one or several real but incorrect cyber identities. That is a very new kind of terrorism. Therefore, tracking down the culprit becomes very difficult and innocent people can often be involved.

On a purely technical basis, chasing down a cyber terrorist requires applicative logging on each and every bouncing point. But this can be done only if the bouncing point owner is aware of the bouncing activity. In the other cases (Trojans or hacked proxies, for

example), it is necessary to log all traffic information in any country, which is hardly feasible, legally and technically. But, with time, it is making headway, for example, in Europe (European Parliament, 2005).

Moreover collaboration of international law enforcement services is essential to sharing logging information. Note that logging is not the final solution. Some powerful analysis tools are necessary to deal with the huge amount of data, which is still an open problem.

REFERENCES

Dingledine, R., Matthewson, R., & Syverson, P. (2004). Tor: The second-generation onion router. *Proceedings of the 13th USENIX Security Symposium* (pp. 303-320).

Edney, J., & Arbaugh, W. A. (2003). *Real 802.11 security: Wi-Fi protected access and 802.11i*. Addison-Wesley Professional.

Erbschloe, M. (2004). *Trojans, worms, and spyware: A computer security professional's guide to malicious code*. Butterworth-Heinemann.

European Parliament. (2005). *Directive of the European Parliament on data retention*. Retrieved from http://ue.eu.int/ ueDocs/cms_Data/docs/pressData/en/jha/88467.pdf

Fluhrer, S., Mantin, I., & Shamir, A. (2001). Weaknesses in the key scheduling algorithm of RC4. *Proceedings of the Eighth Annual Workshop on Selected Areas in Cryptography* (pp. 1-24). Toronto, Canada.

Jones, K. J., Bejtlich, R., & RoseReal, C. W. (2005). *Digital forensics: Computer security and incident response*. Addison-Wesley Professional.

Luotonen, A. (1997). *Web proxy servers*. Prentice Hall PTR.

TERMS AND DEFINITIONS

802.11b/Wi-Fi Networks: This is the first popular wireless networking standard, largely deployed and used by companies and individuals. It provides a security feature, called wired encryption protocol (WEP), which is now known to be easily breakable.

Logs: These are special system files, keeping traces of every important event. There are no general rules specifying what can be found in log files. However, they are a first way of knowing what has happened at a given time.

Trojans: Trojans are malicious programs that are disguised so that they do not appear as they actually are. Typically, Trojans are sent as attachments to e-mails, stating it is a video, an image, or something that make the reader open it. They also can be found on peer-to-peer networks under the form of music files, on so-called *warez* sites (sites that allow for downloading illegal software copies), and so forth.

War Driving: This refers to driving, usually in urban areas, in order to detect wireless networks. Many war drivers use a Wi-Fi laptop connected to a GPS device to locate the networks, for further referencing on special Web sites.

Chapter XLVI
Cyber Forensics

Stéphane Coulondre
University of Lyon, France

ABSTRACT

Nowadays, terrorists master technology. They often use electronic devices that allow them to act without being physically exposed. As a consequence, their attacks are quicker, more precise, and even more disastrous. As cyber-terrorism relies on computers, the evidence is distributed on large-scale networks. Internet providers as well as government agencies around the world have set up several advanced logging techniques. However, this kind of information alone is not always sufficient. It is sometimes paramount to also analyse the target and source computers, if available, as well as some networking elements. This step is called cyber-forensics, and allows for precisely reconstructing and understanding the attack, and sometimes for identifying the intruders. In this paper, we present the basics and well-known issues, and we give some related perspectives.

INTRODUCTION

When a crime is committed, the police resort to scientific methods in order to track down the culprit. These methods largely rely on traces that have been left unconsciously or unintentionally, either on or around the victim. When a suspect has been identified, the very same methods are used to gather proof on the suspect or in his/her environment (home, work, etc.).

Nowadays, electronic devices are extensively used in terrorist attacks. For example, mobile phones are used for bomb ignition; and the chemical industry's computer systems are very often the target of intru-sion attempts in order to launch uncontrolled chemical reactions, either directly or indirectly, by using a specially tailored malicious code sent as Trojans to particular users. As a consequence, a new discipline is born: cyber forensics.

BACKGROUND

In the mid-1980s, various law enforcement agencies began to examine computer evidence. By analogy, examining the traces left by a user in computers and, more generally, in electronic devices (mobile phone, personal digital assistant (PDA), videotapes, etc.) and reconstructing the evidence is called computer forensics (Shinder, 2002). The term computer forensics was coined in the first training session held by the International Association of Computer Investigative Specialists (IACIS) in Portland, OR.

As the FBI states (FBI, 2004):

Computer crimes can be separated into two categories: (1) crimes facilitated by a computer and (2) crimes where a computer or network is the target.

When a computer is used as a tool to aid criminal activity, it may include storing records of fraud, producing false identification, reproducing and distributing copyright material, collecting and distributing child pornography, and many other crimes. Crimes where computers are the targets can result in damage or alteration to the computer system. Computers which have been compromised may be used to launch attacks on other computers or networks. (p. X)

Cyber forensics is a larger term than computer forensics and applies essentially to point 2 of the above definition. Indeed, cyber terrorism very often relies on the networking aspect of forensics. Cyber forensics includes network forensics and focuses on evidence that is distributed on large-scale networks.

Forensics is a paramount step in the investigation that can reveal a lot of precise and useful information, depending on the criminal's skills, for example, the weapons and methods that have been used, the precise attack time, and what has been destroyed, stolen, or hidden. When the terrorist's origin is not known, this step can sometimes reveal both location and identity (Middleton, 2004). Whenever the attacker's electronic devices can be seized, this step enables the collection of trivial evidence.

This chapter will focus on networking aspects of cyber forensics, which are central to cyber terrorism. We first describe the basic types of traces that can be left by a terrorist or an automated process, intentionally, or unintentionally, in a target computer system

or in his/her own computer. We then explain how to gather them and how they can be used, in conjunction with external information sources, to reconstruct precisely the attack scenario and track down the culprit. Then we try to give some perspectives on the future of cyber forensics, especially with reference to encryption and anonymization techniques and identity issues. Note that we do not focus here on dedicated monitoring techniques (which have to be deployed prior to any attack, i.e., intrusion detection systems, traffic recording, etc.) or incident response handling, which are outside the scope of this chapter.

DATA LIFE

A computing device (computer, PDA, digital camera, smart phone) can manipulate four types of data (Jones, Bejtlich, & RoseReal, 2005):

- Active data, which is recorded willingly and can be hidden willingly
- Temporary data, which is recorded by the system itself
- Latent data, which is considered as useless or erasable
- Archival data, which is located on an isolated media

Most computer users think that accessible data is only composed of active and archival data. Indeed, for sake of usability and simplicity, most operating systems do not mention to users the existence of temporary or latent data. However this data is of great importance.

Virtually any computing activity generates temporary and latent data. Internet browsers, word processors, mailers, games, music players, video edition software, and even intrusions or malicious code (spyware, viruses, Trojans, etc.), all leave traces of activity. The amount of disseminated information depends on the kind and duration of activity. It is important to notice that temporary and, especially,

Table 1. Examples of extractable temporary and latent data

- Deleted or rewritten files
- Data in unallocated sectors or in allocated file slacks
- Date and time of file creation, deletion, modification, and execution
- Information on previously installed applications
- Downloaded files
- Web browsing history, including local copies of visited pages
- Cookies
- Forms information, including some passwords
- Sent and deleted e-mails
- System logs

latent data has a limited lifetime and will eventually be deleted, unless the computer activity is stopped.

Moreover, a part of those computing activities can unwillingly leave traces on other computing systems. It is the case, for example, for Internet surfing, chatting, mailing, operating system upgrading, and so forth. This data also can be remotely active, temporary, latent, or archival, for example, when browsing activity is monitored on a special computer. Therefore, even if particular data has been securely deleted from a computer, it can still be active on another.

Table 1 enumerates some types of temporary and latent data that can be extracted from a computer system. Extraction is sometimes not entirely possible, depending on numerous parameters.

CYBER FORENSICS BASICS

Many computer forensic tools are available that are able to access all major electronic devices' memory areas. These tools allow for extracting and analyzing temporary and latent data, but also for dealing with active and archival data (e-mails, contacts, calendar entries, etc). Some examples of commercial software are Guidance Software Encase and AccessData Forensic Toolkit, and examples of free software are The Sleuth Kit and Autopsy Browser (Carrier, 2005).

These computer forensics tools cannot only extract and analyze temporary and latent data, but also perform advanced operations by deduction. For example, they can deduce, from date and time file stamps, the sequence of events that occurred at a given moment, for example, the time of an attack, or the time a document has been hidden. The investigator can see that a file transfer program has been launched and that new files have been written to disk only a few seconds after, executed, and then deleted. By retrieving these files, he or she may notice that a malicious program has been downloaded from the Internet, installed, and that the installation files have been deleted. An example of timeline reconstruction, within the Autopsy browser, is shown in Figure 1. These tools also can retrieve files or file chunks in unallocated disk sectors or file slacks, and detect their type by comparing their content with a set of signatures. This is very useful when a disk partition has been formatted or when files have been rewritten.

Retrieving and analyzing temporary and latent data is just a step towards understanding an attack, tracking down the author, and gathering proof. Indeed, this information has to be analyzed as a whole by the investigators, and this step cannot be automatic.

In every case, external sources of information are necessary in an inquiry. Indeed, for example, when investigators only have a compromised machine at

Figure 1. A reconstructed timeline of activity using Autopsy

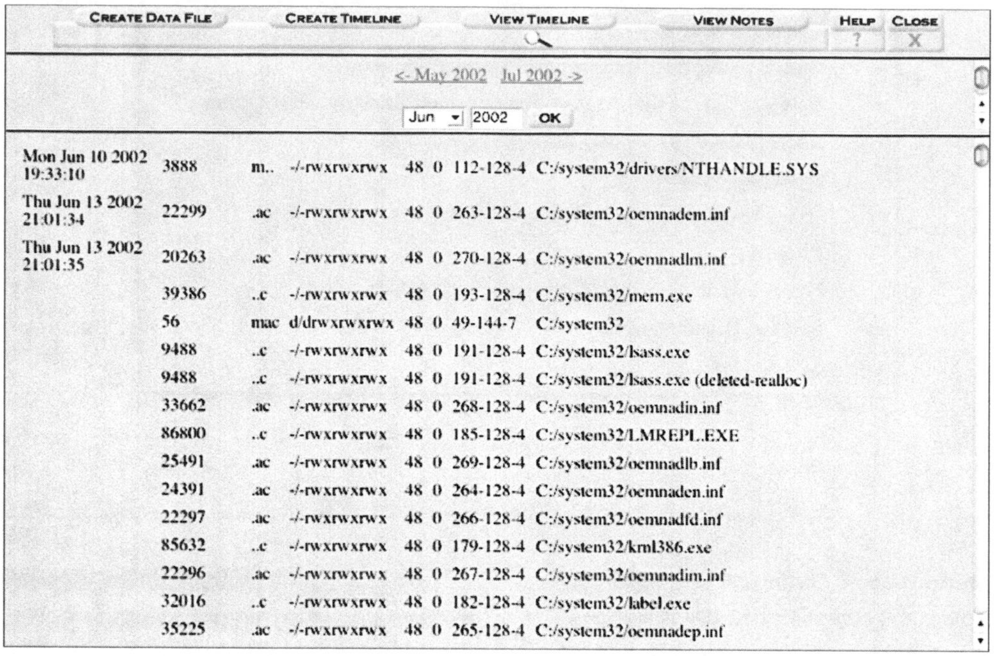

their disposal, they need to find the Internet addresses from which the attack has been launched. This can only be achieved by using information that forensic tools have extracted, in conjunction with information located on distant systems. That makes up the essence of cyber forensics.

One of the primary sources is managed by Internet service providers (ISPs). In European countries, for instance, ISPs are required by law to keep connection information, that is, dynamically or statically assigned Internet addresses, together with date, time, and duration of each connection, for a given delay (usually three months to 1 year). This enables the retrieval of any customer identity, based on a given Internet address and date/time, and thus further forensic analysis of his or her computer after seizure. Note, as a consequence, that in the case of international lawsuit, including terrorism, collaboration between countries is essential. Often, the origin of the cyber attack is not trivial, and extra sources of information are necessary when bouncing techniques have been used (see below).

In a case of a passive attack (i.e., when malicious code is detected on a computer), only a highly skilled computer scientist can analyze the purpose, means, and internal specifications of this code. Indeed, spyware, Trojans, and viruses can be very useful for a cyber terrorist for gathering information prior to launching an attack, which may not necessarily be electronic, or to take distant control of a sensitive computer. The origin of malicious code is harder to locate, especially if the code has been made for a special purpose (i.e., spying on a given company or institution). In general, a malicious code's origin can be tracked down, if it is widely spread, by studying the spreading dynamics of the code. This includes gathering logs from private- and public-sector institutions.

CYBER FORENSICS ISSUES

The size of current storage media increases every month. Indeed, a forensic analysis requires copying the exact media content on a dedicated hard disk, in order to protect the original from the investigator making mistakes. This leads to frequent dedicated hardware upgrades. Moreover, the amount of data to analyze, and especially the number of computing devices people use also grows (laptop, PDA, online services, Internet cafés, etc.). Future forensic tools, therefore, should be able to help investigators to deal with all of these new devices, to quickly focus on relevant data, and to detect relations between distributed data. This is still an active research area.

Encryption is now available for everybody, after being considered as a weapon for a long time by many governments. As a consequence, analyzing an encrypted device (i.e., hard disk) can become very difficult if at all possible (Menezes, 2001). Many forensic tools include password cracking or bypassing primitives (e.g., Encase includes an optional module for accessing Microsoft's encrypting file system), but in some cases, it can be nearly impossible, especially when the criminal has used special-purpose privacy enhancing techniques (PETs). These techniques can be divided into four groups: encryption tools, policy tools, filtering tools, and anonymous tools. Encryption and anonymous tools are really an obstacle to forensic analysis; the two other kinds of tools are especially tailored for legitimate users' privacy protection. Encryption techniques are numerous. While necessary for common data protection, encryption tools can provide a very secure way for hiding illegal data, even from forensic investigators.

Anonymous techniques (Shields& Levine, 2000) are discussed more in-depth in the article entitled *Bouncing Techniques*. They allow for hiding not only the content of communications, but also provide extended privacy, hiding personal information. This is possible in two ways: centralized (i.e., anonymizing Web sites, proxies, or poorly secured WiFi access points) (Pointcheval, 2000) and decentralized (i.e., onion routing) (Dingledine, Matthewson & Syverson, 2004). When an attacker uses this kind of tool, forensic analysis will return the Internet address of the centralized anonymizing computer (proxy), or one of the computers that make up the onion routing network. This depends on the logging features of each of them, and on the legal possibility of getting this information. This dramatically increases the chances of the attacker not getting caught. In practical terms, a skilled attacker prefers to use these techniques instead of properly erasing all the traces left by an intrusion, which can be hard, but still possible.

This leads us to the more general problem of identity usurpation in cyber forensics. Investigators are confronted by this when bouncing techniques are used; evidence refers to a culprit, who is, in fact, not the right one, for example, in the case of wireless networks hijacking. Therefore, an important question has to be answered by investigators: Are we sure that a given digital identity always refers to the right physical person? A thorough discussion can be found on the FIDIS Web site (FIDIS, 2006).

Finally, there is an important legal aspect in forensic analysis (Smith & Bace, 2002). As this greatly differs according to local laws, we do not detail here the peculiarities of each judicial system, but a general rule for any evidence to be valid in court is to prove that nothing has been tampered with during the analysis, that integrity is preserved as well as a person's right to privacy, and that the evidence is valid, technically, and legally.

CONCLUSION

Forensic analysis of computing devices and networks is now an important aspect of investigations and a fundamental aspect of cyber warfare. It must be carried out by specialized investigators whose competences are twofold: judiciary and technical. It is not only a domain of computer specialists.

Future tools should find a way to tackle the current issues that can develop into real challenges. It is very important that investigators keep in touch with new tools and techniques, as cyber criminals will certainly always try to use technical and scientific breakthroughs to their advantage.

REFERENCES

Carrier, B. (2005). *File system forensic analysis*. Addison-Wesley Professional.

Dingledine, R., Matthewson, R., & Syverson, P. (2004). Tor: The second-generation onion router. *Proceedings of the 13th USENIX Security Symposium* (pp. 303-320).

FBI. (2004). *How the FBI investigates computer crime*. Retrieved from http://www.cert.org

FIDIS. (2006). *Forensic implications of identity management systems*. Retrieved from http://www.fidis.net

Jones K. J., Bejtlich R., & RoseReal C. W. (2005). *Digital forensics: Computer security and incident response*. Addison-Wesley Professional.

Meneze,s A. (2001). *Handbook of applied cryptography* (5th ed.). CRC Press.

Middleton, B. (2004). *Cyber crime investigator's field guide*. Auerbach.

Pointcheval, D. (2000). Self-scrambling anonymizers. *Proceedings of the Financial Cryptography Conference* (LNCS 1962, pp. 259-275).

Shields, C., & Levine, B. (2000). A protocol for anonymous communication over the Internet. *Proceedings of the ACM Computer and Communication Security Conference* (pp. 33-42). ACM Press: New York

Shinder, D. L. (2002). *Scene of the cybercrime: Computer forensics handbook*. Syngress.

Smith, F. C., & Bace, R. G. (2002). *A guide to forensic testimony: The art and practice of presenting testimony as an expert technical witness*. Addison-Wesley Professional.

TERMS AND DEFINITIONS

File Slack: This specific area on a storage device is located between the end of a file and the end of the corresponding sector. A storage device is divided into logical sectors (typically 512 bytes). When a file is, for example, 520 bytes long, it uses two sectors, leaving 504 bytes called file slack, which is not used nor initialized. This means that it is possible to find data from a previous file.

Forensic: Forensic science (often shortened to forensics) is the application of a broad spectrum of sciences to answer questions of interest to the judicial system. This may be in relation to a crime or to a civil action.

Formatted: Formatting a storage format means making it entirely available for new use. This does not mean erasing. The most used formatting algorithm only cleans allocation tables, that is, information stating how the data is ordered. The side effect is that data is left on the medium, unordered, but perfectly readable, if the program can guess the erased order.

Logs: These are special system files, which keep traces of every important event. There are no general rules specifying what can be found in log files. However, they are a first way of knowing what has happened at a given time.

Onion Routing: This routing algorithm uses a special network of machines, capable of receiving and forwarding any traffic without knowing its origin or its destination. Only the sender knows the route, and the receiver only knows the last machine that has routed the traffic.

Proxy: This is an entity capable of making connections and/or performing protocol commands in the name of another computer. When a computer connects to a Web site by an anonymous proxy, the Web site cannot know its real Internet address.

Chapter XLVII
Software Component Survivability in Information Warfare

Joon S. Park
Syracuse University, USA

Joseph Giordano
Air Force Research Laboratory, USA

ABSTRACT

The need for software component survivability is pressing for mission-critical systems in information warfare. In this chapter, we describe how mission-critical distributed systems can survive component failures or compromises with malicious codes in information warfare. We define our definition of survivability, discuss the survivability challenges in a large mission-critical system in information warfare, and identify static, dynamic, and hybrid survivability models. Furthermore, we discuss the trade offs of each model. Technical details and implementation of the models are not described in this chapter because of space limitations.

INTRODUCTION

As information systems became ever more complex and the interdependence of these systems increased, the survivability picture became more and more complicated. The need for survivability is most pressing for mission-critical systems in information warfare. When components are exported from a remote system to a local system under different administration and deployed in different environments, we cannot guarantee the proper execution of those remote components in the current run-time environment. Therefore, in the run time, we should consider component failures (in particular, remote components) that may occur due to poor implementation, during integration with other components in the system, or because of cyber attacks. Although advanced technologies and system architectures improve the capability of today's systems, we cannot completely avoid threats to them. This becomes more serious when the systems are integrated with commercial off-the-shelf (COTS) products and services, which typically have both known and unknown vulnerabilities that may cause unexpected problems and that can be exploited by attackers trying to disrupt mission-critical services (Kapfhammer, Michael, Haddox, & Colyer, 2000). Organizations, including the Department of Defense (DoD), use COTS systems and services to provide office productivity, Internet services, and database services, and they tailor these systems and services to satisfy their specific requirements. Using COTS systems and services as much as possible is a cost-effective strategy, but such systems—even when tailored to the specific needs of the implementing organization—also inherit flaws and weaknesses from specific COTS products and services that are used. Therefore, we need reliable approaches to ensure survivability in mission-critical systems that must rely on commercial services and products in a distributed computing environment.

Definitions of survivability were introduced by previous researchers (Knight & Sullivan, 2000; Lipson & Fisher, 1999). We define survivability as the capability of an entity to continue its mission even in the presence of damage to the entity (Park, Chandramohan, Devarajan, & Giordano, 2005). An entity ranges from a single software component (object), with its mission in a distributed computing environment, to an information system that consists of many components to support the overall mission. An entity may support multiple missions.

The damage caused by cyber attacks, system failures, or accidents, and whether a system can recover from this damage (Jajodia, McCollum, & Ammann, 1999; Knight, Elder, & Du, 1998; Liu, Ammann, & Jajodia, 2000), will determine the survivability characteristics of a system. A survivability strategy can be set up in three steps: protection, detection and response, and recovery (Park & Froscher, 2002). To make a system survivable, it is the mission of the system rather than the components of the system. This implies that the designer or assessor should define a set of critical services the system must provide in order to fulfill the mission. In other words, they must understand what services should be survivable by the mission and what

functions of which components in the system should continue to support the system's mission.

In this article, we focus on the survivability of mission-critical software components downloaded on the Internet. We assume that all software components are susceptible to malicious cyber attacks or internal failures. Cyber attacks may involve tampering with existing source code to include undesired functionality (e.g., Trojan horses), or replacing a genuine component with a malicious one. When using such components, particularly in mission-critical applications in information warfare, we must check to see if the component was developed by a trusted source, and whether the code has been modified in an unauthorized manner since it was created. Furthermore, we should check to see if the component is functioning in an expected way. If all these conditions are satisfied, we call it "trusted component sharing."

CHALLENGES TO SOFTWARE SURVIVABILITY IN A MISSION-CRITICAL SYSTEM

Typically, an application running at an enterprise level may span more than one organization. Figure 1 shows an example of a distributed application that spans multiple organizations. The figure depicts three organizations interconnected to form a large enterprise-computing environment. In the real world, there may be more than two or three organizations connected to form a large enterprise, and some of the organizations in the enterprise may provide specialized services that other organizations do not provide (e.g., Department of Homeland Security). In the figure, for example, components in Organizations 1 and 3 are involved in application X. In this example the application running in Organization 3 downloads necessary components for some special features that it lacks. These components are dynamically downloaded from remotely administered hosts (in Organization 1 in the example) and run locally. This situation becomes complex when one must administer components downloaded from disparate administrations. For instance,

Figure 1. A distributed application spanning multiple organizations

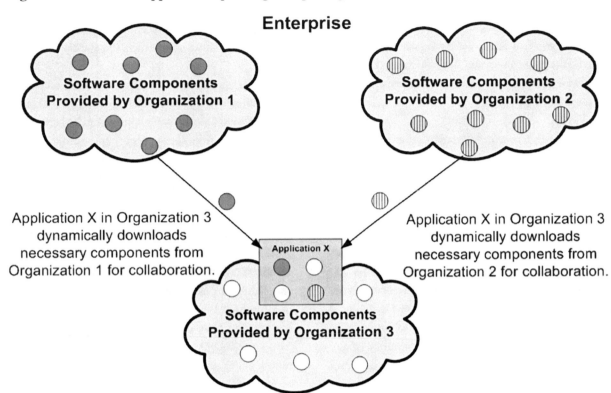

Figure 1 shows that a user under Organization 3's administration can dynamically download software components under Organization 1's administration. From this point forward, the software running in Organization 3 should cooperate with the downloaded components that originated from different administrations. To employ autonomous administration, the local administrator must perform the extra job of dealing with interoperability problems and failures of or attacks via external components.

Based on the typical scenario described above, we identify the following generic challenges for software survivability in large distributed mission-critical systems.

Challenge 1. An autonomous mechanism to support component survivability between different organizations or systems is needed due to the fact that no single administrator can control every aspect (e.g., software component testing and implementation) of the various systems used in an enterprise. This is an inherent challenge because many systems, including those from different organizations, are integrated within current distributed computing environments. This implies that a remote component may have failures or malicious code that could affect a local computing environment. Unfortunately, a remote component cannot be tested in a local environment until runtime.

Challenge 2. Testing software components before deployment cannot detect or anticipate all of the possible failures or attacks that may manifest themselves during run time, especially when external components are integrated. Some failures are detected only when the components are deployed and integrated with other components in the operational environments. Existing faults in one component can be triggered by other components during runtime. Furthermore, since we cannot simply assume that all the participating organizations followed proper testing procedures for their software components, we need a new component-test mechanism that can test the component in the actual run-time environment—especially for components downloaded from different environments. The test criteria can vary, based on current applications or run-time environments, even for the same component. The remote component may cause an interoperability problem in a different run-time environment, although it passed its original test.

Challenge 3. In a distributed mission-critical system, we must check whether a remote component has been altered in an unauthorized manner, especially if it contains malicious codes, such as Trojan Horses, viruses, or spyware, before malicious codes are activated in the run-time environment. For instance, in Figure 1, when different organizations collaborate for a common enterprise but are competitors in the market, each organization should check the components from other organizations before they are used in the local environment. Furthermore, if a component includes any malicious codes, but the functionality of the original code is still needed for the system, we cannot simply reject the entire component. Instead, we should safely retrieve only the original code, enervating the malicious code.

Challenge 4, Currently available redundancy-based static approaches cannot solve the problem completely. If one component has failed because of reason R1, then the rest of the redundant components will fail for the same reason. It is only a matter of time before every redundant component is compromised for the same reason, especially when those components are identical. Furthermore, the strength of the redundancy-based approaches depends on the prepared redundancy, which brings up the question of "how many" redundant components we need to provide. Technically, one could maintain as many redundant components as necessary for a critical service. However, if the initially selected component is running in its normal state—meaning there is no need to use other redundant components as the component is not defective or compromised—the cost for running the redundant components has been wasted. In this situation, the resource efficiency is low, and the maintenance cost is high. Therefore, for

mission-critical systems in information warfare, a dynamic technique is needed to detect and analyze the possible faults and attacks in the components and fix/immunize these components on-the-fly.

Challenge 5. Even if we know the reasons for and the locations of the software failures or attacks, in most currently available recovery approaches in distributed computing environments, changing the component's capability (e.g., for immunization) in run time is difficult, especially when the source code is not available (which is not an uncommon situation). When dealing with component failures, we are concerned with the problem of how to fix these failed components. One possibility is to modify the source code according to the identified failures; however, this approach is possible only if the source code for that component is available. In the case of COTS components and other components downloaded from externally administered systems, the source code is often unavailable. Although some source codes are available to the public, if they are poorly documented, it will hardly be possible to modify the source code effectively. Furthermore, many mission-critical systems do not tolerate the suspension of operation for code debugging and recompilation. One must, therefore, employ other techniques to achieve the goal of fixing failed components on-the-fly—without access to the source code—in order for the mission of the component to continue.

SUPPORT MECHANISMS FOR SOFTWARE SURVIVABILITY

Component Recovery

Barga, Lomet, Shegalov, and Weikum (2004) introduced a framework for an application-independent infrastructure that provides recovery of data, messages, and states in Web-based applications. The framework requires an interaction contract between two components that specifies the joint behavior of those two interacting components. An application component can be replayed from an earlier installed state and arrive at the same state as in its prefailure incarnation. It masks from users the failures of clients, application servers, or data servers only if the replay could recover the component. Unfortunately, however, there are many component failures that cannot be fixed simply by replays. With this approach, a component may go back to the state before the failure; however, it cannot proceed further from that failure point again, unless the reason for the failure is fixed. Therefore, the component is not able to continue its mission. Furthermore, this approach does not consider malicious codes that are already included in the components. Similarly, the state-based recovery approaches for client-server systems were introduced by Freytag Cristian, and KŁhler (1987) and Barga, Lomet, Baby, and Agrawal (2000), and for databases by Liu et al. 2000) and Jajodia et al. (1999).

Ring, Esler, and Cole (2004) introduced self-healing mechanisms for kernel system compromises in run time, which analyze the system call table and enable the compromised addresses to return to their original values, terminate hidden processes, remove hidden files, and block hidden connections. As with state-based recovery, these can recover a compromised system to its state before the failure or attack and prevent the situation from getting worse. However, like the state-based approach, this approach does not fix the fundamental reason for the problem or let the system go to further states. Also, the scope of the work is within a kernel module in Linux.

Dowling and Cahill (2004) introduced the idea of K-components for self-adaptive decentralized systems. By using a component interface definition language called K-IDL, the definitions of component states and adaptation actions are used by decision-making programs to reason about and adapt component operation. Programmers can specify adaptation contracts for their local environments. However, this limits the overall robustness of the adaptive systems because, typically, programmers do not know all the possible adaptive options in various computing environments in which their components will be running. When the components are used in a large distributed application, which is the scope of our work, this approach is especially not scalable.

Helsinger, Kleinmann, and Brinn (2004) introduced a multitiered control framework between high-level observable metrics and low-level control actions for distributed multiagent systems that are composed of distributed autonomous agents interacting on a peer-to-peer basis. The framework imposes intermediate measurers of performance (MOPs) that measure the contributions of different components and actions to higher-level functions. They observe the behaviors at one level and seek to manage those behaviors by taking control actions at a lower level, such as by restarting dead agents or load balancing by moving agents between hosts. Assuming that each agent will be developed correctly and trusted, this framework can improve the availability of agents and may optimize load balancing. However, the framework may not comply properly when the components have internal failures or are compromised by malicious codes, which is not unusual in a real mission-critical distributed system in information warfare.

Component Test

Existing technologies for identifying faulty components are more or less static in nature. One of these approaches employs black-box testing of the components. In this technique, behavioral specifications are provided for the component to be tested in the target system. This technique treats the target component as a black box and can be used to determine how the component behaves anomalously. Traditionally, black-box testing is done without knowledge of the internal workings of the component tested. Normally, black-box testing involves only input and output details of the component, while information on how the output is arrived at is not needed. The main disadvantage of this technique is that the specifications should cover all the details of the visible behavior of the components, which is impractical in many situations. Another approach employs a source-code analysis, which depends on the availability of the source code of the components. Software testability analysis employs a white-box testing technique that determines the locations in the component where a failure is likely to occur. Unlike black-box testing, white-box testing allows the tester to see the inner details of the component, which later helps him to create appropriate test data. Yet another approach is software component dependability assessment, a modification or testability analysis that thoroughly tests each component. These techniques are possible only when the source code of the components is available.

In the past, Kapfhammer et al. (2000) have employed a simple behavioral specification utilizing execution-based evaluation. This approach combines software fault injection (Avresky, Arlat, Laprie, & Crouzet, 1996; Hsueh, Tsai, and Iyer, 1997; Madeira, Costa, and Vieira, 2000) at component interfaces and machine learning techniques to: (1) identify problematic COTS components and (2) to understand these components anomalous behavior. They isolated problematic COTS components, created wrappers, and introduced them into the system under different analysis stages to uniquely identify the failed components and to gather information on the circumstances that surrounded the anomalous component behavior. Finally, they preprocessed the collected data and applied selective machine learning algorithms to generate a finite state machine to better understand and to increase the robustness of faulty components. In other research (Chen, Kiciman, Fratkin, Fox, & Brewer, 2002; Voas & McGraw, 1998), the authors developed a dynamic problem determination framework for a large J2EE platform, employing a fault-detection approach based on data-clustering mechanisms to identify faulty components.

COMPONENT SURVIVABILITY MODELS

In this section, we identify static, dynamic, and hybrid models for software survivability and discuss their trade offs. Technical details and implementation of these models are available in our previous publications (Park & Chandramohan, 2004; Park et al., 2005). We describe our approaches using client and server components in a typical distributed environment.

Static Survivability Model

The survivability of this model is based on redundant components, prepared before the operation, to support critical services continuously in a distributed client-server environment. Redundant servers can be located in the same machine, in different machines in the same domain or even in different domains. Existing approaches, such as dynamic reconfiguration, can be associated with this static model. Although the term "dynamic" is used in the terminology, it belongs to the static model, according to our definition, as long as the available components are generated before the operation starts. The same service can be provided by identical components (e.g., copies of the original servers) or by different components that are implemented in various ways. Isolated redundancy (in different machines or domains) usually provides higher survivability because the replaced component can be running in an uninfected area. For instance, if the redundant components are distributed in different network places, then the services provided by those components can be recovered in the event of network failures, in different environments. However, if there is a failure within a component, replacing that component with an identical copy is not effective, because identical components are vulnerable to the same failure.

Dynamic Survivability Model

In this model, unlike the static model, there is no redundant component. Components with failures or malicious codes are replaced by dynamically generated components on-the-fly and deployed in run time when required. Furthermore, this model allows replacement of the infected components with immunized components, if possible, which enables it to provide more robust services than the static model.

Basically, when failures or malicious codes are detected in a component, the corresponding factory generates an immunized component and deploys it into a safe environment, while the monitor issues a command to shut down the old component. The concept of "factory" was originally introduced as one of the commonly used design patterns in the object-oriented design. If we do not know the exact reason for the failures or types of malicious codes, or if it is hard to immunize components against known failures or malicious codes, we can simply replace the infected component with a new one in a safe environment. We call this a generic immunization strategy, which is effective against cyber attacks. If a component (a machine or a whole domain) is under attack, the generic immunization strategy suggests generating a new copy of the component and deploying it in a new environment that is safe from attack. Although this approach supports service availability continuously, the new component might still be susceptible to the same failures or attacks. Therefore, an immunized component, if possible, would provide a more robust survivability.

The Hybrid Model

The hybrid survivability model combines the features of the above two models. The dynamic model has an inherent disadvantage in terms of service downtime. The recovery process can range from seconds to a few minutes. This downtime drawback will cause major problems in mission-critical systems in information warfare because there will be no service available for clients during the recovery period. On the other hand, the static model has inherent disadvantages in terms of resource efficiency, adaptation, and robustness.

To compensate for the weaknesses in the two models, we incorporated the idea of a hybrid model. At the beginning of the operation, an array of n redundant components is initiated as described in the static model approach. These redundant servers will be used as a buffer while a more robust server is generated and deployed by the dynamic model approach. When a server fails because of an attack or internal failure, the buffer servers will take over the service for a brief period until the new immunized server is initialized. Since all of the buffer servers are susceptible to the same failures or attacks, it is a matter of time before the redundant servers are also infected for the same reason, especially when those

servers are identical. Therefore, if the transition period is long, multiple buffer servers may be used before the immunized server is ready. The hybrid model ensures the availability of service to the client and provides more robust services in the end. However, this model needs more complex implementations than the two models previously discussed.

Trade Offs

In the static survivability model there are n numbers of redundant servers running in parallel that are deployed even before the operation starts. If one server fails, the broker delegates incoming requests to another server in the remaining server pool. Since the redundant components are ready to be used (unlike those in the dynamic model) during the failure or attack, the service downtime is relatively shorter than in the dynamic model. The implementation of the static survivability model is comparatively simpler than the dynamic or the hybrid model. In the static survivability model, it is unnecessary to maintain a server component factory, whose main job is to replace faulty server components with immunized ones. On the other hand, the static model has inherent disadvantages in terms of resource efficiency, adaptation, and robustness.

The hybrid model combines the logic of both the static and dynamic models. Here, if the monitor finds a fault in one of the server components, it informs the factory (as in the dynamic model) to replace the faulty component with an immunized one, and, in the meantime, it also sends a message to the broker to temporarily deploy a redundant component (as in the static model) until the new immunized component is built and deployed. Since the dynamic and hybrid models are able to build immunized components, they are more robust than the static model. The static model uses more memory resources than the dynamic model to maintain the redundant server components, making it less resource-efficient than the dynamic model. But this resource efficiency is accompanied by higher downtime in the dynamic model. The hybrid model is a balance between the static and dynamic models in terms of its resource efficiency.

CONCLUSION

In this chapter, we have described how mission-critical distributed systems can survive component failures or compromises with malicious codes in information warfare. We defined our definition of survivability, discussed the survivability challenges in a large mission-critical system in information warfare, and identified static, dynamic, and hybrid survivability models. Furthermore, we discussed the trade offs of each model. Technical details and implementation of the models are not described here because of space limitations.

Components can be immunized based on the generic or specific strategies provided by the monitors. If the monitor figures out the reasons for the failures or types of attacks on the components, it can provide specific strategies to the corresponding component factories. The level of immunization depends on the monitor's capability. The more powerful monitoring mechanisms and their communication channels between other components can provide more resistance to failures and attacks. Analyzing specific reasons for unexpected failures in run time is another challenge. Monitors can cooperate with other monitors, and different monitors are in charge of different interests. To detect and analyze types of attacks, the monitors can be associated with existing intrusion detection systems, which is also part of our future work.

REFERENCES

Avresky, D. R., Arlat, J., Laprie, J.-C., & Crouzet, Y. (1996). Fault injection for formal testing of fault tolerance. *IEEE Transactions on Reliability, 45*(3), 443-455.

Barga, R. S., Lomet, D. B., Baby, T., & Agrawal, S. (2000). Persistent client-server database sessions. In *Proceedings of the 7th International Conference on Extending Database Technology: Advances in Database Technology* (pp. 462-477). Konstanz, Germany.

Barga, R., Lomet, D., Shegalov, G., & Weikum, G. (2004). Recovery guarantees for Internet applications. *ACM Transactions on Internet Technology (TOIT), 4*(3), 289-328.

Chen, M. Y., Kiciman, E., Fratkin, E., Fox, A., & Brewer, E. (2002). Pinpoint: Problem determination in large, dynamic Internet services. In *Proceedings of International Conference on Dependable Systems and Networks (DSN)* (pp. 595-604). Washington, DC.

Dowling, J., & Cahill, V. (2004). Self-managed decentralized systems using k-components and collaborative reinforcement learning. In *Proceedings of the 1st ACM SIGSOFT workshop on self-managed systems (WOSS)* (pp. 39-43). New York.

Freytag, J. C., Cristian, F., & KŁhler, B. (1987). Making system crashes in database application programs. In *Proceedings of the 13th International Conference on Very Large Data Bases* (pp. 407-416). Brighton, UK.

Helsinger, A., Kleinmann, K., & Brinn, M. (2004). A framework to control emergent survivability of multi agent systems. In *Proceedings of the 3rd International Joint Conference on Autonomous Agents and Multiagent Systems (AAMAS)* (pp. 28-35). Washington, DC.

Hsueh, M.-C., Tsai, T. K., & Iyer, R. K. (1997). Fault injection techniques and tools. *Computer, 30*(4), 75-82.

Jajodia, S., McCollum, C., & Ammann, P. (1999). Trusted recovery. *Communications of the ACM, 42*(7), 71-75.

Kapfhammer, G., Michael, C., Haddox, J., & Colyer, R. (2000). An approach to identifying and understanding problematic cots components. In *Proceedings of the Software Risk Management Conference (ISACC)*. Reston, VA.

Knight, J., Elder, M., & Du, X. (1998). Error recovery in critical infrastructure systems. In *Proceedings of the Computer Security, Dependability, and Assurance (CSDA) Workshop*. Williamsburg, VA.

Knight, J., & Sullivan, K. (2000). Towards a definition of survivability. In *Proceedings of the 3rd Information Survivability Workshop (ISW)*. Boston.

Lipson, H., & Fisher, D. (1999). Survivability: A new technical and business perspective on security. *Proceedings of the New Security Paradigms Workshop (NSPW)*, Caledon Hills, Ontario, Canada.

Liu, P., Ammann, P., & Jajodia, S. (2000). Rewriting histories: Recovering from malicious transactions. *Distributed and Parallel Databases, 8*(1), 7-40.

Madeira, H., Costa, D., & Vieira, M. (2000). On the emulation of software faults by software fault injection. In *Proceedings of the International Conference on Dependable Systems and Networks (DNS)* (pp. 417-426). Washington, DC.

Park, J. S., & Chandramohan, P. (2004). Component recovery approaches for survivable distributed systems. In *Proceedings of the 37th Hawaii International Conference on Systems Sciences (HICSS-37)*. Big Island, HI.

Park, J. S., Chandramohan, P., Devarajan, G., & Giordano, J. (2005). Trusted component sharing by runtime test and immunization for survivable distributed systems. In *Proceedings of the 20th IFIP International Conference on Information Security (IFIP/SEC 2005)*. Chiba, Japan.

Park, J. S., & Froscher, J. N. (2002). A strategy for information survivability. In *Proceedings of the 4th Information Survivability Workshop (ISW)*. Vancouver, Canada.

Ring, S., Esler, D., & Cole, E. (2004). Self-healing mechanisms for kernel system compromises. In *Proceedings of the 1st ACM SIGSOFT workshop on self-managed systems (WOSS)* (pp. 100-104). New York.

Voas, J. M., & McGraw, G. (1998). *Software fault injection: Inoculating programs against errors.* Wiley Computer Publishing.

TERMS AND DEFINTIONS

Commercial Off-the-Shelf (COTS): These software systems are developed to interoperate with existing systems without the need for customization and available for sale to public.

Software Component: This reusable software element provides predefined services and can communicate with other components with relatively little effort.

Spyware: This software program monitors a user's computer activity surreptitiously or collects sensitive information about users or organizations without their knowledge.

Survivability: This refers to the capability of an entity to continue its mission even in the presence of damage to the entity.

Trojan Horse: A rogue software program installed on the victim's machine that can run secretly with the user's privileges.

Trusted Component: This software component has not been modified by an unauthorized manner, since it was created by a trusted source and functions in an expected way.

Virus: This software program attaches itself to other programs, propagating itself in this way, and does something, usually malicious and unexpected.

Chapter XLVIII
Taxonomy for Computer Security Incidents

Stefan Kiltz
Otto-von-Guericke University Magdeburg, Germany

Andreas Lang
Otto-von-Guericke University Magdeburg, Germany

Jana Dittmann
Otto-von-Guericke University Magdeburg, Germany

ABSTRACT

The adaptation and extension is necessary to apply the CERT-taxonomy to malware in order to categorise the threat (e.g., Trojan horses, Viruses etc.) as a basis for countermeasures. For the adaptation of the taxonomy to include malware a new entry in the tools section is needed (malicious software). This entry will cover the Trojan horses mentioned earlier. The proposed extension of the CERT-taxonomy will include the attacker-model, the vulnerability and the objectives. Within the attacker-model a new entry should be added, the security scan. This type of penetration testing by security-experts is similar to the works done by 'white hat'- hackers. However, such penetration testing is done by contractors on request, within strict margins concerning ethics and the assessment of potential damages before such testing takes place. The objectives within the CERT-taxonomy need a supplement, the security evaluation. This of course is the addition necessary to complement the introduction of the security scan. A very important vulnerability, social engineering, should be added to the taxonomy as well. It describes a very effective way to attack an IT-System. Two types can be distinguished, social engineering with the use of computers (e.g. e-mail content, phishing) and social engineering using human-based methods (e.g. dumpster diving, impostors).

INTRODUCTION

Since its introduction in 1998 in Howard and Longstaff (1998), the *CERT-taxonomy* for computer security incidents has been a very useful tool in finding a common language to describe computer security-related incidents. This ability to use a standardized language can be of great use, especially in situations where swift action is required (e.g., during incident response actions).

The authors propose a couple of extensions to this taxonomy, in order to adapt it to the environment that is found in the field of computer security today. Although the general nature of computer security incidents has not changed much, the proposed extension seems necessary to cover a new range of malicious tools, techniques, and motivations for an attack on a computer system or network.

BACKGROUND

The taxonomy was created in order to standardize the terminology used when dealing with incidents. It is useful for computer *security* incidents; *safety* aspects are not yet considered.

Safety deals mostly with incidents that appear at random or are caused by negligence or natural events. They often relate to material damage on physical objects. Security, however, is interested in malicious attacks against mostly immaterial entities like information, such as stored data.

Using the taxonomy, computer- and network security-related incidents can be reconstructed precisely and measures needed to be taken to remedy the situation can be discussed.

MAIN THRUST OF THE CHAPTER

The CERT-Taxonomy

The taxonomy was published in Howard and Longstaff (1998). Its objective was to provide a common language for security experts when dealing with security-related incidents. Their taxonomy classifies a computer security-related incident into the event, the attack, and the whole incident. It lists several items in the categories of attacker, tool, vulnerability, action, target, result, and objective.

The incident, therefore, includes the attacker, the objectives, as well as the attack itself. This attack is then divided into the tools used, the exploited vulnerability, the event, and the (unauthorized) result. The event consists of the action taken and target of the attack. The taxonomy can be interpreted as follows: An attacker using certain tools on a known vulnerability of a computer system that enables him to perform actions on a target. The outcome is the unauthorized result that allows the attacker to achieve his objectives.

It shows that the actual event is only a part of the whole incident. To fully understand the incident, the whole chain of the taxonomy has to be considered. For it can be vital to look at the attacker as well as the objective; this allows for conclusions to be drawn for similar events. Certain characteristics can be considered, for instance, a hacker will most likely leave the system after a successfully breaking in, where as a spy is most likely to gather as much data as possible.

The Attacker

Certain known types of attackers are listed here. Some subcategories can be formed (e.g., the so-called white-hat hackers or the black-hat hackers). Politically or monetarily motivated attackers can be considered highly dangerous who often stop at nothing to achieve their objectives.

The Tools

The taxonomy tries to classify the tools used for a computer security incident. As can be seen in the picture, the tools range from physical access up to *distributed attack tools* (e.g., to be used distributed denial of service attacks).

The Vulnerability

Vulnerabilities are used by exploiters. The hardest one to remedy is design vulnerability, as it can only be overcome by employing a new design, which in turn implies a new implementation. Vulnerabilities based on a false implementation of a correct design are likely to be fixed more easily. Although configuration vulnerabilities do not imply a redesign or r-implementation, fixing them (e.g., in a complex networked environment) is of a nontrivial nature.

The Action

The exploitation of a known vulnerability using an appropriate tool is known as the action. Security aspects as pointed out in Bishop (2005), such as confidentiality, integrity, or availability, or aspects like entity and data authenticity or nonrepudiation, are likely to be violated during the course of such an action.

The Target

Targets of an action are all sorts of resources connected with a computer system, such as data and information stored there. Also a whole, computer, a network of computers, or even a network of networks can be a target of an attack.

The Unauthorized Result

The result is the manifestation of the violation of the security aspects mentioned earlier. It is an attempt to classify the damage resulting from a computer security incident.

The Objective

The objective or motivation is closely tied to the attacker model. A very comprehensive description of both the attacker and the objectives can be found in Scheier (2002).

In the next section an extension to the CERT-taxonomy is proposed.

Figure 1. The extended CERT-taxonomy from Howard and Longstaff (1998) with modifications in the categories of attacker, vulnerability, and objective

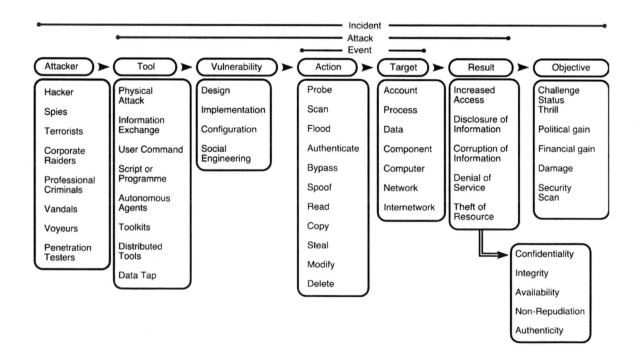

The Extended CERT-Taxonomy

Although the taxonomy is already comprehensible, three new entries are proposed in order to find a common language for the following items (as can be seen in Figure 1).

The Penetration Tester

This item is proposed for addition to the attacker description. The intention of a penetration tester is not to cause damage to a computer system. A *penetration test* is primarily conducted to verify the installed security mechanisms of a given system. Penetration testers are required to have high ethical standards (as they probably data that is confidential in nature) and have to obey the law. In, for example, Tiller (2005) penetration tests are covered in detail.

The Security Scan

The item proposed for addition to the objective section of the taxonomy is the security scan. Such a scan is performed by the penetration tester. Great care must be taken not to unintentionally cause damage while performing a penetration test. In many respects, the security scan is very similar to a common attack. But the security scan does not end with a successful or with an unsuccessful attack. The conclusions drawn from the result of the scan, the thorough planning ahead considering all possible consequences, and the consent of the owner of the computer system set it aside from a malicious attack.

Social Engineering

The vulnerability hardest to address is the user of a computer system. So *social engineering* is proposed to be added to the vulnerabilities section of the taxonomy. Social engineering is finding means to trick or pressure a person into doing things that they would not do under normal circumstances. Thereby certain traits of a person are exploited, such as the willingness to help or the fear of reprisals. Technical measures cannot protect against an attack based on social engineering. The authors of *Trojan horses*, a special category of *malicious software*, for instance, often rely on that method to trick people into installing the program on their computer system.

Attack Results: Violation of Security Aspects

The following security requirements (also called security aspects) are essential for computer and network systems and *security policies* to address and identify the relevant aspects for each entity. Therefore, in an attack evaluation, it is of great interest to know if a security aspect and, consequently, a security policy was violated or not. For example, if the confidentiality of a system is a defined security policy, integrity violations are not of interest, and the attack itself can be ranked less critical. In the following, we, therefore, extend the results taxonomy in accordance to the security aspects enumerated in Bishop (2005) and Dittman and Wohlmacher and Nahrstedt (2001) as follows:

- **Confidentiality:** Confidentiality addresses the secrecy or unauthorized disclosure of resources. In most practical cases, it refers to information, which needs to be treated secret from unauthorized entities. Information has the property of confidentiality with respect to a set of entities, if no member of this set can obtain information about the information. A special aspect of confidentiality is privacy, where data related to a person needs to be protected.
- **Integrity:** Integrity refers to the integrity of resources. It described if the resource for example information is altered or manipulated. Integrity is the quality or condition of being whole and unaltered, and it refers to consistency, accuracy, and correctness.
- **Authenticity:** This security requirement is divided into two aspects: data-origin authenticity and entity authenticity. Data-origin authenticity is the proof of the data's origin, genuineness, originality, truth, and "realness." Entity authen-

ticity is the proof that an entity, like a person or other agent, has been correctly identified as the originator, sender, or receiver; it ensures that an entity is the one it claims to be.

- **Nonrepudiation:** Nonrepudiation mechanisms prove to involved parties and third parties whether or not a particular event occurred or a particular action happened. The event or action can be the generation of a message, the sending of a message, the receipt of a message, and the submission or transport of a message.

- **Availability:** Given a set of entities and a resource, the resource has the property of availability with respect to these entities, if all members of the set can access the resource.

CONCLUSION

Finding a common language to describe computer security incidents is necessary. Especially during the *incident response* where time is of the essence, and everybody involved in the response needs to use the same phrasing for the same entity to avoid costly mistakes.

The CERT-taxonomy is an attempt to find such a common language. The proposals for its update are made in order to enhance an already comprehensive tool kit for the description of security-related incidents.

More often than not, describing incidents precisely leads to countermeasures and to ways to prevent the same attack from happening again. It, therefore, can form the building blocks of a successful solution for a computer security incident.

REFERENCES

Bishop, M. (2005). *Introduction to computer security*.

Dittmann, J., Wohlmacher, P., & Nahrstedt, K. (20010.

Multimedia and security: Using cryptographic and watermarking algorithms. *IEEE MultiMedia, 8*(4), 54-65.

Howard, J. D., & Longstaff, T. A. (1998). *A common language for computer security incidents*.

Scheier, B., (2002). *Securing the network from malicious code*.

Tiller, J. S. (2005). *The ethical hack: a framework for business value penetration testing*.

TERMS AND DEFINITIONS

Authenticity: This area is divided into two aspects: data-origin authenticity and entity authenticity. Data-origin authenticity is the proof of the data's origin, genuineness, originality, truth, and "realness." Entity authenticity is the proof that an entity, like a person or other agent, has been correctly identified as the originator, sender, or receiver; it ensures that an entity is the one it claims to be.

Availability: Given a set of entities and a resource, the resource has the property of availability with respect to these entities, if all members of the set can access the resource.

CERT-Taxonomy: This is a collection of standardized terms to precisely describe computer security incidents.

Confidentiality: This area addresses the secrecy or unauthorized disclosure of resources. In most practical cases, it refers to information that needs to be treated secret from unauthorized entities. Information has the property of confidentiality with respect to a set of entities, if no member of this set can obtain information about the information. A special aspect of confidentiality is privacy, where the person related to the data needs to be protected.

Integrity: This also refers to the integrity of resources. It described if the resource for example information is altered or manipulated. Integrity is the quality or condition of being whole and unaltered, and it refers to consistency, accuracy, and correctness.

Nonrepudiation: This proves to involved parties and third parties whether or not a particular event occurred or a particular action happened. The event or action can be the generation of a message, the sending of a message, the receipt of a message, and the submission or transport of a message.

Safety: This area deals mostly with incidents that appear at random or are caused by negligence or natural events. They often relate to material damage on physical objects.

Security: This deals malicious attacks against mostly immaterial entities like information, such as stored data.

Social Engineering: This refers to finding means to trick or pressure a person into doing things that they would not do under normal circumstances. Thereby certain traits of a person are exploited, such as the willingness to help or the fear of reprisals.

Section VII
Cyber Warfare and Cyber Terrorism:
National and International Responses

Every organization faces the threat from cyber warfare and cyber terrorism. These threats are sometimes high and sometime low, but always need to be taken seriously. The product of these evaluations (though risk analysis) provides guidance, and what to do to mitigate their risks.

Building company defenses will not always be enough to reduce threats. Quite often a wider cooperation is required. This cooperation may be split into two streams.

Stream one would group organization using similar systems or facing similar threats. The best example would be the cooperation between Internet service providers (ISP). The handling of distributed denial of service attacks is much simpler if ISPs are working together on this issue. Such unity assists in removing wider system responses to such threats.

Stream two is to coordinate national and international law. Common sense dictates that if hacking would be made strictly forbidden in each and every country, then the number of hacking attacks would definitely drop across the globe. Reaching a global consensus at times may seem to be nearly impossible, but when the need arises we manage to do just that. There are numerous examples where world-wide cooperation already works. Air traffic control is an example of such global security arrangements.

We have already noticed initial first attempts to standardize national efforts in the field of information technology security. The following section discuss a number of more recent initiatives having national, regional or world-wide effect in relation to cyber crime and cyber terrorism:

Chapter XLIX
Measures for Ensuring Data Protection and Citizen Privacy Against the Threat of Crime and Terrorism:
The European Response

Ioannis P. Chochliouros
Hellenic Telecommunications Organization S.A. and University of Peloponnese, Greece

Anastasia S. Spiliopoulou
Hellenic Telecommunications Organization S.A., Greece

Stergios P. Chochliouros
Independent Consultant, Greece

ABSTRACT

Europe has entered a new phase of growth in its history, and characterized by the fast deployment of modern electronic communications networks and information systems in the broader scope of a competitive, dynamic and knowledge-based economy. Network and information security is an essential evolving concept among current strategic issues. These can impact on a wide range of existing/emerging policies, citizens' concerns, including the protection against crime and terrorist threats, and the adaptation of governance structures to effectively deal with such matters and to preserve national security, public safety and the economic well-being of the State. In this context, several measures (legal, regulatory and technical provisions) have been adopted by the European Union to ensure data protection, citizen privacy and the legitimate interest of legal persons. However, member states preserve the right to carry-out lawful interception of electronic communications, or take other measures such as retention of traffic data, when necessary, for exact and specific purposes, to preserve security and to meet the generally recognised objectives of preventing and combating crime and terrorism. The current work examines the "balance" between these two fundamental policy requirements, with the aim of offering a high level of protection in an area of liberty, security and justice.

INTRODUCTION

Electronic communication networks and information systems are now an essential part of the daily lives of European citizens and are fundamental "tools" to the success of the broader European economy (Chochliouros & Spiliopoulou-Chochliourou, 2005). Networks and information systems are converging and becoming increasingly interconnected, thus creating a variety of potential opportunities for all categories of "players" involved. An overwhelming number of employees use a mobile phone, a laptop, or a similar device to send or retrieve information for work. Such information can represent a considerable value, for instance, describing a business transaction or containing technical knowledge. Moreover, Europe's rapid transition towards an innovative information society is being marked by profound developments in all aspects of human life: work, education, leisure, government, industry, and trade. The new information and communication technologies are having a revolutionary and fundamental impact on our economies and societies. In fact, the success of the information society is important for growth, competitiveness, and employment opportunities and has far-reaching economic, social, and legal implications. However, in the hands of persons acting in bad faith, malice, or grave negligence, information society technologies (ISTs) may become tools for activities that endanger or injure, the life, property, or dignity of individuals or even damage the public interest (European Commission, 2001c).

Despite the many and obvious benefits of the modern electronic communications development, it has also brought with it the worrying threat of intentional attacks against information systems and network platforms/infrastructures. As cyberspace gets more and more complex and its components more and more sophisticated, especially due to the fast development and evolution of (broadband) Internet-based platforms, new and unforeseen vulnerabilities may emerge (European Commission, 2001b). These attacks can take a wide variety of forms including illegal access, spread of malicious code, and denial of service attacks.

Unfortunately, it is possible to launch an attack from anywhere in the world, to anywhere in the world, at any time (Eloff & von Solms, 2000).

Some of the most serious incidents of attacks against information systems are directed against electronic communications network operators and service providers or against electronic commerce companies. More traditional areas also can be severely affected (PriceWaterhouseCoopers, 2001), given the everincreasing amount of interconnectivity in the modern communications environment: manufacturing industries, service industries, hospitals, other public sector organizations, and governments themselves. But victims of attacks are not only organizations; there can be very direct, serious and damaging effects on individuals as well. The economic burden imposed by these attacks on public bodies, companies, and individuals is considerable and threatens to make information systems more costly and less affordable to users. Consequently, as so much depends on networks and information systems, their secure functioning has become a key concern.

BACKGROUND: CURRENT EUROPEAN RESPONSES FOR INCREASED SECURITY

In order to fully support the importance of the transition to a competitive, dynamic, and knowledge-based economy, the European Commission launched the *e*Europe initiative, (accompanied by a proper Action Plan) to ensure that Europeans can reap the benefits of the digital technologies and that the emerging information society is socially inclusive (European Commission, 2002). In particular, the Action Plan highlights the importance of network security and the fight against cybercrime (European Commission, 2001a).

Information and communication infrastructures have become a critical part of the backbone of modern economies. Users should be able to rely on the availability of information services and have the confidence that their communications and data are safe from unauthorized access or modification. However, modern infrastructures have their own vulnerabilities and offer new opportunities for criminal conduct. These criminal activities may take a large variety of forms and may "cross" many borders. Although, for a number of reasons, there are no reliable statistics, there is little doubt that these offences constitute a threat to industry investment and assets, and to safety and confidence in the universal information society. For instance, some recent examples of denial of service and virus attacks have been reported to cause extensive financial damage.

Security is one particular global challenge that has recently come to the fore due to world events and societal changes. Security has therefore become a key enabler for e-businesses and a pre-requisite for privacy. There is scope for significant action both in terms of preventing criminal activity by enhancing the security of information infrastructures and by ensuring that the law enforcement authorities have the appropriate means to act, whilst fully respecting the fundamental rights of individuals. More specifically, the European Union has already taken a number of steps, including, *inter-alia*, initiatives to fight harmful and illegal content on the Internet, to protect intellectual property and personal data, to promote electronic commerce and the use of electronic signatures and to enhance the security of transactions.

Recent initiatives have been mainly focused on two fundamental sectors of activities: the legal interception of communications and the appropriate retention of traffic data for crime investigations (European Parliament and Council of the European Union, 2006).

Among the priorities of the European policies is the support of mutual understanding and interactive co-operation between all parties involved, including law enforcement agencies, Internet Service Providers, telecommunications operators, civil liberties organizations, consumer representatives, data protection authorities, and other interested parties. This can raise public awareness of the risks posed by criminals on the Internet (Akdeniz, Walker, & Wall, 2000); promote best practice(s) for security; identify effective counter-crime tools and procedures to combat computer-related crime; and to encourage further development of early warning and crisis management mechanisms. The new digital and wireless technologies are already all pervasive. As societies become increasingly reliant on these technologies, effective practical and legal means will have to be employed to help manage the associated risks.

The classical security approach (Kaufman, 2002) called for strict organizational, geographical, and structural compartmentalization of information according to sensitivity and category. This is no longer really feasible in this digital world, since information processing is distributed, services follow mobile users, and interoperability of systems is a prerequisite. Innovative solutions relying on emerging technologies are replacing traditional security approaches. Such solutions may involve the use of encryption and digital signatures, new access control and authentication tools, and software filters of all kinds. (In fact, information flows are filtered and controlled at all levels from the firewall that looks at data packets, the filter that looks for malicious software, the e-mail filter that discretely eliminates spam, to the browser filter that prevents access to harmful material.) Ensuring secure and reliable information infrastructures not only requires a range of technologies, but also their correct deployment and effective use. Some of these technologies already exist, but often users are either not aware of their existence, of the ways to use them, or of the reasons why they may even be necessary. Simultaneously, at the European Union level, a variety of legislative actions has taken mainly the form of measures in the fields of the protection of the fundamental right to privacy and data protection, electronic commerce, and electronic signatures.

PRIVACY PROTECTION VS. PRIVACY OFFENSES

The fundamental rights to privacy and data protection constitute substantial issues in contemporary European policy (Kamal, 2005). The principles of protection must be reflected, *on the one hand*, in the obligations imposed on persons, public authorities, enterprises, agencies, or other bodies responsible for processing, in particular, regarding data quality, technical security, notification to the supervisory authority, and the circumstances under which processing can be carried out; and, *on the other hand*, in the right conferred on individuals, on whom the data is being processed, to be informed that processing is taking place, to consult the data, to request corrections, and even to object to processing in certain circumstances. These objectives are mainly expressed through the provisions of European directives, having obligatory character for all member states. The Internet is overturning traditional market structures by providing a common, global infrastructure for the delivery of a wide range of public electronic communications services. Such services, over the Internet, open new possibilities for users, but also new risks for their personal data and privacy.

The latest Directive 2002/58/EC (European Parliament and Council of the European Union, 2002) requires a provider of a publicly available electronic communications service to take appropriate technical and organizational measures to safeguard security of its services and also requires the confidentiality of communications and related traffic data. It has been adapted to conform to developments in the markets and technologies for electronic communications services, in order to provide an "equal level" of protection of the personal data and the privacy for users of publicly available electronic communications services, regardless of the technologies used. The previous Directive 95/46/EC (European Parliament and Council of the European Union, 1995) imposes on member states to provide that the controller must implement appropriate technical and organizational measures to protect personal data against accidental or unlawful destruction, accidental loss, alteration, or unauthorized disclosure or access, in particular, where the processing involves the transmission of data over a network, and against all other unlawful forms of processing. The directive has broadly achieved its aim of ensuring strong protection for privacy, while making it easier for personal data to be moved around the European Union.

Until now, various countries have introduced criminal laws addressing privacy offenses, illegal collection, storage, modification, disclosure or dissemination of personal data. In the European Union, specific regulatory measures have been adopted (mainly in the form of recent directives and decisions) that approximate the national laws on the protection of privacy with regard to the processing of personal data. Among others, several provisions oblige member states to adopt suitable measures to ensure imposition of sanctions in case of related infringements. There is a need for effective substantive and procedural law instruments approximated (*at least*) at the European level to protect the potential victims of electronic- or computer-related crime and to bring the perpetrators to justice (Sieber, 1998). Moreover, multiple forms of criminal or terrorist activities could be prevented or even properly investigated via the appropriate and coordinated control and/or surveillance of all electronic means, used for such illegal purposes. The latter implies that law enforcement agencies should possess the powers to investigate offenses and to respond, drastically, whenever they detect unlawful activities, to preserve security of the state and of individuals (European Commission, 2001b). However, at the same time, it should be guaranteed that personal communications, privacy, data protection, and access to and dissemination of information are fundamental rights in modern democracies. This is why the availability and use of effective prevention measures are desirable, so as to reduce the need to apply enforcement measures. Any legislative measures that might be necessary to tackle electronic-related crime need to strike the right balance between these important interests.

INTERCEPTION OF COMMUNICATIONS

In the European Union, the confidentiality of communications (and related traffic data) is guaranteed in accordance with the international instruments relating to human rights (in particular the European Convention for the Protection of Human Rights and

Fundamental Freedoms) and the constitutions of the member states. The introduction of advanced digital technologies in telecommunications networks, has given rise to specific requirements concerning the protection of personal data and privacy of the end user. Legal, regulatory, and technical provisions adopted by the member states concerning the protection of personal data, privacy, and the legitimate interest of legal persons in the telecommunications sector must be harmonized to avoid obstacles to the internal market (European Parliament and Council of the European Union, 1998).

Interceptions are illegal unless they are authorized by law, when necessary, in specific cases for limited purposes. This mainly follows from Article 8 of the European Convention of Human Rights (Council of Europe, 2003), referred to in Article 6 of the Treaty of the European Union (TEU)—*as it now exists*—and more particularly from relevant official directives, being in force. More specifically, it is predicted that:

there shall be no interference by a public authority with the exercise of this right except such as is in accordance with the law and is necessary in a democratic society in the interests of national security, public safety or the economic well-being of the country, for the prevention of disorder or crime, for the protection of health or morals, or for the protection of the rights and freedoms of others.

Electronic communication can be intercepted and data copied or modified. Interception can be undertaken in a number of ways, including through the physical access of networks.

The protection enjoyed by EU citizens depends on the legal situation in the individual member states, which varies very substantially (in some cases parliamentary monitoring bodies do not even exist), so that the degree of protection can hardly be said to be adequate. EU member states have now a proper legal framework, for example, regarding wire tapping and monitoring radio transmission. The most critical points for the interception of communication traffic are the network management and concentration points, such

as routers, gateways, switches, and network operation servers. In the laws of the member states, there are possibilities for restricting the secrecy of communications and, under certain circumstances, intercepting communications to secure certain purposes (Chochliouros & Spiliopoulou-Chochliourou, 2003). Consequently, various measures that are considered as necessary can be applied for the protection of public security, defense, state security (including the economic well-being and financial interests of the state, when these activities relate to state security matters) and the enforcement of criminal law (prevention, investigation, detection, and prosecution of criminal offenses).

There is a need, when implementing telecommunications interception measures, to observe the right of individuals to privacy as enshrined in the territorially applicable national law. It is quite evident (European Parliament, 2001) that the legally authorized interception of telecommunications is an important tool for the protection of national interests (Walker & Akdeniz, 2003), in particular, national security and the investigation of serious crimes in place to allow law enforcement to obtain judicial orders for the interception of communications on the public telecommunications network. This legislation, which has to be in line with community law to the extent that it applies, contains safeguards protecting individuals' fundamental right to privacy, such as limiting the use of interception to investigations of serious crimes, requiring that interception in individual investigations should be necessary and proportionate, or ensuring that the individual is informed about the interception as soon as it will no longer hamper the investigation. In many member states, interception legislation contains obligations for (public) telecommunications operators to provide suitably designed—and applied—interception capabilities (Council of the European Union, 1995).

Traditional network operators, in particular those offering voice services, have in the past established working relations with law enforcement to facilitate lawful interception of communications. Telecommunications liberalization and the explosion of Internet use have attracted many entrants to the marketplace, who have been confronted afresh with interception requirements. Questions on regulations, technical feasibility, allocation of costs, and commercial impact need to be (re)discussed in government-industry dialogues, with all other parties concerned, including data protection supervisory authorities, dealing with specific requirements concerning the protection of personal data and privacy of the user. New advanced digital technologies make it essential that member states work together, if they are to maintain their capabilities for lawful interception of communications. Wherever new technical interception requirements are to be introduced, these should be coordinated internationally to prevent distortion of the single market, to minimize the costs for industry and to respect privacy and data protection requirements. Measures to be applied should be public and "open," where possible, and should not introduce weaknesses into the communications infrastructure.

In the framework of the EU Convention on Mutual Assistance in Criminal Matters (Council of the European Union, 2000), an approach has been settled on to facilitate collaboration on legal interception. The convention provides for minimal safeguards, concerning the protection of privacy and personal data, and, more specifically, it contains provisions on the interception of satellite telephone communication and on interception of communications of a person in the territory of another member state. The text of the convention is technology neutral. Interception may only be used if the necessary technical provisions have been made (Fink, 1996). Necessary technical conditions have to be established in all member states and the authorities, in accordance with national authorization procedures, actually should obtain access to data, thus being able to exercise the powers granted to them by national law at the technical level.

All related measures must ensure an appropriate level of security, taking into account the state of the art and the costs of their implementation, in relation to the risks inherent in the processing and the nature of the data to be protected. Moreover, law enforcement agencies should require appropriate prerequisites, such as real-time, full-time monitoring capabilities

for the interception of telecommunications and access to all interception subjects operating temporarily or permanently within a telecommunications system. It is remarkable that the European Union has reached proper agreement on the coordination of intelligence gathering by intelligence services as part of the development of its own security and defense policy (Kaufman, 2002).

DATA RETENTION

Data relating to subscribers processed to establish electronic communications contain information on the private life of persons and concern the right to respect for their correspondence or concern the legitimate interests of legal persons (Chochliouros & Spiliopoulou-Chochliourou, 2003). Citizens increasingly perform daily activities and transactions using electronic communications networks and services. These communications generate "traffic data" or "location data" that includes details about the location of the caller, the number called, and the time and duration of the call. When combined with data enabling the identification of the subscriber or user of the service, the availability of such traffic data is important for purposes related to law enforcement and security, such as the prevention, investigation, detection, and prosecution of serious crime, such as terrorism and organized crime. Although attempts to regulate the retention of traffic data for criminal investigations and prosecutions were presented in former European initiatives (European Commission, 2001a), the decisive point for the adoption of a proper European legal instrument, under the form of a directive, was the terrorist attacks in Madrid in 2004. In fact, soon after the attacks took place, the Council of the European Union considered the retention of communications traffic data by service providers, in cooperation with the appropriate authorities, as an adequate measure to combat terrorism and urged for proposals for establishing relevant rules, stressing that priority has to be given to this aim. It is suggested, however, that the actual needs of law enforcement should be taken into consideration for the determination of the retention period or the data that are to be stored.

Location data may refer to the latitude, longitude, and altitude of the user's terminal equipment, to the direction of travel, to the level of accuracy of the location information, to the identification of the network cell in which the terminal equipment is located at a certain point in time, and to the time the location information was recorded. A communication may include any naming, numbering, or addressing information provided by the sender of a communication or the user of a connection to carry out the communication. Traffic data may include any translation of this information by the network over which the communication is transmitted for the purpose of carrying out the transmission. Traffic data may, *inter alia*, consist of data referring to the routing, duration, time, or volume of a communication, to the protocol used, to the location of the terminal equipment of the sender or recipient, to the network on which the communication originates or terminates, and to the beginning, end, or duration of a connection. They also may consist of the format in which the communication is conveyed by the network.

To investigate and prosecute crimes involving the use of communications networks, including the Internet, law enforcement authorities frequently use traffic data when they are stored by service providers for billing purposes (Kamal, 2005). As the price charged for a communication is becoming less and less dependent on distance and destination (due to market liberalization and competition) and service providers move towards flat-rate billing, there will no longer be any need to store traffic data for billing purposes. In fact, with changes in business models and service offerings, such as the growth of flat-rate tariffs, pre-paid, and free electronic communications services, traffic data may not always be stored by all operators to the same extent as they were in recent years, depending on the services they offer.

Law enforcement authorities fear that this will reduce potential material for criminal investigations and, therefore, advocate that service providers keep certain traffic data for at least a minimum period of time so that these data may be used for law enforcement purposes. The necessity to have rules at EU level that guarantee the availability of traffic data for antiterrorism purposes across the 25 member states was confirmed multiple times. Several member states have adopted legislation providing for the retention of data by service providers for the prevention, investigation, detection, and prosecution of crimes and criminal offenses; the provisions of the various national legislations vary considerably. Data relating to the use of electronic communications is particularly important and, therefore, a valuable tool in the prevention, investigation, detection, and prosecution of crimes and criminal offences. So, the retention of traffic communications data is a fundamental tool for law enforcement authorities to prevent and combat crime and terrorism.

According to the adopted approaches, traffic data must be erased or made anonymous immediately after the telecommunications service is provided, unless they are necessary for billing purposes. For flat-rate or free-of-charge access to telecommunications services, service providers are in principle not allowed to preserve traffic data.

A recent European initiative (European Parliament and Council of the European Union, 2006) promotes suitable measures, in the form of a draft directive aiming: (1) to establish, clearly, the purpose for which the data, which are retained, can be used; (2) to limit the categories of data that need to be retained; and (3) to limit the period of retention to an appropriate extent. A further important safeguard is that the suggested measures are not applicable to the content of communications—this would amount to interception of communications, which falls outside the scope of the latter legal instrument. Member states shall ensure that the following categories of data are retained, that is, necessary data: (a) to trace and identify the source and/or the destination of a communication; (b) to identify the date, time, and duration of a communication; (c) to identify the type of communication; (d) to identify the communication device or what purports to be the communication device; and (e) to identify the location of mobile communication equipment.

The categories of information to be retained reflect an appropriate balance between the benefits for the prevention, investigation, detection, and prosecution of the serious offenses and the level of invasion of privacy they will cause. The approach suggests that retention periods of one year for mobile and fixed telephony traffic data and six months for traffic data related to Internet usage will cover the main needs of law enforcement, whilst limiting the associated costs for the industry and the intrusion into the private life of citizens. Any solution on the complex issue of retention of traffic data should be well founded, proportionate, and achieve a fair balance between the different interests. Given the fact that retention of data generates significant additional costs for electronic communication providers, whilst the benefits in terms of public security and its impact on society, in general, it is appropriate that member states reimburse demonstrated additional costs incurred in order to comply with the obligations imposed on them.

CONCLUSION

Europe has entered a new phase in its history, marked by major political, demographic, social, and economic evolutions. The European Union stressed the importance of the transition to a competitive, dynamic, and knowledge-based economy. Security is an evolving concept and presents many challenges to the European Union that impact a wide range of existing and emerging policies, citizen concerns, including the protection against terrorist threats, and the adaptation of governance structures to effectively deal with these matters. Managing electronic security has turned out to be a difficult and complex task, as the user has to deal with the availability, integrity, authenticity, and confidentiality of data and services. Due to the complexity of technology, many components and actors must work together, and human behavior has become a crucial factor. Governments see a widening

responsibility for society and are increasingly making efforts to improve and promote electronic communication security in their territory. They also equip and train law enforcement to deal with computer- and Internet-related crime.

The very nature of computer-related criminal offenses brings procedural issues to the forefront of national and international attention, as different sovereignties, jurisdictions, and laws come into play. Approximation of procedural law powers will improve the protection of victims by ensuring that law enforcement agencies have the powers they need to investigate offenses in their own territory, and will ensure that they are able to respond quickly and effectively to requests from other countries for cooperation. The implementation of security obligations following from the data protection directives contributes to enhancing security of the networks and of data processing. Security of networks and communications is a major area of concern for the development of the digital economy. Networks and information systems are now supporting services and carrying data of great value, which can be vital to other critical infrastructures. Increased protection of the networks and information systems is, therefore, necessary against the various types of attacks on their availability, authenticity, integrity, and confidentiality.

These activities also form part of the European contribution to the response to the threat of a terrorist attack against vital information systems. They supplement measures to approximate laws on terrorism on which political agreement was reached (European Commission, 2001b). Taken together, such instruments can ensure that member states have effective criminal laws in place to tackle cyber terrorism (Sieber, 1998) and will enhance international cooperation against terrorism and organized crime. Legal, regulatory, and technical provisions adopted by the member states concerning the protection of personal data, privacy, and the legitimate interest of legal persons in the electronic communication sector should be harmonized in order to avoid obstacles to the internal market for electronic communication. In the security area, however, all parties involved, *from the state to the individuals*, face serious threats (ranging from the well being of the state and of the economy, to the life and the health of people) (Shoniregun, Chochliouros, Lapeche, Logvynovskiy, & Spiliopoulou-Chochliourou, 2004). It is a priority of the European Union to increase the security level of its electronic communications systems via the establishment of suitable measures, occasionally permitting both telecommunications interception and retention of traffic data. Such measures should be objective, appropriate, and strictly proportionate to their intended purpose to guarantee a reasonable sense of balance for all potential cases and to preserve the benefit of the state and of citizens, as well.

Only approaches that bring together the expertise and capacities of government, industry, data protection supervisory authorities, and users will succeed in meeting such goals. In any case, member states have the full right to carry out lawful interception of electronic communications or take other measures, such as retention of traffic data, when necessary for specific purposes to preserve security and to meet the generally recognized objectives of preventing and combating crime and terrorism. This can be done in the framework of a democratic society, in a way both to satisfy the need for effective tools for prevention, detection, investigation, and prosecution of criminal offenses and the protection of fundamental rights and freedoms of persons and, in particular, their right to privacy, data protection, and secrecy of correspondence (which constitute fundamental freedoms and rights). Consistent approaches by all member states on such complex issues are highly desirable to meet the objectives of both effectiveness and proportionality, and to avoid the situation where both law enforcement and the Internet community would have to deal with a patchwork of diverse technical and legal environments. In the case of public communications networks, specific legal, regulatory, and technical provisions should be made in order to protect fundamental rights and freedoms of persons and legitimate interests of legal persons, in particular with regard to the increasing capacity for automated storage and processing of data relating to subscribers and users.

REFERENCES

Akdeniz, Y., Walker, C., & Wall, D. (2000). *The Internet, law and society.* London: Longman.

Chochliouros, I. P., & Spiliopoulou-Chochliourou, A. S. (2003). Innovative horizons for Europe: The new European telecom framework for the development of modern electronic networks and services. *The Journal of The Communications Network, 2*(4), 53-62.

Chochliouros, I. P., & Spiliopoulou-Chochliourou, A. S. (2005). Broadband access in the European Union: An enabler for technical progress, business renewal and social development. *The International Journal of Infonomics, 1,* 5-21.

Council of Europe. (1950). Article 8. *The European Convention on Human Rights.* Retrieved on May 17, 2007 from http://www.hri.org/docs/ECHR50.html#C.Art8

Council of Europe. (2003). *Convention for Protection of Human Rights and Fundamental Freedoms, as amended by protocol No.11 with Protocol Nos. 1, 4, 6, 7, 12 and 13.* Registry of the European Court of Human Rights.

Council of the European Union. (1995). *Council Resolution of 17 January 1995 on the lawful interception of telecommunications (Official Journal C329, 04.11.1996, pp. 1-6).* Brussels, Belgium: The Council of the European Union.

Council of the European Union. (2000). *Council Act of 29 May 2000 establishing in accordance with Article 34 of the Treaty on European Union the Convention on Mutual Assistance in Criminal Matters between the Member States of the European Union (Official Journal C197, 12.07.2000, pp. 1-2).* Brussels, Belgium: Council of the European Union.

Eloff, M. M., & von Solms, S. H. (2000). Information security management: An approach to combine process certification and product evaluation. *Computers & Security 19*(8), 698-709.

European Commission. (2001a). *Communication on network and information security: Proposal for a European policy approach* [COM(2001) 298 final, 06.06.2001]. Brussels, Belgium: European Commission.

European Commission. (2001b). *Proposal for a council framework decision on combating terrorism* [COM(2001) 521 final, 19.09.2001]. Brussels, Belgium: European Commission.

European Commission. (2001c). *Communication on creating a safer information society by improving the security of information infrastructures and combating computer-related crime (eEurope 2002)* [COM(2000) 890 final, 26.01.2001]. Brussels, Belgium: European Commission.

European Commission. (2002). *Communication on eEurope 2005: An information society for all—An Action plan to be presented in view of the Sevilla European Council, 21/22 June 2002* [COM(2002)263 final, 28.05.2002]. Brussels, Belgium: European Commission.

European Parliament. (2001). *Report on the existence of a global system for the interception of private and commercial communications (ECHELON interception system)* [2001/2098(INI)]. Brussels, Belgium: Temporary Committee on the ECHELON Interception System.

European Parliament and Council of the European Union. (1995). *Directive 95/46/EC of 24 October 1995 on the protection of individuals with regard to the processing of personal data and on the free movement of such data* [Official Journal (OJ) L281, 23.11.1995, pp. 31-50]. Brussels, Belgium: European Parliament and Council of the European Union.

European Parliament and Council of the European Union. (1998). *Directive 97/66/EC of 15 December 1997 concerning the processing of personal data and the protection of privacy in the telecommunications sector* [Official Journal L24, 30.01.1998, pp. 1-8]. Brussels, Belgium: European Parliament and Council of the European Union.

European Parliament and Council of the European Union. (2002). *Directive 2002/58/EC of 12 July 2002 concerning the processing of personal data and the protection of privacy in the electronic communications sector (Directive on privacy and electronic communications).* [Official Journal L201, 31.07.2002, pp. 37-47]. Brussels, Belgium: European Parliament and Council of the European Union.

European Parliament and Council of the European Union. (2006). *Directive 2006/24/EC on the retention of data generated or processed in connection with the provision of publicly available electronic communications services or of public communications networks and amending Directive 2002/58/EC* [Official Journal L105, 13.04.2006, pp. 54-63]. Brussels, Belgium: European Parliament and Council of the European Union.

Fink, M. (1996). *Eavesdropping on the economy: Interception risks and techniques. Prevention and protection.* Richard Boorberg, Verlag.

Kamal, A. (2005). *The Law of cyber-space.* Geneva: United Nations Institute of Training and Research (UNITAR).

Kaufman, C. (2002). *Network security: Private communication in a public world* (2nd ed.). Prentice Hall, USA.

PriceWaterhouseCoopers. (2001). *European economic crime survey 2001. European Report.* Retrieved January 16, 2006, from http://www.pwcglobal.com

Shoniregun, C. A., Chochliouros, I. P., Laperche, B., Logvynovskiy, O L., & Spiliopoulou-Chochliourou, A. S. (Eds.). (2004). *Questioning the boundary issues of Internet security.* London: e-Centre for Infonomics.

Sieber, U. (1998). *Legal aspects of computer-related crime in the information society (COM-CRIME Study).* University of Würzburg, Germany: European Commission, Legal Advisory Board. Retrieved February 1, 2006, from http://europa.eu.int/ISPO/legal/en/comcrime/sieber.html

Walker, C., & Akdeniz, Y. (2003). Anti-terrorism laws and data retention: War is over? *Northern Ireland Legal Quarterly, 54*(2), 159-182. Retrieved January 31, 2006, from http://www.cyber-rights.org/interception/

TERMS AND DEFINITIONS

Availability: It means that data is accessible and services are operational, despite possible disruptive events such as power-supply cuts, natural disasters, accidents, or attacks. This is particularly vital in contexts where communication network failures can cause breakdowns in other critical networks, such as air transport or the power supply.

Communication: This is any information exchanged or conveyed between a finite number of parties by means of a publicly available electronic communications service. This does not include any information conveyed as part of a broadcasting service to the public over an electronic communications network, except to the extent that the information can be related to the identifiable subscriber or user receiving the information.

Confidentiality: It is the protection of communications or stored data against interception and reading by unauthorized persons. It is particularly needed for the transmission of sensitive data and is one of the requirements for addressing privacy concerns of users of communication networks. Systems and networks must enforce this control at all levels.

Electronic communications network: This is a transmission systems and, where applicable, switching or routing equipment and other resources that permit the conveyance of signals by wire, by radio, by optical, or by other electromagnetic means, including satellite networks; fixed (circuit- and packet-switched, including Internet) and mobile terrestrial networks; electric cable systems; and, to the extent that they are used for the purpose of transmitting signals, networks used for radio and television broadcasting and cable television networks, irrespective of the type of information conveyed.

Integrity: It is the confirmation that data that has been sent, received, or stored are complete and unchanged, that is not altered by inappropriate treatment or a malevolent event . This is particularly important in relation to authentication for the conclusion of contracts or where data accuracy is critical (medical data, industrial design, etc.).

Location data: This is any data processed in an electronic communications network, indicating the geographic position of the terminal equipment of a user of a publicly available electronic communications service.

Traffic data: This is any data processed for the purpose of the conveyance of a communication on an electronic communications network or for the billing thereof.

Chapter L
EU Tackles Cybercrime

Sylvia Mercado Kierkegaard
International Association of IT Lawyers (IAITL), Denmark

ABSTRACT

The growing importance of information and communication infrastructure opens up new opportunities for criminal activities. The European Union has therefore taken a number of steps to fight harmful and illegal content on the Internet, protect intellectual property and personal data, promote electronic commerce and tighten up the security of transactions. However, in spite of the EU initiatives, many observers believe that cybercrime requires an international response that should include countries that are havens for cybercriminals.

INTRODUCTION

The European economy is moving from a predominantly industrial society to an information society. Communication networks and information systems are vital in the economic and societal development of the European Union (EU). The development and growth of information and communication technologies have been accompanied by an increase in criminal activities, which have been detrimental to the development of electronic commerce (e-commerce). Network and information security problems continue to grow as information flows freely across national borders. The Internet is increasingly used as a tool and medium by transnational organized crime, undermining user confidence, and generating substantial financial damage. Cognizant of the importance of computing networking and the need for secure communication networks and initiatives, the EU has adopted various instruments to combat criminal activity in the Internet. The following article provides a survey of current EU initiatives on combating cybercrime and an analysis of the council framework decision on attacks against information systems, which will be enforced in the EU in 2007.

BACKGROUND

The growing importance of information and communication infrastructure opens up new opportunities for criminal activities. Since the early '90s, the EU has taken steps to assess cyberthreats and the nature of cybercrime. The EU, therefore, has taken a number of steps to fight harmful and illegal content on the Internet; protect intellectual property and personal data; promote e-commerce; and tighten up the security of transactions. The action program on organized crime, adopted by the council (justice and home affairs) in May 1997 and endorsed by the Amsterdam European Council, called on the commission to carry out a study on computer-related crime.

In 1997, the European Commission commissioned a report to study the legal aspects of computer crime. The study (Sieber, 1998) was prepared under a contract with the European Commission. While this study did not focus specifically on cyberterrorism, it contributed greatly to the understanding of the vulnerability of information technologies to criminal activity. According to the study (known as the COMCRIME study), the various national laws have remarkable differences, uncertainties, or loopholes, especially with respect to the criminal law provision on infringements of privacy, hacking, trade-secret protection, and illegal content. On the international level, there was a lack of coordination among the various organizations, which risks the start of redundant programs. The report recommended that future measures against computer crime must be *international,* since different national strategies with the aim of preventing computer crime would create "data havens" or "computer crime havens," which, in turn, would lead to market restrictions and national barriers to the free flow of information and Europewide services (Sieber, 1998).

In October of 1999, the Tampere Summit of the European Council concluded that high-tech crime should be included in the efforts to agree on common definitions and sanctions. The following year, the European Council adopted a comprehensive eEurope Action Plan that highlighted the importance of network security and the fight against cybercrime.

The commission issued Com 2000 (890), which discussed the need for and possible forms of a comprehensive policy initiative in the context of the broader information society and freedom, security and justice objectives for improving the security of information infrastructures and combating cybercrime, in accordance with the commitment of the EU with respect to fundamental human rights. The communication addressed computer crime in its broadest sense as any crime involving the use of information technology. The terms "computer crime," "computer-related crime," "high-tech crime" and "cybercrime" share the same meaning in that they describe a) the use of information and communication networks that are free from geographical constraints and b) the circulation of intangible and volatile data. Whereas the computer-specific crimes require updates of the definitions of crimes in national criminal codes, the traditional crimes performed with the aid of computers call for improved cooperation and procedural measures.

These characteristics called for a review of existing measures to address illegal activities performed on or using these networks and systems. Other than a council decision on child pornography on the Internet and the framework decision, there are so far no EU legal instruments directly addressing computer-related crime, but there are a number of indirectly relevant legal instruments.

According to the communication, the main offenses covered by existing European and national legislation are:

1. **Privacy offenses:** Illegal collection, storage, modification, disclosure, or dissemination of personal data. Member states are clearly obliged by 95/46/EC to adopt all suitable measures to ensure the full implementation of the provisions of the directive, including sanctions to be imposed in case of infringements of the provisions of

national laws. Directive 2002/58/EC of the European Parliament and of the council of July 12, 2002, concerns the processing of personal data and the protection of privacy in the electronic communications sector. The fundamental rights to privacy and data protection are furthermore included in the Charter of Fundamental Rights of the European Union.

2. **Content-related offenses:** Involve the dissemination, especially via the Internet, of pornography, in particular, child pornography, racist statements, revisionist statements concerning Nazism, and information inciting violence. The commission has supported the view that what is illegal offline should also be illegal online. The author or the content provider may be liable under criminal law. The liability of the intermediary service providers, whose networks or servers are used for the transmission or storage of third-party information, has been addressed by the directive on e-commerce.

3. **Economic crimes:** Related to unauthorized access to computer systems (e.g., hacking, computer sabotage and distribution of viruses, computer espionage, computer forgery, computer fraud, and new forms of committing offenses, such as computer manipulations).

4. **Intellectual property offenses:** Endanger the legal protection of computer programs and databases, copyright, and related rights.[1]

CURRENT INITIATIVES

Legislative

Cybercrime Convention

In 2000, the commission has followed the work of the Council of Europe (CoE) on the Cybercrime Convention. The convention is the first international treaty on crimes committed via the Internet and other computer networks, dealing particularly with infringements of copyright, computer-related fraud, child pornography, and violations of network security. It also contains a series of powers and procedures, such as the search of computer networks and interception. Four categories of criminal offenses are listed in the CoE Cybercrime Convention: (1) offenses against the confidentiality, integrity, and availability of computer data and systems; (2) computer-related offenses; (3) content-related offenses; and (4) offenses related to infringements of copyright and related rights. The Cybercrime Convention requires parties to establish laws against cybercrime, to ensure that their law enforcement officials have the necessary procedural authorities to investigate and prosecute cybercrime offenses. The EU has encouraged the member states to ratify the International Cybercrime Convention. However, the convention has been assailed as fundamentally imbalanced by privacy advocates and civil libertarians as it gives government agencies awesome powers without ensuring minimum human rights and data protection safeguards.

Council Framework Decision 2005/222/JHA of 24 February 2005 on Attacks Against Information Systems

On Feb. 4, 2005, the Council of the European Union adopted Framework Decision 2005/222/JHA on attacks against information systems (hereafter the framework decision). The deadline for implementation of the framework decision into national law is March 16, 2007. The framework decision is a new legal framework intended to close the gaps and differences in member state's laws in this area and to tackle new forms of crime, such as hacking, spreading computer viruses, and other malicious code, and organizing denial of service attacks on Web sites. Thus, the framework decision will cover intentional hacking, distribution of viruses, denial of service attacks, and Web site defacement, among other activities The framework decision was drafted to be consistent with the Cybercrime Convention and aims to align laws between member states.

It has two main objectives: (1) creating a common set of legal definitions and criminal offenses across the EU and (2) improving the effective prosecution of offenders by setting out minimum rules with regards to penalties as well as rules with regards to the judicial cooperation among member states.

The framework decision provides for a common set of legal definitions and criminal offenses across the EU for these activities. Article 1 defines the following terms:

- Information system means any device or group of interconnected or related devices, one or more of which, pursuant to a program, performs automatic processing of computer data, as well as computer data stored, processed, retrieved, or transmitted by them for the purposes of their operation, use, protection, and maintenance.
- Computer data means any representation of facts, information, or concepts in a form suitable for processing in an information system, including a program suitable for causing an information system to perform a function.
- "Legal person" means any entity having such status under the applicable law, except for states or other public bodies in the exercise of state authority and for public international organizations.
- "Without right" means access or interference not authorized by the owner, other right holder of the system or part of it, or not permitted under the national legislation.

According to Article 2 (1), "Each Member State shall take the necessary measures to ensure that the intentional access without right to the whole or any part of an information system is punishable as a criminal offence, at least for cases which are not minor." This includes the notion of hacking an information system. It is intended to cover not only offenses affecting the member states, but also offenses committed in their territory against systems located in the territory of third countries. Each member state may decide that the conduct referred to in paragraph 1 is incriminated only where the offense is committed by infringing a security measure. This is, at present, not the case in all member states.

Article 3 deals with illegal interference of the system. The criminal offense includes the intentional serious hindering or interruption of the functioning of an information system by inputting, transmitting, damaging, deleting, deteriorating, altering, suppressing, or rendering inaccessible computer data, when committed without right, at least, for cases that are not minor. Thus, the framework decision explicitly seeks to strike a balance between punishing acts that are harmful to information systems and "over-criminalization," that is, criminalizing *minor* offenses or criminalizing right-holders and authorized persons. The elements of inputting or transmitting computer data specifically address the problem of so-called denial of service attacks, where there is a deliberate attempt to overwhelm an information system. The offense also covers the interruption of the functioning of an information system, which could be inferred from the phrase hindering, but is included here explicitly for the sake of clarity.

Under section 4, the intentional deletion, damaging, deterioration, alteration, suppression, or rendering inaccessible of computer data on an information system is punishable as a criminal offense when committed without right, at least, for cases which are not minor. The other elements in the offense (damaging, deleting, deteriorating, altering, or suppressing computer data) specifically address the problem of viruses and other types of attacks, such as corruption of wWb sites, which are directed at hindering or interrupting the functions of the information system itself. The term *hindering* or *interruption* is not defined, and each member state is allowed to determine for itself what criteria must be fulfilled for an information system to be considered as seriously hindered.

The phrase "without right" builds on the previous definitions so as to exclude conduct by authorized persons. Without right means that conduct by authorized persons or other conduct recognized as lawful under domestic law is excluded. There are a number of technical issues that arise with the framework decision because the legal language within it differs from that used in some member states, for example, in the United Kingdom. This causes problems when some access is permitted and some is not. For example, the notion of without right will give rise to bones of contention, in particular, concerning the nature and extent of authority required to access a computer.

In R v. Bignell[2], access to data held on the Police National Computer was held not to be unlawful under section 1 of the UK Computer Misuse Act because the police officers involved were authorized to access the system.

However, in the extradition case, R v. Bow Street Magistrates Court and Allison: Ex Parte Government of the United States[3], the House of Lords declined to follow the earlier case of DPP v. Bignall. The defendant was extradited to the United States for fraud. His normal work was to access parts of a database to provide information about credit card accounts. He was approached by a codefendant, Joan Ojomo, to obtain similar details from other parts of the database to enable her to commit fraud. The question was whether, if he had authority to access parts of the database as part of his normal work, he could, in any sense, be unauthorized to access other parts of the database. The court held that although there was an entitlement to access some information about credit cards on a computer system, there was not authorization to access the relevant information, which was subsequently used in the theft of $1 million from U.S. cash machines.

In R v. Raphael Gray, a teenage hacker pleaded guilty to stealing credit card details from e-commerce Web sites by simply invoking insecure access methods that were installed by default and incompetent Web masters had not removed. The accused pleaded guilty, so the possible defense that this was not unauthorized access because there was nothing special about authorized access was not tested (Broersma, 2001).

The term without intention raises difficulties for victims. A jury acquitted Paul Bedworth for reasons that were unclear. During the trial, it was revealed that the perpetrator suffered from a condition that deemed him addicted to hacking. The prosecution was unable to determine intent (a requirement for successful completion). The defense argued that his actions were involuntary, and he was subsequently acquitted. The prosecution failed to show that the defendant had reason of intent or mens rea. His "compulsion" cost an estimated £25,000 in damages, and he also left the European Organisation for the Research and Treatment of Cancer with a £10,000 telephone bill.

Instigating, aiding, abetting, and attempting to commit any of the above offenses also will be liable to punishment (Art. 5) and are considered criminal offenses.

Member states are required to lay down penalties commensurate with the gravity of the offense, which includes custodial sentences with a maximum term of imprisonment of no less than one year in serious cases (Art. 6). Member states are required to have available a maximum penalty of between one and three years of imprisonment for offenses involving interference with information systems and computer data, and a maximum penalty of between two and five years of imprisonment when the offenses are committed in the framework of a criminal organization (Art. 7).[4] Serious cases shall be understood as excluding cases where the conduct resulted in no damage or economic benefit.

The framework decision also contains provisions on legal persons and jurisdiction. The member states need to ensure that legal persons can be held liable for computer-related crime that was committed for their benefit by any person with a leading position within the legal person, or by any other person under its authority, in case that the offense was the result of a lack of supervision or control by the relevant leading persons (Art. 8). Member states should ensure that legal persons also are punishable by "effective, proportionate and dissuasive penalties." These shall include criminal or noncriminal fines, but may also consist of other measures, such as a temporary or permanent disqualification from the practice of commercial activities or an exclusion from entitlement to public aid (Art. 9).

Each member state will have jurisdiction, inter alia, for offenses committed on its territory or by one of its nationals or for the benefit of a legal person that has its head office in that member state. Where several member states consider that they have jurisdiction, they must cooperate with the aim of centralizing proceedings in a single member state. Where an offense would fall under the jurisdiction of more then one member state, and when any of the member states concerned can validly prosecute on the basis of the same facts, the member states shall cooperate and decide which will prosecute the offenders with the aim, if possible, of centralizing proceedings in one member state.

Member states also are required to join the so-called "24/7 network" of operational points of contact for high-tech crime available 24 hours a day, 7 days a week, for the purposes of exchanging information on attacks against information systems (Art. 11).

Non-Legislative

Contact Points to Combat High-Tech Crime

On March 19, 1998, the council invited the member states to join the Group of 8 (G8) 24-hour network for combating high-tech crime. In G8 discussions on high-tech crime, two major categories of threats have been identified.

First, threats to computer infrastructures, which concern operations to disrupt, deny, degrade, or destroy information resident in computers and computer networks, or the computer and networks themselves. Secondly, there are computer-assisted threats, which concern malicious activities, such as fraud, money laundering, child pornography, infringement to intellectual property rights, and drug trafficking, which are facilitated by the use of a computer. This proposal deals with the first category of threats. This network provides the countries that join it with an overview of computer network crime, given that it often occurs simultaneously at different locations in different countries.

Those countries that do not form part of the G8 have joined Interpol's National Central Reference Point System (NCRP), which currently links more

than 60 countries. However, Interpol's national central reference points do not always provide 24-hour readiness. Council recommendation of June 25, 2001, recommended that those member states that have not yet joined the G8 network of contact points do so, and that the national units designated as contact points specialize in combating high-tech crime. The Council also recommended that those units should be able to take operational measure.

G8

The G8 is a multilateral group consisting of the world's major industrial democracies. While the EU is not a member of the G8, EU representatives attend G8 meetings as observers. A group of experts, known as the Lyon Group, was brought together to look for better ways to fight transnational crime. Over time, that mission has expanded to include work with third countries and on such topics as combating terrorist use of the Internet and protection of critical information infrastructures.

To handle the various types of high-tech crime as swiftly and in as highly professional way as possible and to conserve evidence in environments where information can be destroyed rapidly, the EU Council has passed the Council Recommendation of June 25, 2001, to join the G8 24-hour information network for combating high-tech crime. This network provides the countries that join it with an overview of computer network crimes, given that it often occurs simultaneously at different locations in different countries. In order to facilitate cooperation between the member states, a list of 24-hour national contact points and specialized units has been established that currently links more than 60 countries.

European Network and Information Security Agency

In accordance with the procedure laid down in Article 251 of the EC Treaty, Regulation EC No.460/2004 of the European Parliament and of the council established the European Network and Information Security

Agency (ENISA). This was prompted by the growing number of security breaches that has already generated substantial financial damage, undermined user confidence, and was detrimental to the development of e-commerce. The main role of ENISA is to support the internal EU market by facilitating and promoting increased cooperation and information exchange on issues of network and information security, to enhance the capability of the community, the member states, and, consequently, the business community to prevent, address, and respond to network and information security problems.

CONCLUSION

In spite of the EU initiatives, many observers believe that cybercrime requires an international response that should include countries that are havens for cyber criminals. Many of the hacking and cyber criminals operate out of countries in Eastern Europe, particularly Russia, and it is difficult to bring them to justice. The International Cybercrime Convention and the Framework Decision will attain only a minimal effect, unless the countries that host these criminal elements have the necessary resolve to enforce the law and join the convention. Within the EU, while criminal enforcement agencies advocate tougher laws and claim that the framework decision will become an effective tool to fight cybercrime, consumers question whether it will actually deter hardened criminals and whether they will be used as an excuse by law enforcement agencies to conduct illegal surveillance. Any EU initiatives must respect the data protection principles and the principles of the European Human Rights. Abusive and indiscriminate use of interception capabilities, particularly internationally, will raise human rights questions and will undermine citizens' trust in the information society.

The council's framework decision and national laws require "intent," or mens rea, of the crime to make the offender liable. The issue is, of course, what about victim restitution when the culprits are acquitted for lack of intent? The commission must improve its protection of victims and make it a priority in its conclusions.

REFERENCES

Broersma, M. (2001). Gates' credit hacker sentenced. *ZDNet.UK*. Retrieved December 9, 2005, from http://www.zdnetasia.com/

Council framework decision 2005/222/JHA of 24 February 2005 on attacks against information systems [Official Journal L 069, 16/03/2005, pp. 67-71].

Sieber, U. (1998). *Legal aspects of computer related crime in the information society.*. Retrieved June 26, 2006, from the University of Würzburg Web site: http://europa.eu.int/ISPO/legal/en/comcrime/sieber.doc

TERMS AND DEFINITIONS

Communication: This is a soft-law instrument used to signal, in what way the European Commission will use its competencies and how the commission shall perform its tasks within the area of its discretion

Council Framework Decisions: These are binding legislations in the European Union. They were introduced by the 1997 Amsterdam Treaty. Under Article 34 of the amended Treaty on European Union, the council may, by unanimous decision, adopt a framework decision for the purpose of the approximation of the laws of member states. Although framework decisions are stated to be binding upon member states as to the result to be achieved, member states are given the choice as to the form and methods employed to achieve the result and are stated not to have direct effect.

Council of Europe: This is an international organization of 46 member states in the European region, which accept the principle of the rule of law and guarantee fundamental human rights and freedoms to their citizens.

Cybercrime: This is any illegal act involving a computer and all activities done with criminal intent in cyberspace or which are computer-related

Directives: These are general legislation agreed upon by the European Council and Parliament. It is binding on the member states and has to be implemented into national law. However, it is left to individual member states to decide how they are incorporated into national law.

Information System: Any device or group of interconnected or related devices, one or more of which, is pursuant to a program, performs automatic processing of computer data, as well as computer data stored, processed, retrieved, or transmitted by them for the purposes of their operation, use, protection, and maintenance.

International Convention: This is an agreement among many nations. International conventions (also referred to as treaties) are means by which states create international law. Conventions are legally binding agreements, governed by international law, made between states having legal capacity to enter into a convention/treaty.

Legal Person: This means any entity having such status under the applicable law, except for states or other public bodies in the exercise of state authority and for public international organizations.

Mens Rea: This means guilty mind.

Without Right: This means access or interference not authorized by the owner, other right holder of the system or part of it, or not permitted under the national legislation.

ENDNOTES

[1] Two directives have been adopted on the legal protection of computer programs and of databases, relating to the information society and providing for sanctions (Data Base Directive 96/9 EC and Directive 91/250/EEC on the Legal Protection of Computers). Directive 2001 /29/ EC on the harmonization of certain aspects of copyright and related rights in the information society was adopted by the council to reflect technological developments and, in particular, the information society, and to transpose into community law the main international obligations arising from the two treaties on copyright and related rights, adopted within the framework of the World Intellectual Property Organisation (WIPO).

[2] DPP v Bignell [1998] 1 Cr App R

[3] R v Bow Street Magistrates Court Ex p. Allison [1999] 4 All ER 1

[4] The maximum penalty of at least one year imprisonment in serious cases brings these offenses within the scope of the European Arrest Warrant as well as other instruments, such as the Council Framework Decision of June 26, 2001 on money laundering, the identification, tracing, freezing, seizing, and confiscation of the instrumentalities and the proceeds from crime.

Chapter LI
The U.S. Military Response
to Cyber Warfare

Richard J. Kilroy, Jr.
Virginia Military Institute, USA

ABSTRACT

The United States military has taken a number of steps to confront the threat of cyber warfare. These include organizational, operational, and personnel changes by all the armed services, as well as the joint commands, which conduct operational warfare. Many of these changes began before the terrorist attacks of 9/11 as military planners recognized the vulnerabilities the nation faced to asymmetrical warfare conducted in cyberspace, as well as the military's dependency on key critical infrastructures within the United States that were vulnerable to cyber warfare. Although many changes have taken place, to include training new classes of military officers and enlisted specialists in career fields and military doctrine related to cyber warfare (both offensive and defensive), the military continues to remain vulnerable to an adversary's ability to control the informational battlefield. Thus, a key strategic goal of the U.S. military leadership is to achieve information superiority over its current and potential adversaries.

INTRODUCTION

In the mid-1990s, the U.S. military recognized a growing threat to its informational architecture as well as the nation's critical infrastructure from *cyber warfare*. Since Department of Defense (DoD) installations in the United States were dependent on civilian infrastructure for communications, transportation, energy, water, and the full range of logistical support, the DoD recognized that a threat to any of these critical systems would directly impact the military's ability to deploy forces overseas against foreign threats and

actors. This chapter will address the U.S. military response to the threat of cyber warfare, to include organizational and doctrinal changes made to confront the threat, as well as cultural and career force changes that have impacted forces structures, resources, and the war-fighting capability of the armed forces.

In 1995, the chairman of the Joint Chiefs of Staff, Army Gen. John Shalikashvili, released an unclassified document, *Joint Vision 2010*, that laid out his strategic goals for the military for the next 25 years. The document identified four key operational concepts that the chairman viewed as essential for the ability of the

U.S. military to fight as a joint force in an uncertain future. "This vision of future warfighting embodies the improved intelligence and command and control available in the information age and goes on to develop four operational concepts: dominant maneuver, precision engagement, full dimensional protection, and focused logistics" (Shalikashvili, 1995, p. 1).

To achieve such operational success in any future battlefield, military planners realized that their ability to maneuver forces, engage adversaries, protect the force, and even deploy the force to any future conflict was completely dependent on a complex civilian infrastructure, which the DoD had little control over. Critical infrastructures, such as transportation networks, telecommunications, power generation, and even health care and financial resources, were outside of federal oversight when it came to assessing national security and the potential threats to those infrastructures. To make matters worse for military planners, the "operational environment" for these infrastructures was not a series of buildings or "hard sites" that could be secured with concertina wire and a guard force. Rather, these infrastructures were comprised of complex information systems, which presented a whole new set of challenges for security planners who were now faced with the difficult question of how to defend critical infrastructures "over here" in order to even begin to get military forces deployed "over there" for the next conflict.

Recognizing these new challenges, the DoD began a series of training exercises aimed at testing the vulnerabilities of our nation's critical infrastructures and the information systems on which they depended. The first operational-level exercise conducted in June 1997 was called Eligible Receiver. The exercise involved using National Security Agency (NSA) "hackers," operating as an adversary (red-team), to attack defense and other government information systems, while also conducting simulated attacks on civilian infrastructure (Robinson, 2002). The lessons learned from the exercise showed serious problems with defending critical information systems and infrastructures, on which the DoD (and the nation) depended, against cyber attacks by adversaries using

asymmetrical means to defeat (or simply neutralize) our nation's military strength indirectly. The U.S. Atlantic (later Joint Forces) Command in Norfolk, VA, also ran an exercise labeled Evident Surprise, which continued to explore vulnerabilities to cyber warfare in DoD information systems. One example involved a simulated attack on the DoD's electronic medical records that track blood supplies.

If Evident Surprise and Eligible Receiver were not enough to convince defense planners that cyber warfare was a real threat to military operations, a series of incidents in early 1998 provided additional proof. Termed *Solar Sunrise,* an investigation into intrusions into DoD information systems, which appeared to be originating from a Middle Eastern country, coincided with operational planning for Dessert Fox, a series of military attacks against Iraq in February 1998. The cyber intrusions impacted multiple service components and DoD agencies; such that investigators believed they were deliberate attacks being perpetrated by a foreign government. Further criminal investigations later turned up two California teenagers being mentored by an Israeli man, Ehud Tannenbaum, as being behind the attacks (Robinson, 2002). Although no real security breaches of critical DoD information systems occurred, the incidents did further identify significant vulnerabilities, which, if exploited, could have had a significant impact on operational planning and execution utilizing the military's integrated command, control, communications, computers, and intelligence (C4I) architecture.

In December 1998, the DoD took the initiative to stand up an operational unit to specifically deal with the threat toward DoD information systems posed by cyber warfare. The Joint Task Force – Computer Network Defense (JTF-CND) was formed as a field operating agency, based in Arlington, VA, at the Defense Information Systems Agency (DISA). The JTF-CND would later move to operational control of U.S. Space Command (SPACECOM) in Colorado Springs, CO, as a result of changes to the DoD's Unified Command Plan which took effect on Oct. 1, 2000 (Verton, 1999). The JTF-CND originally focused only on the defensive aspects of what would be called information operations (IO) in the military's evolving information warfare doctrine. The JTF-CND would eventually evolve into the JTF-Computer Network Operations (CNO), responsible for both offensive and defensive aspects of IO as the organization changed hands once again in October 2002, to come under operational control of the U.S. Strategic Command (STRATCOM) in Omaha, NE.

Before these operational changes took place, the DoD was moving forward with the development of military doctrine to deal with information-age cyber warfare threats. Although individual service components began considering information warfare as a viable mission area in the mid-1990s (such as the Army's Field Manual FM 100-6), it was a couple years later before the DoD recognized the need to issue joint doctrine with regard to IO. The DoD had previously issued IO policy guidance in the form of a classified DoD directive in 1996. Yet, it was not until the release of Joint Publication 3-13, *Joint Doctrine for Information Operations* on Oct. 9, 1998, that joint commands began to organize their staffs around the need for IO planning and execution, as well as education and training.

IO emerged from previous joint doctrine (JP 3-13.1) involving command and control warfare (C2W), based on lessons learned after the first Gulf War and the effectiveness of new information-based technologies for intelligence collection and targeting. IO expanded on the traditional "pillars" of C2W (psychological operations, military deception, electronic warfare, physical destruction, and operations security), by adding computer network defense and two "related" activities of public affairs and civil affairs (Department of Defense, 1998). IO became the means by which DoD elements would conduct cyber warfare, initially focused on defensive aspects of the cyber threat, but later expanded to include offensive cyber warfare planning and execution under the broader category of CNO (which would also come to include the intelligence gathering required under computer network exploitation in order to actually conduct both offensive and defensive operations).

In June 2000, the chairman of the Joint Chiefs of Staff, Army Gen. Hugh Shelton, issued a follow-on document to *Joint Vision 2010*. Titled *Joint Vision 2020*, the chairman sought to build on the strategic view of his predecessor, while taking into consideration the changes that had occurred organizationally and operationally as a result of the information revolution. For example, as a reason for issuing the new strategic vision, *Joint Vision 2020* includes, "the continued development and proliferation of information technologies will substantially change the conduct of military operations. These changes in the information environment make information superiority a key enabler of the transformation of the operational capabilities of the joint force and the evolution of joint command and control" (Shelton, 2000, p. 3). With Information Superiority as the DoD's strategic enabler, IO is the chief means by which the DoD will take offensive and defensive actions to maintain *information superiority* over the nation's adversaries and achieve the broader goal of full spectrum dominance, as defined in *Joint Vision 2020.*

While the joint commands were beginning to organize themselves to function in the information battle space, the military service components had already begun the transformation doctrinally and organizationally. The Army was the first service component to develop military doctrine with regard to IO and the conduct of cyber warfare. Field Manual 100-6 IO, first appeared in August 1996, two years before the joint community published Joint Publication 3-13. (Since then, the Army reissued its Field Manual to reflect the joint community numbering system; it is now FM 3-13.) The Army's approach to IO, however, was more along the lines of viewing the informational component of warfare as an enabler to further enhance the "hard" power of Army weapons systems, rather than a "soft" power alternative. As one Army officer, once noted, "IO simply helps us to do a better job putting steel on target."

Yet, the Army did make organizational changes reflecting the new doctrine and the integration of IO planning into military operations. The Army's Land Information Warfare Activity (LIWA), located with the U.S. Intelligence and Security Command (IN-SCOM) at Ft. Belvoir, VA, was stood up on May 8, 1995 (Sizer, 1997). It proved its value immediately, providing field support teams to Army components deployed to support the NATO Implementation Force (IFOR) in Bosnia. The Army's first IO planners were a mix of combat arms, signal, and intelligence officers. Field artillery training and the use of the attack guidance matrix using "information weapons" proved particularly useful in planning IO in the theater, since the use of "hard" power, such as physical destruction, was restricted due to the peace-keeping nature of the mission. The LIWA also included the Army's first Computer Emergency Response Team (CERT), which helped to defend Army communications networks against the threat of cyber warfare, as well as other Army elements, which would provide the offensive cyber warfare capability. The Army later changed the LIWA to a new designator as the 1st Information Operations (IO) Command, to bring it in line with organizational changes under the new Unified Command Plan in 2002, which will be discussed later.

The Army also developed a new career field, functional area (FA) 30-IO, for its officer corps. Army officers designed as FA-30s received training in IO at either joint or Army schools and were assigned as IO planners on both Army and joint staffs. Army IO officers filled new positions designed for IO cells on division- and corps-level staffs as well as in the newly formed Independent Brigade Combat Teams. On joint staffs, these officers typically served within the J-3 operations directorate, rather than as a separate staff section designated for IO.

The other military services (Air Force, Navy, and Marines) initially chose not to create new career fields for IO officers, but rather developed special skills identifiers or "codes" to designate certain officers with IO-specific skills and abilities. The Air Force stood up its own training course for teaching IO (to both officers and enlisted personnel) at Hurlburt Field in Florida. The Navy stood up the Fleet Information Warfare Center (FIWC) at Norfolk, VA, which included IO training programs. Most Navy officers working in IO-related positions came from the cryptology community. In

2005, the chief of naval operations decided to recode certain cryptology billets in the Navy to information warfare billets, recognizing the growth of IO as a core competency for all military services (Chief of Naval Operations Message, 2005). The Marines still leverage the other service and joint schools teaching IO for its needs.

Of all services, the Air Force took the most dramatic steps, organizationally, to accommodate the need for IO capability in its operational units. Looking at IO as a weapon system, rather than simply an enabler, the Air Force stood up IO squadrons (IOS) to provide the numbered air forces their own organic IO capability. The IOS provided each unit an integrated IO capability with specialists in each of the IO capabilities, according to the joint and Air Force IO doctrine. The Air Force also stood up the Air Force Information Warfare Center (AFIWC) at Lackland Air Force Base in San Antonio, Texas, as its lead operational unit for IO. The AFIWC further integrates the Air Force's Computer Emergency Response Team (AFCERT), linked with the various *network operations security centers* (NOSC), designated to monitor and protect Air Force C4I systems from cyber attacks. For example, the NOSC at Langley Air Force Base in Hampton, VA, monitors all of the networks for the Air Force's Air Combat Command (ACC) units deployed both in the United States and overseas.

The Navy's FIWC (changed to Navy Information Operations Command (NIOC) in November 2005) also serves a similar function to the AFIWC and Army's 1st IO command, as the operational component for all naval fleet IO activity. In addition to training Navy personnel to serve in IO-related positions in the fleet, the NIOC also contains the Navy's Computer Incident Response Team (NAVCIRT) capability for coordinating the Navy's defensive response to the cyber warfare threat. The NIOC reorganization came about as a result of standup of the Naval Network Warfare Command (NETWARCOM) in Norfolk, VA, in 2002, also as a result of organizational changes at the joint command level. NETWARCOM reflects the "operationalizing" of the Navy's network centric operations concept, which was first proposed by Adm. Arthur Cebrowski in 1998, who recognized then that networks were a "weapons system" and a key component of information-age warfare (See Cebrowski & Gartska, 1998).

The terrorist attacks against the Pentagon and the World Trade Center in September 2001, provided the impetus for broader DoD organizational changes that impacted the military's ability to prosecute and defend against cyber warfare. The threat posed by Al Qaeda and other international terrorist groups to the U.S. homeland caused the DoD to create a new joint command, U.S. Northern Command, which is dedicated to the homeland defense mission of the DoD, in support of the nation's overall homeland security effort. This change to the Unified Command Plan (UCP), signed by President Bush in May 2002, further eliminated the U.S. Space Command in Colorado Springs, CO, moving most of the space and IO roles of the military to STRATCOM in Omaha, NE. Under STRATCOM, operational control for all aspects of IO, including computer network attack and CND, were consolidated into new organizational structures and responsibilities. The JTF-CND came under STRATCOM's control, for example. Each of the services transformed existing IO organizations into IO "commands" in order to provide the service components in support of the joint command structure.

To provide operational control over the diverse components of Information Operations, STRATCOM developed various joint functional component commands. The Joint Functional Component Command (JFCC) for Space and Global Strike includes the Joint Information Operations Center (JIOC), located at Lackland Air Force Base in San Antonio, Texas. The JIOC was previously under the Joint Forces Command prior to the Oct 2002 UCP change. The JIOC is responsible for "the integration of IO (IO) into military plans and operations across the spectrum of conflict" (U.S. Strategic Command, 2006). The JIOC routinely deploys support teams to the other combatant commands (such as U.S. Central Command) to assist their staffs with developing their IO plans and operations. Another component command created by STRATCOM is the JFCC for Network Warfare. This component command is commanded by the director

of the NSA, signaling the merging of computer network defense, offense, and exploitation (intelligence collection) less than one functional command for cyber warfare. Also with this change, the JTF-CNO was designated the JTF-Global Network Operations (GNO), which is now headed by the director of the Defense Information Systems Agency (DISA).

The military's information-age transformation signals recognition that threats to the nation's (and military's) information systems will remain. Whether the threat of cyber warfare comes from a terrorist organization or a nation-state, the DoD's reorganization at the joint combatant command level, as well as service component level, will better position the military to face these information-age threats. One significant problem, however, remains. The DoD does not control access to, nor does it defend, the nation's critical infrastructures on which military power "rides." Whether it is the nation's rail and transport system, global telecommunications architecture, or our nation's power grid, the DoD is dependent on having access to these systems. Even the DoD's logistics system cannot function in getting troops and supplies to Iraq or other future conflict areas without the help of commercial transportation and FEDEX. A cyber attack on any of the information systems that manage these critical infrastructures would have devastating effects on our military's ability to provide for our nation's defense.

In the future, more countries will develop information warfare capabilities as a means to offset the overwhelming military superiority of the United States. Seen as a "cheap fix," nations such as China will employ asymmetric tactics to defeat the United States by crippling our nation's ability to even wage war. In a book published in 1999, two Chinese colonels advocated employing such an approach, using cyber warfare and other means to attack the United States in a future conflict (see Liang & Xiangsui, 1999). The tactics they advocated to undermine our support networks and destroy critical infrastructure digitally were very much in line with classic Eastern military philosophy, seen in Sun Tzu's classic, *The Art of War,* where the ultimate military goal is to defeat an adversary's will to fight without having to actually enter into military combat (Armistead, 2004). What is interesting in the Chinese colonels' text is the assertion that it is not a matter of *if* China goes to war with the United States, but simply *when*.

The U.S. military response to the threat of cyber warfare conducted against the United States by China, or any other adversary is a maturing process, reflecting both organizational and operational changes. The military also is creating new categories of officers and enlisted members who possess unique training and knowledge on how to conduct cyber warfare, both offensively and defensively. As their awareness of the types of cyber threats increases, so will their ability to respond technologically to new challenges. Unlike other forms of warfare, however, a cyber war could break out at anytime; and if these cyber defenders are successful, the public may never even know it happened!

REFERENCES

Armistead, L. (Ed.). (2004). *Information operations: Warfare and the hard reality of soft power.* Potomac Books, Brassey's Inc.

Cebrowski, A., & Gartska, J. J. (1998). Network centric warfare: It's origins and its future." *Proceedings.* U.S. Naval Institute. Retrieved January 6, 2006, from http://www.usni.org/Proceedings/Articles98/PROcebrowski.htm

Chief of Naval Operations Message. (2005). *Subject: Cryptologic officer name change to Information Warfare* (DTG R 151308Z SEP 05).

Department of the Army. (2003). *Information operations: Doctrine, tactics, techniques and procedures* (Field Manual (FM) 3-13) Washington, DC.

Department of Defense. (1998). *Joint doctrine for information operations,* (Joint Publication (JP) 3-13). Washington, DC: U.S. Government Printing Office.

Liang, Q., & Xiangsui, W. (1999). *Unrestricted warfare* (FBIS, Trans., selected chapters). Beijing: PLA Literature and Arts Publishing House.

Robinson, C. (2002). Military and cyber defense: Reactions to the threat. Center for Defense Information. Retrieved September 10, 2005, from http://www.cdi.org/terrorism/cyberdefense-pr.cfm

Shalikashvili, J. (1995). *Joint vision 2010*. Washington, DC: U.S. Government Printing Office and Department of Defense, Office of the Joint Chiefs of Staff.

Shelton, H. H. (2000). *Joint vision 2020.* Washington, DC: U.S. Government Printing Office and Department of Defense, Office of the Joint Chiefs of Staff.

Sizer, R. A. (1997). Land information warfare activity. *Military Intelligence Bulletin, 1997-1.* Retrieved January 6, 2006, from http://www.fas.org/irp/agency/army/tradoc/usaic/mipb/1997-1/sizer.htm

U.S. Strategic Command. (2006). *Functional components.* Retrieved January 6, 2006, from http://www.stratcom.mil/organization-fnc_comp.html

Verton, D. (1999, October 9). DoD boosts IT security role. *Federal Computer Week,.* Retrieved January 9, 2006, from http://www.fcw.com:8443/fcw/articles/1999/FCW_100499_7.asp

TERMS AND DEFINITIONS

Computer Emergency Response Team (CERT): This refers to a group of Internet security experts, whose members study Internet security vulnerabilities, research long-term changes in networked systems, and develop information and training to improve security.

Computer Network Operations (CNO): This is comprised of computer network attack, computer network defense, and related computer network exploitation enabling operations.

Cyber Warfare: This typically involves units organized along nation-state boundaries, in offensive and defensive operations, using computers to attack other computers or networks through electronic means. It also can be conducted by nonstate actors, such as terrorists.

Information Operations (IO): This is the integrated employment of the core capabilities of electronic warfare, computer network operations, psychological operations, military deception, and operations security, in concert with specified supporting and related capabilities, to influence, disrupt, corrupt, or usurp adversarial human and automated decision making, while protecting one's own.

Information Superiority (IS): This is that degree of dominance in the information dimension environment that permits the conduct of operations without effective opposition.

Network Operations Security Center (NOSC): This is a command center that provides situational awareness of the myriad of networks, systems and applications that make up that organization's information infrastructure and determines how to protect and defend that system from potential cyber threats. It also can be called a Network Operations Center (NOC).

Solar Sunrise: This refers to a series of attacks on Department of Defense computer networks that occurred Feb. 1-26, 1998. The attack pattern was indicative of a preparation for a follow-on attack by an adversary nation. The timing of the cyber attacks coincided with U.S. military preparations for an Allied air attack on Iraq, increasing the appearance of an attack by a foreign nation in the Middle East. It turned out to be computer hacking by a couple teenagers in California, being mentored by an Israeli teenager.

Chapter LII
USA's View on
World Cyber Security Issues

Norman Schneidewind
Naval Postgraduate School, USA

ABSTRACT

There is little evidence that the world is more secure from a major cyber attack than in 2000 because attacks on the Internet go on unabated. In addition to calling for new legislation and oversight, this chapter serves as a source of information about cyber security that domestic and international security analysts can use as a resource for understanding the critical issues and as a guide for preparing for hearings and legislative initiatives.

INTRODUCTION

There has been much talk by cyber security officials about plans to protect the world from cyber attacks. Unfortunately, there is little evidence that the world is more secure from a major cyber attack than in 2000 because attacks on the Internet go on unabated (see Table 1). In addition to calling for new legislation and oversight, this chapter serves as a source of information about cyber security that domestic and international security analysts can use as a resource for understanding the critical issues and as a guide for preparing for hearings and legislative initiatives.

This is accomplished by describing and analyzing both the technical and policy issues. With increased understanding of the threat to the nation's cyber space, security analysts will be prepared to determine the adequacy of existing legislation and the possible need for new or amended legislation.

MOTIVATION

Naturally, after the events of 9/11, the world focused on possible further attacks on their physical infrastructure. However, this approach is like "fighting the last war." The enemy knows that we have gone to great lengths to protect our physical infrastructure. The probability is much higher for terrorist attacks on the nation's cyber space. Having focused on fighting the last war, we are much less prepared to protect our network resources, such as the Internet, despite the fact that a successful attack on our cyber space could bring the world's economy to its knees. In addition to security, it is important to recognize that both hardware and software reliability play a vital role in keeping the world's network infrastructure secure and operational. Therefore, the motivation of this chapter is to provide a focus on cyber security and reliability, with an emphasis on determining the extent of actual *implementation* as opposed to plans for implementation.

This chapter addresses various policy issues that have arisen in the debate on the cyber security threat in the U.S. that we believe also has significance worldwide.

POLICY INITIATIVES FOR DEVELOPING AND IMPROVING CYBER SECURITY POLICY

There is much that can be done to enhance the security of the world's critical information infrastructure that include: (1) new thinking about how to solve the cyber security problem and (2) implementation of plans to solve the problem that have been proposed but where action has been lacking.

1. In September 2003, Microsoft Corporation announced three new critical flaws in its latest Windows operating systems software. Security experts predicted that computer hackers might possibly exploit these new vulnerabilities by releasing more attack programs, such as the "Blaster worm" that recently targeted other Windows vulnerabilities causing widespread disruption on the Internet. (Vijayan & Jaikumar, 2003)

Microsoft operating systems and application programs are notorious for having experienced numerous security breaches. Since Microsoft products account for about 90% of the installed base of software nationwide, a great deal of leverage in mitigating user vulnerabilities to attack could be gained by improving the security of Microsoft software. This factor is frequently overlooked in securing the nation's cyber space. The fact is that software vendors, such as Microsoft, *are* the most significant source of security problems. Windows operating systems and application software have been subject to repeated successful attacks for many years. Thus, making the Internet more secure is not going to solve the core problem. A possible partial solution is legislation mandating that federal government acquired software be subject to rigorous security checks by the National Institute for Standards and Technology (NIST) prior to implementation. Of course, there is a political problem in doing this: Congresspersons representing software vendors in their districts would object. However, the problem is so serious that the political risk should be accepted.

A related idea is for Congress to exercise oversight responsibility to prevent Windows operating systems from being used on mission critical government systems and to substitute a more secure system, such as Linux. Again, the political fallout that would result from implementing this idea is recognized.

The NIST would seem to be the logical organization to perform software security certification. The private sector would be required to submit its software to NIST for security certification in order to be eligible for federal IT contracts. However, if analysis revealed that it is neither interested in nor capable of performing this function, a new software certification lab could be legislated to focus on the cyber security threat. This lab would perform research and development in software cyber security in addition to certifying operational software. It is worth noting that the National Information Assurance Partnership (NIAP), the joint venture of NIST and the NSA, with wide international acceptance, is doing exactly this.

It is common to find vulnerabilities in products after they have been put on the market. In some cases, patches are issued at the same time a new product is brought onto the market (Moteff & Parfomak, 2004). A possible approach to mitigating this problem in the federal sector would be for the NIST, or a new software certification lab, to specify security standards that all vendors would have to meet in order to bid on and win software procurements. Accompanying the imposition of standards would be a requirement for federal agencies to maintain records on vendor security performance and to use the history of performance as a factor in the award of contracts.

2. The response to a cyber attack should be predicated on a simultaneous physical attack. For example, a cyber attack on the Internet connectivity of the electric grid control system to regulate voltage could be accompanied by a simultaneous physical attack to blow up the grid's transformers. It is proposed that congressional oversight be augmented to require the Department of Homeland Security (DHS) to integrate cyber and physical threat planning into a single coordinated response plan and that the new Assistant Secretary for Cyber Security be charged with developing the "cyber" part of the plan.

3. Innovative research should be supported to solve the operating system and application software security problems cited previously. Related to this is the need for federal support for fellowships at universities for producing the scientists and engineers who are needed to conceptualize and engineer the next generation of cyber security architecture.

4. The President's Information Technology Advisory Committee (PITAC), now disbanded, has produced the *National Strategy to Secure Cyber Space*. This strategy should be *implemented* by DHS.

5. Congressional oversight should be exercised to require fixes (i.e., patches) be applied without delay in federal IT installations after a vulnerability has been identified or an attack has occurred. The urgency of this recommendation is stimulated by the following statistics: (1) According to the security group www.Attrition. org, failure to keep software patches up-to-date resulted in 99% of 5,823 Web site defacements in 2003. (2) Government observers have stated that approximately 80% of successful intrusions into federal computer systems can be attributed to software errors, or poor software quality. (Krim, 2003)

6. Richard Clarke, former White House cyber space advisor under the Clinton and Bush Administrations (until 2003), has said: That many commercial software products are poorly written, or have poorly configured security features. There is currently no regulatory mechanism or legal liability if a software manufacturer sells a product that has design defects. Often the licensing agreement that accompanies the software product includes a disclaimer protecting the software vendor from all liability.

INHIBITORS TO PREVENTING CYBER ATTACKS

Although these initiatives, if acted on, would significantly improve cyber security and the quality of software in the federal sector, it must be recognized that from a global perspective, it is not feasible to guarantee protection against cyber attacks. The reason is that since Internet service providers (ISPs) control much of the infrastructure of the Internet, they are important players in network security. For example, ISPs' operate routers through which all Internet traffic flows. In addition, they control the domain name servers (DNSs) that provide computer names to Internet protocol (IP) address conversion. By virtue of this control, the ISPs' set policies on message routing through routers and DNSs. These policies have a direct bearing on the level of security achieved on the Internet. Examples of vulnerabilities that can occur in ISP facilities are: hacker attacks to overload routers with bogus messages, engaging in denial-of-service attacks by taking over routers and DNSs', stealing user IP addresses, and rerouting messages so that they never reach their intended recipients. It is not clear how the federal government can affect ISP security policy, since ISPs' operate in the private sector.

The Internet Engineering Task Force (IETF) develops network protocols and Internet security policies that do have a significant effect on ISP security operations. The IETF is comprised of network professionals who develop Internet standards on a voluntary basis. It might be possible for the NIST to set more stringent network security standards and thereby influence the IETF, which, in turn, could strengthen ISP security polices. However, this idea must be tempered by the fact that ISPs' are profit makers and will not install any more security than absolutely necessary.

CYBER SPACE THREATS AND VULNERABILITIES (THE REGENTS OF THE UNIVERSITY OF CALIFORNIA, 2002)

The terrorist attacks against the United States that took place on September 11, 2001, had a profound impact on our nation. The federal government and society as a whole have been forced to reexamine conceptions of security on our home soil, with many understanding only for the first time the lengths to which self designated enemies of our country are willing to go to inflict debilitating damage. We must move forward with the understanding that there are enemies who seek to inflict damage on our way of life. They are ready to attack us on our own soil, and they have shown a willingness to use unconventional means, such as attempts to bring down the entire Internet, to execute those attacks. While the attacks of September 11 were physical attacks, we are facing increasing threats from hostile adversaries in the realm of cyber space as well.

Our economy and national security are fully dependent upon information technology and the information infrastructure. At the core of the information infrastructure upon which we depend is the Internet, a system originally designed to share unclassified research among scientists who were assumed to be uninterested in abusing the network. It is that same Internet that today connects millions of other computer networks that allow the nation's infrastructures to work. These computer networks also control physical objects such as electrical transformers, trains, pipeline pumps, chemical vats, radars, and stock markets. A spectrum of malicious actors can and do conduct attacks against our critical information infrastructures. Of primary concern is the threat of organized cyber attacks capable of causing disruption to our nation's critical infrastructures.

The required technical sophistication to carry out such an attack is high—and partially explains the lack of an attack to date. We should not, however, be too sanguine. There have been instances where organized attackers have exploited vulnerabilities that may be indicative of more destructive capabilities. Uncertainties exist as to the intent and full technical capabilities of several observed attacks. Enhanced cyber threat analysis is needed to address long-term trends related to threats and vulnerabilities. What is known is that the attack tools and methodologies are becoming widely available, and the technical capability and sophistication of hackers bent on causing disruption is improving.

THE PROBLEM OF SECURING COMPUTERS AND NETWORKS

This problem is not easily solved because the great majority of the countermeasures for defeating intrusion are not under the control of the user. The reason is that, unlike the "old days," when organizations developed their own software, and there was no Internet, these days users are dependent on ISPs' and vendors of operating systems and application programs like Microsoft. Furthermore, users no longer employ home-grown software; they rely on packages like Word and Excel. This environment provides a bonanza for hackers who are dismissive of Microsoft products and wish to expose their security holes. In addition, computer criminals enjoy introducing viruses and worms in popular programs like Word, so that there can be maximum damage done, worldwide, because of the ubiquitous use of these programs. Therefore, even though user organizations can apply preventive medicine to mitigate the security problem, the substantive solutions must come from organizations external to the user organization. To illustrate, suppose organizations do engage in security preventive medicine. The patient can still suffer from unsecured vendor operating systems and application software, unsecured facilities operated by ISPs', and hackers bent on corrupting vendor programs. This is not to suggest that users do nothing about security; rather, it is to say that the solution is largely out of the hands of the user. Major improvements in computer and network security must come from changes in both culture and technology as practiced by external organizations.

NATIONAL STRATEGY TO SECURE CYBER SPACE

Next we provide a background on U.S. policy to secure cyber space that, we believe, has application to the international community.

The *National Strategy to Secure Cyber Space* outlines an initial framework for both organizing and prioritizing efforts. It provides direction to federal government departments and agencies that have roles in cyber space security. It also identifies steps that state and local governments, private companies and organizations, and individual Americans can take to improve our collective cyber security. The *Strategy* highlights the role of public and private engagement. The speed and anonymity of cyber attacks makes distinguishing among the actions of terrorists, criminals, and nation-states difficult. Therefore, the *National Strategy to Secure Cyber Space* helps reduce our nation's vulnerability to debilitating attacks against

our critical information infrastructures and the physical assets that support them.

Unfortunately, there is no evidence that these pronouncements have made the nation more secure from cyber attacks. For example, every day 2,500 notifications of damage to Web sites were received at a Web intrusion recording site ("The Internet," 2004). In addition, 55,000 Web site intrusions were chaptered to the same site in December 2004. Web sites were not the only target of attacks. Operating systems were also a favorite target with 54,000 attacks in the same month. Additional evidence of the increasing cyber threat is shown in Table 1, as chaptered by the Carnegie-Mellon University CERT Coordination Center. What is needed to provide greater protection of the nation's cyber space is increased emphasis on the following three fronts.

1. Innovative research in cyber security
2. Technical implementation of the *National Strategy to Secure Cyber Space*

With respect to (2), the President's Information Technology Advisory Committee (PITAC) recommends:

Strengthen the coordination of the Interagency Working Group on Critical Information Infrastructure Protection and integrate it under the Networking and Information Technology Research and Development (NITRD) Program. These actions will lead the way toward improving the Nation's cyber security, thereby promoting the security and prosperity of our citizens. (President's Information Technology Advisory Committee, 2005)

The biggest problem with National Cyber Security Division (NCSD) policy is that there is no requirement for the private sector to chapter threats and attacks. This organization does not think it necessary to have legislation to require this chaptering. However, it would be a serious matter if essential information to countering a cyber attack is not chaptered. To assist the private sector in chaptering cyber security information, PITAC recommends: "Provide increased support for the rapid transfer of Federally developed cutting-edge cyber security technologies to the private sector" (President's Information Technology Advisory Committee, 2005).

An interesting claim of NCSD is that coordination across all sectors of the economy could occur in real-time during a cyber attack. This might be possible with respect to telephonic communication, but this is only part of the story. The other part involves the technical process of attempting to identify the source of the attack, the operations and their locations that are being attacked, and the countermeasures (e.g., temporarily quarantine the affected part of the Internet) to employ to defeat or mitigate the attack. This involves both human decision-making to identify the appropriate countermeasures and the hardware and software network resources to implement it. It is doubtful that this could be accomplished in "real-time," if we use the following definition:

Pertaining to a system or mode of operation in which computation is performed during the actual time that an external process occurs, in order that the computation results can be used to control, monitor, or respond in a timely manner to the external process. (The Institute of Electrical and Electronic Engineers, 1990).

3.   Federal support for fellowships at universities for producing the scientists and engineers who are needed to conceptualize and engineer the next generation of cyber security architecture.

With respect to (3), PITAC recommends:

Intensify Federal efforts to promote recruitment and retention of cyber security researchers and students at research universities, with an aim of doubling this profession's numbers by the end of the decade. Also, increase Federal support for fundamental research in civilian cyber security by $90 million annually at NSF and by substantial amounts at agencies such as DARPA and DHS" (President's Information Technology Advisory Committee, 2005).

SUMMARY

This chapter has addressed a problem in security that while focused on the U.S. cyber security situation, has applicability worldwide because the fundamental problem is universal: how to protect critical infrastructure systems from attack by removing vulnerabilities; and, if attacked, how to mitigate the effects of the attack. We described and analyzed legislation and national strategy executive directives with respect to their efficacy in securing the nation's critical infrastructure. Based on this analysis, recommendations were made for possible additional or amended legislation and strategy. Included were policy and technical discussions of the threats, vulnerabilities, and risks of cyber attacks.

REFERENCES

The Institute of Electrical and Electronic Engineers. (1990). *IEEE standard glossary of software engineering terminology.*

The Internet thermometer. (2004). *Web server intrusion statistics.* www.zone-h.org

Krim, J. (2003). *Security report puts blame on Microsoft.* Washingtonpost.com. Retrieved May 17, 2007, from http://www.washingtonpost.com/wp-dyn/articles/A54872-2003Sep23.html

Moteff, J., & Parfomak, P. (2004*). CRS chapter for congress, critical infrastructure and key assets: Definition and identification.* Resources, Science, and Industry Division.

President's Information Technology Advisory Committee. (2005). *Cyber security: A crisis of prioritization.*

The Regents of the University of California. (2002). *Cyberspace threats and vulnerabilities.*

Vijayan, Jaikumar, (2003). Attacks on new Windows flaws expected soon. *Computerworld*, (37), 1.

Table 1. CERT/CC and other Statistics 19882005

Year	1995	1996	1997	1998	1999
Vulnerabilities	171	345	311	262	417

Source	Date	Frequency	Vulnerabilities	Per Year	Internet Users	Type of Attack
CERT	2004		3780			
CERT	2000		1090			
CERT	195		171			
Symantec	1995-2005		20000	2000		
	2000				429000000	
	1995				45000000	
www.zone-h.org		daily	2,500			web intrusions
www.zone-h.org	Dec-04		55,000			web intrusions
www.zone-h.org	Dec-04		54,000			Operating systems

Vulnerabilities	171	345	311	262	417

2000-2005

Year	2000	2001	2002	2003	2004	1Q,2005
Vulnerabilities	1,090	2,437	4,129	3,784	3,780	1,220

Total vulnerabilities chaptered (1995-1Q,2005): 17,946

Computer and Network Attacks				
Reference	Type of attack	Description	Percent	When
Bob Glass, Software, Jan/Feb 2005	virus	38 of 71 messages: viruses MIME: 17 Netsky: 13 Kriz: 4 Mydoom: 2 Fun Love: 2	53	Fall, 2004
Bob Glass, Software, Jan/Feb 2005	spam		17	Fall, 2004

Chapter LIII
ECHELON and the NSA

D. C. Webb
Leeds Metropolitan University, UK

ABSTRACT

Communication via electronic systems such as telephones, faxes, e-mail, computers, etc., has enormously increased the volume and ease with which people and institutions can exchange messages and information. However, the associated technologies have also enabled the introduction of new sophisticated concepts and methods in interception and analysis for intelligence gatherers. One such method has been dubbed ECHELON and is used by which the United States and its partners in a worldwide intelligence alliance to intercept and analyse messages transmitted electronically from anywhere on Earth. The National Security Agency (NSA), based at Fort Mead in Maryland, is the US organisation most intimately involved in the operation of this covert surveillance system. This is the story of the methods developed and the institutions that adopt them and the debates and arguments that have accompanied their use from domestic surveillance to international commercial and political espionage.

INTRODUCTION

The ECHELON system is widely accepted to be the most pervasive and powerful electronic intelligence gathering system in the world. It was developed and is operated on behalf of the United States and its partners (the United Kingdom, Australia, Canada, and New Zealand) in an intelligence alliance known as UKUSA. The system involves the automatic selection of intercepted electronic messages from target lists using a computer-based system known as DICTIONARY. Those messages, which include specific combina-

tions of names, dates, places, and subjects, matching particular criteria are sent for further processing by analysts at Fort Mead, Maryland—the Headquarters of the U.S. National Security Agency (NSA). The messages can be intercepted at ground-based stations that may link directly into land lines or pick up radio or microwave frequency signals. These signals are broadcast and distributed through radio aerials or a series of microwave towers as part of a local, national, or international network. Microwave signals can also be intercepted in space using specially designed satellites positioned to pick up signals which overshoot receivers and continue in a straight line into space. The satellites then downlink the intercepted signals to ground-based receivers in a number of geographical locations to enable a global coverage.

ECHELON was first revealed by Duncan Campbell in 1988 in an article in the British *New Statesman* political periodical (Campbell, 1988).[1] In 1991, a UK television *World in Action* programme disclosed the presence of a DICTIONARY computer at the Government Communications Headquarters (GCHQ) processing centre in Westminster. In 1993, Campbell produced a documentary for Channel 4 television called *The Hill* describing the ECHELON operation at the Menwith Hill NSA field station near Harrogate in Yorkshire. It is also described in more detail by Nicky Hagar in his book *Secret Power* in 1996 (Hagar, 1996a, b).[2] In his article Campbell described a world wide electronic interception and monitoring network operated by the NSA which makes use of a secret, post-World War II, international agreement to collect and share SIGnals INTelligence (SIGINT) information gathered from a variety of electronic sources (telephone, fax, telex, e-mail, etc.). ECHELON was described as the part of the system that involves satellite interception.

HISTORICAL BACKGROUND

UKUSA Agreement

Perhaps the first public reference to the UKUSA agreement was made in a 1972 article in *Ramparts* magazine (Peck, 1972)[3] which described the NSA global eavesdropping network of stations. The UKUSA Agreement was formed in secret in 1947, to enable intelligence information to be shared between the U.S. and the UK. The agreement brought together personnel and stations from the NSA and the GCHQ in the UK. They were joined soon after by the intelligence networks of three British Commonwealth countries—the Communications Security Establishment (CSE) of Canada, the Australian Defence Security Directorate (DSD), and the Government Communications Security Bureau (GCSB) of New Zealand. Since then other countries,

including Germany, Japan, Norway, Denmark, South Korea, and Turkey, have become "third party" participants in the UKUSA network (Richelson, 1989). In addition, other countries, such as China, may host UKUSA SIGINT stations or share limited SIGINT information.

The network operates by dividing the world up into regions, with each region being allocated to a network member who then takes responsibility for collecting SIGINT in that particular area. Jeffrey Richelson and Desmond Ball have recorded that:

... the current division of responsibility allocates coverage of the eastern Indian Ocean and parts of South East Asia and the South-west Pacific to the DSD; Africa and the Soviet Union east of the Urals to the GCHQ; the northern USSR and parts of Europe to the Canadian CSE; a small portion of the South-west Pacific to the New Zealand GCSB; and all the remaining areas of interest to the NSA and its component service agencies. (Richelson & Ball, 1990)

However, they also note that "the geographical division of the world is, in practice, of course not as clear cut as this" (Richelson & Ball, 1990). For example, although the NSA predominately collects SIGINT information on the former Soviet Union, the UK also monitors activity associated with the Western Soviet Union in which the NSA field station at Menwith Hill plays an important role.

An example of how intelligence agreements can be used is provided by former Canadian agent Mike Frost. He revealed that in 1983 former British Prime Minister Margaret Thatcher did not have full confidence in two of her ministers and requested that they be monitored. Because of legal difficulties associated with domestic spying on high governmental officials, the GCHQ could not perform this task directly and so a request was made to CSE in Ottawa asking them to conduct the surveillance mission, which they did (Gratton, 1994).

This use of the UKUSA alliance for purely political reasons (rather than those of state security) appears to be very easy to arrange. It is unlikely that approval to carry out this exercise was requested from officials high up in the intelligence hierarchy. It was probably thought that checking too much with those at the top might only complicate things unnecessarily.

Frost also claimed that in 1975 he was asked to spy on Margaret Trudeau, the Canadian Prime Minster Pierre Trudeau's wife. Apparently, the Royal Canadian Mounted Police's (RCMP) Security Service division believed that Mrs. Trudeau might be involved in the use of marijuana. However, months of surveillance by the CSE revealed nothing of importance and Frost was concerned that there were political motivations behind the RCMP request:

She was in no way suspected of espionage. Why was the RCMP so adamant about this? Were they trying to get at Pierre Trudeau for some reason or just protect him? Or were they working under orders from their political masters? (Gratton, 1994)

ECHELON

The ECHELON system is directed primarily at the Intelsat and Inmarsat satellites that carry the vast majority of global civilian, diplomatic, and governmental phone and fax communications. Signals from these satellites are intercepted at a number of field stations—a station at Morwenstow in Cornwall, England intercepts signals from satellites transmitting to Europe, Africa, and western Asia from above the Atlantic and Indian Oceans. The Yakima station in Washington state listens in to Pacific Ocean and Far East communications, while signals for North and South America are picked up at Sugar Grove, West Virginia. A DSD facility at Geraldton, Australia and one run by the GCSB at Waihopai, New Zealand cover Asia, the South Pacific countries, and the Pacific Ocean. Another station on Ascension Island is suspected of covering communications meant for the South Atlantic (Poole, 1999/2000).

Some other stations also monitor signals from other satellites that relay information that may be of interest to the UKUSA nations—as do bases at Menwith Hill;

Shoal Bay near Darwin in northern Australia; Leitrim in Canada; Bad Aibling (since moved to Darmstadt) in Germany, and Misawa in Japan.

The NSA and CIA also operate their own satellite networks to pick up microwave signals that leak into space from ground-based transmitters. These satellites then download the intercepted signals to field stations on the ground. They include the first generation of spy satellites launched in the 1960s (known as Ferret), the second generation Canyon, Rhyolite, and Aquacade satellites of the 1970s; a third generation in the 1980s known as Chalet, Vortex, Magnum, Orion, and Jumpseat satellites, the fourth generation Mercury, Mentor and Trumpet satellites of the 1990s and the fifth generation Intruder and Prowler series from 2000 (Darling, n.d.).

In addition, a world wide network of radio listening posts was set up by the UKUSA countries before satellite communications became so important. These are still employed to intercept high frequency (HF) radio frequency signals (used by the military for communications with ships and aircraft) and very high frequency (VHF) and ultra high frequency (UHF) signals (often used for short range tactical military communications).

Each ECHELON station maintains its own DICTIONARY system of key words used in searching the intercepted data. Messages that meet specific criteria are identified with an associated code that represents the source or subject, the date and time, and the receiving station. These messages are then transmitted to each intelligence agency's headquarters via a global computer system named PLATFORM (Bamford, 1983). Messages that go for further processing are organised into different analysis types: reports—which are direct and complete translations of intercepted messages; "gists"—which give basic information on a series of messages within a given category; and summaries—made from compilations of reports and gists (Hagar, 1996a) They are then classified in terms of sensitivity and coded as, for example, MORAY (secret), SPOKE (more secret than MORAY), UMBRA (top secret), GAMMA (Russian intercepts), and DRUID (intelligence forwarded to non-UKUSA parties).

In 1992 former NSA Director William Studeman illustrated the extent of the message selection process through systems like ECHELON:[4]

One [unidentified] intelligence collection system alone can generate a million inputs per half hour; filters throw away all but 6500 inputs; only 1,000 inputs meet forwarding criteria; 10 inputs are normally selected by analysts and only one report is produced. These are routine statistics for a number of intelligence collection and analysis systems which collect technical intelligence.

Much of the information about ECHELON that formed the basis of Campbell's original 1988 article was provided by Margaret Newsham who was a software system support co-ordinator at Menwith Hill in the late 1970s. While working there she witnessed the interception of a telephone call made by U.S. Senator Strom Thurmond but her disclosure of this did not result in any substantive official investigation, although it was reported to the House Committee (Campbell, 2000b).

The full details of ECHELON were described by Nicky Hager following 6 years of painstaking research on the activities of New Zealand's Government Communications Security Bureau and the NSA ECHELON station at Waihopi that started operating in 1989. According to Hagar (1996b):

The ECHELON system is not designed to eavesdrop on a particular individual's e-mail or fax link. Rather, the system works by indiscriminately intercepting very large quantities of communications and using computers to identify and extract messages of interest from the mass of unwanted ones.

In 1998 and 1999 Jeffrey Richelson of the National Security Archive[5] used the Freedom of Information Act to obtain official documents to confirm the existence and wide spread use of the ECHELON system. Its existence was officially confirmed in a report for the European Parliament Scientific and Technological Options office (STOA) by Steve Wright of the Omega

Foundation in January 1998 (Wright, 1998). The disclosure of this surveillance system in NSA-run bases in Europe caused widespread concern and a further series of working documents were produced for STOA in 1999 (Holdsworth, 1999a). These documents brought together the results of four studies, one of which, *Interception Capabilities 2000* by Duncan Campbell (1999b), exposed the political and commercial uses of the system and caused considerable apprehension among European politicians and the media, who paid special attention to the likelihood of commercial intelligence gathering which could give U.S. companies an advantage over European businesses when bidding for lucrative international contracts.

Concern in Europe grew rapidly and, in March 2000, 172 members of the European Parliament (MEP) of all political groups signed up in support of the establishment of a Parliamentary Inquiry Committee on ECHELON. This proposal was at first rejected by the major political groups and instead, on July 5, 2000, the European Parliament decided to set up a *Temporary Committee on the ECHELON Interception System* and appointed 36 MEPs' (rapporteur: Gerhard Schmid)[6] to lead a year-long investigation to verify the existence of the system and to assess any legal implications and commercial risks. A temporary committee is not restricted to dealing only with matters relating to community law (as a committee of enquiry would be) and can investigate, for example, whether the rights of European citizens are adequately protected or determine whether European industry is put at risk by the global interception of communications.

In May 2001, members of the committee visited the U.S. on a fact-finding mission to include discussions with various politicians and intelligence officials. However, noone in the U.S. government would admit that ECHELON even existed and the NSA, the CIA, the State Department, and the Department of Commerce refused to talk to the committee. The MEPs cut their visit short, returning home somewhat angry and frustrated (Perrott, 2001).

A working document for the Temporary Committee was issued in early May 2001[7] and a draft report "On the existence of a global system for the interception of private and commercial communications (ECHELON interception system)" was published later that month.[8] The MEPs' were unable to find conclusive proof of industrial espionage. However, they considered the threat to privacy posed by ECHELON to be more disturbing. They concluded that the system could not be as extensive as initially claimed as it is concerned mainly with the worldwide interception of satellite communications, which forms only a small part of the total global communications. The committee decided that ECHELON had access to a limited proportion of radio and cable communications, although evidence submitted showed that the ECHELON system gave 55,000 British and American operatives access to data gathered by 120 spy satellites worldwide.

The Committee's Final Report and Motion for a Resolution was issued in June 2001.[9] The Temporary Committee found that the conduct of electronic surveillance activities by U.S. intelligence breaches the European Convention of Human Rights even when conducted, allegedly, for law enforcement purposes. It concluded that the British and German governments may be in breach of community law and of human rights treaties if they fail to prevent the improper use of surveillance stations sited on their territory to intercept private and commercial communications. Two of the NSA's largest electronic intelligence stations were located at that time in Bad Aibling, Bavaria, and Menwith Hill, in England.

Duncan Campbell supplied four important submissions to the Committee on *Interception Capabilities—Impact and Exploitation*. These were commissioned by the Committee in December 2000 to update and extend the 1999 report, *Interception Capabilities 2000*. They covered the use of COMmunications INTelligence (COMINT) for economic purposes, legal and human rights issues, and recent political and technological developments and were presented in Brussels on January 22 and 23, 2001. The first paper summarised the role of ECHELON in COMINT (Campbell, 2001a) and pointed out that very few media reports had provided any new information about ECHELON at that time. Campbell claimed that previous statements that had credited ECHELON with

the capacity to intercept "within Europe, all e-mail, telephone, and fax communications" had since proven to be incorrect, although the global NSA SIGINT capability could process most of the world's satellite communications (Campbell, 2000a).

The third paper (Campbell, 2001c) revealed how Britain protects the rights of Americans, Canadians and Australians against interception that would not comply with their own domestic law, but does not offer such protection to Europeans. The fourth study, on new political and technical developments, was presented in the form of a slideshow.[10]

Economic Espionage

The second of Campbell's submissions to the Temporary Committee was on the *COMINT Impact on International Trade* (Campbell, 2001b) and described in detail how, since 1992, Europe could have sustained significant employment and financial loss as a result of the U.S. government's use of ECHELON. Estimates of the damage varied from $13 billion to $145 billion and the paper refers to various annexes which described (among other things) the work of the U.S. Trade Promotion Co-ordinating Committee (TPCC) and the Advocacy Center set up by President Clinton with direct intelligence inputs from the CIA and NSA.

The earlier STOA reports had accused the U.S. of using ECHELON for economic espionage—to help U.S. companies gain an advantage over European competitors in major contracts. In 2000, former CIA director James Woolsey stated in an article in the *Wall Street Journal* that the policy of the U.S. government was to use the U.S. intelligence system to spy on European companies in order to level the playing field by gathering evidence of bribery and unfair trade practices (Woolsey, 2000).

Campbell's paper describes in some detail how U.S. intelligence gathering priorities underwent a major change after the Cold War and how "about 40 percent of the requirements" of U.S. intelligence collection became "economic, either in part or in whole." The new priorities for economic intelligence were approved by President George Bush in a document called NSD-67 (National Security Directive 67), issued on March 20, 1992.

The Temporary Committee did not find new reports of European business losses beyond those appearing in the American media in 1994-1996, however, it did find that, even if bribery was involved, NSA activities of this kind were illegal in Europe and pointed out that "all EU Member States have properly functioning criminal justice systems. If there is evidence that crimes have been committed, the USA must leave the task of law enforcement to the host countries."

The report also stated that: "interference in the exercise of the right to privacy must be proportional and, in addition, the least invasive methods must be chosen" and, because Europeans can only try to obtain legal redress for misconduct in their own national and not American courts, then:

As far as European citizens are concerned, an operation constituting interference carried out by a European intelligence service must be regarded as less serious than one conducted by an American intelligence service.

The draft committee report therefore concluded that:

... there would seem to be good reason ... to call on Germany and the United Kingdom to take their obligations under the ECHR [European Court of Human Rights] seriously and to make the authorisation of further intelligence activities by the NSA on their territory contingent on compliance with the ECHR.

The report also pointed out that: "possible threats to privacy and to businesses posed by a system of the ECHELON type arise not only from the fact that is a particularly powerful monitoring system, but also that it operates in a largely legislation-free area." It consequently called for the development and promotion of European "user-friendly open-source encryption software" and wanted "encryption to become the norm" with "a common level of protection against intelligence operations based on the highest level

which exists in any member state."

The Committee was particularly critical of the UK and some other member states where there is no parliamentary oversight of surveillance. It said that national governments should set up "specific, formally structured monitoring committees responsible for supervising and scrutinising the activities of the intelligence services" and called for the European Parliament to hold an international congress for NGOs from Europe, the U.S. and other countries to provide a forum on the protection of privacy against telecommunications surveillance.

Political Espionage

The European Committee concentrated on the issues of economic espionage, perhaps believing that political activities were too delicate to consider or that they were the prerogative of individual governments. There is no doubt though that the ECHELON surveillance and interception techniques are used for political purposes. In 1992 for example, several former GCHQ officials confidentially told the *London Observer* that organisations such as Amnesty International, Greenpeace, and Christian Aid, were being targeted (Merritt, 1992). Another story in *The Observer* included an admission by Robin Robison, a former employee of the British Joint Intelligence Committee, that Margaret Thatcher had personally ordered the communications interception of Lonrho, the parent company of *The Observer*, following the publication in that newspaper of a 1989 article claiming that bribes had been paid to Mark Thatcher, the Prime Minister's son, in a multi-billion dollar British arms deal with Saudi Arabia. Despite facing legal action for breaking the Official Secrets Act, Robison admitted that he had personally delivered intercepted Lonrho messages to Mrs. Thatcher's office (O'Shaughnessy, 1992).

Although it is not clear that ECHELON or the intelligence agencies of other countries are always involved in examples of domestic surveillance, it is perhaps not a huge assumption that the vast intelligence network of the UKUSA alliance and the sophisticated surveillance techniques offered by ECHELON can be and are often used not only for the purposes of monitoring and detection of national threats but also for the purposes of political control.

The National Security Agency (NSA)[11]

The history and activities of the U.S. National Security Agency (NSA)[12] were first introduced to a worldwide audience through James Bamford's book *The Puzzle Palace* in 1982 (Bamford, 1982). Bamford has enjoyed a somewhat erratic relationship with the NSA who threatened to sue him over his first exposure of their work and then later celebrated him at the publication of his second book on the NSA—*Body of Secrets* (Bamford, 2001).

The NSA was established in secret by President Harry S. Truman in 1952 to act as a focal point for U.S. SIGINT and Communications Security (COMSEC) activities. SIGINT is subdivided into Communications Intelligence (COMINT) and Electronics Intelligence (ELINT). Its headquarters have been at Fort George G. Meade, Maryland (approximately ten miles or 16 km northeast of Washington, DC) since 1957.

The controlling National Security Council Intelligence Directive defines COMINT as: "technical and intelligence information derived from foreign communications by other than the intended recipients" and the same NSC directive also states that COMINT: "shall not include…any intercept and processing of unencrypted written communications, press and propaganda broadcasts, or censorship."

Communications signals (e-mail, fax, telephone intercepts) are collected at NSA field stations around the world and after some initial processing those of interest are passed on to Fort Meade for further analysis. The results are then presented to other agencies such as the CIA or DIA (Defense Intelligence Agency). The NSA is staffed by a mixture of civilians and military personnel although it provides operational guidance for SIGINT collection for stations maintained by the military intelligence services, collectively known as the Central Security Service (CSS).

Two NSA analysts, Vernon Mitchell and William Martin, who had defected to the Soviet Union, told the world what the NSA was doing at a press conference in Moscow as long ago as September 1960:

We know from working at NSA [that] the United States reads the secret communications of more than forty nations, including its own allies ... Both enciphered and plain text communications are monitored from almost every nation in the world, including the nations on whose soil the intercept bases are located. [13]

The NSA and Political Espionage

The NSA has frequently been accused of being involved in political spying. For example, John Ehrlichman revealed that Henry Kissinger used the NSA to intercept messages of then Secretary of State William P. Rogers (Ehrlichman, 1982). Kissinger was said to use this information to convince President Nixon of Rogers' incompetence. However, Kissinger himself became a victim of the NSA's spy network when President Richard Nixon was informed of his secret diplomatic dealings with foreign governments (Shane & Bowman, 1995).

In 1969, people thought to be involved in *subversive* domestic activities were organized into *watch lists* under an operation called MINARET. The lists included people such as Martin Luther King, Malcolm X, Jane Fonda, Joan Baez, and Dr. Benjamin Spock. The NSA instructed its personnel to "restrict the knowledge" that it was collecting this information and to keep its name off any disseminated information.[14] The watch lists were determined to be of "questionable legality" in October 1973 by the Assistant Attorney General Henry Petersen and Attorney General Elliot Richardson.

The NSA had therefore already been secretly spying on Americans for some time when, in 1970, President Nixon directed the NSA "to program for coverage the communications of US citizens using international facilities" and, in particular, to target a number of Vietnam war protestors. No warrant was needed for these actions and the NSA could decide on who they could spy on, where and when their operations should take place (Poole, 1999/2000).

Concerns that antiwar protestors were being spied upon led to the formation of select committee hearings in both chambers in the mid-1970s. Investigations determined that the NSA had intercepted communications under an operation known as SHAMROCK. A number of American citizens were targeted and the information obtained had been disseminated to the FBI, CIA, Secret Service, Bureau of Narcotics and Dangerous Drugs (BNDD), and the Department of Defense.[15]

During the hearings conducted by the Senate Select Committee (chaired by Senator Frank Church), Lt. General Lew Allen, Jr., the Director of NSA, testified in open session and gave a public overview of NSA's responsibilities, stating:

This mission of NSA is directed to foreign intelligence, obtained from foreign electrical communications and also from other foreign signals such as radars. Signals are intercepted by many techniques and processed, sorted and analyzed by procedures which reject inappropriate or unnecessary signals. The foreign intelligence derived from these signals is then reported to various agencies of the government in response to their approved requirements for foreign intelligence.[16]

In August 1975, Lt. General Allen told the Select Committee of the U.S. House of Representatives (the Pike Committee) that the "NSA systematically intercepts international communications, both voice and cable" and that "messages to and from American citizens have been picked up in the course of gathering foreign intelligence."

The final report of the Pike Committee recommended that the Agency should be held accountable for their actions and proposed that they be made subject to legal constraints. Their recommendations contributed to the establishment of the Foreign Intelligence Surveillance Act (FISA) of 1978 which created the Foreign Intelligence Surveillance Court (FISC) to which requests were to be made to authorise electronic

surveillance and physical search. The FISC issued about 500 FISA warrants per year from 1979 to 1995, and then slowly increased them until 2004 when some 1,758 were issued.

Legislation concerning the intelligence community is complicated, and takes a long time to formulate and the NSA did not receive a functional charter until 1992. However, guidance was provided by a series of executive orders issued by President Gerald Ford on February 18, 1976 (requiring the government to acquire a warrant to conduct electronic surveillance within the U.S. for foreign intelligence purposes)[17] and President Jimmy Carter in 1979 (authorising the Attorney General to approve warrantless electronic surveillance so as to obtain foreign intelligence as long as the conditions required by the FISA are met—that the means of communication are exclusively between or among foreign powers or the objective is under the "open and exclusive" control of a foreign power, and that there is no substantial likelihood that the surveillance will acquire the contents of any communication involving a U.S. citizen).[18] In December 1981 President Ronald Reagan signed an order to assign responsibility for the NSA to the Secretary of Defense.[19]

It was also the Reagan Administration that directed the NSA to intercept phone calls placed to Nicaraguan officials by Congressman Michael Barnes of Maryland. A conversation he had with the Foreign Minister of Nicaragua where he protested about the imposition of martial law there was leaked to reporters (Poole, 1999/2000).

CURRENT ISSUES

Spying on the UN

On March 2, 2003, *The Observer* newspaper published the contents of a leaked NSA memorandum, dated January 31, 2003, that showed that the U.S. had developed an "aggressive surveillance operation, which involves interception of the home and office telephones and the e-mails of UN delegates." The purpose of the memo was "to win votes in favour of war against Iraq" and it had been circulated to senior agents in the NSA and to Britain's GCHQ (Bright, Vulliamy, & Beaumont, 2003).

The Observer report explained that:

The leaked memorandum makes clear that the target of the heightened surveillance efforts are the delegations from Angola, Cameroon, Chile, Mexico, Guinea and Pakistan at the U.N. headquarters in New York—the so-called "Middle Six" delegations whose votes are being fought over by the pro-war party, led by the U.S. and Britain, and the party arguing for more time for U.N. inspections, led by France, China and Russia.

Katharine Gunn, a GCHQ translator, was later arrested and charged under the Official Secrets Act in connection with the leak. She stated her intention to plead not guilty on the grounds that her actions were justified to prevent an illegal war. The UK government eventually dropped the charges against her. During this time the story was hardly covered at all in the U.S. media and, as Norman Solomon has said:

In contrast to the courage of the lone woman who leaked the NSA memo—and in contrast to the journalistic vigour of the Observer team that exposed it—the most powerful U.S. news outlets gave the revelation the media equivalent of a yawn. Top officials of the Bush administration, no doubt relieved at the lack of U.S. media concern about the NSA's illicit spying, must have been very encouraged (Solomon, 2005).

Five days after the date of the leaked memo, on February 5, U.S. Secretary of State Colin Powell gave a dramatic presentation to the UN Security Council during which he played NSA intercepts of Iraqi field commanders and showed satellite photographs in an attempt to present a case for military intervention in Iraq. SIGINT was also seen to play a significant role during the execution of the Gulf War.[20]

ECHELON, The NSA, and Terrorism

The U.S. "war against terror" has allowed the NSA to develop and expand their programmes of spying and surveillance. The government and intelligence agencies use events such as the bombing in Oklahoma City, attacks on the World Trade Center in New York, and the bombings of the American embassies in Dar es Salaam, Tanzania, and Nairobi, Kenya, to justify the continued monitoring of people and organisations around the world.

ECHELON systems have been employed successfully in monitoring international and domestic communications to detect international criminals. Among the claimed successes are:

- The discovery of missile sites in Cuba in 1962.
- The capture of the Achille Lauro terrorists in 1995.
- The uncovering of the involvement of Libya in the Berlin discotheque bombing that killed one American (and resulted in the bombing of Tripoli in 1996).

Incidents such as these, and some others that have been prevented from happening, are used to add credibility to arguments that a large scale and free ranging surveillance system is necessary for the sake of national security.

The United States has never aspired to be a country where the state continually spies on its citizens and is not accountable to them for its actions, in fact the Constitution goes to some lengths to limit the powers of government and protect the rights of individuals in this respect. However, there are always difficulties when a country is in a state of war or siege. The state and/or military are then often tempted to justify a temporary loss of civil liberties in exchange for a general feeling of increased national and/or personal security. President George W. Bush has stated that the U.S. is currently involved in a "war against terror" which, if not perpetual, may last a long time against an "enemy" that is difficult to identify and monitor. In this case, the temptation to cut corners, to become misleading as far as concepts of security and freedom are concerned, and to conceal certain actions and intentions, is likely to be strong on a number of occasions.

For example, just a few days after the September 11 attacks on New York and the Pentagon, the Justice Department lawyer, John Yoo, wrote a memo arguing that the government might use "electronic surveillance techniques and equipment that are more powerful and sophisticated than those available to law enforcement agencies in order to intercept telephonic communications and observe the movement of persons but without obtaining warrants for such uses." He noted that while such actions could raise constitutional issues, in the face of devastating terrorist attacks "the government may be justified in taking measures which in less troubled conditions could be seen as infringements of individual liberties" (Isikoff, 2004; Risen & Lichtblau, 2005).

Also around this time, President George W. Bush issued a secret executive order authorizing the NSA to conduct phone-taps on anyone suspected of links with terrorism without the need to issue warrants from a special court, as required by the Foreign Intelligence Surveillance Act. This programme of surveillance was concealed from the public until December 2005, when the *New York Times* reported it. The article contained a statement that the newspaper had delayed publication for a year at the request of the White House who asked that the article not be published "arguing that it could jeopardize continuing investigations and alert would-be terrorists that they might be under scrutiny."

The article emphasises that:

The previously undisclosed decision to permit some eavesdropping inside the country without court approval was a major shift in American intelligence-gathering practices, particularly for the National Security Agency, whose mission is to spy on communications abroad.

And also that:

Nearly a dozen current and former officials, who were granted anonymity because of the classified nature of the program, discussed it with reporters for The New York Times because of their concerns about the operation's legality and oversight (Isikoff, 2004; Risen & Lichtblau, 2005).

The article refers to statements made by officials familiar with the program that the NSA eavesdrops without warrants on up to 500 people in the U.S. at any one time and from 5,000 to 7,000 people overseas. It was also claimed that the eavesdropping programme had helped uncover a plot by Iyman Faris (who pleaded guilty in 2003 to supporting Al Qaeda and planning to bring down the Brooklyn Bridge) and also helped to expose a possible plot to attack British pubs and train stations in 2004. Even so, it seems that most people monitored by the NSA have never actually been charged at all.

Political Espionage

It was also revealed in April 2005 that, under the previously mentioned programme, recent NSA Director General Michael Hayden approved intercepts of phone conversations made by past and present U.S. government officials. These intercepts played a major role in the controversy surrounding the nomination of Undersecretary of State John R. Bolton as ambassador to the United Nations (Madsen, 2005).

During Bolton's Senate Foreign Relations Committee nomination hearing, Senator Christopher Dodd from Connecticut revealed that Bolton had requested transcripts of 10 intercepts of conversations between named U.S. government officials and foreign persons. Later, it was revealed that U.S. companies (treated as "U.S. persons" by the NSA) were identified in an additional nine intercepts requested by Bolton. NSA insiders reported that Hayden approved special intercept operations on behalf of Bolton and had them masked as "training missions" in order to get around internal NSA regulations that normally prohibit such eavesdropping on U.S. citizens.

The response to the revelations that the NSA had engaged in warrantless domestic surveillance was immediate and dramatic. Following a considerable amount of media coverage in the U.S., a congressional hearing examined the legality of the program in February 2006. Evidence suggests that the NSA had already begun these activities before President Bush had granted formal approval and that the operation involved cooperation from American telecommunication companies, and information shared with other agencies, including the DIA.

In February 2006, the National Security Archive, the American Civil Liberties Union (ACLU), and the Electronic Privacy Information Center (EPIC) filed a Freedom of Information Act lawsuit against the Department of Justice to compel the immediate disclosure of the internal legal justifications for the surveillance programme. As a consequence the Justice Department conceded that it could begin releasing the internal legal memos used to set up the programme imminently. The results and further investigations may have dramatic repercussions for the intelligence community, the Bush Administration and the people of the United States.

CONCLUSION

Spying is often referred to as the "second oldest profession" and it is well known that throughout history governments have not always fully trusted each other (even those supposed to be allies) and often go to considerable lengths to find out what others may be doing in secret while at the same time concealing their own secrets. Perhaps what comes as a big surprise to many people (especially in democracies) is the extent of state surveillance of its own citizens—including its own elected officers and servants—and that they too may be a target for state security systems without ever knowing why and what records have been made and kept on them and their activities.

ECHELON and the activities of the NSA are just the latest developments in a long history of surveillance activities developed and executed by those in authority and/or those who see thmselves as protectors

of the status quo and/or the well-being of the general public. Problems arise when these activities are seen to be carried out for personal or political advantage. This is why accountabilty for security activities must be assured and legal protection available. The general public and their watchdogs need to be continually alert to ensure that their rights are protected and their systems of governance are improved. This is especially true in a time of upheaval produced by national emergencies and widespread security concerns.

The *New York Times'* disclosure of warrantless surveillance by the NSA on U.S. citizens and officials has led to a major national controversy in which a number of related issues have been discussed and debated. These include:

- The legality of the warrantless wiretaps on U.S. citizens (Eggen, 2006; Halperin, 2006)
- The U.S. citizens' right to privacy [21]
- Constitutional issues concerning presidential powers and the separation of powers (Dreazen, 2006)
- The effectiveness (Bergman, Lichtblau, Shane & van Natta, 2006) and scope (Gellman, Linzer, & Leonning, 2006) of the program
- The legality of the publication of highly classified information[22]
- Implications for U.S. national security[23]

It is clear that the capabilities and practices of the NSA have resulted in suspicion and resentment from overseas and U.S. citizens alike. Whether or not the methods employed by the NSA are legal, U.S. officials justify the NSA's activities as being necessary to acquire information about threats to national security, international terrorism, and the narcotics trade.

Rapid advances in new professions of computer science and electronic communications have heavily influenced the way that procedures and techniques have developed in the "second oldest profession." New technologies have been embraced and exploited rapidly and effectively. Sometimes these developments move more quickly than the legal structures and guidance in place to protect individuals' rights. Perhaps the greatest test for any society is how it responds to and deals with these new situations and challenges?

REFERENCES

Bamford, J. (1982). *The puzzle palace: Inside the National Security Agency, America's most secret intelligence organization.* Boston: Houghton Mifflin.

Bamford, J. (2001). *Body of secrets: Anatomy of the ultra-secret National Security Agency.* New York: Doubleday.

Bergman, L., Lichtblau, E., Shane, S., & van Natta, D., Jr. (2006, January 17). Spy agency data after Sept. 11 led FBI to dead ends. *The New York Times.* http://www.commondreams.org/headlines06/0117-01.htm

Bright, M., Vulliamy, E., & Beaumont, P. (2003, March 2). Revealed: US dirty tricks to win vote on Iraq war: Secret document details American plan to bug phones and emails of key security council members. *The Observer.* http://observer.guardian.co.uk/iraq/story/0,12239,905936,00.html

Campbell, D. (1988, August 12). They've got it taped: Somebody's listening. *New Statesman.* http://www.gn.apc.org/duncan/echelon-dc.htm

Campbell, D. (1999b, October). *Interception capabilities 2000.* European Parliament Scientific and Technological Options office (STOA) report, PE 168.184/Vol 2/5. http://www.europarl.eu.int/stoa/publi/pdf/98-14-01-2_en.pdf

Campbell, D. (2000a, July 25). Inside Echelon. *Telopolis, Hannover.* http://www.telepolis.de/english/inhalt/te/6929/1.html

Campbell, D. (2000b, February 25). Making history: The original source for the 1988 first Echelon report steps forward. http://cryptome.org/echelon-mndc.htm

Campbell, D. (2001a, May 27). *Interception capabilities: Impact and exploitation: Paper 1: Echelon and its role in COMINT.* http://www.heise.de/tp/r4/artikel/7/7747/1.html

Campbell, D. (2001b, May 27). *Interception capabilities: Impact and exploitation: Paper 2: COMINT impact on international trade.* http://www.heise.de/tp/r4/artikel/7/7752/1.html

Campbell, D. (2001c, May 27). *Interception capabilities: Impact and exploitation: Paper 3: COMINT, privacy and human rights.* http://www.heise.de/tp/r4/artikel/7/7748/1.html

Darling, D. (n.d.). *SIGINT satellites.* In *The encyclopedia of astrobiology astronomy and spaceflight, the worlds of David Darling.* http://www.daviddarling.info/encyclopedia/S/SIGINT.html

Dreazen, Y. J. (2006, February 9). Expert on Congress's power claims he was muzzled for faulting Bush. *The Wall Street Journal.*

Eggen, D. (2006, January 19). Congressional agency questions legality of wiretaps. *The Washington Post.* http://www.washingtonpost.com/wp-dyn/content/article/2006/01/18/AR2006011802158.html

Ehrlichman, J. (1982). *Witness to power: The Nixon years.* Pocket Books.

Gellman, B., Linzer, D., & Leonnig, C. D. (2006, February 5). Surveillance net yields few suspects: NSA's hunt for terrorists scrutinizes thousands of Americans, but most are later cleared. *The Washington Post.* http://www.washingtonpost.com/wp-dyn/content/article/2006/02/04/AR2006020401373.html

Gratton, M. (1994). *Spyworld: Inside the Canadian and American intelligence establishments.* Canada: Doubleday.

Hagar, N. (1996a). *Secret power: New Zealand's role in the international spy network.* New Zealand: Craig Potton Publishing. http://www.fas.org/irp/eprint/sp/sp_c2.htm

Hagar, N. (1996b, December). Exposing the global surveillance system. *Covert Action Quarterly, 59.* http://caq.com/CAQ/CAQ59GlobalSnoop.html

Halperin, M. H. (2006, January 6). *A legal analysis of the NSA warrantless surveillance program*. Center for American Progress.http://www.americanprogress.org/site/pp.asp?c=biJRJ8OVF&b=1334469

Holdsworth, D. (Ed.). (1999a, October). *Development of surveillance technology and risk of abuse of economic information*. European Parliament Scientific and Technological Options office (STOA) report. http://www.europarl.eu.int/stoa/publi/pop-up_en.htm

Isikoff, M. (2004, December 18). 2001 memo reveals push for broader presidential powers. *Newsweek*. Retrieved May 21, 2007 from http://www.msnbc.msn.com/id/6732484/site/newsweek/

Madsen, W. (2005, April 25). NSA intercepts for Bolton masked as "training missions." *Online Journal Contributing*.http://www.onlinejournal.org/Special_Reports/042505Madsen/042505madsen.html

Merritt, J. (1992, June 18). UK: GCHQ spies on charities and companies—fearful whistleblowers tell of massive routine abuse. *The Observer (London)*.

O'Shaughnessy, H. (1992, June 28). Thatcher ordered Lonrho phone-tap over Harrods affairs. *The Observer (London)*.

Peck, W. (1972, August). .U.S. electronic espionage: A memoir. *Ramparts, 11*(2), 3550. http://jya.com/nsa-elint.htm

Perrott, A. (2001, June 7). Echelon: Spying chain's cover blown. *New Zealand Herald*. http://www.commondreams.org/headlines01/0607-03.htm

Poole, P. S. (1999/2000). *ECHELON: America's secret global surveillance network*.http://fly.hiwaay.net/~pspoole/echelon.html

Richelson, J. (1989). *The U.S. intelligence community* (2nd ed.). Ballinger.

Richelson, J., & Ball, D. (1990). *The ties that bind: Intelligence cooperation between the UKUSA countries: The United Kingdom, the United States of America, Canada, Australian and New Zealand* (2nd ed.). Boston: Unwin Hyman.

Risen, J., & Lichtblau, E. (2005, December 16). Bush lets U.S. spy on callers without courts. *The New York Times*. Retrieved May 21, 2007 from http://select.nytimes.com/gst/abstract.html?res=F00F1FFF3D540C758DDDAB0994DD404482

Shane, S., & Bowman, T. (1995, December 12). Catching Americans in NSA's net. *The Baltimore Sun*.

Solomon, N. (2005). *War made easy: How presidents and pundits keep spinning us to death*. NJ: John Wiley & Sons.

Woolsey, R. J. (2000, March 17). Why we spy on our allies. *The Wall Street Journal*. http://cryptome.org/echelon-cia2.htm

Wright, S. (1998, January). *An appraisal of technologies of political control*. European Parliament Scientific and Technological Options office (STOA) report. http://mprofaca.cronet.com/atpc2.html

TERMS AND DEFINITIONS

ACLU: American Civil Liberties Union

BNDD: United States Bureau of Narcotics and Dangerous Drugs

CIA: Central Intelligence Agency of the United States

COMINT (Comunications Intelligence): A major component of SIGINT. Technical and intelligence information derived from foreign communications by other than the intended recipients.

COMSEC: Communications Security

CSE: Communications Security Establishment of Canada

CSS: Central Security Services of the U.S.

DIA: Defense Intelligence Agency of the U.S.

DICTIONARY: Computer-based system for the automatic selection of intercepted electronic messages that may include combinations of specific names, dates, places, subjects, and so forth, from target lists.

DRUID: Code word for intelligence forwarded to non-UKUSA parties.

DSD: Defence Security Directorate of Australia

ECHELON: The part of the SIGINT system that involves satellite interception.

ECHR: European Court of Human Rights

EPIC: United States Electronic Privacy Information Centre

EU: European Union

FBI: Federal Bureau of Investigation of the United States

FISA: United States Foreign Intelligence Surveillance Act of 1978

FISC: United States Foreign Intelligence Surveillance Court which would authorise electronic surveillance and searches.

GAMMA: Code word for Russian intercepts.

GCHQ: Government Communications Head Quarters in the UK, headquarters in Cheltenham.

GCSB: Government Communications Security Bureau of New Zealand

MEP: Member of the European Parliament

MINARET: U.S. surveillance operation in and around 1969, which kept track of people suspected of being involved in subversive domestic activities.

MORAY: Code word for secret documents.

NGO: Non Governmental Organistion

NSA: National Security Agency of the United States, headquarters in Fort Mead, Maryland.

NSD: National Security Directive of the United States

PLATFORM: Global computer system used by U.S. Intelligence.

RCMP: Royal Canadian Mounted Police

SHAMROCK: U.S. 1970s operation which targeted a number of U.S. citizens.

SIGINT (Signal Intelligence): Information gathered from a variety of electronic sources (telephone, fax, telex, email, etc.). SIGINT is subdivided into "Communications Intelligence" (COMINT) and "Electronics Intelligence" (ELINT).

SPOKE: Code word for documents more secret than MORAY.

STOA: Scientific and Technological Options Office of the European Parliament

TPCC: Trade Promotion Coordinating Committee of the United States

UMBRA: Code word for top secret documents.

UKUSA: An intelligence alliance bringing together personnel and stations from the NSA in the U.S., and the GCHQ in the UK. Later joined by the intelligence networks of three British Commonwealth countries—the Communications Security Establishment (CSE) of Canada, the Australian Defence Security Directorate (DSD), and the General Communications Security Bureau (GCSB) of New Zealand.

ENDNOTES

[1]   Available at: http://www.gn.apc.org/duncan/echelon-dc.htm

[2]   Secret Power - New Zealand's Role in the International Spy Network is available at: http://www.fas.org/irp/eprint/sp/sp_c2.htm - and Exposing the Global Surveillance System is available at: http://caq.com/CAQ/CAQ59GlobalSnoop.html

3   Available at: http://jya.com/nsa-clint.htm

4   Address to the Symposium on "National Security and National Competitiveness : Open Source Solutions" by Vice Admiral William Studeman, Deputy Director of Central Intelligence and former director of NSA, 1 December 1992, McLean, Virginia.

5   See: "Making history: the original source for the 1988 first Echelon report steps forward", London, Friday 25 February, 2000 by Duncan Campbell – available at http://cryptome.org/echelon-mndc.htm

6   See details at: http://www.europarl.eu.int/comparl/tempcom/echelon/mandate_en.htm

7   "Working Document in preparation for a report on the existence of a global system for intercepting private and commercial communications (ECHELON interception system)", Temporary Committee on the ECHELON Interception System, DT\437638EN.doc, Rapporteur: Gerhard Schmid, May 8, 2001 - available at http://fas.org/irp/program/process/europarl_draft.pdf

8   "Draft Report on the existence of a global system for the interception of private and commercial communications (ECHELON interception system)", European Parliament Temporary Committee on the ECHELON Interception System, PR/439868EN.doc, Rapporteur: Gerhard Schmid, 18 May, 2001 - available at http://www.fas.org/irp/program/process/prechelon_en.pdf

9   "Report on the existence of a global system for the interception of private and commercial communications (ECHELON interception system), Motion for a Resolution ", European Parliament Temporary Committee on the ECHELON Interception System, Report 2001/2098(INI), Rapporteur: Gerhard Schmid, 11 July 2001 - available at http://cryptome.org/echelon-ep-fin.htm

10   See: "ECHELON Violates Human Rights Treaties: Echelon system identified as "legislation-free zone", Nizkor Int. Human Rights Team, Derechos Human Rights, Serpaj Europe, 10

June 2001 - available at http://www.cndyorks.gn.apc.org/yspace/articles/echelon22.htm

11   Up to-date news and information on the activities of the NSA can be obtained from "The National Security Archive" of the George Washington University - available at http://www.gwu.edu/~nsarchiv/ and from NSA watch at http://www.nsawatch.org/

12   Official web-site: http://www.nsa.gov/history/index.cfm

13   The New York Times, 7 September 1960 quoted in "Inside Echelon: The history, structure und function of the global surveillance system known as Echelon" by Duncan Campbell, 25 July 2000 – available at http://www.heise.de/tp/r4/artikel/6/6929/1.html

14   MINARET Charter, 7/1/69, Hearings, Vol. 5, Exhibit No. 3, pp. 149-150.

15   "Supplementary Detailed Staff Reports on Intelligence Activities and the Rights of Americans: Book III", Final Report of the Select Committee to Study Governmental Operations with respect to Intelligence Activities, United States Senate, April 23 (under authority of the order of April 14), 1976 - available at http://www.icdc.com/~paulwolf/cointelpro/churchfinalreport IIIj.htm

16   Testimony of Lt. Gen. Lew. Allen, Jr., Director, National Security Agency in U.S. Congress, 94th Congress, 1st session, Senate, Select Committee to Study Governmental Operations with Respect to Intelligence Activities, Hearings, vol 5. The National Security Agency and Fourth Amendment Rights, 1976, p. 17.

17   Gerald R. Ford's Executive Order 11905: "United States Foreign Intelligence Activities", February 18, 1976, text available from the Weekly Compilation of Presidential Documents, Vol. 12, No. 8, February 23, 1976

18   Jimmy Carter, Executive Order 12139, "Foreign Intelligence Electronic Surveillance", May 23, 1979. Unclassified. Source: Federal Register, 44, 103, May 25, 1979

[19]   Ronald Reagan, "Executive Order 12333, "United States Intelligence Activities", December 4, 1981 – available at http://www.fas.org/irp/offdocs/eo12333.htm

[20]   See for example, "SIGINT and Warfighting", on the Yorkshire CND web site - available at http://cndyorks.gn.apc.org/mhs/mhswar.htm

[21]   See for example, "The Electronic Privacy Information Centre" - http://www.epic.org/

[22]   See for example the American Civil Liberties Union" - http://www.aclu.org/

[23]   See for example, "The National Security Archive", George Washington University - http://www.gwu.edu/~nsarchiv/

Chapter LIV
International Cybercrime Convention

Sylvia Mercado Kierkegaard
International Association of IT Lawyers (IAITL), Denmark

ABSTRACT

The Internet's global character and the increasing pressure from industries have prompted legislators to sort-out cross border cybercrime issues with a legislative solution—the CoE Convention on Cybercrime. The Convention on Cybercrime is the first international treaty on crimes committed via the Internet and other computer networks, dealing particularly with infringements of copyright, computer-related fraud, child pornography and violations of network security. Its main objective, set out in the preamble, is to pursue a common criminal policy aimed at the protection of society against cybercrime, especially by adopting appropriate legislation and fostering international co-operation. The convention is cause for concern as it gives governments too much power without any system of check and balance, and without protecting the civil liberties of web users.

INTRODUCTION

Information technology, in particular the Internet, provides great benefits for society. However, organized crime has become well established in cyberspace, using the Internet for human trafficking and other crimes. Governments and private sector officials from around the world are seeking ways to jointly combat cybercrime. Cyber criminals engage in activities such as selling access to networks of hacked personal computers (PCs) to send spam or launch attacks, or selling details of new security vulnerabilities so systems can be compromised. Security experts are increasingly concerned about the growing sophistication of the technology and techniques used by organized gangs of computer hackers and other criminals. The growth of cybercrime underscores the vulnerability of Internet users at a time when more and more people rely on the Web.

National boundaries are still too much of an obstacle to law enforcement. The paradox of the Internet—a worldwide computer network designed by visionaries and scientists—succumbing to hacking, phising and other forms of multijurisdictional cybercrime committed by teenagers and organized criminal elements riles law enforcement agents and government leaders. There is little doubt that computer crime and computer misuse is a growing malaise and has contributed to loss of business, competitive advantage, and privacy. The Internet's global character and the increasing pressure from industries have prompted legislators to sort out cross border cybercrime issues with a legislative solution—the Council of Europe (CoE) Convention on Cybercrime. This chapter will discuss the convention, its salient provisions, and possible impact on the cyber community. The aim of this chapter is to determine whether the treaty is an effective and rapid response to the growing threat of cybercrime, and whether these threats prompted by the borderless Web eventually could be resolved by a treaty.

CYBERCRIME

While "the emergence of new forms of computer crime has been widely noted in the press" (Michalowski, 1996), there is still no accepted definition of what really constitutes cybercrime. The 2005 *Oxford Dictionary of Law* defines cybercrime as "crime committed over the Internet. No specific laws exist to cover the Internet, but such crimes might include hacking, defamation over the Internet, copyright infringement, and fraud." *Encyclopaedia Britannica* defines it as "any use of a computer as an instrument to further illegal ends, such as committing fraud, trafficking in child pornography and intellectual property, stealing identities, or violating privacy."

The definition of cybercrime is still evolving and has now been expanded to cover any illegal act involving a computer and to all the activities done with criminal intent in cyberspace or are computer related. There is a sharp disagreement among legal experts on whether cybercrime should only include new forms of crimes that have no offline equivalent.

Jurisprudence and Internet legislations are just emerging for managing computer-related crimes. Cybercrime is neither fully nor partially covered by most existing laws. For example, Reonel Ramones,

authored the Love Bug virus, but was not prosecuted because the Philippines did not have then a law to deal with computer crime. The absence of uniform law is an issue that has crime fighters up in arms and has led the CoE and the United States to confront the legal problems at a multinational level through the harmonization of substantive criminal law and a coordinated approach.

Is Cybercrime Really a Menace?

Results from the 2005 E-Crime Watch survey reveals the fight against electronic crimes (e-crimes) may be paying off. The 2005 E-Crime Watch survey was conducted by *CSO* magazine in cooperation with the U.S. Secret Service and Carnegie Mellon University. The research was conducted to unearth e-crime fighting trends and techniques, including best practices and emerging trends. Respondents' answers were based on the 2004 calendar year.[1] Thirteen percent of the 819 survey respondents—more than double the 6% from the 2004 survey—reported that the total number of e-crimes (and network, system, or data intrusions) decreased from the previous year; 35% reported an increase in e-crimes; and 30% reported no change. Almost onethird (32%) of respondents experienced fewer than 10 e-crimes (versus the 25% reported in 2004), while the average number of e-crimes per respondent decreased to 86 (significantly less than 136 average reported in the 2004 survey). Respondents reported an average loss of $506,670 per organization due to e-crimes and a sum total loss of $150 million. While the average number of e-crimes decreased from 2003 to 2004, 68% of respondents reported at least one e-crime or intrusion committed against their organization in 2004; and 88% anticipated an increase in e-crime during 2005. More than half (53%) expected monetary losses to increase or remain the same. When asked what e-crimes were committed against their organizations in 2004, respondents cited virus or other malicious code as most prevalent (82%), with spyware (61%), phishing (57%), and illegal generation of spam e-mail (48%) falling close behind. Phishing jumped from 31% in the 2004 survey to 57%, the largest single percent increase of an e-crime year to year.

According to the Tenth Annual Computer Crime and Security Survey conducted by the CSI with the help of San Fran Francisco's FBI Computer Security Institute, average financial losses caused by cybercrime decreased by 61% (Loeb et al., 2005). The results confirm that the total dollar amount of financial losses resulting from security breaches is decreasing, with an average loss of $204,000 per respondent in 2004, down 61% from the average loss of $526,000 in 2003. Virus attacks were again the source of the greatest financial losses, accounting for 32% of the overall losses reported, but losses resulting from unauthorized access leapt into second place, accounting for 24% of overall reported losses and overtaking those caused by denial of service attacks. Losses from the theft of proprietary information—especially as hackers pursue databases full of online identities—rose dramatically. The fastest-growing computer-security threat to organizations was Web site defacement. A whopping 95% of respondents reported more than 10 Web site incidents.

Hi-tech crime cost Britain's business millions of pounds in 2004, according to the latest survey conducted by market research firm NOP for the National Hi-Tech Crime Unit. Using the data, total estimated minimum cost of the impact of hi-tech crime on United Kingdom-based companies with more than 1,000 employees is £2.45 billion. In Germany, cybercrimes accounted for just 1.3% of recorded crimes, but 57%—or € 6.8bn ($8.3bn)—of the financial damages arising from criminal activity (Leyden, 2004).

The various surveys indicate that threats designed to facilitate cybercrime are increasing. The tools of cybercrime are increasingly sophisticated, and businesses and governments are at risk of attack. The international aspects and national economic implications of cyber threats prompted the CoE together with other nonmember states, specifically the United States, to work together and to put an international treaty in place to ensure a coordinated response to cybercrime.

A GLOBAL TREATY

The Convention on Cybercrime is the first international treaty on crimes committed via the Internet and other computer networks, dealing particularly with infringements of copyright, computer-related fraud, child pornography, and violations of network security. Its main objective, set out in the preamble, is to pursue a common criminal policy aimed at the protection of society against cybercrime, especially by adopting appropriate legislation and fostering international cooperation.

The Council of Europe (CoE) has been working since 1989 to address threats posed by hacking and other computer-related crimes. In 1997, the CoE formed a Committee of Experts on Crime in Cyberspace and met behind closed doors for several years drafting an international treaty entitled the Convention on Cybercrime. The convention is the product of several years of work by CoE experts led by Holland's Henrik Kaspersen, and also by the United States, Canada, Japan, and other countries, which are not members of the organization. The treaty was drafted under strong pressure from the United States, which has been active behind the scenes in developing and promoting these efforts. Draft 19 was released in April 2000 for public comment. It attracted a storm of criticism from civil liberties organizations, human rights advocates, and computer industry organizations. Several more drafts were later released, culminating in the final draft released on June 29, 2001. The convention was adopted by the ministers for foreign affairs of the 43 member states of the CoE in Budapest, Hungary, on Nov. 23, 2001. It followed the approval of the 27th and final version in September 2001 by the council's deputy ministers.

The convention has so far been signed by 38 of the 46 member states of the CoE, including the United Kingdom, France, Germany, and Norway. Four nonmember states—Canada, Japan, South Africa, and the United States—also have signed the treaty. However, for the convention to work, it must not only be signed but also ratified. This means that for the convention to have the force of law, its provisions must be implemented in national laws of the participating country, by five of those states, three of which must be members of the CoE (a body that should not be confused with the Council of Ministers of the European Union).

Following the ratification of Lithuania, the CoE's Convention on Cybercrime entered into force on July 1, 2004. Lithuania joins Albania, Croatia, Estonia, and Hungary in ratifying the convention. Only nineteen states have now ratified the convention. This group of first-movers may be surprising: Albania, Bulgaria, Croatia, Cyprus, Denmark, Estonia, Hungary, Lithuania, Romania, Slovenia, and the former Yugoslav Republic of Macedonia.

The convention aims to harmonize laws on crimes, such as hacking and online piracy, fraud, and child pornography. The convention faced much criticism from privacy groups during its long drafting process. CoE representatives dismissed these criticisms, dubbing the convention as the first ever international treaty to address criminal law and procedural aspects of various types of criminal behaviour directed against computer systems, networks or data and other types of similar misuse.

However, the Cybercrime Convention is the result of a process that excluded legal experts and human rights advocates. Civil libertarians charge that it is a one-sided document that fails to reflect the broad commitment to the rule of law and the protection of democratic institutions that has otherwise characterized the treaties proposed by the CoE. As a result, the vast majority of the countries of the CoE have thus far failed to ratify the Cybercrime Convention.

On November 17, 2003, U.S. President Bush transmitted the convention, along with the state department's report on the treaty, to the U.S. Senate with a view to receiving its advice and consent for ratification. The U.S. Senate Committee on Foreign Relations approved the Cybercrime Convention in July of 2005, despite claims from human rights group that the CoE's treaty threatens civil liberties. With the committee's approval, the United States has taken the first steps towards ratification. To become binding on the United States, the treaty requires approval of two-thirds of the senate. The treaty will now go to a vote in the full senate.

THE CYBERCRIME CONVENTION

The convention deals, in particular, with offenses related to infringements of copyright, computer-related fraud, child pornography, and offenses connected with network security. It also covers a series of procedural powers, such as searches of and interception of material on computer networks. The convention is divided into the following sections: (1) definition of terms, (2) substantive law, (3) procedural law, and (4) international cooperation. Parties agree to ensure that their domestic laws criminalize such offenses and establish the procedural tools necessary to investigate such crimes described in Articles 2-11 under their own national laws when there is mens rea (guilty mind) or committed "intentionally" or "wilfully." It must be pointed out that the convention does not give a definition of the crimes, which it seeks to criminalize. Instead, it would criminalize the following activities.

Substantive Law

- Illegal access (Art. 2)—by infringing security measures with the intent of obtaining computer data, such as hacking.
- Illegal interception (Art. 3).
- Data interference (Art. 4)—causes the damaging, deterioration, or suppression of computer data such as malicious codes.
- System interference (Art. 5)—computer sabotage, including Trojan horses, worms, and malicious codes; cracking; denial of service attack; and dissemination of viruses.
- Misuse of device (Art. 6)—cracking device and tools for hacking. It makes it a crime to create, possess, or acquire any computer program designed to crack or disrupt systems illegally. It would not impose criminal liability when the program in question was not created or transferred "for the purpose of committing an offence, such as for testing or the protection of a computer system."
- Computer-related fraud and forgery (Arts. 7 and 8)—These articles are too broad and could make

it illegal to give inauthentic data to protect one's privacy.

- Child pornography (Art. 9).
- Copyright infringement (Art. 10).
- Aiding and abetting (Art. 11).
- Corporate liability (Art. 12)—The treaty imposes criminal liability on businesses if they, through lack of supervision, permit users to commit potentially illegal acts.

Procedural Laws

- Article 14 requires parties to establish legislative and other measures to be applied to the powers established in Articles 16-21 and expands these powers to include other criminal offenses not even defined by the convention, provided it is committed by means of a computer system.
- Articles 16-21 require each participating nation to grant new powers of search and seizure to its law enforcement authorities, including the power to force an Internet service provider (ISP) to preserve a citizen's Internet usage records or other data for up to 90 days (data retention); to submit specified existing computer data and subscriber's information; to search and seize the computer system and data stored therein; to monitor a citizen's online activities in real time; to capture in real time the time and origin of all traffic on a network, including telephone networks; and to search and intercept the actual content of the communications on computer networks.

International Cooperation

Articles 23-35 define the principles relating to international cooperation through extradition, acquisition and preservation of data on behalf of another party. It would permit international access to such information by governmental authorities in different jurisdictions. A "mutual assistance" provision then obligates the country to use those tools to help out other signatory countries in cross-border investigations.

Protocol

An addition to the treaty would make it illegal to distribute or publish anything online that "advocates, promotes or incites hatred (or) discrimination." It covers "distributing, or otherwise making available, racist and xenophobic material to the public through a computer system," defined as "any written material, any image or any other representation of ideas or theories, which advocates, promotes or incites hatred, discrimination or violence, against any individual or group."

Benefits of the Convention

The Convention on Cybercrime is a ground-breaking agreement that will play a key role in fighting computer-related crime. Cybercrime is a major global challenge that requires cooperation and a coordinated international response.

The convention will result in a uniform law among member states. This would require every member state to enact legislation in accordance with the provisions of the treaty. Member states must adopt similar criminal laws against hacking, infringements of copyrights, computer-facilitated fraud, child pornography, and other illicit cyber activities. For example, Romania has already implemented the treaty with law No. 64. Under Romanian law, even just the intent to commit illegal access and interception is already a crime. The first casualty of the new law is a student who was arrested for releasing a modified version of the Blaster Worm via the a university's intranet and faces between three and 15 years for unlawful possession of a program and disturbing it on a computer system.

The International Cybercrime Convention can make things easier for law enforcement. For example, U.S. law enforcement agencies will be able to go into businesses registered in Lithuania to access information that could aid an investigation. Law enforcement officers often hit a barred gate when dealing with such companies. The businesses can insist on due judicial process, which can take six to 10 months to obtain—before they will comply with providing data for investigations. On top of this, there are also the chances of flip-flops. For example, FBI agents who used hacking techniques to find two hackers in Russia were countercharged with cybercrime offenses.

Organized crime is well established in cyberspace, using the Internet for human trafficking and economic crimes. A lot of crime is international. Effective prosecution with national remedies is all but impossible in a global space. The Cybercrime Convention enables prosecution of cybercrime due to cross-border cooperation. The Cybercrime Convention will serve as an important tool in the global fight against those who seek to disrupt computer networks, misuse private or sensitive information, or commit traditional crimes utilizing Internet-enabled technologies.

According to U.S. President George Bush, "The treaty would remove or minimize legal obstacles to international cooperation that delay or endanger U.S. investigations and prosecutions of computer-related crime" (Poulse, 2004).

Although it lacks the so-called "dual criminality" provisions, other language in the pact would prevent abuses. One clause in the treaty allows a country to refuse to cooperate in an investigation if its "essential interests" are threatened by the request. This would allow, for example, the United States to be excluded from investigations protected by the U.S. Constitution. Moreover, political offenses are specifically excluded from some types of mutual assistance requests available under the treaty.

Countries will be able to obtain electronic evidence in cases involving money laundering, conspiracy, racketeering, and other offenses that may not have been criminalized in all other countries.

The treaty would benefit copyright owners, especially the American movie and recording industry, and software companies as participating nations must enact criminal laws targeting Internet piracy and circumvention devices committed willfully, on a commercial scale and by means of a computer system.

Problems with the Convention

Notwithstanding the benefits that the Cybercrime Convention provides in battling cybercrime, the treaty is unfortunately fundamentally imbalanced. It gives law enforcement agencies powers of computer search and seizure and government surveillance, but no correspondingly procedural safeguards to protect privacy and limit government use of such powers. ISPs are worried about becoming surveillance arms for despotic regimes. The industry is not assured that the treaty's awesome powers will never be misused.

Aside from the Preamble, Article 15 is the only part of the Cybercrime Convention that makes reference to human rights and privacy of the individual, and thus illustrating the imbalance in the convention between security and privacy. It does not ensure that minimum standards or safeguards consistent with the European Convention on Human Rights and other international human rights instruments will be implemented.[2] Parties who have obligations under the previous human rights treaty would have to adhere to human rights principles, while those who have not ratified any human rights treaties, such as the non-CoE countries, may determine their own safeguards without having to adhere to the standards imposed by the European Convention on Human Rights or other international treaties. Data protection safeguards are also not included in Article 15.

The treaty lacks a dual criminality clause. Article 25 (5) states that "the requested party *is permitted* to make mutual assistance conditional upon the existence of dual criminality, and that conditions shall be deemed fulfilled, irrespective of whether its laws place the offence within the same category of offence" provided the conduct is criminal offense under its laws. This implies that dual criminality is not a requisite for mutual assistance but is permitted if the other party insists. Some fear that it could put, for example, the UK surveillance capabilities at the disposal of foreign governments with poor human rights records, who may be investigating actions that are not considered crimes elsewhere. There is no requirement that the act that is being investigated be a crime both in a nation that is asking for assistance and the nation that is providing assistance. An acceptable condition would have been that requests for interception could only take place if it is permitted under the relevant criminal law as an offense that merits interception in both countries. Requests also should have a specified level of authorization, that is, where warrants are only acted upon if they are received from a judicial authority in the requested country.

The convention includes a requirement that participating nations outlaw Internet-based copyright infringement as a "criminal offence" even if it is not done for a profit, and prohibiting, in some cases, the "distribution" of computer programs that can be used for illicit purposes. It makes copyright violations into extraditable offenses, without allowing exemptions, such as fair use and parodies.

The treaty was drafted behind closed doors. The drafters ignored the pernicious influence of hundreds, if not thousands, of individual computer users, security experts, civil liberties groups, ISPs, computer companies, and others outside of their select circle of law enforcement representatives who expressed their concerns about the treaty.

According to privacy advocate Banisar (2000):

The main gap is a lack of limits on cybercrimes, surveillance powers, and assistance that are created in the convention. The treaty did not include any procedural safeguards for limiting surveillance power. The sections on searches still force individuals to disclose encryption keys and other data at the direction of law enforcement officials, in violation of protections against self-incrimination guaranteed by US, Canadian and European laws; wiretap powers remain broadly defined and cover all computer devices down to the smallest local area network (and perhaps even smaller); provisions on real-time data collection remain Carnivore-friendly; and local authorities will still be required to assist law enforcement agencies from other countries, even when investigating actions that are not crimes under local law.

When asked publicly why the treaty did not include any procedural safeguards for limiting surveillance powers, the chair of the committee that drafted the convention said that determining privacy standards was too hard and controversial for the committee and had to be left to the national governments of the CoE and signatory countries (Banisar, 2000).

CONCLUSION

Many think the problems prompted by the borderless Web eventually could be resolved by a treaty, but with the conundrum posed by the CoE's cybercrime treaty, it is anyone's guess. The convention is cause for concern as it gives governments too much power without any system of checks and balances and without protecting the civil liberties of Web users. Many have expressed anxiety that jurisdictional disputes could set off a firestorm of recrimination, where prosecution of a foreign company in one country prompts retaliatory laws in another, escalating isolated scuffles into all-out war. Or what would be the consequences when countries with harsher laws, such as those governed by military dictators or countries without a strong human rights commitment, weigh in with judgments of their own and reach across borders to try to enforce them? Other countries have different histories and different cultural sensitivities.

On the other hand, without treaties or consistent case law, the question remains: What constitutes doing business on the Web?

Many hope that the Cybercrime Convention would bring many countries into the international fold, and then, through the pact, enable a coordinated response by law enforcement agencies in the global fight against those who seek to disrupt computer networks. However, is it worth sacrificing basic freedoms and respect for individual rights in favor of a criminal crackdown?

Combating cybercrime should not lead to the crime of violating the fundamental rights of privacy and data protection of cyber users.

REFERENCES

Banisar, D. (2000). International cybercrime remains horrid. *The Register*. Retrieved from http://www.theregister.co.uk/

Council of Europe Report. (2004). *The threat of cybercrime: Situation report 2004*. Strasbourg, France: Council of Europe Pub.

Encyclopedia Britannica. (n.d.). Retrieved from www.britannica.com

Leyden, J. (2004). Sign the cybercrime convention, urge secureocrats. *The Register*. Retrieved from http://www.theregister.com/2004/09/17/euro_cybercrime_conference/

Michalowski, R. (1996). White collar crime, computers, and the legal construction of property. In *Definitional dilemma: Can and should there be a universal definition of white collar crime?* (pp. 173-203). Morgantown, WV: National White Collar Crime Center.

Oxford Dictionary of Law. (2004). *Mobipocket ebook*. Oxford University Press.

Poulse, K. (2004). *US defends cybercrime treaty. Security focus.* The Register Retrieved December 9, 2005, from http://www.theregister.com/2004/04/24/

TERMS AND DEFINITIONS

Carnivore: This is a surveillance tool for data networks. It can tap into networks to intercept anything done on the Internet. It is a computer program designed by the FBI to intercept Internet communications.

Dual Criminality: An accused person can be only if the conduct complained of is considered criminal by the juris prudence or under the laws of both the requesting and requested nations.

Extradition: This refers to the surrender by one state to another of a person charged with a crime.

Procedural Law: This is the law that concerns how to enforce and defend the rights and obligations.

Protocol: This is either an additional agreement or the first copy of a treaty or other such document before its ratification.

Substantive Law: This is the statutory law that governs rights and obligations of those who are subject to it.

Surveillance: This is close observation of a person or group, especially one under suspicion.

Xenophobic: This means to be unduly fearful or contemptuous of that which is foreign, especially of strangers or foreign peoples.

ENDNOTES

[1] A similar version of this survey was also conducted in 2004 with corresponding answers from the 2003 calendar year. Trending data is provided where relevant. The online survey of *CSO* magazine subscribers and members of the U.S. Secret Service's Electronic Crimes Task Force was conducted from March 3 to March 14, 2005. Results are based on 819 completed surveys, up from 500 for the 2004 survey. A sample size of 819 at a 95% confidence level has a margin of error of +/- 3.4%.

[2] It states that "each party shall insure the establishment, implementation and application of the powers and procedures, subject to the conditions and safeguards provided for under its domestic law including rights and obligations it has undertaken under the European Human Rights Convention, the 1996 UN Intl. Covenant on Civil and Political Rights, and other applicable international human rights treaty "and "which shall incorporate the principle of proportionality."

Epilogue

Awareness of security is increasing in an ever more threatening world. Whether these threats reside in the physical world, the electronic world, or both, our constant vigilance is required to ensure our own respective futures. The content provided in this text may serve to further the efforts to secure our organizational, national, and international information infrastructures in addition to our critical proprietary and personal information from the threat of cyber warfare and cyber terrorism.

With this epilogue, we would like to offer an over-arching perspective towards the security of our information infrastructures that may put much of the detail that has been offered into context.

If we consider that most nations no longer use gold and silver backed money, but instead have embraced negotiated currencies, and these currencies are now in digital form, then we must also consider the viability that lesser economically, politically, and militarily equipped nations and their respective actors will focus their competitive efforts on such a critical economic foundation. Why wouldn't they?

Currency is now traded around the world 24 hours a day, 7 days a week through electronic marketplaces alongside commodities, stocks, bonds, futures, and options. The digital universe has come to structure our reality and impacts the world in ways that most people are only beginning to understand. Brokerages, banks, and the like have already experienced breaches resulting in financial thefts and infrastructure losses. The notion that any true competitor would ignore the implications of exploiting and/or destabilizing these systems is just plain delusional. In addition, all of the systems that support and/or utilized these digital markets are now also subject to exploitation and/or destabilization. Add to this all the disassociated systems and organizations that simply rely on a stable currency and commodity market, and the consequences of an insecure infrastructure that is critical to everyday life is enormous. This means there truly are not many organizations and individuals in any industry around the world that can ignore this fundamental threat, nor can the governments and militaries that are sustained by these organizations and individuals. The unprecedented electronic attacks of Estonia in May of 2007 clearly display our meaning.

One of the elements of the "de-communization" of East European countries is the removal of the visible symbols of Soviet domination. Of course such removal may not always be welcomed. When Estonian authorities began removing a bronze statue depicting a World War II-era Soviet soldier in Tallinn (i.e. the capital of Estonia), the internal protests were insignificant compared to the external response and far exceeded their wildest expectations.

What followed was what some have described as the first war in cyberspace, a month-long campaign that has forced Estonian authorities to defend their nation from a data flood that they claim was initiated by orders from Russia. The Russian government has denied any involvement to the attacks that came close to shutting down the country's critical digital infrastructure by clogging the websites of the President, the Prime Minister, Parliament and other government agencies, as well as staggering Estonia's biggest bank and the sites of several daily newspapers.

Most of the attacks were of the DDoS type (Distributed Denial of Service) using a giant network of zombies machines or so-called botnets that included perhaps as many as one million computers. These botnets greatly amplify the impact of this type of assault. As a sign of their considerable resources, there is evidence that the attackers rented time on other botnets.

According to sources, the 10 largest assaults blasted streams of 90 megabits of data per second at Estonia's networks, lasting up to 10 hours each. That is a data load equivalent to downloading the entire Windows XP operating system every six seconds for 10 hours.

Estonia is a NATO and EU member and member states have offered help. Computer security experts converged on Tallinn to offer assistance and to learn what they can about cyber war in the digital age. For NATO, the attack may lead to a discussion of whether it needs to modify its policies related to collective defense of the North Atlantic Treaty Organization member states.

The scope of the problem is simply too scary to casually be addressed by a few, limited individuals with decision powers and no creativity or propensity to actually solve the core problems. Nor can the scope of the problem be contemplated only by those residing in ivory towers with no direct access to decision makers. The resolutions and solutions reside in everyone with merit and excellence in thought. Creative thinkers and implementers, power brokers and resource allocaters, technology evangelists, and congregations all must come together towards the exclusive goal to secure our organizational, national, and international information infrastructures and the information they collect, store, and transmit around the world. This is a goal worthy of a progressive culture.

In the meantime, we must collectively act on the proposals and corrective actions that have been offered in this text and others.

Security is an ongoing endeavor that must continually improve against a dynamic environment of threats. In this book, the authors have discussed many of the issues and consequences of cyber-based attacks, and have proposed solutions for permitting organizations to endure such assaults through protecting their information resources. Information resources are a key objective to an organization surviving an attack, and thus they are also a fundamental target. In order to respond to a threat, people generally must first be made aware of its existence and alerted to it. We believe that one of this text's main contributions is to do just that: alert the world of the seriousness of cyber warfare and cyber terrorism. We also believe that the authors' works have also provided some new thought and innovation towards minimizing the threats imposed by the threat of cyber warfare and cyber terrorism.

AC & LJ

Glossary

Application encryption: Cryptographic functions built into the communications protocols for a specific application, like e-mail. Examples include PEM, PGP, and SHTTP.

Authentication: The ability to ensure that the given information is produced by the entity whose name it carries and that it was not forged or modified.

Availability: It means that data is accessible and services are operational, despite possible disruptive events such as power-supply cuts, natural disasters, accidents, or attacks. This is particularly vital in contexts where communication network failures can cause breakdowns in other critical networks, such as air transport or the power supply.

Buffer overflow: This means techniques by which large inputs are given to software to induce it to do things it normally does not.

Carnivore: This is an FBI system that is used to analyze the e-mail packets of suspected criminals.

Certificate, public key: This is a specially formatted block of data that contains a public key and the name of its owner. The certificate carries the digital signature of a certification authority to authenticate it.

Collateral damage: This is damage from an attack to other than the intended targets.

Communication: This is any information exchanged or conveyed between a finite number of parties by means of a publicly available electronic communications service. This does not include any information conveyed as part of a broadcasting service to the public over an electronic communications network, except to the extent that the information can be related to the identifiable subscriber or user receiving the information.

Computer forensics: This includes methods for analyzing computers and networks to determine what happened to them during a cyber attack, with the hope of repairing the damage and preventing future similar attacks.

Confidentiality: It is the protection of communications or stored data against interception and reading by unauthorized persons. It is particularly needed for the transmission of sensitive data and is one of the requirements for addressing privacy concerns of users of communication networks. Systems and networks must enforce this control at all levels.

Covert channel: This is a concealed communications channel.

Critical infrastructure protection: This means security of those physical and cyber-based systems that are essential to the minimum operations of the economy and government by ensuring protection of information systems for critical infrastructure, including emergency preparedness communications, and the physical assets that support such systems.

Cryptography: The practice and study of encryption and decryption—encoding data so that it can only be decoded by specific individuals. A system for encrypting and decrypting data is a cryptosystem.

Cyber attack: This refers to offensive acts against computer systems or networks.

Cyber war: This is attacks on computer systems and networks by means of software and data.

Cyber weapon: Software designed to attack computers and data.

Denial of service: This refers to an attack that overwhelms a cyberspace resource with requests so as to prevent authorized persons from using the resource.

Department of Homeland Security (DHS): The Homeland Security Act of 2002, which created the Department of Homeland Security (DHS), brought together 22 diverse organizations to help prevent terrorist attacks in the United States, reduce the vulnerability of the United States to terrorist attacks, and minimize damage and assist in recovery from attacks that do occur.

Digital watermarks: Much like a watermark on a letterhead, a digital watermark is used to assist in identifying ownership of a document or other file. It includes embedded unique strings of data that do not alter the sensory perception of the image file, music file, or other data file.

Echelon: This is a putative system of analysis of international communications. The details of the system are difficult to obtain because many government officials often deny or ignore reports regarding the existence of Echelon.

Electronic communications network: This is a transmission systems and, where applicable, switching or routing equipment and other resources that permit the conveyance of signals by wire, by radio, by optical, or by other electromagnetic means, including satellite networks; fixed (circuit- and packet-switched, including Internet) and mobile terrestrial networks; electric cable systems; and, to the extent that they are used for the purpose of transmitting signals, networks used for radio and television broadcasting and cable television networks, irrespective of the type of information conveyed.

Encryption: This is a reversible method of encoding data, requiring a key to decrypt. Encryption can be used in conjunction with steganography to provide another level of secrecy.

Encryption: This is a systematic and reversible way of making a message unintelligible by using secret keys.

Escalation of privileges: This is exploiting security weaknesses to increase one's abilities on a computer system.

Financial services information sharing and analysis centers (FS-ISAC): The FS-ISAC, established in response to PDD-63, is a not-for-profit organization formed to serve the needs of the financial services industry for the dissemination of physical and cyber security, threat, vulnerability, incident, and solution information.

Hacker: This refers to an amateur attacker of computers or sites on the Internet.

Hacktivism: This refers to politically motivated attacks on publicly accessible Web pages/resources or e-mail servers.

Information sharing and analysis centers: Presidential Decision Directive 63 (PDD-63) in 1998 resulted in creation of information sharing and analysis centers to allow critical sectors to share information and work together to help better protect the economy.

Information warfare: This means the use and management of information in pursuit of a competitive advantage over an opponent.

Integrity: It is the confirmation that data that has been sent, received, or stored are complete and unchanged, that is not altered by inappropriate treatment or a malevolent event . This is particularly important in relation to authentication for the conclusion of contracts or where data accuracy is critical (medical data, industrial design, etc.).

Jus in bello: These are international laws for conducting warfare.

Location data: This is any data processed in an electronic communications network, indicating the geographic position of the terminal equipment of a user of a publicly available electronic communications service.

Pacifism: An ethical position opposed to warfare and violence.

Patch: This means a modification of software to fix vulnerabilities that a cyber attack could exploit.

Phishing: This type of e-mail tries to steal secrets by directing users to a counterfeit Web site.

Presidential Decision Directive (PDD) 63: In 1998, the Clinton Administration issued Presidential Decision Directive 63 (PDD-63), to meet the demands of national security interests in cyberspace and to help protect the critical infrastructure of the United States.

Private key: Key used in public key cryptography that belongs to an individual entity and must be kept secret.

Public key system: A public key system is one which uses two keys, a public key known to everyone and a private key that only the recipient of message uses.

Rootkit: This replacement code for the operating system of a computer is placed on a compromised system by an attacker to ensure that their malicious activities will be hidden and to simplify future access to the system by them.

RSA: A popular, highly secure algorithm for encrypting information using public and private keys, obscurely named for the initials of its creators (Massachusetts Institute of Technology (MIT) professors Ron Rivest, Adi Shamir, and Leonard Adleman).

Secure sockets layer (SSL): Cryptography protocol applied to data at the socket interface. It is often bundled with applications and widely used to protect World Wide Web traffic.

Social engineering: This refers to methods to trick or manipulate people into providing sensitive information or performing a task.

SpamMimic: A Web site located at http://www.spam-mimic.com can be used to send a message that appears to be spam when in reality the message is just a cover for sending secret content. The use of spam as a cover will likely increase the workload of FBI systems, such as Carnivore and Echelon.

Steganalysis: This is the process of detecting hidden data in other files. Steganalysis is typically done by searching for small deviations in the expected pattern of a file.

Steganography: In general, it is the process of hiding information or "covered writing." More specifically, in the digital environment, steganography involves hiding data or images within other files, so they appear unaltered to persons unaware of the secret content.

Steganography: This means concealed messages within others.

Traffic data: This is any data processed for the purpose of the conveyance of a communication on an electronic communications network or for the billing thereof.

Virtual fingerprint: This is a unique digital watermark that can be used to uniquely identify a particular file.

Zero-day attack: This is a type of cyber attack that has not been used before.

Compilation of References

404 tonnes. (2004, December 16). *The Economist.* Retrieved December 27, 2004, from http://www.economist. com/displaystory.cfm?story_id=3503931

A multi-level defense against social engineering. (2003). David Gragg. Retrieved January 30, 2006, from http:// www.sans.org/rr/whitepapers/engineering/920.php

A proactive defense to social engineering. (2001). Wendy Arthurs. Retrieved January 30, 2006, from http://www. sans.org/rr/whitepapers/engineering/511.php

Abrams, M. D., & Jajodia, S., & Podell, H. J. (1995, February). *Information security: An integrated collection of essays* (Essay 21, p. 768). Los Alamitos, CA: IEEE Computer Society Press.

ACLU. (2004). *Privacy in America: Electronic monitoring.* Retrieved 14 May, 2005 from http://archive.aclu. org/library/pbr2.html

Act 328 of 1931, Michigan Penal Code. §750.540c (2004).

Adam, N. R., Atluri, V., Bertino, E., & Ferrari, E. (2002). A content-based authorization model for digital libraries. *IEEE Transactions Knowledge and Data Engineering, 14*(2), 296-315.

Adams, C., & Lloyd, S. (2002). *Understanding PKI: Concepts, standards, and deployment Considerations.* Addison-Wesley Professional.

Adams, J. (2001, May/June). Virtual defense. *Foreign Affairs.* Retrieved May 11, 2007 from http://www. foreignaffairs.org/20010501faessay4771/james-adams/ virtual-defense.html

Agrawal, R., Imielinski, T., & Swami, A. (1993). Mining association rules between sets of items in large databases. In P. Buneman & S. Jajodia (Eds.), *Proceedings of the 1993 International Conference on Management of Data, (ACM SIGMOND), 22*(2), 207-216.

AirDefense. (2003). *Wireless LAN security: What hackers know that you don't.* Retrieved from http://ssl.salesforce. com/servlet.Email/AttachmentDownload?q=00m00000 00003Pr00D00000000hiyd00500000005k8d5

Akdeniz, Y., Walker, C., & Wall, D. (2000). *The Internet, law and society.* London: Longman.

Akritidis, P., Anagnostakis, K., & Markatos, E. (2005). Efficient content-based fingerprinting of zero-day worms. *Proceedings of the International Conference on Communications (ICC 2005).*

Alberts, C. J., & Dorofee, A. J. (2001). *OCTAVE method implementation guide version 2.0.* Retrieved February 27, 2006, from Carnegie Mellon Software Engineering Institute Web site: http://www.cert.org/octave/download/intro.html

Alger, J. I. (1996). *Introduction.* In W. Schwartau (Ed.), *Information warfare: Cyberterrorism: Protecting your personal security in the information age* (2nd ed., pp. 814). New York: Thunder's Mouth Press.

Allen, J. H., Mikoski Jr., E. F., Nixon, K. M., & Skillman, D. L. (2002). *Common sense guide for senior managers: Top ten recommended information security practices.* Arlington, VA: Internet Security Alliance.

Alvesson, M., & Willmott, H. (1996). *Making sense of management: A critical introduction.* SAGE Publications.

American Civil Liberties Union. (2003). *Privacy and technology.* Retrieved October 29, 2003, from http://www.aclu.org/Privacy/PrivacyMain.cfm

Andersen, H. B., Garde, H., & Andersen, V. (1998). MMS: An electronic message management system for emergency response. *IEEE Transactions on Engineering Management, 45*(2), 132-140.

Anderson, D., Lunt, T. F., Javitz, H., Tamaru, A., & Valdes, A. (1995). Detecting unusual program behavior using the statistical component of the next generation intrusion detection expert system (NIDES). *Computer Science Laboratory SRI-CSL 95-06.*

Anderson, J. P. (1980). *Computer security threat monitoring and surveillance* (Technical Report). Fort Washington, PA.

Anderson, P. (2001). *Deception: A healthy part of any defense in-depth strategy.* Retrieved February 25, 2006, from SANS Institute Web site: www.sans.org/rr/white-papers/policyissues/506.php

Anderson, R. (2001). *Why information security is hard.* Mimeo.

Anderson, R. J., & Petitcolas, F. A. P. (1998). On the limits of steganography. *IEEE Journal on Selected Areas in Communications, 16*(4), 474-481.

Andrews, C., Litchfield, D., Grindlay, B., & NGS Software. (2003). *SQL server security.* McGraw-Hill/Osborne.

Andrews, S., & Palaniappan, R. (2004). Extracting single trial evoked potential signals using spectral power ratio principal components. *Proceedings of Annual Fall Meeting BMES 2004 (Biomedical Engineering Society),* Philadelphia.

Andrews, S., Kamel, N., & Palaniappan, R. (2005). Overcoming accuracy deficiency of filtrations in source separation of visual evoked potentials by adopting principal component analysis. *Proceedings of International Science Congress (ISC),* Malaysia (p. 344).

Andrews, S., Palaniappan, R., & Asirvadam, V. S. (2004). Single trial source separation of VEP signals using selec-tive principal components. *Proceedings of IEE MEDSIP 2004, International Conference on Advances in Medical Signal Processing,* Malta G.C, EU (pp. 51-57).

Andrews, S., Palaniappan, R., & Kamel, N. (2005). Single trial VEP source separation by selective eigen rate principal components. *Transactions on Engineering, Computing and Technology, Enformatika, 7, 330-333.*

Androutsopoulos, I., Koutsias, J., Chandrinos, K., & Spyropoulos, D. (2000). An experimental comparison of naive Bayesian and keyword-based anti-spam filtering with personal email messages. In *Proceedings of the 23ʳᵈ ACM SIGIR Annual Conference* (pp. 160-167). Athens, Greece.

Ang, P., & Nadarajan, B. (1996, June). Censorship and the internet: A Singapore perspective. *Communications of the ACM, 39*(6), 7278.

Anupam, V., & Mayer, A. (1998). Security of web browser scripting languages: Vulnerabilities, attacks, and remedies. In *Proceedings of the 7ᵗʰ USENIX Security Symposium* (pp. 187-200).

Ariely, G. (2003). Knowledge is the thermonuclear weapon for terrorists in the information age. In *ICT at the Interdisciplinary Center Herzlia.*

Ariely, G. (2006) Operational Knowledge Management in the Military. In Schwartz, D. G. (Ed.) *Encyclopedia of Knowledge Management.* Hershey: Idea Group Inc. pp. 713-720.

Arkin, W. (1999, January 26). Phreaking hacktivists *The Washington Post.* Retrieved from http://www.washingtonpost.com/wp=srv/national/dotmil/arkin.htm

Armistead, L. (Ed.). (2004). *Information operations: Warfare and the hard reality of soft power.* Potomac Books, Brassey's Inc.

Årnes, A., Sallhammar, K., Haslum, K., Brekne, T., Moe, M. E. G., & Knapskog, S. J. (2005). Real-time risk assessment with network sensors and intrusion detection systems. *Proceedings of the International Conference on Computational Intelligence and Security (CIS 2005).*

Arora, A., Krishman, R., Telang, R., & Yang, Y. (2005). *An empirical analysis of vendor response to software vulnerability disclosure.* Mimeo.

Arora, A., Nandkumar, A., Krishman, R., Telang, R. & Yang, Y. (2004, May 13-15). *Impact of vulnerability disclosure and patch availability—An empirical analysis.* Presented at the Third Workshop on Economics and Information Security, Minneapolis, MN.

Arora, A., Telang, R., & Xu, H. (2004). *Optimal policy for software vulnerability disclosure.* Working paper, Carnegie-Mellon.

Arquilla, J. (1999). Ethics and information warfare. In Z. Khalilzad, J. White, & A. Marsall (Eds.), *Strategic appraisal: The changing role of information in warfare* (pp. 379-401). Santa Monica, CA: Rand Corporation.

Arquilla, J., Ronfeldt, D. F., Rand Corporation, & National Defense Research Institute (U.S.). (2001). *Networks and netwars : The future of terror, crime, and militancy.* Santa Monica, CA: Rand.

Arterton, C. (1989). Teledemocracy: Can technology protect democracy? In T. Forester (Ed.), *Computers in the human context* (pp. 438450). Cambridge, MA: MIT Press.

Asokan, N., Janson, P. A., Steiner, M., & Waidner, M. (1997). The state of the art in electronic payment systems. *IEEE Computer, 30*(9), 2835.

Associated Press. (2005, December 18). *Bush says domestic surveillance a 'vital tool'.* Retrieved May 18, 2007 from http://www.msnbc.msn.com/id/10505574/

Atwood, M. (2004). The art of governance. *Outsourcing Center.* Retrieved December 27, 2004, from http://www.outsourcing-requests.com/center/jsp/requests/print/story.jsp?id=4616

August, T., & Tunca, T. (2005). *Network software security and user incentives.* Mimeo.

Australian, The. (2004, August 3). Officials break up Russian extortion ring. *The Australian,* p. C03.

Avresky, D. R., Arlat, J., Laprie, J.-C., & Crouzet, Y. (1996). Fault injection for formal testing of fault tolerance. *IEEE Transactions on Reliability, 45*(3), 443-455.

Axelsson, S. (2000). *Intrusion detection systems: A survey and taxonomy* (Tech. Rep. No. 99-15). Chalmers University, Sweden.

Bagchi, K., & Udo, G. (2003). An analysis of the growth of computer and internet security breaches. *Communications of the Association for Information Systems, 12*(46), 129.

Bailey, K., Curran, K., & Condell, J. (2004). An evaluation of pixel based steganography and stegodetection methods. *The Imaging Science Journal, 52*(3), 131-150.

Baily, M. N., & Farrell, D. (2004, July). Exploding the myths of offshoring. *The McKinsey Quarterly.*

Baird, L., & Henderson, J. C. (2001). *The knowledge engine: How to create fast cycles of knowledge-to-performance and performance-to-knowledge.* San Francisco: BK.

Bala, J. W., Baik, S., Hadjarian, A., Gogia, B. K., & Manthorne, C. (2002). Application of a distributed data mining approach to network intrusion detection. *AAMAS 2002,* 1419-1420.

Balasubramaniyan, J. S., Garcia-Fernandez, J. O., Isacoff, D., Spafford, E., & Zamboni, D. (1998). An architecture for intrusion detection using autonomous agents. *Proceedings of the 14ᵗʰ Annual Computer Security Applications Conference,* IEEE Computer Society, p. 13.

Bamford, J. (1982). *The puzzle palace: Inside the National Security Agency, America's most secret intelligence organization.* Boston: Houghton Mifflin.

Bamford, J. (2001). *Body of secrets: Anatomy of the ultra-secret National Security Agency.* New York: Doubleday.

Banisar, D. (2000). International cybercrime remains horrid. *The Register.* Retrieved from http://www.theregister.co.uk/

Barabasi, A.-L. (2000, July 26). *Strength is weakness on the internet*. Retrieved from http://physicsweb.org/articles/news/4/7/10/1

Barbara, D. (2002). *Applications of data mining in computer security* (S. Jajodia, Ed.). Norwell, MA: Kluwer Academic Publishers.

Barbara, D., Wu, N., & Jajodia, S. (2001, April). Detecting novel network intrusions using bayes estimators. *Proceedings of the First SIAM Conference on Data Mining*, Chicago.

Barga, R. S., Lomet, D. B., Baby, T., & Agrawal, S. (2000). Persistent client-server database sessions. In *Proceedings of the 7th International Conference on Extending Database Technology: Advances in Database Technology* (pp. 462-477). Konstanz, Germany.

Barga, R., Lomet, D., Shegalov, G., & Weikum, G. (2004). Recovery guarantees for Internet applications. *ACM Transactions on Internet Technology (TOIT), 4*(3), 289-328.

Barnes, V. (2004). *An hour with Kevin Mitnick, Part 2*. Retrieved March 1, 2006, http://www.enterpriseitplanet.com/security/features/article.php/3337141

Barquin, R., LaPorte, T., & Weitzner, D. (1995, April 28). Democracy in cyberspace. *Presented at the 4th National Computer Ethics Institute Conference*, Washington, DC.

Barr, D. (1996). RFC 1912: Common DNS operational and configuration errors.

Barron, A., Rissanen, J., & Yu, B. (1998). The minimum description length principle in coding and modelling. *IEEE Transactions on Information Theory, 44*, 2743-2760.

Barton, L., & Hardigree, D. (1995). Risk and crisis management in facilities: Emerging paradigms in assessing critical incidents. *Facilities Journal, 13*(9), 10-11.

Basel Committee on Banking Supervision (BCBS). (2003). *Initiatives by the BCBS, IAIS and IOSCO to combat money laundering and the financing of terrorism.*. Retrieved February 15, 2006, from http://www.bis.org/publ/joint05.pdf

Baskerville, R. (1993). Information systems security design methods: Implications for information systems development. *ACM Computing Surveys, 25*(4), 375-414.

Bass, T., & Robichaux, R. (2002). *Defense in depth revisited: Qualitative risk analysis methodology for complex network-centric operations*. Retrieved February 26, 2006, from http://www.silkroad.com/papers/pdf/archives/defense-in-depth-revisited-original.pdf

Bayles, W. (2001). Network attack. *Parameters, US Army War College Quarterly, 31*, 44-58.

BBC. (2002, February 5). Move towards compulsory ID cards. *BBC News Online*. Retrieved May 25, 2004, from http://news.bbc.co.uk/1/hi/uk_politics/1802847.stm

BBC. (2004, February 27). UN bugging scandal widens. *BBC News*. http://news.bbc.co.uk/2/hi/asia-pacific/3492146.stm

Bejtlich, R. (2004). *The tao of network security monitoring: Beyond intrusion detection*. Addison Wesley Professional.

Bell, D. E., & LaPadula, L. J. (1973). *Secure computer systems: Mathematical foundations and model*. The Mitre Corporation.

Bell, J., & Whaley, B. (1991). *Cheating and deception*. New Brunswick, NJ: Transaction Publishers.

Bellardo, S., Karwan, K. R., & Wallace, W. A. (1984). Managing the response to disasters using microcomputers. *Interfaces, 14*(2), 29-39.

Bellare, M., Garay, J. A., Hauser, R., Herzberg, A., Krawczyk, H., Steiner, M., et al. (1995). iKP—A family of secure electronic payment protocols. *Usenix Electronic Commerce Workshop*.

Belokosztolszki, A., & Eyers, D. (2003). Shielding the OASIS RBAC infrastructure from cyber-terrorism. In *Research Directions in Data and Applications Security: Proceedings of the Sixteenth Annual IFIP WG 11.3 Conference on Data and Application Security*, (pp. 3-14).

Bendor-Samuel, P. (2004). Lou Dobbs: Here's why you're wrong! *Outsourcing Center*. Retrieved December 20, 2004, from http://www.outsourcing-requests.com/center/jsp/requests/print/story.jsp?id=4565

Ben-Dov, M., Wu, W., Feldman, R., & Cairns, P. A. (2004). Improving knowledge discovery by combining text-mining and link analysis techniques. *Workshop on Link Analysis, Counter-Terrorism, and Privacy, in Conjunction with SIAM International Conference on Data Mining.*

Benjamin, D., McNamara, T. E., & Simon, S. (2004). *The neglected instrument: Multilateral counterterrorism. Prosecuting terrorism: The global challenge.* Presented at the Center for Strategic and International Studies (CSIS), Florence, Italy.

Berger, A. L., Della Pietra, S. A., & Della Pietra, V. J. (1996). A maximum entropy approach to natural language processing. *1996 Association for Computational Linguistics, 22*(1), 1-36.

Bergman, L., Lichtblau, E., Shane, S., & van Natta, D., Jr. (2006, January 17). Spy agency data after Sept. 11 ledFBI to dead ends. *The New York Times.* http://www.commondreams.org/headlines06/0117-01.htm

Berinato, S. (2002, March). The truth about cyberterrorism. *CIO Magazine.*

Bertino, E., Castano, S., & Ferrari, E. (2001). Securing XML documents with author-X. *IEEE Internet Computing, 5*(3), 21.

Bertino, E., Catania, B., Damiani, M. L., & Perlasca, P. (2005). GEO-RBAC: A spatially aware RBAC. *10th Symposium on Access Control Models and Technologies,* 29-37.

Bertino, E., Ferrari, E., & Perego, A. (2002). MaX: An access control system for digital libraries and the web. *COMPSAC 2002,* 945-950.

Bertino, E., Hammad, M., Aref, W. G., & Elmagarmid, A. K.(2000). Access control model for video database systems. *Proceedings of the 9th International Conference on Information Knowledge Management, CIKM* (pp. 336-343).

Biba, K. J. (1977). *Integrity considerations for secure computer systems.* The Mitre Corporation.

Bishop, M. (1989, December). A model of security monitoring. *Proceedings of the Fifth Annual Computer Security Applications Conference,* Tucson, AZ.

Bishop, M. (2005). *Introduction to computer security.*

Bissett, A. (2004). High technology war and "surgical strikes." *Computers and Society (ACM SIGCAS), 32*(7), 4.

Bloys, D. (2006, January 22). Online records linked to identity theft and worse. *News for Public Officials.* Retrieved August 25, 2006, from http://www.davickservices.com/Online_Records_Linked_To_Crime.htm

Bocij, P. (2004). *Corporate cyberstalking: An invitation to build theory.* http://www.firstmonday.dk/issues/issues7_11/bocij/

Bocij, P., & McFarlane, L. (2002, February). Online harassment: Towards a definition of cyberstalking. [HM Prison Service, London]. *Prison Service Journal,* 139.

Boeing Company. (2006). *JDAM information.* www.boeing.com/defence-space/missiles/jadam/news/index.html

Bok, S. (1978). *Lying: Moral choice in public and private life.* New York: Pantheon.

Bok, S. (1986). *Secrets.* Oxford, UK: Oxford University Press.

Boley, D. L. (1998). Principal direction divisive partitioning. *Data Mining and Knowledge Discovery, 2*(4), 325-344.

Bombs. (2005). Retrieved from http://www.bluemud.org/article/11606

Bongard, K. (2001). *Wirtschaftsfaktor Geldwäsche.* Wiesbaden, Germany: Deutscher Universitäts-Verlag.

Borland, J., & Bowman, L. (2002, August 27). E-terrorism: Liberty vs. security. *ZDNet.com.* Retrieved 22 May, 2005 from http://zdnet.com.com/2100-1105-955493.html

Bosworth, S., & Kabay, M. E. (2002). *Computer security handbook* (4th ed.). John Wiley & Sons.

Boyd, C., & Mathuria, A. (2003). *Protocols for key establishment and authentication.* Germany: Springer-Verlag, Berlin and Heidelberg GmbH & Co.

Boyd, S., & Keromytis, A. (2004, June 8-11). SQLrand: Preventing SQL injection attacks. In *Proceedings of the Second Applied Cryptography and Network Security (ACNS) Conference,* Yellow Mountain, China (LNCS 2121, pp. 292-302). Heidelberg, Germany: Springer-Verlag.

Brands, S. A. (2000). *Rethinking public key infrastructures and digital certificates: Building in privacy.* MIT Press.

Braverman, M. (2003). Managing the human impact of crisis. *Risk Management, 50*(5), 10-19.

Breidenbach, B. (2002). *Guarding your website against SQL injection attacks* (e-book). Apress.

Brekne, T., & Årnes, A. (2005). Circumventing IP-address pseudonymization in O(n2) time. *Proceedings of IASTED Communication and Computer Networks (CCN 2005).*

Brekne, T., Årnes, A., & Øslebø, A. (2005). Anonymization of IP traffic monitoring data: Attacks on two prefix-preserving anonymization schemes and some proposed remedies. *Proceedings of the Privacy Enhancing Technologies Workshop (PET 2005).*

Brewer, D., & Nash, M. (1989). The Chinese wall security policy. *Proceedings of the IEEE Computer Society Symposium on Research in Security and Privacy* (pp. 215-228).

Briere, D. (2005). *Wireless network hacks and mods for dummies* (for Dummies S.). Hungry Minds, Inc.

Bright, M., Vulliamy, E., & Beaumont, P. (2003, March 2). Revealed: US dirty tricks to win vote on Iraq war: Secret document details American plan to bug phones and emails of key security council members. *The Observer.* http://observer.guardian.co.uk/iraq/story/0,12239,905936,00.html

Broersma, M. (2001). Gates' credit hacker sentenced. *ZDNet.UK.* Retrieved December 9, 2005, from http://www.zdnetasia.com/

Brooks, C. C. (2000). Knowledge management and the intelligence community. *Defense Intelligence Journal 9*(1), 15-24.

Brownstein, A. (2000). In the campus shadows, women are stalkers as well as the stalked. *The Chronicle of Higher Education, 47*(15), 40-42.

Brustoloni, J. C. (2002). Protecting electronic commerce from distributed denial-of-service attacks. *Proc. 11th International WWW Conference, Honolulu.* Retrieved from http://wwwconf.ecs.soton.ac.uk/archive/00000333/01

BSI Bundesamt für Sicherheit in der Informationstechnik BSI. Erkennung und Behandlung von Angriffen aus dem Internet. Retrieved from http://www.bsi.bund.de/fachthem/sinet/webserv/angriff.htm

Buchholz, S., Hamann, Th. & Hübsch, G. (2004). Comprehensive Structured Context Profiles (CSCP): Design and Experiences. In *Proceedings of PerCom Workshops* (pp. 43-47).

Burgess, G., Clark, T. D., Hauser, R. D. Jr., & Zmud, R. W. (1992). The application of causal maps to develop a collective understanding of complex organizational contexts in requirements analysis. *Accounting, Management and Information Technology, 2*(3), 143-164.

Burgess, J., Pattison, E., & Goksel, M., (2000) *Public key cryptography.* Stanford University. Retrieved from http://cse.stanford.edu/classes/sophmore-college/projects-97/cryptography/history.html

Burnett, I., Van de Walle, R., Hill, K., Bormans, J., & Pereira, F. (2003). MPEG-21: Goals and achievements. *IEEE MultiMedia, 10*(4), 6070.

Burroughs, P. A. (1986). *Principles of geographic information systems for land resources assessment.* Oxford: Claredon Press.

Burtner, W. (1991). Hidden pressures. *Notre Dame Magazine,* 29-32.

Byrnes, N. (2005, January 1). Green eyeshades never looked so sexy. *BusinessWeek Online.* Retrieved January 5, 2005, from http://www.businessweek.com/@@ na*EhYQQxu80VAkA/magazine/content/05_02/ b3915041_mz011.htm

Callamari, P., & Reveron, D. (2003). China's use of perception management. *International Journal of Intelligence & Counter Intelligence, 16*(1), 115.

Camp, L. J., & Wolfram, C. (2004). Pricing security. In L.J. Camp & S. Lewis (Eds.). *Economics of information security* (Vol. 12). *Advances in information security*. Springer-Kluwer.

Campbell, D. (1988, August 12). They've got it taped: Somebody's listening. *New Statesman*. http://www.gn.apc.org/duncan/echelon-dc.htm

Campbell, D. (1999, October). *Interception capabilities 2000*. European Parliament Scientific and Technological Options office (STOA) report, PE 168.184/Vol 2/5. http://www.europarl.eu.int/stoa/publi/pdf/98-14-01-2_en.pdf

Campbell, D. (2000, July 25). Inside Echelon. *Telopolis, Hannover*. http://www.telepolis.de/english/inhalt/te/6929/1.html

Campbell, D. (2000, February 25). Making history: The original source for the 1988 first Echelon report steps forward. http://cryptome.org/echelon-mndc.htm

Campbell, D. (2001, May 27). *Interception capabilities: Impact and exploitation: Paper 1: Echelon and its role in COMINT*. http://www.heise.de/tp/r4/artikel/7/7747/1.html

Campbell, D. (2001, May 27). *Interception capabilities: Impact and exploitation: Paper 2: COMINT impact on international trade*. http://www.heise.de/tp/r4/artikel/7/7752/1.html

Campbell, D. (2001, May 27). *Interception capabilities: Impact and exploitation: Paper 3: COMINT, privacy and human rights*. http://www.heise.de/tp/r4/artikel/7/7748/1.html

Carrier, B. (2005). *File system forensic analysis*. Addison-Wesley Professional.

Caruso, J.T. (2002). Congressional Testimony. Testimony before the House Subcommittee on National Security, Veterans Affairs, and International Relations, March 21, 2002. Last accessed electronically January 30, 2006, from http://www.fbi.gov/congress/congress02/caruso032102.htm

Carver, C. A., Jr., Hill, J. M., Surdu, J. R., & Pooch, U. W. (2000, June 6-7). A methodology for using intelligent agents to provide automated intrusion response. *Proceedings of the IEEE Systems, Man, and Cybernetics Information Assurance and Security Workshop*, West Point, NY.

Cashell, B., Jackson, W. D., Jickling, M., & Webel, B. (2004). *The economic impact of cyber-attacks*. CRS Report for Congress, Congressional Research Service, The Library of Congress. April 1, 2004.

CC/PP. (n.d.). *Composite capability/preference profiles*. http://www.w3.org/Mobile/CCPP

Cebrowski, A., & Gartska, J. J. (1998). Network centric warfare: It's origins and its future." *Proceedings*. U.S. Naval Institute. Retrieved January 6, 2006, from http://www.usni.org/Proceedings/Articles98/PROcebrowski.htm

Center for International Security and Co-operation. *Proposal for an international convention on cyber crime and terrorism*. Retrieved February 3, 2006, from http://www.iwar.org.uk/cyberterror/#cyber

Cerf, V. G. (2005). Spam, spim, and spit. *Communications of the ACM, 48*(4), 39-43.

Cerrudo, C. (2004). *Manipulating Microsoft SQL server using SQL injection* (Tech. Rep.). Application Security, Inc.

CERT. (2002). *CERT vulnerability note VU#282403*. Retrieved from http://www.kb.cert.org/vuls/id/282403

CERT/CC. (2005). *CERT/CC Statistics, 1988-2005*. Retrieved February 15, 2006, from www.cert.org/stats/cert_stats.html

Cesarano, C., d'Acierno, A., & Picariello, A. (2003, November 7-8). An intelligent search agent system for semantic information retrieval on the internet. *Proceedings of the Fifth ACM International Workshop on Web Information and Data Management,* New Orleans, LA (pp. 111-117).

Chakrabarti, A., & Manimaran, G. (2002, November/December). *Internet infrastructure security: A taxonomy.* Iowa State University, IEEE Network.

Chalhoub, G., Saad, S., Chbeir, R., & Yétongnon, K. (2004). Towards fully functional distributed multimedia DBMS. *Journal of Digital Information Management (JDIM), 2*(3), 116-121.

Chand, V., & Orgun, C. O. (2006). Exploiting linguistic features in lexical steganography: Design and proof-of-concept implementation. *Proceedings of the 39th Annual Hawaii International Conference on System Sciences (HICSS).*

Chang, G., Healey, M. J., McHugh, J. A. M., & Wang, J. T. L. (2001). *Mining the World Wide Web: An information search approach.* Norwell, MA: Kluwer Academic Publishers.

Charny, B. (2001). *Disposable cell phones spur debates.* Retrieved October 29, 2003, from http://news.com.com/2102-1033_3-273084.html?tag=st_util_print

Chaum, D. (1981). Untraceable electronic mail, return addresses, and digital pseudonyms. *Communications of the ACM, 24*(2), 84-88.

Chaum, D. (1988). The dining cryptographers problem: Unconditional sender and recipient untraceability. *Journal of Cryptology, 1*(1), 65-75.

Chen, M. Y., Kiciman, E., Fratkin, E., Fox, A., & Brewer, E. (2002). Pinpoint: Problem determination in large, dynamic Internet services. In *Proceedings of International Conference on Dependable Systems and Networks (DSN)* (pp. 595-604). Washington, DC.

Cheng, G., & Greiner, R. (1999). Comparing Bayesian network classifiers. *Proceedings of the Fifteenth Conference on Uncertainty in Artificial Intelligence.* San Francisco: Morgan Kaufmann Publishers.

Cheng, T. (2004). Recent international attempts to can spam. *Computer Law & Security Report, 20*(6), 472-479.

Cheswick, B. (1990). An evening with Berferd in which a cracker is lured, endured, and studied. *Proceedings of USENIX* (pp. 163174).

Chief of Naval Operations Message. (2005). *Subject: Cryptologic officer name change to Information Warfare* (DTG R 151308Z SEP 05).

Chisholm, P. (2005, December 19). *Protect our electronics against EMP attack.* Retrieved from www.csmonitor.com/2005/1219/p25s02-stct.html

Chochliouros, I. P., & Spiliopoulou, A. S. (2003). Perspectives for achieving competition and development in the European information and communications technologies (ICT) markets. *The Journal of the Communications Network, 2*(3), 42-50.

Chochliouros, I. P., & Spiliopoulou, A. S. (2005). Broadband access in the European Union: An enabler for technical progress, business renewal and social development. *The International Journal of Infonomics, 1,* 5-21.

Chochliouros, I. P., & Spiliopoulou-Chochliourou, A. S. (2003). Innovative horizons for Europe: The new European telecom framework for the development of modern electronic networks and services. *The Journal of The Communications Network, 2*(4), 53-62.

Choi, J., Fershtman, C., & Gandal, N. (2007). *Network Security: Vulnerabilities and Disclosure Policy* (CEPR Working Paper #6134).

Chokhani, S., & Ford, W. (1999). *Internet X.509 public key infrastructure: Certificate policy and certification practices framework, RFC 2527.* Sterling, VA: Internet Engineering Task Force (IETF).

Choucri, N., Madnick, S. E., Moulton, A., Siegel, M. D., & Zhu, H. (2004). Activities: Requirements for context mediation, MIT Sloan School of Management. In *IEEE Aerospace Conference Proceedings Information Integration for Counter Terrorism.*

Chua, C. E. H., & Wareham, J. (2004). Fighting internet auction fraud: An assessment and proposal. *IEEE Computer, 37*(10), 31-37.

Church, J., & Gandal, N. (2006). Platform competition in telecommunications. In M. Cave, S. Majumdar, & I. Vogelsang (Eds.), *The handbook of telecommunications* (Vol. 2, pp. 117-153). Elsevier.

CipherTrust. (2004, November 18). *Maximizing Email Security ROI*. Retrieved from http://www.ciphertrust.com/resourses/articles/articles/roi_2_virus.php

Claise, B. (2005). IPFIX protocol specification. *IETF Internet Draft.*

Clark, D. D., & Wilson, D. R. (1987). A comparison of commercial and military computer security policies. *IEEE Symposium of Security and Privacy,* 184-194.

Clark, E. (2001). A reason to love spam. *Network Magazine, 16,* 20.

Clarke, I., Flaherty, T., & Zugelder, M. (2005). The CAN-SPAM act: New rules for sending commercial e-mail messages and implications for the sales force. *Industrial Marketing Management, 34*(4), 399-405.

Claypoole Jr., R. L., Gunsch, G. H., & Jackson, J. T. (2003). Blind steganography detection using a computational immune system: A work in progress. *International Journal of Digital Evidence, 4*(1), 1-19.

Clear, T. (2002). Design and ysability in security systems: Daily life as a context of use? *Inroads SIGCSE Bulletin, 34*(4).

Clemens, P. L. (2002). *Energy flow/barrier analysis* (3rd ed.). Retrieved February 26, 2006, from http://www.sverdrup.com/safety/energy.pdf

CMC (2005) *Watch Your Identity: Tips for reducing the risk of identity theft*. Retrieved May 17, 2007 from http://www.cmcweb.ca/epic/site/cmc-cmc.nsf/en/fe00040e.html

Cobb, C. (2004). *Cryptography for dummies.* Dummies Series.

Cohen, A. (2001, November 12). When terror hides oOnline. *Time, 158,* 65-69.

Cohen, F., & Koike, D. (2004). Misleading attackers with deception. In *Proceedings of the.5th Information Assurance Workshop*, West Point, NY (pp. 30-37).

Cohen, W. (2001, March 6). *Former Defense Secretary Cohen's remarks at the 2001 summit*. George Mason University. Retrieved August 10, 2005, from http://www.gmu.edu/departments/law/////techcenter/programs/summit/cohen's_2001_remarks.html

Cole, E. (2003). *Hacking: What the future holds. Computer and hacker exploits.* SANS Publishers.

Cole, E. (2003). *Hiding in plain sight: Steganography and the art of covert communication*. Indianapolis, IN: Wiley Publishing, Inc.

Colwell, R. N. (1997). History and place of photogrammetric interpretation. In W. R. Philipson (Ed.), *Manual of photographic interpretation* (2nd ed., pp. 3348). Bethesda: American Society for Photogrammery and Remote Sensing.

Colwell, R. N. (Ed.). (1983). *Manual of remote sensing* (2nd ed.). Falls Church, VA: American Society of Photogrammetry.

Commission of the European Communities. (2003). *Proposal for a directive of the European Parliament and of the council on measures and procedures to ensure the enforcement of intellectual property rights* (Brussels, 30.1.2003). Retrieved February 15, 2006, from http://europa.eu.int/eur-lex/en/com/pdf/2003/com2003_0046en01.pdf

Completewhois Project, The. (2004). Questions and answers on IP hijacking. Retrieved on July 31, from www.completewhois.com/hijacked/hijacked_qa.htm

Computer Economics. (2005). Retrieved from http://http://www.computereconomics.com/article.cfm?id=1090

Computer Security Institute. (2005). 2005 CSI/FBI computer crime and security survey. *Computer Security Issues and Trends*. Retrieved February 26, 2006, from http://www.gocsi.com

Computers and Crime. (2000). IT law lecture notes (Rev. ed.). http://www.law.auckland.ac.nz/itlaw/itlawhome.htm

Conner, B., Noonan, T. & Holleyman, R.W., II. (2003). *Information security governance: Toward a framework for action.* Business Software Alliance.

Coombs, W. T. (2000). Designing post crisis messages: Lesson for crisis response strategies. *Review of Business, 21*(3/4), 37-41.

Coppens, J., Markatos, E., Novotny, J., Polychronakis, M., Smotlacha, V., & Ubik, S. (2004). Scampi: A scaleable monitoring platform for the internet. *Proceedings of the 2nd International Workshop on Inter-domain Performance and Simulation (IPS 2004).*

Coppersmith, D. (1994). The data encryption standard (DES) and its strength against attacks. *IBM Journal of Research and Development, 38*(3), 243-250.

Corera, G. (2004, October 6). Web wise terror network. *BBC NEWS.* Retrieved October 9, 2004, from http://news.bbc.co.uk/go/pr/fr/-/1/hi/world/3716908.stm

Council framework decision 2005/222/JHA of 24 February 2005 on attacks against information systems [*Official Journal L 069, 16/03/2005, pp. 67-71].*

Council of Europe Report. (2004). *The threat of cybercrime: Situation report 2004.* Strasbourg, France: Council of Europe Pub.

Council of Europe. (1950). Article 8. *The European Convention on Human Rights.* Retrieved on May 17, 2007 from http://www.hri.org/docs/ECHR50.html#C.Art8

Council of Europe. (2003). *Convention for Protection of Human Rights and Fundamental Freedoms, as amended by protocol No. 11 with Protocol Nos. 1, 4, 6, 7, 12 and 13.* Registry of the European Court of Human Rights.

Council of the European Union. (1995). *Council Resolution of 17 January 1995 on the lawful interception of telecommunications (Official Journal C329, 04.11.1996, pp. 1-6).* Brussels, Belgium: The Council of the European Union.

Council of the European Union. (2000). *Council Act of 29 May 2000 establishing in accordance with Article 34 of the Treaty on European Union the Convention on Mutual Assistance in Criminal Matters between the Member States of the European Union (Official Journal C197, 12.07.2000, pp. 1-2).* Brussels, Belgium: Council of the European Union.

Cournane, A., & Hunt, R. (2004). An analysis of the tools used for the generation and prevention of spam. *IEEE Computers & Security, 23*(2), 154-166.

Courtney, R. (1997). Security risk assessment in electronic data processing. *AFIPS Proceedings of the National Computer Conference, 46* (pp. 97-104).

Cousins, D. B., & Weishar, D. J. (2004, March). Intelligence collection for counter terrorism in massive information content. In *2004 IEEE Aerospace Conference Proceedings* (pp. 3273-3282) Vol.5

Cranor, I., & LaMacchia, B. (1998). Spam! *Communications of the ACM, 41*(11), 74-84.

Cronin, B., & Crawford, H. (1999). Information warfare: Its applications in military and civilian contexts. *Information Society, 15*(4), 257264.

Crowe, D. (1990). *Root cause training course for Catawba nuclear station.* General Physics Corporation.

Cruikshank, C. G. (1979). *Deception in World War Two.* New York: Oxford.

Cunningham, W. (2005). *Wiki history.* Retrieved October 29, 2005, from http://c2.com/cgi/wiki?WikiHistory

Cyber Crime in India. (2004). *Cyber stalking—online harassment.* http://www.indianchild.com/cyberstalking.htm

Cyber Security: A Crisis of Prioritization. (2005, February). President's Information Technology Advisory Committee.

Cyber terrorism and critical infrastructure protection. (2002) (testimony of Ronald L. Dick). Retrieved from www.fbi.gov/congress/congress02/nipc072402.htm

CyberAngels. (1999). http://cyberangels.org

'*Cyberterrorism' testimony before the House Special Oversight Panel on Terrorism Committee on Armed Services.* (2000). (testimony of D. E. Denning). Retrieved February 3, 2006, from http://www.cs.georgetown.edu/~denning/infosec/cyberterror.html

D'Arcy, J. (2005). *Improving IS security through procedural and technical countermeasures: An analysis of organizational security measures* (Research report). Temple University, Irwin L. Gross e-business Institute.

Dagon, D., Qin, X., Gu, G., Lee, W., Grizzard, J. B., Levine, J. G., et al. (2004). Honeystat: Local worm detection using honeypots. *Proceedings of the Seventh International Symposium on Recent Advances in Intrusion Detection (RAID 2004).*

Daigle, L. (2004). WHOIS protocol specification, RFC 3912. IETF.

Dain, O., & Cunningham, R. (2001). Fusing a heterogeneous alert stream into scenarios. *Proceedings of the 2001 ACM Workshop on Data Mining for Security Applications, 113.*

Damiani, E., De Capitani di Vimercati, S., Fernández-Medina, E., & Samarati, P. (2002). Access control of SVG documents. *DBSec 2002,* 219-230.

Damiani, E., De Capitani di Vimercati, S., Fugazza, C., & Samarati, P. (2004). Extending policy languages to the Semantic Web. *ICWE 2004,* 330-343.

Damiani, E., De Capitani di Vimercati, S., Paraboschi, S., & Samarati, P. (2000). Securing XML documents. *EDBT 2000,* 121-135.

Damiani, E., De Capitani di Vimercati, S., Paraboschi, S., & Samarati, P. (2002). A fine-grained access control system for XML documents. *ACM Transactions on Information and System Security (TISSEC), 5*(2), 169-202.

Danchev, D. (2005, December 19). Cyberterrorism—don't stereotype and it's there! *Mind streams of information security knowledge blog.* Retrieved from http://ddanchev.blogspot.com/2005/12/cyberterrorism-dont-stereotype-and-its.html

Danchev, D. (2005, December 19). Cyberterrorism—don't stereotype and it's there! *Mind Streams of Information Security Knowledge blog.* Retrieved 12 May, 2005 from http://ddanchev.blogspot.com/2005/12/cyberterrorism-dont-stereotype-and-its.html

Danchev, D. (2006, January 9). Malware: Future trends. *Mind streams of information security knowledge blog.* Retrieved May 17, 2007 from http://ddanchev.blogspot.com/2006_02_01_archive.html

Darling, D. (n.d.). *SIGINT satellites.* In *The encyclopedia of astrobiology astronomy and spaceflight, the worlds of David Darling.* http://www.daviddarling.info/encyclopedia/S/SIGINT.html

Datz, T. (2002, December 1). Integrating America. *CIO Magazine.*

David, J. (2002). Policy enforcement in the workplace. *Computers and Security, 21*(6), 506513.

Davies, S. (2002). A year after 9/11: Where are we now? *Communications of the ACM, 45***(9), 35-39.**

Davis, K. E., Coker, L., & Sanderson, M. (2002, August). Physical and mental health effects of being stalked for men and women. *Violence Vict 2002, 17*(4), 429-43.

De Capitani di Vimercati, S., & Samarati, P. (2005). *New directions in access control, in cyberspace security and defense: Research issues.* Kluwer Academic Publisher.

Dean, K. (2000). The epidemic of cyberstalking. *Wired News* http://www.wired.com/news/politics/0,1283,35728,00.html

Dearth, D. H. (1998). Imperatives of information operations and information warfare. In A. D. Campen & D. H. Dearth (Eds.), *Cyberwar 2.0: Myths, mysteries, and reality.* Fairfax, VA: AFCEA International Press.

Debar, H., Becker, M., & Siboni, D. (1992). A neural network component for an intrusion detection system. *Proceedings, IEEE Symposium on Research in Computer Security and Privacy.*

Debar, H., Curry, D., & Feinstein, B. (2005). Intrusion detection message exchange format (IDMEF). *IETF Internet-Draft.*

Deloitte Global Security Survey. (2004). *Global financial services industry.*

Deloitte Global Security Survey. (2005). *Global financial services industry.*

DelZoppo, R., Browns, E., Downey, M., Liddy, E. D., Symonenko, S., Park, J. S., et al. (2004). A multi-disciplinary approach for countering insider threats. *Workshop on Secure Knowledge Management (SKM)*, Amherst, NY.

DeMarrais, K. (2003, September 4). Identity theft on the rise, FTC warns. *Knight Ridder Business News*, pp. 14.

Dénes, T. (2002). *Cardan and cryptography—The mathematics of encryption grids.* Hungary. Retrieved from http://www.komal.hu/lap/2002-ang/cardano.e.shtml

Denning, D. (1999). *Information warfare and security.* Boston: Addison-Wesley.

Denning, D. (2000, May 23). Cyberterrorism. *Testimony before the Special Oversight Panel on Terrorism, Committee on Armed Services U.S. House of Representatives*, Georgetown University.

Denning, D. E. (1987, February). An intrusion-detection model. *IEEE Transactions on Software Engineering, 3*(2), 222-232.

Denning, P. J. (1992). Electronic junk. *Communications of the ACM, 25*(3), 163-165.

Department of Defense (DoD) National Computer Security Center. (1985). *Department of Defense trusted computer systems evaluation criteria* (DoD 5200.28-STD).

Department of Defense. (1998). *Joint doctrine for information operations,* (Joint Publication (JP) 3-13). Washington, DC: U.S. Government Printing Office.

Department of the Army. (2003). *Information operations: Doctrine, tactics, techniques and procedures* (Field Manual (FM) 3-13) Washington, DC.

Devost, M., & Pollard, N. (2002). *Taking cyber terrorism seriously—Failing to adapt to threats could*

have dire consequences. Retrieved from http://www.terrorism.com

DHS (2003). *The national strategy to secure cyberspace.* Department of Homeland Security, February 2003. Last accessed January 30, 2006, from http://www.dhs.gov/interweb/assetlibrary/National_Cyberspace_Strategy.pdf

DHS (2003). *The national strategy for the physical protection of critical infrastructures and key assets.* The United States Whitehouse, February, 2003. Last accessed January 30, 2006, from http://www.dhs.gov/interweb/assetlibrary/Physical_Strategy.pdf

Dierks, T., & Allen, C. (1999). *The TLS protocol version 1.0.* Internet Engineering Task Force, Request For Comments: 2246.

Diffie, W., & Hellman, M. (1976). New directions in cryptography. *IEEE Transactions on Information Theory, 22*(6), 644-654.

Dingledine, R., Mathewson, N., & Syverson, P. (2004). Tor: The second-generation onion router. *Proceedings of the 13th USENIX Security Symposium.*

Dingledine, R., Matthewson, R., & Syverson, P. (2004). Tor: The second-generation onion router. *Proceedings of the 13th USENIX Security Symposium* (pp. 303-320).

Dittmann, J., & Lang, A. (2004). *Lecture selected aspects of IT-security (WS 04/05)* (Internal Rep.).

Dittmann, J., Wohlmacher, P., & Nahrstedt, K. (20010. Multimedia and security: Using cryptographic and watermarking algorithms. *IEEE MultiMedia, 8*(4), 54-65.

Doak, J. (1992). *Intrusion detection: The application of feature selection, a comparison of algorithms, and the application of a wide area network analyzer.* PhD thesis, University of California, Davis.

Dolan, A. (2004). *Social engineering* (GSEC Option 1 version 1.4b). Retrieved March 1, 2006, from http://sans.org/rr

Donchin, E., Spencer, K. M., & Wijesinghe R. (2000). The mental prosthesis: Assessing the speed of a P300-

based brain-computer interface. *IEEE Trans. Rehabil. Eng., 8*, 174-179.

Douligeris, C., & Mitrokotsa, A. (2004). DDoS attacks and defense mechanisms: Classification and state-of-the-art. *Computer Networks: The International Journal of Computer and Telecommunications Networking Archive, 44*(5), 643-666.

Dowling, J., & Cahill, V. (2004). Self-managed decentralized systems using k-components and collaborative reinforcement learning. In *Proceedings of the 1st ACM SIGSOFT workshop on self-managed systems (WOSS)* (pp. 39-43). New York.

Doyle, E. (2004, November/December). Spam rules—And there's nothing you can do. *Elsevier Infosecurity Today*, pp. 24-28.

Dreazen, Y. J. (2006, February 9). Expert on Congress's power claims he was muzzled for faulting Bush. *The Wall Street Journal*.

Dr-K. (2000). *Complete hacker's handbook*. London: Carlton Book Limited.

Duda, R. O., & Hart, P. E. (1973). *Pattern classification and scene analysis*. New York: Wiley.

Dunnigan, J. F., & Nofi, A. A. (2001). *Victory and deceit: Deception and trickery in war* (2nd ed.). San Jose, CA: Writers Press Books.

Dwork, C., & Naor, M. (1992). Pricing via processing or combating junk mail. In *Proceedings of the 12th Annual International Cryptology Conference on Advances in Cryptology* (pp. 139-147). Santa Barbara, CA.

Dyer, S. C. (1995). Getting people into the crisis communication plan. *Public Relations Quarterly, 40*(3), 38-41.

Early, J. P., & Brodley, C. E. (2003, September 24-26). Decision trees for server flow authentication. *Workshop on Statistical and Machine Learning Techniques in Computer Intrusion Detection*, George Mason University.

Eastlake, D., III, Boesch, B., Crocker, S., & Yesil, M. (1996). *Cybercash credit card protocol version 0.8.* RFC 1898.

Edney, J., & Arbaugh, W. A. (2003). *Real 802.11 security: Wi-Fi protected access and 802.11i*. Addison-Wesley Professional.

Eggen, D. (2006, January 19). Congressional agency questions legality of wiretaps. *The Washington Post*. http://www.washingtonpost.com/wp-dyn/content/article/2006/01/18/AR2006011802158.html

e-gold Ltd. (n.d.). *What is e-gold?* Retrieved February 3, 2006, from http://www.e-gold.com/unsecure/qanda.html

Ehrlichman, J. (1982). *Witness to power: The Nixon years*. Pocket Books.

Ellison, C. (1999). *SPKI requirement, RFC2692*. Sterling, VA: Internet Engineering Task Force (IETF).

Ellison, L. (1999). Cyberspace 1999: Criminal, criminal justice and the internet. *Fourteenth BILETA Conference*, York, UK. http://www.bileta.ac.uk/99papers/ellison.html

Ellison, L., & Akdeniz, Y. (1998). Cyber-stalking: The regulation of harassment on the internet (Special Edition: Crime, Criminal Justice and the Internet). *Criminal Law Review, 2948.* http://www.cyber-rights.org/documents/stalking

Eloff, M. M., & von Solms, S. H. (2000). Information security management: An approach to combine process certification and product evaluation. *Computers & Security 19*(8), 698-709.

Elovici, Y., Kandel, A., Last, M., Shapira, B., Zaafrany, O., Schneider, M., & Friedman, M. (2004). Terrorist detection system. *Proceedings of the 8th European Conference on Principles and Practice of Knowledge Discovery in Databases (PKDD 2004)*, Pisa, Italy (LN in Artificial Intelligence 3202, pp. 540-542). Springer-Verlag.

Elovici, Y., Shapira, B., Last, M., Zaafrany, O., Friedman, M., Schneider, M., & Kandel, A. (2005, May 19-20). Content-based detection of terrorists browsing the web using an advanced terror detection system (ATDS). *Proceedings of the IEEE International Conference on*

Intelligence and Security Informatics (IEEE ISI-2005), Atlanta, GA (pp. 244-255).

Encyclopedia Britannica. (n.d.). Retrieved from www. britannica.com

EPA. (2003). *Information management branch update.* http://www.epa.gov/OGWDW/imb_update/february2003.htm

Erbschloe, M. (2005). *Trojans, worms, and spyware: A computer security professional's guide to malicious code.* Amsterdam: Elsevier.

Erdie, P, & Michael, J. (2005, June). Network-centric strategic-level deception. In *Proceedings of the 10ᵗʰ International Command and Control Research and Technology Symposium.* McLean, VA.

Ericsson, E. (1999). Information warfare: Hype or reality? *The Nonproliferation Review, 6*(3), 57-64.

Ernst & Young. (2004). *Global information security survey.* Retrieved from http://www.ey.com

Ertoz, L., Eilertson, E., Lazarevic, A., Tan, P., Dokes, P., Kumar, V., et al. (2003, November). Detection of novel attacks using data mining. *Proceedings of the IEEE Workshop on Data Mining and Computer Security.*

Estes, J. (1999). *History of remote sensing.* Santa Barbara, CA: National Center for Geographic Information and Analysis.

Estevez-Tapiador, J. M. (2004). The emergence of cyberterrorism. *IEEE Distributed Online System, 5*(1).

EURO Kartensysteme. (2006). *Kartenarten.* Retrieved February 15, 2006, from http://www.geldkarte.de/ww/de/pub/rund_um_die_geldkarte/hintergruende/karten_arten.htm

Europäische Zentralbank. (EZB). (2003). *Elektronisierung des Zahlungsverkehrs in Europa* (Monatsbericht, S. 65-78).

European Commission. (2001). *Communication on network and information security: Proposal for a European policy approach* [COM(2001) 298 final, 06.06.2001]. Brussels, Belgium: European Commission.

European Commission. (2001). *Proposal for a council framework decision on combating terrorism* [COM(2001) 521 final, 19.09.2001]. Brussels, Belgium: European Commission.

European Commission. (2001). *Communication on creating a safer information society by improving the security of information infrastructures and combating computer-related crime (eEurope 2002)* [COM(2000) 890 final, 26.01.2001]. Brussels, Belgium: European Commission.

European Commission. (2002). *Communication on eEurope 2005: An information society for all—An Action plan to be presented in view of the Sevilla European Council, 21/22 June 2002* [COM(2002)263 final, 28.05.2002]. Brussels, Belgium: European Commission.

European Commission. (2003). *Communication on electronic communications: The road to the knowledge economy* [COM(2003) 65 final, 11.02.2003]. Brussels, Belgium: European Commission.

European Commission. (2004). *Communication on connecting Europe at high speed: Recent developments in the sector of electronic communications* [COM(2004) 61 final, 03.02.2004]. Brussels, Belgium: European Commission.

European Institute for Research and Strategic Studies in Telecommunications (Eurescom) GmbH. (2000). *EURESCOM Project P944: Impact of PKI on the European telecommunications business. deliverable* [1, Main Rep.]. Heidelberg, Germany: Eurescom GmbH.

European Parliament and Council of the European Union. (1995). *Directive 95/46/EC of 24 October 1995 on the protection of individuals with regard to the processing of personal data and on the free movement of such data* [Official Journal (OJ) L281, 23.11.1995, pp. 31-50]. Brussels, Belgium: European Parliament and Council of the European Union.

European Parliament and Council of the European Union. (1998). *Directive 97/66/EC of 15 December 1997 concerning the processing of personal data and the protection of privacy in the telecommunications sector* [Official Journal

L24, 30.01.1998, pp. 1-8]. Brussels, Belgium: European Parliament and Council of the European Union.

European Parliament and Council of the European Union. (1999). *Directive 1999/93/EC of 13 December 1999, on a community framework for electronic signatures* [Official Journal (OJ) L13, 19.01.2000, pp. 12-20]. Brussels, Belgium: European Parliament and Council of the European Union.

European Parliament and Council of the European Union. (2002). *Directive 2002/58/EC of 12 July 2002 concerning the processing of personal data and the protection of privacy in the electronic communications sector (Directive on privacy and electronic communications).* [Official Journal L201, 31.07.2002, pp. 37-47]. Brussels, Belgium: European Parliament and Council of the European Union.

European Parliament and Council of the European Union. (2006). *Directive 2006/24/EC on the retention of data generated or processed in connection with the provision of publicly available electronic communications services or of public communications networks and amending Directive 2002/58/EC* [Official Journal L105, 13.04.2006, pp. 54-63]. Brussels, Belgium: European Parliament and Council of the European Union.

European Parliament and of the Council. (2001). *Directive 2001/97/EC.* Retrieved February 15, 2006, from http://europa.eu.int/eurlex/pri/en/oj/dat/2001/l_344/l_34420011228en00760081.pdf

European Parliament, The. (2005). Electronic communications: Personal data protection rules and availability of traffic data for anti-terrorism purposes (amend. direct. 2002/58/EC).

European Parliament. (2001). *Report on the existence of a global system for the interception of private and commercial communications (ECHELON interception system)* [2001/2098(INI)]. Brussels, Belgium: Temporary Committee on the ECHELON Interception System.

European Parliament. (2005). *Directive of the European Parliament on data retention.* Retrieved from http://ue.eu.int/ ueDocs/cms_Data/docs/pressData/en/jha/88467. pdf

Fagnot, I. J., & Stanton, J. M. (2006). Using security assessment interviews to predict organizational security status. *The Security Conference,* Las Vegas, NV.

Fahlman, S. E. (2002). Selling interrupt rights: A way to control unwanted e-mail and telephone calls. *IBM Systems Journal, 41*(4), 759-766.

Farnham, F. R., James, D. V., & Cantrell, P. (2000). Association between violence, psychosis, and relationship to victim in stalkers. *The Lancet, 355*(9199), 199.

Fawcett, T. & Provost, F. (1999). Activity monitoring: Noticing interesting changes in behavior. *Proceedings of the Fifth ACM SIGKDD International Conference on Knowledge Discovery and Data Mining,* San Diego, CA (pp. 53-62).

Fayyad, U., Piatetsky-Shapiro, G., & Smyth, P. (1996). From data mining to knowledge discovery: An overview. In U. Fayyad, G. Piatetsky-Shapiro, P. Smyth, & R. Uthurusamy (Eds.), *Advances in knowledge discovery and data mining* (pp. 134). Menlo Park, CA: AAAI/MIT Press.

FBI. (2004). *How the FBI investigates computer crime.* Retrieved from http://www.cert.org

Federal News Service. (2003, May 16). Press Conference with Attorney General John Ashcroft, FBI Director Robert Mueller, and FTC Chairman Timothy J. Muris. *Federal News Service Inc.*

Feghhi, J., Williams, P., & Feghhi J. (1998). *Digital certificates: Applied Internet security.* MA: Addison-Wesley.

Ferraiolo, D. F., Barkley, J. F., & Kuhn, D. R. (1999). A role-based access control model and reference implementation within a corporate intranet. *ACM Transactions on Information and System Security, 2*(1), 34-64.

Ferraiolo, D. F., Chandramouli, R., Ahn, G. J., & Gavrila, S. I. (2003). The role control center: Features and case studies. *8th Symposium on Access Control Models and Technologies,* 12-20.

Ferraiolo, D. F., Kuhn, R., & Chandramouli, R. (2003).

Role-based access controls. Artech House.

Ferrari-Trecate, G., Muselli, M., Liberati, D., & Morari, M. (2003). A clustering technique for the identification of piecewise affine systems. *Automatica, 39,* 205-217.

Fetterly, D., Manasse, M., & Najorket, M. (2004, June 17-18). Spam, damn spam, and statistics—Using statistical analysis to locate spam web pages. In *Proceedings of the 7th International Workshop on the Web and Databases (WebDB 2004)*, Paris (p. 16).

FIDIS. (2006). *Forensic implications of identity management systems.* Retrieved from http://www.fidis.net

Fighel, J. (2003). *Hamas calls for "economic Jihad" against the US.* ICT Website, ICT.

Fighel, J., & Kehati, Y. (2002). *Analysis of al-qaida documents.* ICT Website, ICT.

Financial Action Task Force on Money Laundering (FATF). (2004). *Report on money laundering typologies, 2003-2004.* Retrieved February 3, 2006, from http://www.fatf-gafi.org/dataoecd/19/11/33624379.pdf

Financial Action Task Force on Money Laundering (FATF). (2004). *Report on money laundering and terrorist financing typologies, 2003-2004* (FATF-XV). Retrieved February 3, 2006, from http://www1.oecd.org/fatf/pdf/TY2004_en.PDF

Financial Action Task Force on Money Laundering (FATF). (2005). *Typologies report 2004-2005.* Retrieved February 15, 2006, from http://www.fatf-gafi.org/dataoecd/41/25/34988062.pdf

Financial services information sharing and analysis centers (FS-ISAC) brochure. (n.d.). Retrieved January 28, 2006, from http://www.fsisac.com/docs/FSISAC.pdf

Fink, M. (1996). *Eavesdropping on the economy: Interception risks and techniques. Prevention and protection.* Richard Boorberg, Verlag.

FIPS PUB 186. (1994). FIPS 186: Federal Information Processing Standard: Digital Signature Standard (DSS). National Institute of Standards and Technology (NIST). Retrieved from http://www.taugh.com/epostage.pdf

Firesmith, D. (2003). Engineering security requirements. *Journal of Object Technology, 2*(1), 53-64.

Fischer, H. W. (1998). The role of the new information technologies in emergency mitigation, planning, response, and recovery. *Disaster Prevention and Management, 7*(1), 28-37.

Fisher, R. (1984). *Information systems security.* Englewood Cliffs, NJ: Prentice-Hall.

Fluhrer, S., Mantin, I., & Shamir, A. (2001). Weaknesses in the key scheduling algorithm of RC4. *Proceedings of the Eighth Annual Workshop on Selected Areas in Cryptography* (pp. 1-24). Toronto, Canada.

Ford, C. V. (1996). *Lies! Lies!! Lies!!! The psychology of deceit.* Washington, DC: American Psychiatric Press.

Foresman, T. (Ed.). (1998*). The history of geographic information systems: Perspectives from the pioneers.* Prentice Hall.

Forest, J. (2005). *The making of a terrorist: Recruitment, training and root causes.* Westport, CT: Praeger Publishers.

Forgas, J. P. (Ed.). (2001). *Handbook of affect and social cognition.* Lawrence Erlbaum Associates.

Fossen, E. A. (2005). *Principles of internet investigation: Basic reconnaissance, geopositioning, and public information sources.* Unpublished master's thesis, Norwegian University of Science and Technology.

Fossen, E. A., & Årnes, A. (2005). Forensic geolocation of internet addresses using network measurements. *Proceedings of the Nordic Workshop on IT-Security (NORDSEC 2005).*

Frambach, R. T. (1993). An integrated model of organizational adoption and diffusion of innovations. *European Journal of Marketing, 27*(5), 22-41.

Frank, J. (1994). Artificial intelligence and intrusion detection: Current and future directions. *Proceedings of the 17th National Computer Security Conference,* Baltimore (pp. 22-33).

Frank, T. (2003). *Zur strafrechtlichen Bewältigung des Spamming, Würzburg , Diss.*, p. 177.

Freier, A. O., Karlton, P., & Kocher, P. C. (1996). *The SSL protocol version 3.0*. Internet Engineering Task Force, Internet Draft.

Fremauw, W. J., Westrup, D., & Pennypacker, J. (1997). Stalking on campus: The prevalence and strategies for coping with stalking. *Journal of Forensic Sciences, 42*(4), 666-669.

Freytag, J. C., Cristian, F., & KŁhler, B. (1987). Making system crashes in database application programs. In *Proceedings of the 13th International Conference on Very Large Data Bases* (pp. 407-416). Brighton, UK.

Friedman, N., Geiger, D., & Goldszmidt, M. (1997). Bayesian network classifiers. *Machine Learning, 29*, 131-161.

FS-ISAC dashboard. (n.d.). Retrieved January 29, 2006, from https://core.fsisac.com/dashboard/

Funk, A., Zeifang, G., Johnson, D., & Spessard, R. (2003). Unsolicited commercial e-mails in the jurisdictions of Germany and the USA. *CRi* 5, p. 141.

Fussell, J., Rundquist, D.C., & Harrington, J. A., Jr. (1986). On defining remote sensing. *Photogrammetric Engineering and Remote Sensing, 52*(9), 15071511.

FX, Craig, P., Grand, J., Mullen, T., Fyodor, Russell, R., & Beale, J. (2004). *Stealing the network: How to own a continent*.

Fyodor. (2006). *Nmap (network mapper) documentation (including zombie scanning technique)*. Retrieved from http://www.insecure.org/nmap/docs.html

Gabillon, A., & Bruno, E. (2001). *Regulating access to XML documents. Proceedings of the 15th Annual IFIP WG 11.3 Working Conference on Database and Application Security,* Niagara on the Lake, Ontario, Canada (pp. 299-314).

Gadomski, A. M., Bologna, S., Costanzo, G. D., Perini, A., & Schaerf, M. (2001). Towards intelligent decision support systems for emergency managers: The IDS approach. *International Journal of Risk Assessment and Management, 2*(3/4), 224-242.

Gandal, N. (2002). Compatibility, standardization, & network effects: Some policy implications. *Oxford Review of Economic Policy, 18*, 8091.

Ganor, B. (2001). *Defining terrorism: Is one man's terrorist another man's freedom fighter?* www.ict.org.il

Ganor, B. (2001). *The world is not coming to an end, however ... .* ICT.

Ganor, B. (2004). The international counter-terrorism academic community. In *Proceedings of the ICTAC Inauguration Conference*, Athens, Greece. ICT.

Garatti, S., Savaresi, S., & Bittanti, S. (2004). On the relationships between user profiles and navigation sessions in virtual communities: A data-mining approach. *Intelligent Data Analysis, 8*(6), 576-600.

Garg, A., Curtis, J., & Halper, H. (2003). Quantifying the financial impact of IT security breaches. *Information Management and Computer Security, 11*(2), 74-83.

Garrett, P., & Lieman, D. (2005). Public-key cryptography. In *Proceedings of Symposia in Applied Mathematica.*

Garten, J. E. (2004, June 21). Offshoring: You ain't seen nothin' yet. *BusinessWeek Online*. Retrieved December 30, 2004, from http://businessweek.com/print/magazine/content/04_25/b3888024_mz007.htm

Gatignon, H., & Robertson, T. (1985). A prepositional inventory for new diffusion research. *Journal of Consumer Research, 11*(March), 849-867.

Gaudin, S. (2003). *Smarter 'blended threats' replacing simple viruses*. Retrieved March 2, 2006, from http://www.winplanet.com/article/2310-.htm

Gaudin, S. (2003, November 19). Offshoring IT jobs expected to accelerate. *ClickZ*. Retrieved November 30, 2004, from http://www.clickz.com/stats/sectors/b2b/print.php/3111321

Gavrilenko, K. (2004) *WI-FOO: The secrets of wireless hacking.* Addison Wesley.

Gburzynski, P., & Maitan, J. (2004). Fighting the spam wars: A remailer approach with restrictive aliasing. *ACM Transactions on Internet Technology, 4*(1), 1-30.

Gehani, A., & Kedem, G. (2004). Rheostat: Real-time risk management. *Proceedings of the 7th International Symposium on Recent Advances in Intrusion Detection (RAID 2004).*

Gellman, B., Linzer, D., & Leonnig, C. D. (2006, February 5).Surveillance net yields few suspects: NSA's hunt for terrorists scrutinizes thousands of Americans, but most are later cleared. *The Washington Post.* http://www.washingtonpost.com/wp-dyn/content/article/2006/02/04/AR2006020401373.html

Gentry, C., & Powers, F. G. (2003). *A memoir of the U@ incident.* Potomac Books, Inc.

Geospatial Solutions. (2003, February). Satellite imagery: History through the keyhole. *Geospatial Solutions Magazine,* (Feb), 19.

Gerard, G., Hillison, W., & Pacini, C. (2004, May/June). What your firm should know about identity theft. *The Journal of Corporate Accounting & Finance,* 311.

Gertz, B. (2000). *The China threat* (1st ed.). Regnery Publishing.

Gerwehr, S., Weissler, R., Medby, J. J., Anderson, R. H., & Rothenberg, J. (2000). *Employing deception in information systems to thwart adversary reconnaissance-phase activities* (Project Memorandum, PM-1124-NSA). National Defense Research Institute, Rand Corp.

Gheorghe, A. V., & Vamanu, D. V. (2001). Adapting to new challenges: IDSS for emergency preparedness and management. *International Journal of Risk Assessment and Management, 2*(3/4), 211-223.

Ghiglieri, M. P. (1999). *The dark side of man: Tracing the origins of male violence.* Perseus Books.

Ghosh, A. K. (1998). *E-commerce security: Weak links, best defenses.* John Wiley & Sons.

Ghosh, A. K. (2002). E-commerce vulnerabilities. In S. Bosworth & M. E. Kabay (Eds.), *Computer security handbook* (4th ed., chap. 13, pp. 13-113-21). John Wiley & Sons.

Gilad, B. (2004). *Early warning: Using competitive intelligence to anticipate market shifts, control risk, and create powerful strategies.* AMACOM.

Gilmer, C. (2006, February 15). Worms prey on Google for victims. *The unofficial Google weblog.* retrieved on May 17, 2007 from http://google.weblogsinc.com/2006/02/15/worms-prey-on-google-for-victims/

GIS. (2005). *Discussion of GIS system requirements.* www.gis.com/implementing_gis/sysrequirements.html

GlobalSecurity. (2005). *Eligible receiver.* Retrieved from http://www.globalsecurity.org/miliatary/ops/eligible-receiver.htm

Gold-ATM. *Debit and prepaid cards for digital currencies users.* Retrieved February 13, 2006, from http://www.gold-atm.biz/cards.php

Goldschlag, D., Reed, M., & Syverson, P. (1999). Onion routing. *Communications of the ACM, 42*(2), 3941.

Goldsmith, D., & Schiffman, M. (1998). *Firewalking: A traceroute-like analysis of IP packet responses to determine gateway access control lists.* Retrieved July 31, 2006, from http://packetstormsecurity.org/UNIX/audit/firewalk/

Golub, G. H., & van Loan, C. F. (1996). *Matrix computations.* Johns Hopkins University Press.

Goodchild, M. (2000). Remote sensing. In R. J. Johnston et al. (Eds.), *The dictionary of human geography* (4th ed., pp. 699701). Oxford, UK: Blackwell.

Goode, M. (1995). Stalking: Crime of the nineties? *Criminal Law Journal, 19,* 21-31.

Goolsby, K. (2001). Healthcare's biggest challenge. *Outsourcing Center.* Retrieved December 12, 2004, from http://www.outsourcing-requests.com/center/jsp/requests/print/story.jsp?id=1660

Goolsby, K. (2001). How to get ready for HIPAA. *Outsourcing Center*. Retrieved December 12, 2004, from http://www.outsourcing-requests.com/center/jsp/requests/print/story.jsp?id=1686

Goolsby, K. (2001). Nobody does it better. *Outsourcing Center*. Retrieved December 12, 2004, from http://www.outsourcing-requests.com/center/jsp/requests/print/story.jsp?id=1816

Goolsby, K. (2001). *Perspectives on HIPAA*. Dallas, TX: Outsourcing Center.

Goolsby, K. (2003). *Governing attitudes: 12 best practices in managing outsourcing relationships.*

Gordon, L. A., Loeb, M. P., Lucyshyn, W., & Richardson, R. (2005). *Tenth Annual, 2005 CSI/FBI Computer Crime and Security Survey*. San Francisco: Computer Security Institute (www.gocsi.com).

Gordon, L. A., Loeg, M. P., Lucyshyn, W., & Richardson, R. (2005). *2005 CSI/FBI computer crime and security survey*. Computer Security Institute. Last accessed January 30, 2006, from http://i.cmpnet.com/gocsi/db_area/pdfs/fbi/FBI2005.pdf

Gordon, L., & Loeb, M. (2005). *Managing aging cybersecurity resources: a cost-benefit analysis* (1st ed.). McGraw-Hill.

Gordon, S. L. (2002). *Israel against terror—A national assessment*. Efi Meltzer.

Government Information July 9, 2002 Hearing On S. 2541, "The Identity Theft Penalty Enhancement Act". *Federal Bureau of Investigation*. Retrieved February 12, 2006, from http://www.fbi.gov/congress/congress02/idtheft.htm

Grady, M., & Francesco, P. (2006, in press). *The law and economics of cybersecurity: An introduction*. Cambridge University Press.

Graham, B. (2005, August 25). Hackers attack via Chinese Web sites, U.S. agencies' networks are among targets. *The Washington Post*, p. A1.

Granger, S. (2001). *Social engineering fundamentals,*

part I: Hacker tactics. Retrieved March 1, 2006, from http://www.securityfocus.com/infocus/1527

Granger, S. (2002). *Social engineering fundamentals, part II: Combat strategies*. Retrieved March 1, 2006, from http://www.securityfocus.com/infocus/1533

Gratton, M. (1994). *Spyworld: Inside the Canadian and American intelligence establishments*. Canada: Doubleday.

Grazioli, S., & Jarvenpaa, S. (2003). Deceived: Under target online. *Communications of the ACM, 46* (12), 196-205.

Green, H. (2003, August 25). We all knew better. *BusinessWeek Online*. Retrieved from http://www.businessweek.com/magazine/toc/03_34/B38460333futuretech.htm

Greene, R. W. (2002). *Confronting catastrophe: A GIS handbook*. Redlands, CA: ESRI Press.

Grimes, A., Hough, M., & Signorella, M. (in press). E-mail end users and spam: Relations of gender and age group to attitudes and actions. *Computers in Human Behavior.*

Gritzalis, S. (2005). Public key infrastructure: Research and applications. *International Journal of Information Security, 5*(1), 1-2.

Grove, G. D., Goodman, S. E., & Lukasik, S. J. (2000). Cyber-attacks and international law. *Survival, 42*(3), 89-103.

Grubb, L. (2004). *Survey of network weapons: part 1: weapons for profiling*. Consortium for Computing Sciences in Colleges (CCSC).

Gueye, B., Ziviani, A., Crovella, M., & Fdida, S. (2004). Constraint-based geolocation of internet hosts. *Proceedings of ACM/SIGCOMM Internet Measurement Conference (IMC 2004).*

Gustin, J. F. (2004). *Cyber terrorism: A guide for facility managers*. Fairmont Press.

Gutman, R., & Rieff, D. (1999). *Crimes of war: What the public should know*. New York: Norton.

Hachez, G. (2003). *A comparative study of software protection tools suited for e-commerce with contributions to software watermarking and smart cards.* Unpublished doctoral dissertation, Louvain-la-Neuve.

Hackers attacked parliament using WMF exploit. (2006). Tom Espiner. Retrieved January 30, 2006, from http://news.zdnet.co.uk/internet/security/0,39020375,39248387,00.htm

Haddad, D., Walter, S., Ratley R., & Smith, M. (2002). *Investigation and evaluation of voice stress analysis technology* (NIJ 193832). Washington, DC: Office of Justice Programs, National Institute of Justice, Department of Justice.

Haddon Jr., W. (1973). Energy damage and the ten countermeasure strategies. *Human Factors Journal, 15,* 355-365.

Hagar, N. (1996). *Secret power: New Zealand's role in the international spy network.* New Zealand: Craig Potton Publishing. http://www.fas.org/irp/eprint/sp/sp_c2.htm

Hagar, N. (1996, December). Exposing the global surveillance system. *Covert Action Quarterly, 59.* http://caq.com/CAQ/CAQ59GlobalSnoop.html

Halperin, M. H. (2006, January 6). *A legal analysis of the NSA warrantless surveillance program.* Center for American Progress.http://www.americanprogress.org/site/pp.asp?c=biJRJ8OVF&b=1334469

Han, J., & Kamber, M. (2001). *Data mining: Concepts and techniques.* Morgan Kaufmann.

Hand, D., Mannila, H., & Smyth, P. (2001). *Principles of data-mining.* Cambridge, MA: MIT Press.

Handerson, J. C., & Venkatraman, N. (1993). Strategic alignment: Leveraging information technology for transforming organizations. *IBM Systems Journal, 32*(1), 472-483.

Hansell, S. (2004, August 26). U.S. tally in online-crime sweep: 150 charged. *New York Times.*

Hardjono, T., & Lakshminath R. D. (2005). *Security in wireless LANs and MANs.* Artech House Books.

Harl. (1997). *People hacking: The psychology of social engineering* (text of Harl's talk at Access All Areas III). Retrieved March 1, 2006, from http://packetstormsecurity.nl/docs/social-engineering/aaatalk.html

Harrington, D., Presuhn, R., & Wijnen, B. (2002, December). An architecture for describing simple network management protocol (SNMP) management frameworks, RFC 3411. IETF.

Harris, S., Harper, A., Eagle, C., Ness, J., & Lester, M. (2005). *Gray hat hacking: The ethical hacker's handbook.* McGraw-Hill Publishing Co.

Harrison, M., Ruzzo, W., & Ullman, J. (1976). Protection in operating systems. *Communication of the ACM, 19*(8), 461-471.

Hartman, S. (2001). *Securing e-commerce: An overview of defense in-depth.* Retrieved February 26, 2006, from http://www.giac.org/certified_professionals/practicals/gsec/0592.php

Hassler, V. (2001). *Security fundamentals for e-commerce.* Artech House.

Hauptman, R. (1996). Cyberethics and social stability. *Ethics and Behavior, 6*(2), 161-163.

Hawkinson, J., & Bates, T. (1996, March). Guidelines for creation, selection, and registration of an autonomous system (AS). RFC1930. IETF.

Haydon, F. (2000). *Military ballooning during the Civil War.* Johns Hopkins University Press.

Haydon, M. V. (1999). *The insider threat to U.S. government information systems* [INFOSEC 1-99]. National Security Telecommunications and Information Systems Security Committee. Retrieved June 4, 2006 from http://www.nstissc.gov/Assets/pdf/NSTISSAM_INFOSEC1-99.pdf

Helmer, G., Wong, J. S. K., Honavar, V. G., Miller, L., & Wang, Y. (2003). Lightweight agents for intrusion detection. *Journal of Systems and Software, 67*(2), 109122.Internet Society, The. (2005). 20 DNS root name servers—frequently asked questions. *ISOC Member Briefing #20.* Retrieved July 31, 2006, from http://www.

isoc.org/briefings/020/

Helsinger, A., Kleinmann, K., & Brinn, M. (2004). A framework to control emergent survivability of multi agent systems. In *Proceedings of the 3rd International Joint Conference on Autonomous Agents and Multiagent Systems (AAMAS)* (pp. 28-35). Washington, DC.

Hidalgo, J., Opez, M., & Sanz, E. (2000). Combining text and heuristics for cost-sensitive spam filtering. In *Proceedings of the 4th Computational Natural Language Learning Workshop (CoNLL)* (pp. 99-102). Lisbon, Portugal.

Himma, K. (2004). The ethics of tracing hacker attacks through the machines of innocent persons. *International Journal of Information Ethics, 2*(11), 1-13.

Hitchcock, J. A. (2000). Cyberstalking. *Link-Up, 17*(4). http://www.infotoday.com/lu/ju100/hitchcock.htm

Hoffman, B. (2003). The leadership secrets of Osama bin Laden: The terrorist as CEO. *The Atlantic Monthly.*

Hoffman, B. (2003). Modern terrorism trends: Re-evaluation after 11 September. In *Proceedings of the ICT'S 3rd International Conference on Post Modern Terrorism: Trends, Scenarios, and Future Threats*, Herzliya. ICT.

Holdsworth, D. (Ed.). (1999, October). *Development of surveillance technology and risk of abuse of economic information.* European Parliament Scientific and Technological Options office (STOA) report. http://www.europarl.eu.int/stoa/publi/pop-up_en.htm

Hollnagel, E. (1999). *Accident analysis and barrier functions.* Retrieved July 3, 2005, from http://www.hai.uu.se/projects/train/papers/accidentanalysis.pdf

Holz, T., & Raynal, F. (2005). *Defeating honeypots: System issues* (Parts 1 and 2). Retrieved October 25, 2005, from www.securityfocus.com/infocus/1826

Homeland security: Information sharing responsibilities, challenges, and key management issues [GAO-03-715T]. (2003, May 8). Presented to Committee on Government Reform, House of Representatives.

Homer-Dixon, T. (2002). The rise of complex terrorism. *Foreign Policy.*

Hook, D. (2005). *Beginning cryptography with Java.* Wrox.

Housley, R., Ford, W., Polk, W., & Solo, D. (1999). *Internet X.509 public key infrastructure. Certificate and CRL profile, request for comments (RFC) 2459.* Sterling, VA: Internet Engineering Task Force (IETF).

Howard, J. D., & Longstaff, T. A. (1998). *A common language for computer security incidents.*

HR 3162 (2001). Uniting and Strengthening America by Providing Appropriate Tools Required to Intercept and Obstruct Terrorism (USA PATRIOT ACT) Act of 2001. United States Senate.

Hsueh, M.-C., Tsai, T. K., & Iyer, R. K. (1997). Fault injection techniques and tools. *Computer, 30*(4), 75-82.

Huang, Y. A., & Lee, W. (2003). A cooperative intrusion detection system for ad hoc Networks. *Proceedings of the 1st ACM Workshop Security of Ad Hoc and Sensor Networks* (pp. 135-147).

Hughes, B. (2002, November 21). A functional definition of critical infrastructure: making the problem manageable. *ACM Workshop on Scientific Aspects of Cyber Terrorism (SACT)*, Washington DC.

Hutchings, R. (2004). *Terrorism and economic security.* Talk given at the International Security Management Association meeting, Scottsdale, AZ, 14 January 2004. Last accessed January 30, 2006, from http://www.cia.gov/nic/PDF_GIF_speeches/terror_and_econ_sec.pdf

Hutchings, R. L. (2004). *Looking over the horizon: Assessing America's strategic challenges.* Talk given at the Department of State/INR/World Affairs Council Seminar, Washington, DC, March 9, 2004. Last accessed January 30, 2006, from http://www.cia.gov/nic/PDF_GIF_speeches/strategic_challenges.pdf

Hutchinson, W. (2002). Concepts in information warfare. *Logistics Information Management, 15*(5/6), 410413.

Hutchinson, W., & Warren, M. (2001). *Information warfare: Corporate attack and defense in a digital world.*

London: Butterworth-Heinemann.

Hutchinson, W., & Warren, M. J. (2001). *Information Warfare: Corporate attack and defence in a digital world*. London: Butterworth-Heinemann.

Hutter, D. (2002). *Security engineering.* Retrieved July 3, 2005, from http://www.dfki.de/~hutter/lehre/sicherheit/securityengineering.ppt

Iakovou, E. & Douligeris, C. (2001). An information management system for the emergency management of hurricane disasters. *International Journal of Risk Assessment and Management, 2*(3/4), 243-262.

IBM Corporation. (2002). *Enterprise security architecture using IBM Tivoli security solutions.*

IBM. (2005). *The future of crime.* Retrieved from http://www.306.ibm.com/innovation/us/pointofview/cybercrime/jan23/IBM_Future_Crime.html

ICSA/TruSecure. (2002). *Virus stats.* Retrieved from http://www.ICSAlabs.com; also at http://www.cit.cornell.edu/computer/security/seminarspast/virus

IEEE standard glossary of software—Engineeringterminology [Standard 610.12-1990]. (n.d.).

Imai, H. (Ed.). (2005). *Wireless communications security.* Artech House Books.

Immen, W. (2004, April 28). Workplace privacy gets day in court. *The Globe and Mail.* Retrieved 12 May, 2005 from http://www.theglobeandmail.com

Innella, P. (2001). *The evolution of intrusion detection systems.* Retrieved from http://www.securityfocus.com/printable/infocus/1514

International Organization for Standardization (ISO). (2005). *ISO/IEC 17799: Information technology—Security techniques: Code of practice for information security management*. Geneva, Switzerland: ISO.

Introna, L. (2000, December). Workplace surveillance, privacy and Distributive justice. *ACM SIGCAS Computers and Society, CEPE 2000, 30*(4), 33-39.

Ioannidis, J. (2003). Fighting spam by encapsulating policy in email addresses. In *Proceedings of the 10ᵗʰ Annual Network and Distributed System Security Symposium (NDSS).* San Diego, CA.

Ioannidis, J., & Bellovin, S. M. (2002). *Implementing pushback: Router-based defense against DDoS attacks.* Retrieved from http://www.isoc.org/isoc/conferences/ndss/02/proceedings/papers/ioanni.pdf

Ironwalker, (2004). *Does IPv6 introduce new security vulnerabilities?* (#9464). Retrieved from http://www.dslreports.com/faq/9464

ISE. (n.d.). *The internet no1 close protection resource.* http://www.intel-sec.demon.co.uk

Isikoff, M. (2004, December 18). 2001 memo reveals push for broader presidential powers. *Newsweek.* Retrieved May 21, 2007 from http://www.msnbc.msn.com/id/6732484/site/newsweek/

Jackson, O. A., Baker, J. C., Cragin, K., Parachini, J., Trujillo, H. R. & Chalk, P. (2005) *Aptitude for destruction: Organizational learning in terrorist groups and its implications for combating terrorism.* RAND.

Jain, A. K., Murty, M. N., & Flynn, P. J. (1999). Data clustering: A review. *ACM Computing Surveys, 31*(3), 264-323.

Jajodia, S., & Johnson, N. F. (1998). Exploring steganography: Seeing the unseen. *IEEE Computer, 31*(2), 26-34.

Jajodia, S., McCollum, C., & Ammann, P. (1999). Trusted recovery. *Communications of the ACM, 42*(7), 71-75.

Jennex, M. E. (2003). Information security in the era of terrorist attacks. *Information Resource Management Association International Conference Panel.*

Jennex, M. E. (2003). *Security design.* Unpublished system design lecture [IDS 697]: San Diego State University.

Jennex, M. E. (2004). Emergency response systems: The utility Y2K experience. *Journal of IT Theory and Application (JITTA), 6*(3), 85-102.

Jennex, M. E. (2005). What is knowledge management? *International Journal of Knowledge Management, 1*(4), iiv.

Jennex, M. E. (2006). Open source knowledge management. *International Journal of Knowledge Management, 2*(4), iiv.

Jennex, M. E., & Walters, A. (2003). A comparison of knowledge requirements for operating hacker and security tools. *The Security Conference,* Information Institute.

Jensen, J. (2000). *Remote sensing of the environment.* Upper Saddle River, NJ: Prentice-Hall.

Jensen, J. (2005). *Introductory digital image processing.* Prentice Hall.

Jenson, B. (1996). *Cyberstalking: Crime, enforcement and personal responsibility of the on-line world.* S.G.R. MacMillan. http://www.sgrm.com/art-8.htm

Johnson, A. C., & Tesch, B. (2005). *US e-commerce: 2005 to 2010: A five-year forecast and analysis of US online retail sales.* Forrester Research.

Jones, A., Kovacich, G. L., & Luzwick, P. G. (2002). *Global information warfare: How businesses, governments, and others achieve objectives and attain competitive advantages.* New York: Auerbach Publications.

Jones, K. J., Bejtlich, R., & RoseReal, C. W. (2005). *Digital forensics: Computer security and incident response.* Addison-Wesley Professional.

Jonietz, E. (2003). Total information overload. *MIT Technology Review, 106*(6), 68.

Joshi, J., Bhatti, R., Bertino, E., & Ghafoor, A. (2004). Access-control language for multidomain environments. *IEEE Internet Computing, 8*(6), 40-50.

Joshi, J., Li, K., Fahmi, H., Shafiq, C., & Ghafoor, A. (2002). A model for secure multimedia document database system in a distributed environment. *IEEE Transactions on Multimedia: Special Issue of on Multimedia Datbases, 4*(2), 215-234.

Juels, A., & Brainhard, J. (1999). Client puzzles: A cryptographic countermeasure against connection depletion attacks. In *Proceedings of the Conference Networks and Distributed Security Systems* (pp. 151-165). San Diego, CA. Retrieved from http://www.isoc.org/isoc/conferences/ndss/99/proceedings/papers/juels.pdf

Julian, D., Rowe, N., & Michael, J. (2003). Experiments with deceptive software responses to buffer-based attacks. In *Proceedings of the IEEE-SMC Workshop on Information Assurance* (pp. 43-44). West Point, NY.

Julisch, K. (2003, November). Clustering intrusion detection alarms to support root cause analysis. *ACM Transactions on Information and System Security (TISSEC), 6*(4), 443-471.

Jung, J., & Smit, E. (2004, October 25-27). An empirical study of spam traffic and the use of DNS black lists. *Proceedings of The Internet Measurement Conference (IMC'04)*, Taormina, Italy.

Jupitermedia Corporation. (2003). *Steganography.* Retrieved August 31, 2003, from http://www.webopedia.com/TERM/S/steganography.html

Kahn, A. (2005, December 13). *Quanta computer to manufacture $100 laptop.* Retrieved from http://www.laptop.org/2005-1213.olpc.pdf

Kamal, A. (2005). *The Law of cyber-space.* Geneva: United Nations Institute of Training and Research (UNITAR).

Kamien, D. (2006). *The McGraw-Hill homeland security handbook.* McGraw-Hill.

Kamphuis, J. H., & Emmelkamp, P. M. G. (2000). Stalking—A contemporary challenge for forensic and clinical psychiatry. *British Journal of Psychiatry, 176,* 206-209.

Kannan, K., & Telang, R. (2004). *Market for software vulnerabilities? Think again.* Working paper, Carnegie-Mellon.

Kapfhammer, G., Michael, C., Haddox, J., & Colyer, R. (2000). An approach to identifying and understanding problematic cots components. In *Proceedings of the Software Risk Management Conference (ISACC).* Reston, VA.

Kargl, F., Maier, J., & Weber, M. (2001). Protecting Web servers from distributed denial of service attacks. In *Proceedings 10th International WWW Conference* (pp. 514-524). Hong Kong. Retrieved from http://www.www10.org/cdrom/papers/p409.pdf

Kaspersky. (2006). *Virus statistics.* Retrieved from http://www.kasprsky.com/press?chapter=146437529

Kasprzycki, D. (2004). Trends in regulating unsolicited commercial communication. *CRi* 3, p. 77.

Kaufman, C. (2002). *Network security: Private communication in a public world* (2nd ed.). Prentice Hall, USA.

Kaza, S., Murthy, S., & Hu, G. (2003). Identification of deliberately doctored text documents using frequent keyword chain (FKC) model. In *Proceedings of the IEEE International Conference on Information Reuse and Integration*, Las Vegas, NV (pp. 398-405).

Keeney, M., Kowalski, E., Cappelli, D., Moore, A., Shimeall, T., & Rogers, S. (2005). *Insider threat study: Computer system sabotage in critical infrastructure sectors.* National Threat Assessment Center, U.S. Secret Service, and CERT® Coordination Center/Software Engineering Institute, Carnegie Mellon. Retrieved from http://www.cert.org/archive/pdf/insidercross051105.pdf

Keller, S., Powell, A., Horstmann, B., Predmore, C., & Crawford, M. (2005). Information security threats and practices in small businesses. *Information Systems Management, 22*(2), 719.

Kennedy, H. (2001). *Dictionary of GIS terminology.* Redlands, CA: ESRI Press.

Keogh, E., & Pazzani, M. J. (2002). Learning the structure of augmented Bayesian classifiers. *International Journal on Artificial Intelligence Tools, 11*(4), 587-601.

Khattab, S. M., & Sangpachatanaruk, C. (2003). Melhem, R.; Mosse, D.; Znati, T.: Proactive server roaming for mitigating denial-of-service attacks. In *Proceedings 1st Int. Conference on International Technology: Research and Education ITRE* (pp. 500-504). Newark, NJ. Retrieved from http://www.cs.pitt.edu/NETSEC/publications_files/itre03.pdf

Khong, W. (2001). Spam law for the internet. *The Journal of Information, Law and Technology (JILT)*, (3). http://elj.warwick.ac.uk/jilt

Kim, E., Massey, D., & Ray, I. (2005). Global internet routing forensics: Validation of BGP paths using ICMP traceback. *Proceedings of IFIP International. Conference on Digital Forensics.*

Kim, L. (1998). Crisis construction and organizational learning: Capability building in catching-up at Hyundai Motor. *Organization Science, 9*(4), 506-521.

Kitamato, A. (2005). Digital typhoon: Near real-time aggregation, recombination and delivery of typhoon-related information. *Proceeding of the 4th International Symposium on Digital Earth.* Retrieved October 26, 2005, from http://www.cse.iitb.ac.in/~neela/MTP/Stage1-Report.pdf

Klusch, M. (2001). Information agent technology for the internet: A survey [Special Issue on Intelligent Information Integration. D. Fensel (Ed.)]. *Journal on Data and Knowledge Engineering, 36*(3), 337-372.

Knight, J., & Sullivan, K. (2000). Towards a definition of survivability. In *Proceedings of the 3rd Information Survivability Workshop (ISW)*. Boston.

Knight, J., Elder, M., & Du, X. (1998). Error recovery in critical infrastructure systems. In *Proceedings of the Computer Security, Dependability, and Assurance (CSDA) Workshop.* Williamsburg, VA.

Kodali, N. B., Farkas, C., & Wijesekera, D. (2004). An authorization model for multimedia digital libraries (Special Issue on Security). *Journal of Digital Libraries, 4*(3), 139-155.

Kodali, N. B., Farkas, C., & Wijesekera, D. (2004). Specifying multimedia access control using RDF (Special Issue on Trends in XML Technology). *International Journal of Computer Systems, Science and Engineering, 19*(3), 129-141.

Koerner, B. (2006). Terrorist groups relying on identity theft for funding operations. *About.com.* Retrieved September 1, 2006, from http://idtheft.about.com/od/useofstolenidentity/p/IDTheftTerror.htm

Kononenko, I. (1995). On biases in estimating multi-valued attributes. In *Proceedings of the International Joint Conference on Artificial Intelligence* (IJCA195)(pp. 1034-1040).

Kosloff, T., Moore, T., Keller, J., Manes, G., & Shenoi, S. (2002, November 21). SS7 messaging attacks on public telephone networks: Attack scenarios and detection. *ACM Workshop on Scientific Aspects of Cyber Terrorism (SACT)*, Washington DC.

Kotulic, A. G., & Clark, G. J. (2004). Why there aren't more information security research studies. *Information & Management, 41*, 597-607.

Krasavin, S. (2000). *What is cyber-terrorism?* Computer Crime Research Center. Retrieved February 3, 2006, from http://www.crime-research.org/library/Cyber-terrorism.htm

Kratt, H. (2004). *The inside story: A disgruntled employee gets his revenge.* Retrieved March 1, 2006, from http://sans.org/rr

Krawetz, N. (2004). Anti-honeypot technology. *IEEE Security and Privacy, 2*(1), 76-79.

Krebs, V. (2002). Mapping networks of terrorist cells. *Connections 24*(3), 4352.

Krim, J. (2003). *Security report puts blame on Microsoft.* Washingtonpost.com. Retrieved May 17, 2007, from http://www.washingtonpost.com/wp-dyn/articles/A54872-2003Sep23.html

Kriss, A. (1993). Recording technique. In A. M. Halliday (Ed.), *Evoked potentials in clinical testing* (2nd edition) (pp. 1-56). New York: Churchill Livingstone.

Kruegel, C., & Vigna, G. (2003, October 27-31). Anomaly detection of web-based attacks. *Proceedings of the 10th ACM Conference on Computer and Communications Security (CCS'03)*, Washington, DC (pp. 251-261).

Kruegel, C., Mutz, D., Robertson, W., & Valeur, F. (2003). Topology-based detection of anomalous BGP messages. *Proceedings of the International Symposium on Recent Advances in Intrusion Detection (RAID 2003).*

Kruegel, C., Valeur, F., & Vigna, G. (2005). *Intrusion detection and correlation: challenges and solutions* (Vol. 14). Springer.

Kruse, F. A., Lefkoff, A. B., Boardman, J. W., Heidebrecht, K. B., Shapiro, A. T., & Barloon, P. J. et al. (1992). The spectral image processing system (SIPS): Interactive visualization and analysis of imaging spectrometer data. In *Proceedings of the International Space Year Conference,* Pasadena, CA.

Kuhnhauser, W. (2004). Root kits: an operating systems viewpoint. *ACM SIGOPS Operating Systems Review, 38*(1), 12-23.

Kumar, V., Lazarevic, A., Ertoz, L., Ozgur, A., & Srivastava, J. (2003, May). A comparative study of anomaly detection schemes in network intrusion detection. *Proceedings of the Third SIAM International Conference on Data Mining,* San Francisco.

Kuznetsov, V., Sandstrom, H., & Simkin, A. (2002). An evaluation of different IP traceback approaches. *In ICICS '02: Proceedings of the 4th International Conference on Information and Communications Security (ICICS 2002).*

Kwan, M.-P., & Lee, J. (2005). Emergency response after 9/11. *Computers, Environment and Urban Systems, 29*(2).

Lalopoulos, G. K., Chochliouros, I .P., & Spiliopoulou, A. S. (2004). Challenges and perspectives for Web-based applications in organizations. In M. Pagani (Ed.), *The encyclopedia of multimedia technology and networking* (pp. 82-88). Hershey, PA: IRM Press.

Lampson, B. (1974). Protection. *ACM Operating System Reviews, 8*(1), 18-24.

Lancaster, J. (1998, June). Cyber-stalkers: The scariest growth crime of the 90's is now rife on the net. *The Weekend Australian,* 20-21.

Landgrebe, D. (1999). *An introduction to MULTISPEC.* West Lafayette, IN: Purdue University.

Landwehr, C. E. (1981). Formal models of computer security. *ACM Comput. Surv., 13*(3), 247-278.

Lankewicz, L., & Benard, M. (1991). Realtime anomaly detection using a nonparametric pattern recognition approach. *Proceedings of the 7th Annual Computer Security Applications Conference.*

Last, M. (2005). Computing temporal trends in web documents. *Proceedings of the Fourth Conference of the European Society for Fuzzy Logic and Technology (EUSFLAT 2005)* (pp. 615-620).

Last, M., & Kandel, A. (1999). Automated perceptions in data mining. *Proceedings of the 1999 IEEE International Fuzzy Systems Conference, Part I* (pp. 190-197).

Last, M., & Kandel, A. (2005). Fighting terror in cyberspace. *Singapore: World Scientific, Series in Machine Perception and Artificial Intelligence, Vol. 65.*

Last, M., & Maimon, O. (2004). A compact and accurate model for classification. *IEEE Transactions on Knowledge and Data Engineering, 16*(2), 203215.

Last, M., Markov, A., & Kandel, A. (2006, April 9). Multi-lingual detection of terrorist content on the web. *Proceedings of the PAKDD'06 Workshop on Intelligence and Security Informatics (WISI'06),* Singapore (LN in Computer Science, Vol. 3917) (pp. 16-30). Springer

Laughren, J. (2000). *Cyberstalking awareness and education.* http://www.acs.ucalgary.ca/~dabrent/380/webproj/jessica.html

Lazarus, D. (2004, April 2). Extortion threat to patients' records: Clients not informed of India staff's breach. *San Francisco Chronicle.* Retrieved March 1, 2005, from http://sfgate.com/cgi-bin/article.cgi?file=/c/a/2004/04/02/MNGI75VIEB1.DTL

Lazarus, D. (2004, March 28). Looking offshore: Outsourced UCSF notes highlight privacy risk. *San Francisco Chronicle.* Retrieved March 1, 2005, from http://www.sfgate.com/cgi-bin/article.cgi?file=/chronicle/archive/2004/03/28/MNGFS3080R264.DTL

Leavitt, N. (2005). Mobile phones: The next frontier for hackers? *IEEE Computer, 38*(4), 20-23.

LeClaire, J. (2004, December 29). Netherland issues its first fines against spammers. *E-commerce Times.*

Ledeen, M. (2000). Blame the United States for India's Nukes: Indian nuclear testing program and CIA intelligence failure. *Journal of the American Enterprise Institute.* http://www.aei.org/publications/pubID.9068/pub_detail.asp

Lee, J., & Bui, T. (2000). A template-based methodology for disaster management information systems. *Proceedings of the 33rd Hawaii International Conference on System Sciences.*

Lee, W., & Stolfo, S. (1998). Data mining approaches for intrusion detection. *Proceedings of the 7th USENIX Security Symposium.* San Antonio, TX, 2004.

Lee, W., & Stolfo, S. (2000). A framework for constructing features and models for intrusion detection systems. *ACM Transactions on Information and System Security, 3*(4), 227-261.

Lee, W., & Stolfo, S. J. (1998). Data mining approaches for intrusion detection. *Proceedings of the Seventh USENIX Security Symposium,* San Antonio, TX.

Lee, W., Stolfo, S. J., & Kwok, K. W. (1998). Mining audit data to build intrusion detection models. *Proceedings of the Fourth International Conference on Knowledge Discovery and Data Mining,* NY.

Lee, W., Stolfo, S. J., & Kwok, K. W. (1999, May). A data mining framework for building intrusion detection models. *IEEE Symposium on Security and Privacy, Berkeley, CA,* 120-132.

Lee, Y., Lee, Z., & Lee, C. K. (2002). A study of integrating the security engineering process into the software lifecycle process standard [IEEE/EIA 12207]. *6th Americas conference on information systems, AMCIS* (pp. 451-457).

Legard, D. (2003, May 14). *Fake bank web site scam reaches U.S.* Retrieved August 10, 2005, from http://www.itworld.com/Tech/2987/030514fakebank

Leipnik, M. R., & Albert, D. (Eds.). (2003). *GIS in law enforcement.* London: Taylor and Francis

Lemos, R. (2002, August 26). What are the real risks of cyberterrorism? *ZDNet.*

Leng, R. (1994). Interstate crisis escalation and war. In M. Portegal & J. Knutson (Eds.), *The dynamics of aggression* (pp. 307-332). Hillsdale, NJ: Lawrence Erlbaum.

Lewis, J. (2002). *Assessing the risks of cyber-terrorism, cyber war, and other cyber threats.* Washington, DC: Center for Strategic and International Studies. Retrieved November 23, 2005, from http://www.csis.org

Lewis, J. (2003). Cyber terror: Missing in action. *Knowledge, Technology, & Policy, 16*(2), 34-41.

Lewis, J. A. (2002). Assessing the risks of cyber terrorism, cyber war and other cyber threats. Center for Strategic and International Studies, December 2002. Last accessed January 30, 2006, from http://www.csis.org/media/csis/pubs/021101_risks_of_cyberterror.pdf

Lewis, S. F., Fremouw, W. J., Ben, K. D., & Farr, C. (2001). An investigation of the psychological characteristics of stalkers: Empathy, problem-solving, attachment and borderline personality features. *Journal of Forensic Sciences, 46*(1), 8084.

Leyden, J. (2004). Sign the cybercrime convention, urge secureocrats. *The Register.* Retrieved from http://www.theregister.com/2004/09/17/euro_cybercrime_conference/

Li, J., Dou, D., Wu, Z., Kim, S., & Agarwal, V. (2005). An internet routing forensics framework for discovering rules of abnormal BGP events. *SIGCOMM Computer Communication Review, 35*(5), 5566.

Liang, Q., & Xiangsui, W. (1999). *Unrestricted warfare* (FBIS, Trans., selected chapters). Beijing: PLA Literature and Arts Publishing House.

Libicki, M. C. (1995). *What is information warfare?* Washington, DC: National Defense University, Institute for National Strategic Studies.

Liedtke, M. (2005, January 24). Google agrees to censor results in China. *BREITBART.COM.* Retrieved 12 May, 2005 from http://www.breitbart.com/article.php?id=2006-01-25_D8FBONMG7&show_article=1&cat=breaking

Liepens, G., & Vacaro, H. (1989). Anomaly detection: purpose and framework. *Proceedings of the 12th National Computer Security Conference.*

Lipson, H. F. (2002). Tracking and tracing cyber-attacks: Technical challenges and global policy (Technical Report). CERT Coordination Center.

Lipson, H., & Fisher, D. (1999). Survivability: A new technical and business perspective on security. *Proceedings of the New Security Paradigms Workshop (NSPW),* Caledon Hills, Ontario, Canada.

Lipton, E., & Lichtblau, E. (2004, September 23). Even near home, a new front is opening in the terror battle. *The New York Times.*

Litan, A. (2005). *Increased phishing and online attacks cause dip in consumer confidence.* Gartner Group.

Liu, P., Ammann, P., & Jajodia, S. (2000). Rewriting histories: Recovering from malicious transactions. *Distributed and Parallel Databases, 8*(1), 7-40.

Loia, V., Senatore, S., & Sessa, M. (2004). Combining agent technology and similarity-based reasoning for targeted e-mail services. *Fuzzy Sets and Systems, 145*(1), 29-56.

Long, J., Skoudis, E., & Van Eijkelenborg, A. (Eds.). (2001). *Google hacking for penetration testers..*

Longley, P. A., McGuire, D. J., Goodchild, M. F., & Rhind, D. (Eds.). (1999). *GIS principles and applications.* London: Longmans.

Lormel, D. M. (2002, July 9). Testimony of Dennis M. Lormel, Chief, Terrorist Financial Review Group, FBI before the Senate Judiciary Committee Subcommittee on Technology, Terrorism and

Lougheed, K., & Rekhter, Y. (1991). Border gateway protocol 3 (BGP-3). RFC 1267 (Historic), IETF.

Luftman, J. (2003). *Managing the information technology resource.* Prentice Hall.

Lukaszewski, J. E. (1987). Anatomy of a crisis response: A checklist. *Public Relations Journal.*

Luotonen, A. (1997). *Web proxy servers*. Prentice Hall PTR.

Machlis, A. (2000, April 21). *Protecting the net*. Retrieved May 17, 2007 from http://www.jewishjournal.com/old/hackers.4.21.0.htm

MacQueen, J. (1967). Some methods for classification and analysis of multivariate observations. *Proceedings of the Fifth Berkeley Symposium on Mathematical Statistics and Probability* (pp. 291-297).

Madeira, H., Costa, D., & Vieira, M. (2000). On the emulation of software faults by software fault injection. In *Proceedings of the International Conference on Dependable Systems and Networks (DNS)* (pp. 417-426). Washington, DC.

Madinger, J., & Zalopany, S. A. (1999). *Money laundering. A guide for criminal investigators*. Boca Raton, FL: CRC Press.

Madsen, W. (2005, April 25). NSA intercepts for Bolton masked as "training missions." *Online Journal Contributing*. http://www.onlinejournal.org/Special_Reports/042505Madsen/042505madsen.html

Mahoney, M., & Chan, P. (2002). Learning nonstationary models of normal network traffic for detecting novel attacks. *Proceedings of the SIGKDD*, Edmonton, Alberta (pp. 376-385).

Maimon, O., & Rokach, L. (2005). *Introduction to knowledge discovery in databases*. In *The data mining and knowledge discovery handbook 2005* (pp. 117).

Mandia, K., & Prosise, C. (2003). *Incident response and computer forensics*. New York: McGraw-Hill/Osborne.

Manganaris, S., Christensen, M., Zerkle, D., & Hermiz, K. (2000). A data mining analysis of RTID alarms. *Computer Networks, 34*, 571-577.

Manion, M., & Goodrum, A. (2000). Terrorism or civil disobedience: toward a hacktivist ethic. *Computers and Society (ACM SIGCAS), 30*(2), 14-19.

Mankins, D., Krishnan, R., Boyd, C., Zao, J., & Frentz, M. (2004). *Mitigating distributed denial of service attacks with dynamic resource pricing*. Retrieved from http://www.ir.bbn.com/~krash/pubs/mankins_acsac01.pdf

Marchette, D. J. (2001). *Computer intrusion detection and network monitoring: A statistical viewpoint*. Springer-Verlag.

Massey, J. E. (2001). Managing organizational legitimacy: Communication strategies for organizations in crisis. *Journal of Business Communications, 38*(2), 153-182.

Mastercard Int. *Frequently asked questions*. Retrieved February 15, 2006, from http://www.mondex.com/faq.html#q07

Mattison, D. (2003). Quickwiki, swiki, twiki, zwiki and the plone wars: Wiki as PIM and collaborative content tool, searcher. *The Magazine for Database Professionals, 11*(4), 32.

Maxwell, A. (2001). *Cyberstalking*. Masters' thesis, http://www.netsafe.org.nz/ie/downloads/cyberstalking.pdf

McAfee. (2005). *Virtual criminology report: North American study into organized crime and the Internet*. Santa Clara, CA.

McArdle, D. (2004). Myfip packing trait worries virus experts. *Electricnews*, Retrieved July 15, 2006, from http://www.electricnews.net/news.html?code=9561560

McCaffrey, J. (2003, November). Keep your data secure with the new advanced encryption standard. *MSDN Magazine*. Retrieved from http://msdn.microsoft.com/msdnmag/issues/03/11/AES/

McCann, J. T. (2000). A descriptive study of child and adolescent obsessional followers. *Journal of Forensic Sciences, 45*(1), 195-199.

McCarty, B. (2003). The honeynet arms race. *IEEE Security and Privacy, 1*(6), 79-82.

McClure, S., Scambray, J., & Jurtz, G. (2003). *Hacking exposed: network security secrets and solutions* (4th ed.). New York: McGraw-Hill; Osborne.

McClure, S., Scambray, J., & Kurtz, G. (2005). *Hacking exposed* (5th ed.). New York: McGraw-Hill; Osborne.

McClure, S., Scambray, J., & Kurtz, G. (2005). *Hacking exposed: Network security secrets & solutions* (5th ed.). New York: McGraw-Hill; Osborne.

McClure, S., Shah, S., & Shah, S. (2002). *Web hacking: Attacks and defense*. Addison-Wesley.

McGuiness, T. (2001). *Defense in depth*. Retrieved February 25, 2006, from SANS Institute Web site: http://www.sans.org/rr/whitepapers/basics/525.php

McKitterick, D., & Dowling, J. (2003). *State of the art review of mobile payment technology* (Tech. Rep.). The University of Dublin, Trinity College. Retrieved February 15, 2006, from http://www.cs.tcd.ie/publications/tech-reports/reports.03/TCD-CS-2003-24.pdf

McLuhan, M. (1960). Effects of the improvements of communication media. *The Journal of Economic History 20*(4), 566575.

Meall, L. (1989). Survival of the fittest. *Accountancy (UK), 103*(1147), 140141.

Meikle, G. (2002). *Future active: Media activism and the internet*. Routledge.

Meloy, J. R. (1996). Stalking (obsessional following): A review of some preliminary studies. *Aggressive and Violent Behaviour, 1*(2), 147-162.

Meloy, J. R., & Gothard, S. (1995). Demographic and clinical comparison of obsessional followers and offenders with mental disorders. *American Journal of Psychiatry, 152*(2), 25826.

Mena, J. (2003). *Investigative data mining for security and criminal detection*. Butterworth Heinemann.

Mena, J. (2004). *Homeland security techniques and technologies*. Charles River Media.

Mendez-Torreblanca, A., Montes-y-Gomez, M., & Lopez-Lopez, A. (2002). A trend discovery system for dynamic web content mining. *Proceedings of CIC-2002*.

Menezes, A. (2001). *Handbook of applied cryptography* (5th ed.). CRC Press.

Merkle, R. C. (1978). Secure communications over insecure channels. *Communications of the ACM, 21*(4), 294-299.

Merritt, J. (1992, June 18). UK: GCHQ spies on charities and companies—fearful whistleblowers tell of massive routine abuse. *The Observer (London)*.

MessageLabs. (2005). *Annual security report*. Retrieved February 8, 2006, from www.messagelabs.com/publishedcontent/publish/threat_watch_dotcom_en/intelligence_reports/2005_annual_security_report/DA_123230.chp.html

Messmer, E. (1999, September 13). Threat of "infowar" brings CIA warnings. *Network World Fusion*. Retrieved from http://www.nwfusion.com/archive/1999/75306_09-13-1999.html

Michael, C. C., & Ghosh, A. (2002). Simple, state-based approaches to program-based anomaly detection. *ACM Transactions on Information and System Security, 5*(3), 203-237.

Michael, J. B., Fragkos, G., & Auguston, M. (2003). An experiment in software decoy design: intrusion detection and countermeasures via system call instrumentation. In *Proceedings of the IFIP 18th International Information Security Conference*, Athens, Greece (pp. 253-264).

Michael, J., Wingfield, T., & Wijiksera, D. (2003). Measured responses to cyber attacks using Schmitt analysis: a case study of attack scenarios for a software-intensive system. In *Proceedings of the 27th IEEE Computer Software and Applications Conference*, Dallas, TX.

Michalowski, R. (1996). White collar crime, computers, and the legal construction of property. In *Definitional dilemma: Can and should there be a universal definition of white collar crime?* (pp. 173-203). Morgantown, WV: National White Collar Crime Center.

Middleton, B. (2004). *Cyber crime investigator's field guide*. Auerbach.

Midwinter, J. E. (1979). *Optical fibres for transmission*. John Wiley & Sons.

Miller, G. (1999). Gore to release cyberstalking report, call for tougher laws. *Latimes.com*. http://www.latimes.

com/news/ploitics/elect2000/pres/gore

Miller, G. R., & Stiff, J. B. (1993). *Deceptive communications*. Newbury Park, UK: Sage Publications.

Miller, R. (1991). *Interpretations of conflict: ethics, pacifism, and the just-war tradition*. Chicago, IL:: University of Chicago Press.

Minami, N., & Kasahara, M. (2005). A new decoding method for digital watermark based on error correcting codes and cryptography. *Electronics and Communications in Japan (Part III: Fundamental Electronic Science), 88*(8), 9-17.

Mitchell, T. M. (1997). *Machine learning*. McGraw-Hill.

Mitnick, K. (2002). *The art of deception: Controlling the human element of security*. New York: John Wiley & Sons.

Mockapetris, P. (1987). Domain names concepts and facilities. RFC 1034 (Standard). IETF. (Updated by RFCs 1101, 1183, 1348, 1876, 1982, 2065, 2181, 2308, 2535, 4033, 4034, 4035, 4343)

Mockapetris, P. (1987). RFC 1035: Domain names—Implementation and specification.

Molander, R., & Siang, S. (1998). The legitimization of strategic information warfare: Ethical considerations. *AAAS Professional Ethics Report, 11*(4). Retrieved November 23, 2005, from http://www.aaas.org/spp/sfrl/sfrl.htm

Mollin, R. (2002). *RSA and public-key cryptography*. Chapman & Hall/CRC.

Moniz, D. (2002). U.S. fine tunes its air war capabilities. *USA Today* 12/06/2002.

Monmonier, M. (1982). *Computer assisted cartography, principles and prospects*. Eaglewood Cliffs, NJ: Prentice-Hall.

Monmonier, M. (2002). *Spying with maps*. New York: University of Chicago Press.

Mookhey, K. K., & Burghate, N. (2003). *Detection of*

SQL injection and cross-site scripting attacks (Tech. Rep.). Retrieved from http://www.securityfocus.com/infocus/1768

Moore, D., Shannon, C., & Brown, J. (2002). *Code-Red: A case study on the spread and victims of an Internet worm*. Retrieved from http://www.caida.org/outreach/papers/2002/codered/codered.pdf

Moore, D., Shannon, C., Brown, D., Voelker, G. M., & Savage, S. (2006). Inferring internet denial-of-service activity. *ACM Transactions on Computer Science, 24*(2), 115-139.

Moore, D., Voelker, G. M., & Savage, S. (2001). Inferring internet denial-of-service activity. *Proceedings of the 2001 USENIX Security Symposium*.

MOR. (1996). Ministry of Research. *The global short-circuit and the explosion of information*. Retrieved 15 May, 2005 from http://www.fsk.dk/fsk/publ/info2000-uk/chap01.html

Mork, L. (2002). Technology tools for crisis response. *Risk Management, 49*(10), 44-50.

Moteff, J., & Parfomak, P. (2004*). CRS chapter for congress, critical infrastructure and key assets: Definition and identification*. Resources, Science, and Industry Division.

Moulin, P., & O'Sullivan, J. A. (2003). Information-theoretic analysis of information hiding. *IEEE Transactions on Information Theory, 49*(3), 563-593.

Mullen, P. E., & Pathe, M. (1997). The impact of stalkers on their victims. *British Journal of Psychiatry, 170*, 12-17.

Mullen, P. E., Pathe, M., Purcell, R., & Stuart, G. W. (1999). Study of stalkers. *The American Journal of Psychiatry, 156*(8), 1244-1249.

Mundie, C., de Vries, P., Haynes, P., & Corwine, M. (2002). *Trustworthy computing*. Microsoft White Paper.

Murphy, T., & Jennex, M. E. (2006). Knowledge management systems developed for Hurricane Katrina response. *Third International Conference on Information Systems for Crisis Response and Management.*

Muselli, M., & Liberati, D. (2000). Training digital circuits with Hamming clustering. *IEEE Transactions on Circuits and Systems – I: Fundamental Theory and Applications, 47,* 513-527.

Muselli, M., & Liberati, D. (2002). Binary rule generation via Hamming clustering. *IEEE Transactions on Knowledge and Data Engineering, 14,* 1258-1268.

Nakhjiri, M. (2005). *AAA and network security for mobile access: Radius, diameter, EAP, PKI and IP mobility.* John Wiley & Sons.

Nardin, T. (Ed.). (1998). *The ethics of war and peace.* Princeton, NJ: Princeton University Press.

Natarajan, A., & Hossain, L. (2004). Towards a social network approach for monitoring insider threats to information security. *Proceedings of the Second NSF/NIJ Symposium on Intelligence and Security Informatics,* Tucson, AZ.

National Institute of Standards and Technology (NIST). (2004) *Role-based access control* (NIST Standard 359-2004). Retrieved from http://csrc.nist.gov/rbac

National Research Council. (1991). *Computers at risk.* National Academy Press.

National strategy for combating terrorism. (2003, February) Submitted by the White House.

Negroponte, N. (2005). *Being Digital,* p. 11, New York: Alfred A. Knopf, Inc.

Neumann, P. G. (1997). Computer security in aviation: Vulnerabilities, threats, and risks. In *Proceedings of the International Conference in Aviation Safety and Security in the 21ˢᵗ Century, White House Commission on Safety and Security, and George Washington University.* Retrieved from http://www.csl.sri.com/neumann/air.html

Neumann, P. G. (1998). Identity-related misuse. In D. E. Denning & P. J. Denning (Eds.), *Internet Besieged.* Reading, MA: ACM Press.

Neumann, P., & Weinstein, L. (1997). Inside risks: Spam, spam, spam! *Communications of the ACM, 40*(6), 112.

NGIF. (2005). National geospatial intelligence foundation. *Proceedings of the Technologies for Critical Incident Response Conference and Exposition,* San Diego, CA.

Nguyen, N., Reiher, P., & Kuenning, G. H. (2003). Detecting insider threats by monitoring system call activity. *Proceedings of the 2003 IEEE Workshop on Information Assurance.*

NIAC (2004). Prioritizing cyber vulnerabilities: Final report and recommendations by the Council. National Infrastructure Advisory Council. October 12, 2004.

NIAC (2004). Hardening the Internet: Final report and recommendations by the Council. National Infrastructure Advisory Council. October 12, 2004.

Nikolaidis, N., & Pitas, I. (1996). Copyright protection of images using robust digital signatures. *IEEE International Conference on Acoustics, Speech and Signal Processing, 4,* 2168-2171.

Ning, P., & Xu, D. (2003). Learning attack strategies from intrusion alerts. *Proceedings of the ACM Computer and Communications Security Conference.*

Ning, P., Cui, Y., & Reeves, D. S. (2002). Constructing attack scenarios through correlation of intrusion alerts. *Proceedings of the ACM Computer and Communications Security Conference.*

NIPC. (2003). *Encourages heightened cyber security as Iraq—US tensions increase* (Advisory 03-002). Washington, DC.

Nir, S., Or, S., Bareket, Y., & Ariely, G. (2002). Implications of characteristics of low intensity conflict on the issue of learning and operational knowledge management. In *Learning throughout fighting.* School of Command, IDF.

Nisbet, C. (2003). Cybercrime and cyber terrorism. In S. Paulus, N. Pohlmann, & H. Reimer (Eds.), *Securing electronic business processes—Highlights of the information security solutions conference 2003.* Vieweg. Retrieved February 3, 2006, from http://www.qinetiq.com/home_enterprise_security/conference_papers_index.Par.0001. File.pdf%5D

Nisha de Silva, F. (2001). Providing spatial decision support for evacuation planning: a challenge in integrating technologies. *Disaster Prevention and Management, 10*(1), 11-20.

Nitzberg, S. (1998). Conflict and the computer: Information warfare and related ethical issues. In *Proceedings of the 21ˢᵗ National Information Systems Security Conference*, Arlington, VA (p. D7).

Nizovtsev, D., & Thursby, M. (2005). *Economic analysis of incentives to disclose software vulnerabilities.* Mimeo.

NN. (2004). Attracting hackers. *Communications of the ACM, 48*(11), 9.

No Law to Tackle Cyberstalking. (2004). *The Economic Times.* http://ecoonomictimes.indiatimes.com/articleshow/43871804.cms

Noble, J. J. I. (1999). Cyberterrorism hype. *Jane's Intelligence Review.*

Noe, D (2007). *The near escape: The Jonathan Jay Pollard spy case.* Retrieved May 18, 2007 from http://www.crimelibrary.com/terrorists_spies/spies/pollard/1.html

Nolte, W. M. (2000). Information control is dead. What's next? The knowledge management challenge for the intelligence community in the 21st century. *Defense Intelligence Journal 9*(1), 513.

Northcutt, S. J. N. (2002). *Network intrusion detection* (3ʳᵈ ed.). Sams.

NRC. (2003). *NRC initiates additional security review of publicly available records.* Nuclear Regulatory Commission News, No. 04-135, Office of Public Affairs. www.nrc.gov

Nugent, J. (2005). *RF energy as an attack medium for digitally stored data.* Unpublished working conceptual research paper, University of Dallas Center for Information Assurance, Irving, TX.

Nuke, L. (2002). *A brief history of unmanned aerial vehicles.* American Institute of Aeronautics and Astronautics.

O'Connel, M. J. (1974). Search program for significant variables. *Computational Physic Commumications, 8,* 49.

O'Mahony, D., Peirce, A. M., & Tewari, H. (2001). *Electronic payment systems for e-commerce* (2ⁿᵈ ed.). Artech House.

O'Rourke, M. (2004). Cyber-extortion evolves. *Risk Management, 51*(4), 1012.

O'Shaughnessy, H. (1992, June 28). Thatcher ordered Lonrho phone-tap over Harrods affairs. *The Observer (London).*

Oba, T. (2004, April). *Cyberterrorism seen as future threat* (Computer Crime Research Centre Tech. Report). Retrieved from http://www.crime-research.org/news/2003/04/Mess0103.html

Ogilvie, E. (2000). *Cyberstalking, trends and issues in crime and criminal justice.* 166. http://www.aic.gov.au

Ollman, G. (2004). *Passive information gathering: The analysis of leaked network security information* (Tech. paper). Next Generation Security Software Ltd.

Organization for the Advancement of Structured Information Standards (OASIS). (2005). *eXtensible access control markup language* (XACML 2.0).

Orwant, C. (1994). EPER ethics. In *Proceedings of the Conference on Ethics in the Computer Age*, Gatlinburg, TN (pp. 105-108).

Orwell, G. (1949). *Nineteen eighty-four.* New York: Harcourt Brace Javanovich.

OSSTMM: Open source security testing methodology manual. (2006). Pete Herzog. Retrieved January 30, 2005, from http://www.isecom.org/osstmm/

Oxford Dictionary of Law. (2004). *Mobipocket ebook.* Oxford University Press.

Ozment, A. (2004). *Bug auctions: Vulnerability markets reconsidered.* Mimeo.

Padmanabhan, V. N., & Subramanian, L. (2001). An investigation of geographic mapping techniques for internet hosts. *Proceedings of the 2001 conference on Applications, technologies, architectures, and protocols for computer communications (SIGCOMM 2001).*

Palaniappan, R., Anandan, S., & Raveendran, P. (2002, December 25). Two level PCA to reduce noise and EEG from evoked potential signals. *Proceedings of 7th International Conference on Control, Automation, Robotics and Vision,* Singapore (pp. 1688-1693).

Pankanti, P. J. (2001, December). On the individuality of fingerprints. *Proceedings of the IEEE Conference on Computer Vision and Pattern Recognition.*

Panko, R. R. (2003). SLAMMER: The first blitz worm. *Communications of the AIS, CAIS, 11*(12).

Pant, G., Srinivasan, P., & Menczer, F. (2004). Crawling the web. In M. Levene & A. Poulovassilis (Eds.), *Web dynamics.* Springer.

Park, J. S., & Chandramohan, P. (2004). Component recovery approaches for survivable distributed systems. In *Proceedings of the 37th Hawaii International Conference on Systems Sciences (HICSS-37).* Big Island, HI.

Park, J. S., & Deshpande, A. (2005). Spam detection: Increasing accuracy with a hybrid solution. *Journal of Information Systems Management (ISM), 23*(1).

Park, J. S., & Froscher, J. N. (2002). A strategy for information survivability. In *Proceedings of the 4th Information Survivability Workshop (ISW).* Vancouver, Canada.

Park, J. S., & Ho, S. M. (2004). Composite role-based monitoring (CRBM) for countering insider threats. *Proceedings of Second Symposium on Intelligence and Security Informatics (ISI),* Tucson, Arizona.

Park, J. S., Chandramohan, P., Devarajan, G., & Giordano, J. (2005). Trusted component sharing by runtime test and immunization for survivable distributed systems. In *Proceedings of the 20th IFIP International Conference on Information Security (IFIP/SEC 2005).* Chiba, Japan.

Parker, D. B. (1976). *Crime by computer.* New York: Scribners.

Parlament of Victoria. (2005). *Victorian electronic democracy—Final report.* Retrieved October 29, 2005, from http://www.parliament.vic.gov.au/sarc/E-Democracy/Final_Report/Glossary.htm

Pastor-Satorras, R., & Vespignani, A. (2001, April 4). *Internet aids the spread of computer viruses.* Retrieved from http://www.physicsweb.org/article/news/5/4/2/1

Patton, D., & Flin, R. (1999). Disaster stress: An emergency management perspective. *Disaster Prevention and Management, 8*(4), 261-267.

PayPal Corporation. (n. d.). Retrieved from http://www.paypal.com

PCWorld. (2001, November 19). Timeline: A 40-year history of hacking. *IDG News Service.* Retrieved August 10, 2005, from http://www.cnn.com/2001/TECH/internet/11/19/hack.history.idg/

Pearson Education, Inc., Information Please Database. (2005). *History of viruses.* Retrieved from http://www.factmonster.com/pages/copyright.html

Pearson, C. M., Misra, S. K., Clair, J. A., & Mitroff, I. I. (1997). Managing the unthinkable. *Organizational Dynamics, 26,* 51-64.

Peck, W. (1972, August). .U.S. electronic espionage: A memoir. *Ramparts, 11*(2), 3550. http://jya.com/nsa-elint.htm

Peikary, C., & Fogie, S. (2003). *Guarding against SQL server attacks: Hacking, cracking and protection techniques* (Tech. Rep.). AirScanner.

Peng, T., Leckie, C., & Ramamohanarao, K. (2003). Protection from distributed denial of service attack using history-based IP filtering. *Proc. of IEEE Int. Conference of Communication ICC,* Anchorage. Retrieved from http://www.ee.mu.oz.au/staff/caleckie/icc2003.pdf

Peng, Z.-R., & Tsou, M.-H. (2003). *Internet GIS: Distributed GIS for the internet and wireless networks.* Hoboken, NJ: John Wiley & Sons.

Perez, E. (2005, February 18). Identity theft puts pressure on data sellers. *Wall Street Journal.*

Perrott, A. (2001, June 7). Echelon: Spying chain's cover blown. *New Zealand Herald*. http://www.commondreams.org/headlines01/0607-03.htm

Peterson, B. L. (2002). Information security in outsourcing agreements. *Outsourcing Center*. Retrieved December 27, 2004, from http://www.outsourcing-requests.com/center/jsp/requests/print/story.jsp?id=2355

Pfleeger, C. P. (1997). *Security in computing* (2nd ed.). Upper Saddle River, NJ: Prentice Hall PTR.

Pfleeger, C. P., & Pfleeger, S. L. (2003). *Security in computing* (3rd ed.). Upper Saddle River, NJ: Prentice-Hall.

PGP Corporation. (2005). *PGP Corporation source code*. Retrieved from http://www.pgp.com/downloads/sourcecode/index.html

Phung, M. (2000, October 24). *Data mining in intrusion detection*. http://www.sans.org/resources/idfaq/data_mining.php

PICS. (n.d.). *Platform for internet content selection*. http://www.w3.org/pics/

Platt, A. F. (2002). Physical threats to the information infrastructure. In S. Bosworth & M. E. Kabay (Eds.), *Computer security handbook* (4th ed., chap. 14, pp. 14-114-25). John Wiley & Sons.

Pointcheval, D. (2000). Self-scrambling anonymizers. *Proceedings of the Financial Cryptography Conference*.

Polich, J. (1991). P300 in clinical applications: Meaning, method and measurement. *American Journal of EEG Technology, 31*, 201-231.

Pollitt, M. M. (1997). A cyberterrorism fact or fancy? In *Proceedings of the 20th National Information Systems Security Conference, 1997* (pp. 285-289). Retrieved February 3, 2006, from http://www.cs.georgetown.edu/~denning/infosec/pollitt.html

Poole, P. S. (1999/2000). *ECHELON: America's secret global surveillance network*. http://fly.hiwaay.net/~pspoole/echelon.html

Popp, R., Pattipati, K., Wille, P., Serfaty, D., Stacy, W.,

Carley, K., et al. (2004). Collaboration and modeling tools for counter-terrorism analysis. *CIHSPS2004—IEEE International Conference on Computational Intelligence for Homeland Security and Personal Safely*, Venice, Italy.

Portnoy, L., Eskin, E., & Stolfo, S. J. (2001). Intrusion detection with unlabeled data using clustering. *Proceedings of ACM Workshop on Data Mining Applied to Security*.

Postel, J. (1982). *RFC 821: Simple mail transfer protocol*.

Poulse, K. (2004). *US defends cybercrime treaty. Security focus*. The Register Retrieved December 9, 2005, from http://www.theregister.com/2004/04/24/

Poulsen, K. (2004, September 27). U.N. warns of nuclear cyber attack risk. *SecurityFocus*. Retrieved August 10, 2005, from http://www.securityfocus.com/news/9592

President's Information Technology Advisory Committee. (2005). *Cyber security: A crisis of prioritization*.

PriceWaterhouseCoopers. (2001). *European economic crime survey 2001. European Report*. Retrieved January 16, 2006, from http://www.pwcglobal.com

Proctor, P. E. (2001). *Practical intrusion detection handbook*. Upper Saddle River, NJ: Prentice-Hall PTR.

Pruitt, E. L. (1979). The office of naval research and geography. *Annals, Association of American Geographers, 69*(1), 106.

Quinlan, J. R. (1994). *C4.5: Programs for machine learning*. San Francisco: Morgan Kaufmann.

Ralston, B. (2004). *GIS and public data*. Clifton Park, NY: Thompson/Delmar Press.

Raman, M., Ryan, T., & Olfman, L. (2006). Knowledge management systems for emergency preparedness: The Claremont University Consortium experience. *International Journal of Knowledge Management, 2*(3), 33-50.

Ranum, M. (2002). Intrusion detection: Challenges and myths. *Network Flight Recorder, Inc.* Retrieved July

31, 2006, from http://www.windowsecurity.com/white-papers/

Ranum, M. (2004). *The myth of homeland security.* Indianapolis: Wiley.

Rattray, G. J. (2001). *Strategic warfare in cyberspace.* Cambridge, MA: MIT Press.

Raymond, E. (1996). *The new Hacker's dictionary* (3rd ed.). The MIT Press.

Raz, O., Koopman, P., & Shaw, M. (2002). Enabling automatic adaptation in systems with under-specified elements. *WOSS'02.*

Raz, O., Koopman, P., & Shaw, M. (2002). Semantic anomaly detection in online data sources. In Proceedings of the *ICSE'02* (pp. 302-312).

Regan, K. (2005). *Fraud seen rising among large e-commerce companies.* http://www.ecommercetimes.com/story/47260.html

Rekhter, Y., Li, T., & Hares, S. (2006). A border gateway protocol 4 (BGP-4). RFC 4271 (Draft Standard). IETF.

Renaud, R., & Phillips, S. (2003). Developing an integrated emergency response programme for facilities: The experience of public works and government services Canada. *Journal of Facilities Management, 1*(4), 347-364.

Report of the joint inquiry into the terrorist attacks of September 11, 2001. (2003, July). Submitted by the House Permanent Select Committee on Intelligence (HPSCI) and the Senate Select Committee on Intelligence (SSCI).

Report on Cyberstalking. (1999, August). *Cyberstalking: A new challenge for law enforcement and industry.* A Report from the Attorney General to The Vice President. http://www.usdoj.gov/criminal/cybercrime/cyberstalking.htm

Reporter. (2004, November 14). Mol in AIVD gaf tekens op website. *De Telegraaf.*

Reuters. (2004, July 18). France outsources, Senegal calls.

Wired. Retrieved September 20, 2004, from http://www.wired.com/news/print/0,1294,64262,00.html

Reuters. (2004, July 7). Scotland Yard and the case of the Rent-A-Zombies. *Online News.* Retrieved 16 May, 2007 from http://news.zdnet.com/2100-1009_22-5260154.html

Reuters. (2004, September 2). Outsourcing's next big thing—Malaysia? *News.Com.* Retrieved September 7, 2004, from http://news.com.com/2100-1011-5344618.html

Rhem, K. T. (2005, July 20). China investing in information warfare technology, doctrine. *American Forces Press Service.* Retrieved August 10, 2005, from http://www.pentagon.gov/news/jul2005/20050720_2171.html

Richelson, J. (1989). *The U.S. intelligence community* (2nd ed.). Ballinger.

Richelson, J., & Ball, D. (1990). *The ties that bind: Intelligence cooperation between the UKUSA countries: The United Kingdom, the United States of America, Canada, Australian and New Zealand* (2nd ed.). Boston: Unwin Hyman.

Richmond, R. (2004, January 22). Netware associates to attack spyware with new products. *Wall Street Journal,* p. B5.

Ring, S., Esler, D., & Cole, E. (2004). Self-healing mechanisms for kernel system compromises. In *Proceedings of the 1st ACM SIGSOFT workshop on self-managed systems (WOSS)* (pp. 100-104). New York.

Ringelestijn, T. V. (2004, March 23). *Technologie buiten schot in zaak toetjesterrorist.* Retrieved June 30, 2006, from http://www.netkwesties.nl/editie86/artikel3.php

Riordan, J., Wespi, A., & Zamboni, D. (2005). How to hook worms. *IEEE Spectrum.*

Risen, J., & Lichtblau, E. (2005, December 16). Bush lets U.S. spy on callers without courts. *The New York Times.* Retrieved May 21, 2007 from http://select.nytimes.com/gst/abstract.html?res=F00F1FFF3D540C758DDDAB0994DD404482

Ritter, J. B., & Money, M. (2002). E-commerce safeguards. In S. Bosworth & M. E. Kabay (Eds.), *Computer security handbook* (4th ed., chap. 19, pp. 19-119-31). John Wiley & Sons.

Rivest, R. L. (1992). *The MD5 message-digest algorithm.* MIT LCS and RSA Data Security, Inc. RFC 1321. Retrieved from http://www.faqs.org/rfcs/rfc1321.html

Rivest, R. L., Shamir, A., & Adleman, L. M. (1978). A method for obtaining digital signatures and public key cryptosystems. *Communications of the ACM, 21*(2), 120-126.

Robertson, T. S., & Gatignon, H. (1986). Competitive effects on technology diffusion. *Journal of Marketing, 50*(July), 1-12.

Robinson, C. (2002). Military and cyber defense: Reactions to the threat. Center for Defense Information. Retrieved September 10, 2005, from http://www.cdi.org/terrorism/cyberdefense-pr.cfm

Robinson, G. (2003, January 3). Statistical appoach to the spam problem—Using Bayesian statistics to detect an e-mail's spamminess. *ACM Linux Journal.*

Roeckle, H., Schimpf, G., & Weidinger, R. (2000). Process-oriented approach for role-finding to implement role-based security administration in a large industrial organization. *Proceedings of the Fifth ACM Workshop on Role-Based Access Control,* 103-110.

Roesch, M. (1999, November). Snort-lightweight intrusion detection for networks. *Proceedings of the. USENIX Lisa '99,* Seattle, WA.

Rogers, E. M. (1995). *Diffusion of innovations* (4th ed.). New York: The Free Press.

Rosenoer, J. (2002). Safeguarding your critical business information. *Harvard Business Review, 80*(2), 2021.

Rosenthal, B. E. (2004). How real estate choices affect offshoring decisions. *Outsourcing Center.* Retrieved December 12, 2004, from http://www.outsourcing-requests.com/center/jsp/requests/print/story.jsp?id=4718

Rosenthal, B. E. (2004). META predicts offshoring will continue to grow at 20 percent clips through 2008. *Outsourcing Center.* Retrieved December 27, 2004, from http://www.outsourcing-requests.com/center/jsp/requests/print/story.jsp?id=4714

Rosenthal, B. E. (2004). Why the US and UK are calling South African call centers. *Outsourcing Center.*

Rosenthal, B. E. (2005). New outsourcing risks in 2005 and how to mitigate them. *Outsourcing Center.* Retrieved January 2, 2005, from http://www.outsourcing-requests.com/center/jsp/requests/print/story.jsp?id=4721

Ross, S. (2005). *A guide to social engineering* (vol. 1 and 2). Astalavista.

Rowe, N. (2004). Designing good deceptions in defense of information systems. In *Proceedings of the Computer Security Applications Conference,* Tucson, AZ (pp. 418-427).

Rowe, N. (2006). Measuring the effectiveness of honeypot counter-counterdeception. In *Proceedings of the Hawaii International Conference on Systems Sciences,* Koloa, HI.

Rowe, N. (2006, March). *A taxonomy of deception in cyberspace.* Presented at the International Conference on Information Warfare and Security, Princess Anne, MD.

Rowe, N., & Rothstein, H. (2004). Two taxonomies of deception for attacks on information systems. *Journal of Information Warfare, 3*(2), 27-39.

Rowe, N., Duong, B., & Custy, E. (2006). Fake honeypots: A defensive tactic for cyberspace. In *Proceedings of the 7th IEEE Workshop on Information Assurance,* West Point, NY.

Ruffner, K. (2005). *Corona: Americas first satellite program.* Morgan James Publishing, LLC.

Sahami, M., Dumais, S., Heckerman, D., & Horovitz, E. (1998). A Bayesian approach to filtering junk email. In *AAAI Workshop on Learning for Text Categorization* (pp. 26-27). Madison, WI.

Salkever, A. (2004, July 7). Racing to cure sickly medical

security. *BusinessWeek Online*. Retrieved December 30, 2004, from http://www.businessweek.com/print/technology/content/jul2004/tc2004077_9847_tc_171

Sandhu, R. S., Bhamidipati, V., & Munawer, Q. (1999). The ARBAC97 model for role-based administration of roles. *ACM Transactions on Information System Security, 2*(1), 105-135.

Sandhu, R. S., Coyne, E. J., Feinstein, H. L., & Youman C. E. (1996). Role-based access control models. *Computer, IEEE Computer Society Press, 29*(2), 38-47.

Sasse, M. A., Brostoff, S., & Weirich, D. (2001). Transforming the "weakest link": A human/computer interaction approach to usable and effective security. *BT Technology Journal, 19*(3), 122-131.

Savage, S., Wetherall, D., Karlin, A., & Anderson, T. (2001). Network support for IP traceback. *Transactions on Networking, 9*(3), 226-237.

Savaresi, S. M., & Boley, D. L. (2004). A comparative analysis on the bisecting K-means and the PDDP clustering algorithms. *International Journal on Intelligent Data Analysis, 8*(4), 345-363

Schechter, S. (2004). *Computer security, strength and risk: A quantitative approach*. Mimeo.

Scheier, B., (2002). *Securing the network from malicious code*.

Schmitt, M. (1998). Bellum Americanum: The U.S. view of twenty-first century war and its possible implications for the law of armed conflict. *Michigan Journal of International Law, 19*(4), 1051-1090.

Schmitt, M. (2002). Wired warfare: computer network attack and jus in bello. *International Review of the Red Cross, 84*(846), 365-399.

Schneider, K.-M. (2003). A comparison of event models for naive Bayes anti-spam e-mail filtering. In *Proceedings of the 10th Conference of the European Chapter of the Association for Computational Linguistics (EACL)* (pp. 307-314). Budapest, Hungary.

Schneier, B. (1995). *Applied cryptography: Protocols, algorithms and source code in C*. John Wiley & Sons.

Schneier, B. (n.d.). *Natural advantages of defense: What military history can teach network security* (Part 1).

Schoonover, G. (2005). Enhancing customer security: Built-in versus bolt-on. *DoD Software Tech News, Secure Software Engineering, 8*(2).

Schultz, E. E. (2002). A framework for understanding and predicting insider attacks. *Computers and Security, 21*(6), 526-531.

Schwartau, W. (1998). Something other than war. In A. D. Campen & D. H. Dearth (Eds.), *Cyberwar 2.0: Myths, mysteries, and reality*. Fairfax, VA: AFCEA International Press.

SearchSecurity.com's definitions: Social engineering. (2005). Retrieved March 2, 2006, from http://searchsecurity.techtarget.com/sDefinition/0,290660,sid14_gci531120,00.html

Sequeira, K. & Zaki, M. (2002). ADMIT: Anomaly-based data mining for intrusions. *Proceedings of the Eighth ACM SIGKDD International Conference on Knowledge Discovery and Data Mining* (pp. 386-395).

SET—Secure Electronic Transaction LLC. (1999). *The SET™ specification*. Retrieved from http://www.setco.org/

Shahar, Y. (1997). *Information warfare*. Retrieved from www.ict.org.il

Shalikashvili, J. (1995). *Joint vision 2010*. Washington, DC: U.S. Government Printing Office and Department of Defense, Office of the Joint Chiefs of Staff.

Shane, S., & Bowman, T. (1995, December 12). Catching Americans in NSA's net. *The Baltimore Sun*.

Shelton, H. H. (2000). *Joint vision 2020*. Washington, DC: U.S. Government Printing Office and Department of Defense, Office of the Joint Chiefs of Staff.

Sheridan, L., Davies, G. M., & Boon, J. C. W. (2001). Stalking: Perceptions and prevalence. *Journal of Interpersonal Violence, 16*(2), 151-167.

Shields, C., & Levine, B. (2000). A protocol for anonymous communication over the Internet. *Proceedings of the ACM Computer and Communication Security Conference.*

Shinder, D. L., & TittelScene, E. (2002). *Scene of the cybercrime: Computer forensics handbook.* Syngress.

Shoniregun, C. A., Chochliouros, I. P., Laperche, B., Logvynovskiy, O L., & Spiliopoulou-Chochliourou, A. S. (Eds.). (2004). *Questioning the boundary issues of Internet security.* London: e-Centre for Infonomics.

Shroder, J. (2005). Remote sensing and GIS as counterterrorism tools in the Afghanistan war: Reality, plus the results of media hyperbole. *The Professional Geographer, 57*(4).

Shy, O. (2001). *The Economics of Network Industries.* Cambridge University Press.

Sieber, U. (1998). *Legal aspects of computer-related crime in the information society (COM-CRIME Study).* University of Würzburg, Germany: European Commission, Legal Advisory Board. Retrieved February 1, 2006, from http://europa.eu.int/ISPO/legal/en/comcrime/sieber.html

Sieberg, D. (2001, September 21). Expert: Hijackers likely skilled with fake IDs. *CNN.com.* Retrieved August 28, 2006, from http://archives.cnn.com/2001/US/09/21/inv.id.theft/

Simons, B., & Spafford, E. H. (2003, March). Inside Risks 153. *Communications of the ACM, 46*(3).

Sims. (2002). *How much info 2000?* Retrieved from http://sims.berkeley.edu/research/projects/how-much-info/summary.html

Singhal, A., & Jajodia, S. (2005). *Data mining for intrusion detection.* In *The data mining and knowledge discovery handbook 2005* (pp. 1225-1237). Springer.

Sink or Schwinn. (2004, November 11). *The Economist.* Retrieved December 6, 2004, from http://www.economist.com/printedition/PrinterFriendly.cfm?Story_ID=3351542

Sinwelski, S., & Vinton, L. (2001). Stalking: The constant threat of violence. *Affilia, 16,* 46-65.

Sipior, J. C., Ward, B. T., & Roselli, G. R. (2005). The ethical and legal concerns of spyware. *Information Systems Management, 22*(2), 3949.

Siponen, M., Baskerville, R. (2001). A new paradigm for adding security into IS development methods. *8th Annual Working Conference on Information Security Management and Small Systems Security.*

Sizer, R. A. (1997). Land information warfare activity. *Military Intelligence Bulletin, 1997-1.* Retrieved January 6, 2006, from http://www.fas.org/irp/agency/army/tradoc/usaic/mipb/1997-1/sizer.htm

Smart, C. F., & Vertinsky, I. (1977). Designs for crisis decision units. *Administrative Science Quarterly, 22,* 639-657.

Smart, C. F., & Vertinsky, I. (1984). Strategy and environment: A study of corporate response to crises. *Strategic Management Journal, 5,* 199-213.

Smart, C. F., Thompson, W., & Vertinsky, I. (1978). diagnosing corporate effectiveness and susceptibility to crises. *Journal of Business Administration, 9*(2), 57-96.

Smetannikov, M. (2001, June 4). Cyberspies protect the virtual business world. *Interactive Week.* Retrieved from http://www.zdnet.com/zdnn/stories/news/0,4586,2767657.00.html

Smith, C. A. P., & Hayne, S. (1991). A distributed system for crisis management. *Proceedings of the 24th Hawaii International Conference on System Sciences, HICSS, 3,* 72-81.

Smith, F. C., & Bace, R. G. (2002). *A guide to forensic testimony: The art and practice of presenting testimony as an expert technical witness.* Addison-Wesley Professional.

Smith, G. (2004). *Control and security of e-commerce.* John Wiley & Sons.

Smith, L. (2004, June 30). Web amplifies message of primitive executions. *Los Angeles Times.*

Snapp, S. R., Brentano, J., Dias, G. V., Goan, T. L., Heberlein, L. T., Ho, C.lin, et al. (1991). DIDS (distributed intrusion detection system) motivation, architecture, and an early prototype. *Proceedings of the 14ᵗʰ National Computer Security Conference.* Washington, DC.

Snoeren, A. C., Partridge, C., Sanchez, L. A., Jones, C. E., Tchakountio, F., Kent, S. T.; & Strayer, W. T. (2001). Hash-based IP traceback. In *Proceedings of the ACM SIGCOMM 2001 Conference on Applications, Technologies, Architectures, and Protocols for Computer Communication* (pp. 3-14). New York.

Social engineering. (2006). In *Wikipedia: The free encyclopedia.* Retrieved December 18, 2005, from http://en.wikipedia.org/wiki/Social_engineering

Solomon, N. (2005). *War made easy: How presidents and pundits keep spinning us to death.* NJ: John Wiley & Sons.

Somayaji, A., & Forrest, S., (2000). Automated response using system-call delays. In *Proceedings of the 9ᵗʰ Usenix Security Symposium*, Denver, CO (pp. 185-198).

Spertus, E. (1996). *Social and technical means for fighting on-line harassment.* http://ai.mit.edu./people/ellens/Gender/glc

Spett, K. (2002). *SQL injection: s your Web application vulnerable?* (Tech. Rep.). SPI Dynamics Inc.

Spitzner, L. (2002). *Honeypots: Tracking hackers.* Addison Wesley.

Spitzner, L. (2003). *Honeypots: Tracking hackers.* Boston: Addison-Wesley.

Spitzner, L. (2004). *Know your enemy: Learning about security threats* (2ⁿᵈ ed.). Addison Wesley.

Srikant, R. & Agrawal, R. (1996). Mining quantitative association rules in large relational tables. *Proceedings of the 1996 ACM SIGMOD International Conference on Management of Data,* Montreal, Quebec, Canada (pp. 1-12).

Stafford, T. F., & Urbaczewski, A. (2004). Spyware: The ghost in the machine. *Communications of the Association for Information Systems, 14*, 291306.

Stallings, W. (2005). *Cryptography and network security* (4ᵗʰ ed.). Prentice Hall.

Stam, K., Guzman, I., Fagnot, I., & Stanton, J. (2005). *What's your password? The experience of fieldworkers using ethnographic methods to study information technology in work organizations.* Paper presented at the 2005 American Anthropological Association Annual Meetings, Washington, DC.

Staniford, S., Hoagland, J. A., & McAlerney, J. M. (2002). Practical automated detection of stealthy portscans. *J. Comput. Secur., 10*(12), 105-136.

Staniford-Chen, S., Cheung, S., Crawford, R., Dilger, M., Frank, J., Hoagland, J., et al. (1996). GrIDS: A graph-based intrusion detection system for large networks. *Proceedings of the 19ᵗʰ National Information Systems Security Conference.*

Stanton, J. & Fagnot, I. (2006). Extracting useful information from security assessment interviews. *Proceedings of the 39th Annual Hawaii International Conference on System Sciences (HICSS).*

Stanton, J. M., Stam, K. R., Mastrangelo, P., & Jolton, J. (2005). An analysis of end user security behaviors. *Computers and Security, 24*, 124-133.

Stanton, J. M., Yamodo-Fagnot, I., & Stam, K. R. (2005). The madness of crowds: Employees beliefs about information security in relation to security outcomes. *The Security Conference,* Las Vegas, NV.

Sterling, B. (2004, August). The other war on terror. *Wired, 12*(8). Retrieved August 10, 2005, from http://www.wired.com/wired/archive/12.08/view.html?pg=4

Stevenson, Jr. R. B. (1980). *Corporations and information: Secrecy, access, and disclosure.* The John Hopkins University Press.

Stewart, T. A. (1997). *Intellectual capital: The new wealth of organizations.* New York: Doubleday/Currency.

Stewart, T. A. (2001). Six degrees of Mohamed Atta. *Business 2.0.*

Stickel, E., & Woda, K. (2005): Electronic money. In E. Petzel (Ed.), *E-finance* (pp. 831-860). Gabler Verlag.

Stienberg, S., & Stienberg, S. (2006). *GIS for the social sciences*. Thousand Oaks, CA: Sage Publications.

STMicroelectronics, Proton PRISMA. (n.d.). Retrieved February 15, 2006, from http://www.st.com/stonline/products/promlit/pdf/flprotongen-1003.pdf

Stoll, C. (1989). *The cuckoo's egg: Tracking a spy through the maze of computer espionage*. New York: Doubleday.

Stoll, C. (2000). *The cuckoo's egg: Tracking a spy through the maze of computer espionage*. New York: Pocket Books.

Strassmann, P. A. (2001). *Government should blaze global information warfare trails*. Retrieved August 10, 2005, from http://www.strassmann.com/pubs/searchsecurity/2001-8.php

Straub, K. R. (2003). *Managing risk with defense in depth*. Retrieved February 25, 2006, from SANS Institute Web site: http://www.sans.org/rr/whitepapers/infosec/1224.php

Sukhai, N. B. (2004). Hacking and cybercrime. *Computer Society, 5*(10), 128-132.

Sullivan, B. (2004, August 4). 9/11 report light on ID theft issues. *MSNBC*. Retrieved January 2, 2006, from http://www.msnbc.msn.com/id/5594385

Sun, Z., & Wang, R. (2003). Research on mixed encryption authentication. *The Journal of China Universities of Posts and Telecommunications, 10*(4), 90-94.

Sunday Times. (1996, June 9). Secret DTI inquiry into cyber terror. *The (London) Sunday Times*, pp. 18.

Sushma, M., & Dhillon, G. (2006). information systems security governance research: A behavioral perspective. *NYS Cyber Security Conference (NYS CSIS)*, Albany, NY.

Svensson, P. (2003, March 25). Al-Jazeera site experiences hack attack. *The Associated Press*.

Swann, P., & Gill, J. (1993). *Corporate vision and rapid technology change: The revolution of market structure*. New York: Routledge.

Swartz, N. (2005). Britain warns of Trojan horse computer attacks. *Information Management Journal*, Retrieved July 15, 2006, from http://www.findarticles.com/p/articles/mi_qa3937/is_200509/ai_n15350562

Swire, P. P., & Litan, R. E. (1998). *None of your business: World data flows, electronic commerce, and the European privacy directive*. Washington DC: Brookings Institution Press.

Symantec Internet sescurity threat report, volume IX: March 2006 (Highlights). (2006). Retrieved March 5, 2006, from http://www.symantec.com/enterprise/threatreport/index.jsp

Symantec. (2004). Internet security threat report Vol. VI, Cupertino. Retrieved from http://www.enterprise-security.symantec.com

Symantec. (2005). Internet security threat report Vol. VIII, Cupertino. Retrieved from http://www.enterprise-security.symantec.com

Symonenko, S., Liddy, E. D., Yilmazel, O., Del Soppo, R., Brown, E., & Downey, M. (2004). *Semantic analysis for monitoring insider threats*. Presented at The Second NSF/NIJ Symposium on Intelligence and Security Informatics (ISI). Tucson, AZ.

Szor, P. (2005). *The art of computer virus research and defense*.

Taha, I., & Ghosh, J. (1999). Symbolic interpretation of artificial neural networks. *IEEE Tranactions on Knowledge and Data Engineering., 11*, 448-463.

Talbot, D. (2005, February). Terror's server. *Technology Review*. Retrieved March 17, 2005, from http://www.technologyreview.com/articles/05/02/issue/feature_terror.asp

Tannenbaum, A. (1996). *Computer networks* (3th ed.). Prentice Hall.

Taylor, C., Krings, A., & Alves-Foss, J. (2002, November 21). Risk analysis and probabilistic survivability assessment (RAPSA): An assessment approach for power substation hardening. *ACM Workshop on Scientific Aspects of Cyber Terrorism (SACT)*, Washington DC.

Tee, C., Teoh, A., Goh, M., & Ngo, D. (2004). Palm hashing: A novel approach to cancelable biometrics. *Information Processing Letter, 93*(1), 15.

Teoh, S. T., Zhang, K., Tseng, S. M., Ma, K. L., & Wu, S. F. (2004). Combining visual and automated data mining for rear-real-time anomaly detection and analysis in BGP. *VizSEC/DMSEC '04.*

The Honeynet Project. (2004) *Know your enemy* (2nd ed.). Boston: Addison-Wesley.

The Institute of Electrical and Electronic Engineers. (1990). *IEEE standard glossary of software engineering terminology.*

The Internet thermometer. (2004). *Web server intrusion statistics.* www.zone-h.org

The Regents of the University of California. (2002). *Cyberspace threats and vulnerabilities.*

Theriault, M., & Newman, A. (2001). Oracle security handbook. In *Firewalls and oracle.* Osborne/McGraw-Hill.

Thomas, T. L. (2003). Al Qaeda and the Internet: The danger of "cyberplanning". *Parameters,* 11223.

Thompson, R. (2005). Why spyware poses multiple threats to security. *Communications of the ACM, 48*(8), 41-43.

Thornburgh, N. (2005, August 29). The Invasion of the chinese cyberspies (and the man who tried to stop them). *Time Magazine.* Retrieved from http://www.time.com/time/magazine/article/0,9171.1098961,00html

Thuraisingham, B. (2002, December). Data mining, national security, privacy and civil liberties. *ACM SIGKDD Explorations Newsletter, 4*(2), 1-5.

Tiller, J. S. (2005). *The ethical hack: a framework for business value penetration testing.*

Tinnel, L. S., Sami Saydjari, O., & Farrell, D. (2002, June). An analysis of cyber goals, strategies, tactics, and techniques. In *Proceedings of the 2002 IEEE Workshop on Information Assurance,* United States Military Academy, West Point, NY.

Tippett, P. (2002). The future of information security. In S. Bosworth & M. E. Kabay (Eds.), *Computer security handbook* (4th ed., chap. 54, pp. 54-154-18). John Wiley & Sons.

Tirenin, W., & Faatz, D. (1999). A concept for strategic cyber defense. In *Proceedings of the Conference on Military Communications* (Vol. 1, pp. 458-463).

Tjaden, P., & Thoennes, N. (1997). Stalking in America: Findings from the National Violence

Toffler, A. (1970). *Future shock.* New York: Random House.

Toffler, A. (1981). *The third wave.* New York: Bantam Books.

Townsend, F. F. (2006). *The federal response to Hurricane Katrina, lessons learned.* Department of Homeland Security, United States of America.

Trappe, W., & Washington, L. (2005). *Introduction to cryptography with coding theory* (2nd ed.). Prentice Hall.

Treasury Board of Canada Secretariat. (1999). *Digital signature and confidentiality—Certificate policies for the government of Canada public key infrastructure* [Government of Canada (GOC), PKI Certificate Policies version 3.02].

Treurniet, J. (2004). *An overview of passive information gathering techniques for network security* (Tech. memo.). Defence R&D Canada.

Trojan War. (2005). In *Britannica.com.* Retrieved from http://www.britannica.com/ebc/article-9381198?query=trojan\%horse&ct=

Trost, W. A., & Nertney, R. J. (1995). *Barrier analysis.* Retrieved July 3, 2005, from http://ryker.eh.doe.gov/analysis/trac/29/trac29.html

Turoff, M. (2002). Past and future emergency response information systems. *Communications of the ACM, 45*(4), 29-32.

Turoff, M., Chumer, M., Van de Walle, B., & Yao, X. (2004). The design of a dynamic emergency response management information system (DERMIS). *The Journal of Information Technology Theory and Application (JITTA), 5*(4), 135.

Tzu, S. (1910). *Sun Tzu on the art of war, the oldest military treatise in the world* (L. Giles, Trans.). Retrieved from http://classics.mit.edu/Tzu/artwar.html

U.S. Computer Emergency Response Team (US-CERT). (2004). Cyber security tip ST04-014: Avoiding social engineering and phishing attacks. Carnegie Mellon University, U.S. Computer Emergency Readiness Team National Cyber Alert System. Retrieved March 2, 2006, from http://www.us-cert.gov/cas/tips/ST04-014.html

U.S. Health Insurance Portability and Accountability Act (HIPAA). (1996). Retrieved from http://cms.hhs.gov/hipaa

U.S. Navy. (2004). *Patterns of global yerrorism*. Monterey, CA: Naval Postgraduate School. http://library.nps.navy.mil/home/terrorism.htm

U.S. Patriot Act of 2001. §§ 1956, 981.

U.S. Strategic Command. (2006). *Functional components*. Retrieved January 6, 2006, from http://www.stratcom.mil/organization-fnc_comp.html

U.S. Treasury—The Office of Terrorism and Financial Intelligence (TFI). (2003). *National money laundering strategy.* Retrieved February 3, 2006, from http://www.treas.gov/offices/enforcement/publications/ml2003.pdf

URISA. (2003). Initial response and recovery at the World Trade Center. *Urban and Regional Information Systems Association Journal, January-February 2003.* www.URISA.org

Valeur, F., Vigna, G., Kruegel, C., & Kemmerer, R. A. (2004). A comprehensive approach to intrusion detection alert correlation. *IEEE Transactions on Dependable and Secure Computing, 1*(3), 146169.

Varon, E. (2000). The Langley files. *CIO Magazine.*

Vaughan, T. M., Wolpaw, J. R., & Donchin, E. (1996). EEG based communications: Prospects and problems, *IEEE Transactions on Rehabilitation Engineering, 4*(4), 425-430.

Venkatesan, R ., Koon, S. -M., Jakubowski, M. H., & Moulin, P. (2000 September). *Proceedings of the IEEE ICIP.* Vancouver.

Venkatesan, R., & Jakubowski, M. H. (2000). *Image watermarking with better resilience.* Presented at the IEEE International Conference on Image Processing (ICIP 2000).

VeriSign. (n. d.). *PayFlow Pro, how it works.* Retrieved from http://www.verisign.com/products-services/payment-processing/online-payment/payflow-pro/how-it-works.html

Verton, D. (1999, October 9). DoD boosts IT security role. *Federal Computer Week,.* Retrieved January 9, 2006, from http://www.fcw.com:8443/fcw/articles/1999/FCW_100499_7.asp

Verton, D. (2003). *Black ice: The invisible threat of cyber-terrorism* (1st ed.). New York: McGraw-Hill; Osborne Media.

Verton, D. (2004). CIA to publish cyberterror intelligence estimate. *ComputerWeekly.com.*

Verton, D. (2004, August 30). *Organized crime invades cyberspace.* Retrieved August 10, 2005, from http://www.computerworld.com/securitytopics/security/story/0,10801,95501,00.html

Vijayan, Jaikumar, (2003). Attacks on new Windows flaws expected soon. *Computerworld,* (37), 1.

Vines, R. D. (2002). *Wireless security essentials, defending mobile systems from data piracy.* IN: Wiley Publishing.

Voas, J. M., & McGraw, G. (1998). *Software fault injection: Inoculating programs against errors.* Wiley Computer Publishing.

Vrij, A. (2000). *Detecting lies and deceit: The psychology of lying and the implications for professional practice.* Chichester, UK: Wiley.

Wagner, D., & Dean, D. (2001). Intrusion detection via static analysis. In *Proceedings of the IEEE Symposium on Security and Privacy*, Washington, DC (pp. 156-169).

Walker, C., & Akdeniz, Y. (2003). Anti-terrorism laws and data retention: War is over? *Northern Ireland Legal Quarterly, 54*(2), 159-182. Retrieved January 31, 2006, from http://www.cyber-rights.org/interception/

Wallace, B. (2000, July 10). Stalkers find a new tool—The Internet e-mail is increasingly used to threaten and harass, authorities say. *SF Gate News*. http://sfgate.com/cgi-bin/article_cgi?file=/chronicle/archive/2000/07/10/MN39633.DTL

Wang, F. (2005). *GIS and crime analysis.* IGI Global.

Wang, J., & Osborn, S. L. (2004). A role-based approach to access control for XML databases. *SACMAT 2004*, 70-77.

Warren, M. J. (2003). *The impact of hackers.* Presented at the Second European Information Warfare Conference, Reading, UK.

Warren, M. J. (2005). *Cyber terrorism.* Presented at the Annual Police Summit, Melbourne, Australia.

Warren, M. J., & Hutchinson, W. (2002). *Will new laws be effective in reducing web sponsorship of terrorist groups.* Presented at the Third Australian Information Warfare and Security Conference, Perth, Australia.

Warren, M.J., & Furnell, S.M. (1999). *Cyber-terrorism: The political evolution of the computer hacker.* Australian Computer Ethics Conference, July 1999. Last accessed January 30, 2006, from http://www.cissr.com/whitepapers/cyberterrorism4.pdf

Watel, J. (2001). Le problème du Spamming ou comment guérir le cancer de l' Internet, JurPC Web-Dok. 163/2001.

Wayner, P. (2002). *Disappearing cryptography: Information hiding: Steganography and watermarking.* San Francisco: Morgan Kaufmann.

Wayner, P. (2006). *Disappearing cryptography: Information hiding, steganography and water marking.* Morgan Kaufman.

Weaver, N., & Paxson, V. (2004). *A worst case worm.* Mimeo.

Webopedia: Trojan horse. (2006). Retrieved March 2006, from http://www.webopedia.com/TERM/T/Trojan_horse.html

Weir, L. (2004, August 24). Boring game? Outsource it. *Wired.* Retrieved September 20, 2004, from http://www.wired.com/news/print/0,1294,64638,00.html

Weissel, J. (1990). Remote sensing entry. *Remote sensing Glossary.* Retrieved from http://rst.gsfc.nasa.gov/AppD/glossary.html

Westrup, D., Fremouw, W. J., Thompson, R. N., & Lewis, S. F. (1999). The psychological impact of stalking on female undergraduates. *Journal of Forensic Sciences, 44*, 554-557.

Westwood, C. (1997). *The future is not what it used to be: Conflict in the information age.* Fairbairn, Australia: Air Power Studies Center.

While progress has been made, managers and employees are still susceptible to social engineering techniques (2005). U.S. Department of Treasury. Retrieved December 15, 2005, from http://www.treas.gov/tigta/auditreports/2005reports/200520042fr.html

Whine, M. (1999). *Cyberspace: A new medium for communication, command and control for extremists.* ICT.

Whitman, M. E., & Mattord, H. J. (2004). *Management of information security.* Boston: Thomson Course Technology.

Whitworth, B., & Whitworth, E. (2004). Spam and the social-technical gap. *IEEE Computer, 37*(10), 38-45.

Wikipedia. (2006). Retrieved from http://en.wikipedia.org/wiki/Cryptography

Wikipedia. (2006). Social engineering (computer security). Retrieved March 6, 2006, from http://en.wikipedia.org/wiki/Social_engineering_%28computer_security%29

Wikipedia. (2006). Social engineering (political science). Retrieved March 6, 2006, from http://en.wikipedia.org/wiki/Social_engineering_(political_science)

Wikipedia. (2006). *Wiki*. Retrieved March 30, 2006, from http://en.wikipedia.org/wiki/Wiki

Wilkinson, P. (1976). *Political terrorism*. MacMillan Press Ltd.

Wilson, J. (2001). E-bomb. *Popular Mechanics, 178*(9), 5054.

Wilson, S. (2002). *Combating the lazy user: An examination of various password policies and guidelines*. Retrieved March 1, 2006, http://sans.org/rr

Wired China. (2000, July 22). *The Economist*, pp. 24-28.

Wired News. (2003). *Internet phone calls stymie FBI*. Retrieved October 27, 2003, from http://www.wired.com/news/print/0,1294,58350,00.html

Wong, M. (2006). *Sender policy framework (SPF) for authorizing use of domains in e-mail*. Network Working Group. RFC 4408. Retrieved from http://tools.ietf.org/html/4408

Woolsey, R. J. (2000, March 17). Why we spy on our allies. *The Wall Street Journal*. http://cryptome.org/echelon-cia2.htm

Working to Halt Online Abuse. (WHO). (2003). Online harrassment statistics. http://www.haltabuse.org/

Wright, J. (2003). *Detecting wireless LAN MAC address spoofing*. Retrieved from http://home.jwu.edu/jwright/papers/wlan-mac-spoof.pdf

Wright, S. (1998, January). *An appraisal of technologies of political control*. European Parliament Scientific and Technological Options office (STOA) report. http://mprofaca.cronet.com/atpc2.html

XACML. (n.d.). *eXtensible access control markup language*. http://www.oasis-open.org/committees/tc_home.php?wg_abbrev=xacml

Xu, J., Fan, J., Ammar, M., & Moon, S. B. (2002). Prefix-preserving IP address anonymization: Measurement-based security evaluation and a new cryptography-based scheme. *Proceedings of the 10th IEEE International Conference on Network Protocols (ICNP 2002)*.

Yamaguchi, T., Hashiyama, T., & Okuma, S. (2005). The proposal of power analysis for common key cryptography implemented on the FPGA and its countermeasure. *Electronics and Communications in Japan (Part III: Fundamental Electronic Science), 88*(8), 28-37.

Yarmus, J. S. (2003). *ABN: A fast, greedy Bayesian network classifier*. Retrieved from http://otn.oracle.com/products/bi/pdf/adaptive_bayes_net.pdf

Yeh, A. (2004). China now world's number two spam recipient, after United States. *Privacy and Security Law Report, 3*(13), 361.

Yen, J. (2003, September). Emerging technologies for homeland security. *Communications of the ACM, 46*(9).

Yoshihara, T. (2005). *Chinese information warfare: A phantom menace or emerging threat?* Retrieved December 2005 from www.strategicstudiesinstitute.army.mil/pubs/display.cfm?PubID=62

Yu, E. S., Koo, P. C., & Liddy, E. D. (2000). Evolving intelligent text-based agents. *Proceedings of the Fourth International Conference on Autonomous agents*, Barcelona, Spain (pp. 388-395).

Yuan, E., & Wenzel, G. (2005, March). Assured counter-terrorism information sharing using: Attribute based information security (ABIS). In *Proceedings of IEEE Aerospace Conference* (pp. 1-12). 5-12 March 2005.

Yurcik, W., & Doss, D. (2001). *Internet attacks: A policy framework for rules of engagement*. Department of Applied Computer Science, Illinois State University.

Yurcik, W., Loomis, D., & Korzyk, Sr., A. D. (2000, September). Predicting Internet attacks: On developing an effective measurement methodology. In *Proceedings of the 18ᵗʰ Annual International Communications Forecasting Conference*.

Zalewski, M. (2005). *Silence on the wire: A field guide to passive reconnaissance and indirect attacks*.

Zhang, Y., & Lee, W. (2000) Intrusion detection in wireless ad-hoc networks. *MOBICOM 2000*.

Zhang, Y., Lee, W., & Huang, Y. A. (2003). *Intrusion detection techniques for mobile wireless networks*. The Netherlands: Kluwer Academic Publishers.

Zheng, L., & Myers, A. C. (2005). *End-to-end availability policies and noninterference*. Presented at the 18ᵗʰ IEEE Computer Security Foundations Workshop, Aix-en-Provence, France.

Zhou, L., Twitchell, D., Qin, T., Burgoon, J., & Nunamaker, J. (2003). An exploratory study into deception detection in text-based computer-mediated communication. In *Proceedings of the 36ᵗʰ Hawaii International Conference on Systems Sciences*, Waikoloa, HI (p. 10).

Zimmermann, P. (2004). *Philip Zimmermann—Creator of PGP*. Retrieved from http://www.philzimmermann.com

Zimmermann, P. (2005). *Why do you need PGP?* Retrieved from http://www.pgpi.org/doc/whypgp/en/

Zimmermann, P. R. (1995). *The official PGP user's guide*. Cambridge, MA: MIT Press.

Zona, M. A., Sharma, K. K., & Lone, J. (1993). A comparative study of erotomanic and obsessional subjects in a forensic sample. *Journal of Forensic Sciences, 38*, 894-903.

Zou, C. C., Gong, W., Towsley, D., & Gao, L. (2005, October). The monitoring and early detection of internet worms. *IEEE/ACM Transactions on Networking, 13*(5).

About the Editors

Lech J. Janczewski has over 35 years experience in information technology. He is an associate professor at the University of Auckland, Department of Information Science and Operations Management. His area of research includes management of IS resources with the special emphasis on data security. Dr. Janczewski has written more than 100 publications that have been presented in scientific journals, conference proceedings, and books. He is the chairperson of the New Zealand Information Security Forum, a fellow of the New Zealand Computer Society, and the secretary of the IFIP's Technical Committee on Security and Protection in Information Processing Systems (TC-11).

Andrew M. Colarik has accumulated over 25 years experience of knowledge utilizing computer information systems. This includes systems analysis and design, network administration, university level teaching, and the justification, specification, and implementation of factory and office automation. He is the holder of a PhD in information systems from the University of Auckland, and a Master of Business Administration from Kent State University. As a researcher, author, and inventor, Dr. Colarik has been published in top-tier security conferences, authored several information security books, and is an inventor of both utility and design patents.

Index